COMPOSING KNOWLEDGE
Readings for College Writers

COMPOSING KNOWLEDGE
Readings for College Writers

Rolf Norgaard

University of Colorado at Boulder

Bedford/St. Martin's

Boston ◆ New York

For Bedford/St. Martin's

Senior Developmental Editor: John E. Sullivan III
Production Editor: Kendra LeFleur
Senior Production Supervisor: Nancy Myers
Marketing Manager: Karita dos Santos
Editorial Assistant: Jennifer Lyford
Production Assistants: Lidia MacDonald and Amy Derjue
Copyeditor: Mary Lou Wilshaw-Watts
Text Design: Anne Carter
Cover Design: Wiley Design Studio
Cover Art: Particular Times. Painting courtesy of Martina Nehrling, © Martina Nehrling. Photo courtesy of Zg Gallery, Chicago.
Composition: Pine Tree Composition
Printing and Binding: R.R. Donnelly & Sons Company

President: Joan E. Feinberg
Editorial Director: Denise B. Wydra
Editor in Chief: Karen S. Henry
Director of Marketing: Karen Melton Soeltz
Director of Editing, Design, and Production: Marcia Cohen
Managing Editor: Elizabeth M. Schaaf

Library of Congress Control Number: 2006933435

Manufactured in the United States of America.

1   0   9   8   7   6
f   e   d   c   b   a

For information, write: Bedford/St. Martin's, 75 Arlington Street, Boston, MA 02116 (617-399-4000)

ISBN-10: 0–312–15313–9
ISBN-13: 978–0–312–15313–7

Acknowledgments

David Bartholomae. "Inventing the University." From *When A Writer Can't Write* by David Bartholomae. Copyright © 1985. Reprinted by permission of the Guilford Press.

Charles Bazerman. "Where Is the Classroom?" From *English Basics*, Winter 1992. A Houghton Mifflin newsletter. Copyright © 1992 by Houghton Mifflin Company. Reprinted with permission.

PREFACE

Higher education has its own rules — rules about who is heard, what counts as knowledge, what works as persuasion. For students who don't know these rules, college can be a confusing place. In college courses, students learn more than facts or topics in a discipline. They are exposed, often indirectly, to assumptions and conventions about how language and inquiry work together. Writing courses afford a special opportunity to explore this process. With its focus on the role of writing in inquiry, and its goal of helping students join a community of inquiring minds, *Composing Knowledge* embraces this challenge and enables you to make this process of education more explicit for your students.

Composing Knowledge first asks students to step back and examine their assumptions about learning. Then it provides them with a training ground for higher education, giving them tools with which to think deeply about and understand their learning experiences. By considering how we "compose" knowledge, this anthology also helps students gain some "composing knowledge." That is, it helps them become better thinkers and writers, able to join the conversations that shape what we know and how we know it. Ultimately, students are better positioned to contribute to the many conversations of academic and civic life.

Students often wonder what holds their college education together. Aware that facts or topics in this or that course do not make for an education, students are eager to explore questions that might connect their academic experience and integrate their intellectual lives. Initially, these questions are straightforward: How do we read a syllabus? How do we respond to a sophisticated piece of writing? The questions progress in complexity: How do we enter the college community, the community of our chosen discipline, civic communities, or for that matter electronic communities? How are ways of knowing shaped by communities, and how are those communities themselves shaped by language? And as we enter those communities, how do we connect our work to the larger discussions of civic life? Taking up these questions, *Composing Knowledge* offers provocative, wide-ranging readings and apparatus that help students explore and understand their experiences in higher education.

The organization of *Composing Knowledge* encourages students to reflect on writing their way into — and beyond — a community. Chapters One and Two, "Joining the Conversation," and "Inventing the University," take up the challenge faced by so many students, even the best: that of joining a conversation where that very conversation is precisely what "invents" a university. Chapter Three, "Persuading Each Other," takes a closer look at those conversations and their hidden (and often perplexing) discursive moves. The remaining chapters bring into the classroom current discussions that are changing the ways we learn and write in communities: Chapter Four, "Engagements," encourages discussions about our collaborative way of working; Chapter Five, "(En)gendering Knowledge," examines issues surrounding gender and knowing; Chapter Six, "Learning Technology," takes on debates about technology as it shapes our learning and writing; and Chapter Seven, "Seeing and Believing," explores new interest in visual rhetoric.

Composing Knowledge supports fruitful classroom instruction in a number of distinctive ways:

- It helps students to master the habits of reflective thinking, active reading, and critical writing essential to success in college and professional life.
- It offers our best current thinking on writing and learning in communities — communities that are themselves organized through language.
- It addresses contemporary issues that are reshaping the writing and learning we do in those communities.
- It encourages students to reflect on ways of knowing from across the curriculum, and to connect those ways to broader issues of literacy and community.
- It lends relevance to the writing classroom by having students develop writing projects that take them "into the field" to reflect on and respond to their own situated learning and writing experiences.
- It links the college writing classroom to professional and civic life by having students write in genres that extend beyond the academic essay to include letters, editorials, and proposals.

Provocative Readings from Experts and Insiders

The readings in *Composing Knowledge* differ in some respects from standard anthology fare. Open most any composition reader, and you are likely to find selections driven by topical concerns. The text operates on a "field coverage" principle, with essays on this or that topic, from one or another discipline or area of life. Such anthologies reinforce the assumption, common in other courses, that knowledge is a given, that what students consume is a bundle of views or information on certain topics. Even controversy tends to come prepackaged as a static set of opposing opinions on a given subject.

The readings in *Composing Knowledge* are driven by a different concern: open questions grounded in the lived learning experience of students as they find their way in new communities. Moreover, the readings are not meant to be consumed but rather engaged. Each invites reflection, interaction, and response — that is, each invites the work of readers. The readings are also provocations in that they ask students to test insights in and through their own writing and learning experiences.

The questions that drive *Composing Knowledge* are explored in essays that vary in both style and difficulty. Each section opens with short, accessible — and often personal — essays and then moves to essays of greater length, complexity, and range. Many of the authors, renowned writers and prominent intellectuals, will be welcomingly familiar: Amy Tan, Stephen Jay Gould, George Orwell, Katha Pollitt, Jared Diamond, Malcolm Gladwell, Susan Sontag, and Neil Postman, to name but a few. Others, less likely to be known to students, will help them participate in discussions now shaping the academy: Mary Louise Pratt, Deborah Tannen, bell hooks, Gerald Graff, Paulo Freire, Louis Menand, Mike Rose, George Lakoff, Kenneth A. Bruffee, Thomas S. Kuhn, and Jane Tompkins. Still others will be our own voices, the voices of our colleagues in rhetoric and composition, who broach issues of compelling interest and relevance to undergraduates themselves: Nancy Sommers, David Bartholomae, Wayne C. Booth, Lisa Ede, Andrea Lunsford, Charles Bazerman, David Russell, Gregory G. Colomb, and Joseph Williams. All too often withheld from the very students taking our courses, these voices remind students that our own knowledge in and of composition is, like their own, always constructed, always "composed," and provide a uniquely informed perspective on the way knowledge is produced in the writing classroom.

Flexible Organization

Composing Knowledge is designed to assist you in composing your own course. Because each of the seven chapters is made up of two smaller units of readings, for a total of fourteen sets, the book is eminently adaptable. Students might be asked to sample several essays from each unit, or to delve into several chapters in depth, or to link sets of readings in novel ways. This flexible text is thus meant to serve the several ways you might organize your own course:

- **Courses that focus on critical reading** will find a range of selections, some quite challenging, that encourage students to read both with and against the grain of the text. The book's apparatus supports this focus through headnotes, questions and short assignments, and longer writing projects that help students interact with texts on several levels and in several ways.
- **Courses that focus on academic writing** will find a wide array of readings (many of which are documented) that exemplify or discuss the

multifaceted nature of academic writing. The book's own writing instruction supports this focus with questions, short assignments, and writing projects that address those skills critical to academic writing, among them defining, summarizing, analyzing, and arguing.

- **Courses that include extensive research and writing projects** will find a host of innovative project ideas that connect readings with ethnographic fieldwork that has students exploring engaging issues drawn from their own situated learning and writing experiences.
- **Courses that focus on writing across the curriculum** will find a wide range of readings that set academic, professional, and civic issues in the context of disciplinary communities. Questions associated with the readings and a host of writing projects encourage students to develop the kinds of documents that speak to various disciplines and to professional and civic audiences, among them letters and memos, proposals, reports, executive summaries, newsletters, commentaries, and reviews.

Rich Editorial Apparatus

A number of editorial and pedagogical features complement the readings themselves, supporting their effective use in writing classrooms. These features help you compose a classroom that encourages critical reading and engaged discussion, leading to innovative writing projects. They include:

A CHAPTER-LONG GENERAL INTRODUCTION. The general introduction to *Composing Knowledge* establishes the rhetorical context for the book and the student's own work. The first of three parts in the introduction acquaints students with the several ways in which literacy, community, and inquiry intersect. It reveals how contested those terms are and makes the case why exploring those intersections matters in their development as mature writers. The second section helps students view the readings themselves and their critical engagement with them as conversations that occur in a community. It outlines specific strategies (from previewing and annotating to uncovering argumentative structure) that help students both honor and challenge texts as they work with the readings in the collaborative setting of the writing classroom. The final section helps students see their own lived experience in academic and civic communities as an important dimension of this collection. It introduces the concept of writing projects as "fieldwork" and offers specific "how to" strategies for conducting various kinds of fieldwork projects. This work connects the readings with students' own sustained reflection on how they compose—and are composed by—writing and learning in the academy and beyond.

INTRODUCTIONS TO EACH UNIT OF READINGS. For each of the fourteen units of readings, a short introduction sets the stage for the various concerns raised in and by the selections.

PREWRITING ACTIVITIES. Each unit introduction is followed by a group of questions under the heading "Reflecting on Prior Knowledge." Designed to encourage prewriting activities, the questions remind students that they do not come to the readings "cold"; their own experiences in and out of college have been shaped by the very issues they will soon engage in the readings.

HEADNOTES. Contextual information prior to each selection introduces the readers to the author and places the reading as a contribution to an ongoing conversation.

WRITING ON READINGS. Two sets of questions and writing assignments follow each reading selection, offering an opportunity to build rhetorically informed writing instruction into the students' engagement with the readings. The first set of questions and short assignments, "Working with the Text," encourages students to uncover core issues and arguments in ways that prepare them for a closer second reading. The second set of questions and short assignments, "From Text to Field," raises connections and intersections with other texts in the collection and with contemporary issues on campus and in the community. This second set of activities often prepares the ground for the more extensive "Into the Field: Options for Writing Projects."

FIELDWORK PROJECTS. These assignments, titled "Into the Field: Options for Writing Projects," are located at the end of each of the fourteen units of readings. Here, students are encouraged to engage in their own fieldwork. Approximately ten to twelve questions and scenarios at the end of each chapter prompt students to develop more extended writing projects that link the issues raised in the readings with their own experience in academic and civic communities.

Often drawing on local documents and students' own close observation, these options for writing projects have students reflect on courses and curricula, teaching and learning, syllabi and assignments, disciplines and departments, classroom and workplace cultures. Students might examine their own required curriculum to uncover the assumptions that drive how their college constructs their education. Or they might analyze recruiting and admissions materials from their own and other colleges to analyze what images they construct of college living and learning.

You might think of the various "Into the Field" options as helping students to pursue their own ethnographic projects, to explore their college, their newly chosen discipline, and their immediate community as an ethnographer might explore an unfamiliar and fascinating culture.

RESOURCES FOR TEACHING *COMPOSING KNOWLEDGE*. This instructor's manual includes a sample syllabus and teaching tips for each of the four kinds of courses noted above. Entries for each of the readings provide guidance and anticipate possible classroom issues.

COMPANION WEB SITE. Located at bedfordstmartins.com/composingknowledge, the site provides research links for each unit in *Composing Knowledge*, helping students to make connections among the text, their academic and personal lives, and issues in the world at large.

Acknowledgments

This book would not have seen the light of day were it not for the sustained interest, friendly persistence, and Job-like patience of John Sullivan, development editor at Bedford/St. Martin's. He continued to support the project, even when personal and professional lives intervened (everything from hand surgery to heavy administrative duties as I helped establish a new Program for Writing and Rhetoric on our campus). His insightful and creative suggestions and his attention to detail have made this a far better book than I could have produced on my own.

I would also like to thank others at Bedford/St. Martin's who believed in and worked on *Composing Knowledge*, in particular Jimmy Fleming, humanities specialist, who signed the project; Joan Feinberg, president; Chuck Christensen, president emeritus; Denise Wydra, editorial director; Karen Henry, editor in chief; Steve Scipione, executive editor; and Jennifer Lyford, editorial assistant, who helped during its development; Kendra LeFleur, production editor, and Elizabeth Schaaf, managing editor, who saw the book through production; Martha Friedman and Naomi Kornhauser, for handling art permissions; Sandy Schechter and Diane Kraut, for clearing text permission; and Karita dos Santos, marketing manager.

I would also like to thank those reviewers who examined portions of the manuscript and provided helpful feedback on it: Valerie Balester, Texas A&M; William A. Covino, Florida Atlantic University; Van Hillard, Duke University; Roxanne Mountford, University of Arizona; Christine Murray, University of Texas, Arlington; and Thomas A. Wallis, North Carolina State University. I am also grateful to those reviewers who have chosen to remain anonymous.

The support and interest of my colleagues in the Program for Writing and Rhetoric at the University of Colorado at Boulder have enriched me intellectually and sustained me personally, and thus served, in ways too numerous to mention, as midwives for this book. I owe a special debt of gratitude to Paula Wenger, whose invaluable assistance on headnotes and text questions kept the project moving forward when administrative duties threatened to overwhelm me. Faculty and graduate students in a campuswide Rhetoric Workshop offered a forum for scholarly discussion and writing that enriched the conception and pedagogy of this book. Administrators on campus helped support this project through their renewed commitment to writing and rhetoric as cornerstones for educational excellence.

First and last, I owe an enormous debt to my students over the years. Their spirited discussion, insightful comments, and engaged writing have taught me even as I was teaching them. Born in the classroom, not the private study, this book is as much theirs as mine. My thanks to you all.

Thus, the history of my debts becomes the tale of my good fortune. Nowhere more so than at home. Andrea has been at once my most perceptive reader and my unfailing muse. Stefan and Lara have come to share my passion for ideas and language, growing inch by inch as this book grew chapter by chapter.

CONTENTS

1. Joining the Conversation   *33*

2. Inventing the University   *147*

sacrosanct, a demilitarized zone; to whom margins, with their white blanketed space, whisper 'Don't tread on me.'"

5. (En)gendering Knowledge   *491*

"Fascinated and excited, tens of millions of Americans stared at their screens, sharing the experience of these missiles and bombs unerringly guided by the wonders of American technology to a target identified by a narrator as an important military installation. The generation raised in video arcades and on Nintendo could hardly be more satisfied."

"The globalization of terror is something new. It goes hand in hand with the globalization of the media. The creation of new media technology has created a public space in which political actors may perform: terrorists are some of the actors who can now play on a global stage."

CONTENTS BY THEMES AND DISCIPLINES

DISCOURSE CONVENTIONS

EDUCATION

GENDER STUDIES AND RHETORICS OF DIFFERENCE

LANGUAGE AND LITERACY

MEDIA AND TECHNOLOGY

COMPOSING KNOWLEDGE
Readings for College Writers

INTRODUCTION

> Imagine that you enter a parlor. You come late. When you arrive, others have long preceded you, and they are engaged in a heated discussion, a discussion too heated for them to pause and tell you exactly what it is about. In fact, the discussion had already begun long before any of them got there, so no one present is qualified to retrace all the steps that had gone before. You listen for a while, until you decide that you have caught the tenor of the argument; then you put in your oar. Someone answers; you answer him; another comes to your defense; another aligns himself against you. . . . However, the discussion is interminable. The hour grows late, you must depart. And you do depart, with the discussion still vigorously in progress.
>
> — KENNETH BURKE, *The Philosophy of Literary Form*

Knowing and Composing

When you enter the university, or enter advanced course work in your major, you are entering the sort of parlor that Kenneth Burke describes. While the conversation can certainly be engaging, and the ideas stimulating, the experience of entering a new setting can be quite unsettling. Who are these folks who are deep in conversation, and what are they getting so worked up about? On what basis are they taking sides? What does it take to join the conversation and become one of "them"? And what are the "moves" involved in having a voice in the conversation and in having that voice heard?

We would do well to think of the university as a kind of Burkean parlor or rather a set of overlapping parlors, for no one parlor could ever be sufficient to capture all of the conversations that go on in various disciplines or on campus. Although we may think of a college or university as a collection of buildings, or our own education as a list of courses completed or of expertise gained, the conversational metaphor is actually quite apt. The university is a house of argument. The university represents an ongoing conversation about questions that are genuinely at issue. An essential part of your college education is not just learning facts but also learning how to make sense of and join that conversation—a conversation that is not limited to classrooms but also extends to larger civic spaces. This book, and the writing course you are taking, can play a helpful role in that process.

If we look more closely at Burke's parlor, we find three concerns in play. Those three concerns, and the various intersections among them, inform the readings in the chapters that lie ahead. By exploring the intersections of literacy, community, and inquiry, this collection can help you enter the many conversations of academic and civic life.

LITERACY. Although Burke's description of the parlor foregrounds conversation, we can hardly imagine that this conversation could be effective without reading and writing—without, in short, literacy. Indeed, conversation itself—the give and take among various voices—becomes a way of better understanding how and why we read and write. Yet literacy is a vexed concept. Does Burke's parlor, and your own first attempts to participate in it, presume the mere ability to read and write (that is, functional literacy) or some kind of critical engagement or critical literacy?

COMMUNITY. On a first reading, Burke's description of parlor conversation might suggest that those in the room form a cohesive, homogeneous community. But the more we look about in that parlor, the more fraught that term *community* becomes. The community of your own writing class may be a case in point. Although community may first seem a warm and fuzzy concept, membership also implies exclusion. Who is silenced in Burke's parlor? Who decides when and whether you can "put in your oar"? And how do the conversations in one parlor intersect with those in the next room?

INQUIRY. Heated conversation seems to be the norm in Burke's parlor, yet participants seem to be doing more than *having* an argument. They are *making* arguments. What does that distinction mean for your own reading and writing? How do you know how to participate if no one ever pauses and shows you the hidden moves needed to foster and support genuine inquiry and to develop and shape an argument?

Composing Knowledge locates you at the crossroads of these three contested concepts, most especially at the site of your own practice. The readings in this collection help you reflect on your own situated writing and learning experiences. Those readings, and above all your own writing, suggest that knowledge doesn't come prepackaged. It's not something to consume and then regurgitate. *Knowledge is composed.* Knowledge is shaped by language and by communities of knowers that organize themselves through language. And as we work together to explore this notion, we will also uncover *knowledge that can help you compose.*

But first, let's consider a bit more closely the three contested terms at play in Burke's parlor and how they intersect with each other and with your own writing and reading experiences in college, the site of our practice.

Literacy

When my son Stefan entered kindergarten and began to engage writing and reading in a school setting, he took a greater interest in my own work. "What do you do at the university?" he asked one day. "I teach writing," I replied. Flush with the self-confidence that only a precocious kindergartner can have, he offered, "I can do that!" "Well, it's a bit more complicated," I said. He paused, and then his eyes grew large. "Oh, you mean cursive!"

Writing and reading are indeed complicated acts, and at the university we have no foolproof Palmer Method for learning the strokes. Yet the tendency to reduce the advanced literacy needed for college work back to a basic mechanical skill—the ability to read and write—persists to this day. Some still presume, for example, that a first-year writing course is but a prelude to the real intellectual work of college.

Literacy has traditionally been seen as a neutral, mechanical skill, an ability one picks up, much like riding a bike, that requires little further development or nuanced application. No wonder more than a few students chafe at college writing courses, especially when they are required. Standard definitions of *literacy* tend to stress this focus on basic competence, implying that literacy is a rather unproblematic term and that it can be easily measured—and just as easily learned or taught. But even as levels of literacy have changed over the centuries, the focus on measurement and competence persists. This perception is reinforced with each election cycle, when we hear cries that our country is in the midst of a "literacy crisis." Johnny, we are told, cannot read. And if schools haven't done the job, college must step in to remediate.

College writing courses suffer from this legacy, from definitions of literacy that are themselves far too literal—and remedial. That needn't be the case. Through this book, and through your collaboration with fellow readers and writers in class, I hope you will begin to explore—and question—what it means to read and write in the Burkean parlors of your college or university.

One move that can help you get under way is to look beyond writing and reading as merely individual or private acts. That is, literacy sheds light on how individual acts of writing are connected to larger cultural, historical, social, and political systems. Paulo Freire, the Brazilian educator who spurred much of the discussion of literacy in this century, put it this way: "Reading the word" cannot be separated from "reading the world." If literacy involves reading the world, then we need to look beyond mere individual competence in encoding and decoding texts. Far from being a merely personal matter, literacy involves cultural contexts. These cultural contexts are often multiple and can overlap or even become fraught with tensions.

One such context is the culture of the university itself. By familiarizing students with academic discourse, professors seek to help students understand and participate in the conversations that shape the university. The goal here is to "learn the language" and master the secret handshake of this community. Yet the term *academic literacy* remains highly contested even inside the ivory tower. How broadly or narrowly can or should one define academic writing? Can a focus on academic writing draw on your own experiences beyond the academy and on other avenues for literacy development, such as civic discourse or home and community discourse? How can one accommodate disciplinary differences in academic writing? And does an interest in socializing you to academic literacy amount at some point to exerting undue influence on or authority over you?

Asking such questions requires not just literacy in the usual sense but a "critical literacy," one that helps you become aware of how authority and power work in and through language. Literacy is inherently tied to membership and belonging, with all their implications regarding exclusion and access. To be critical of the heated discussions in Burke's parlor, one still has to get inside the door and join the conversation.

Traditional literacy models all too often assume a print culture—the culture of the book—that is seen in isolation from broader and alternative experiences with literacy. Recent advances in electronic communication, for example, raise a host of questions about how the supposed primacy of the written word is mediated by, or at times supplanted by, multimedia environments. Computers and the Web have changed in some fundamental ways how we read, write, and circulate the written word—and how such words interact with the world of images. We need today a "cyberliteracy" that encourages critical reflection on the role of technology in literacy, just as that same critical reflection is needed in discussions of traditional print literacy.

In your own writing class, and in other classes across campus, you will find invoked, directly or perhaps subtly, one or more of these competing and contested definitions of *literacy*. This book and especially your own literate activities in this and other courses offer an opportunity to question those definitions yourself. Whatever consequences literacy brings will be the result of the social practices with which it is associated. Those social practices have to do with the nitty gritty of your own situated writing, reading, and learning experiences. In short, *what literacy does to you depends on what you do with literacy*. That is the challenge afforded in and through this book.

For Writing and Discussion

During the course of one day, inventory your own literacy practices. In other words, create a "literacy log." What do you count as literacy, and what do others seem to value? What various (and perhaps competing) definitions of *literacy* are implied in your log?

Community

Let's slip once again into Burke's parlor. The heated discussion that goes on in the parlor can help us distinguish several elements of that context. We have, of course, the speakers or writers. And once we have caught the tenor of the arguments in play, we can "put in [our] oar" and join that discussion. We also have an audience: those to whom the speakers address their comments. As the conversation evolves, they will, in turn, take up their own roles as speakers. And we have the forum itself, the parlor, the place or context for this discussion. Several general terms have been used to describe this constellation of elements: speech community, interpretive community, or, perhaps best for our purposes, *discourse community*. By that term we mean the site or social group that is shaped and defined by shared assumptions about communicative practices such as speaking or writing. The boundaries and character of that site or group are set by those communicative practices, along with the shared norms and values of its members.

Discourse communities are not static. Recall that at some point every participant in Burke's parlor slips in and slips out. But the conversation continues — and evolves. The norms or ground rules for that discussion are not set once and for all but take shape in and through the conversation. Moreover, discourse communities are not exclusive. We can belong to several such communities simultaneously, and they can overlap. Discourse communities can be relatively local, such as the discourse community of your writing classroom or the English department on your campus or the corporate office down the road. In such communities, the day-to-day contact of its members helps shape shared norms of behavior and habits of thought. But discourse communities can also be much more global, as in the worldwide community of physicists who study subatomic particles. These participants may never actually meet everyone in the community, but that community is held together through a commitment to a shared intellectual enterprise and through a set of common expectations and methods. Recent advances in electronic communication make virtual communities more real by the day. The term *discourse community* reminds us that society is held together by discourse and that, in turn, discourse has a social dimension.

Implicit in all this talk about community is a warm, comforting sense of like-mindedness. Indeed, *community* is one of the very few terms that does not seem to have any negative connotations. Just think of all the instances in which this term has come up in your life: community center, campus community, community of friends, community fund-raiser, community values. The list can go on, but what is common among these phrases is a sense of homogeneity, a sense of cohesiveness, of shared values and purposes. For this reason, community is a seductive and powerful concept. Hear it mentioned and it tugs at you. And for that very reason, it is a concept that we ought to interrogate.

The discourse communities in which we participate are often invisible or transparent to us, so second nature do they become. Only when we are thrust into a new setting do such communities become opaque and puzzling. Consider the disorienting first few weeks on your college campus, for example, or that difficult course in your new academic major. Although the term *community* would have us believe that everybody is of like mind, that everybody lives in a shared community, the concept becomes a bit problematic when we notice just how many communities we participate in and how they overlap and conflict.

Because of its relatively small size, your own writing class may seem to offer your best shot at a like-minded, cohesive academic community. Or so it might seem. Look about you, and it doesn't take long for the internal tensions to emerge. You and your classmates have been thrown together in one room, or parlor, through course requirements and the luck of academic scheduling. As the term progresses, many of you will surely become friends, perhaps close friends. Even so, membership in this classroom community becomes problematic. In your classroom dealings, who is included, and who may be subtly excluded? What counts as authority and expertise in this setting? What is foregrounded in the conversation, and what are the taboos, the things you cannot speak about openly? What kind of social ethos or character is it best to adopt? Who are the insiders and the outsiders? And what are the subtle and not so subtle forms of academic and social gatekeeping? Much of your work in the writing classroom will surely call upon good-spirited collaboration, the sort of cooperation that is essential when writers share work in progress. Even so, these sorts of questions alert us to an aspect of community that is often hidden beneath the more public focus on consensus and shared norms. Community can also be a site where competing beliefs intersect and come into conflict.

Our brief reflection on community in the writing classroom can point us to some general observations about this strange academic culture in which you are trying to find your way. Whether we think of the university as one monolithic community or as a "multiversity," a group of somewhat fragmented disciplinary communities, that community is not just about subject matter. True, we often think of the university as a collection of subject-matter communities, with biology here, sociology across the way, and engineering over on the other side of campus. But beneath these tidy, received distinctions, we can begin to see how language practices define the activities of social groups, including disciplines.

As a venue for overlapping (and sometimes competing) language practices, the university is really a stage for various styles of interacting with questions, claims, and evidence. It offers a kaleidoscope of manifestations of authority and expertise, each manifestation dependent on specific traditions or ways of knowing. Knowledge appears less and less to be a given, something you merely consume. Linguistic formations drive and direct the organization and production of knowledge. Seen in this light, your college education shouldn't end with mastering the facts in this or that course. Your college education is just as much about figuring out Burke's parlor, about knowing how to join the heated conversations themselves. Knowledge emerges as something composed — something that you yourself can and must compose.

As you try to orient yourself to this new setting, you may face pressure (from the institution, from your instructors, and perhaps from your parents or peers) to take up and make your own the voice of the academy. You want to talk the talk but not if it becomes an unnatural act of ventriloquism. You want to appropriate new ways of writing and thinking but without becoming appropriated by the university. The challenge is how to find new aspects of yourself without losing yourself — to try on new voices without losing your voice.

This book offers a way to negotiate these competing claims as you enter the Burkean parlor that is the university. In the chapters that follow, you will read and write about the very community you find yourself in, with all its contradictions and tensions. (And if you haven't noticed yet, it can be a very strange community.) In a sense, you will explore this community as if you were an ethnographer trying to figure out the culture on some South Seas island. With this critical and purposeful awareness of community, and of the ways literate practices shape community, this book and your writing course can also serve as an introduction to college learning. Welcome to University 101.

For Writing and Discussion

Team up with one or two other members of your writing class and exchange your perceptions about what makes a community in this and other classes. How and why might your perceptions of community differ from those of your classmates? Explore both the "seams" and the "ruptures" that lie along the borders between, and even within, communities.

Inquiry

At heart, inquiry is a process of asking questions and trying out answers. The "heated conversations" in the Burkean parlor might first give the impression that participants are *having* arguments. But to be true to the process of inquiry, they must be *making* arguments — that is, crafting both questions and answers in ways that have us test and revise our ideas. If, in the spirit of Burke's parlor, we might see the university as a house of argument, inquiry lies at its center. For this very reason, surely all of your professors will exhort you to think critically. Writing instructors especially will press you at each turn, for the great virtue of writing is that it makes thinking visible.

If critical thinking is the capacity to see relationships methodically, it is little wonder that teachers have sought a way to teach that kind of seeing. For some years, the focus was on developing critical thinking through skills that could be objectified, codified, and easily taught. Yet a series of "steps" or measurable subskills had the effect of making critical thinking into a mechanical calculus. It also translated critical thinking into the pursuit of "true" knowledge, of stable if not eternal truths that remain unsullied by the uncertainty around us. If mention of critical thinking or inquiry makes your eyes glaze over, you are experiencing firsthand the legacy of making thinking into some abstract skill, remote from your immediate writing, reading, and learning, remote from your daily life, your communities, your language.

Composing Knowledge invites you, by contrast, to ground inquiry in literacy and community. Your own knowledge is "composed" through language and through the conversations that shape and maintain your communities. These conversations often have to do not with absolute truth or verifiable fact but with knowledge that is to some degree contingent, uncertain, rooted in particular contexts and in the transactions we have with others. Knowledge becomes something that is not "out there" in the material and social world, just as it is not "in here" in the personal or private world of the individual. It emerges only through the interactions among material, social, and personal worlds. The vehicle for that interaction is rhetoric, the available means of persuasion that we find as we converse in and among communities.

Especially when linked to inquiry, such conversations should not be viewed as a "shouting match" or a "debate" whose purpose is to "win" by "pounding the opposition into the ground." These characterizations have in common a rather simplistic confrontational understanding of argument. That's not to say that argument doesn't involve some degree of conflict or the presence of a skeptical audience. Yet if the university is a house of argument, we should argue about questions at issue in ways that offer the best possible response to shared concerns, with reasons that will prompt our audience to consider, accept, and act on our claims. In this sense, argument has an inherently social dimension, one grounded in belief and assent. Claims are not merely *claims that* something is so but rather *claims on* us and on our fellow citizens to believe that something is so.

To garner that belief, that assent, we had best not be too hasty to write from preconceived positions. If writing is an avenue for making thinking visible, accessible, and revisable, we should not just believe and defend but also ask and inquire. If our work in the university is about reaching conclusions, we need to make and defend those conclusions in ways that permit us, throughout, to test and revise them. We also need to make them in ways that speak to the communities (disciplinary and otherwise) in which we find ourselves. Your education in college consists not just of the facts you learn about certain subjects but also of the conversations you join. That is, your education is not just topical; it is also rhetorical.

Conversations, however, are inherently unstable and uncertain, making inquiry a risky business. It's not so much that you may be proven wrong (although that possibility is always there). Rather, it's that you—and your positions—must certainly grow and evolve. The test of true inquiry is that it doesn't stop, just as the heated conversations in Burke's parlor precede us and continue long after we are gone. Inquiry grounded in literacy and community, in language and conversation, can meet this test. After all, as Burke's parlor suggests, good argument and good inquiry have all the virtues of good conversation.

Composing Knowledge seeks to support your conversations by having you explore your own situated writing, reading, and learning experiences. The readings in the chapters, and the fieldwork they can launch, are offered as provocations and opportunities.

For Writing and Discussion

At the opening of every term, professors usually offer some statements about the importance of inquiry, critical thinking, or argument in their courses. Catalog a few of these statements—garnered from classroom lectures or conversations, assignment sheets, and syllabi—and share them with your classmates. What commonalities do you detect? To what extent do expectations differ among the disciplines?

Reading the Conversation

To enter and take an active role in Burke's parlor, or in the conversations on your campus and in your discipline, you'll need to figure out the implicit, unstated rules for how people go about talking and arguing. In college, as in the professional world, much of this conversation occurs in and through written texts. Although there are surely general patterns or guidelines to academic conversations, you'll need to alert yourself to the subtle but telling differences between how conversation partners handle themselves in different contexts or disciplinary spaces. Beyond the obvious differences in topic, conversations in the science parlor proceed in a slightly different way than those in the humanities parlor. All the more reason, then, that you read the conversation before you step into it. "Reading the conversation" means reading texts in what might be new and unfamiliar ways.

As you enter college or your particular major, you already have a long and rich reading life behind you. What's more, you are already familiar with various kinds of reading. There's beach reading, of course, where you delight in the page-turner. And you have also become well practiced in what we might call sponge reading: soaking up as much information as you can prior to a test. You've become adept at focused reading, as when you study a bus schedule for the exact information you need. And of course you have often skimmed reading material, as when you flip through a magazine to find an article that interests you.

Yet for all of the variety in your reading habits, they tend to focus on using or consuming texts. The academic conversations you are now entering into require something more: savvy reading, rhetorical reading. You'll need to read texts *as* conversations, noting not just what is being said but also how and why the conversation proceeds as it does.

Savvy Reading, Rhetorical Reading

Academic reading distinguishes itself not only by the sheer volume and difficulty of the texts but also by the expectations that accompany reading tasks and assignments. You've braced yourself for a lot of reading, and difficult reading it will be, but what may be unexpected is that you'll need to read in new and different ways.

Nearly all of the reading you do for research and for course work requires that you work simultaneously at two levels. On one level, the level you are probably most familiar with, you'll need to read for content. We can think of this kind of knowledge as *conceptual knowledge*. Here, your focus is on understanding terms, concepts, and formulas—the body of knowledge itself. This kind of reading focuses on the mastery of domain content, on the facts of the discipline. Most introductory textbooks for a discipline work primarily at this level.

But a good deal of academic reading also requires you to work at a second level. Here, your focus is not only on the body of knowledge but also on how bodies of knowers—people in that discipline—use this body of knowledge to pose new questions or to apply their expertise to new problems. We might think of this second kind of knowledge as *procedural knowledge*. Reading at this second level helps you to understand disciplinary "ways of knowing"— how people in a disciplinary community wrap their minds around problems. You are not only learning *what* biologists or sociologists know but also *how* biologists or sociologists think—not just *what* experts say in texts but *how* experts do their work in and through texts and *why* they construct their texts as they do. To become a savvy academic reader means reading rhetorically, with an eye to purpose and persuasion. It means reading not just for the "what" but also for the "how" and the "why." It means reading in two dimensions at once.

To enter Burke's parlor as a fully participating member, you need to know the conversational and textual "moves." The best way to become attuned to those moves and to begin to make them your own is to understand reading as a conversation—a conversation that you will join. Although the mute and static words on the printed page might first give you quite a different impression, reading is in fact a layered and dynamic exchange.

The first and most immediate layer lies in your interaction with the text itself. It's tempting to presume that the process of reading black marks on a white page is entirely passive or that it is a one-way process of decoding. But even as you seem to be consuming or devouring a text, you are also constructing a mental model of the text and its meaning. We tend to think of composing a text as something that the author does, but as a reader you are also sharing in that act of composition. In reading a text, you are composing a reading of the text. You are bringing your understanding and contextual awareness to the text in order to construct its meaning. Among the many joys of reading is that the words on the page may prompt you to make private associations, based on your own individual experiences. However, as a rhetorical reader, you must focus, first and foremost, on the public meaning of a text — a meaning that must be accessible to and shared by many readers, based on the text you have in common. Even as you compose a reading of the text, you need to be able to test and defend that reading within and before a community of readers.

What also makes reading such a layered and dynamic exchange is that the text you have in front of you is the result of the author's choices. Those choices are driven by the author's purposes and are shaped by the rhetorical context in which he or she writes. To read a text is, then, to read the rhetorical context in which the text was first written and read. As you compose your reading of a text, you'll need to understand and respect the potential difference between the author's purposes for writing and your purposes for reading. When you read a text, you find yourself in and responding to a rhetorical situation that may not be identical to the one in which the author wrote. This double focus on the author's situation and your own situation is part of what makes academic reading both challenging and engaging.

A third layer in the dynamic exchange has to do with the text's place in a larger conversation of texts. The author's voice is invariably calling upon, engaging, and responding to a variety of voices. Although words on a page may give the impression of a monologue, reading in a savvy, rhetorical fashion means picking up on the various clues about the hidden conversation that is going on. These clues can be found in the way a text may quote or reference other authors or previous works or even in the way a text may make subtle allusions to history or culture. A rhetorical reading means appreciating a text's place in and use of a web of texts. Given your many years of schooling, you may be accustomed to thinking of references in a text as an author's way of signaling his or her debt and thus of avoiding plagiarism. But that is only part of the complex ways references to texts and authors are deployed. Writers cite other authors to convince us that their reading is broad and current; they signal alliances and disagreements; they establish the problem or identify the research gap they are filling; they frame issues and contending positions; they engage skeptical questions and counterarguments; and they marshal support and credibility for their own position. Savvy reading enables you to understand how authors make rhetorical use of this larger web of texts.

Reading for the conversation has its real payoff in preparing you to join that conversation—to extend it, disagree with it, or take it in new directions. Reading becomes a prelude to and an invitation for your own writing. Having paid attention to the rhetoric of reading, you are now in a much better position to write in rhetorically effective ways for other readers. Your own purposes, and the rhetorical situation in which you write, may well be quite different from those of the authors whom you have read. But your reflection on your own reading process and on the nature of the conversation you are joining will surely make your contributions all the more valuable.

For Writing and Discussion

Working in small groups, discuss your prior reading life and the training (or lack of training) you have had in academic reading. What misconceptions, old habits, fears, or worries seem to plague your reading life in college?

Dialogue, Argument, Collaboration

To develop and apply specific strategies for reading rhetorically, let's consider in some detail how you might approach one particular text. Deborah Tannen's short article "Agonism in the Academy: Surviving Higher Learning's Argument Culture" provides an interesting opportunity, in that the author is discussing her views on the kinds of conversations students and faculty have in academic settings. So, not only will we be practicing how to read Tannen's text as a kind of conversation, but we will also be considering Tannen's views on academic conversations.

It's tempting to start reading by . . . well, starting to read the text's first paragraph. But in the very first moments when we come upon and enter a text, we are making crucial—if sometimes unconscious—decisions about our reading strategies. The more we can become conscious of and reflect on these first moments, the more likely it is that we can become savvy rhetorical readers. Five strategies are crucial in these early moments.

DEVELOP A CONTEXT FOR YOUR READING BY LOOKING FOR TEXTUAL CUES. Savvy readers don't dive into their reading without first surveying the rhetorical landscape. Where was the article published, and when? Tannen's piece first appeared in March of 2000 in the *Chronicle of Higher Education*, a weekly newspaper whose audience is college faculty and administrators. Who is the author? With a quick glance you should try to identify who the author is (Deborah Tannen) and to locate any information about the author (the brief note at the end of the article identifies her as a professor at Georgetown University and the author of a book titled *The Argument Culture*). The most important cue is perhaps the article's title. Because titles often signal the focus or even the central claim of a text, you can use titles to help shape your reading process and to make early predictions about the text's meaning. In the case of Tannen's article, you know that she will address "argument culture" and that it is something one must "survive." Even at this early stage, before reading that first paragraph, you can begin developing questions that can guide your inquiry. What, for example, does *agonism* mean? By beginning to survey the rhetorical context of the text, you are able to call upon and better utilize whatever background or prior knowledge you may have.

A second strategy follows from the first. Having glanced at the text and considered where it was published, you already have some important clues about the kind of text it is—its *genre*—and thus the general kind of reading required.

LINK YOUR READING STRATEGY TO THE GENRE OF THE TEXT. Although we tend to think of genre as the outward appearance of a text (poems and novels and academic articles do look a bit different, after all), genre is actually an important indicator of how readers and writers carry on their conversations. Before diving in to read sentence after sentence, you'll want to consider how the structure and the style of the piece, and what use it makes of evidence or citations, offer guidance on ways the selection is best read. For example, Tannen's article is relatively short and offers no footnotes or bibliography. It was published in a newspaper about higher education that often presents opinion pieces or short, nontechnical articles that capture the leading ideas of a longer work or book. By understanding its genre, you can adapt your reading strategies appropriately. In this case, you can expect that the article will try to interest and address a fairly wide academic audience with arguments drawn from a more detailed study. In your college and professional career, you will encounter any number of different textual genres, from literary analysis to scientific research articles, each with its own conventions, its own distinctive conversational handshake.

How, then, should you read Tannen's article? It all depends on your immediate purpose in reading. And thus we come to a third strategy.

UNDERSTAND AND ADAPT YOUR READING STRATEGY IN LIGHT OF YOUR OWN CHANGING PURPOSES. Your purposes and goals for reading any text can vary, from a quick skim to determine your interest in reading further to a moderately paced reading to understand the gist of the argument to a detailed study of the text in preparation for your writing. Because no one style of reading can meet very different goals, you'll want to become accustomed to rereading material. Rereading doesn't mean that you somehow didn't "get" the article. It means that what you did get on a first reading can now prepare you to read again in a somewhat new fashion, with different and more specific goals and questions in mind. Savvy readers are readers who adapt.

Because the words on the page are your crucial resource for composing a reading of the text, it's important to stay close to those words. Here is a further strategy.

WORK WITH (AND ON) THE PAGE BY ANNOTATING YOUR TEXT. Annotating a text with your notes, comments, and queries is a way to make the text your own, to talk back to the text even as it talks to you. For a text to make an impression on us, it is often helpful to make an impression (literally) on the text. (If you are working from a library copy, you will of course need to keep the text clean and record your annotations in a reading notebook.) Annotations are a way to focus your attention, to probe and question, and to record the evolution of your reading of the text over time. You'll need to adopt your own annotation style, but be sure that your annotations are helpful and informative for future readings. Simple underlining, especially of whole passages, may not tell you enough when you return to the text. Likewise, broad swatches of text highlighted in some neon color may look impressive but may do little to enlighten you about the text or your own response to it. When annotating, focus on some of the following: key or unfamiliar terms and concepts, formulations of the issue, statements of purpose, indications about the organization or structure of the text or its line of reasoning, connections among ideas, and, of course, questions about or objections to the author's views.

In general, annotations, like the reading process itself, should reflect the two basic movements or rhythms of any conversation: We both listen and respond.

BALANCE SYMPATHETIC LISTENING TO THE TEXT WITH SKEPTICAL QUESTIONING OF THE TEXT. Annotations can help you read both with and against the grain of the text. They can prompt you to listen attentively as you seek to understand the text. In turn, annotations can help you interrogate the text as you develop avenues for responding to it. You'll need to balance both approaches, and each is enriched by the other. Only by listening can you ask more probing questions. And those very questions can help send you back to the text for a closer and more informed reading of what the author is saying. Savvy, rhetorical reading has all of the give-and-take qualities of good conversation.

To illustrate these strategies for listening and responding, I have annotated Tannen's article. It's important to remember that annotations aren't all made on a first reading. In fact, most evolve from continued rereading and the ongoing give and take of listening and responding.

For Writing and Discussion

Locate your reading notes or annotations for an article you read in another course from a previous semester or from high school. Coming back to these annotations, what do you find to be helpful or unhelpful about them? What would you like to change or adapt as you refine how you interact with texts on the page?

Agonism in the Academy: Surviving Higher Learning's Argument Culture

Key term — look this up.

Deborah Tannen

A reading group that I belong to, composed of professors, recently discussed a memoir by an academic. I came to the group's meeting full of anticipation, eager to examine the insights I'd gained from the book and to be enlightened by those that had intrigued my fellow group members. As the meeting began, one member announced that she hadn't read the book; four, including me, said they'd read and enjoyed it; and one said she hadn't liked it because she does not like academic memoirs. She energetically criticized the book. "It's written in two voices," she said, "and the voices don't interrogate each other."

Quickly, two other members joined her critique, their point of view becoming a chorus. They sounded smarter, seeing faults that the rest of us had missed, making us look naive. We credulous three tried in vain to get the group talking about what we had found interesting or important in the book, but our suggestions were dull compared to the game of critique.

I know how this feels.

Effective phrase

I left the meeting disappointed because I had learned nothing new about the book or its subject. All I had learned about was the acumen of the critics. I was especially struck by the fact that one of the most talkative and influential critics was the member who had

Engaging story. What's its rhetorical function?

Key term/ concept

Can't debate be helpful and instructive?

Need more on naturally; arising argument; Tannen doesn't follow up on this.

Sounds like this could be Tannen's claim—check out "endemic."

General road map for Tannen's article?

Yes, I've seen this happen. Well put!

not read the book. Her unfamiliarity with the work had not hindered her, because the critics had focused more on what they saw as faults of the genre than on faults of the particular book.

The turn that the discussion had taken reminded me of the subject of my most recent book, *The Argument Culture.* The phenomenon I'd observed at the book-group meeting was an example of what the cultural linguist Walter Ong calls "agonism," which he defines in *Fighting for Life* as "programmed contentiousness" or "ceremonial combat." Agonism does not refer to disagreement, conflict, or vigorous dispute. It refers to ritualized opposition—for instance, a debate in which the contestants are assigned opposing positions and one party wins, rather than an argument that arises naturally when two parties disagree.

In *The Argument Culture,* I explored the role and effects of agonism in three domains of public discourse: journalism, politics, and the law. But the domain in which I first identified the phenomenon and began thinking about it is the academic world. I remain convinced that agonism is endemic in academe—and bad for it.

The way we train our students, conduct our classes and our research, and exchange ideas at meetings and in print are all driven by our ideological assumption that intellectual inquiry is a metaphorical battle. Following from that is a second assumption, that the best way to demonstrate intellectual prowess is to criticize, find fault, and attack.

Many aspects of our academic lives can be described as agonistic. For example, in our scholarly papers, most of us follow a conventional framework that requires us to position our work in opposition to someone else's, which we prove wrong. The framework tempts— almost requires—us to oversimplify or even misrepresent others' positions; cite the weakest example to make a generally reasonable work appear less so; and ignore facts that support others' views, citing only evidence that supports our own positions.

The way we train our students frequently reflects the battle metaphor as well. We assign scholarly work for them to read, then invite them to tear it apart. That is helpful to an extent, but it often means that they don't learn to do the harder work of integrating ideas, or of considering the work's historical and disciplinary context. Moreover, it fosters in students a stance of arrogance and narrow-mindedness, qualities that do not serve the fundamental goals of education.

In the classroom, if students are engaged in heated debate, we believe that education is taking place. But in a 1993 article in *The*

History Teacher, Patricia Rosof, who teaches at Hunter College High School in New York City, advises us to look more closely at what's really happening. If we do, she says, we will probably find that only a few students are participating; some other students may be paying attention, but many may be turned off. Furthermore, the students who are arguing generally simplify the points they are making or disputing. To win the argument, they ignore complexity and nuance. They refuse to concede a point raised by their opponents, even if they can see that it is valid, because such a concession would weaken their position. Nobody tries to synthesize the various views, because that would look indecisive, or weak.

I've had this experience, but is Tannen overgeneralizing? Isn't Tannen being agonistic in her own attack on agonism? She offers few concessions.

If the class engages in discussion rather than debate—adding such intellectual activities as exploring ideas, uncovering nuances, comparing and contrasting different interpretations of a work—more students take part, and more of them gain a deeper, and more accurate, understanding of the material. Most important, the students learn a stance of respect and open-minded inquiry.

Is debate all that bad? I've learned a lot from debate experiences.

Academic rewards—good grades and good jobs—typically go to students and scholars who learn to tear down others' work, not to those who learn to build on the work of their colleagues. In *The Argument Culture,* I cited a study in which communications researchers Karen Tracy and Sheryl Baratz examined weekly colloquia attended by faculty members and graduate students at a large university. As the authors reported in a 1993 article in *Communication Monographs,* although most people said the purpose of the colloquia was to "trade ideas" and "learn things," faculty members in fact were judging the students' competence based on their participation in the colloquia. And the professors didn't admire students who asked "a nice little supportive question," as one put it —they valued "tough and challenging questions."

My best classes use inquiry. But I've sat through really lame discussions too. Much depends on the teacher.

Can't challenging questions also play a helpful and supportive role?

One problem with the agonistic culture of graduate training is that potential scholars who are not comfortable with that kind of interaction are likely to drop out. As a result, many talented and creative minds are lost to academe. And, with fewer colleagues who prefer different approaches, those who remain are more likely to egg each other on to even greater adversarial heights. Some scholars who do stay in academe are reluctant to present their work at conferences or submit it for publication because of their reluctance to take part in adversarial discourse. The cumulative effect is that nearly everyone feels vulnerable and defensive, and thus less willing to suggest new ideas, offer new perspectives, or question received wisdom.

Yes. Self-selection. Cultures include & exclude people.

But ideas do need to be tested. And American culture is competitive.

Although scholarly attacks are ritual—prescribed by the conventions of academe—the emotions propelling them can be real. Jane Tompkins, a literary critic who has written about the genre of the western in modern fiction and film, has compared scholarly exchanges to shootouts. In a 1988 article in the *Georgia Review*, she noted that her own career took off when she published an essay that "began with a frontal assault on another woman scholar. When I wrote it I felt the way the hero does in a western. Not only had this critic argued *a*, *b*, and *c*, she had held *x*, *y*, and *z*! It was a clear case of outrageous provocation." Because her opponent was established and she was not, Tompkins felt "justified in hitting her with everything I had."

Later in her career, as she listened to a speaker at a conference demolish another scholar's work, she felt that she was witnessing "a ritual execution of some sort, something halfway between a bullfight, where the crowd admires the skill of the matador and enjoys his triumph over the bull, and a public burning, where the crowd witnesses the just punishment of a criminal. For the academic experience combined the elements of admiration, bloodlust, and moral self-congratulation."

At a deeper level, the conceptual metaphor of intellectual argument as a battle leads us to divide researchers into warring camps. Just about any field can provide examples. For instance, many disciplines are affected—and disfigured—by a stubborn nature/nurture dichotomy, although both biology and culture obviously influence all of us. Such divisiveness encourages both students and scholars to fight about others' work rather than trying to understand it. And those whose work is misrepresented end up using creative energy to defend their past work—energy that they could use more productively in other ways.

Agonism has still another serious effect: It is one of the reasons scholars have a hard time getting policymakers to pay attention to their research. Policymakers who come across relevant academic research immediately encounter opposing research. Lacking the expertise to figure out who's right, they typically conclude that they cannot look to academe for guidance.

Our agonistic ideology seems so deeply embedded in academe that one might wonder what alternatives we have. In *Embracing Contraries*, the English professor Peter Elbow calls the ways we approach ideas a "doubting game"—a method for sniffing out faults. What we need, he says, is an additional approach—a "believing game," to sniff out strengths. The two games would complement

---

Marginal notes:

Note use of war/battle metaphors.

Again, concepts of ritual and game.

Interesting. Effects go beyond individuals to whole disciplines.

Yes. Academics seem never to agree. True of global-warming debate?

Note that both games needed.

each other. Although we wouldn't end up agreeing with all the authors we read, by suspending disbelief we would be more likely to learn something from them.

Suspend—when and for how long? Don't we need doubt?

In my view, we need new metaphors through which to think about our academic enterprise, or to conceptualize intellectual interchange. We could learn much more if we thought of theories not as static structures to be shot down or falsified, but as sets of understandings to be questioned and reshaped. The sociologist Kerry Daly, in the introduction to his book *Families and Time*, suggests that "theories should be treated like bread dough that rises with a synergetic mix of ingredients only to be pounded down with the addition of new ingredients and human energy."

Transition—focus now on metaphors.

Nice metaphor!

In the realm of teaching, Don McCormick and Michael Kahn, in a 1982 article in *Exchange: The Organizational Behavior Teaching Journal*, suggest that critical thinking can be taught better if we use the metaphor of a barn raising, instead of that of a boxing match. We should think of "a group of builders constructing a building, or a group of artists fabricating a creation together."

Another effective metaphor. What do these new metaphors have in common?

McCormick and Kahn make another point that, as I wrote in *The Argument Culture*, I came to believe is the most crucial and damaging aspect of the culture of agonism. Living, working, and thinking in ways shaped by the battle metaphor produces an atmosphere of animosity that poisons our relations with each other at the same time that it corrupts the integrity of our research. Not only is the agonistic culture of academe not the best path to truth and knowledge, but it also is corrosive to the human spirit.

Well put. But is all of academe agonistic in bad ways? Are all disciplines the same? Don't sciences combine debate with collaboration and teamwork?

After my reading group had discussed the academic memoir, I expressed my frustration to a group member. She commented, "It turns out that book wasn't the best example of the genre."

"But we didn't read an example of a genre," I protested. "We read a book by a person."

Return to opening story. Story serves as bookends for article.

Refocusing our attention in that way is the greatest gain in store if we can move beyond critique in its narrow sense. We would learn more from each other, be heard more clearly by others, attract more varied talents to the scholarly life, and restore a measure of humanity to ourselves, our endeavor, and the academic world we inhabit.

Effective summary statement.

Deborah Tannen is a university professor at Georgetown University. Her most recent book is The Argument Culture *(Random House, 1998; Ballantine paperback, 1999).*

Look up Tannen on Georgetown Website for more info.

Rhetorical Deep Structure

As you work with the text and experience its tug and pull through your own listening and questioning, you are doing more than reading word for word. Looking beyond the surface features of the text, you are locating and assessing what we might think of as the text's "rhetorical deep structure." Your annotations can help you uncover this deep structure, as can developing a rhetorical outline of the text or writing a brief summary.

To join the conversation that this text has initiated for you, you'll need to look beyond the flow of words and the array of topics covered to find core arguments and underlying reasoning. Here are some of the issues or concerns that you'll want to be alert to. Use the following questions as an informal checklist that can help develop more depth and nuance in your reading process.

WHAT IS THE QUESTION AT ISSUE? WHAT PROBLEM IS BEING ADDRESSED? Although most textbooks do a good job of hiding from your view the open issues that drive current work in a particular discipline, much of the actual writing and reading that gets done in the university is really about finding, framing, and pursuing questions at issue. Review your reading text to see how the author states or frames the question at issue. What kind of question is it? Does it concern issues of definition or questions about consequences and results? Or do the questions concern issues of value or issues of policy and action? Note that the question at issue may be implied. For example, Deborah Tannen does not pose her question at issue in blunt or direct terms, but as you read and reread her article, it becomes clear that the question or problem that motivates her is the presumption that agonism is the appropriate and preferred approach to teaching, learning, and scholarship. Her article seeks to question that presumption.

WHO IS THE AUDIENCE? HOW DOES THE TEXT CONSTRUCT OR POSITION ITS AUDIENCE? WHAT KIND OF CONVERSATION IS BEING PRESUMED BY THE TEXT? Questions at issue are rarely abstract and disembodied. Depending on how they are framed, questions at issue become questions for someone. In some of your reading, you'll find that the author addresses a very specific audience. In other texts, you may find that the audience is a bit more general. You should also be alert that some texts will have both a primary and a secondary audience. Rarely, however, will the audience simply be "the general reader." Consider where or by what means the text has been published, and you'll quickly get a handle on matters of audience. Given that it was published in the *Chronicle of Higher Education*, Tannen's article, for example, speaks to college faculty and administrators but has a broader secondary audience that can include students and all those interested in education. In the texts that you read, ask yourself if you are an insider or an outsider to the community addressed by the text. Beyond identifying who the audience is, you'll want to consider how the text positions or characterizes the audience. Is the audience assumed to be sympathetic, hostile, uncommitted, or skeptical? How is the audience expected to react, or what action does the text presume the audience should take? What is the audience's role in the conversation, and what use will it make of the text? Tannen, for example, encourages her audience to think more broadly about teaching and learning and to question the presumed virtues of agonism. Her examples and stories are intended to establish a common bond of experience with her audience.

WHAT IS THE AUTHOR'S PURPOSE? Authors have aims that they set for themselves, and those aims are forged out of the relationship that authors have to the subject matter and the audience. Some aims can be pursued through several different genres, other aims lend themselves to certain kinds of genres. Some purposes can overlap, and some texts can have multiple purposes, each one building or laying the foundation for the next. Here are some of the common purposes you will encounter in your college reading:

> expressing or reflecting
> inquiring or exploring
> explaining or informing
> analyzing or interpreting
> arguing, deliberating, or taking a stand
> evaluating, judging, or critiquing
> proposing solutions
> finding common ground or consensus building

Tannen's article focuses on evaluating, judging, or critiquing, even as it may pursue other purposes in specific paragraphs to help support her critique and even as she touches on possible solutions.

WHAT IS THE AUTHOR'S CLAIM OR THESIS? WHAT LINE OF REASONING DOES THE AUTHOR PURSUE? DOES THE AUTHOR ENGAGE SKEPTICAL QUESTIONS? If much of the work in the university centers on finding, framing, and pursuing questions at issue, then it follows that many of the texts will offer and support answers to such questions. Some of the texts you will read in college will be very explicit about the claim being made; others will only offer such a claim implicitly; and still others, depending on the author's purpose, will not stake out one particular claim. A claim or thesis is an arguable opinion; it not only states a proposition but also makes a claim on our belief. Given that they are arguable, claims are potentially refutable (they can't be merely personal expressions of preference or self-evident statements) and thus demand explanation, support, and a consideration of potential skeptical questions or counterarguments. So, as a rhetorically savvy reader, your job is to ask what the author wishes you to believe, how the author attempts to elicit or persuade you of that belief, and what assumptions are made in the process. In much academic writing and reading, those attempts are grounded in reasoning and evidence and are pursued through lines of reasoning that build or work toward the author's conclusions. Specific disciplines, however, have differing conventions and expectations about what kinds of evidence are acceptable and how such evidence is to be collected and presented. Tannen's article claims that "agonism is endemic in academe—and bad for it." She pursues this claim through a line of reasoning that she summarizes in paragraph six, which in turn gives us some clues about the organizational structure of her article. But along with the obligation to explain herself and support her claim comes the obligation (perhaps only partially met) to consider skeptical questions about her own positions.

HOW DOES THE AUTHOR ENGAGE THE INTERESTS, EMOTIONS, VALUES, AND COMMITMENTS OF THE AUDIENCE? Although academic writing and reading place a high premium on appeals to reason and evidence, we can ill afford to overlook the ways in which texts appeal to our interests, emotions, and commitments. In many respects, such appeals can be very powerful, for they have to do with the often hidden ways in which we and others identify with certain experiences, values, and beliefs, and with certain communities and causes. In Tannen's article, she calls on stories and examples that appeal to the audience's potentially negative prior experiences with agonism. Emotionally laden terms and the careful choice of evidence tend to paint agonism in a very negative light and collaborative learning in a very positive light.

HOW DOES THE AUTHOR ESTABLISH HIS OR HER CREDIBILITY? Authors elicit our belief not only by the reasoning they offer but also by who they are and by the character that they establish for themselves on the page. Academic credentials and positions, the nature of the publication in which their work appears, and references to their own research and the work of others are among the many ways that authors win your belief. The voice of the author in the text and the degree to which the text exhibits evenhandedness and fairness all contribute to the judgments a reader invariably makes about the author—and what the author is saying. In the case of Tannen's article, we know from the note about the author that she is a professor at Georgetown University (and as it turns out a well-published and highly regarded sociolinguist). Although the *Chronicle of Higher Education* is not a place where authors publish new research, she does gain credibility by mentioning her full-length book on the subject. She also gains credibility by mentioning other well-regarded scholars (among them Walter Ong, Karen Tracy, and Peter Elbow), thereby demonstrating how her work builds on the efforts of others. Tannen demonstrates, in short, that she is active in and is advancing an ongoing conversation. But her voice and style also indicate that she is successful in reaching beyond a merely academic audience (her books are popular well beyond the classroom). She is an insider in Burke's parlor who has also developed a knack for welcoming newbies to the conversation.

WHAT WORLDVIEW OR IDEOLOGY DOES THE TEXT SUBSCRIBE TO? WHAT HAS BEEN FOREGROUNDED OR EMPHASIZED, AND WHAT HAS BEEN DE-EMPHASIZED OR OMITTED? Texts do more than present ideas; they offer a glimpse into a worldview out of which those ideas have grown. Individual ideas and beliefs are invariably part of a network or system of truth claims— what we might call an ideology. As a savvy, rhetorical reader, you will want to locate a given text within such a larger system. You can thereby gain a sense of the premises or beliefs that inform an author's view but are rarely announced or questioned themselves. You might think of worldviews or ideologies as filters that highlight some issues and concerns, while screening out others. Asking what a text neglects or omits altogether is often as important as focusing on what is written on the page. In the article on agonism, we gain insight into a set of pedagogical commitments and values that Tannen seems to have, although she may not discuss such commitments directly. For example, we can gather that her pedagogical worldview places high priority on teamwork and collaborative teaching and learning.

Two preliminary writing activities can help you build on your annotations and answer the questions that were enumerated above.

DEVELOP A RHETORICAL OUTLINE OF THE TEXT. You are surely familiar with outlines, especially as a way of organizing information prior to and during your own writing process. But a reverse outline—an outline of an already written text or draft—can help you refine both your reading and your writing skills. A rhetorical outline has two parts describing what is happening in each paragraph or section of a text. The first part describes what the author *says*. Here your focus is on identifying the content or topic of that section of text. The second part of a rhetorical outline describes what the author *does* in that section. Here your focus is on how what the author is saying does something rhetorically. Examples of *does* statements might include the following: frames the question at issue, summarizes prior research; offers his or her claim, provides evidence for an assertion, answers a skeptical question or counterargument; signposts the organization of the text, provides a transition from one section of the text to the next, and so on. A rhetorical outline can help you look beyond the content of a text so that you can uncover how the author orchestrates the conversation. This strategy can also help you as a writer, especially when you have a promising but unruly and chaotic rough draft. The *does* statements help you clarify in your own mind what you hope to accomplish at each stage in your own writing as you join and sustain a conversation.

WRITE A SUMMARY OF THE TEXT. Summaries challenge you to portray the ideas of another piece of writing in a brief text that must itself acquire shape and serve a purpose. Although summaries seem merely descriptive, they challenge even the most accomplished writers because they ask you to comprehend and render the rhetorical deep structure of what you summarize. Summaries must be fair, balanced, concise, and accurate. Most importantly, you must discern what is essential to the line of argument and how individual statements relate to the thrust and function of the whole. The rhetorical deep structure of the source text can help you shape your summary of it, as you reflect the author's question, claim, and line of reasoning in your own text. Summaries can serve as powerful aids for reading rhetorically. Moreover, because they help you identify key rhetorical issues, they can also invite you to assess texts and join the conversation. Summaries can take many forms in your academic and professional life. To be sure, a common assignment might be to write a summary or to write a summary that is followed up by a short response. But summaries also have further and varied applications. Summaries can help you write an annotated bibliography or a review of research on a particular question. You will often see summaries serve as abstracts for a published article. In the business world, an executive summary offers a nontechnical, action-oriented condensation of a long report to busy managers and executives. Promissory abstracts serve as summaries for long works still on the drawing board. Summaries most often appear not as stand-alone documents but as integral elements in your own writing. Any time you are responding to or critiquing a text, or calling on another text to further your own point, you owe it to your audience to first summarize it in a fair manner. As you stand on the shoulders of other authors and build on their research, you need to characterize their work even as you draw on it for your own rhetorical purposes.

For Writing and Discussion

Drawing on a reading in this collection, try your hand at annotating the text, answering questions about its rhetorical structure, developing a rhetorical outline, and writing a summary. These tools will serve you well in a variety of coming reading and writing assignments. Circulate copies of your summary in small groups, each of whose members have worked with the same text. Compare each other's work and discuss the challenges of writing a summary. Given that you read the same text, how similar are your summaries? What might account for the differences? What can you learn about your writing and about your reading habits by reviewing the summaries written by others in your group?

Joining the Conversation

When you enter the parlor that Kenneth Burke describes—the house of argument that is the university—you must first "read" the conversation in order to understand its ebb and flow and its conversational rules. But the larger purpose of reading the conversation is to participate, to add your voice. As Burke notes, "You listen for a while, until you decide that you have caught the tenor of the argument; then you put in your oar."

"Putting in your oar" requires that you think of yourself a bit differently than many high school and college courses may have thought of you. Other courses often position you as a consumer of what other people already know. *Composing Knowledge* and the course you may be using it in serve as an invitation to think of yourself as a writer in a community of writers and most especially as a producer of knowledge. Writing becomes an opportunity to compose knowledge both for yourself and for others. Through your own acts of reading and writing, criticism and research, you learn firsthand the ways that knowledge is composed, beliefs are formed, values are sustained, and a corner of the world is transformed. I hope you learn, above all, that your own voice can make a difference.

For your voice to make a difference, you need to establish your authority even as you work with and call on the authority of others. The texts you are reading may loom as authoritative, the authors as beyond question. But as you read closely and are drawn into conversation with the texts, you will find opportunities to make claims about the texts, to extend the conversation, and to apply insights to your own situated learning experience. You will find, in short, your own voice, and you will discover the grounds for your own authority. Such authority can be won through the manner in which you engage the text, through your ability to integrate other voices and texts into your conversation, and through your own expertise and experience. But even as you "author-ize" your own voice, you will want to keep in play and rely on the voices of others. You'll discover that the tug and pull between your voice and the voices of others, your authority and the authority of others, is part of what makes conversation productive and genuinely worthwhile.

Strategies for Engaging the Conversation

Your own contributions to an ongoing conversation don't start with a long and full-blown speech. They often start with a question, a comment, and, perhaps only in response to someone else's comment, a somewhat longer reply. It's much the same with your writing. Your formal written essays in college often find their most productive early moments in informal writing. These moments, in turn, can give you the impetus to develop more formal essays that analyze or argue with the text or that extend or apply insight you have about the text in new ways. Here are three strategies for engaging the conversation in ways that can lead you to make valuable contributions and produce work that you are especially proud of.

START WITH INFORMAL WRITING THAT CAN SPUR RHETORICAL INVENTION. Informal writing can often help you find your best ideas because it gives you permission not to censor them prematurely. What is known as "freewriting" is one such kind of informal exercise in invention. After freewriting for, let's say, ten or fifteen minutes, you can then return to the rambling text you have produced to locate issues and ideas that you can then develop in a more systematic manner. A reading log or a learning log can help you ground your response to specific moments in the text, preparing you to then develop that response into a fuller and more ambitious text. One specific kind of reading log is what is known as a double-entry notebook, in which you literally draw a line down the middle of the page as a way of connecting specific quotes or passages from the text, recorded in one column, with your responses and reflections, noted in the parallel column. Short response papers (sometimes preceded by a summary) allow you to build on informal and often private exploratory writing in a more systematic and formal way. These response papers can in turn become a prelude to a longer project.

Composing Knowledge supports your informal writing by inviting you to "reflect on your prior knowledge" at the beginning of each chapter. Each selection, in turn, poses questions for "Working with the Text" that can draw on your textual annotations and send you back into the text for a second reading with new questions and perspectives.

MAKE AND REFINE CLAIMS ABOUT THE TEXT THAT LEAD TO ANALYSIS OR ARGUMENT. Having worked closely with a text through annotations and through informal exploratory writing, you will have developed a sharper sense of the way the text is crafted and whether or not you agree or disagree with the claims made by the author. A common college writing assignment is to advance a claim about a written text because in many disciplines (literature, history, religion, and law, among them) close, critical reading of a text is a fundamental skill. Your focus will be on the rhetorical methods and strategies employed by the author; in turn, you will call upon rhetorical strategies of your own as you support the thesis or claim you are making, drawing on textual evidence and analysis. Having looked for the rhetorical deep structure of the text, you are in a good position to draft your own text that calls upon those very features: an engaging question at issue, an arguable claim, a line of reasoning that explores and supports that claim, and a willingness to engage skeptical questions that may seem to be inconvenient to the very case you are building.

Accompanying each reading in *Composing Knowledge*, you will find questions that can help you in the section "Working with the Text." These questions by no means exhaust the interesting issues you can pose about a text, but they do offer you a start and represent an invitation for you to pose—and answer—such questions on your own.

EXTEND OR APPLY THE CONVERSATION, OFTEN TO YOUR OWN SITUATED EXPERIENCES. Another common writing assignment in college calls for you to draw on texts as part of a larger conversation—one in which you take the primary role. Here the focus is on your contribution and on your ability to extend or apply the voices of others to a new issue or problem. College research papers have received a deservedly bad reputation, especially when they are produced simply to describe the arguments of others. But at heart, such assignments call on much more creative work than may seem apparent. You must read and synthesize the work of others and evaluate what contributions they might make to your own new argument, one that addresses a question you have formulated. In essence, the work of others serves as a provocation or springboard for your own ideas. You will use the voices of others to frame questions, to position yourself in the conversation, and to raise questions regarding and offer support for your own line of reasoning. As you extend or apply the work of others, you must draw on your own specialized knowledge and fieldwork. For this reason, projects that address your own lived experience or areas of expertise are especially appropriate.

Following each reading in *Composing Knowledge*, you will find questions under the heading "From Text to Field" that help you shift your focus from the text itself to questions or issues that invite you to extend or apply the conversation. At the end of each of the seven chapters in the book, you will find a large portfolio of more ambitious project ideas, "Into the Field," that can launch you into your own original work.

For Writing and Discussion

1. As you meet in small groups, reflect back on a writing opportunity in high school or college, in whatever discipline, in which you felt you most successfully engaged texts and composed knowledge. Discuss what it was in your reading and writing that helped to account for this success. How do the keys for your prior success relate to the strategies discussed here, and how might these strategies build on and refine some techniques you may already be using? How do you think you can leverage your prior successful experience and take your work to the next higher level?

2. Now that you have read and considered the annotations on Tannen's short article on "Agonism in the Academy," ask yourself what your own opinion on the matter is. Do you agree or disagree with Tannen? Is there one aspect of her argument that you'd like to consider in detail? Or would you like to extend or apply Tannen's work in light of your own learning experiences? You can work through a series of short papers that draw on the progression from informal writing to analysis and argument and on to essays that apply or extend the issues raised in her essay. Alternatively, you can focus on just one kind of academic assignment as you consider your own response to Tannen's views on the kinds of conversations we have in the academy.

Into the Field

Composing Knowledge takes seriously the proposition that you are far more than a consumer of knowledge—a role that many of your courses may unwittingly have you adopt. As a writer, you are shaping, composing, and sharing knowledge. You draw on the work of others, to be sure, but also on your own close observation and experience. Little wonder, then, that the writing projects suggested in this book place a premium on original fieldwork—fieldwork that invites you to reflect on, extend, and apply the various readings in this volume.

Why fieldwork? Issues broached in the readings come alive as you see their connection to your own situated learning experience in college. And the writing process itself becomes more relevant as you include not only library research but also close observation of your own classrooms, curricula, and campus. Fieldwork positions you not as a novice but as an expert-in-the-making. Moreover, because you bring to bear experience and observation that is situated and drawn from local contexts, you can make distinctive and original contributions to a larger, ongoing conversation.

Varieties of Fieldwork

Composing Knowledge offers fieldwork that draws on various disciplines and on the varied settings, methods, and issues that arise in your own education.

Each of the seven chapters in the book takes on a different facet of composing knowledge in college.

We begin where you begin: with the challenges inherent in entering the college community and joining its many conversations. These challenges include "learning the language" (academic and otherwise) of your campus and figuring out how to "dance" with your professors as you engage with them in the classes you take. Here, fieldwork may involve a profile of the very rituals and traditions you need to learn if you are to become an insider on campus or an examination of the various texts (cartoons, announcements, and so on) that are displayed on or near the doors of your professors' offices.

The second chapter of *Composing Knowledge* invites you to consider how, through your own activities, you are inventing the university for yourself. We'll look at how classrooms, courses, and curricula are constructed and what role language and writing have in shaping the university. Fieldwork will include studying documents that you may not immediately recognize as having archival value. Syllabi, for example, can tell you a good deal not just about the course you are taking but also about how the course positions you as a student and about what kind of teaching and learning will be valued. You might also read the physical classroom as a kind of text, observing how learning spaces are designed and how they distribute authority and power. Alternatively, you may find yourself looking into historical documents that describe the evolution of any writing requirements on your campus.

In Chapter 3, you'll consider how we go about persuading each other in an academic setting. It turns out that frames of reference or the kinds of conceptual glasses we wear on our noses go a long way in influencing what and how we see. In turn, we'll consider how arguments occur in the contexts of communities, each of which has slightly different conventions and expectations about how members talk to each other. Your fieldwork will encourage you to think about what academic research methods both include and exclude and about the metaphors we use when describing that work. You'll also consider whether the various academic disciplines on your campus contribute to one common academic community or fracture your campus into a series of academic fiefdoms.

Although we may be tempted at times to think of academic life in college as essentially solitary, even lonely, Chapter 4 makes the argument that college requires of us a series of ongoing engagements with others. Our work is inherently social. We find ourselves collaborating at every turn and crossing a variety of cultural borders. Your fieldwork will invite you to explore the benefits—and the tensions—in such collaborations, whether in a writing class or in your particular major. You might also find yourself exploring the cultural divides on your campus and the ways in which college forces us to reflect on various borderland experiences.

Chapter 5—"(En)gendering Knowledge"—explores how the creation and communication of knowledge invariably raises issues of gender and identity. The first unit of the chapter, "Speaking of Gender," addresses issues of gender and language. The second unit, "Minding Gender," asks us to pay attention to how gender roles and concepts influence us at a very deep level, affecting our minds and emotions, even our scientific study of brains and biology. This chapter will send you into the field to study the dynamics of classroom conversation and gendered roles as captured by campus graffiti. You'll consider how histories of your academic field are gendered and assess the role of gender issues in shaping the very climate of your campus.

The sixth chapter explores the role of technology in education. Even as we focus on learning the latest technology, we all too easily forget just how much influence technology has as we learn about and encounter the world. By loosening the bonds of time and place, technology lets us rethink our notions of community. Likewise, we must be mindful that technology can influence and even create new tools for thinking. Fieldwork opportunities include assessing the role of technology in wired classrooms and in the creation of a sense of community on campus. You'll take a critical look at how PowerPoint is used—or misused—in your classes, and you'll ponder how your campus library is reconceiving itself in the late age of print.

The final chapter of *Composing Knowledge* explores how, in our increasingly visual culture, text and image are intertwined. Here we explore the connections between seeing and believing and how our "mind's eye" contributes to our vision. And we'll ponder what it means to witness our world and to witness the images by which we sometimes know our world. Fieldwork will send you out on your campus to see its nooks and crannies and even its famous landmarks afresh. We'll consider how schemas (visual and otherwise) influence what we see and know. We'll even explore how campus image making influences high school students and has itself become a big business. We'll ask ourselves why we tend to believe images, and we'll ponder the global reach of an image-saturated media.

These many opportunities for fieldwork will lead to far more than the usual academic essay. Based on your fieldwork and involvement in actual communities, you will find yourself writing diverse documents (from profiles to reports to proposals). Most importantly, based on your fieldwork, you'll find real audiences and discover that your voice and your writing matter. You'll come to know that by composing your knowledge well you can contribute to and even change what and how we know.

Launching Your Fieldwork

Although you won't need a pith helmet to carry out the fieldwork that *Composing Knowledge* invites, you will need to be savvy about your work in the field. This book invites you to become aware of your own situated learning and living environment. It asks that you become more aware as you observe, participate in, reflect on, and question the world of your college experience — and the larger world beyond. You'll come to look closely at your everyday experiences in class, on campus, and in the community. And in so doing, you'll discover texts, artifacts, and resources that may have escaped your notice.

How can you work effectively in the field and draw on that experience as you read and write? Here are some tips:

- Be willing to observe and question what might at first seem normal or habitual. Consider how events and artifacts become part of a culture — part of a web of behaviors, patterns, and (often unspoken) rules that a group of people or a community shares.
- Keep detailed and accurate field notes on what you observe and on the artifacts that you are analyzing. Expand on those field notes when you are not in the field or at your research site.
- Draw on the evidence of the everyday. Although you may be tackling large issues, everyday artifacts of the classroom, campus, or community can often be telling and invaluable resources.
- Question your assumptions. What untested attitudes, beliefs, or cultural values might you project onto your work in the field?
- Acknowledge your role as both a participant and an observer. You are both looking at a culture or community and participating in that culture or community. Be aware of your own position or stance in relation to what you are studying.
- Be willing to step outside of a group or situation with which you may be quite familiar. Likewise, be willing to step into a group or situation that may seem foreign. Be willing to make the familiar strange and the strange familiar.
- Respect your fellow students and the various citizens on your campus and in your community. Consult with your instructor as you engage in your fieldwork to determine if any special permission or approval may be needed.

Composing Knowledge invites you to explore your own learning, the teaching and learning cultures of college, and the connections of your college experience to the larger community. The readings in the coming chapters will help you make sense of the many conversations that occur in the Burkean parlor that is your college or university. Those readings will also serve as provocations for your own response and invitations for extending and applying the issues discussed to your own lived experience. Framed by these readings, the original fieldwork you conduct positions you not as the novice but as the expert-in-the-making. Even as you draw on the work of others, you have your own knowledge to compose. Your journey through the following chapters will offer you knowledge for composing well.

1

Joining the Conversation

LEARNING THE LANGUAGE

You and I belong to a community to the extent that we are able to join in its conversations. But to join those conversations, we need to learn the language of that community. That process, explored in this chapter's readings, is not nearly as straightforward as it may seem.

Learning a language surely conjures up memories of our French or German or Spanish classes. We recall the vocabulary quizzes and the grammar tests and our early, awkward attempts to carry on the most basic of conversations. Yet if we think of "learning the language" at this level, the level of verb endings and subjunctives, we surely miss the vital connection between language and community or culture. Even as we slog through the daily homework routine of learning a foreign language, we know that in time learning this language will allow us to participate in the conversations of a community at a far deeper level. We may try to imitate cultural practices or wear our French beret at just the right slight angle. But only through learning a language can we understand the common, but unspoken, assumptions and the hidden attitudes and beliefs that hold a community together. And in so doing, we hope to enter that community without immediately being singled out as the newcomer, the foreigner.

As a college student, you too are joining a community or, to be more precise a whole host of communities—some disciplinary, some social, each overlapping with others. The process is at once exciting and challenging, all the more so because to join these communities you must learn their languages. Here, too, no one wants to be singled out as the newcomer, the foreigner. The common language seems to be English: the academic version of English. You expect to be inundated with new technical vocabulary, especially in the sciences. But what may come as a particular surprise is that each disciplinary community, even composition, has something of its own language. It would be relatively easy if learning this language were simply a matter of learning the buzzwords, the jargon. But at a deeper level, the languages you are encountering carry with them new attitudes and behaviors, new assumptions and values, new ways of thinking about and seeing the world.

Writing class holds a special place among the various classes in that it offers an opportunity to reflect on—and not merely to use or imitate—the languages of the academy. A writing class has us look *at* language and literacy, not merely *through* them, to the concerns of this or that field. And as we become more aware of our own continuing attempts to learn the language, we become more aware of our several identities and of our hopes and fears and likewise more aware of how we move in and between several communities.

The six readings included in this chapter explore the process of learning the language from several perspectives. Each perspective bears in some way on your own entry into language and community on campus.

Because life in the academy assumes advanced literacy, it is important to begin by recalling that an assumption even about basic literacy does not hold for millions of our fellow citizens. In the chapter's first selection, Jonathan Kozol reveals what is the enormous human cost of illiteracy.

Perri Klass recalls her education in medical school as being an education in a new language and, through that language, an initiation into a new community. In addition to learning a host of new technical terms, she also picks up on the attitudes and behaviors carried in the language she now hears in the hospital corridors.

Our entry into a community has not only to do with language but also with rituals and traditions. As David Berreby reminds us, "Students don't just attend a college; they join its tribes." And in so doing, they become involved in a process that, at whatever level, separates "us" from "them."

For novelist Amy Tan, knowing more than one language and more than one culture means that we begin to realize that social settings are easily misunderstood in translation. As we learn new languages and join new communities, we become more aware that language becomes "the peg and the shelf that enables us to sort out and categorize the world."

The language that holds us together, that creates commonalities, say, in high school classrooms across the country, is not what many educators might presume. Formal academic learning—the literacy we acquire in school—has far less influence than we might realize. More important by far, argues Theodore Sizer, is the public literacy that shapes our national culture.

For Barbara Mellix, learning the new language of the academy is also an occasion for reflecting on our cultural roots. As we learn that new language, we will never quite have the same relationship with our other voices. Like the other five authors, Mellix comes to realize that the languages we learn and the conversations we join shape who we are.

Reflecting on Prior Knowledge

1. In a journal entry, recall the experience of being an outsider joining a new group. What was unfamiliar in the language—and behavior—of that group? How did your own attitudes and behavior begin to change as you grew to be accepted within that new community? How was that change captured in your language?

2. Think back to a time when you modified how you spoke or wrote given the particular setting or audience. In a journal entry, recall the scenario and begin exploring why you changed your language behavior. What was your relationship to your audience that prompted this change?

3. In a journal entry, recall the experience of some newcomer trying to enter your community or trying to appropriate and use your language. How did you feel or react? What does it mean to "own" language, and what is entailed in "taking" or "adopting" a language or a set of rituals and traditions?

4. Recall an experience when some misunderstanding occurred in a bicultural or multicultural context despite everyone trying to be well intentioned and polite. In a journal entry, explore what it was about the social context that failed "in translation."

5. Describe the "proper" way to act, speak, or write in a particular situation, be it social or academic, on campus or off. How do we come to learn such proprieties, especially if there are no explicit rules?

The Human Cost
of an Illiterate Society

Jonathan Kozol

An activist and well-known writer on issues of education and home-lessness, Jonathan Kozol has stirred the conscience of America with his incisive and moving critiques. For some four decades, Kozol has sought to end illiteracy, to put a human face on homelessness, to draw attention to continuing segregation in America's schools, and through such issues to prick the conscience of an affluent America that squanders its wealth and ingenuity by failing to address these issues.

Educated at Harvard University, where he graduated summa cum laude, and chosen as a Rhodes scholar, Kozol found that his career plans took a turn in 1964, when the political and social tumult of the 1960s moved him to become a public-school teacher in some of our nation's poorest schools. His account of teaching in a segregated school system, *Death at an Early Age: The Destruction of the Hearts and Minds of Negro Children in the Boston Public Schools,* won the National Book Award in 1968. *Illiterate America* (1985) offers a profoundly troubling exposé of the ways in which millions of Americans are excluded from our society because they cannot read or write. In *Rachel and Her Children: Homeless Families in America* (1988), Kozol offers a moving, detailed portrait of homeless families living in a New York City shelter. In 1991, in what is arguably his most well-known book, *Savage Inequalities: Children in America's Schools,* Kozol reveals the fundamental disparities in school quality from district to district. Two books then followed that offer a personal portrait of children growing up in Mott Haven, the poorest neighborhood in New York City: *Amazing Grace: The Lives of Children and the Conscience of a Nation* (1995) and *Ordinary Resurrections: Children in the Years of Hope* (2000). In his latest book, *Shame of a Nation: The Restoration of Apartheid Schooling in America* (2005), Kozol delivers a scathing indictment of public-education policy that preserves inequities along lines of race and class.

"The Human Cost of an Illiterate Society" is a chapter from *Illiterate America*. Here Kozol discusses how illiteracy forecloses worlds of possibility and renders millions at best "half-citizens."

PRECAUTIONS. READ BEFORE USING.
Poison: Contains sodium hydroxide (caustic soda-lye).
Corrosive: Causes severe eye and skin damage, may cause blindness.
Harmful or fatal if swallowed.
If swallowed, give large quantities of milk or water.
Do not induce vomiting.
Important: Keep water out of can at all times to prevent contents from violently erupting. . . .
— Warning on a Can of Drano

We are speaking here no longer of the dangers faced by passengers on Eastern Airlines or the dollar costs incurred by U.S. corporations and tax-payers. We are speaking now of human suffering and of the ethical dilemmas that are faced by a society that looks upon such suffering with qualified concern but does not take those actions which its wealth and ingenuity would seemingly demand.

Questions of literacy, in Socrates' belief, must at length be judged as matters of morality. Socrates could not have had in mind the moral compromise peculiar to a nation like our own. Some of our Founding Fathers did, however, have this question in their minds. One of the wisest of those Founding Fathers (one who may not have been most compassionate but surely was more prescient than some of his peers) recognized the special dangers that illiteracy would pose to basic equity in the political construction that he helped to shape.

"A people who mean to be their own governors," James Madison wrote, "must arm themselves with the power knowledge gives. A popular government without popular information or the means of acquiring it, is but a prologue to a farce or a tragedy, or perhaps both."

Tragedy looms larger than farce in the United States today. Illiterate citizens seldom vote. Those who do are forced to cast a vote of questionable worth. They cannot make informed decisions based on serious print information. Sometimes they can be alerted to their interests by aggressive voter education. More frequently, they vote for a face, a smile, or a style, not for a mind or character or body of beliefs.

The number of illiterate adults exceeds by 16 million the entire vote cast for 5 the winner in the 1980 presidential contest. If even one-third of all illiterates could vote, and read enough and do sufficient math to vote in their self-interest, Ronald Reagan would not likely have been chosen president. There is, of course, no way to know for sure. We do know this: Democracy is a mendacious term when used by those who are prepared to countenance the forced exclusion of one-third of our electorate. So long as 60 million people are denied significant participation, the government is neither of, nor for, nor by, the people. It is a government, at best, of those two-thirds whose wealth, skin color, or parental privilege allows them opportunity to profit from the provocation and instruction of the written word.

The undermining of democracy in the United States is one "expense" that sensitive Americans can easily deplore because it represents a contradiction that endangers citizens of all political positions. The human price is not so obvious at first.

Since I first immersed myself within this work I have often had the following dream: I find that I am in a railroad station or a large department store within a city that is utterly unknown to me and where I cannot understand the printed words. None of the signs or symbols is familiar. Everything looks strange: like mirror writing of some kind. Gradually I understand that I am in the Soviet Union. All the letters on the walls around me are Cyrillic. I look for my pocket dictionary but I find that it has been mislaid. Where have I left it? Then I recall that I forgot to bring it with me when I packed my bags in Boston. I struggle to remember the name of my hotel. I try to ask somebody for directions. One person stops and looks at me in a peculiar way. I lose the nerve to ask. At last I reach into my wallet for an ID card. The card is missing. Have I lost it? Then I remember that my card was confiscated for some reason, many years before. Around this point, I wake up in a panic.

This panic is not so different from the misery that millions of adult illiterates experience each day within the course of their routine existence in the U.S.A.

Illiterates cannot read the menu in a restaurant.

They cannot read the cost of items on the menu in the *window* of the   10
restaurant before they enter.

Illiterates cannot read the letters that their children bring home from their teachers. They cannot study school department circulars that tell them of the courses that their children must be taking if they hope to pass the SAT exams. They cannot help with homework. They cannot write a letter to the teacher. They are afraid to visit in the classroom. They do not want to humiliate their child or themselves.

Illiterates cannot read instructions on a bottle of prescription medicine. They cannot find out when a medicine is past the year of safe consumption; nor can they read of allergenic risks, warnings to diabetics, or the potential sedative effect of certain kinds of nonprescription pills. They cannot observe preventive health care admonitions. They cannot read about "the seven warning signs of cancer" or the indications of blood-sugar fluctuations or the risks of eating certain foods that aggravate the likelihood of cardiac arrest.

Illiterates live, in more than literal ways, an uninsured existence. They cannot understand the written details on a health insurance form. They cannot read the waivers that they sign preceding surgical procedures. Several women I have known in Boston have entered a slum hospital with the intention of obtaining a tubal ligation and have emerged a few days later after having been subjected to a hysterectomy. Unaware of their rights, incognizant of jargon, intimidated by the unfamiliar air of fear and atmosphere of ether that so many of us find oppressive in the confines even of the most attractive and expensive medical facilities, they have signed their names to documents they could not read and which nobody, in the hectic situation that prevails so often in those overcrowded hospitals that serve the urban poor, had even bothered to explain.

Childbirth might seem to be the last inalienable right **We are speaking now of** of any female citizen within a civilized society. Illiterate **human suffering.** mothers, as we shall see, already have been cheated of the power to protect their progeny against the likelihood of demolition in deficient public schools and, as a result, against the verbal servitude within which they themselves exist. Surgical denial of the right to bear that child in the first place represents an ultimate denial, an unspeakable metaphor, a final darkness that denies even the twilight gleamings of our own humanity. What greater violation of our biological, our biblical, our spiritual humanity could possibly exist than that which takes place nightly, perhaps hourly these days, within such overburdened and benighted institutions as the Boston City Hospital? Illiteracy has many costs; few are so irreversible as this.

Even the roof above one's head, the gas or other fuel for heating that protects the residents of northern city slums against the threat of illness in the winter months become uncertain guarantees. Illiterates cannot read the lease that they must sign to live in an apartment which, too often, they cannot afford. They cannot manage check accounts and therefore seldom pay for anything by mail. Hours and entire days of difficult travel (and the cost of bus or other public transit) must be added to the real cost of whatever they consume. Loss of interest on the check accounts they do not have, and could not manage if they did, must be regarded as another of the excess costs paid by the citizen who is excluded from the common instruments of commerce in a numerate society.

"I couldn't understand the bills," a woman in Washington, D.C., reports, "and then I couldn't write the checks to pay them. We signed things we didn't know what they were."

Illiterates cannot read the notices that they receive from welfare offices or from the IRS. They must depend on word-of-mouth instruction from the welfare worker—or from other persons whom they have good reason to mistrust. They do not know what rights they have, what deadlines and requirements they face, what options they might choose to exercise. They are half-citizens. Their rights exist in print but not in fact.

Illiterates cannot look up numbers in a telephone directory. Even if they can find the names of friends, few possess the sorting skills to make use of the yellow pages; categories are bewildering and trade names are beyond decoding capabilities for millions of nonreaders. Even the emergency numbers listed on the first page of the phone book—"Ambulance," "Police," and "Fire"—are too frequently beyond the recognition of nonreaders.

Many illiterates cannot read the admonition on a pack of cigarettes. Neither the Surgeon General's warning nor its reproduction on the package can alert them to the risks. Although most people learn by word of mouth that smoking is related to a number of grave physical disorders, they do not get the chance to read the detailed stories which can document this danger with the vividness that turns concern into determination to resist. They can see the handsome cowboy or the slim Virginia lady lighting up a filter cigarette; they cannot heed the words that tell them that this product is (not "may be") dangerous to their health. Sixty million men and women are condemned to be the unalerted, high-risk candidates for cancer.

Illiterates do not buy "no-name" products in the supermarkets. They must 20 depend on photographs or the familiar logos that are printed on the packages of brand-name groceries. The poorest people, therefore, are denied the benefits of the least costly products.

Illiterates depend almost entirely upon label recognition. Many labels, however, are not easy to distinguish. Dozens of different kinds of Campbell's soup appear identical to the nonreader. The purchaser who cannot read and does not dare to ask for help, out of the fear of being stigmatized (a fear which is unfortunately realistic), frequently comes home with something which she never wanted and her family never tasted.

Illiterates cannot read instructions on a pack of frozen food. Packages sometimes provide an illustration to explain the cooking preparations; but illustrations are of little help to someone who must "boil water, drop the food—*within* its plastic wrapper—in the boiling water, wait for it to simmer, instantly remove."

Even when labels are seemingly clear, they may be easily mistaken. A woman in Detroit brought home a gallon of Crisco for her children's dinner. She thought that she had bought the chicken that was pictured on the label. She had enough Crisco now to last a year—but no more money to go back and buy the food for dinner.

Recipes provided on the packages of certain staples sometimes tempt a semiliterate person to prepare a meal her children have not tasted. The longing to vary the uniform and often starchy content of low-budget meals provided to the family that relies on food stamps commonly leads to ruinous results. Scarce funds have been wasted and the food must be thrown out. The same applies to distribution of food-surplus produce in emergency conditions. Government inducements to poor people to "explore the ways" by which to make a tasty meal from tasteless noodles, surplus cheese, and powdered milk are useless to nonreaders. Intended as benevolent advice, such recommendations mock reality and foster deeper feelings of resentment and of inability to cope. (Those, on the other hand, who cautiously refrain from "innovative" recipes in preparation of their children's meals must suffer the opprobrium of "laziness," "lack of imagination. . . .")

Illiterates cannot travel freely. When they attempt to do so, they encounter 25 risks that few of us can dream of. They cannot read traffic signs and, while they often learn to recognize and to decipher symbols, they cannot manage street names which they haven't seen before. The same is true for bus and subway stops. While ingenuity can sometimes help a man or woman to discern directions from familiar landmarks, buildings, cemeteries, churches, and the like, most illiterates are virtually immobilized. They seldom wander past the streets and neighborhoods they know. Geographical paralysis becomes a bitter metaphor for their entire existence. They are immobilized in almost every sense we can imagine. They can't move up. They can't move out. They cannot see beyond. Illiterates may take an oral test for drivers' permits in most sections of America. It is a questionable concession. Where will they go? How will they get there? How will they get home? Could it be that some of us might like it better if they stayed where they belong?

Travel is only one of many instances of circumscribed existence. Choice, in almost all of its facets, is diminished in the life of an illiterate adult. Even the printed TV schedule, which provides most people with the luxury of preselection, does not belong within the arsenal of options in illiterate existence. One consequence is that the viewer watches only what appears at moments when he happens to have time to turn the switch. Another consequence, a lot more common, is that the TV set remains in operation night and day. Whatever the program offered at the hour when he walks into the room will be the nutriment that he accepts and swallows. Thus, to passivity, is added frequency—indeed, almost uninterrupted continuity. Freedom to select is no more possible here than in the choice of home or surgery or food.

"You don't choose," said one illiterate woman. "You take your wishes from somebody else." Whether in perusal of a menu, selection of highways, purchase of groceries, or determination of affordable enjoyment, illiterate

Americans must trust somebody else: a friend, a relative, a stranger on the street, a grocery clerk, a TV copywriter.

"All of our mail we get, it's hard for her to read. Settin' down and writing a letter, she can't do it. Like if we get a bill . . . we take it over to my sister-in-law. . . . My sister-in-law reads it."

Billing agencies harass poor people for the payment of the bills for purchases that might have taken place six months before. Utility companies offer an agreement for a staggered payment schedule on a bill past due. "You have to trust them," one man said. Precisely for this reason, you end up by trusting no one and suspecting everyone of possible deceit. A submerged sense of distrust becomes the corollary to a constant need to trust. "They are cheating me . . . I have been tricked . . . I do not know. . . ."

Not knowing: This is a familiar theme. Not knowing the right word for the   30
right thing at the right time is one form of subjugation. Not knowing the world that lies concealed behind those words is a more terrifying feeling. The longitude and latitude of one's existence are beyond all easy apprehension. Even the hard, cold stars within the firmament above one's head begin to mock the possibilities for self-location. Where am I? Where did I come from? Where will I go?

"I've lost a lot of jobs," one man explains. "Today, even if you're a janitor, there's still reading and writing. . . . They leave a note saying, 'Go to room so-and-so. . . .' You can't do it. You can't read it. You don't know."

"The hardest thing about it is that I've been places where I didn't know where I was. You don't know where you are. . . . You're lost."

"Like I said: I have two kids. What do I do if one of my kids starts choking? I go running to the phone. . . . I can't look up the hospital phone number. That's if we're at home. Out on the street, I can't read the sign. I get to a pay phone. 'Okay, tell us where you are. We'll send an ambulance.' I look at the street sign. Right there, I can't tell you what it says. I'd have to spell it out, letter for letter. By that time, one of my kids would be dead. . . . These are the kinds of fears you go with, every single day. . . .

"Reading directions, I suffer with. I work with chemicals. . . . That's scary to begin with. . . ."

"You sit down. They throw the menu in front of you. Where do you go   35
from there? Nine times out of ten you say, 'Go ahead. Pick out something for the both of us.' I've eaten some weird things, let me tell you!"

Menus. Chemicals. A child choking while his mother searches for a word she does not know to find assistance that will come too late. Another mother speaks about the inability to help her kids to read: "I can't read to them. Of course that's leaving them out of something they should have. Oh, it matters. You *believe* it matters! I ordered all these books. The kids belong to a book club. Donny wanted me to read a book to him. I told Donny: 'I can't read.' He said: 'Mommy, you sit down. I'll read it to you.' I tried it one day, reading from the pictures. Donny looked at me. He said, 'Mommy, that's not right.' He's only five. He knew I couldn't read. . . .

A landlord tells a woman that her lease allows him to evict her if her baby cries and causes inconvenience to her neighbors. The consequence of challenging his words conveys a danger which appears, unlikely as it seems, even more alarming than the danger of eviction. Once she admits that she can't read, in the desire to maneuver for the time in which to call a friend, she will have defined herself in terms of an explicit impotence that she cannot endure. Capitulation in this case is preferable to self-humiliation. Resisting the definition of oneself in terms of what one cannot do, what others take for granted, represents a need so great that other imperatives (even one so urgent as the need to keep one's home in winter's cold) evaporate and fall away in face of fear. Even the loss of home and shelter, in this case, is not so terrifying as the loss of self.

"I come out of school. I was sixteen. They had their meetings. The directors meet. They said that I was wasting their school paper. I was wasting pencils. . . ."

Another illiterate, looking back, believes she was not worthy of her teacher's time. She believes that it was wrong of her to take up space within her school. She believes that it was right to leave in order that somebody more deserving could receive her place.

Children choke. Their mother chokes another way: on more than   40
chicken bones.

People eat what others order, know what others tell them, struggle not to see themselves as they believe the world perceives them. A man in California speaks about his own loss of identity, of self-location, definition:

"I stood at the bottom of the ramp. My car had broke down on the freeway. There was a phone. I asked for the police. They was nice. They said to tell them where I was. I looked up at the signs. There was one that I had seen before. I read it to them: ONE WAY STREET. They thought it was a joke. I told them I couldn't read. There was other signs above the ramp. They told me to try. I looked around for somebody to help. All the cars was going by real fast. I couldn't make them understand that I was lost. The cop was nice. He told me: 'Try once more.' I did my best. I couldn't read. I only knew the sign above my head. The cop was trying to be nice. He knew that I was trapped. 'I can't send out a car to you if you can't tell me where you are.' I felt afraid. I nearly cried. I'm forty-eight years old. I only said: 'I'm on a one-way street. . . .'"

Perhaps we might slow down a moment here and look at the realities described above. This is the nation that we live in. This is a society that most of us did not create but which our President and other leaders have been willing to sustain by virtue of malign neglect. Do we possess the character and courage to address a problem which so many nations, poorer than our own, have found it natural to correct?

The answers to these questions represent a reasonable test of our belief in the democracy to which we have been asked in public school to swear allegiance.

Working with the Text

1. Jonathan Kozol opens this chapter from *Illiterate America* by citing the set of warnings on a can of Drāno. Why do you think Kozol chooses this strategy? What effect do you think he is hoping to achieve? How did this opening affect you as a reader? How does your ability to read the warnings bring home to you the dangers that might be encountered by someone who can't read those warnings?

2. For the first six paragraphs of this chapter, Kozol focuses on the costs of illiteracy to democratic institutions and to political and civic participation. He then transitions to a perspective that highlights the "human price" of illiteracy, a perspective that he maintains for much of the chapter. Then, in the final two paragraphs, Kozol again returns to a broader perspective and calls on us to act—in ways both civic and political—on our growing awareness of the "human price" that he has revealed. What purposes lie behind Kozol's structural decisions in his organization of this chapter? What does Kozol accomplish by framing specific examples of the human cost of illiteracy with broader reflections on democracy and ethics?

3. Kozol's discussion of the human costs of illiteracy relies in large measure on specific examples. Indeed, the very cascade of examples, their sheer number, carries an important rhetorical effect. How does the ever-increasing number of examples contribute to the persuasiveness of Kozol's argument? Does the copiousness of evidence contribute to a sense of the magnitude and scope of the problem?

From Text to Field

1. As Jonathan Kozol turns to catalog the "human price" of illiteracy, he recounts a dream. "I find that I am in a railroad station or a large department store within a city that is utterly unknown to me and where I cannot understand the printed words" (par. 7). Kozol argues that the panic he experiences from this dream is "not so different from the misery that millions of adult illiterates experience each day within the course of their routine existence in the U.S.A." Reflect on your experiences and nightmares, and recall a situation (real or

dreamt) in which you experienced panic of the kind Kozol describes. To what extent does that situation parallel the plight of illiterate Americans? Why does Kozol relate a dream to his audience? Does the dream story succeed in personalizing the succeeding real-life examples, which may be beyond the immediate experience of those in his audience?

2. Kozol's discussion of illiteracy relies on examples and concrete scenarios. What additional examples or stories might you contribute to those Kozol has offered? Consider offering examples that stem from your immediate surroundings: your campus and your community. How would someone who is illiterate handle even the most basic of jobs on your campus? Likewise, find a consumer item in a store that would prove difficult for an illiterate to understand, or describe an activity or task not mentioned by Kozol that would prove daunting for someone who cannot read. In a short essay, discuss what aspects of Kozol's argument your own examples have reinforced or what new perspectives your examples might shed light on.

3. The experience of being in a foreign country where you do not know even the most basic aspects of the language is at best an imperfect analogue to the experiences of being illiterate. If you have traveled abroad in countries where you did not know the language, or perhaps even the alphabet, what was the experience like? To what extent is such an experience helpful in understanding illiteracy? Likewise, in what ways is such an experience fundamentally different from the experiences encountered by those who are illiterate?

Learning the Language

Perri Klass

As a medical student, Perri Klass had to learn a new code, a new language, a new set of attitudes and behaviors. Although most of us will never learn that particular language, her initiation into the language of the medical community parallels what happens when any one of us enters a new group. Whether that new group is a family or a fraternity/sorority, a discipline or profession, or a new workplace culture, Perri Klass calls to our attention both the rewards and dangers of "learning the language." To use a medical euphemism, she might say the process is "a not entirely benign procedure."

With her own diverse background as a pediatrician, writer, and mother, Perri Klass is sensitive to the ways in which we come into language. She was born in Trinidad in 1958, where her father (an anthropologist) and her mother (a writer) lived at the time. She received her MD from Harvard Medical School in 1986 and has gone on to specialize in pediatric medicine. Even with the demands of medical training and practice, not to mention family, she has published three novels, *Recombinations* (1985), *Other Women's Children* (1990), and *The Mystery of Breathing* (2004), as well as two short-story collections, *I Am Having an Adventure* (1986) and *Love and Modern Medicine: Stories* (2001). She has also written two collections of essays about medical training, *Baby Doctor: A Pediatrician's Training* (1992) and *A Not Entirely Benign Procedure: Four Years as a Medical Student* (1987), in which the following selection appears as a chapter. Her latest book, written with Eileen Costello, is *Quirky Kids* (2004). Perri Klass's interest in "learning the language" continues, as she now serves as the medical director of the national literacy program Reach Out and Read, dedicated to promoting literacy as part of pediatric primary care.

"Mrs. Tolstoy is your basic LOL in NAD, admitted for a soft rule-out MI," the intern announces. I scribble that on my patient list. In other words, Mrs. Tolstoy is a Little Old Lady in No Apparent Distress who is in the hospital to make sure she hasn't had a heart attack (rule out a Myocardial Infarction). And we think it's unlikely that she has had a heart attack (a *soft* rule-out).

If I learned nothing else during my first three months of working in the hospital as a medical student, I learned endless jargon and abbreviations. I started out in a state of primeval innocence, in which I didn't even know that "sCP, SOB, N/V" meant "without chest pain, shortness of breath, or nausea and vomiting." By the end I took the abbreviations so much for granted that I would complain to my mother the English professor, "And can you believe I had to put down *three* NG tubes last night?"

"You'll have to tell me what an NG tube is if you want me to sympathize properly," my mother said. NG, nasogastric—isn't it obvious?

I picked up not only the specific expressions but also the patterns of speech and the grammatical conventions; for example, you never say that a patient's blood pressure fell or that his cardiac enzymes rose. Instead, the patient is always the subject of the verb. "He dropped his pressure." "He bumped his enzymes." This sort of construction probably reflects the profound irritation of the intern when the nurses come in the middle of the night to say that Mr. Dickinson has disturbingly low blood pressure. "Oh, he's gonna hurt me bad tonight," the intern might say, inevitably angry at Mr. Dickinson for dropping his pressure and creating a problem.

When chemotherapy fails to cure Mrs. Bacon's cancer, what we say is, "Mrs. Bacon failed chemotherapy." 5

"Well, we've already had one hit today, and we're up next, but at least we've got mostly stable players on our team." This means that our team (group of doctors and medical students) has already gotten one new admission today, and it is our turn again, so we'll get whoever is admitted next in emergency, but at least most of the patients we already have are fairly stable; that is, unlikely to drop their pressures or in any other way get suddenly sicker and hurt us bad. Baseball metaphor is pervasive. A no-hitter is a night without any new admissions. A player is always a patient—a nitrate player is a patient on nitrates, a unit player is a patient in the intensive care unit, and so on, until you reach the terminal player.

It is interesting to consider what it means to be winning, or doing well, in this perennial baseball game. When the intern hangs up the phone and announces, "I got a hit," that is not cause for congratulations. The team is not scoring points; rather, it is getting hit, being bombarded with new patients. The object of the game from the point of view of the doctors, considering the players for whom they are already responsible, is to get as few new hits as possible.

This special language contributes to a sense of closeness and professional spirit among people who are under a great deal of stress. As a medical student,

I found it exciting to discover that I'd finally cracked the code, that I could understand what doctors said and wrote, and could use the same formulations myself. Some people seem to become enamored of the jargon for its own sake, perhaps because they are so deeply thrilled with the idea of medicine, with the idea of themselves as doctors.

I knew a medical student who was referred to by the interns on the team as Mr. Eponym because he was so infatuated with eponymous terminology, the more obscure the better. He never said "capillary pulsations" if he could say "Quincke's pulses." He would lovingly tell over the multinamed syndromes—Wolff-Parkinson-White, Lown-Ganong-Levine, Schönlein-Henoch—until the temptation to suggest Schleswig-Holstein or Stevenson-Kefauver or Baskin-Robbins became irresistible to his less reverent colleagues.

You move closer and closer to being a doctor instead of just talking like one.

And there is the jargon that you don't ever want to hear yourself using. You know that your training is changing you, but there are certain changes you think would be going a little too far. 10

The resident was describing a man with devastating terminal pancreatic cancer. "Basically he's CTD," the resident concluded. I reminded myself that I had resolved not to be shy about asking when I didn't understand things. "CTD?" I asked timidly.

The resident smirked at me. "Circling The Drain."

The images are vivid and terrible. "What happened to Mrs. Melville?"

"Oh, she boxed last night." To box is to die, of course.

Then there are the more pompous locutions that can make the beginning medical student nervous about the effects of medical training. A friend of mine was told by his resident, "A pregnant woman with sickle-cell represents a failure of genetic counseling." 15

Mr. Eponym, who tried hard to talk like the doctors, once explained to me, "An infant is basically a brainstem preparation." The term "brainstem preparation," as used in neurological research, refers to an animal whose higher brain functions have been destroyed so that only the most primitive reflexes remain, like the sucking reflex, the startle reflex, and the rooting reflex.

And yet at other times the harshness dissipates into a strangely elusive euphemism. "As you know, this is a not entirely benign procedure," some doctor will say, and that will be understood to imply agony, risk of complications, and maybe even a significant mortality rate.

The more extreme forms aside, one most important function of medical jargon is to help doctors maintain some distance from their patients. By reformulating a patient's pain and problems into a language that the patient doesn't even speak, I suppose we are in some sense taking those pains and problems under our jurisdiction and also reducing their emotional impact. This linguistic separation between doctors and patients allows conversations to go on at the bedside that are unintelligible to the patient. "Naturally, we're worried about adeno-CA," the intern can say to the medical student, and lung cancer need never be mentioned.

I learned a new language this past summer. At times it thrills me to hear myself using it. It enables me to understand my colleagues, to communicate effectively in the hospital. Yet I am uncomfortably aware that I will never again notice the peculiarities and even atrocities of medical language as keenly as I did this summer. There may be specific expressions I manage to avoid, but even as I remark them, promising myself I will never use them, I find that this language is becoming my professional speech. It no longer sounds strange in my ears—or coming from my mouth. And I am afraid that as with any new language, to use it properly you must absorb not only the vocabulary but also the structure, the logic, the attitudes. At first you may notice these new and alien assumptions every time you put together a sentence, but with time and increased fluency you stop being aware of them at all. And as you lose that awareness, for better or for worse, you move closer and closer to being a doctor instead of just talking like one.

Working with the Text

1. Why do doctors use medical jargon? Perri Klass offers several reasons in her essay. First list those reasons, and then write a short response essay in which you tease out how those reasons might be related. From your perspective as a patient, are there reasons that Klass might have neglected to mention?

2. Klass reflects on both the benefits and the drawbacks of specialized medical language. Develop a two-column list of those benefits and drawbacks. Whose interests and perspectives does that list represent? Are there other benefits and drawbacks you would add to that list? Working from your lists, write a short response essay on whether the language of any community is inevitably partial and inevitably speaks to certain interests. Does specialized language imply a user's particular view of the world?

3. Two figures make cameo appearances in the essay: the mother and a fellow medical student whom Klass names "Mr. Eponym." What functions do these two characters serve? How do the mother and Mr. Eponym relate to the implied reader of the essay? In what ways are groups defined as much by outsiders as by members? Write a short analysis of the essay in which you tease out connections between the structure of Klass's essay and the dynamics of entering a community.

From Text to Field

1. Reflecting on her medical education, Klass says "you must absorb not only the vocabulary but also the structure, the logic, the attitudes" (par. 19). What do you think Klass means by this statement? What arguments do you think Klass is making by telling her story as she does? In a brief autobiographical essay, analyze your own early apprenticeship in an academic field or in an area of interest, such as sports or music or a hobby. Consider what the veiled argument might be behind your own story.

2. Klass ends her essay by commenting on the relationship between "talking like" a doctor and "being a doctor." How do you see this relationship between language and identity in your own college life? How does that relationship change as you move from home to campus, from friends to class, even from discipline to discipline? Write a short exploratory or reflective essay on language and identity from your perspective as a student.

3. Consider some specialty, discipline, or sphere of activity with a language of its own, perhaps one far removed from your own interests. You may refer to books (even essays in this book) or to your experiences in the classroom. As you offer examples of that specialized language, write an essay in which you consider what uses of jargon are appropriate or inappropriate and for whom. Is jargon natural or even beneficial, or does it offer an unwelcome barrier? Does jargon offer a means for regulation or control, for the "disciplining" of a community's members?

It Takes a Tribe

David Berreby

What is it about the human mind that makes us believe in categories like race, gender, and ethnicity? Why is it that we form groups, dividing ourselves into "us" and "them"?

These are the questions that sent David Berreby on a quest that resulted in his recent book *Us and Them: Understanding Your Tribal Mind* (2005). Berreby pursues answers to those questions by spanning a number of disciplines and drawing on a wide range of sources, from classical texts to the most current research. A science journalist and nonfiction writer, David Berreby has written regularly about science and culture for such publications as the *New York Times,* the *New Republic,* the *Sciences, Discover,* and *Slate.*

In his article "It Takes a Tribe," which appeared in the *New York Times* in 2004, David Berreby explores why and how we become so thoroughly identified with the universities we attend. What Berreby discovers is that "[s]tudents don't just attend a college; they join its tribes." It turns out that we want to live in tribes, and we are keen on figuring out the rules of membership, initiation, and exclusion. We're eager to belt out the school song—just as soon as we learn what the words are.

When the budding pundit Walter Lippmann coined the term *stereotype* back in 1922, he offered several examples from the America of his time: *Agitator. Intellectual. South European. From the Back Bay.* You know, he told the reader, when a glimpse and a word or two create a full mental picture of a whole group of people. As in *plutocrat.* Or *foreigner.* Or *Harvard man.*

Harvard man? We know, thanks to Lippmann, that stereotypes are part of serious problems like racism, prejudice, and injustice. What is Lippmann's alma mater doing on such a list? (He even added: "How different from the statement, 'He is a Yale man.'")

Spend time on a campus in coming weeks, though, and you'll see what he meant.

At colleges across the country, from Ivy League to less exclusive state schools, students who are mispronouncing the library's name this month will soon feel truly and deeply a part of their college. They'll be singing their school songs and cherishing the traditions (just as soon as they learn what they are). They'll talk the way "we" do. (Going to Texas A & M? Then greet people with a cheerful "howdy.") They'll learn contempt for that rival university—Oklahoma to their Texas, Sacramento State to their UC Davis, Annapolis to their West Point.

They may come to believe, too, that an essential trait separates them from the rest of humanity—the same sort of feeling most Americans have about races, ethnic groups, and religions. As the writer Christopher Buckley said recently in his college's alumni magazine: "When I run into a Yale man I somehow feel that I am with a kindred spirit. A part of that kindred-ness comes from his gentility and his not being all jumped up about it. It's a certain sweetness of character." 5

All this sentiment comes on fast (a study last year at Ivy League campuses found freshmen even more gung-ho than older students). Yet college loyalty, encouraged by alumni relations offices, can last a lifetime—as enduring as the Princeton tiger tattooed on the buttock of former Secretary of State George P. Shultz, or the Yale sweater sported by evil Mr. Burns on *The Simpsons*, a number of whose writers went to Harvard.

New identities are forged within the university as well, in elite groups like Skull and Bones at Yale or the Corps of Cadets at Texas A & M, or Michigamua at the University of Michigan; in sororities and fraternities; even in particular majors and particular labs. Students don't just attend a college; they join its tribes.

"What endlessly impresses me is people losing sight of how arbitrary it is," says Robert M. Sapolsky, a Stanford biologist who specializes in the links between social life and stress. "Students understand how readily they could have wound up at another school or wound up in another lab." Yet every year, he adds, "they fall for it." For most, what Professor Sapolsky calls that "nutty but palpable" onset of college tribalism is just a part of campus life. For social scientists, it's an object of research, offering clues to a fundamental and puzzling aspect of human nature: People need to belong, to feel a part of *us*. Yet a sense of *us* brings with it a sense of *them*.

Human beings will give a lot, including their lives, for a group they feel part of—for *us*, as in *our nation* or *our religion*. They will also harm those labeled "them," including taking their lives. Far as genocide and persecution seem from fraternity hazings and Cal versus Stanford, college tribes may shed light on the way the mind works with those other sorts of groups, the ones that shape and misshape the world, like nation, race, creed, caste, or culture.

After all, a college campus is full of people inventing a sense of *us* and a   10
sense of *them*. As one junior at the University of California, Los Angeles, told her school paper before a game against the University of Southern California: "School spirit is important because it gives us a sense of belonging and being a part of something bigger. Besides," she said, "USC sucks in every way."

In an e-mail interview, Professor Sapolsky writes that "Stanford students (and faculty) do tons of this, at every possible hierarchical level." For instance, he says, they see Stanford versus Harvard, and Stanford versus the University of California at Berkeley. "Then, within Stanford, all the science wonks doing tribal stuff to differentiate themselves from the fuzzies—the humanities/social science types. Then within the sciences, the life science people versus the chemistry/physics/math geeks." Within the life sciences, he adds, the two tribes are "bio majors and majors in what is called 'human biology'—former deprecated as being robotic premeds, incapable of thinking, just spitting out of factoids; latter as fuzzies masquerading as scientists."

Recent research on students suggests these changes in perception aren't trivial. A few years ago, a team of social psychologists asked students at the University of California at Santa Barbara to rank various collections of people in terms of how well they "qualify as a group." In their answers, "students at a university" ranked above "citizens of a nation." "Members of a campus committee" and "members of a university social club" ranked higher than "members of a union" or "members of a political party," "romantic couples," or "office colleagues working together on a project." For that matter, "students at a university" and "members of a campus committee" ranked well above blacks and Jews in the students' estimation of what qualifies as a group.

Students . . . will soon feel truly and deeply a part of their college.

Much of this thinking, researchers have found, is subconscious. We may think we care about our college ties for good and sensible reasons—wonderful classes! dorm-room heart-to-hearts! job connections!—when the deeper causes are influences we didn't notice.

Some twenty years ago, researchers asked students at Rutgers to describe themselves using only words from a set of cards prepared in advance. Some cards contained words associated with Rutgers, like *scarlet*, the school color, and *knight*, the name of its athletic teams. Others, like *orange*, were associated with archrival Princeton. Some students took the test in a room decorated with a Rutgers pennant; others took it under a Princeton flag. A third group saw only a New York Yankees banner.

Students who saw a Princeton or Rutgers emblem were more likely to use 15 Rutgers-related words to describe themselves. They also mentioned that they were students at Rutgers earlier than those who saw only the neutral flag. They didn't consciously decide to stand up for Rutgers. Outside their conscious minds, though, that identity was in place, ready to be released by symbols of the tribe.

More recently, three social psychologists at Harvard looked at another example of subconscious tribal beliefs. Mahzarin R. Banaji, who led the study, argues that people in similar, equivalent groups will place those groups into a hierarchy, from best to worst, even when there is no rational basis for ranking them. The psychologists tested Yale sophomores, juniors, and seniors, who live and eat together in "residential colleges." Students know that these colleges are effectively all alike and that people are assigned to them at random. Still, the team found, Yalies did indeed rank them from best to worst. (In the interests of peace and comity, the colleges were kept anonymous.) Moreover, students assigned to the less prestigious units were less enthusiastic about their homes than those from the ones with a better reputation.

What this suggests, Professor Banaji says, is that taking one's place in a tribe and accepting the tribe's place in a larger society are mental acts that happen regardless of the group's purpose or meaning. Once people see that they've been divided into groups, they'll act accordingly, even if they know that the divisions are as meaningless as, oh, the University of Arizona versus Arizona State. "We know that human beings identify with social groups, sometimes sufficiently to kill or die on their behalf," she says. "What is not as well known is that such identity between self and group can form rapidly, often following a psychological route that is relatively subconscious. That is, like automata, we identify with the groups in which we are accidentally placed."

Not all researchers agree that people care about so-called nonsense groups with the same passion they give to religion, politics, or morals. Another theory holds that the subconscious mind can distinguish which groups matter and how much. One example comes from a much-cited experiment, performed, naturally, on college students.

In 1959, the social psychologists Elliot Aronson and Judson Mills asked undergraduate women to join a discussion group after a short initiation. For one set of participants the initiation required reciting a few mild sexual words. The other group had to say a list of much saltier words about sex, which embarrassed them to no end (remember, this was 1959). The discussion group was dull as dishwater, but the women who suffered to join rated it as much more valuable than those who had a mild initiation (and higher than a control group that didn't have to do anything).

A subconscious clue for perceiving a tribe as real and valuable, then, may 20 be expending sweat, tears, and embarrassment to get in. The political activist

Tom Hayden recently recalled just such a rite at the University of Michigan, in an article on the left-wing Web site alternet.org. He was complaining about the lock that Skull and Bones has on November's election (President Bush and the Democratic nominee, Senator John Kerry, are members).

"As a junior, I was tapped for the Druids," Mr. Hayden wrote about his own campus clan, "which involved a two-day ritual that included being stripped to my underpants, pelted with eggs, smeared with red dye, and tied to a campus tree. These humiliations signified my rebirth from lowly student journalist to Big Man on Campus."

As for Professor Aronson, had he not wanted tight control over the experiment, he writes in his widely used textbook, *The Social Animal*, he and Professor Mills could simply have studied an initiation outside the lab—at a campus fraternity or sorority.

That kind of lumping together—studying one group to explain another—drives scholars in other fields to distraction. To them, a pep rally is different from a political rally. Historians, trained to see big generalizations as meaningless, are often aghast at the way psychologists' theories about groups ignore the difference between, say, today's two-gendered, multiethnic, and meritocratic Harvard College and the one that gave Lippmann his degree in 1909. And anthropologists for generations have disdained psychology for ignoring cultural differences.

But one fact is clear, and college groups exemplify it well: While many creatures live in groups, humanity's are unlike anything else found in nature. Peter Richerson, a biologist at Sacramento State's rival, the University of California at Davis, likes to point out that his students, sitting quietly together on the first day of class, are an amazing exception to the general rules of animal behavior. Put chimpanzees or monkeys that don't know one another in a room, and they would be in hysterics. People team up with strangers easily.

Professor Richerson and his longtime collaborator, Robert Boyd, an   25 anthropologist at USC's hated enemy, UCLA, argue that we will sign up for membership in tribelike groups for the same reason birds sing: It feels right because we evolved to do it. "We want to live in tribes," Professor Richerson says. Humans are "looking to be told what group they belong to, and then once they do that, they want to know, 'What are the rules?'"

The tricky part, says Professor Sapolsky of Stanford, Cal-Berkeley's bitter rival, is that humans alone among animals can think about what a tribe is and who belongs. "Humans actually think about who is an 'us' and who is a 'them' rather than just knowing it," he says. "The second it becomes a cognitive process, it is immensely subject to manipulation."

And, of course, studying the phenomenon won't make you immune. "I'm true blue," says Professor Banaji, who taught at Yale from 1986 until 2002, when she joined the Harvard faculty. "I was physically unable to sit through a women's basketball game between Harvard and Yale on the Harvard side."

Working with the Text

1. Although the subject of group allegiance in college may lend itself to anecdotal treatment, David Berreby organizes this article by citing various experts and moving from one research study to the next. What advantages does this strategy hold? Given the subject of the article, why does Berreby lend his voice to the voices of others? Are there any disadvantages to Berreby's strategy?

2. Many of the examples and research studies cited by Berreby highlight the early moments when tribal affiliations are formed. What is distinctive and important about these early moments? Why does the nature of our initiation into a group carry such continuing significance?

3. College rituals and traditions do more than create a sense of community and belonging. They also function as a means of exclusion—a way not just to foster a sense of "us" but also to create a sense of "them," a sense of the "other." Review Berreby's article for references to this us/them dichotomy. Why is the creation of a sense of "us" implicated in the creation of "them"?

4. Berreby suggests at several points that the distinctions that help us create a tribal identity are often not terribly real or essential. Indeed, some distinctions seem to be fictions of our own creation. In what ways do our tribal impulses lead us to create questionable distinctions among ourselves? According to Berreby, what accounts for this impulse?

From Text to Field

1. In his article, David Berreby makes frequent references to the rituals and traditions of campus life. What rituals and traditions on your campus seem to be most important to you and your fellow students? How might these compare to the rituals and traditions important to faculty members and alumni?

2. As you recall the first several weeks you spent on campus, what role did orientation programs or dorm life or sports have in fostering a sense of belonging? Berreby notes that studies have shown that first-year students are especially "gung-ho" about college loyalty. Why do you think this may be the case?

3. On your own campus, do you observe instances when tribal loyalties and initiation into a particular "tribe" seem to have gotten out of hand? To what extent are hazing and other initiation rituals driven by this tribal impulse? Do various groups on your campus—sororities and fraternities among them—balance the impulse to form tribes with an awareness of its possible dangers?

4. Berreby notes that we do more than place ourselves and others in tribes; we also place these tribes in hierarchies. What kind of hierarchies exist on your campus—whether among majors, dorms or residential colleges, and clubs? How did you learn about these hierarchies, and how did they evolve?

5. In this particular article, David Berreby focuses exclusively on tribal instincts on college campuses. Are campuses unique or distinctive in this respect, or do such instincts play themselves out in other arenas, such as in the business world or in community and social activities? Discuss examples of tribalism that are not tied to a college campus. Do you see these examples as supporting essentially the same arguments that Berreby makes, or do these examples raise new issues?

The Language of Discretion

Amy Tan

> Raised in California by her immigrant parents from China, Amy Tan understands firsthand the issues of language use and translation that come from living in a bicultural or multicultural environment. A good part of learning any language (even the academic languages of various disciplines) involves understanding "the language of discretion." You might think of discretion as "cautious reserve in speech" or, in the context of Tan's essay, the set of expectations and understandings that needn't be verbalized in speech because they are shared within a community. Learning those silent or tacit expectations is a challenge for all of us, as we move in and among communities.
>
> Tan began writing short stories while working as a freelance writer in San Francisco specializing in corporate communications. Those stories were collected in her immensely popular first novel, *The Joy Luck Club* (1989), which was later produced as a motion picture. Tan's other fiction includes *The Kitchen God's Wife* (1991), *The Hundred Secret Senses* (1995), and most recently *Saving Fish from Drowning* (2005) as well as two children's books, *The Moon Lady* (1992) and *The Chinese Siamese Cat* (1994). She has also published a collection of essays, *The Opposite of Fate* (2003). In "The Language of Discretion" (1989) you hear Tan's voice as an essayist, reflecting on the very issues that drive her works of fiction.

At a recent family dinner in San Francisco, my mother whispered to me: "Sau-sau [Brother's Wife] pretends too hard to be polite! Why bother? In the end, she always takes everything."

My mother thinks like a *waixiao*, an expatriate, temporarily away from China since 1949, no longer patient with ritual courtesies. As if to prove her point, she reached across the table to offer my elderly aunt from Beijing the last scallop from the Happy Family seafood dish.

Sau-sau scowled. *"B'yao, zhen b'yao!"* (I don't want it, really I don't!) she cried, patting her plump stomach.

"Take it! Take it!" scolded my mother in Chinese.

"Full, I'm already full," Sau-sau protested weakly, eyeing the beloved scallop. 5

"Ai!" exclaimed my mother, completely exasperated. "Nobody else wants it. If you don't take it, it will only rot!"

At this point, Sau-sau sighed, acting as if she were doing my mother a big favor by taking the wretched scrap off her hands.

My mother turned to her brother, a high-ranking communist official who was visiting her in California for the first time: "In America a Chinese person could starve to death. If you say you don't want it, they won't ask you again forever."

My uncle nodded and said he understood fully: Americans take things quickly because they have no time to be polite.

I thought about this misunderstanding again—of social contexts failing in translation—when a friend sent me an article from the *New York Times Magazine* (24 April 1988). The article, on changes in New York's Chinatown, made passing reference to the inherent ambivalence of the Chinese language. 10

Language enables us to sort out and categorize the world.

Chinese people are so "discreet and modest," the article stated, there aren't even words for "yes" and "no."

That's not true, I thought, although I can see why an outsider might think that. I continued reading.

If one is Chinese, the article went on to say, "One compromises, one doesn't hazard a loss of face by an overemphatic response."

My throat seized. Why do people keep saying these things? As if we truly were those little dolls sold in Chinatown tourist shops, heads bobbing up and down in complacent agreement to anything said!

I worry about the effect of one-dimensional statements on the unwary and guileless. When they read about this so-called vocabulary deficit, do they also conclude that Chinese people evolved into a mild-mannered lot because the language only allowed them to hobble forth with minced words? 15

Something enormous is always lost in translation. Something insidious seeps into the gaps, especially when amateur linguists continue to compare, one-for-one, language differences and then put forth notions wide open to misinterpretation: that Chinese people have no direct linguistic means to make decisions, assert or deny, affirm or negate, just say no to drug dealers, or behave properly on the witness stand when told, "Please answer yes or no."

Yet one can argue, with the help of renowned linguists, that the Chinese are indeed up a creek without "yes" and "no." Take any number of variations on the old language-and-reality theory stated years ago by Edward Sapir: "Human beings . . . are very much at the mercy of the particular language which has become the medium for their society. . . . The fact of the matter is that the 'real world' is to a large extent built up on the language habits of the group."[1]

This notion was further bolstered by the famous Sapir-Whorf hypothesis, which roughly states that one's perception of the world and how one functions in it depends a great deal on the language used. As Sapir, Whorf, and new carriers of the banner would have us believe, language shapes our thinking, channels us along certain patterns embedded in words, syntactic structures, and intonation patterns. Language has become the peg and the shelf that enables us to sort out and categorize the world. In English, we see "cats" and "dogs"; what if the language had also specified *glatz*, meaning "animals that leave fur on the sofa," and *glotz*, meaning "animals that leave fur and drool on the sofa"? How would language, the enabler, have changed our perceptions with slight vocabulary variations?

And if this were the case—of language being the master of destined thought—think of the opportunities lost from failure to evolve two little words, *yes* and *no*, the simplest of opposites! Ghenghis Khan could have been sent back to Mongolia. Opium wars might have been averted. The Cultural Revolution could have been sidestepped.

There are still many, from serious linguists to pop psychology cultists, [20] who view language and reality as inextricably tied, one being the consequence of the other. We have traversed the range from the Sapir-Whorf hypothesis to est° and neurolinguistic programming, which tell us "you are what you say."

I too have been intrigued by the theories. I can summarize, albeit badly, ages-old empirical evidence: of Eskimos and their infinite ways to say "snow," their ability to *see* the differences in snowflake configurations, thanks to the richness of their vocabulary, while non-Eskimo speakers like myself founder in "snow," "more snow," and "lots more where that came from."

I too have experienced dramatic cognitive awakenings via the word. Once I added "mauve" to my vocabulary I began to see it everywhere. When I learned how to pronounce *prix fixe*, I ate French food at prices better than the easier-to-say *à la carte* choices.

But just how seriously are we supposed to take this?

Sapir said something else about language and reality. It is the part that often gets left behind in the dot-dot-dots of quotes: ". . . No two languages are ever sufficiently similar to be considered as representing the same social reality. The worlds in which different societies live are distinct worlds, not merely the same world with different labels attached."

---

est: Erhard Seminars Training, a program for large group awareness training founded by Werner Erhard and popular in the 1970s.

When I first read this, I thought, Here at last is validity for the dilemmas I 25 felt growing up in a bicultural, bilingual family! As any child of immigrant parents knows, there's a special kind of double bind attached to knowing two languages. My parents, for example, spoke to me in both Chinese and English; I spoke back to them in English.

"Amy-ah!" they'd call to me.

"What?" I'd mumble back.

"Do not question us when we call," they scolded me in Chinese. "It is not respectful."

"What do you mean?"

"Ai! Didn't we just tell you not to question?" 30

To this day, I wonder which parts of my behavior were shaped by Chinese, which by English. I am tempted to think, for example, that if I am of two minds on some matter it is due to the richness of my linguistic experiences, not to any personal tendencies toward wishy-washiness. But which mind says what?

Was it perhaps patience—developed through years of deciphering my mother's fractured English—that had me listening politely while a woman announced over the phone that I had won one of five valuable prizes? Was it respect—pounded in by the Chinese imperative to accept convoluted explanations—that had me agreeing that I might find it worthwhile to drive seventy-five miles to view a time-share resort? Could I have been at a loss for words when asked, "Wouldn't you like to win a Hawaiian cruise or perhaps a fabulous Star of India designed exclusively by Carter and Van Arpels?"

And when this same woman called back a week later, this time complaining that I had missed my appointment, obviously it was my type A language that kicked into gear and interrupted her. Certainly, my blunt denial—"Frankly I'm not interested"—was as American as apple pie. And when she said, "But it's in Morgan Hill," and I shouted, "Read my lips. I don't care if it's Timbuktu," you can be sure I said it with the precise intonation expressing both cynicism and disgust.

It's dangerous business, this sorting out of language and behavior. Which one is English? Which is Chinese? The categories manifest themselves: passive and aggressive, tentative and assertive, indirect and direct. And I realize they are just variations of the same theme: that Chinese people are discreet and modest.

Reject them all! 35

If my reaction is overly strident, it is because I cannot come across as too emphatic. I grew up listening to the same lines over and over again, like so many rote expressions repeated in an English phrasebook. And I too almost came to believe them.

Yet if I consider my upbringing more carefully, I find there was nothing discreet about the Chinese language I grew up with. My parents made everything abundantly clear. Nothing wishy-washy in their demands, no compromises accepted: "Of course you will become a famous neurosurgeon," they told me. "And yes, a concert pianist on the side."

In fact, now that I remember, it seems that the more emphatic outbursts always spilled over into Chinese: "Not that way! You must wash rice so not a single grain spills out."

I do not believe that my parents—both immigrants from mainland China—are an exception to the modest-and-discreet rule. I have only to look at the number of Chinese engineering students skewing minority ratios at Berkeley, MIT, and Yale. Certainly they were not raised by passive mothers and fathers who said, "It is up to you, my daughter. Writer, welfare recipient, masseuse, or molecular engineer—you decide."

And my American mind says, See, those engineering students weren't able to say no to their parents' demands. But then my Chinese mind remembers: Ah, but those parents all wanted their sons and daughters to be *pre-med*. 40

Having listened to both Chinese and English, I also tend to be suspicious of any comparisons between the two languages. Typically, one language—that of the person doing the comparing—is often used as the standard, the benchmark for a logical form of expression. And so the language being compared is always in danger of being judged deficient or superfluous, simplistic or unnecessarily complex, melodious or cacophonous. English speakers point out that Chinese is extremely difficult because it relies on variations in tone barely discernible to the human ear. By the same token, Chinese speakers tell me English is extremely difficult because it is inconsistent, a language of too many broken rules, of Mickey Mice and Donald Ducks.

Even more dangerous to my mind is the temptation to compare both language and behavior *in translation*. To listen to my mother speak English, one might think she has no concept of past or future tense, that she doesn't see the difference between singular and plural, that she is gender blind because she calls my husband "she." If one were not careful, one might also generalize that, based on the way my mother talks, all Chinese people take a circumlocutory route to get to the point. It is, in fact, my mother's idiosyncratic behavior to ramble a bit.

Sapir was right about differences between two languages and their realities. I can illustrate why word-for-word translation is not enough to translate meaning and intent. I once received a letter from China which I read to non-Chinese-speaking friends. The letter, originally written in Chinese, had been translated by my brother-in law in Beijing. One portion described the time when my uncle at age ten discovered his widowed mother (my grandmother) had remarried—as a number three concubine, the ultimate disgrace for an honorable family. The translated version of my uncle's letter read in part:

> In 1925, I met my mother in Shanghai. When she came to me, I didn't have greeting to her as if seeing nothing. She pull me to a corner secretly and asked me why didn't have greeting to her. I couldn't control myself and cried, "Ma! Why did you leave us? People told me: one day you ate a beancake yourself. Your sister in-law found it and sweared at you, called your names. So . . . is it true?" She clasped my hand and answered immediately, "It's not true, don't say what like this." After this time, there was a few chance to meet her.

"What!" cried my friends. "Was eating a beancake so terrible?"

Of course not. The beancake was simply a euphemism; a ten-year-old boy did not dare question his mother on something as shocking as concubinage. Eating a beancake was his equivalent for committing this selfish act, something inconsiderate of all family members, hence, my grandmother's despairing response to what seemed like a ludicrous charge of gluttony. And sure enough, she was banished from the family, and my uncle saw her only a few times before her death.

While the above may fuel people's argument that Chinese is indeed a language of extreme discretion, it does not mean that Chinese people speak in secrets and riddles. The contexts are fully understood. It is only to those on the *outside* that the language seems cryptic, the behavior inscrutable.

I am, evidently, one of the outsiders. My nephew in Shanghai, who recently started taking English lessons, has been writing me letters in English. I had told him I was a fiction writer, and so in one letter he wrote, "Congratulate to you on your writing. Perhaps one day I should like to read it." I took it in the same vein as "Perhaps one day we can get together for lunch." I sent back a cheery note. A month went by and another letter arrived from Shanghai. "Last one perhaps I hadn't writing distinctly," he said. "In the future, you'll send a copy of your works for me."

I try to explain to my English-speaking friends that Chinese language use is more *strategic* in manner, whereas English tends to be more direct; an American business executive may say, "Let's make a deal," and the Chinese manager may reply, "Is your son interested in learning about your widget business?" Each to his or her own purpose, each with his or her own linguistic path. But I hesitate to add more to the pile of generalizations, because no matter how many examples I provide and explain, I fear that it appears defensive and only reinforces the image: that Chinese people are "discreet and modest"—and it takes an American to explain what they really mean.

Why am I complaining? The description seems harmless enough (after all, the *New York Times Magazine* writer did not say "slippery and evasive"). It is precisely the bland, easy acceptability of the phrase that worries me.

I worry that the dominant society may see Chinese people from a limited 50 —and limiting—perspective. I worry that seemingly benign stereotypes may be part of the reason there are few Chinese in top management positions, in mainstream political roles. I worry about the power of language: that if one says anything enough times—in *any* language—it might become true.

Could this be why Chinese friends of my parents' generation are willing to accept the generalization?

"Why are you complaining?" one of them said to me. "If people think we are modest and polite, let them think that. Wouldn't Americans be pleased to admit they are thought of as polite?"

And I do believe anyone would take the description as a compliment — at first. But after a while, it annoys, as if the only things that people heard one say were phatic remarks: "I'm so pleased to meet you. I've heard many wonderful things about you. For me? You shouldn't have!"

These remarks are not representative of new ideas, honest emotions, or considered thought. They are what is said from the polite distance of social contexts: of greetings, farewells, wedding thank-you notes, convenient excuses, and the like.

It makes me wonder though. How many anthropologists, how many soci- 55 ologists, how many travel journalists have documented so-called "natural interactions" in foreign lands, all observed with spiral notebook in hand? How many other cases are there of the long-lost primitive tribe, people who turned out to be sophisticated enough to put on the stone-age show that ethnologists had come to see?

And how many tourists fresh off the bus have wandered into Chinatown expecting the self-effacing shopkeeper to admit under duress that the goods are not worth the price asked? I have witnessed it.

"I don't know," the tourist said to the shopkeeper, a Cantonese woman in her fifties. "It doesn't look genuine to me. I'll give you three dollars."

"You don't like my price, go somewhere else," said the shopkeeper.

"You are not a nice person," cried the shocked tourist, "not a nice person at all!"

"Who say I have to be nice," snapped the shopkeeper.   60

"So how does one say 'yes' and 'no' in Chinese?" ask my friends a bit warily.

And here I do agree in part with the *New York Times Magazine* article. There is no one word for "yes" or "no"—but not out of necessity to be discreet.

If anything, I would say the Chinese equivalent of answering "yes" or "no" is dis*crete*, that is, specific to what is asked.

Ask a Chinese person if he or she has eaten, and he or she might say *chrle* (eaten already) or perhaps *meiyou* (have not).

Ask, "So you had insurance at the time of the accident?" and the response would be *dwei* (correct) or *meiyou* (did not have).

Ask, "Have you stopped beating your wife?" and the answer refers directly   65 to the proposition being asserted or denied: stopped already, still have not, never beat, have no wife.

What could be clearer?

As for those who are still wondering how to translate the language of discretion, I offer this personal example.

My aunt and uncle were about to return to Beijing after a three-month visit to the United States. On their last night I announced I wanted to take them out to dinner.

"Are you hungry?" I asked in Chinese.

"Not hungry," said my uncle promptly, the same response he once gave   70 me ten minutes before he suffered a low-blood-sugar attack.

"Not too hungry," said my aunt. "Perhaps you're hungry?"

"A little," I admitted.

"We can eat, we can eat," they both consented.

"What kind of food?" I asked.

"Oh, doesn't matter. Anything will do. Nothing fancy, just some simple   75 food is fine."

"Do you like Japanese food? We haven't had that yet," I suggested.

They looked at each other.

"We can eat it," said my uncle bravely, this survivor of the Long March.

"We have eaten it before," added my aunt. "Raw fish."

"Oh, you don't like it?" I said. "Don't be polite. We can go somewhere   80 else."

"We are not being polite. We can eat it," my aunt insisted.

So I drove them to Japantown and we walked past several restaurants featuring colorful plastic displays of sushi.

"Not this one, not this one either," I continued to say, as if searching for a Japanese restaurant similar to the last. "Here it is," I finally said, turning into a restaurant famous for its Chinese fish dishes from Shandong.

"Oh, Chinese food!" cried my aunt, obviously relieved.

My uncle patted my arm. "You think Chinese."   85

"It's your last night here in America," I said. "So don't be polite. Act like an American."

And that night we ate a banquet.

Note

1. Edward Sapir, *Selected Writings*, ed. D. G. Mandelbaum (Berkeley and Los Angeles, 1949).

Working with the Text

1. In "The Language of Discretion," Amy Tan remarks that "the Chinese equivalent of answering 'yes' or 'no' is dis*crete*, that is, specific to what is asked" (par. 62). Look up the terms *discreet* and *discrete* in a college dictionary. Then review the essay with these two terms in mind, and consider what ideas and arguments those two terms enable her to develop. Write a short one-page summary of the essay that casts its argument in terms of those two words.

2. Early in the essay, Tan clarifies that her focus is on "social contexts failing in translation." Drawing on her discussions elsewhere in the essay, clarify what she means. Then write a short response essay in which you analyze the connection between "social context" and "translation" (language use as it moves across communities). Why do social contexts necessarily raise issues of translation and language?

3. Tan writes, "As any child of immigrant parents knows, there's a special kind of double bind attached to knowing two languages" (par. 25). What does Tan mean by "double bind"? In a journal or together with a classmate, use your own acquaintance with two languages (two dialects of English, English and a foreign language, or your native language and the English you have acquired) to come up with one or more scenarios of the sort that Tan describes. In one paragraph, offer that scenario. In a second paragraph, analyze your scenario in light of the arguments that Tan makes.

From Text to Field

1. After Tan writes "language has become the peg and the shelf that enables us to sort out and categorize the world" (par. 18), she goes on to offer a whimsical example: a new way of talking about cats and dogs. As you survey your own initiation into one aspect of the college community, have you stumbled across some important distinctions or categories that our existing language fails to capture? Write your own humorous, whimsical, or satirical essay in which you develop the new vocabulary to capture one such distinction. As you draft and revise this essay, think about the underlying argumentative point you are making and about the audience to whom you are making it.

2. Tan discusses what we might think of as "complimentary" stereotypes about the Chinese. In an essay, explore the problems associated with naïve characterizations of a group that you belong to or a discipline you are studying. Think about how stereotypes arise and why they persist with such strength.

3. Discretion is as much about silence as it is about overt language use. That is, discretion has to do with what needn't or shouldn't be said. Discretion involves expectations, rules or conventions that often become visible only when they are violated. Reflect on such "silent" conventions in a particular community or group or in a particular discipline or classroom. Write an essay in which you articulate the unspoken, in which you reveal the often puzzling "discretions" of a community you belong to or are now just entering.

Public Literacy: Puzzlements of a High School Watcher

Theodore R. Sizer

A paradox of American culture is that even as we place so much emphasis on diversity, we bemoan the fact that our cities, interstates, and institutions tend to look very much alike. For all of our emphasis on local control, our public schools are themselves astonishingly similar to one another. Public literacy—the shared experience expressed in our language, images, and symbols—has become a common subject of academic study in recent years, but when Theodore Sizer delivered his "Public Literacy" presentation in 1988, academics were largely silent on the issue. The following essay is based on Sizer's presentation at the Modern Language Association's "Right to Literacy" Conference, where the focus was on addressing illiteracy. In his essay, Sizer addresses the question, "But what of the shared symbol systems, the public literacy, that we already have? It is shaping, in an unprecedented way, a national culture."

Theodore Sizer has spent most of his academic career "watching" education, particularly secondary education. In the early 1980s, he led a study of the practices in American high schools. After teaching at Harvard and serving as dean of the Harvard Graduate School of Education, he was headmaster of Phillips Academy. Currently Sizer is University Professor Emeritus at Brown University and has been chairman of the Coalition of Essential Schools as well as visiting professor of education at Harvard. Among a number of publications focusing on secondary education is his 1999 book, *The Students Are Watching: Schools and the Moral Contract,* which he wrote with his wife, Nancy Sizer.

To visit among American high schools is to be struck by how similar these venerable social institutions are. Certainly, there is variety, best explained by differences in social class and, to a small extent, the race and the ethnicity of the students. The feel of a school serving the poor is profoundly different from the feel of its cousin in a Gold Coast suburb. However, it is the similarities that impress—the ubiquitous routines, the seven-period day, the bells, homecoming, school defined as English-math-science-social studies-language, each purveyed to students in isolation from every other. There are the texts, the sequence of topics, the testing, and, most important, the assumptions about learning and teaching and schooling that undergird these practices and the wry, usually genial cynicism of the teachers. In a nation priding itself on its local schooling, the consistencies are surprising. And the consistencies are exhibited by the students themselves—their clothing, lingo, enthusiasms, symbols. Again, class counts here, as does geography But the wonder is why the differences are not far greater. Americans are mesmerized by their differences. Perhaps they should reflect a bit more on their similarities.

There is a wealth of shared knowledge reflected in high school regimens. Kids can move from Bangor to Butte and lose few steps. Not only are the language and the school routines relatively the same, but the nuances and the gestures of getting along remarkably transcend geography. The starker differences among Americans portrayed in basic training barrack scenes from World War II movies seem quaint today to most of us The fact is that we clearly have a pervasive and powerful public literacy, a set of widely accepted symbols and ideas that give meaning to being American.

At a recent seminar my Brown University colleague Robert Scholes neatly demonstrated this public literacy by asking us to examine carefully what we must already know if we are to understand a twenty-eight-second Budweiser beer television commercial. The spot portrayed a fledgling black baseball umpire. In the half minute he moves from a scruffy minor-league ballpark to a major-league stadium to a close play at third and the resultant tirade from an offended, beefy white manager to the predictable smoke-filled bar where, with a glamorous black woman dutifully at his side, he accepts the tip of a bottle across the room from that same manager. It's all about making it, with Bud. The segment is redolent with assumed meanings. Most foreigners would miss most of it, as Scholes found. We Americans share a culture so completely that we are barely aware of it.

During the week of 19 June 1988, a typical early-summer span, the television sets that reside in more than 95 percent of America's 89 million homes were on some seven hours a day; 14.5 million households tuned in to *Night Court* and *Cheers*; *The Cosby Show* and *Sixty Minutes* drew barely fewer. Earlier that year, 37 million households watched the football Super Bowl. Shared experience, necessarily articulated in widely shared language and symbols, is a stunning reality. This shared experience shapes our expectations and discourse. It is no wonder that our adolescents are so much more alike than we, considering the expanse and the heterogeneous ethnicity of this country, might otherwise expect.

One might easily mock the results of this shared experience, this ⁵ American public literacy. It is better to test it undefensively and perhaps try to harness it. Our public literacy is characterized by at least four properties. First, it is centrally driven, usually for purposes of merchandising. Whether with jeans or biology textbooks, the name of the commercial game is national saturation. Only large companies survive in this big league, even if they appear to be little companies. For example, in the textbook field, Silver Burdett, Ginn, Allyn and Bacon, Simon and Schuster, and Prentice Hall are all Gulf and Western satraps. National symbols are expertly crafted. We have a substantial national curriculum, one with few professional educators' or elected school boards' fingerprints on it.

Second, our public literacy is commercial. The vehicle for our shared culture emerges from the selling of things, usually products or services of some sort but also people, in electoral campaigns, and even ideas, as Jim and Tammy Bakker and their kin would have us believe. Much of the message is about demands in the making, provoking us to want things we previously didn't even know about. Thus, it's expansive, broadening. If you've never tried oat bran, you haven't lived. Move up to a Buick.

Third, our public literacy simplifies, synthesizes, unifies, focuses. *USA Today*. The McDonald's arches. Stylized logos. The *Harpers* short-essay format. The point is to be made simply, easily, quickly, and, above all, effectively. The sound bite. The powerful metaphor: an iron curtain. The utterly memorable modern version of Confucian analects. The reduction of a full life-style to the snapshot of a celebrity: *People* magazine.

Finally, our public literacy is pedagogically sophisticated, using understandings about human learning and a range of technologies far beyond the school-teacher's ken. There are tie-ins—film to **We clearly have a pervasive** video to books to T-shirts. Clustered media charac**and powerful public literacy.** terize this pedagogy, the carefully coordinated use of sight and sound and print in artful, powerful combination. It is tough for your average French teacher to compete with MTV. As teachers, we school and college folk limp far behind our cousins in the communications industry.

The questions all this provokes are as demanding as they are obvious. Is this shared experience, this public literacy, a good thing? Is it tasteless? Is some of it, in fact, a vicious form of "acceptable" lying? Or is it modestly more benign, merely purveying corrupting fictions? Does it, with an artfulness that provokes acceptance and passivity, undermine habits of thoughtfulness? Is it undemocratic?

Why do we have it? Or, put more cogently, who wants it? (Public accept- 10
ance to date seems to be almost universal.) Should it be changed? That is,
should there be rules of public discourse, as well as rules of the road, or is the
First Amendment the inevitable protector of tawdriness and dishonesty, as
well as free expression? Can, in fact, a public literacy be changed? What are
the costs in trying to change it? Who should change it? Government? If so,
by direct regulation, a national assessment of all the educating media? Or by
indirection, through the tax code, with great business advantages given to
alternative or public (not-for-profit) enterprises? Or do we leave change to
the market, hoping that an aroused public will clean up mindlessness and
worse in the common domain, somewhat as it appears to be doing to rid publicly shared air of cigarette-smoke pollution?

There must be answers to these questions. My concern here, however, is
not to pursue these but to express some puzzlements. Why aren't we talking
much about this ubiquitous public literacy? The intense and visible concern
for illiteracy, for the inability of many to read and to find meaning in that
reading—as reflected in this conference— is as sincere and important as it is
conventional; folks have to be able to read, understand, and articulate to survive in this society. But what of the shared symbol systems, the public literacy, that we already have? It is shaping, in an unprecedented way, a national
culture. Its power seems greater in some important respects than the formal
teaching in schools and colleges.

The academy itself accepts the megaculture, the machine for public literacy, in a revealing way: It barely studies the matter. Higher education has
been largely mute, for example, about the threat to academic freedom implicit in national testing or a de facto nationalized and virtually monopolistic textbook industry. The effects of television on American thought are remarkably
little studied. We accept cultural gigantism, little reflecting on its meaning. By
contrast, our savage little debates about critical theory rarely focus on the texts
that saturate our cultural life but turn around intense little obscurities that,
while perhaps of intellectual merit, have no cultural significance.

I am puzzled by how easily we rely on quick fixes in these matters—
acceptance of a single score on a forty-minute machine-graded test to rate a
school or to rank a student against hundreds of thousands of others; a glib
dismissal of the mass media, one resting on precious little empirical data; an
avoidance of that army of people in the communications industry who are,
in fact, teaching our people their shared values; concession to the encroachments on individual freedom implicit in the increasingly centralized character of our institutions. We aren't paying enough attention, and a charge of
myopia against the academy is not too strong. However, there is not just
inattention; there is in all too many quarters active hostility to studying the

popular culture in general, much less its aspect as a form of literacy. Such concerns are considered soft, unworthy activity for the bright person seeking tenure. It is both strange and sad.

The academy must recognize the reality of a public literacy, see it in perspective, and study it carefully. We must adopt a rich definition of this public literacy. As E. D. Hirsch has reminded us, it has a content, and we must see it as a content in context—gregarious, changeable, reflected and used in a rich variety of media. But content is only a part; no functioning literacy is merely facts; it is the ways of using those facts, of using style, of exhibiting habits. This use or exhibition arises from incentives, and the incentives that a culture presents its citizens shape their willingness to use and to be in the habit of using the values, content, and symbols that tie that culture together. Incentives arise from politics, both formal and informal, and the social system in which those politics proceed. Americans need to know more about the real content of our literacy, about its exhibition, and about the incentives and the politics that produce such incentives, that provoke that exhibition. It is the duty of the academy to pursue these complex issues.

In sum, we have an unprecedented wide public literacy in this country. All   15 those adolescents roiling through their schools' standardized routines and responding collectively to mass media's messages are evidence enough of that. Let us pay close attention to this new phenomenon, this product of affluence and technology. And if we find it wanting, let us be about changing it.

Working with the Text

1. The title of Theodore Sizer's essay presents an odd combination: It mixes the public with the academic. Write a brief essay in which you comment on Sizer's strategic use of his title. How does his "puzzlement" provide a key to a fresher understanding of why academics should pay more attention to public literacy?

2. To illustrate how "pervasive and powerful" our public literacy is, Sizer describes an exercise led by Brown University's Robert Scholes, in which he asked his colleagues to identify "what we must already know . . . to understand" a beer commercial (par. 3). To reflect on the point Scholes wanted to make, choose a commercial that you find especially effective or entertaining. With Sizer's essay in mind, write a brief essay in which you identify what a viewer would have to already know to interpret the message of the commercial. What images, actions, phrases, and assumed values would only an American be likely to understand?

3. Sizer analyzes our public literacy by claiming that it is "characterized by at least four properties" (par. 5). As you reread the essay, review those properties. In a brief essay, use the properties to analyze an artifact in our culture—an image,

an object, a phrase, a gesture, an icon—that you consider to be part of our "public literacy."

4. The purpose of Sizer's argument, which was originally an address for a Modern Language Association conference, is to persuade his colleagues to study and critique our public literacy. Reread the final segment of the essay, starting with "The academy itself accepts the megaculture, the machine for public literacy, in a revealing way: It barely studies the matter" (par. 12). From your perspective as a student, write a brief proposal to academics persuading them to study an aspect of our public literacy that raises an issue or issues identified by Sizer that are also concerns for you.

From Text to Field

1. Sizer challenges his audience to analyze our public literacy by asserting, "The questions all this provokes are as demanding as they are obvious" (par. 9). What follows are two paragraphs of those questions. Based on your own knowledge, observations, and experience, write an essay in which you answer one or more of the questions that interest you most.

2. One of Sizer's deepest concerns is that the power of our public literacy "seems greater in some important respects than the formal teaching in schools and colleges" (par. 11). From your perspective as a student, write an essay in which you reflect on whether this has been the case for you. If aspects of our public literacy have been more powerful for you than your formal education, what are they, and why have they had a greater influence? If your formal education has been more powerful, in what ways, and why?

3. Sizer indicts academics for accepting "quick fixes" in the face of what he considers to be serious challenges from the "megaculture." Review the examples of issues that concern Sizer along these lines, listed in the paragraph that begins, "I am puzzled by how easily we rely on quick fixes in these matters" (par. 13). Write an essay in which you explore how one of these "matters" is manifesting itself in our culture. For example, you might explore a way or ways in which the "army of people in the communications industry" are "teaching our people their shared values." Or you might analyze particular "encroachments on individual freedom implicit in the increasingly centralized character of our institutions."

From Outside, In

Barbara Mellix

Each one of us, at varying points in life and career, will find ourselves moving, as in the title of this essay, "From Outside, In." This entry can also be, in some sense, a leave-taking, and as such can involve several communities. It also may involve complicated relationships between language and power and may require a new awareness of what is "proper" in each community. No easy move, this stepping "from outside, in." It forces us to rethink who we are and may prompt us to discover both the limits and the resourcefulness of language.

Raised in Greeleyville, South Carolina, Barbara Mellix draws on her own vexed relationship to multiple languages and communities in this essay, published in the *Georgia Review* in 1987. The essay recounts her experiences from early childhood through her first college writing courses that she took as a working mother. Mellix went on to receive her MFA in creative writing in 1986 from the University of Pittsburgh. In addition to teaching writing in the English department at the University of Pittsburgh, she serves as executive assistant dean in the College of Arts and Sciences, where she edits the college's alumni magazine.

Two years ago, when I started writing this paper, trying to bring order out of chaos, my ten-year-old daughter was suffering from an acute attack of boredom. She drifted in and out of the room complaining that she had nothing to do, no one to "be with" because none of her friends were at home. Patiently I explained that I was working on something special and needed peace and quiet, and I suggested that she paint, read, or work with her computer. None of these interested her. Finally, she pulled up a chair to my desk and watched me, now and then heaving long, loud sighs. After two or three minutes (nine or ten sighs), I lost my patience. "Looka here, Allie," I said, "you are too old for this kinda carryin' on. I done told you this is important. You wronger than dirt to be in here haggin' me like this and you know it. Now git on outta here and leave me off before I put my foot all the way down."

I was at home, alone with my family, and my daughter understood that this way of speaking was appropriate in that context. She knew, as a matter of fact, that it was almost inevitable; when I get angry at home, I speak some of my finest, most cherished black English. Had I been speaking to my daughter in this manner in certain other environments, she would have been shocked and probably worried that I had taken leave of my sense of propriety.

Like my children, I grew up speaking what I considered two distinctly different languages—black English and standard English (or as I thought of them then, the ordinary everyday speech of "country" coloreds and "proper" English)—and in the process of acquiring these languages, I developed an understanding of when, where, and how to use them. But unlike my children, I grew up in a world that was primarily black. My friends, neighbors, minister, teachers—almost everybody I associated with every day—were black. And we spoke to one another in our own special language: *That sho is a pretty dress you got on. If she don' soon leave me off I'm gon tell her head a mess. I was so mad I could'a pissed a blue rod. He all the time trying to low-rate somebody. Ain't that just about the nastiest thing you ever set ears on?*

Then there were the "others," the "proper" blacks, transplanted relatives and one-time friends who came home from the city for weddings, funerals, and vacations. To these we spoke standard English. "Ain't?" my mother would yell at me when I used the term in the presence of "others." "You *know* better than that." And I would hang my head in shame and say the "proper" word.

I remember one summer sitting in my grandmother's house in ₅ Greeleyville, South Carolina, when it was full of the chatter of city relatives who were home on vacation. My parents sat quietly, only now and then volunteering a comment or answering a question. My mother's face took on a strained expression when she spoke. I could see that she was being careful to say just the right words in just the right way. Her voice sounded thick, muffled. And when she finished speaking, she would lapse into silence, her proper smile on her face. My father was more articulate, more aggressive. He spoke quickly, his words sharp and clear. But he held his proud head higher, a signal that he, too, was uncomfortable. My sisters and brothers and I stared at our aunts, uncles, and cousins, speaking only when prompted. Even then, we hesitated, formed our sentences in our minds, then spoke softly, shyly.

My parents looked small and anxious during those occasions, and I waited impatiently for our leave-taking when we would mock our relatives the moment we were out of their hearing. "Reeely," we would say to one another, flexing our wrists and rolling our eyes, "how dooo you stan' this heat? Chile, it just too hyooo-mid for words." Our relatives had made us feel "country," and this was our way of regaining pride in ourselves while getting a little revenge in the bargain. The words bubbled in our throats and rolled across our tongues, a balming.

As a child I felt this same doubleness in uptown Greeleyville where the whites lived. "Ain't that a pretty dress you're wearing!" Toby, the town policeman, said to me one day when I was fifteen. "Thank you very much," I replied, my voice barely audible in my own ears. The words felt wrong in my mouth, rigid, foreign. It was not that I had never spoken that phrase before—it was common in black English, too—but I was extremely conscious that this was an occasion for proper English. I had taken out my English and put it on as I did my church clothes, and I felt as if I were wearing my Sunday best in the middle of the week. It did not matter that Toby had not spoken grammatically correct English. He was white and could speak as he wished. I had something to prove. Toby did not.

Speaking standard English to whites was our way of demonstrating that we knew their language and could use it. Speaking it to standard-English-speaking blacks was our way of showing them that we, as well as **I write and continually give** they, could "put on airs." But when we spoke stan-**birth to myself.** dard English, we acknowledged (to ourselves and to others—but primarily to ourselves) that our customary way of speaking was inferior. We felt foolish, embarrassed, somehow diminished because we were ashamed to be our real selves. We were reserved, shy in the presence of those who owned and/or spoke *the* language.

My parents never set aside time to drill us in standard English. Their forms of instruction were less formal. When my father was feeling particularly expansive, he would regale us with tales of his exploits in the outside world. In almost fluent English, complete with dialogue and flavored with gestures and embellishment, he told us about his attempt to get a haircut at a white barbershop; his refusal to acknowledge one of the town merchants until the man addressed him as "Mister"; the time he refused to step off the sidewalk uptown to let some whites pass; his airplane trip to New York City (to visit a sick relative) during which the stewardess and porters—recognizing that he was a "gentleman"—addressed him as "Sir." I did not realize then—nor, I think, did my father—that he was teaching us, among other things, standard English and the relationship between language and power.

My mother's approach was different. Often, when one of us said, "I'm gon wash off my feet," she would say, "And what will you walk on if you wash them off?" Everyone would laugh at the victim of my mother's "proper" mood. But it was different when one of us children was in a proper mood. "You think you are so superior," I said to my oldest sister one day when we were arguing and she was winning. "Superior!" my sister mocked. "You mean I am acting 'biggidy'?" My sisters and brothers sniggered, then joined in teasing me. Finally, my mother said, "Leave your sister alone. There's nothing wrong with using proper English." There was a half-smile on her face. I had gotten "uppity," had "put on airs" for no good reason. I was at home, alone with the family, and I hadn't been prompted by one of my mother's proper moods. But there was also a proud light in my mother's eyes; her children were learning English very well.

Not until years later, as a college student, did I begin to understand our ambivalence toward English, our scorn of it, our need to master it, to own and be owned by it—an ambivalence that extended to the public-school classroom. In our school, where there were no whites, my teachers taught standard English but used black English to do it. When my grammar-school teachers wanted us to write, for example, they usually said something like, "I want y'all to write five sentences that make a statement. Anybody get done before the rest can color." It was probably almost those exact words that led me to write these sentences in 1953 when I was in the second grade:

> The white clouds are pretty.
> There are only 15 people in our room.
> We will go to gym.
> We have a new poster.
> We may go out doors.

Second grade came after "Little First" and "Big First," so by then I knew the implied rules that accompanied all writing assignments. Writing was an occasion for proper English. I was not to write in the way we spoke to one another: The white clouds pretty; There ain't but 15 people in our room; We going to gym; We got a new poster; We can go out in the yard. Rather I was to use the language of "other": clouds *are*, there *are*, we *will*, we *may*.

My sentences were short, rigid, perfunctory, like the letters my mother wrote to relatives:

> Dear Papa,
> How are you? How is Mamie? Fine I hope. We are fine. We will come to see you Sunday. Cousin Ned will give us a ride.
>   Love,
>   Daughter

The language was not ours. It was something from outside us, something we used for special occasions.

But my coloring on the other side of that second-grade paper is different. I drew three hearts and a sun. The sun has a smiling face that radiates and envelops everything it touches. And although the sun and its world are enclosed in a circle, the colors I used—red, blue, green, purple, orange, yellow, black—indicates that I was less restricted with drawing and coloring than I was with writing standard English. My valentines were not just red. My sun was not just a yellow ball in the sky.

By the time I reached the twelfth grade, speaking and writing standard English had taken on new importance. Each year, about half of the newly graduated seniors of our school moved to large cities—particularly in the North—to live with relatives and find work. Our English teacher constantly corrected our grammar: "Not 'ain't,' but 'isn't.'" We seldom wrote papers, and even those few were usually plot summaries of short stories. When our teacher returned the papers, she usually lectured on the importance of using standard English: "I *am*; you *are*; he, she, or it *is*," she would say, writing on the chalkboard as she spoke. "How you gon git a job talking about 'I is,' or 'I isn't' or 'I ain't'?"

In Pittsburgh, where I moved after graduation, I watched my aunt and   15
uncle—who had always spoken standard English when in Greeleyville — switch from black English to standard English to a mixture of the two, according to where they were or who they were with. At home and with certain close relatives, friends, and neighbors, they spoke black English. With those less close, they spoke a mixture. In public and with strangers, they generally spoke standard English.

In time, I learned to speak standard English with ease and to switch smoothly from black to standard or a mixture, and back again. But no matter where I was, no matter what the situation or occasion, I continued to write as I had in school:

> Dear Mommie,
> How are you? How is everybody else? Fine I hope. I am fine. So are Aunt and Uncle. Tell everyone I said hello. I will write again soon.
> 　　Love,
> 　　Barbara

At work, at a health insurance company, I learned to write letters to customers. I studied form letters and letters written by coworkers, memorizing the phrases and the ways in which they were used. I dictated:

> Thank you for your letter of January 5. We have made the changes in your coverage you requested. Your new premium will be $150 every three months. We are pleased to have been of service to you.

In a sense, I was proud of the letters I wrote for the company: They were proof of my ability to survive in the city, the outside world—an indication of my growing mastery of English. But they also indicate that writing was still mechanical for me, something that didn't require much thought.

Reading also became a more significant part of my life during those early years in Pittsburgh. I had always liked reading, but now I devoted more and more of my spare time to it. I read romances, mysteries, popular novels. Looking back, I realized that the books I liked best were simple, unambiguous: good versus bad and right versus wrong with right rewarded and wrong punished, mysteries unraveled and all set right in the end. It was how I remembered life in Greeleyville.

Of course I was romanticizing. Life in Greeleyville had not been so very uncomplicated. Back there I had been—first as a child, then as a young woman with limited experience in the outside world—living in a relatively closed-in society. But there were implicit and explicit principles that guided our way of life and shaped our relationships with one another and the people outside—principles that a newcomer would find elusive and baffling. In Pittsburgh, I had matured, become more experienced: I had worked at three different jobs, associated with a wider range of people, married, had children. This new environment with different prescripts for living required that I speak standard English much of the time, and slowly, imperceptibly, I had ceased seeing a sharp distinction between myself and "others." Reading romances and mysteries, characterized by dichotomy, was a way of shying away from change, from the person I was becoming.

But that other part of me—that part which took great pride in my ability to hold a job writing business letters—was increasingly drawn to the new developments in my life and the attending possibilities, opportunities for even greater change. If I could write letters for a nationally known business, could I not also do something better, more challenging, more important? Could I not, perhaps, go to college and become a school teacher? For years, afraid and a little embarrassed, I did no more than imagine this different me, this possible me. But sixteen years after coming north, when my younger daughter entered kindergarten, I found myself unable—or unwilling—to resist the lure of possibility. I enrolled in my first college course: Basic Writing, at the University of Pittsburgh.

For the first time in my life, I was required to write extensively about 20 myself. Using the most formal English at my command, I wrote these sentences near the beginning of the term:

> One of my duties as a homemaker is simply picking up after others. A day seldom passes that I don't search for a mislaid toy, book, or gym shoe, etc. I change the Ty-D-Bol, fight "ring around the collar," and keep our laundry smelling "April fresh." Occasionally, I settle arguments between my children and suggest things to do when they're bored. Taking telephone messages for my oldest daughter is my newest (and sometimes most aggravating) chore. Hanging the toilet paper is my most insignificant.

My concern was to use "appropriate" language, to sound as if I belonged in a college classroom. But I felt separate from the language—as if it did not and could not belong to me. I couldn't think and feel genuinely in that language, couldn't make it express what I thought and felt about being a housewife. A part of me resented, among other things, being judged by such things as the appearance of my family's laundry and toilet bowl, but in that language I could only imagine and write about a conventional housewife.

For the most part, the remainder of the term was a period of adjustment, a time of trying to find my bearings as a student in a college composition class, to learn to shut out my black English whenever I composed, and to prevent it from creeping into my formulations; a time for trying to grasp the language of the classroom and reproduce it in my prose; for trying to talk about myself in that language, reach others through it. Each experience of writing was like standing naked and revealing my imperfection, my "otherness." And each new assignment was another chance to make myself over in language, reshape myself, make myself "better" in my rapidly changing image of a student in a college composition class.

But writing became increasingly unmanageable as the term progressed, and by the end of the semester, my sentences sounded like this:

> My excitement was soon dampened, however, by what seemed like a small voice in the back of my head saying that I should be careful with my long awaited opportunity. I felt frustrated and this seemed to make it difficult to concentrate.

There is a poverty of language in these sentences. By this point, I knew that the clichéd language of my Housewife essay was unacceptable, and I generally recognized trite expressions. At the same time, I hadn't yet mastered the language of the classroom, hadn't yet come to see it as belonging to me. Most notable is the lifelessness of the prose, the apparent absence of a person behind the words. I wanted those sentences—and the rest of the essay—to convey the anguish of yearning to, at once, become something more and yet remain the same. I had the sensation of being split in two, part of me going into a future the other part didn't believe possible. As that person, the student writer at that moment, I was essentially mute. I could not—in the process of composing—use the language of the old me, yet I couldn't imagine myself in the language of "others."

I found this particularly discouraging because at midsemester I had been writing in a much different way. Note the language of this introduction to an essay I had written then, near the middle of the term:

> Pain is a constant companion to the people in "Footwork." Their jobs are physically damaging. Employers are insensitive to their feelings and in many cases add to their problems. The general public wounds them further by treating them with disgrace because of what they do for a living. Although the workers are as diverse as they are similar, there is a definite link between them. They suffer a great deal of abuse.

The voice here is stronger, more confident, [with] appropriate terms like "physically damaging," "wounds them further," "insensitive," "diverse"—terms I couldn't have imagined using when writing about my own experience—and shaping them into sentences like "Although the workers are as diverse as they are similar, there is a definite link between them." And there is the sense of a personality behind the prose, someone who sympathizes with the workers. "The general public wounds them further by treating them with disgrace because of what they do for a living."

What causes these differences? I was, I believed, explaining other people's thoughts and feelings, and I was free to move about in the language of "others" so long as I was speaking *of* others. I was unaware that I was transforming into my best classroom language my own thoughts and feelings about people whose experiences and ways of speaking were in many ways similar to mine.

The following year, unable to turn back or to let go of what had become   25 something of an obsession with language (and hoping to catch and hold the sense of control that had eluded me in Basic Writing), I enrolled in a research writing course. I spent most of the term learning how to prepare for and write a research paper. I chose sex education as my subject and spent hours in libraries, searching for information, reading, taking notes. Then (not without messiness and often demoralizing frustration) I organized my information into categories, wrote a thesis statement, and composed my paper—a series of paragraphs and quotations spaced between carefully constructed transitions. The process and results felt artificial, but as I would later come to realize I was passing through a necessary stage. My sentences sounded like this:

> This reserve becomes understandable with examination of who the abusers are. In an overwhelming number of cases, they are people the victims know and trust. Family members, relatives, neighbors, and close family friends commit seventy-five percent of all reported sex crimes against children, and parents, parent substitutes, and relatives are the offenders in thirty to eighty percent of all reported cases. While assault by strangers does occur, it is less common, and is usually a single episode. But abuse by family members, relatives, and acquaintances may continue for an extended period of time. In cases of incest, for example, children are abused repeatedly for an average of eight years. In such cases, "the use of physical force is rarely necessary because of the child's trusting, dependent relationship with the offender. The child's cooperation is often facilitated by the adult's position of dominance, an offer of material goods, a threat of physical violence, or a misrepresentation of moral standards."

The completed paper gave me a sense of profound satisfaction, and I read it often after my professor returned it. I know now that what I was pleased with was the language I used and the professional voice it helped me maintain. "Use better words," my teacher had snapped at me one day after reading the notes I'd begun accumulating from my research, and slowly I began taking on the language of my sources. In my next set of notes, I used the word "vacillating"; my professor applauded. And by the time I composed the final draft, I felt at ease with terms like "overwhelming number of cases," "single episode," and "reserve," and I shaped them into sentences similar to those of my "expert" sources.

If I were writing the paper today, I would of course do some things differently. Rather than open with an anecdote—as my teacher suggested—I would begin simply with a quotation that caught my interest as I was researching my paper (and which I scribbled, without its source, in the margin of my notebook): "Truth does not do so much good in the world as the semblance of truth does evil." The quotation felt right because it captured what was for me the central idea of my essay—an idea that emerged gradually during the making of my paper—and expressed it in a way I would like to have said it. The anecdote, a hypothetical situation I invented to conform to the information in the paper, felt forced and insincere because it represented—to a great degree—my teacher's understanding of the essay, *her* idea of what in it was most significant. Improving upon my previous experiences with writing, I was beginning to think and feel in the language I used, to find my own voices in it, to sense that how one speaks influences how one means. But I was not yet secure enough, comfortable enough with the language to trust my intuition.

Now that I know that to seek knowledge, freedom, and autonomy means always to be in the concentrated process of becoming—always to be venturing into new territory, feeling one's way at first, then getting one's balance, negotiating, accommodating, discovering one's self in ways that previously defined "others"—I sometimes get tired. And I ask myself why I keep on participating in this highbrow form of violence, this slamming against perplexity. But there is no real futility in the question, no hint of that part of the old me who stood outside standard English, hugging to herself a disabling mistrust of a language she thought could not represent a person with her history and experience. Rather, the question represents a person who feels the consequences of her education, the weight of her possibilities as a teacher and writer and human being, a voice in society. And I would not change that person, would not give back the good burden that accompanies my growing expertise, my increasing power to shape myself in language and share that self with "others."

"To speak," says Frantz Fanon, "means to be in a position to use a certain syntax, to grasp the morphology of this or that language, but it means above all to assume a culture, to support the weight of civilization."[1] To write means to do the same, but in a more profound sense. However, Fanon also says that to achieve mastery means to "get" in a position of power, to "grasp," to "assume." This I have learned both as a student and subsequently as a teacher—can involve tremendous emotional and psychological conflict for those attempting to master academic disclosure. Although as a beginning student writer I had a fairly good grasp of ordinary spoken English and was proficient at what Labov calls "code-switching" (and what John Baugh in *Black Street Speech* terms "style shifting"), when I came face to face with the demands of academic writing, I grew increasingly self-conscious, constantly aware of my status as a black and a speaker of one of the many black English vernaculars—a traditional outsider. For the first time, I experienced my sense of doubleness as something menacing, a built-in enemy. Whenever I turned inward for salvation, the balm so available during my childhood, I found instead this new fragmentation which spoke to me in many voices. It was the voice of my desire to prosper, but at the same time it spoke of what I had relinquished and could not regain: a safe way of being, a state of powerlessness which exempted me from responsibility for who I was and might be. And it accused me of betrayal, of turning away from blackness. To recover balance, I had to take on the language of the academy, the language of "others." And to do that, I had to learn to imagine myself as a part of the culture of that language, and therefore someone free to manage that language, to take liberties with it. Writing and rewriting, practicing, experimenting, I came to comprehend more fully the generative power of language. I discovered—with the help of some especially sensitive teachers—that through writing one can continually bring new selves into being, each with new responsibilities and difficulties, but also with new possibilities. Remarkable power, indeed. I write and continually give birth to myself.

Note

1. *Black Skin, White Masks* (1952; rpt. New York: Grove Press, 1967), pp. 17–18.

Working with the Text

1. Even as Barbara Mellix tells us a story, she is making an argument. How would you rephrase her argument as one core assertion? As you reread the essay, try out several such assertions. Choose one that seems to capture her argument and build a one-paragraph summary of the essay's argument (not its chronological story) around that statement. In a second paragraph, reflect on what the summary has brought to light and what it now hides from view. What is persuasive about the narrative or story that is difficult to capture in a summary of the argument?

2. Early in the essay, Mellix uses the term *propriety*, a term that continues to be central throughout her essay. Look up *propriety* in a college dictionary, and

then reread Mellix in light of this concept. In a short essay, clarify what you think to be Mellix's attitude toward propriety. What is the relationship between propriety and community? propriety and power?

3. Given the title of Mellix's essay, "From Outside, In," write a one-page characterization of her rhetorical situation. That is, consider how Mellix has incorporated her speaking "selves" into the essay, who her intended audience seems to be, and how both affect her take on the subject of advanced literacy.

From Text to Field

1. Underlying much of Mellix's essay is the complex relationship between speaking and writing, between orality and literacy. Write an essay in which you analyze the difficulties of developing more advanced literacy in a world that leaves less time for books and accords more prominence to oral/spoken technologies such as television and radio.

2. At several points in her essay, Mellix raises the connection between language and power. Review the essay in light of that relationship. What several dimensions of power (institutional, social, pedagogical, personal) come into play? Can power both constrain and empower? Given your reading of Mellix's essay, turn your attention to the role of writing in your own college education. Write an essay in which you analyze the several ways power exerts itself over your writing or develops through your writing.

3. Mellix speaks of a "doubleness," of both a loss and a gain, that she experiences as she learns standard English. She also notes an "ambivalence toward English, our scorn of it, our need to master it, to own and be owned by it" (par. 11). In a short essay, comment on that doubleness, the reasons that occasion it, and the consequences of it. How is this doubleness related to the role of the mature Mellix as narrator or to your own role as a college student as you look back on your development as a writer? What are her, and your, challenges in dealing with several communities at once, each one bleeding into others? Can one distinguish "outside" and "inside" as clearly as Mellix's title seems to suggest?

INTO THE FIELD: Options for Writing Projects

1. The Languages of Community: An Ethnographic Report

Consider a nonacademic community to which you belong that is organized around some activity—a volunteer organization, for example, or perhaps a fraternity or sorority. How does language help constitute or regulate that community? Given your community, what is the relationship between language and consensus? Between language and social activity? Does language identify insiders and outsiders and thus serve a kind of "gatekeeping" function, a kind of "secret handshake"?

Describe and analyze this community as if you were an ethnographer who came upon this culture on some remote island. (An ethnographer is a field researcher who lives, observes, describes, and analyzes the daily life, behaviors, and language of a group of people over a period of time.) You may wish to focus on one particular social event or one "text" to help focus your analysis.

2. Literacy and Illiteracy in Your Community

Illiteracy is a difficult problem to address because it is invisible: No outward signs will single out this or that person. But illiteracy is also difficult to address because our ignorance of the prevalence of the issue can render it invisible. We might assume, for example, that our college town—because it is a "college" town—couldn't possibly have a literacy problem among its residents. But even the most prosperous communities often have a hidden problem with literacy.

This field project invites you to learn more about literacy and illiteracy in your hometown or in the community where you go to college. The local public library or your university's community outreach office can probably provide information about existing literacy programs, the literacy demographics of your community, and opportunities for volunteer work or service learning that can aid literacy efforts.

For this project, you may find it useful to write a profile of community efforts to improve literacy or you may wish to write a proposal for an initiative to help students become involved in literacy education in the community.

3. Insider's Guide to a Course

Recently you may have taken a class in a discipline previously unfamiliar to you, perhaps for general-education requirements or as a gateway course into your major. Analyze what might be the seemingly "foreign" language of a specific "text" in that course: the remarks made by your professor during one class, the preface or introduction to a textbook, the syllabus for the course, or a particular assignment. How does that language reflect the community you are entering, be it the disciplinary community or the classroom community? What are the means of exclusion and inclusion that separate insiders from outsiders? How does the language used imply a particular view of the world? How does language serve as a means of exerting power?

For your project, write an "Insider's Guide" to the text you have chosen from that course. Your goal is to help a student not otherwise familiar with the hidden assumptions present in the language.

4. Codes of Speech and Conduct

Explore whether your college or university has a code of conduct, some statement about civility, or some codes regulating speech. Examine the actual language of the document and the relationships it suggests among language, conduct, and community. You might also examine statements in course syllabi, or comments by your instructor or by classmates, that communicate expectations about conduct in the classroom community. You may also wish to examine documents circulated in your dorm by your resident advisor or by the campus housing office. Be sure to discuss the language of the document in the context of actual behavior in the dorms, classrooms, or on campus. You may also wish to conduct an interview with faculty or officials who may have had a hand in drafting the documents so that you better understand their intentions and the purposes of the documents.

For your project, write an analysis of one such document. What assumptions does it make about the role of language in building community and regulating behavior? In what ways is language a means to regulate and form a community?

Or, if your fieldwork uncovers problems with the document or problems in its enforcement or acceptance, consider writing a letter to the appropriate campus office in which you analyze those problems and propose changes to the document.

5. Literacy Narrative

The essay "From Outside, In" (p. 76), by Barbara Mellix, offers what amounts to her own "literacy narrative." Perri Klass (p. 48) likewise offers, albeit in more abbreviated fashion, her own story about learning a new language. For your project, offer your own literacy narrative.

Think about what goes into constructing such a narrative. In what respect is it a "construction," shaped by your mature, literate self? What is the argument behind your narrative? Consider writing a second, parallel essay that articulates those very argumentative issues more directly. You may also wish to examine literacy narratives in literature (e.g., *Pygmalion*) or in film (e.g., *Educating Rita, Wild Child, Children of a Lesser God*).

6. An Assignment "Rule Book"

At one point in her essay, Barbara Mellix (p. 76) speaks of the "rules of assignments." Take a close look at the "rules of assignments" in your composition course or in a course you are taking in a different discipline. For your project, develop an assignment rule book. Your goal is to develop a set of rules, conventions, or procedures for the assignment that may not be explicit but nonetheless inform the purpose and evaluation of the assignment. In that respect, your goal is to develop a document that could help the professor explain the assignment in more detail the next time he or she gives it or that can help future students meet the challenge of that assignment.

Here are some questions you may wish to consider: Are the rules explicit or only implied? What status and function do those rules have? Are they absolute or relative and flexible? For whom are those rules written? When can they be broken and by whom? What purpose do they serve? What is the connection between a set of specific rules and what we might call the "literacy activities" in that field? That is, does the assignment serve as a kind of miniapprenticeship, socializing you to the ways of that community? If so, why and how? In what ways do the tacit rules for the assignment reflect the culture of that particular discipline—its ways of knowing, thinking, and arguing?

7. Social Contexts in Translation

Amy Tan (p. 60) points out that social contexts often fail in translation. Choose from among the following three scenarios and explore the connection between language and community, focusing on difficulties in translation.

- If you are bilingual or if you are a literature or foreign-language major, consider analyzing the difficulties in translating a particular passage from a literary or nonliterary text. If you can, compare several translations. Write an essay in which you analyze the manner in which issues of translation often involve social assumptions or hidden understandings about culture.
- If you are a business major or if you are interested in new technologies, consider exploring handheld electronic translators or Web site services that promise to translate documents. Imagine that you have been hired as a consultant by a company that is expanding its international operations. Write a consultant's report in which you analyze the ability of pocket translating machines and/or Web sites to capture the social contexts of business practices.
- Find out if your campus has an ESL or English as a second language program. Interview one or more nonnative speakers of English, or volunteer as a "conversation partner" for the program (you'll find it immensely rewarding). Focus on a specific country of origin and write an analysis of some of the difficulties that foreign students encounter as they try to "learn the

language" of social contexts on your campus. You may wish to focus on just one particular aspect of social context (for example, interactions between students and professors).

8. "Tribalism" on Campus

David Berreby's article "It Takes a Tribe" (p. 53) invites you to take stock of rituals and traditions on your campus. How does one become an insider on campus—a "Spartan," or an "Aggie," or a "Buffalo"? Likewise, how does one become identified with one or the other group or club, fraternity or sorority, on campus?

This field project asks you to consider what prompts students—especially new students—to form such affiliations and to examine the means and methods of initiation. You may also wish to explore how various groups maintain themselves over time. You can focus on sports as a key means for identity formation, but don't forget academic majors or, for that matter, the role of the alumni office.

Develop your research and ethnographic fieldwork into a profile of tribal rituals and traditions on your campus, one that could be submitted as a chapter in a (hypothetical) book *Alma Mater: An Insider's Guide to College Rituals and Traditions*.

9. Curricular Narratives

In the course of Barbara Mellix's essay (p. 76), she comments on several different writing classes that she has taken and on the expectations and writing processes involved in each. For your project, become familiar with the writing courses your college offers. Be sure to consult course catalogs and syllabi; you also may wish to interview several instructors. Once you become familiar with those course offerings, analyze the implied narrative or the expected path of intellectual or career development that those writing courses may assume. Do those assumptions or expectations hold true most of the time? Or does the implied literacy narrative governing those courses pose some problem for students and faculty? For additional context, you may wish to consider what assumptions other courses in your university make about your development as a writer.

Your project may take one of several forms. You may wish to write a document that explains to students entering the course what they might expect during the first few weeks and how this course might fit into their other writing courses or college courses with a substantial commitment to writing. This document could take the form of a letter to new students or a preface to a handbook your writing program might provide its students.

If, during your fieldwork, you uncover problems or tensions in the way one or more courses are conceived, consider writing a letter to the department's curriculum committee in which, from your perspective as a student, you offer your views and recommendations. If you choose this option, be sure you are well informed and that you understand the "state of the conversation" about these courses and what agendas and values may be in play.

10. Dramatic Cognitive Awakenings

At one point in her essay, Amy Tan speaks of her own "dramatic cognitive awakenings via the word" (par. 22). This project asks you to focus on one key term or concept of interest to you that has importance to your field of study. It is especially helpful if you choose a term that is somehow "contested" or that is subject to varying interpretations.

For this project, write an essay in which you analyze both your chosen term and your cognitive awakening to it. First, consider naïve or uninformed interpretations of the term or how a newcomer to the field might misunderstand the complexities surrounding the term. Next, offer a fuller interpretation of the term that captures its contested life. How does the term fit into disciplinary conversations? What hidden agendas or values might accompany various interpretations of the term? Finally, reflect on your own "cognitive awakening" to the term. What has enabled you to see the term in a richer, more complex context? In what ways did "learning this language" require you to learn or adopt certain attitudes or behaviors of your disciplinary community?

11. Taking Stock of Your Literacy: Academic and Public

When it comes to literacy in narrow terms (reading and writing), we tend to think of our literacy education as something that happens at home or in school. And yet, our reading and writing, and especially the cultural knowledge that informs our reading and writing, tend to be influenced by a broader social and public literacy.

This field project invites you to take an introspective look at the influences that have guided your growth as a reader and writer. Drawing on Theodore Sizer's article (p. 70) in this chapter, consider whether school literacy or public literacy has had more influence in your life. Can one cleanly and clearly separate the two? Do these two kinds of literacy reinforce one another, or do they compete and potentially undermine one another?

You may wish to frame your project as a personal essay that responds to Sizer's article.

12. The Language of Community on the Net

Entering a community requires that you learn its language and with that language a host of attitudes, assumptions, and expectations. As we become habituated to moving from this to that community in real life, we tend not to notice their distinctive language behaviors. The Internet provides an interesting vehicle for exploring the connections between language, behavior, and community precisely because so much of the interaction is explicitly verbal.

For this project, choose one Internet site or one community with a presence on the Web. Monitor and analyze how this community uses language to maintain itself. What accommodation does this site or this community make for newcomers? Or does the site or community presume to speak only to "true believers"? How does language function on this site or in this community to uphold certain beliefs, assumptions, or agendas. To what extent does the language of this site or community welcome debate or criticism? You will probably find that the language of community on the Net becomes more pronounced as the community adopts what are regarded as more radical or extreme positions.

Write your project as an ethnographic report. That is, based on the specific language of this community as available on an Internet site, what can you infer about its practices and beliefs, its attitudes and values?

DANCING WITH PROFESSORS

The title for this unit is drawn from one of the readings, an essay by historian Patricia Nelson Limerick. Writing in the *New York Times Book Review,* she wonders why it is that so many professors "write bad prose." For Limerick, the apt answer can be found in a remark she recalls being made by a classics professor some years ago: "We must remember that professors are the ones nobody wanted to dance with in high school."

Now that you are in college, however, you do find yourself dancing with professors—intellectually, at least—be it in the seminar room or the lecture hall. Gone are the crepe-paper streamers in the high school gym, yet the notion that you might have to "dance" with your professor, or that he or she might have to dance with you, remains unsettling. Instead of eyeing each other warily from across the gym floor, you'll find that the seminar room and the lecture hall now become the venues for those sometimes awkward steps together.

What can we make of this "dance" between student and professor, and why might it be helpful to step out onto the dance floor and try out a few basic steps? It's tempting to think of your education as a solo number, as something you do by and for yourself. After all, you're the one who's getting the grade. Yet the dance metaphor holds and can shed some light on your experience in college and in the writing classroom.

Teaching and learning occur together and influence each other in often unexpected ways. Moreover, both teaching and learning are inherently social. We think and write at our best in the company of others. Although no one may literally strike the dance-floor pose, there is surely a good deal of dancing going on. You might be tempted to think of your professor as the one who is "leading," and often times he or she is, but the expected roles, the assumed positions, can change. You might take the lead as you work on a project, and surely, especially in smaller classes, you may find that your partner is a fellow student or a group of students.

We dance with each other—at times awkwardly, but surely with ever-increasing confidence—because college is all about learning "the moves." We might think that our days are filled with the demands of teaching and learning what might be called "domain content"—the factual information of any one field. But beyond or underlying that explicit and visible education is a more subtle but telling one: You are learning the moves of thinking and writing so essential to success in college and in your chosen field. You are imitating, practicing, and trying out—on your own and with each other—a variety of dance steps that show a mind in action.

The dance floor, in this respect, can extend well beyond the classroom. We are dancing in the library or in our respective dorms and offices. We are dancing when we read or listen attentively, not just when we write or speak. We are dancing when we engage each other and ourselves. We are, all of us, dancing in and with our minds.

The writing classroom has a special role in helping you learn those moves, those habits of mind that inform your work with professors and with each other. Because writing renders visible and malleable the ways in which we think, a writing class can help you reflect on the connections between language and inquiry. Moreover, because writing classes are inherently collaborative, they offer an opportunity for all of us, as we entertain different ideas and various audiences, to step out of our own skins. You may not find black footprints placed on the classroom floor as a guide to the latest swing or salsa, but you will be learning nevertheless some key moves.

The four readings included on this unit's "dance card" touch on the different kinds of partnerships that come into play as you write and learn in college. For Mike Rose, entering the conversation that is college relied in good measure on the support of faculty mentors. Coming as he did from South L.A., Rose encountered a very different set of expectations on campus. His mentors—the ones you yourself might find—played a crucial role in helping to explain the moves that occur, but are often not explained, in the college classroom.

Gerald Graff found his favorite dance partner not in books themselves—he found he disliked them at an early age—but in the critical debates that swirled around the famous books he felt he was obliged to like. Those critical debates offered a chance to join a conversation that was not always readily apparent in the books themselves.

Patricia Nelson Limerick explores the very metaphor of the dance and questions why it is that college professors seem to neglect the needs of their partners, be they the readers of their own prose or the students they are teaching. Limerick offers, in the end, a useful reminder that, for all of us, professors and students alike, egos can get in the way of a good dance.

Nancy Sommers reminds us that we are our own best—and severest—partners. In an essay that explores the interplay between personal and external authority that unfolds in our written drafts, Sommers challenges us never to leave ourselves behind, even as we write academic essays.

Reflecting on Prior Knowledge

1. In a journal entry, or working collaboratively in a small group, recall why you first became interested in going to college. What role did an academic program, sports, mentor, or teacher have in developing this interest? What have been your own expectations—or those of your family and high school friends—about the role of college in your life and career?

2. In what you might title "A Brief Personal History of the Book," reflect on the role of books in your life. You may wish to focus on one key period in your reading life or on one kind of book. Have you ever disliked books or a certain kind of book? If so, what might have accounted for that attitude? Have you found your relationship with books changing for better or for worse? What instigated that change—a teacher, an issue or a debate, a friend, or a particular book?

3. In American culture, certain stereotypes tend to define the image of the college professor. Briefly recall what you see as the most salient of those stereotypes, and then describe an encounter or a situation (in college or in the past) in which those stereotypes were either confirmed or challenged.

4. In a journal entry, reflect on what you see as the ideal educational relationship (intellectual and/or interpersonal) with a professor. In short, what kind of "dance" would you like to have? Consider what would need to change—in professors, in yourself, in the institution—in order for that educational relationship to come about. What rewards do you see in your idealized relationship, and what risks or challenges?

5. Reflect on an opportunity you might have had in the past to connect your academic and personal commitments. Did that opportunity lead to the kind of successful integration that you hoped for? What might have accounted for that success or for an outcome that was short, perhaps well short, of being successful? How did you handle the competing claims of establishing your academic authority and calling upon the authority of lived experience?

Entering the Conversation

Mike Rose

School, especially a college or a university, can make students feel unintelligent, threatened, and angry when they encounter conversations that use unfamiliar terms and foreign-sounding logic. It was only through the insight and effort of his teachers that Mike Rose moved from the language and culture of South L.A., where he grew up, into the conversations of his liberal-arts course work at Loyola University.

The importance of his mentors, and the worlds they helped him enter, led Rose first into teaching then into the study of teaching. With degrees from Loyola University, the University of Southern California, and UCLA, Rose has taught public school, undergraduate, and graduate students. His research into effective teaching focuses on recognizing the social, cultural, linguistic, and cognitive factors that influence how students learn. His books on language and learning include *Possible Lives: The Promise of Public Education in America* (1995), based on four years of searching across the nation for public school classrooms that work. "Entering the Conversation" is from his landmark book, *Lives on the Boundary: The Struggles and Achievements of America's Underprepared* (1989). The range of his interests is reflected in two recent publications, *Widening the Lens on Standardized Patient Assessment: What the Encounter Can Reveal about the Development of Clinical Competence* (2001) and *The Working Life of a Waitress: Mind, Culture, and Activity* (2001). His most recent book is *The Mind at Work* (2004).

Mike Rose is currently a professor of social research methodology in the UCLA graduate school of education and an instructor for the UCLA writing program.

It is an unfortunate fact of our psychic lives that the images that surround us as we grow up—no matter how much we may scorn them later—give shape to our deepest needs and longings. Every year Loyola men elected a homecoming queen. The queen and her princesses were students at the Catholic sister schools: Marymount, Mount St. Mary's, St. Vincent's. They had names like Corinne and Cathy, and they came from the Sullivan family or the Mitchells or the Ryans. They were taught to stand with toe to heel, their smiles were inviting, and the photographer's flash illuminated their eyes. Loyola men met them at fraternity parties and mixers and "CoEd Day," met them according to rules of manner and affiliation and parental connection as elaborate as a Balinese dance. John and I drew mustaches on their photographs, but something about them reached far back into my life.

Growing up in South L.A. was certainly not a conscious misery. My neighborhood had its diversions and its mysteries, and I felt loved and needed at home. But all in all there was a dreary impotence to the years, and isolation, and a deep sadness about my father. I protected myself from the harsher side of it all through a life of the mind. And while that interior life included spaceships and pink chemicals and music and the planetary moons, it also held the myriad television images of the good life that were piped into my home: Robert Young sitting down to dinner, Ozzie Nelson tossing the football with his sons, the blond in a Prell commercial turning toward the camera. The images couldn't have been more trivial—all sentimental phosphorescence—but as a child tucked away on South Vermont, they were just about the only images I had of what life would be without illness and dead ends. I didn't realize how completely their message had seeped into my being, what loneliness and sorrow was being held at bay—didn't realize it until I found myself in the middle of Loyola's social life without a guidebook, feeling just beyond the superficial touch of the queen and her princesses, those smiling incarnations of a television promise. I scorned the whole silly show and ached to be embraced by one of these mythic females under the muted light of a paper moon.

So I went to school and sat in class and memorized more than understood and whistled past the academic graveyard. I vacillated between the false potency of scorn and feelings of ineptitude. John and I would get in his car and enjoy the warmth of each other and laugh and head down the long strip of Manchester Boulevard, away from Loyola, away from the palms and green, green lawns, back to South L.A. We'd throw the ball in the alley or lag pennies on Vermont or hit Marty's Liquor. We'd leave much later for a movie or a football game at Mercy High or the terrible safety of downtown Los Angeles. Walking, then, past the *discotecas* and pawnshops, past the windows full of fried chicken and yellow lamps, past the New Follies, walking through hustlers and lost drunks and prostitutes and transvestites with rouge the color of bacon—stopping, finally, before the musty opening of a bar where two silhouettes moved around a pool table as though they were underwater.

I don't know what I would have found if the flow of events hadn't changed dramatically. Two things happened. Jack MacFarland privately influenced my course of study at Loyola, and death once again ripped through our small family.

The coterie of MacFarland's students—Art Mitz, Mark Dever, and me—   5
were still visiting our rumpled mentor. We would stop by his office or his apartment to mock our classes and the teachers and all that "'Loyola man' bullshit." Nobody had more appreciation for burlesque than Jack MacFarland, but I suppose he saw beneath our caustic performances and knew we were headed for trouble. Without telling us, he started making phone calls to some of his old teachers at Loyola—primarily to Dr. Frank Carothers, the chairman of the English Department—and, I guess, explained that these kids needed to be slapped alongside the head with a good novel. Dr. Carothers volunteered to look out for us and agreed to some special studies courses that we could substitute for a few of the more tradi-tional requirements, courses that would enable us to read and write a lot under the close supervision of a faculty member. In fact, what he promised were tutorials—and that was exceptional, even for a small college. All this would start up when we returned from summer vacation. Our sophomore year, Jack MacFarland finally revealed, would be different.

When Lou Minton rewired the trailer, he rigged a phone line from the front house: A few digits and we could call each other. One night during the summer after my freshman year, the phone rang while I was reading. It was my mother and she was screaming. I ran into the house to find her standing in the kitchen hysterical—both hands pressed to her face—and all I could make out was Lou's name. I didn't see him in the front of the house, so I ran back through the kitchen to the bedroom. He had fallen back across the bed, a hole right at his sideburn, his jaw still quivering. They had a fight, and some ugly depth of pain convulsed within him. He left the table and walked to the bedroom. My mother heard the light slam of a .22. Nothing more.

That summer seems vague and distant. I can't remember any specifics, though I had to take care of my mother and handle the affairs of the house. I probably made do by blunting a good deal of what I saw and navigating with intuitive quadrants. But though I cannot remember details, I do recall feel-ings and recognitions: Lou's suicide came to represent the sadness and dead time I had protected myself against, the personal as well as public oppres-siveness of life in South Los Angeles. I began to see that my escape to the trailer and my isolationist fantasies of the demimonde would yield another kind of death, a surrender to the culture's lost core. An alternative was some-how starting to take shape around school and knowledge. Knowledge seemed . . . was it empowering? No, that's a word I would use now. Then I felt freed, as if I were untying fetters. There simply were times when the pain and confusion of that summer would give way to something I felt more than I knew: a lightness to my body, an ease in breathing. Three or four months later I took an art history course, and one day during a slide show on Gothic architecture I felt myself rising up within the interior light of Mont-Saint-Michel. I wanted to be released from the despair that surrounded me on South Vermont and from my own troubled sense of exclusion.

Jack MacFarland had saved me at one juncture—caught my fancy and revitalized my mind—what I felt now was something further, some tentative recognition that an engagement with ideas could foster competence and lead me out into the world. But all this was very new and fragile, and given what I know now, I realize how easily it could have been crushed. My mother, for as long as I can remember, always added onto any statement of intention—hers or others'—the phrase *se vuol Dio*, if God wants it. The fulfillment of desire, no matter how trivial, required the blessing of the gods, for the world was filled with threat. "I'll plant the seeds this weekend," I might say. "Se vuol Dio," she would add. *Se vuol Dio*. The phrase expressed several lifetimes of ravaged hope: my grandfather's lost leg, the failure of the Rose Spaghetti House, my father laid low, Lou Minton, the landscapes of South L.A. *Se vuol Dio*. For those who live their lives on South Vermont, tomorrow doesn't beckon to be defined from a benign future. It's up to the gods, not you, if any old thing turns out right. I carried within me no history of assurances that what I was feeling would lead to anything.

> Words piled up like cars in a serial wreck.

Because of its size and because of the kind of teacher who is drawn to small liberal arts colleges, Loyola would turn out to be a very good place for me. For even with MacFarland's yearlong tour through ideas and language, I was unprepared. English prose written before the twentieth century was difficult, sometimes impossible, for me to comprehend. The kind of reasoning I found in logic was very foreign. My writing was okay, but I couldn't hold a candle to Art Mitz or Mark Dever or to those boys who came from good schools. And my fears about science and mathematics prevailed: Pereira Hall, the Math and Engineering Building, was only forty to fifty yards from the rear entrance to the English Department but seemed an unfriendly mirage, a malevolent castle floating in the haze of a mescaline dream.

We live, in America, with so many platitudes about motivation and self-reliance and individualism—and myths spun from them, like those of Horatio Alger—that we find it hard to accept the fact that they are serious nonsense. To live your early life on the streets of South L.A.—or Homewood or Spanish Harlem or Chicago's South Side or any one of hundreds of other depressed communities—and to journey up through the top levels of the

American educational system will call for support and guidance at many, many points along the way. You'll need people to guide you into conversations that seem foreign and threatening. You'll need models, lots of them, to show you how to get at what you don't know. You'll need people to help you center yourself in your own developing ideas. You'll need people to watch out for you. There is much talk these days about the value of a classical humanistic education, a call for an immersion in the humanities, a return to the great books. These appeals raise lots of suspicions, for such curricula have traditionally served to exclude working-class people from the classroom. It doesn't, of necessity, have to be that way. The teachers that fate and Jack MacFarland's crisis intervention sent my way worked at making the humanities truly human. What transpired between us was the essence of humane liberal education, and it enabled me to move far beyond the cognitive charade of my freshman year.

From the midpoint of their freshman year, Loyola students had to take one philosophy course per semester: Logic, Philosophy of Nature, Philosophy of Man, General Ethics, Natural Theology, and so on. Logic was the first in the series, and I had barely gotten a C. The rest of the courses looked like a book fair of medieval scholasticism with the mold scraped off the bindings, and I dreaded their advent. But I was beginning my sophomore year at a time when the best and brightest of the Jesuit community were calling for an intellectually panoramic, socially progressive Catholicism, and while this lasted, I reaped the benefits. Sections of the next three courses I had to take would be taught by a young man who was studying for the priesthood and who was, himself, attempting to develop a personal philosophy that incorporated the mind and the body as well as the spirit.

Mr. Johnson could have strolled off a Wheaties box. Still in his twenties and a casting director's vision of those good looks thought to be all-American, Don Johnson had committed his very considerable intelligence to the study and teaching of philosophy. Jack MacFarland had introduced me to the Greeks, to Christian scholasticism, eighteenth-century deism, and French existentialism, but it was truly an introduction, a curtsy to that realm of the heavens where the philosophers dwell. Mr. Johnson provided a fuller course. He was methodical and spoke with vibrance and made connections between ancients and moderns with care. He did for philosophy what Mr. MacFarland had done for literary history: He gave me a directory of key names and notions.

We started in a traditional way with the Greek philosophers who preceded Socrates—Thales, Heraclitus, Empedocles—and worked our way down to Kant and Hegel. We read a little Aquinas, but we also read E. A. Burtt's *The Metaphysical Foundations of Modern Science*, and that gave me entry to Kepler, Copernicus, Galileo (which I was then spelling *Galelao*), and Newton.

As he laid out his history of ideas, Mr. Johnson would consider aloud the particular philosophical issue involved, so we didn't, for example, simply get an outline of what Hegel believed, but we watched and listened as Don Johnson reasoned like Hegel and then raised his own questions about the Hegelian scheme. He was a working philosopher, and he was thinking out loud in front of us.

The Metaphysical Foundations of Modern Science was very tough going. It assumed not only a familiarity with Western thought but, as well, a sophistication in reading a theoretically rich argument. It was, in other words, the kind of book you encounter with increased frequency as you move through college. It combined the history of mathematics and science with philosophical investigation, and when I tried to read it, I'd end up rescanning the same sentences over and over, not understanding them, and, finally, slamming the book down on the desk—swearing at this golden boy Johnson and angry with myself. Here's a typical passage, one of the many I marked as being hopeless:

> We begin now to glimpse the tremendous significance of what these fathers of modern science were doing, but let us continue with our questions. What further specific metaphysical doctrines was Kepler led to adopt as a consequence of this notion of what constitutes the real world? For one thing, it led him to appropriate in his own way the distinction between primary and secondary qualities, which had been noted in the ancient world by the atomist and skeptical schools, and which was being revived in the sixteenth century in varied form by such miscellaneous thinkers as Vives, Sanchez, Montaigne, and Campanella. Knowledge as it is immediately offered the mind through the senses is obscure, confused, contradictory, and hence untrustworthy; only those features of the world in terms of which we get certain and consistent knowledge open before us what is indubitably and permanently real. Other qualities are not real qualities of things, but only signs of them. For Kepler, of course, the real qualities are those caught up in this mathematical harmony underlying the world of the senses, and which, therefore, have a causal relation to the latter. *The real world is a world of quantitative characteristics only; its differences are differences of number alone.*

I couldn't get the distinction that was being made between primary and secondary qualities, and I certainly didn't have the background that would enable me to make sense of Burtt's brief historical survey: from "atomist and skeptical schools [to] . . . Campanella." It is clear from the author's italics that the last sentence of the passage is important, so I underlined it, but because Burtt's discussion is built on a rich intellectual history that I didn't know, I was reading words but not understanding text. I was the human incarnation of language-recognition computer programs; able to record the dictionary meanings of individual words but unable to generate any meaning out of them.

"What," I asked in class, "are primary and secondary qualities? I don't get it." And here Don Johnson was very good. "The answer," he said, "can be found in the passage itself. I'll go back through it with you. Let's start with primary and secondary qualities. If some qualities are primary and others secondary, which do you think would be most important?"

"Primary?"

"Right. Primary qualities. Whatever they are. Now let's turn to Kepler, since Kepler's the subject of this passage. What is it that's more important to Kepler?"

I pause and say tentatively, "Math." Another student speaks up, reading from the book: "Quantitative characteristics."

"All right. So primary qualities, for Kepler, are mathematical, quantitative. But we still don't know what this primary and secondary opposition really refers to, do we? Look right in the middle of the paragraph. Burtt is comparing mathematical knowledge to the immediate knowledge provided by—what?"   20

My light bulb goes on: "The senses."

"There it is. The primary-secondary opposition is the opposition between knowledge gained by pure mathematical reasoning versus knowledge gained through our five senses."

We worked with *The Metaphysical Foundations of Modern Science* for some time, and I made my way slowly through it. Mr. Johnson was helping me develop an ability to read difficult texts—I was learning how to reread critically, how to tease out definitions and basic arguments. And I was also gaining confidence that if I stayed with material long enough and kept asking questions, I would get it. That assurance proved to be more valuable than any particular body of knowledge I learned that year.

For my second semester, I had to take Philosophy of Man, and it was during that course that Mr. Johnson delivered his second gift. We read Gabriel Marcel and Erich Fromm, learning about phenomenology and social criticism. We considered the human animal from an anthropological as well as philosophical perspective. And we read humanistic psychologist Abraham Maslow's *Toward a Psychology of Being*. Maslow wrote about "the 'will to health,' the urge to grow, the pressure of self-actualization, the quest for one's identity." The book had a profound effect on me. Six months before, Lou Minton's jaw quivered as if to speak the race's deepest sorrow, and through the rest of that summer I could only feel in my legs and chest some fleeting assurance that the world wasn't a thin mask stretched over nothingness. Now I was reading an articulation of that vague, hopeful feeling. Maslow was giving voice to some delicate possibility within me, and I was powerfully drawn to it. Every person is, in part, "'his own project' and makes himself." I had to know more, so I called Mr. Johnson up and asked if I could visit with him. "Sure," he said, and invited me to campus. So one Saturday morning I took a series of early buses and headed west.

Mr. Johnson and the other initiates to the priesthood lived in an old white residence hall on the grassy east edge of campus, and the long walk up Loyola Boulevard was quiet and meditative: Birds were flying tree to tree and a light breeze was coming in off Playa del Rey. I walked up around the gym, back behind Math-Engineering to his quarters, a simple one-story building with those Spanish curves that seem simultaneously thick and weightless. The sun had warmed the stucco. A window by the door was open, and a curtain had fluttered out. I rang the bell and heard steps on a hardwood floor. Mr. Johnson opened the door and stepped out. He was smiling and his eyes were attentive in the light . . . present . . . there. They said, "Come, let's talk."

Dr. Frank Carothers taught what is generally called the sophomore survey, a yearlong sequence of courses that introduces the neophyte English major to the key works in English literary history. Dr. Carothers was tall and robust. He wore thick glasses and a checkered bow tie and his hairline was male Botticelli, picking up somewhere back beyond his brow. As the year progressed, he spread English literary history out in slow time across the board, and I was introduced to people I'd never heard of: William Langland, a medieval acolyte who wrote the dream-vision *Piers Plowman*; the sixteenth-century poet Sir Thomas Wyatt; Elizabethan lyricists with peculiar names like Orlando Gibbons and Tobias Hume (the author of the wondrous suggestion that tobacco "maketh lean the fat men's tumour"); the physician Sir Thomas Browne; the essayist Joseph Addison; the biographer James Boswell; the political philosopher Edmund Burke, whose prose I could not decipher; and poets Romantic and Victorian (Shelley and Rossetti and Algernon Charles Swinburne). Some of the stuff was invitingly strange ("Pallid and pink as the palm of the flag-flower . . ."), some was awfully hard to read, and some was just awful. But Dr. Carothers laid it all out with his reserved passion, drew for us a giant conceptual blueprint onto which we could place other courses, other books. He was precise, thorough, and rigorous. And he started his best work once class was over.

Being a professor was, for Frank Carothers, a profoundly social calling: He enjoyed the classroom, and he seemed to love the more informal contacts with those he taught, those he once taught, and those who stopped by just to get a look at this guy. He stayed in his office until about four each afternoon, leaning back in his old swivel chair, hands clasped behind his head, his bow tie tight against his collar. He had strong opinions, and he'd get irritated if you missed class, and he sometimes gave quirky advice—but there he'd be shaking his head sympathetically as students poured out their troubles. It was pure and primary for Frank Carothers: Teaching allowed him daily to fuse the joy he got from reading literature—poetry especially—with his deep pleasure in human community. What I saw when I was around him—and I hung out in his office from my sophomore year on—was very different from the world I had been creating for myself, a far cry from my withdrawal into an old house trailer with a silent book.

One of Dr. Carothers's achievements was the English Society. The English Society had seventy-eight members, and that made it just about the biggest organization on campus: jocks, literati, C-plus students, frat boys, engineers, mystics, scholars, profligates, bullies, geeks, Republicans—all stood side by side for group pictures. The English Society sponsored poetry readings, lectures, and card games, and best of all, barbecues in the Carotherses' backyard. We would caravan out to Manhattan Beach to be greeted by Betsy, the youngest of the seven Carothers children, and she'd walk us back to her father who, wrapped now in an apron, was poking coals or unscrewing the tops from jugs of red wine.

Vivian Carothers, a delicate, soft-spoken woman, would look after us and serve up trays of cheese and chips and little baked things. Students would knock on the redwood gate all through the late afternoon, more and more finding places for themselves among flowers and elephant ears, patio furniture, and a wizened pine. We would go on way past sunset, talking to Dr. Carothers and to each other about books and sports and currently despised professors, sometimes letting off steam and sometimes learning something new. And Frank Carothers would keep us fed, returning to the big, domed barbecue through the evening to lift the lid and add hamburgers, the smoke rising off the grill and up through the telephone lines stretching like the strings of Shelley's harp over the suburbs of the South Bay.

When I was learning my craft at Jack MacFarland's knee, I continually mis-used words and wrote fragments and run-on sentences and had trouble making my pronouns agree with whatever it was that preceded them. I also produced sentences like these: 30

> Some of these modern-day Ramses are inherent of their wealth, others are self-made.

> An exhibition of will on the part of the protagonist enables him to accom-plish a subjective good (which is an element of tragedy, namely: the pro-tagonist does not fully realize the objective wrong that he is doing. He feels objectively justified if not completely right.)

I was struggling to express increasingly complex ideas, and I couldn't get the language straight: Words, as in my second sentence on tragedy, piled up like cars in a serial wreck. I was encountering a new language—the language of the academy—and was trying to find my way around in it. I have some more examples, written during my first year and a half at Loyola. There was inflated vocabulary:

> I conjectured that he was the same individual who had arrested my attention earlier.
>
> In his famed speech, "The American Scholar," Ralph Waldo Emerson posed several problems that are particularly germane to the position of the young author.

There were clichés and mixed and awkward metaphors:

> In 1517, when Luther nailed his 95 theses to the door of Wittenburg Cathedral, he unknowingly started a snowball rolling that was to grow to tremendous reprocussions.

And there was academic melodrama:

> The vast realm of the cosmos or the depths of a man's soul hold questions that reason flounders upon, but which can be probed by the peculiar private insight of the seer.

Pop grammarians and unhappy English teachers get a little strange around sentences like these. But such sentences can be seen as marking a stage in linguistic growth. Appropriating a style and making it your own is difficult, and you'll miss the mark a thousand times along the way. The botched performances, though, are part of it all, and developing writers will grow through them if they are able to write for people who care about language, people who are willing to sit with them and help them as they struggle to write about difficult things. That is what Ted Erlandson did for me.

Dr. Erlandson was one of the people who agreed to teach me and my Mercy High companions a seminar—a close, intensive course that would substitute for a larger, standard offering like Introduction to Prose Literature. He was tall and lanky and had a long reddish brown beard and lectured in a voice that was basso and happy. He was a strong lecturer and possessed the best memory for fictional detail I'd ever witnessed. And he cared about prose. The teachers I had during my last three years at Loyola assigned a tremendous amount of writing. But it was Ted Erlandson who got in there with his pencil and worked on my style. He would sit me down next to him at his big desk, sweep books and pencils across the scratched veneer, and go back over the sentences he wanted me to revise.

He always began by reading the sentence out loud: "Camus ascented to a richer vision of life that was to characterize the entirety of his work." Then he would fiddle with the sentence, talking and looking up at me intermittently to comment or ask questions: "'Ascent'. That sounds like 'assent', I know, but look it up, Mike." He'd wait while I fluttered the dictionary. "Now, 'the entirety of his work' . . . try this instead: 'his entire work.' Let's read it.

'Camus assented to a richer vision of life that would characterize his entire work.' Sounds better, doesn't it?"

And another sentence. "'Irregardless of the disastrous ending of *Bread and Wine*, it must be seen as an affirmative work.' 'Irregardless' . . . people use it all the time, but 'regardless' will do just fine. Now, I think this next part sounds a little awkward; listen: 'Regardless of the disastrous ending of *Bread and Wine*, it . . .' Hear that? Let's try removing the 'of' and the 'it': 'Regardless of the disastrous ending, *Bread and Wine* must be seen as an affirmative work.' Hmmm. Better, I think."

And so it would go. He rarely used grammatical terms, and he never got   35 technical. He dealt with specific bits of language: "Try this here" or "Here's another way to say it." He worked as a craftsman works, with particulars, and he shuttled back and forth continually between print and voice, making me breathe my prose, making me hear the language I'd generated in silence. Perhaps he was more directive than some would like, but, to be truthful, direction was what I needed. I was easily frustrated, and it didn't take a lot to make me doubt myself. When teachers would write "no" or "awkward" or "rewrite" alongside the sentences I had worked so hard to produce, I would be peeved and disappointed. "Well, what the hell *do* they want?" I'd grumble to no one in particular. So Ted Erlandson's linguistic parenting felt just right: a modeling of grace until it all slowly, slowly began to work itself into the way I shaped language.

When Father Albertson lectured, he would stand pretty much in one spot slightly to the left or right of center in front of us. He tended to hold his notes or a play or a critical study in both hands, releasing one to emphasize a point with a simple gesture. He was tall and thin, and his voice was soft and tended toward monotone. When he spoke, he looked very serious, but when one of us responded with any kind of intelligence, a little smile would come over his face. Jack MacFarland had told me that it was Clint Albertson's Shakespeare course that would knock my socks off.

For each play we covered, Father Albertson distributed a five- to ten-page list of questions to ask ourselves as we read. These study questions were of three general types.

The first type was broad and speculative and was meant to spark reflection on major characters and key events. Here's a teaser on *Hamlet*:

> Would you look among the portrait-paintings by Raphael, or Rembrandt, or Van Gogh, or El Greco, or Rouault for an ideal representation of Hamlet? Which painting by which of these men do you think most closely resembles your idea of what Hamlet should look like?

The second type focused on the details of the play itself and were very specific. Here are two of the thirty-eight he wrote for *As You Like It*:

ACT I, SCENE 2
How is Rosalind distinguished from Celia in this scene? How do you explain the discrepancy between the Folio version of lines 284–287 and Act I, scene 3, line 117?

ACT II, SCENES 4–6:
It has been said these scenes take us definitely out of the world of reality into a world of dream. What would you say are the steps of the process by which Shakespeare brings about this illusion?

The third kind of question required us to work with some historical or critical study. This is an example from the worksheet on *Romeo and Juliet*:

Read the first chapter of C. S. Lewis's *Allegory of Love*, "Courtly Love." What would you say about Shakespeare's concept of love in relation to what Lewis presents as the traditional contradictory concepts in medieval literature of "romantic love" vs. "marriage."

Father Albertson had placed over 150 books on the reserve shelf in the library, and they ranged from intellectual history to literary criticism to handbooks on theater production. I had used a few such "secondary sources" to quote in my own writing since my days with Jack MacFarland, but this was the first time a teacher had so thoroughly woven them into a course. Father Albertson would cite them during lectures as naturally as though he were recalling a discussion he had overheard. He would add his own opinions and, since he expected us to form opinions, would ask us for ours.

I realize that this kind of thing—the close, line-by-line examination, the citing of critical opinion—has given rise to endless parodies of the academy: repressed schoolmen clucking along in the land of lost language. It certainly can be that way. But with Clint Albertson, all the learning furthered my comprehension of the play. His questions forced me to think carefully about Shakespeare's choice of words, about the crafting of a scene, about the connections between language and performance. I had to read very, very closely, leaning over the thin Formica desk in the trailer, my head cupped in my hands with my two index fingers in my ears to blot out the noise from the alley behind me. There were times when no matter how hard I tried, I wouldn't get it. I'd close the book, feeling stupid to my bones, and go find John. Over then to the liquor store, out into the night. The next day I would visit Father Albertson and tell him I was lost, ask him why this stuff was so damned hard. He'd listen and ask me to tell him why it made me so angry. I'd sputter some more, and then he'd draw me to the difficult passage, slowly opening the language up, helping me comprehend a distant, stylized literature, taking it apart, touching it.

I would then return to a classroom where a historically rich conversation   40
was in progress. Other readers of Shakespeare—from Samuel Johnson to the

contemporary literary critic Wylie Sypher—were given voice by Father Albertson, and we were encouraged to enter the dialogue, to consider, to take issue, to be seated amid all that potentially intimidating shoptalk. We were shown how to summarize an opinion, argue with it, weave it into our own interpretations. Nothing is more exclusive than the academic club: Its language is highbrow, it has fancy badges, and it worships tradition. It limits itself to a few participants who prefer to talk to each other. What Father Albertson did was bring us inside the circle, nudging us out into the chatter, always just behind us, whispering to try this step, then this one, encouraging us to feel the moves for ourselves.

Those four men collectively gave me the best sort of liberal education, the kind longed for in the stream of blue-ribbon reports on the humanities that now cross my desk. I developed the ability to read closely, to persevere in the face of uncertainty and ask questions of what I was reading—not with downcast eyes, but freely, aloud, realizing there is no such thing as an open book. My teachers modeled critical inquiry and linguistic precision and grace, and they provided various cognitive maps for philosophy and history and literature. They encouraged me to make connections and to enter into conversations—present and past—to see what talking a particular kind of talk would enable me to do with a thorny philosophical problem or a difficult literary text. And it was all alive. It transpired in backyards and on doorsteps and inside offices as well as in the classroom. I could smell their tobacco and see the nicks left by their razors. They liked books and ideas, and they liked to talk about them in ways that fostered growth rather than established dominance. They lived their knowledge. And maybe because of that their knowledge grew in me in ways that led back out to the world. I was developing a set of tools with which to shape a life.

Working with the Text

1. Mike Rose makes his argument by telling a story based on two pivotal events—the intervention of a mentor and a death in the family—that dramatically change his experience of getting a university education. In a short essay, explore how these two events worked together to bring Rose into a pursuit of knowledge.

2. Why does Rose use narrative to make his argument? What does storytelling lend to his argument that other forms of writing could not? Mark the passages in which Rose interprets the story for the reader—explains to the reader what the settings and events meant to him. Reread the essay, skipping over the interpretive passages. What other meanings might a reader give to the events? In a

short essay, reflect on the roots of Rose's argument and why it emerged as a combination of storytelling and meaning telling.

3. Rose opens the essay asserting, "It is an unfortunate fact of our psychic lives that the images that surround us as we grow up—no matter how much we may scorn them later—give shape to our deepest needs and longings." He then presents images of the homecoming queen and her princesses. Why does he introduce the essay with these images? Beginning with these images, write a short essay tracing the "deepest needs and longings" that eventually lead Rose into an academic life.

4. Through each of the mentors Rose describes, he learned particular approaches to entering the academic community. List the mentors and identify what each of them brought to Rose's undergraduate experience. Reread the final paragraph of the essay. Write a short response essay comparing Rose's experience—or select elements of his experience—to your own. Where there are differences, analyze why those differences might exist.

5. Describing his efforts to understand difficult material, Rose writes, "There were times when no matter how hard I tried, I wouldn't get it. I'd close the book, feeling stupid to my bones, and go find John. Over then to the liquor store, out into the night" (par. 39). As you reread the essay, note Rose's emotional responses to the obstacles he faced. In a short essay, reflect on those responses and the behaviors that came out of them. What was he feeling? Why?

From Text to Field

1. Write an essay in which you invent a mentor for yourself. In what specific ways would this mentor contribute to your university learning experience? How would this mentor fulfill roles that are currently missing from your university experience?

2. Does the fact that you know Rose's reputation as a teacher and scholar color your sense of his narrative? His story has a happy ending. Consider other people from similar backgrounds who don't make it. Write a response to Rose's essay in which you address the factors that lead to other than happy endings. To what extent can those factors be changed to increase the chances of success? To what extent do those factors inevitably—or most often—lead to failure?

3. Find passages in the essay that describe ways Rose's mentors taught him to read and write like an academic. Using those passages as prompts, write an essay that describes and analyzes your own academic reading or writing process. What elements of your process have advanced your ability to enter

into the academic conversation? In what ways does your process fall short of what you would like to be able to do? What would you like to learn to make your process more effective?

4. Rose describes his early attempts to write academically as "words . . . piled up like cars in a serial wreck" (par. 30). Have you ever felt that way about your academic writing? Write a paragraph in which you try to reproduce the language of a field you would like to enter or a course you are required to take. Follow the paragraph with an analysis of why the language is difficult. Is the vocabulary unfamiliar or obscure? Is the sentence structure difficult to master? Every field or discipline has hidden intellectual moves and strategies that express the field's distinctive way of thinking and making arguments. Are those moves and strategies difficult to enter into?

5. In this essay, Rose describes only those mentors who were his teachers. In an essay, reflect on whether peers can serve as mentors. Analyze the role of upperclassmen in orientation, advisement, or study settings, such as a writing center. Consider the influence of other students whose behavior you simply observe for clues on language, attitudes, and other moves expected of students on your campus.

6. Loyola, the university Rose attended as an undergraduate, is a Catholic university. In an essay, reflect on the differences in mentoring offered by a state university versus a religious university dedicated to the larger spiritual well-being of students. What might be the advantages of each institution? What might be the disadvantages?

Disliking Books at an Early Age

Gerald Graff

Gerald Graff has enjoyed a long and distinguished career studying and teaching literature, in spite of the fact that he feared and avoided books well into his undergraduate years as an English major. It was debate among the literary critics, not the literature itself, that gradually drew him in. He remembers in particular *The Adventures of Huckleberry Finn:* He made no connection with Huck's adventures until critical debate over the ending gave him a reason to think about the text. This undergraduate experience informed his career to such an extent that he recently coedited an edition of *Huckleberry Finn* focused on the literary debates that have surrounded it for several decades.

Graff believes his early aversion to reading has given him special insight as a teacher. "[M]any of the students I teach," writes Graff, "seem to have grown up as the same sort of nonintellectual, nonbookish person I was. . . . I like to think it is an advantage for a teacher to know what it feels like to grow up being indifferent to literature and intimidated by criticism and what it feels like to overcome a resistance to talking like an intellectual."

"Disliking Books at an Early Age" is an excerpt from *Beyond the Culture Wars,* which won the American Book Award in 1993. A second excerpt, "Other Voices, Other Rooms," appears on page 163. Gerald Graff is professor of English and dean of curriculum and instruction in the College of Liberal Arts and Sciences at the University of Illinois at Chicago. His most recent book is titled *Clueless in Academe: How Schooling Obscures the Life of the Mind* (2005).

I like to think I have a certain advantage as a teacher of literature because when I was growing up I disliked and feared books. My youthful aversion to books showed a fine impartiality, extending across the whole spectrum of literature, history, philosophy, science, and what by then (the late 1940s) had come to be called social studies. But had I been forced to choose, I would have singled out literature and history as the reading I disliked most. Science at least had some discernible practical use, and you could have fun solving the problems in the textbooks with their clear-cut answers. Literature and history had no apparent application to my experience, and any boy in my school who had cultivated them—I can't recall one who did—would have marked himself as a sissy.

As a middle-class Jew growing up in an ethnically mixed Chicago neighborhood, I was already in danger of being beaten up daily by rougher working-class boys. Becoming a bookworm would have only given them a decisive reason for beating me up. Reading and studying were more permissible for girls, but they, too, had to be careful not to get too intellectual, lest they acquire the stigma of being "stuck up."

In *Lives on the Boundary*, a remarkable autobiography of the making of an English teacher, Mike Rose describes how the "pain and confusion" of his working-class youth made "school and knowledge" seem a saving alternative. Rose writes of feeling "freed, as if I were untying fetters," by his encounters with certain college teachers, who helped him recognize that "an engagement with ideas could foster competence and lead me out into the world."[1] Coming at things from my middle-class perspective, however, I took for granted a freedom that school, knowledge, and engagement with ideas seemed only to threaten.

My father, a literate man, was frustrated by my refusal to read anything besides comic books, sports magazines, and the John R. Tunis and Clair Bee sports novels. I recall his once confining me to my room until I finished a book on the voyages of Magellan, but try as I might, I could do no better than stare bleakly at the pages. I could not, as we would later say, "relate to" Magellan or to any of the other books my father brought home—detective stories, tales of war and heroism, adventure stories with adolescent heroes (the *Hardy Boys, Hans Brinker,* or *The Silver Skates*), stories of scientific discovery (Paul de Kruif's *Microbe Hunters*), books on current events. Nothing worked.

It was understood, however, that boys of my background would go to college and that once there we would get serious and buckle down. For some, "getting serious" meant prelaw, premed, or a major in business to prepare for taking over the family business. My family did not own a business, and law and medicine did not interest me, so I drifted by default into the nebulous but conveniently noncommittal territory of the liberal arts. I majored in English. 5

At this point the fear of being beaten up if I were caught having anything to do with books was replaced by the fear of flunking out of college if I did not learn to deal with them. But though I dutifully did my homework and made good grades (first at the University of Illinois, Chicago branch, then at the University of Chicago, from which I graduated in 1959), I continued to find "serious" reading painfully difficult and alien. My most vivid recollections of college reading are of assigned classics I failed to finish: *The Iliad* (in the Richmond Lattimore translation); *The Autobiography of Benvenuto Cellini*, a major disappointment after the paperback jacket's promise of "a lusty classic of Renaissance ribaldry"; E. M. Forster's *Passage to India*, sixty agonizing pages of which I managed to slog through before giving up. Even Hemingway, Steinbeck, and Fitzgerald, whose contemporary world was said to be "close to my own experience," left me cold. I saw little there that did resemble my experience.

Even when I had done the assigned reading, I was often tongue-tied and embarrassed when called on. What was unclear to me was what I was supposed to *say* about literary works, and why. Had I been born a decade or two earlier, I might have come to college with the rudiments of a literate vocabulary for talking about culture that some people older than I acquired through family, high school, or church. As it was, "cultured" phrases seemed effete and sterile to me. When I was able to produce the kind of talk that was required in class, the intellectualism of it came out sounding stilted and hollow in my mouth. If *Cliffs Notes* and other such crib sheets for the distressed had yet come into existence, with their ready-to-copy summaries of widely taught literary works, I would have been an excellent customer. (As it was, I did avail myself of the primitive version then in existence called *Masterplots*.)

> Getting into immediate contact with the text was for me a curiously triangular business.

What first made literature, history, and other intellectual pursuits seem attractive to me was exposure to critical debates. There was no single conversion experience, but a gradual transformation over several years, extending into my first teaching positions, at the University of New Mexico and then Northwestern University. But one of the first sparks I remember was a controversy over *The Adventures of Huckleberry Finn* that arose in a course during my junior year in college. On first attempt, Twain's novel was just another assigned classic that I was too bored to finish. I could see little connection between my Chicago upbringing and Huck's pre–Civil War adventures with a runaway slave on a raft up the Mississippi.

My interest was aroused, however, when our instructor mentioned that the critics had disagreed over the merits of the last part of the novel. He quoted Ernest Hemingway's remark that "if you read [the novel] you must stop where the nigger Jim is stolen by the boys. This is the real end. The rest is cheating." According to this school of thought, the remainder of the book trivializes the quest for Jim's freedom that has motivated the story up to that point. This happens first when Jim becomes an object of Tom Sawyer's slapstick humor, then when it is revealed that unbeknownst to Huck, the reader, and himself, Jim has already been freed by his benevolent owner, so that the risk we have assumed Jim and Huck to be under all along has been really no risk at all.

Like the critics, our class divided over the question: Did Twain's ending   10 vitiate the book's profound critique of racism, as Hemingway's charge of cheating implied? Cheating in my experience up to then was something students did, an unthinkable act for a famous author. It was a revelation to me that famous authors were capable not only of mistakes but of ones that even lowly undergraduates might be able to point out. When I chose to write my term paper on the dispute over the ending, my instructor suggested I look at several critics on the opposing sides, T. S. Eliot and Lionel Trilling, who defended the ending, and Leo Marx, who sided with Hemingway.

Reading the critics was like picking up where the class discussion had left off, and I gained confidence from recognizing that my classmates and I had had thoughts that, however stumbling our expression of them, were not too far from the thoughts of famous published critics. I went back to the novel again and to my surprise found myself rereading it with an excitement I had never felt before with a serious book. Having the controversy over the ending in mind, I now had some issues *to watch out for* as I read, issues that reshaped the way I read the earlier chapters as well as the later ones and focused my attention. And having issues to watch out for made it possible not only to concentrate, as I had not been able to do earlier, but to put myself in the text—to read with a sense of personal engagement that I had not felt before. Reading the novel with the voices of the critics running through my mind, I found myself thinking of things that I might say about what I was reading, things that may have belonged partly to the critics but also now belonged to me. It was as if having a stock of things to look for and to say about a literary work had somehow made it possible for me to read one.

One of the critics had argued that what was at issue in the debate over *Huckleberry Finn* was not just the novel's value but its cultural significance: If *Huckleberry Finn* was contradictory or confused in its attitude toward race, then what did that say about the culture that had received the novel as one of its representative cultural documents and had made Twain a folk hero? This critic had also made the intriguing observation—I found out only later it was a critical commonplace at that time—that judgments about the novel's aesthetic value could not be separated from judgments about its moral substance. I recall taking in both this critic's arguments and the cadence of the phrases in which they were couched; perhaps it would not be so bad after all to become the sort of person who talked about "cultural contradictions" and the "inseparability of form and content." Perhaps even mere literary-critical talk could give you a certain power in the real world. As the possibility dawned on me that reading and intellectual discussion might actually have something to do with my real life, I became less embarrassed about using the intellectual formulas.

The Standard Story

It was through exposure to such critical reading and discussion over a period of time that I came to catch the literary bug, eventually choosing the vocation of teaching. This was not the way it is supposed to happen. In the standard story of academic vocation that we like to tell ourselves, the germ is first planted by an early experience of literature itself. The future teacher is initially inspired by some primary experience of a great book and only subsequently acquires the secondary, derivative skills of critical discussion. A teacher may be involved in instilling this inspiration, but a teacher who seemingly effaces himself or herself before the text. Any premature or excessive acquaintance with secondary critical discourse, and certainly with its sectarian debates, is thought to be a corrupting danger, causing one to lose touch with the primary passion for literature.

This, as we have seen, is the charge leveled against the current generation of literature teachers, who are said to have become so obsessed with sophisticated critical theories that they have lost the passion they once had for literature itself. They have been seduced by professionalism, drawn away from a healthy absorption in literature to the sickly fascination with analysis and theory and to the selfish advancement of their careers. This hostility to recent theory would not be so powerful, however, if it were not overlaid on a set of older resentments which long predate the rise of deconstruction and post-structuralism, resentments at literature's having become an academic "field" to begin with. Today's attacks on literary theory are often really attacks on literary criticism, or at least on criticism of the intensely analytic kind that academics practice, which has always been suspected of coming between readers (and students) and the primary experience of literature itself. This resentment is rooted in anxieties about the increasing self-consciousness of modern life, which often leaves us feeling that we are never quite living but only endlessly talking about it, too often in some abstract professional vocabulary. The anxieties are expressed in our romantic literary tradition, which protests against urban forms of sophistication that, it is believed, cause us to lose touch with the innocence of childhood and with our creative impulses.

To those who have never reconciled themselves to the academicization of 15 literature, the seeming overdevelopment of academic criticism with its obtrusive methodology and its endless disputes among interpretations and theories seems a betrayal not just of literature and the common reader but of the professor's own original passion for literature. In a recent letter to an intellectual journal one writer suggests that we should be concerned less about the often-lamented common reader whom academic critics have deserted than about "the souls of the academics and literati themselves, who, as a result of social and professional pressures, have lost touch with the inner impulses that drew them to the world of books in the first place."[2] What this writer cannot imagine is that someone might enter academic literary study because he actually *likes* thinking and talking in an analytical or theoretical way about books and that such a person might see his acceptance of "professional pressures" not as a betrayal of the "inner impulses" that drew him "to the world of books in the first place" but as a way to fulfill those impulses.

The standard story ascribes innocence to the primary experience of literature and sees the secondary experience of professional criticism as corrupting. In my case, however, things had evidently worked the other way around: I had to be corrupted first in order to experience innocence. It was only when I was introduced to a critical debate about *Huckleberry Finn* that my helplessness in the face of the novel abated and I could experience a personal reaction to it. Getting into immediate contact with the text was for me a curiously triangular business; I could not do it directly but needed a conversation of other readers to give me the issues and terms that made it possible to respond.

As I think back on it now, it was as if the critical conversation I needed had up to then been withheld from me, on the ground that it could only interfere with my direct access to literature itself. The assumption was that leaving me alone with literary texts themselves, uncontaminated by the interpretations and theories of professional critics, would enable me to get on the closest possible terms with those texts. But being alone with the texts only left me feeling bored and helpless, since I had no language with which to make them mine. On the one hand, I was being asked to speak a foreign language—literary criticism—while on the other hand, I was being protected from that language, presumably for my own safety.

The moral I draw from this experience is that our ability to read well depends more than we think on our ability to *talk well* about what we read. Our assumptions about what is "primary" and "secondary" in the reading process blind us to what actually goes on. Many literate people learned certain ways of talking about books so long ago that they have forgotten they ever had to learn them. These people therefore fail to understand the reading problems of the struggling students who have still not acquired a critical vocabulary.

How typical my case was is hard to say, but many of the students I teach seem to have grown up as the same sort of nonintellectual, nonbookish person I was, and they seem to view literature with some of the same aversions, fears, and anxieties. That is why I like to think it is an advantage for a teacher to know what it feels like to grow up being indifferent to literature and intimidated by criticism and what it feels like to overcome a resistance to talking like an intellectual.

Notes

1. Mike Rose, *Lives on the Boundary* (New York: Free Press, 1989), pp. 46–47.
2. John Toren, letter, *New Republic* 201, no. 9 (August 28, 1989): 6, 41.

Working with the Text

1. As a professor of English at a prominent university, Gerald Graff confesses that when he was growing up, he "disliked and feared books." Throughout the essay, he continues to draw his argument from personal experience. In a short essay, distill his argument and reflect on why he would choose personal experience as the basis for the assertions he makes. Who is his audience? Why is he making this argument? Why is his personal experience significant?

2. In moving through his argument, Graff relates the reasons behind his resistance to reading as well as the reasons behind his "gradual transformation" into an intellectual and a literary critic. Make two lists of those reasons: one for his resistance and another for his transformation. Based on those lists, write a short essay analyzing the relationship between his resistance and his transformation. Why was reading hard for him? How did he respond to it? In what ways did his university experience meet his resistance and transform it?

3. Graff advocates debate as a point of entering into demanding texts with excitement. Given his assertions on debate, how do you think he conducts his own classroom? Referring to the specific approaches, experiences, and ways of thinking he describes, write a short essay in which you imagine the progression of activities in one of his courses. What role would secondary sources play? What would the relationship between class discussion and writing be? What would you learn?

From Text to Field

1. In this essay, Graff describes texts he was supposed to like, but didn't. He also describes "serious" reading that excited him and the approaches to reading that made this possible. In an autobiographical essay, analyze your own relationship to the reading you do in your university studies. What kinds of reading do you resist? Why? What form does your resistance take? What kinds of reading are exciting for you? Why? What happens to create the excitement? What activities or experiences have made reading that was once hard for you easier and more compelling?

2. Graff describes "the standard story of academic vocation" for literature professors, in which "the germ is first planted by an early experience of literature itself" (par. 13). In Graff's own story, he resisted literature for years but

was gradually drawn into the profession by critical debates over the texts. Graff's observations suggest contrasting ways of entering into any new area of inquiry and choosing to pursue it as a profession or an area of specialization. Consider an area of inquiry or specialization you have been required to enter or have chosen to pursue. Did you enter in a way similar to Graff's "standard story," by being exposed to primary texts or materials? Or did you enter as Graff prefers, by being drawn into the current debates? Write an essay in which you reflect on your own experience and describe the path you would prefer to take in mastering the subject matter. Which approach has been or would be most productive for you? Can you imagine a different approach that would be more useful and compelling to you?

3. In key passages, Graff emphasizes the importance of discussion in learning to write about and engage the debates associated with any discipline. Why does he think talking is critical? What is gained that cannot be gained by reading and writing alone? Write an essay from personal experience in which you analyze the contribution class discussion, study groups, or face-to-face conferences with a teacher have made—or not made—to your academic development. In what ways has discussion helped you learn the critical language of a specialty area? In what ways might the requirement to enter into discussion hamper your progress?

4. Have you taken college courses you think would have been more compelling if you had had the opportunity to learn the material through engaging in debate? Have any of your courses given you such an opportunity? Choose one course from your own experience to analyze in light of Graff's argument for critical debate as a way of learning. For a course that offered little or no debate, write an essay that describes how the material was presented and imagine ways that differing points of view might have been introduced to enliven the material. For a course that drew upon differing points of view as a means for exploring the material, describe how this was accomplished.

Dancing with Professors: The Trouble with Academic Prose

Patricia Nelson Limerick

In 1987, at her own request, Patricia Nelson Limerick, professor of history at the University of Colorado at Boulder and chair of the board of the Center of the American West, was named University Fool. Each year on April 1, she tours the campus to remind people to stop taking themselves so seriously.

Limerick's widely circulated article, "Dancing with Professors: The Trouble with Academic Prose," was first published in 1993 in a nonacademic publication—the *New York Times Book Review*. An academic insider, she bases her argument on the observation (borrowed from a classics professor) that "'professors are the ones nobody wanted to dance with in high school.'" The article is an ultimately serious plea for academics to write in such a way that nonspecialists as well as specialists can engage in open discussion, bridging scholarly research with public concerns.

Limerick demonstrated how this could be done in her 1987 revisionist history of the West, *The Legacy of Conquest: The Unbroken Past of the American West* (1987). The book attracted a wide readership among general audiences at the same time it challenged academics inside and outside of history departments to see the West through a new lens. Her books have established her as one of the principal architects of the New Western History, with special interests in the ethnic and environmental aspects of that history.

Among Limerick's numerous accomplishments, she was named a MacArthur Fellow in 1995 and served on the board of advisors for the eight-part PBS series *The West*. Her most recent book is *Something in the Soil: Legacies and Reckonings in the New West* (2001).

In ordinary life, when a listener cannot understand what someone has said, this is the usual exchange:

> *Listener:* I cannot understand what you are saying.
> *Speaker:* Let me try to say it more clearly.

But in scholarly writing in the late twentieth century, other rules apply. This is the implicit exchange:

> *Reader:* I cannot understand what you are saying.
> *Academic Writer:* Too bad. The problem is that you are an unsophisticated and untrained reader. If you were smarter, you would understand me.

The exchange remains implicit, because no one wants to say: "This doesn't make any sense," for fear that the response, "It would, if you were smarter," might actually be true.

While we waste our time fighting over ideological conformity in the scholarly world, horrible writing remains a far more important problem. For all their differences, most right-wing scholars and most left-wing scholars share a common allegiance to a cult of obscurity. Left, right, and center all hide behind the idea that unintelligible prose indicates a sophisticated mind. The politically correct and the politically incorrect come together in the violence they commit against the English language.

University presses have certainly filled their quota every year, in dreary monographs, tangled paragraphs, and impenetrable sentences. But trade publishers have also violated the trust of innocent and hopeful readers. As a prime example of unprovoked assaults on innocent words, consider the verbal behavior of Allan Bloom in *The Closing of the American Mind* published by a large mainstream press. Here is a sample:

> If openness means to "go with the flow," it is necessarily an accommodation to the present. That present is so closed to doubt about so many things impeding the progress of its principles that unqualified openness to it would mean forgetting the despised alternatives to it, knowledge of which makes us aware of what is doubtful in it.

Is there a reader so full of blind courage as to claim to know what this sentence means? Remember, the book in which this remark appeared was a lamentation over the failings of today's students, a call to arms to return to tradition and standards in education. And yet, in twenty years of paper grading, I do not recall many sentences that asked, so pathetically, to be put out of their misery.

Jump to the opposite side of the political spectrum from Allan Bloom, and literary grace makes no noticeable gains. Contemplate this breathless, indefatigable sentence from the geographer Allan Pred, and Mr. Pred and Bloom seem, if only in literary style, to be soul mates:

If what is at stake is an understanding of geographical and historical variations in the sexual division of productive and reproductive labor, of contemporary local and regional variations in female wage labor and women's
work outside the formal economy, of on-the-ground variations in the everyday content of women's lives, inside and outside of their families, then it
must be recognized that, at some nontrivial level, none of the corporal
practices associated with these variations can be severed from spatially and
temporally specific linguistic practices, from languages that not only
enable the conveyance of instructions, commands, role depictions, and
operating rules, but that also regulate and control, that normalize and spell
out the limits of the permissible through the conveyance of disapproval,
ridicule, and reproach.

In this example, 124 words, along with many ideas, find themselves 5
crammed into one sentence. In their company, one starts to get panicky.
"Throw open the windows; bring in the oxygen tanks!" one wants to shout.
"These words and ideas are nearly suffocated. Get them all!" And yet the
condition of this desperately packed and crowded sentence is a perfectly
familiar one to readers of academic writing, readers who have simply learned
to suppress the panic.

Everyone knows that today's college students cannot write, but few seem
willing to admit that the professors who denounce them are not doing much
better. The problem is so blatant there are signs that students are catching
on. In my American history survey course last semester, I presented a few
writing rules that I intended to enforce inflexibly. The students looked more
and more peevish; they looked as if they were about to run down the hall,
find a telephone, place an urgent call, and demand that someone from the
ACLU rush up to campus to sue me for interfering with their First
Amendment rights to compose unintelligible, misshapen sentences.

Finally one aggrieved student raised her hand and said, "You are telling
us not to write long, dull sentences, but most of our assigned reading is full
of long, dull sentences."

As this student was beginning to recognize, when professors undertake to
appraise and improve student writing, the blind are leading the blind. It is,
in truth, difficult to persuade students to write well when they find so few
good examples in their assigned reading.

The current social and political context for higher education makes this
whole issue pressing. In Colorado, as in most states, the legislators are convinced that the university is neglecting students and wasting state resources
on pointless research. Under those circumstances, the miserable writing
habits of professors pose a direct and concrete danger to higher education.
Rather than going to the state legislature, proudly presenting stacks of the
faculty's compelling and engaging publications, you end up hoping that the

lawmakers stay out of the library and stay away, especially, from the periodical room, with its piles of academic journals. The habits of academic writers lend powerful support to the impression that research is a waste of the writers' time and of the public's money.

Why do so many professors write bad prose? 10

Ten years ago, I heard a classics professor say the single most important thing—in my opinion—that anyone has said about professors: "We must remember," he declared, "that professors are the ones nobody wanted to dance with in high school."

This is an insight that lights up the universe—or at least the university. It is a proposition that every entering freshman should be told, and it is certainly a proposition that helps to explain the problem of academic writing. What one sees in professors, repeatedly, is exactly the manner that anyone would adopt after a couple of sad evenings sidelined under the crepe-paper streamers in the gym, sitting on a folding chair while everyone else danced. Dignity, for professors, perches precariously on how well they can convey this message: "I am immersed in some very important thoughts, which unsophisticated people could not even begin to understand. Thus, I would not want to dance, even if one of you unsophisticated people were to ask me."

Think of this, then, the next time you look at an unintelligible academic text. "I would not want the attention of a wide reading audience, even if a wide audience were to ask for me." Isn't that exactly what the pompous and pedantic tone of the classically academic writer conveys?

Professors are often shy, timid, and even fearful people, and under those circumstances, dull, difficult prose can function as a kind of protective camouflage. When you write typical academic prose, it is nearly impossible to make a strong, clear statement. The benefit here is that no one can attack your position, say you are wrong or even raise questions about the accuracy of what you have said, if they cannot tell what you have said. In those terms, awful, indecipherable prose is its own form of armor, protecting the fragile, sensitive thoughts of timid souls.

The best texts for helping us understand the academic world are, of 15 course, Lewis Carroll's *Alice's Adventures in Wonderland* and *Through the Looking Glass*. Just as devotees of Carroll would expect, he has provided us with the best analogy for understanding the origin and function of bad academic writing. Tweedledee and Tweedledum have quite a heated argument over a rattle. They become so angry that they decide to fight. But before they fight, they go off to gather various devices of padding and protection: "bolsters, blankets, hearthrugs, tablecloths, dish covers, and coal scuttles." Then, with Alice's help in tying and fastening, they transform these household items into armor. Alice is not impressed: " 'Really, they'll be more like bundles of old clothes than anything else, by the time they're ready!' she said to herself, as she arranged a bolster round the neck of Tweedledee, 'to keep his head from being cut off, as he said.'" Why this precaution? Because, Tweedledee explains, "'it's one of the most serious things that can possibly happen to one in a battle—to get one's head cut off.'"

Here, in the brothers' anxieties and fears, we have an exact analogy for the problems of academic writing. The next time you look at a classically professorial sentence—long, tangled, obscure, jargonized, polysyllabic—think of Tweedledum and Tweedledee dressed for battle, and see if those timid little thoughts, concealed under layers of clauses and phrases, do not remind you of those agitated but cautious brothers, arrayed in their bolsters, blankets, dish covers, and coal scuttles. The motive, too, is similar. Tweedledum and Tweedledee were in terror of being hurt, and so they padded themselves so thoroughly that they could not be hurt; nor, for that matter, could they move. A properly dreary, inert sentence has exactly the same benefit; it protects its writer from sharp disagreement, while it also protects him from movement.

Why choose camouflage and insulation over clarity and directness? Tweedledee, of course, spoke for everyone, academic or not, when he confessed his fear. It is indeed, as he said, "'one of the most serious things that can possibly happen to one in a battle—to get one's head cut off.'" "Under those circumstances, logic says: Tie the bolster around the neck, and add a protective hearthrug or two. Pack in another qualifying clause or two. Hide behind the passive-voice verb. Preface any assertion with a phrase like "it could be argued" or "a case could be made." Protecting one's neck does seem to be the way to keep one's head from being cut off.

Graduate school implants in many people the belief that there are terrible penalties to be paid for writing clearly, especially writing clearly in ways that challenge established thinking in the field. And yet, in academic warfare (and I speak as a veteran), your head and your neck are rarely in serious danger. You can remove the bolster and the hearthrug. Your opponents will try to whack at you, but they seldom, if ever, land a blow—in large part because they are themselves so wrapped in protective camouflage and insulation that they lose both mobility and accuracy.

So we have a widespread pattern of professors protecting themselves from injury by wrapping their ideas in dull prose, and yet the danger they try to fend off is not a genuine danger. Express yourself clearly, and it is unlikely that either your head—or, more important, your tenure—will be cut off.

How, then, do we save professors from themselves? Fearful people are not made courageous by scolding; they need to be coaxed and encouraged. But how do we do that, especially when this particular form of fearfulness masks itself as pomposity, aloofness, and an assumed air of superiority? 20

Fortunately, we have available the world's most important and illuminating story on the difficulty of persuading people to break out of habits of timidity, caution, and unnecessary fear. I borrow this story from Larry McMurtry, one of my rivals in the interpreting of the American West, though I am putting this story to a use that Mr. McMurtry did not intend.

In a collection of his essays, *In a Narrow Grave*, Mr. McMurtry wrote about the weird process of watching his book *Horseman, Pass By* being turned into the movie *Hud*. He arrived in the Texas Panhandle a week or two after filming had started, and he was particularly anxious to learn how the buzzard scene had gone. In that scene, Paul Newman was supposed to ride up and discover a dead cow, look up at a tree branch lined with buzzards and, in his distress over the loss of the cow, fire his gun at one of the buzzards. At that moment, all of the other buzzards were supposed to fly away into the blue Panhandle sky.

But when Mr. McMurtry asked people how the buzzard scene had gone, all he got, he said, were "stricken looks."

The first problem, it turned out, had to do with the quality of the available local buzzards—who proved to be an excessively scruffy group. So more appealing, more photogenic buzzards had to be flown in from some distance and at considerable expense.

But then came the second problem: how to keep the buzzards sitting on 25 the tree branch until it was time for their cue to fly.

That seemed easy. Wire their feet to the branch, and then, after Paul Newman fires his shot, pull the wire, releasing their feet, thus allowing them to take off. But, as Mr. McMurtry said in an important and memorable phrase, the filmmakers had not reckoned with the "mentality of buzzards." With their feet wired, the buzzards did not have enough mobility to fly. But they did have enough mobility to pitch forward.

So that's what they did: With their feet wired, they tried to fly, pitched forward and hung upside down from the dead branch, with their wings flapping.

I had the good fortune a couple of years ago to meet a woman who had been an extra for this movie, and she added a detail that Mr. McMurtry left out of his essay: Namely, the buzzard circulatory system does not work upside down, and so, after a moment or two of flapping, the buzzards passed out.

Twelve buzzards hanging upside down from a tree branch: This was not what Hollywood wanted from the West, but that's what Hollywood had produced.

And then we get to the second stage of buzzard psychology. After six or 30 seven episodes of pitching forward, passing out, being revived, being replaced on the branch, and pitching forward again, the buzzards gave up. Now, when you pulled the wire and released their feet, they sat there, saying in clear, non-verbal terms: "We tried that before. It did not work. We are not going to try it again." Now the filmmakers had to fly in a high-powered animal trainer to restore buzzard self-esteem. It was all a big mess; Larry McMurtry got a wonderful story out of it; and we, in turn, get the best possible parable of the workings of habit and timidity.

How does the parable apply? In any and all disciplines, you go to graduate school to have your feet wired to the branch. There is nothing inherently wrong with that: Scholars should have some common ground, share some background assumptions, hold some similar habits of mind. This gives you, quite literally, your footing. And yet, in the process of getting your feet wired, you have some awkward moments, and the intellectual equivalent of pitching forward and hanging upside down. That experience—especially if you do it in a public place like a graduate seminar—provides no pleasure. One or two rounds of that humiliation and the world begins to seem like a very treacherous place. Under those circumstances, it does indeed seem to be the choice of wisdom to sit quietly on the branch, to sit without even the thought of flying, since even the thought might be enough to tilt the balance and set off another round of flapping, fainting, and embarrassment.

> **Professors are the ones nobody wanted to dance with in high school.**

Yet when scholars get out of graduate school and get PhDs, and, even more important, when scholars get tenure, the wire is truly pulled. Their feet are free. They can fly wherever and whenever they like. Yet by then the second stage of buzzard psychology has taken hold, and they refuse to fly. The wire is pulled, and yet the buzzards sit there, hunched and grumpy. If they teach in a university with a graduate program, they actively instruct young buzzards in the necessity of keeping their youthful feet on the branch.

This is a very well-established pattern, and it is the ruination of scholarly activity in the modern world. Many professors who teach graduate students think that one of their principal duties is to train the students in the conventions of academic writing.

I do not believe that professors enforce a standard of dull writing on graduate students in order to be cruel. They demand dreariness because they think that dreariness is in the students' best interests. Professors believe that a dull writing style is an academic survival skill because they think that is what editors want, both editors of academic journals and editors of university presses. What we have here is a chain of misinformation and misunderstanding, where everyone thinks that the other guy is the one who demands dull, impersonal prose.

Let me say again what is at stake here: Universities and colleges are currently embattled, distrusted by the public and state funding institutions. As distressing as this situation is, it provides the perfect setting and the perfect timing for declaring an end to scholarly publication as a series of guarded conversations between professors.

The redemption of the university, especially in terms of the public's appraisal of the value of research and publication, requires all the writers who have something they want to publish to ask themselves the question: Does this have to be a closed communication, shutting out all but specialists willing to fight their way through thickets of jargon? Or can this be an open communication, engaging specialists with new information and new thinking, but also offering an invitation to nonspecialists to learn from this study, to grasp its importance and, by extension, to find concrete reasons to see value in the work of the university?

This is a country desperately in need of wisdom, and of clearly reasoned conviction and vision. And that, at the bedrock, is the reason behind this campaign to save professors from themselves and to detoxify academic prose. The context is a bit different, but the statement that Willy Loman made to his sons in *Death of a Salesman* keeps coming to mind: "The woods are burning, boys, the woods are burning." In a society confronted by a faltering economy, racial and ethnic conflicts, and environmental disasters, "the woods are burning," and since we so urgently need everyone's contribution in putting some of those fires out, there is no reason to indulge professorial vanity or timidity.

Ego is, of course, the key obstacle here. As badly as most of them write, professors are nonetheless proud and sensitive writers, resistant to criticism. But even the most desperate cases can be redeemed and persuaded to think of writing as a challenging craft, not as existential trauma. A few years ago, I began to look at carpenters and other artisans as the emotional model for writers. A carpenter, let us say, makes a door for a cabinet. If the door does not hang straight, the carpenter does not say, "I will not change that door; it is an expression of my individuality; who cares if it will not close?" Instead, the carpenter removes the door and works it until it fits. That attitude, applied to writing, could be our salvation. If we thought more like carpenters, academic writers could find a route out of the trap of ego and vanity. Escaped from that trap, we could simply work on successive drafts until what we have to say is clear.

Colleges and universities are filled with knowledgeable, thoughtful people who have been effectively silenced by an awful writing style, a style with its flaws concealed behind a smoke screen of sophistication and professionalism. A coalition of academic writers, graduate advisers, journal editors, university press editors, and trade publishers can seize this moment—*and pull the wire*. The buzzards *can* be set free—free to leave that dead tree branch, free to regain their confidence, free to soar.

Working with the Text

1. The key passage in Patricia Nelson Limerick's essay characterizes academic prose by quoting a classics professor: " 'We must remember . . . that professors are the ones nobody wanted to dance with in high school'" (par. 11). The first part of the title of the essay is "Dancing with Professors." How do the quotation and the title work together to identify the problem posed by academic writing? In a short essay, tease out the meaning of this double use of the dance metaphor. Who is dancing with professors? How does the dance proceed? Why? In what ways does the dance influence what happens within the university?

2. As you reread the essay, note Limerick's own writing style, especially her use of extended metaphor and humor. Why does Limerick use this style in making her argument? Write a short essay that analyzes the general relationship between Limerick's use of language and the argument she is making. As an alternative essay, choose one of the extended metaphors and study the details Limerick includes in it. Write a short essay in which you analyze the effect of each of the details Limerick selects. Why does she include that detail? How does the detail contribute to her argument?

3. Limerick asserts that the "habits of academic writers lend powerful support to the impression that research is a waste of the writers' time and of the public's money" (par. 9). As you reread the essay, mark other passages where Limerick addresses "the trouble with academic prose" from the point of view of the public. In a short essay, analyze Limerick's concern. Exactly what problem does she think poor academic writing causes for the public? What kind of academic writing does she advocate, and why does she think it will address this problem?

From Text to Field

1. In the first part of her essay, Limerick asserts that while "today's college students cannot write . . . the professors who denounce them are not doing much better" (par. 6). She quotes a passage from a book published by a prominent academic and denounces it by claiming that "in twenty years of paper grading, I do not recall many sentences that asked, so pathetically, to be put out of their misery" (par. 3). In a short essay, respond to these and similar passages in Limerick's essay. Consider your own encounters with academic writing or with the language used in another field that has high expectations for those who enter it.

2. Choose a passage from a reading in your discipline or in a course you are taking that exemplifies the kind of academic writing Limerick describes. Write an essay in which you first critique the writing and then translate the passage into the kind of direct, lively prose Limerick recommends.

3. Have you ever used language—in the form of either writing or speaking—as armor, padding, or a weapon to protect yourself? In an essay, analyze the situation that prompted you to use language in this way. What demands of the situation and responses on your part drew you into this use of language? What kind of language did you use, and how did you use it? How effective was it in protecting you? What effect did it have on the dynamics of the situation?

4. Some university professors require students to eliminate *I* from their academic writing. Other professors invite students to include themselves in their writing. In an essay, explore the effects of writing yourself out of versus writing yourself into a piece of academic writing. Within an academic field or discipline, what are the disciplinary politics of self-disclosure? When and why is self-disclosure used or not used?

Between the Drafts

Nancy Sommers

In this essay, "Between the Drafts," Nancy Sommers realizes the deeply personal engagement with "authority" that underlies a writer's ability to accomplish "real revision"—a clearer vision of what the "self" has to say.

Nancy Sommers recalls growing up with parents who had escaped Nazi Germany but had passed on to their children a deference to authority that negated personal experience: "I guess it never occurred to them to reflect or to make connections between generations of German children . . . being instructed from early childhood to honor and defer to the parental authority of the state, and the Nazis' easy rise to power." As Sommers works to understand the stalemate she has reached in revising her own writing, she learns neither to defer to nor to escape authority but rather to find her voice by engaging in "a conversation with all the voices I embody."

Nancy Sommers is the Sosland Director of Writing at Harvard University, where she directs the Expository Writing Program, the Harvard Writing Project, and the Harvard Study of Undergraduate Writing. She recently completed a longitudinal study in which she followed the Harvard class of 2001 through their college years to understand the role writing plays in undergraduate education. She has coauthored or coedited four textbooks, authored numerous articles on the practice and theory of teaching writing, and published a number of personal essays. Throughout her career, Sommers has been particularly fascinated with the process of revision, a fascination that stems from always believing that a new vision is possible and from a commitment to explore how a writer's life and written work can come together in fruitful and unexpected ways. "Between the Drafts" won the 1993 Braddock Award, granted by the Conference on College Composition and Communication (CCCC), for the best article of the year published in its journal, *College Composition and Communication*.

I cannot think of my childhood without hearing voices, deep, heavily-accented, instructive German voices.

I hear the voice of my father reading to me from *Struvelpater*, the German children's tale about a messy boy who refuses to cut his hair or his fingernails. Struvelpater's hair grows so long that birds nest in it, and his fingernails grow so long that his hands become useless. He fares better, though, than the other characters in the book who don't listen to their parents. Augustus, for instance, refuses to eat his soup for four days, becomes as thin as a thread, and on the fifth day he is dead. Fidgety Philip tilts his dinner chair like a rocking horse until his chair falls backwards; the hot food falls on top of him and suffocates him under the weight of the table cloth. The worst story by far for me is that of Conrad, an incorrigible thumb-sucker, who couldn't stop sucking his thumb and whose mother warned him that a great, long, red-legged scissor-man would—and, yes, did—snip both his thumbs off.

As a child, I hated these horrid stories with their clear moral lessons, exhorting me to listen to my parents: Do the right thing, they said; obey authority, or else catastrophic things—dissipation, suffocation, loss of thumbs—will follow. It never occurred to me as a child to wonder why my parents, who had escaped Nazi Germany in 1939, were so deferential to authority, so beholden to sanctioned sources of power. I guess it never occurred to them to reflect or to make any connections between generations of German children reading *Struvelpater*, being instructed from early childhood to honor and defer to the parental authority of the state, and the Nazis' easy rise to power.

When I hear my mother's voice, it is usually reading to me from some kind of guidebook showing me how different *They*, the Americans, were from us, the German Jews of Terre Haute. My parents never left home without their passports; we had roots somewhere else. When we traveled westward every summer from our home in Indiana, our bible was the AAA tour guide, giving us the officially sanctioned version of America. We attempted to "see" America from the windows of our 1958 two-tone green Oldsmobile. We were literally the tourists from Terre Haute, those whom Walker Percy describes in "The Loss of the Creature," people who could never experience the Grand Canyon because it had already been formulated for us by picture postcards, tourist folders, guidebooks, and the words *Grand Canyon*.

Percy suggests that tourists never see the progressive movement of depths,   5 patterns, colors, and shadows of the Grand Canyon, but rather measure their satisfaction by the degree to which the canyon conforms to the expectations in their minds. My mother's AAA guidebook directed us, told us what to see, how to see it, and how long it should take us to see it. We never stopped anywhere serendipitously, never lingered, never attempted to know a place.

As I look now at the black-and-white photographs of our trips, seeing myself in ponytail and pedal pushers, I am struck by how many of the photos were taken against the car or, at least, with the car close enough to be included in the photograph. I am not sure we really saw the Grand Canyon or the Painted Desert or the Petrified Forest except from the security of a parking lot. We were traveling on a self-imposed visa that kept us close to our parked car; we lacked the freedom of our own authority and stuck close to each other and to the book itself.

My parents' belief that there was a right and a wrong way to do everything extended to the way they decided to teach us German. Wanting us to learn the correct way, not trusting their own native voices, they bought language-learning records with an officially sanctioned voice of an expert language teacher; never mind that they spoke fluent German.

It is 1959; I am eight years old. We sit in the olive-drab living room with the drapes closed so the neighbors won't see in. What the neighbors would have seen strikes me now as a scene out of a *Saturday Night Live* skit about the Coneheads. The children and their parental-unit sitting in stiff, good-for-your-posture chairs that my brother and I call the electric chairs. Those chairs are at odd angles to each other so we all face the fireplace; we don't look at each other. I guess my parents never considered pulling the chairs around, facing each other, so we could just talk in German. My father's investment was in the best 1959 technology he could find; he was proud of the time and money he had spent, so that we could be instructed in the right way. I can still see him there in that room removing the record from its purple package, placing it on the hi-fi:

Guten Tag.
Wie geht es Dir?
Wie geht es Werner/Helmut/Dieter?
Werner ist heute krank.
Oh, das tut mir Leid.
Gute Besserung.°

We are disconnected voices worrying over the health of Werner, Dieter, and Helmut, foreign characters, names, who have no place in our own family. We go on and on for an eternity with that dialogue until my brother passes gas, or commits some other unspeakable offense, something that sets my father's German sensibility on edge, and he finally says, "We will continue another time." He releases us back into another life, where we speak English, forgetting for yet another week about the health of Werner, Helmut, or Dieter.

Good morning. How are you? How is Werner/Helmut/Dieter? Werner is sick today. Oh, that's too bad. Get well.

I thought I had the issue of authority all settled in my mind when I was in   10
college. My favorite T-shirt, the one I took the greatest pleasure in wearing,
was one with the bold words *Question Authority* inscribed across my chest. It
seemed that easy. As we said then, either you were part of the problem or you
were part of the solution; either you deferred to authority or you resisted it by
questioning. Twenty years later, it doesn't seem that simple. I am beginning
to get a better sense of my legacy, beginning to see just how complicated and
how far-reaching is this business of authority. It extends into my life and
touches my students' lives, reminding me again and again of the delicate
relationship between language and authority.

In 1989, thirty years after my German lessons at home, I'm having dinner
with my daughters in an Italian restaurant. The waiter is flirting with eight-
year-old Rachel, telling her she has the most beautiful name, that she is *una
ragazza bellissima*. Intoxicated with this affectionate attention, she turns to
me passionately and says, "Oh, Momma, Momma, can't we learn Italian?" I,
too, for the moment am caught up in the brio of my daughter's passion. I say,
"Yes, yes, we must learn Italian." We rush to our favorite bookstore where we
find Italian language-learning tapes packaged in thirty-, sixty-, and ninety-day
lessons, and in our modesty buy the promise of fluent Italian in thirty lessons.
Driving home together, we put the tape in our car tape player, and begin lesson number 1:

> Buon giorno.
> Come stai?
> Come stai Monica?°

As we wind our way home, our Italian lessons quickly move beyond prelim-
inaries. We stop worrying over the health of Monica, and suddenly we are in
the midst of a dialogue about Signor Fellini who lives at 21 Broadway Street.
We cannot follow the dialogue. Rachel, in great despair, betrayed by the
promise of being a beautiful girl with a beautiful name speaking Italian in
thirty lessons, begins to scream at me: "This isn't the way to learn a language.
This isn't language at all. These are just words and sentences; this isn't about
us; we don't live at 21 Broadway Street."

And I am back home in Indiana, hearing the disembodied voices of my
family, teaching a language out of the context of life.

In 1987, I gave a talk at CCCC entitled "New Directions for Researching
Revision." At the time, I liked the talk very much because it gave me an
opportunity to illustrate how revision, once a subject as interesting to our

---

Good morning. How are you? How is Monica?

profession as an autopsy, had received new body and soul, almost celebrity status, in our time. Yet as interesting as revision had become, it seemed to me that our pedagogies and research methods were resting on some shaky, unquestioned assumptions.

I had begun to see how students often sabotage their own best interests when they revise, searching for errors and assuming, like the eighteenth-century theory of words parodied in *Gulliver's Travels*, that words are a load of things to be carried around and exchanged. It seemed to me that despite all those multiple drafts, all the peer workshops that we were encouraging, we had left unexamined the most important fact of all: Revision does not always guarantee improvement; successive drafts do not always lead to a clearer vision. You can't just change the words around and get the ideas right.

Here I am four years later, looking back on that abandoned talk, thinking   15 of myself as a student writer, and seeing that successive drafts have not led me to a clearer vision. I have been under the influence of a voice other than my own.

I live by the lyrical dream of change, of being made anew, always believing that a new vision is possible. I have been gripped, probably obsessed, with the subject of revision since graduate school. I have spent hundreds of hours studying manuscripts, looking for clues in the drafts of professional and student writers, looking for the figure in the carpet. The pleasures of this kind of literary detective work, this literary voyeurism, are the peeps behind the scenes, the glimpses of the process revealed in all its nakedness, of what Edgar Allan Poe called "the elaborate and vacillating crudities of thought, the true purposes seized only at the last moment, the cautious selections and rejections, the painful erasures."

My decision to study revision was not an innocent choice. It is deeply satisfying to believe that we are not locked into our original statements, that we might start and stop, erase, use the delete key in life, and be saved from the roughness of our early drafts. Words can be retracted; souls can be reincarnated. Such beliefs have informed my study of revision, and yet, in my own writing, I have always treated revising as an academic subject, not a personal one. Every time I have written about revision, I have set out to argue a thesis, present my research, accumulate my footnotes. By treating revision as an academic subject, by suggesting that I could learn something only by studying the drafts of other experienced writers, I kept myself clean and distant from any kind of scrutiny. No Struvelpater was I; no birds could nest in my hair; I kept my thumbs intact. I have been the bloodless academic creating taxonomies, creating a hierarchy of student writers and experienced writers, and never asking myself how I was being displaced from my own work. I never asked, "What does my absence *signify?*"

In that unrevised talk from CCCC, I had let Wayne Booth replace my father. Here are my words:

> Revision presents a unique opportunity to study what writers know. By studying writers' revisions we can learn how writers locate themselves within a discourse tradition by developing a persona—a fictionalized self. Creating a persona involves placing the self in a textual community, seeing oneself within a discourse, and positing a self that shares or antagonizes the beliefs that a community of readers shares. As Wayne Booth has written, "Every speaker makes a self with every word uttered. Even the most sincere statement implies a self that is at best a radical selection from many possible roles. No one comes on in exactly the same way with parents, teachers, classmates, lovers, and IRS inspectors."

What strikes me now, in this paragraph from my own talk, is that fictionalized self I invented, that anemic researcher, who set herself apart from her most passionate convictions. In that paragraph, I am a distant, imponderable, impersonal voice—inaccessible, humorless, and disguised like the packaged voice of Signor Fellini giving lessons as if absolutely nothing depends on my work. I speak in an inherited academic voice; it isn't mine.

I simply wasn't there for my own talk. Just as my father hid behind his language-learning records and my mother behind her guidebooks, I disguised myself behind the authority of "the researcher," attempting to bring in the weighty authority of Wayne Booth to justify my own statements, never gazing inward, never trusting my own authority as a writer.

Looking back on that talk, I know how deeply I was under the influence 20 of a way of seeing: Foucault's "Discourse on Language," Barthes's *S/Z*, Scholes's *Textual Power*, and Bartholomae's "Inventing the University" had become my tourist guides. I was so much under their influence that I remember standing in a parking lot of a supermarket, holding two heavy bags of groceries, talking with a colleague who was telling me about his teaching. Without any reference, except to locate my own authority somewhere else, I felt compelled to suggest to him that he read Foucault. My daughter Alexandra, waiting impatiently for me, eating chocolate while pounding on the hood of the car with her new black patent-leather party shoes, spoke with her own authority. She reminded me that I, too, had bumped on cars, eaten Hershey Bars, worn party shoes without straps, never read Foucault, and knew, nevertheless, what to say on most occasions.

One of my colleagues put a telling cartoon on the wall of our Xerox room. It reads "Breakfast Theory: A morning methodology." The cartoon describes two new cereals: Foucault Flakes and Post-Modern Toasties. The slogan for Foucault Flakes reads: "It's French so it must be good for you. A breakfast commodity so complex that you need a theoretical apparatus to digest it. You don't want to eat it; you'll just want to read it. Breakfast as text." And

Post-Modern Toasties: "More than just a cereal, it's a commentary on the nature of cerealness, cerealism, and the theory of cerealtivity. Free decoding ring inside."

I had swallowed the whole flake, undigested, as my morning methodology, but, alas, I never found the decoding ring. I was lost in the box. Or, to use the metaphor of revision, I was stuck in a way of seeing: reproducing the thoughts of others, using them as my guides, letting the post-structuralist vocabulary give authority to my text.

Successive drafts of my own talk did not lead to a clearer vision because it simply was not my vision. I, like so many of my students, was reproducing acceptable truths, imitating the gestures and rituals of the academy, not having confidence enough in my own ideas, nor trusting the native language I had learned. I had surrendered my own authority to someone else, to those other authorial voices.

Three years later, I am still wondering: Where does revision come from? Or, as I think about it now, what happens **I must bring a voice** between the drafts? Something has to happen or else we are **of my own.** struck doing mop and broom work, the janitorial work of polishing, cleaning, and fixing what is and always has been. What happens between drafts seems to be one of the great secrets of our profession.

Between drafts, I take lots of showers, hot showers, talking to myself as I 25 watch the water play against the gestures of my hands. In the shower, I get lost in the steam. There I stand without my badges of authority. I begin an imagined conversation with my colleague, the one whom I told in the parking lot of the grocery store, "Oh, but you must read Foucault." I revise our conversation. This time I listen.

I understand why he showed so much disdain when I began to pay homage to Foucault. He had his own sources aplenty that nourished him. Yet he hadn't felt the need to speak through his sources or interject their names into our conversation. His teaching stories and experiences are his own; they give him the authority to speak.

As I get lost in the steam, I listen to his stories, and I begin to tell him mine. I tell him about my father not trusting his native voice to teach me German, about my mother not trusting her own eyes and reading to us from guidebooks, about my own claustrophobia in not being able to revise a talk about revision, about being drowned out by a chorus of authorial voices. And I surprise myself. I say, Yes, these stories of mine provide powerful evidence; they belong to me; I can use them to say what I must about revision.

I begin at last to have a conversation with all the voices I embody, and I wonder why so many issues are posed as either/or propositions. Either I suck my thumb *or* the great long-legged scissor-man will cut it off. Either

I cook two chickens *or* my guests will go away hungry. Either I accept authority *or* I question it. Either I have babies and be in service of the species *or* I write books and be in service of the academy. Either I be personal *or* I be academic.

These either/or ways of seeing exclude life and real revision by pushing us to safe positions, to what is known. They are safe positions that exclude each other and don't allow for any ambiguity, uncertainty. Only when I suspend myself between either *and* or can I move away from conventional boundaries and begin to see shapes and shadows and contours—ambiguity, uncertainty, and discontinuity, moments when the seams of life just don't want to hold; days when I wake up to find, once again, that I don't have enough bread for the children's sandwiches or that there are no shoelaces for their gym shoes. My life is full of uncertainty; negotiating that uncertainty day to day gives me authority.

Maybe this is a woman's journey, maybe not. Maybe it is just my own, but   30 the journey between home and work, between being personal and being authoritative, between the drafts of my life, is a journey of learning how to be both personal and authoritative, both scholarly *and* reflective. It is a journey that leads me to embrace the experiences of my life, and gives me the insight to transform these experiences into evidence. I begin to see discontinuous moments as sources of strength and knowledge. When my writing and my life actually come together, the safe positions of either/or will no longer pacify me, no longer contain me and hem me in.

In that unrevised talk, I had actually misused my sources. What they were saying to me, if I had listened, was pretty simple: Don't follow us, don't reproduce what we have produced, don't live life from secondary sources like us, don't disappear. I hear Bob Scholes's and David Bartholomae's voices telling me to answer them, to speak back to them, to use them and make them anew. In a word, they say: Revise me. The language lesson starts to make sense, finally: By confronting these authorial voices, I find the power to understand and gain access to my own ideas. Against all the voices I embody—the voices heard, read, whispered to me from off-stage—I must bring a voice of my own. I must enter the dialogue on my own authority, knowing that other voices have enabled mine, but no longer can I subordinate mine to theirs.

The voices I embody encourage me to show up as a writer and to bring the courage of my own authority into my classroom. I have also learned about the dangers of submission from observing the struggles of my own students. When they write about their lives, they write with confidence. As soon as they begin to turn their attention toward outside sources, they too lose confidence, defer to the voice of the academy, and write in the voice of Everystudent to an audience they think of as Everyteacher. They disguise themselves in the weighty, imponderable voice of acquired authority: "In today's society," for instance, or "Since the beginning of civilization mankind has . . ." Or, as one student wrote about authority itself, "In attempting to investigate the origins of authority of the group, we must first decide exactly what we mean by authority."

In my workshops with teachers, the issue of authority, or deciding exactly what we mean by authority, always seems to be at the center of many heated conversations. Some colleagues are convinced that our writing programs should be about teaching academic writing. They see such programs as the welcome wagon of the academy, the Holiday Inn where students lodge as they take holy orders. Some colleagues fear that if we don't control what students learn, don't teach them to write as scholars write, we aren't doing our job and some great red-legged scissor-man will cut off our thumbs. Again it is one of those either/or propositions: Either we teach students to write academic essays or we teach them to write personal essays—and then who knows what might happen? The world might become uncontrollable: Students might start writing about their grandmother's death in an essay for a sociology course. Or even worse, something more uncontrollable, they might just write essays and publish them in professional journals claiming the authority to tell stories about their families and their colleagues. The uncontrollable world of ambiguity and uncertainty opens up, my colleagues imagine, as soon as the academic embraces the personal.

But, of course, our students are not empty vessels waiting to be filled with authorial intent. Given the opportunity to speak their own authority as writers, given a turn in the conversation, students can claim their stories as primary source material and transform their experiences into evidence. They might, if given enough encouragement, be empowered not to serve the academy and accommodate it, not to write in the persona of Everystudent, but rather to write essays that will change the academy. When we create opportunities for something to happen between the drafts, when we create writing exercises that allow students to work with sources of their own that can complicate and enrich their primary sources, they will find new ways to write scholarly essays that are exploratory, thoughtful, and reflective.

I want my students to know what writers know—to know something no   35
researchers could ever find out no matter how many times they pin my students to the table, no matter how many protocols they tape. I want my students to know how to bring their life and their writing together.

Sometimes when I cook a chicken and my children scuffle over the one wishbone, I wish I had listened to my grandmother and cooked two. Usually, the child who gets the short end of the wishbone dissolves into tears of frustration and failure. Interjecting my own authority as the earth mother from central casting, I try to make their life better by asking: On whose authority is it that the short end can't get her wish? Why can't both of you, the long and the short ends, get your wishes?

My children, on cue, as if they too were brought in from central casting, roll their eyes as children are supposed to do when their mothers attempt to impose a way of seeing. They won't let me control the situation by interpreting it for them. My interpretation serves my needs, temporarily, for sibling compromise and resolution. They don't buy my story because they know something about the sheer thrill of the pull that they are not going to let *me* deny *them*. They will have to revise my self-serving story about compromise, just as they will have to revise the other stories I tell them. Between the drafts, as they get outside my authority, they too will have to question, and begin to see for themselves their own complicated legacy, their own trail of authority.

It *is* in the thrill of the pull between someone else's authority and our own, between submission and independence that we must discover how to define ourselves. In the uncertainty of that struggle, we have a chance of finding the voice of our own authority. Finding it, we can speak convincingly . . . at long last.

Working with the Text

1. In her essay, Nancy Sommers explores the interplay between authority and the self in moving from one draft to another during the process of writing. She writes, "It *is* in the thrill of the pull between someone else's authority and our own, between submission and independence that we must discover how to define ourselves" (par. 38). In a short essay, analyze her conception of this interplay.

2. From the beginning of the essay to the end, Sommers moves from a limiting experience of authority to a freeing experience of authority. Write a short essay that explores and articulates this movement. How does she think authority can be limiting? How does she think it can be freeing? What happened to move her out of one concept of authority into another?

3. Analyzing Sommers's essay requires you to engage and respond to her ideas and experiences. In responding to her ideas and experiences, you are positioning her as an authority. Consider Sommers's descriptions of engaging authority as she works to come to her conclusions. In a short essay, reflect on how you are using her as an authority in the process of coming to your own conclusions about her ideas.

From Text to Field

1. Sommers opens her essay with an extensive description of experiences she had growing up that influenced her approach to writing and revision. Reread, in particular, her description of the German language lessons and the role of parental authority in determining how those lessons were carried out. Reflect on the authority figures inside and outside your family who have influenced you intellectually or personally. Such influences can be both enabling and disabling; we often both honor and distance ourselves from them. In an essay, explore how you write and revise and how these authority figures have influenced the way you approach the process. In what ways have they enabled you? In what ways have they disabled you? What is your concept and experience of authority, and how does it influence the way you write? How and to what extent do you bring your own experience and perspectives into your writing?

2. Although Sommers offers a conceptual framework for revision in this essay, she doesn't provide specific descriptions of how revision might take place. In an essay, analyze your approach to revision in writing courses you are taking or have taken. Do you merely "fix" errors in the text? Do you rethink or re-envision the argument itself? Do you set aside a draft for a period of time before you revise it? If so, why? What happens in the interim? How effective is your revision process? What do you want to continue doing? What do you want to change? Consider Sommers's description of an unsuccessful revision of her own: "Successive drafts . . . did not lead to a clearer vision because it simply was not my vision" (par. 23).

3. As Sommers was growing up, her family's vacations were dictated by the AAA guidebook. She describes her family as "people who could never experience the Grand Canyon because it had already been formulated for us by picture postcards, tourist folders, guidebooks, and the words *Grand Canyon*" (par. 4). Reflect on the ways in which authority, in the form of an authoritative text, influenced their manner of seeing. Consider your own experience of being guided by an authoritative text, such as a travel guide, movie or music reviews, sports commentators, or the program for a museum exhibit. Choose one such text that guided or influenced you. Write an essay in which you reflect on your ability to break away from the authority of the text to form your own perspective. To what extent did you form your own experience? What happened to break you away from the text? Look up the word *dissonance*. Does it apply to the experience you're describing?

4. "Between drafts," Sommers says, "I take lots of showers. . . . I get lost in the steam. There I stand without my badges of authority" (par. 25). In the shower,

she can speak freely in her imagination about her own stories and her struggle to revise. The essay indicates that while she searches for the revision that eludes her, she is free to give the process whatever amount of time it requires. Reflect on this process given the demands of your college or university's institutional structure. In other words, to what extent does the university calendar, course timelines, and pace of an assignment facilitate or undermine revision? Why does that structure make it difficult for teachers and students to approach revision the way Sommers suggests? Conversely, what is it about deadlines and the intense focus on a task that can be enabling, even necessary, to the creative process at times?

INTO THE FIELD: Options for Writing Projects

1. A Gallery of Office Doors

Think of the door to a professor's office as a threshold, as a place where contact with students is encouraged, discouraged, or regulated. The office door, and the surrounding wall space, may also have an array of verbal and visual texts: cartoons, pictures, posters, and announcements. For your fieldwork, develop a project in which you study the office doors of several professors, with a special focus on what this space (and its accompanying texts) communicates to students. You may wish to study several doors in one department or doors in several departments. What does the door say about the professor and his or her character or ethos? Likewise, what does the door tell you about the department or discipline? In what ways might a professor overcome or handle the constraints of the space he or she is occupying (remember, not every office is ideal or to a professor's liking)? Consider interviewing some of the professors whose doors you have studied. Based on your research, develop an essay or a report that describes what you found, draws some inferences or conclusions, and then supports those inferences based on the doors and texts you have studied (and, if possible, the professors you have interviewed).

2. Professors on the Web

Many professors maintain a Web page, which you can often access through a link from their department's Web page. For this field project, study several faculty Web pages in one department (ideally, the department that is or might become your major) or compare faculty Web pages across two or more departments. Pay attention to how the professors present themselves and whom they see as the potential audience(s) of their site. As you review several sites, consider how you might categorize them and what criteria you might use to do so. Are there several basic kinds or genres of faculty Web sites? What kind of access to the professors do these sites encourage, if any? If the sites offer any personal information about the professor, what function might such information have, and what relationship does the personal have to the professional? If you know or have taken classes with the professor, how does the Web site compare to the character or ethos that the professor projects in the classroom or in his or her office? How might students make better use of a faculty member's Web presence?

3. Professors in the Press

As you might expect, most if not all of your professors lead an active life as writers and scholars. Yet not all of their work is destined for obscure academic journals. Some of them may write books or magazine articles for a larger audience, pen an occasional column in the local newspaper, or even host a local public radio show. For this fieldwork project, explore the work of one or more of your professors who have ventured beyond academic publishing. To find out who might have done so on your campus, contact your professors directly, query a department secretary, or check in with your college or university's public relations office. Your project may involve an analysis of the published material, with an eye to the strategies they have used to meet the needs of the more public audience.

Alternatively, interview a faculty member on your campus who writes well and frequently for the public. Write a profile of the faculty member that describes this aspect of his or her career. In what publications does his or her work most frequently appear? Who is the audience? What are the issues or topics? From what point of view are they presented? Why does this faculty member write for the public? What does he or she hope to accomplish through this work? Look for reviews of or responses to his or her work; how is it regarded? What are the rewards and the risks of writing beyond one's immediate community?

As a third option, write an essay in which you argue for the role you think academic research and writing should play in your university education and in the world outside the university. What types of research are valuable, and in what ways? How do you think that research should be conveyed to students and to the public? (As part of your inquiry, you may wish to see if your campus has a program that encourages undergraduates to collaborate with faculty on some form of research activity.)

4. Finding a Dance at the Mixer

Opportunities to meet with faculty on your campus may seem restricted to class time itself or to office hours. Both venues can seem intimidating. For your field project, investigate what opportunities exist on your campus for faculty and students to get to know one another more informally. In other words, how might you be able to interact with faculty outside of a more formal classroom structure? And why might you want to? In the spirit of the title for this unit— "Dancing with Professors"—consider how you might go about finding a dance at the mixer. Explore the opportunities offered through dorm programs, advisement, student groups, and receptions at various campus-sponsored events. If you find that such opportunities are rare, you may wish to propose how—and why—your campus might want to develop better ways for students to meet with faculty.

5. Assessing Orientation

Among your very first exposures to college life and learning is surely the orientation you went to on your campus. Whether orientation lasts only for several hours or extends over several days, this program can offer a wealth of information about how to get off to a successful start in college. For your field project, assess what your orientation program offered to you and what messages (subtle or not so subtle) were sent. Did you notice any contradictions between what was said and what life on campus is like? In retrospect, what would you have liked to have heard that was never discussed? Consider writing a letter to the director of orientation, or submitting a more formal proposal, in which you note the program's successes, air your concerns, and propose improvements that might better meet students' needs and the needs of the campus.

6. First Generations

Going to college can represent a major change in your life, all the more so if you or someone you know is the first generation of the family to attend college. This field project offers an opportunity (through a personal essay or a brief memoir) to explore the thoughts of a first generation college student and their continuing relevance today. This project may well start at home, perhaps with an older relative who was the first in the family to go to college, perhaps with a good friend, perhaps even with yourself. Ask what it meant/means to go to college, and what obstacles and fears presented themselves. Who were the mentors who stood by, supporting this person (or you) on this new journey? What remains relevant and fresh about this tale, even though years may separate that person's experience from your own? What remains universal? Remember that each of us, in our own way, is (or has been) a first-generation student.

7. Campus Outreach

Entering the college conversation can be difficult for anyone but all the more so if members of the community tend not to see your campus as part of their lives. This field project offers you a chance to explore and assess one of several outreach programs your campus may have. These programs may involve students in area schools (K–12) or students and families of underrepresented minorities. The focus of these programs may involve academics but also may involve the arts, sports, or a variety of other public programs. (A good first contact might be the office of community relations on your campus.) How has your campus articulated the goals of a particular outreach program, and how might such a program make a difference, both for the community and for your campus? In turn, why might such a program encounter difficulties or be misperceived? What steps has the program taken to prevent any misunderstanding and to capitalize on existing goodwill? What kind of program would you like to have participated in, and why?

8. Service Learning

Joining the conversation in and about college often entails that we find a way to connect our academic and personal commitments. One means can be through what is known as "service learning"—an approach to learning that moves the student outside of the traditional classroom to perform and then reflect on service in and for the community. This fieldwork project encourages you to think about the broader possibilities of fieldwork in your college or university. (For some initial information, you may wish to contact the administrator or faculty member who is coordinating service learning on your campus.) Consider how a college course you have taken might have been improved or fruitfully augmented if it called on service learning. Did you have a high school course that called on service learning in some fashion? What possibilities are there for a writing course to incorporate service learning into its assignments and activities? What special challenges, misunderstandings, and risks might be associated with service learning, both for students and for faculty? As you discover more about service learning opportunities on your campus, nominate one course that would benefit from such an approach, and develop a proposal that captures the rationale for your nomination. Be sure to consider counterarguments or skeptical questions that may arise.

9. Teaching and Learning the Debates

Gerald Graff discusses the importance of learning about a field not through facts and information but through the debates that occur within that field. Write an essay in which you capture one or two critical key terms that define a field, a community, or an area of specialty you belong to or are just now entering. What is expressed or implied by those terms? In other words, what does the field consider to be important? What is, or isn't, debatable? How might such a debate prove to be a good introduction to the field? Why might such a debate prove to be an inadequate or a misleading introduction?

10. Revision Across the Curriculum

The work of revising a written draft may seem the special province of a writing course, with the rest of the university operating in a "first-draft" universe. Yet a good many courses in other fields may encourage or require you to submit drafts that you then revise or continue to develop. For this fieldwork project, consider courses you have taken, or are now taking, that either encouraged a helpful attitude toward revision or failed to do so when it might have been useful. You also may wish to poll members of your writing class about their experiences in other courses regarding the emphasis (or lack of emphasis) on revision. How was this attitude communicated: on the syllabus or in the professor's own words? Do you think this attitude had more to do with the professor's teaching style and inclinations, or might it reflect a more general attitude toward revision in that discipline? What do you think accounts for the activity of revision being more or less invisible in some fields? You may wish to frame your project as a close reading of one course, as a study of disciplinary attitudes and assumptions about revision, or as a proposal that the design for a particular course be changed to better incorporate revision.

11. Authority: How Have You Been "Author"-ized to Write?

Different disciplines construct and use authority in different ways. Consider the writing you do for a course that is not explicitly a writing course, in a field outside of English or the humanities. Write an essay in which you analyze what counts as authoritative in that class or field, and how you are expected to gain and use authority in your own writing. In other words, as a student in that course or in that discipline, what are the ways in which you have been "author"-ized to write? How have you managed to negotiate the connection between personal authority and external authority in that class or field? This project can take one of several directions. You may wish to write a personal essay about the tensions you have experienced between writing yourself into a text and writing yourself out of a text. Alternatively, you may wish to examine several representative scholarly articles in that field for clues about its attitudes toward and use of authority.

2

Inventing the University

CONSTRUCTING CLASSROOMS

Tu/Th, 9:30–10:45. Hellems Hall, Room 230.

Although the day and time, building name, and room number may be different, you know through years of schooling that these are the coordinates, in time and space, for an academic classroom. Whatever department may be offering the class, the classroom itself possesses a familiarity that cuts across subject matter, even teaching styles. When you enter the door of your classroom, you know the space. You recognize this world both from your long acquaintance with classrooms and from the sediment of teaching practices and learning behaviors that have formed in that space.

Classrooms, it turns out, are recognizable because they are conventional or typical. We know them because they are "types." They are recurrent spaces—spaces in which we happen to be (again and again) and spaces in which things happen (again and again). What happens are rhetorical actions and language practices that are themselves recognizable. You know the moves as well as anybody: teacher talk, and student talk, and how that talk is orchestrated through questions and answers and discussion. You know the classroom as if it were a stage. Even though the particular classroom "script" may change from course to course and teacher to teacher, you do know that there is a script. Even the physical moves are blocked out on stage in advance: You know who enters, when, and how, and what positions they assume. Classrooms are places, but they also put us all, teacher and student, in our places. The time and space of the classroom project a world of relationships and norms—a world of its own.

All of us would like to reinvent that world, to reinvent classrooms that more ideally match our aspirations for the best possible learning environment. And, indeed, classrooms are changing. Classrooms are becoming networked to other spaces, whether through technology or through curricular models like service learning that take students out into the community. Classrooms are likewise becoming more student centered and more collaborative. Even so, we recognize these innovations for what they are precisely because we remember, somewhere deep down in our bones and in our collective social memory, the archetype of the classroom.

As much as we remember, we would also like to forget. When we enter the door of our classroom on the first day of the new term, we invoke a fiction that we all, teacher and student alike, maintain to some degree: the fiction of the fresh classroom. We are eager to put any bad experiences behind us and to anticipate better ones. Through that classroom door lies a new territory and a new period of time. This fiction is an enabling fiction, for in forgetting the prior histories of classrooms (histories that are at once personal and institutional) we are all disposed to teach and learn afresh.

Whether you are just beginning your studies in college or have several college terms behind you, it is important to reflect on the time/space that is the classroom. Forget as we might, we'll try to listen to what classrooms whisper in our ears. In the process, we'll recognize what is conventional—yes, oh so conventional—about classrooms. We will surely become aware of what may be right or wrong in any given classroom and why we may wish to reinvent some classrooms. But by looking *at* classrooms, not just *through* them to the subject matter taught, we can also clear a space for the fresh, opportune moments that we all prize in our learning and teaching—moments when magic does happen, even in settings that might seem conventional. This unit helps us realize that classrooms are always invented, always constructed, always saturated with both memory and possibility.

The five readings included in this unit help us reflect on classrooms from several perspectives. They alert us that classrooms are by no means neutral sites, the mere givens of a college education. Classrooms are where time thickens, where space becomes charged.

Sharon Rubin asks that we take a second look at the course syllabus before filing it away in our notebooks. Syllabi should ideally help explain and create the model classroom that a course might envision, but more often than not syllabi fail to become a meeting place between professor, student, and course.

Alexander Calandra turns his attention to the conventional answers that are expected in many classrooms, answers that often turn students off to learning. He recounts the story of a student who turns the table on his professors, offering unexpected answers that are nevertheless correct.

Gerald Graff broadens the discussion by noting the failure of classrooms to connect with one another. Unless each classroom takes into account other voices in other classrooms, he fears a loss of both coherence and community.

Another perspective on community is offered by bell hooks, who explores how language in the classroom can be a tool for both oppression and resistance. Classrooms are worlds created by words. And as we seek to heal ourselves and each other, we need new words and the new worlds those words might create.

For Charles Bazerman, the classroom is something that is constructed, shaped through the perspectives of teachers, students, and the institution. In asking the question "Where is the classroom?" he prompts us to question the notion that classrooms exist apart from students, teachers, and institutions. Classrooms, it turns out, are not neutral or empty sites; they are charged with and created through our experiences in them.

Reflecting on Prior Knowledge

1. In a journal entry, recall a prior classroom in which you felt discouraged as a learner. Likewise, recall a moment that excited you, a moment that captured what is best about classrooms and learning in classrooms. What might account for these experiences? Is there something about classrooms that might create the conditions for both of your experiences?

2. In classrooms, you are asked to assume positions that are not just intellectual but also physical and spatial, even discursive (in the sense that classrooms position when and how you speak and write). How do classrooms position you? How would you like to position yourself?

3. When you enter the college classroom, you bring with you years of experience, from classroom after classroom, from elementary school through high school. What kind of mind-set might you bring, and how might that influence your view of your current classrooms? What mind-sets might instructors have developed over the years? What role do you think you might have in shaping—and reshaping—classrooms?

4. In your experience, what marks a room as being a classroom? Use concrete examples to begin to fashion a list of objects, spatial arrangements, and architectural details. What relationships and norms do these various elements help create?

5. Enter a classroom at night or during the day when it is not being used. Settle yourself in a seat, and pause to let your mind relax. Imagine the classroom whispering in your ear. What would you hear if the walls could speak? After a few minutes, move around the room and then to the front of the classroom. What difference does perspective make as you continue to listen to those whispers? Why do you think classrooms carry such powerful social memories?

Professors, Students, and the Syllabus

Sharon Rubin

When Sharon Rubin was assistant dean for undergraduate studies at the University of Maryland, she reviewed dozens of syllabi as part of the process of approving general-education courses. She learned that for most courses, the syllabus presented an incomplete, often confusing, picture of what students could expect. From this evidence she came to the conclusion that "the inadequate syllabus is a symptom of a larger problem—the lack of communication between teachers and students" (par. 8).

"Professors, Students, and the Syllabus" proposes a "place of meeting," sought by students and faculty alike. For Rubin, the answers to the questions a syllabus should address add up to the message that teachers want their students to master the material.

After her assistant deanship at the University of Maryland, Rubin became dean of liberal arts at Salisbury University, part of the University of Maryland system. She continued her work as an administrator at Ramapo College of New Jersey, where she served as the vice president for academic affairs. At Ramapo College, she returned to teaching and is currently professor of American studies in the School of American and International Studies.

For the past two years I've been sitting in on the meetings of a committee charged with approving courses for the University of Maryland's general-education program. Very often the committee members leave those meetings mystified and exasperated. It's not that the courses proposed are inadequate; it's just that the syllabi submitted with the proposals are so often virtually impossible to decode.

I've listened while a faculty member from a related discipline has tried to guess what a syllabus might possibly mean. I've seen carefully worded letters from the dean requesting clarification—and then looked on as the committee has tried to relate a three-page response to the original syllabus. The committee has even developed a new cover sheet for all proposals, which requests detailed information about objectives and asks for samples of test questions and paper assignments. Yet sufficiently informative syllabi are still so rare that when one appears it elicits audible sighs of relief around the conference table.

The syllabi our committee gets are not much different from the ones I've picked up at conferences or seen attached to grant proposals. In other words, I don't believe the problem is local or idiosyncratic; rather, it seems to be basic to the teaching endeavor. We keep forgetting that what we know—about our disciplines, about our goals, about our teaching methods—is not known (or agreed upon) by everyone. We seem to assume that our colleagues and our students will intuitively be able to reconstruct the creature we see in our mind's eye from the few bones we give them in the syllabus.

The worst syllabi seem to fall into one of two categories.

The "listers" merely specify which books or chapters will be read during   5
which weeks, without a hint about the principles behind the selection. The most puzzling of this type assign chapters in the textbooks in an order considerably different from the order intended by the authors. At best, such modification gives students the impression that the teacher is improving on the original organization for some as yet unrevealed purpose, at worst, it gives students the idea that one order is no less logical or coherent than another, and that all parts are interchangeable and equally valid.

The "scolders" give brief descriptions of content and lengthy sets of instruction detailing what will happen if a student comes in late or leaves early, hands in a paper after the deadline, misses an exam, fails to follow the rules for margins and double-spacing, does not participate in class discussion. The scolders often sound more like lawyers than professors. Undoubtedly the syllabus as legal document has evolved because so often students demand that their teachers provide a set of rules, probably to give the students something concrete to cling to as they struggle with the content of the course. If even sophisticated scholars fall into the trap of equating quantitative data with significance, it's not surprising that students mistake the rules for the meaning.

Here are some questions our committee often finds unanswered even in wonderful syllabi for wonderful courses:

- Why should a student want to take this course? How does it make a difference as part of the discipline? How does it fit into the general-education program?

- What are the objectives of the course? Where does it lead, intellectually and practically? Students should be able to find out what they will know by the end of the course, and also what they will be able to do better afterward than before. Is the purpose of the course to increase their problem-solving abilities, improve their communication skills, sharpen their understanding of moral ambiguities, allow them to translate knowledge from one context to another? Why are the objectives important, and how will different parts of the course help students accomplish those objectives?

- What are the prerequisites? Students should be given some idea about what they should already know and what skills they should already have before taking the course, so they can realistically assess their readiness. Will they be expected to know how to compare and contrast, to analyze and synthesize, or will they be taught those skills during the course?

- Why do the parts of the course come in the order they do? Most syllabi note the order in which topics will be discussed, but make no attempt to explain the way the professor has chosen to organize the course. Sections of the syllabus are usually titled, but only infrequently are questions provided for students to help them put the reading assignments and homework into context.

- Will the course be primarily lectures, discussions, or group work? When a percentage of the grade is for "class participation," what does the professor expect from the students—regular attendance? questions? answers to questions? Will the students be given alternative ways to achieve success in the class, based on different learning styles?

- What is the purpose of the assignments? Students are frequently told how much an assignment will "count" and how many pages long it must be, but they are rarely given any idea about what it will demand of them or what the goal is. Will students be required to describe, discuss, analyze, provide evidence, criticize, defend, compare, apply? To what end? If students are expected to present a project before the class, are the criteria for an excellent presentation made clear?

- What will the tests test?—memory? understanding? ability to synthesize? To present evidence logically? To apply knowledge in a new context?

- Why have the books been chosen? What is their relative importance in the course and in the discipline? Is the emphasis in the course on primary or secondary materials and why?

"Well," you may say, "the syllabus isn't the course—everything will be made clear as the semester progresses." Or, "I can't ask my overworked secretary to type a twelve-page syllabus." Or, "Students are interested only in the numbers—of books, of pages to read, of written assignments, of questions on the exam." Or, "A syllabus with all that information is too static—it doesn't allow me the flexibility to be creative on the spur of the moment." Maybe those are relevant objections—and maybe they are excuses for badly thought-out, hurriedly patched-together efforts. Whatever the rationale, I believe that the inadequate syllabus is a symptom of a larger problem—the lack of communication between teachers and students.

Most of the latest reports on undergraduate education have in common the criticism that faculty members and the students no longer seem to be connecting. Our students do not **What we know is not known** seem to be involved in learning, they say. We seem to **(or agreed upon) by everyone.** have lost the ability to create a shared community of values; we have substituted diversity for coherence and cannot find our way back to integrating principles. However, these reports all seem to ignore a very real wish among students and faculty members to find a place of meeting.

In 1982–83, Lee Knefelkamp of the University of Maryland asked 217 faculty members at eight colleges what they worried about most the first day of class. Their three most common concerns were, "Will the students get involved?" "Will they like me?" "Will the class work well as a class?" 10

When 157 students at those institutions responded to the same question, their three most common concerns were, "Will I be able to do the work?" "Will I like the professor?" "Will I get along with my classmates?"

The notion of relationship between teachers and students and material to be learned is clear in the answers from both groups. However, when the faculty members were asked what they thought students worried about the first day of class, they responded, "Will I get a good grade?" "Will the work be hard?" "Will the class be interesting?" When the students were asked what they thought teachers worried about, they generally couldn't answer the question at all.

The survey showed that there was a real desire on the part of both students and teacher for connectedness, but neither group realized that the other shared that desire. If the participants on both sides don't understand how to develop their relationship, learning will be diminished.

The syllabus is a small place to start bringing students and faculty members back together, of course, and its improvement is not the revolutionary gesture that curriculum reform seems to be. But if students could be persuaded that we are really interested in their understanding the material we offer, that we support their efforts to master it, and that we take their intellectual struggles seriously, they might respond by becoming more involved in our courses, by trying to live up to our expectations, and by appreciating our concern.

Then the real work of learning can begin. 15

Working with the Text

1. Sharon Rubin provides a list of questions that often go unanswered on even well-constructed syllabi. At the end of her essay, she asserts that "if students could be persuaded that we are really interested in their understanding the material we offer, that we support their efforts to master it, and that we take their intellectual struggles seriously, they might respond by becoming more involved in our courses, by trying to live up to our expectations. . . ." (par. 14). In a short essay, explore the connections between her list of questions and her closing assertion. In what ways might a syllabus that answers those questions persuade students that the teacher is interested in helping them master the course material?

2. Commenting on the survey conducted by the University of Maryland, Rubin interprets the findings as showing "that there was a real desire on the part of both students and teacher for connectedness, but neither group realized that the other shared that desire" (par. 13). As evidence, Rubin quotes survey responses from both students and teachers. Write a brief essay analyzing how these answers to the survey support Rubin's interpretation. What can you infer from these answers about the desire for connectedness on the part of both teachers and students? How do the answers indicate that neither group recognized that the desire for connectedness was mutual?

3. Rubin's essay presents evidence that teachers actively resist producing the kind of syllabus she recommends. Based on Rubin's evidence, write a brief essay analyzing how teachers show their resistance and why they might resist. Drawing on your own experience, as well as on Rubin's text, indicate whether or not you agree with Rubin's assessment. Why or why not?

From Text to Field

1. In her essay, Rubin makes a number of assertions about how students read and interpret syllabi. Do any of her assertions reflect your own experience with course syllabi? In a personal essay, analyze yourself as a syllabus reader. How do you read a syllabus? What are you looking for? What do you expect (or want) a syllabus to tell you? To what extent do you look to the syllabus to define the course for you? In addition to the time the teacher spends in class going over the syllabus, do you read it on your own? Do you refer back to it later in the term? If not, why not? If so, for what kind of information?

2. In her description of "scolders," Rubin asserts, "Undoubtedly the syllabus as legal document has evolved because so often students demand that their teachers provide a set of rules, probably to give the students something concrete to cling to as they struggle with the content of the course" (par. 6). Do

you agree with her assertion? What does she mean by the phrase, "something concrete to cling to as they struggle with the content of the course"? How does she define "the rules" of a course? In a brief essay, explore your own attitude toward knowing the rules, as defined by Rubin. Do you demand that teachers provide a set of rules? Do you "cling" to rules as a means for controlling your "struggle with the content of the course"?

3. Review the student responses Rubin quotes from the University of Maryland survey. Do the "first day" worries of these students reflect your own early worries about a course? Write an essay in which you re-create yourself or imagine yourself on the first day of a particular class. What are you thinking and feeling? Where do you look for clues to address your worries about the course? Whether or not you have ever experienced it, imagine that the teacher passes out a syllabus that addresses your worries. What does the syllabus provide to do this?

4. Choose a syllabus from one course—your writing course, another course you are taking or have taken, a course you will take or would take if you could—to analyze in terms of Rubin's essay, in particular the "unanswered" questions from syllabi she has reviewed. Write a brief essay in which you use the syllabus to analyze the course. What is the purpose of the course? What are its objectives? How does it fit into your course of study and your personal development? What are the teacher's values and research interests? What can you tell about the teacher's personality and approach to teaching?

Angels on a Pin:
The Barometer Story

Alexander Calandra

A professor emeritus of physics at Washington University in St. Louis, Alexander Calandra first published the story of the student and the barometer problem in his 1961 textbook, *The Teaching of Elementary Science and Mathematics*. Since then, this parable of playful, creative, even defiant thinking has reappeared several times in various incarnations, one featuring the Nobel Prize–winning Neils Bohr as the young protagonist.

The final paragraph of the *Saturday Review* version (1968) says that the student is reacting to the "*Sputnik*-panicked classrooms of America." *Sputnik 1,* launched by the Soviets in 1957 as the earth's first artificial satellite, sent the United States scrambling to overcome the Soviet Union in the space race. The failure of the United States to beat the Soviets into space was blamed in part on a lax educational system. The National Defense Education Act (NDEA), passed in 1958, poured federal dollars into reforming math and science education from elementary- through graduate-school levels. Although the nation's top scientists urged reforms that encouraged students to think creatively, efforts to bring rigor to the classroom often focused on teaching the *right* methodologies to get the *right* answers.

Born in New York in 1911, Calandra received his PhD from New York University in 1935. Prior to teaching at Washington University, Calandra taught at Brooklyn College, where he had received his undergraduate degree, as well as at the University of Chicago. Concurrently with his professorship at Washington University, he served as chair of the science department at Webster College in St. Louis, starting in 1969. His reputation as an outstanding lecturer who used humor in his teaching is reflected in the barometer story.

In 1979, the American Association of Physics Teachers awarded Calandra the Millikan Medal for "notable and creative contributions to the teaching of physics." He retired in 1981 and passed away in March 2006.

Some time ago, I received a call from a colleague who asked if I would be the referee on the grading of an examination question. He was about to give a student a zero for his answer to a physics question, while the student claimed he should receive a perfect score and would if the system were not set up against the student. The instructor and the student agreed to submit this to an impartial arbiter, and I was selected.

I went to my colleague's office and read the examination question: "Show how it is possible to determine the height of a tall building with the aid of a barometer."

The student had answered: "Take the barometer to the top of the building, attach a long rope to it, lower the barometer to the street, and then bring it up, measuring the length of the rope. The length of the rope is the height of the building."

I pointed out that the student really had a strong case for full credit, since he had answered the question completely and correctly. On the other hand, if full credit were given, it could well contribute to a high grade for the student in his physics course. A high grade is supposed to certify competence in physics, but the answer did not confirm this. I suggested that the student have another try at answering the question. I was not surprised that my colleague agreed, but I was surprised that the student did.

I gave the student six minutes to answer the question, with the warning that his answer should show some knowledge of physics. At the end of five minutes, he had not written anything. I asked if he wished to give up, but he said no. He had many answers to this problem; he was just thinking of the best one. I excused myself for interrupting him, and asked him to please go on. In the next minute, he dashed off his answer, which read:

The student claimed he should receive a perfect score.

"Take the barometer to the top of the building and lean over the edge of the roof. Drop the barometer, timing its fall with a stopwatch. Then, using the formula $S = \frac{1}{2}at^2$, calculate the height of the building."

At this point, I asked my colleague if *he* would give up. He conceded, and I gave the student almost full credit.

In leaving my colleague's office, I recalled that the student had said he had other answers to the problem, so I asked him what they were. "Oh, yes," said the student. "There are many ways of getting the height of a tall building with the aid of a barometer. For example, you could take the barometer out on a sunny day and measure the height of the barometer, the length of its shadow, and the length of the shadow of the building, and by the use of a simple proportion, determine the height of the building."

"Fine," I said. "And the others?"

"Yes," said the student. "There is a very basic measurement method that you will like. In this method, you take the barometer and begin to walk up the stairs. As you climb the stairs, you mark off the length of the barometer along the wall. You then count the number of marks, and this will give you the height of the building in barometer units. A very direct method. 10

"Of course, if you want a more sophisticated method, you can tie the barometer to the end of a string, swing it as a pendulum, and determine the value of 'g' at the street level and at the top of the building. From the difference between the two values of 'g,' the height of the building can, in principle, be calculated."

Finally, he concluded, there are many other ways of solving the problem. "Probably the best," he said, "is to take the barometer to the basement and knock on the superintendent's door. When the superintendent answers, you speak to him as follows: 'Mr. Superintendent, here I have a fine barometer. If you will tell me the height of this building, I will give you this barometer.' "

At this point, I asked the student if he really did not know the conventional answer to this question. He admitted that he did, but said that he was fed up with high school and college instructors trying to teach him how to think, to use the "scientific method," and to explore the deep inner logic of the subject in a pedantic way, as is often done in the new mathematics, rather than teaching him the structure of the subject. With this in mind, he decided to revive scholasticism as an academic lark to challenge the *Sputnik*-panicked classrooms of America.

Working with the Text

1. In Alexander Calandra's essay, the student gives a number of alternative answers to a physics question that has a "conventional answer." (Given this problem, physics students would be expected to calculate the altitude from measurements of the barometric pressure at the top and at the bottom of the building.) As you reread the essay, note the logic behind each of the answers. In a brief essay, analyze the author's intention in using the number and kinds of answers that he assigns to the student. Beyond demonstrating that the conventional answer is not necessarily the only answer, what is Calandra trying to point out? What is the effect of this particular accumulation of alternative

answers on the tone and attitude of the piece? Why would Calandra choose such an effect? Note in particular that the student says that "probably the best" answer is to offer the barometer to the building superintendent.

2. The narrator of the piece, who calls himself the "impartial arbiter," gives the student "almost full credit" for one of his answers, after saying at the outset that the student "had a strong case for full credit" (par. 4). In a brief essay, reflect on how *credit* is used in the story. How is credit significant to the meaning of the story? What factors determine how much credit is given? Do you agree with the arbiter's decision? Why or why not?

3. The first part of the selection title, "Angels on a Pin," refers to an intricate and protracted argument among medieval scholars and clerics over how many angels could stand on the head of a pin. Why would Calandra choose this as the title for his story? Write a brief essay in which you explore the connections between the title and the meaning of the story. In what ways is the title consistent with the meaning of the story? In what ways might the title be a contradiction of the more specific points of the story?

4. In the final paragraph of the story, the student says he is "fed up" with being taught to think in a "pedantic way." Look up the word *pedantic*. Reflecting on what the student does in the rest of the story, write a brief essay in which you analyze what he means by thinking in a "pedantic way." Through the student's behaviors and answers, what argument do you think Calandra is making about science and math instruction?

From Text to Field

1. Calandra uses humor to question the emphasis educators tend to place on "the right answer." Write an essay using a form of humor, such as parody or satire, to send up an aspect of education that you have personally found to be questionable (or ridiculous or absurd). Using "Angels on a Pin" as a model, be aware of how your comic details pinpoint and critique the questionable elements of the aspect of education you have chosen to address.

2. Calandra's story implies that the physics professor expects his students to use particular methods to show their "competence in physics." Taking a position counter to the story, write an essay in which you speculate on the reasons teachers in certain fields might expect you to use certain methods to find "conventional" answers. In what ways might an emphasis on "conventional answers" support, or undermine, the values of the discipline.

3. "Angels on a Pin" was published in 1961 in a book by Calandra, entitled *The Teaching of Elementary Science and Mathematics,* and again in 1968 in the *Saturday Review*. Based on the title of the 1961 book, who do you think was

the intended audience for the book? The *Saturday Review* was a popular weekly magazine for many decades before it ceased publication in 1973. Who do you think was the intended audience for that publication? Write an essay in which you analyze why a story published for the audience of the 1961 book would be republished in 1968 for the audience of the *Saturday Review*.

4. Calandra's story captures a student's rebellion against "the conventional answer." In a personal essay, reflect on your own stance on conventional answers. Do you tend to pursue the conventional answer, or do you look for alternative methods and answers? Might there be value in knowing the conventional answer? In your course work, why do you approach answering questions the way that you do? What would you change about your approach? What about your approach do you value and intend to keep? What effect do you anticipate your approach will have on who you are as a person and as a professional?

Other Voices, Other Rooms

Gerald Graff

A professor at the University of Illinois at Chicago, Gerald Graff has made a career of seeking coherence through controversy. His hotly debated book, *Literature against Itself: Literary Ideas in Modern Society* (1979), argues against trends in literary criticism that have driven academic research for some years. "Other Voices, Other Rooms" is taken from *Beyond the Culture Wars: How Teaching the Conflicts Can Revitalize American Education* (1992), which challenges institutional structures and ideological stances that discourage dialogue within the academy. *Beyond the Culture Wars* won the American Book Award in 1993.

From his vantage point as a teacher of undergraduates, Graff views the curriculum, especially the general-education curriculum, as disjointed and confusing. The "cognitive dissonance" undergraduates experience could be the source of a deeper, more coherent education, Graff believes, if the intellectual and cultural debates that drive academic research were brought into the classroom. "Contrast," says Graff, "is fundamental to understanding, for no subject, idea, or text is an island." Although such contrasts can sometimes be brought into the classroom by exceptional teachers, Graff is convinced that the surer source is an institutional atmosphere and structure that encourages dialogue among scholars.

For Graff the goal is not consensus, but the kind of coherence that is won through genuine and explicit conversation: "One of the oddest things about the university is that it calls itself a community of scholars yet organizes its curriculum in a way that conceals the links of the community from those who are not already aware of them."

An undergraduate tells of an art history course in which the instructor observed one day, "As we now know, the idea that knowledge can be objective is a positivist myth that has been exploded by postmodern thought." It so happens the student is concurrently enrolled in a political science course in which the instructor speaks confidently about the objectivity of his discipline as if it had not been "exploded" at all. What do you do? the student is asked. "What else can I do?" he says. "I trash objectivity in art history, and I presuppose it in political science."

A second undergraduate describes a history teacher who makes a point of stressing the superiority of Western culture in developing the ideas of freedom, democracy, and free-market capitalism that the rest of the world is now rushing to imitate. She also has a literature teacher who describes such claims of Western supremacy as an example of the hegemonic ideology by which the United States arrogates the right to police the world. When asked which course she prefers, she replies, "Well, I'm getting an A in both."

To some of us these days, the moral of these stories would be that students have become cynical relativists who care less about convictions than about grades and careers. In fact, if anything is surprising, it is that more students do not behave in this cynical fashion, for the established curriculum encourages it. The disjunction of the curriculum is a far more powerful source of relativism than any doctrine preached by the faculty.

One of the oddest things about the university is that it calls itself a community of scholars yet organizes its curriculum in a way that conceals the links of the community from those who are not already aware of them. The courses being given at any moment on a campus represent any number of rich potential conversations within and across the disciplines. But since students experience these conversations only as a series of monologues, the conversations become actual only for the minority who can reconstruct them on their own. No self-respecting educator would deliberately design a system guaranteed to keep students dependent on the whim of the individual instructor. Yet this is precisely the effect of a curriculum composed of courses that are not in dialogue with one another.

Ships in the Night

The problem deepens when teachers are further apart. A student today can go from a course in which the universality of Western culture is taken for granted (and therefore not articulated) to a course in which it is taken for granted (and therefore not articulated) that such claims of universality are fallacious and deceptive. True, for the best students the resulting cognitive dissonance is no great problem. The chance to try on a variety of clashing ideas, to see what they feel like, is one of the most exciting opportunities an education can provide; it can be especially rewarding for students who come to the university with already developed skills at summarizing and weighing arguments and synthesizing conflicting positions on their own.

Many students, however, become confused or indifferent and react as the above two students did by giving their teachers whatever they seem to want even though it is contradictory.

Then, too, when their teachers' conflicting perspectives do not enter into a common discussion, students may not even be able to infer what is wanted. Like everyone else, teachers tend to betray their crucial assumptions as much in what they do *not* say, what they take to go without saying, as in what they say explicitly. To students who are not at home in the academic intellectual community, the significance of these silences and exclusions is likely to be intimidating, if it does not elude them entirely.

Furthermore, in an academic environment in which there is increasingly less unspoken common ground, it may not even be clear to students that their teachers are in conflict, for different words may be used by several teachers for the same concepts or the same words for different concepts. If students do not know that "positivism" has in some quarters become a derogatory buzzword for any belief in objectivity, they may not become aware that the art history and political science teachers in the above example are in disagreement. A student who goes from one humanist who speaks of "traditional moral themes" to another who speaks of "patriarchal discursive practices" may not become aware that the two teachers are actually referring to the same thing. Students in such cases are being exposed to some of the major cultural debates of their time, but in a way that makes it difficult to recognize them *as* debates.

Note, too, that the instructors in these situations are protected by the insularity of their classrooms, which makes it unnecessary, if not impossible, for them to confront the challenges to their assumptions that would be represented by their colleagues. Professors do not expect such immunity from peer criticism when they publish their work or appear at professional conferences. It is only in the classroom that such immunity is taken for granted as if it were a form of academic freedom. Since students enjoy no such protection, one can hardly blame them if they, too, protect themselves by compartmentalizing the contradictions to which they are exposed, as my first student did when he became an objectivist in one course and an antiobjectivist in the other.

I recall a semester late in college when I took a course in modern poetry taught by a New Critic, a follower of T. S. Eliot, and a course in seventeenth-century English literature taught by an older scholar who resented Eliot and the New Critics, who had attacked John Milton for his grandiloquence and lack of irony. Three days a week between ten and eleven I listened with dutiful respect to the New Critic's theories of irony and paradox, and between eleven and twelve I listened with dutiful respect to the argument that these New Critical theories had no application whatsoever to Milton, Dryden, and their contemporaries. What was really odd, however, is that I hardly focused at the time on the fact that my two teachers were in disagreement.

Was I just ridiculously slow to comprehend the critical issues that were at stake? Perhaps so, but since no one was asking me to think about the relationship between the two courses, I did not. If my teachers disagreed, this was their business—a professional dispute that did not concern me. Each course was challenging enough on its own terms, and to have raised the question of how they related would have only risked needlessly multiplying difficulties for myself. Then, too, for me to ask my teachers about their differences might have seemed impertinent and ill-mannered—who was I to impugn their authority? Only later did it dawn on me that studying different centuries and clashing theories without having them brought together had made things much *harder* since it removed the element of contrast.

Contrast is fundamental to understanding, for no subject, idea, or text is an island. In order to become intelligible "in itself," it needs to be seen in its relation to other subjects, ideas, and texts. When this relation of interdependence is obscured because different courses do not communicate, subjects, ideas, and texts become harder to comprehend, if not unintelligible. We think we are making things simpler for students by abstracting periods, texts, and authors from their relationships with other periods, texts, and authors so that we can study them closely in a purified space. But the very act of isolating an object from its contrasting background and relations makes it hard to grasp. Since we cannot talk about everything all at once, subjects do have to be distinguished and to that extent isolated from one another. But this isolation does not have to preclude connections and relations. It is hard to grasp the modernity of modern literature unless one can compare it with something that is not modern.

The university conceals the links of the community.

That is why teachers in modern periods need nonmodernists (and vice versa) in order to make their subjects intelligible to their students, just as teachers who defend the culture of the West need the teachers who criticize it (and vice versa). Without the criticisms, after all, there would be no need to defend the West to begin with. Insofar as neither a defense nor a critique of tradition makes sense apart from the dialogue these positions are engaged in, a curriculum which removes that dialogue from view defeats the goals of traditionalists and revisionists alike. It is true that fundamental conflicts like these may turn out to be nonnegotiable. But no one knows this in advance, and even if a dispute proves to be nonnegotiable, to learn that this is the case is not worthless.

I noted earlier that among the factors that make academic culture more confusing today than in the past is not only that there is more controversy but that there is even controversy about what can legitimately be considered controversial. Traditionalists are often angry that there should even *be* a debate over the canon, while revisionists are often angry that there should even be a debate over "political correctness," or the relevance of ideology and politics to their subjects. A recent feminist critic says she finds it "astonishing" that it still needs repeating at this late date that "the perspective assumed to be 'universal' which has dominated knowledge . . . has actually been male and culture-bound."[1] Since the feminist argument, however, is that we still fail to see how culture-bound our thinking is, it is hard to see why this critic should be astonished that she still needs to make the point. Another political critic writes that "we are perhaps already weary of the avalanche of papers, books, and conferences entitled 'The Politics of X,' and we have recently begun to question that most hallowed of all political slogans on the left, 'everything is political.' "[2] Yet the idea of politics that this critic and her audience are already "weary of" is one that most people have not yet encountered and might well find incomprehensible. The "advanced" academic and the layperson (or the traditional academic) are so far apart that what is already old news to one has not yet become intelligible to the other.

Imagine how this affects students who, at the moment they are negotiating the difficult transition from the lay culture to the academic culture, must also negotiate the unpredictable and unfathomable discrepancies between academic departments and factions. When there is no correlation of the different discourses to which students are exposed, it becomes especially difficult for them to infer which assumptions are safe and which are likely to be challenged. The problem is that knowledge of what is and is not considered potentially or legitimately controversial cannot be learned a priori; you cannot get it out of E. D. Hirsch's *Dictionary of Cultural Literacy*. Such knowledge comes only through interaction with a community, and that interaction is precisely what is prevented by a disconnected system of courses. Then, too, assumptions about what is and is not potentially controversial tend to change from one moment to the next and one subcommunity to the next, and they are changing at a faster rate today than in the past.

Thomas S. Kuhn in *The Structure of Scientific Revolutions* describes moments of crisis or "paradigm shift" in the sciences, when "a law that cannot even be demonstrated to one group of scientists may . . . seem intuitively obvious to another."[3] The fate of Kuhn's own book is an interesting case in point. Even as his sociological account of scientific paradigm change has been treated as virtual holy writ by many literary theorists (for a while it seemed almost obligatory to begin every book or essay with a respectful bow to Kuhn), his work has often been ignored or dismissed by scientists and philosophers of science, who accuse him of subverting the concept of objective truth in reducing scientific discovery to "mob psychology." As the controversy over Kuhn has revealed, both the literati and the scientists have remained largely walled up within their clashing assumptions about objectivity, the smugness of which might have been punctured had these parties been forced to argue with each other in their teaching. This mutual smugness has persisted in the sniper fire that continues to be exchanged over the concept of objectivity and the extent to which knowledge is independent of the social situation of the knower; revisionists sneer at the concept and traditionalists sneer at the very idea of questioning it.

The question neither group seems to ask is what it must be like to be a student caught in the crossfire between these conflicting views of objectivity, each one prone to present itself as "intuitively obvious" and uncontroversial. A rhetoric scholar, Gregory Colomb, has studied the disorientation experienced by a bright high school graduate who, after doing well in a humanities course as a freshman at the University of Chicago, tried to apply her mastery to a social science course, only to come up with a grade of C.[4] Imagine trying to write an academic paper when you sense that almost anything you say can be used against you and that the intellectual moves that got you an A in existentialist philosophy may get you a C minus and a dirty look in Skinnerian behaviorism.

Consider the fact that the passive voice that is so standard in sociology writing ("it will be contended in this paper . . .") has been perennially rebuked in English courses.[5] Or consider something so apparently trivial as the convention of using the present tense to describe actions in literature and philosophy and the past tense to describe them in history. Plato *says* things in literary and philosophical accounts while in historical accounts he *said* them. Experienced writers become so accustomed to such tense shifting that it seems a simple matter, but it reflects deep-rooted and potentially controversial differences between disciplines. Presumably, Plato speaks in the present in literary and philosophical contexts because ideas there are considered timeless; only when we move over to history does it start to matter that the writer is dead.[6] We English teachers write "tense shift" in the margin when student writers betray uncertainty about this convention, but how do we expect them to "get" it when they pass from the very different time zones of history and philosophy / English with no engagement of the underlying issues?

One of the most frequent comments teachers make on student papers is "What's your evidence?" But nobody would ever finish a piece of writing if it were necessary to supply evidence for everything being said, so in order to write, one must acquire a sense of which statements have to be supported by evidence (or further argument) and which ones a writer can get away with because they are already taken for granted by the imagined audience. What happens, then, when a writer has no way of knowing whether an assumption that he or she got away with with audience A will also be conceded by audience B? It is no wonder that students protect themselves from the insecurity of such a situation by "psyching out" each course as it comes—and then forgetting about it as soon as possible after the final exam in order to clear their minds for the seemingly unrelated demands of the next set of courses.

It is only ideas and reasoning processes but the recall of basic information as well that figure to be impaired by disjunctive curricular organization. To use the jargon of information theory, an information system that is experienced as an unrelated series of signals will be weak in the kind of redundancy that is needed for information to be retained. Faced with a curriculum overloaded with data and weak in redundancy, students may find it difficult to know which items of information they are supposed to remember. Then, too, a student may be exposed to the same information in several courses while failing to recognize it as "the same," since it is contextualized differently in each course. When students fail to identify a cultural literacy item on a test, the problem may be not that they don't know the information but that they don't know they know it; they may have learned it in a context whose relevance to the test question they don't recognize. What is learned seems so specific to a particular course that it is difficult for students to see its application beyond.

The critic Kenneth Burke once compared the intellectual life of a culture to a parlor in which different guests are forever dropping in and out. As the standard curriculum represents the intellectual life, however, there is no parlor; the hosts congregate in separate rooms with their acolytes and keep their differences and agreements to themselves. Making one's way through the standard curriculum is rather like trying to comprehend a phone conversation by listening at only one end.[7] You can manage it up to a point, but this is hardly the ideal way to do it. 20

To venture a final comparison, it is as if you were to try to learn the game of baseball by being shown a series of rooms in which you see each component of the game separately: pitchers going through their windups in one room; hitters swinging their bats in the next; then infielders, outfielders, umpires, fans, field announcers, ticket scalpers, broadcasters, hot-dog vendors, and so on. You see them all in their different roles, but since you see them separately you get no clear idea of what the game actually looks like or why the players do what they do. No doubt you would come away with a very imperfect understanding of baseball under these conditions. Yet it does not seem far-fetched to compare these circumstances with the ones students face when they are exposed to a series of disparate courses, subjects, and perspectives and expected not only to infer the rules of the academic-intellectual game but to play it competently themselves.

Notes

1. Gayle Green, "The Myth of Neutrality, Again?" in *Shakespeare Left and Right*, ed. Ivo Kamps (New York: Routledge, 1991), p. 24.
2. Diana Fuss, *Essentially Speaking: Feminism, Nature and Difference* (New York: Routledge, 1989), p. 105.
3. Thomas S. Kuhn, *The Structure of Scientific Revolutions*, 2d ed. (Chicago: University of Chicago Press, 1970), p. 150.
4. Gregory Colomb, *Disciplinary "Secrets" and the Apprentice Writer: The Lessons for Critical Thinking* (Upper Montclair, N.J.: Montclair State College, Institute for Critical Thinking, 1988), pp. 2–3.
5. For this point I am indebted to an unpublished talk by Susan Lowry.
6. I am indebted for this point to Susan H. McLeod, "Writing across the Curriculum: An Introduction," forthcoming in *Writing across the Curriculum: A Guide to Developing Programs*, eds. McLeod and Margot Soven (Newberry Park, Calif.: Sage, 1992).
7. I adapt an observation made in a somewhat different context by Mary Louise Pratt, "Humanities for the Future: Reflections on the Western Culture Debate at Stanford," in *Politics of Liberal Education* (Durham: Duke University Press, 1992), p. 19.

Working with the Text

1. In this selection from *Beyond the Culture Wars,* Gerald Graff describes what he considers to be the student experience of the undergraduate curriculum in most American colleges and universities. As you reread Graff's argument, note the specific ways he characterizes the undergraduate experience. In a brief essay, develop a portrait of the student Graff is describing. What does the student encounter? How does the student respond? Consider the terms Graff uses. For instance, what does he mean by "cognitive dissonance" (par. 5)? What connection does he say that dissonance has to the tendency of students to "psych out" (par. 18) a course? What does he think "psyching out" a course involves?

2. Graff weaves examples and personal reminiscence into his discussion of how isolated the individual classroom is on college campuses. What effect do these examples have on Graff's credibility? Do the examples and stories help elicit belief in Graff's argument?

3. Graff titles a section in the excerpt presented here with the phrase "Ships in the Night." Explain the idiomatic expression that Graff is using here. In what ways is the title appropriate as a metaphor for the argument that Graff presents?

4. When discussing how difficult students find it to know what their professors expect, Graff observes: "Like everyone else, teachers tend to betray their crucial assumptions as much in what they do *not* say, what they take to go

without saying, as in what they say explicitly. To students who are not at home in the academic intellectual community, the significance of these silences and exclusions is likely to be intimidating, if it does not elude them entirely" (par. 6). Drawing on examples from your own attempts to figure out those expectations, write a brief explanation of what Graff means by his statement.

From Text to Field

1. Graff, in a part of this selection not reprinted here, asserts that "students have trouble making sense of the disparate and clashing materials with which the curriculum bombards them". Has this been your experience? Write an essay in which you reflect on your ability to "make sense" of the materials you have encountered in your undergraduate education. Have you found the materials to be "disparate and clashing"? Do you see them as separate units of knowledge? Do you play them off of each other or try to reconcile them? Do they seem coherent or fragmented to you?

2. The curriculum Graff describes is commonly found in undergraduate general-education requirements. Examine the requirements for your institution, and consider the general-education courses you have already taken. In an essay, analyze the effectiveness of your general-education curriculum. What is the rationale for that curriculum? In what ways does the curriculum—the rationale, the approach, the courses and their sequence—seem sound to you? In what ways does the curriculum seem questionable?

3. Throughout the selection, Graff refers to the academic debate over Western culture and the debate over objectivity, which are in many ways interrelated. What aspects of these debates have you encountered in your own education or in reading and discussion outside an educational setting? In a personal essay, reflect on those encounters, including your reading of Graff's references to the academic debate. Based on what you know so far, what is your position on the debate over Western culture, objectivity, or both? In what ways do you think they are significant? Over time, how has your position been reinforced or changed? What questions do the debates raise for you?

4. Given Graff's interest in dialogue among courses and among the materials or readings taught in those courses, offer a proposal in which you rethink the design of a course, or of a set of courses, so that the dialogue that Graff has in mind can occur.

Teaching New Worlds/
New Words

bell hooks

In her call for classrooms that encourage students to use the language they "know most intimately," bell hooks takes us back to the violence and oppression that gave birth to black English. Hooks describes how Africans who were brought to America as slaves were forced to replace their own languages with standard English, which they in turn "remade" into a tool of resistance.

As a descendant of slaves who grew up speaking the Southern black vernacular of Kentucky, hooks began to challenge the repressiveness of standard English by drawing the vernacular into her classroom, professional writing, and social life. She believes that through listening to each other's first language, "we may disrupt that cultural imperialism that suggests one is worthy of being heard only if one speaks in standard English."

Gloria Watkins writes under the pseudonym bell hooks, her grandmother's name, using the lowercase to draw attention away from her own authorship and to the unheard voices that drive her explorations of identity and culture. A professor at City College in New York, she has taught at Yale University and Oberlin College. As an educator, a writer, and a speaker, she is one of the most provocative and important voices of her generation of intellectuals. "Teaching New Worlds/New Words" first appeared as a chapter in hooks's book *Teaching to Transgress: Education as the Practice of Freedom* (1994).

Like desire, language disrupts, refuses to be contained within boundaries. It speaks itself against our will, in words and thoughts that intrude, even violate the most private spaces of mind and body. It was in my first year of college that I read Adrienne Rich's poem, "The Burning of Paper Instead of

Children." That poem, speaking against domination, against racism and class oppression, attempts to illustrate graphically that stopping the political persecution and torture of living beings is a more vital issue than censorship, than burning books. One line of this poem that moved and disturbed something within me: "This is the oppressor's language yet I need it to talk to you." I've never forgotten it. Perhaps I could not have forgotten it even if I tried to erase it from memory. Words impose themselves, take root in our memory against our will. The words of this poem begat a life in my memory that I could not abort or change.

When I find myself thinking about language now, these words are there, as if they were always waiting to challenge and assist me. I find myself silently speaking them over and over again with the intensity of a chant. They startle me, shaking me into an awareness of the link between languages and domination. Initially, I resist the idea of the "oppressor's language," certain that this construct has the potential to disempower those of us who are just learning to speak, who are just learning to claim language as a place where we make ourselves subject. "*This is the oppressor's language yet I need it to talk to you.*" Adrienne Rich's words. Then, when I first read these words, and now, they make me think of standard English, of learning to speak against black vernacular, against the ruptured and broken speech of a dispossessed and displaced people. Standard English is not the speech of exile. It is the language of conquest and domination; in the United States, it is the mask which hides the loss of so many tongues, all those sounds of diverse, native communities we will never hear, the speech of the Gullah, Yiddish, and so many other unremembered tongues.

Reflecting on Adrienne Rich's words, I know that it is not the English language that hurts me, but what the oppressors do with it, how they shape it to become a territory that limits and defines, how they make it a weapon that can shame, humiliate, colonize. Gloria Anzaldúa reminds us of this pain in *Borderlands/La Frontera* when she asserts, "So, if you want to really hurt me, talk badly about my language." We have so little knowledge of how displaced, enslaved, or free Africans who came or were brought against their will to the United States felt about the loss of language, about learning English. Only as a woman did I begin to think about these black people in relation to language, to think about their trauma as they were compelled to witness their language rendered meaningless with a colonizing European culture, where voices deemed foreign could not be spoken, were outlawed tongues, renegade speech. When I realize how long it has taken for white Americans to acknowledge diverse languages of Native Americans, to accept that the speech their ancestral colonizers declared was merely grunts and gibberish was indeed *language*, it is difficult not to hear in standard English always the sound of slaughter and conquest. I think now of the grief of displaced "homeless" Africans, forced to inhabit a world where they saw folks like themselves, inhabiting the same skin, the same condition, but who had no shared language to talk with one another, who needed "the oppressor's language." *"This is the oppressor's language yet I need it to talk to you."* When I imagine the terror of Africans on board slave ships, on auction blocks, inhabiting the unfamiliar architecture of plantations, I consider that this terror extended beyond fear of punishment, that it resided also in the anguish of hearing a language they could not comprehend. The very sound of English had to terrify. I think of black people meeting one another in a space away from the diverse cultures and languages that distinguished them from one another, compelled by circumstance to find ways to speak with one another in a "new world" where blackness or the darkness of one's skin and not language would become the space of bonding. How to remember, to reinvoke this terror. How to describe what it must have been like for Africans whose deepest bonds were historically forged in the place of shared speech to be transported abruptly to a world where the very sound of one's mother tongue had no meaning.

I imagine them hearing spoken English as the oppressor's language, yet I imagine them also realizing that this language would need to be possessed, taken, claimed as a space of resistance. I imagine that the moment they realized the oppressor's language, seized and spoken by the tongues of the colonized, could be a space of bonding was joyous. For in that recognition was the understanding that intimacy could be restored, that a culture of resistance could be formed that would make recovery from the trauma of enslavement possible. I imagine, then, Africans first hearing English as "the oppressor's language" and then re-hearing it as a potential site of resistance. Learning English, learning to speak the alien tongue, was one way enslaved Africans began to reclaim their personal power within a context of domination. Possessing a shared language, black folks could find again a way to make community, and a means to create the political solidarity necessary to resist.

Needing the oppressor's language to speak with one another they nevertheless also reinvented, remade that language so that it would speak beyond the boundaries of conquest and domination. In the mouths of black Africans in the so-called New World, English was altered, transformed, and became a different speech. Enslaved black people took broken bits of English and made of them a counterlanguage. They put together their words in such a way that the colonizer had to rethink the meaning of the English language. Though it has become common in contemporary culture to talk about the messages of resistance that emerged in the music created by slaves, particularly spirituals, less is said about the grammatical construction of sentences in these songs. Often, the English used in the song reflected the broken, ruptured world of the slave. When the slaves sang "nobody knows de trouble I see —" their use of the word "nobody" adds a richer meaning than if they had used the phrase "no one," for it was the slave's *body* that was the concrete site of suffering. And even as emancipated black people sang spirituals, they did not change the language, the sentence structure, of our ancestors. For in the incorrect usage of words, in the incorrect placement of words, was a spirit of rebellion that claimed language as a site of resistance. Using English in a way that ruptured standard usage and meaning, so that white folks could often not understand black speech, made English into more than the oppressor's language.

An unbroken connection exists between the broken English of the displaced, enslaved African and the diverse black vernacular speech black folks use today. In both cases, the rupture of standard English enabled and enables rebellion and resistance. By transforming the oppressor's language, making a culture of resistance, black people created an intimate speech that could say far more than was permissible within the boundaries of standard English. The power of this speech is **Words impose themselves, take root in our memory against our will.** not simply that it enables resistance to white supremacy, but that it also forges a space for alternative cultural production and alternative epistemologies—different ways of thinking and knowing that were crucial to creating a counterhegemonic worldview. It is absolutely essential that the revolutionary power of black vernacular speech not be lost in contemporary culture. That power resides in the capacity of black vernacular to intervene on the boundaries and limitation of standard English.

In contemporary black popular culture, rap music has become one of the spaces where black vernacular speech is used in a manner that invites dominant mainstream culture to listen—to hear—and, to some extent, be transformed. However, one of the risks of this attempt at cultural translation is that it will trivialize black vernacular speech. When young white kids imitate this speech in ways that suggest it is the speech of those who are stupid or who are only interested in entertaining or being funny, then the subversive power of speech is undermined. In academic circles, both in the sphere of teaching and that of writing, there has been little effort made to utilize black vernacular—or, for that matter, any language other than standard English. When I asked an ethnically diverse group of students in a course I was teaching on black women writers why we only hear standard English spoken in the classroom, they were momentarily rendered speechless. Though many of them were individuals for whom standard English was a second or third language, it had simply never occurred to them that it was possible to say something in another language, in another way. No wonder, then, that we continue to think "This is the oppressor's language yet I need it to talk to you."

I have realized that I was in danger of losing my relationship to black vernacular speech because I too rarely use it in the predominantly white settings that I am most often in, both professionally and socially. And so I have begun to work at integrating into a variety of settings the particular Southern black vernacular speech I grew up hearing and speaking. It has been hardest to integrate black vernacular in writing, particularly for academic journals. When I first began to incorporate black vernacular in critical essays, editors would send the work back to me in standard English. Using the vernacular means that translation into standard English may be needed if one wishes to reach a more inclusive audience. In the classroom setting, I encourage students to use their first language and translate it so they do not feel that seeking higher education will necessarily estrange them from that language and culture they know most intimately. Not surprisingly, when students in my Black Women Writers class began to speak using diverse language and speech, white students often complained. This seemed to be particularly the case with black vernacular. It was particularly disturbing to the white students because they could hear the words that were said but could not comprehend their meaning. Pedagogically, I encouraged them to think of the moment of not understanding what someone says as a space to learn. Such a space provides not only the opportunity to listen without "mastery," without owning or possessing speech through interpretation, but also the experience of hearing non-English words. These lessons seem particularly crucial in a multicultural society that remains white supremacist, that uses standard English as a weapon to silence and censor. June Jordan reminds us of this in *On Call* when she declares:

> I am talking about majority problems of language in a democratic state, problems of a currency that someone has stolen and hidden away and then homogenized into an official "English" language that can only express non-events involving nobody responsible, or lies. If we lived in a democratic state our language would have to hurtle, fly, curse, and sing, in all the common American names, all the undeniable and representative participating voices of everybody here. We would not tolerate the language of the powerful and, thereby, lose all respect for words, per se. We would make our language conform to the truth of our many selves and we would make our language lead us into the equality of power that a democratic state must represent.

That the students in the course on black women writers were repressing all longing to speak in tongues other than standard English without seeing this repression as political was an indication of the way we act unconsciously, in complicity with a culture of domination.

Recent discussions of diversity and multiculturalism tend to downplay or   10
ignore the question of language. Critical feminist writings focused on issues of difference and voice have made important theoretical interventions, calling

for a recognition of the primacy of voices that are often silenced, censored, or marginalized. This call for the acknowledgment and celebration of diverse voices, and consequently of diverse language and speech, necessarily disrupts the primacy of standard English. When advocates of feminism first spoke about the desire for diverse participation in women's movement, there was no discussion of language. It was simply assumed that standard English would remain the primary vehicle for the transmission of feminist thought. Now that the audience for feminist writing and speaking has become more diverse, it is evident that we must change conventional ways of thinking about language, creating spaces where diverse voices can speak in words other than English or in broken, vernacular speech. This means that at a lecture or even in a written work there will be fragments of speech that may or may not be accessible to every individual. Shifting how we think about language and how we use it necessarily alters how we know what we know. At a lecture where I might use Southern black vernacular, the particular patois of my region, or where I might use very abstract thought in conjuction with plain speech, responding to a diverse audience, I suggest that we do not necessarily need to hear and know what is stated in its entirety, that we do not need to "master" or conquer the narrative as a whole, that we may know in fragments. I suggest that we may learn from spaces of silence as well as spaces of speech, that in the patient act of listening to another tongue we may subvert that culture of capitalist frenzy and consumption that demands all desire must be satisfied immediately, or we may disrupt that cultural imperialism that suggests one is worthy of being heard only if one speaks in standard English.

Adrienne Rich concludes her poem with this statement:

> I am composing on the typewriter late at night, thinking of today. How well we all spoke. A language is a map of our failures. Frederick Douglass wrote an English purer than Milton's. People suffer highly in poverty. There are methods but we do not use them. Joan, who could not read, spoke some peasant form of French. Some of the sufferings are: It is hard to tell the truth; this is America; I cannot touch you now. In America we have only the present tense. I am in danger. You are in danger. The burning of a book arouses no sensation in me. I know it hurts to burn. There are flames of napalm in Cantonsville, Maryland. I know it hurts to burn. The typewriter is overheated, my mouth is burning, I cannot touch you and this is the oppressor's language.

To recognize that we touch one another in language seems particularly difficult in a society that would have us believe that there is no dignity in the experience of passion, that to feel deeply is to be inferior, for within the dualism of Western metaphysical thought, ideas are always more important than language. To heal the splitting of mind and body, we marginalized and oppressed people attempt to recover ourselves and our experiences in language. We seek to make a place for the intimacy. Unable to find such a place in standard English, we create the ruptured, broken, unruly speech of the vernacular. When I need to say words that do more than simply mirror or address the dominant reality, I speak black vernacular. There, in that location, we make English do what we want it to do. We take the oppressor's language and turn it against itself. We make our words a counterhegemonic speech, liberating ourselves in language.

Working with the Text

1. "Teaching New Worlds/New Words" is a meditation on a line from an Adrienne Rich poem: "This is the oppressor's language yet I need it to talk to you." Write a short essay in which you reflect on hooks's interpretation of this line. Why does bell hooks believe that the speakers of standard English are "oppressors"? Who needs to use the oppressor's language, and why? How do they use it?

2. In her description of ways slaves restructured standard English to reflect their own experience, hooks points out that "it was the slave's *body* that was the concrete site of suffering" (par. 5). As you reread the essay, imagine what is happening to and inside of the bodies of Africans as they are brought to a strange land where their language is nullified. Consider the senses—especially hearing—and the sensations of emotion as well as the effects of physical force. In a brief essay, reflect on the relationship between language and the body for people who find themselves in what hooks calls "this terror." As an alternative to a reflective essay, you might write a short narrative or descriptive essay in which you re-create a scene—using people, places, and actions—to make concrete the experience of either being threatened by a dominant language or using that language as a tool of resistance.

3. Reread hooks's description of her classroom, imagining yourself in it. Write a brief essay that analyzes hooks's approach from your perspective as a student. What, exactly, would she be asking you to do? How would you respond? How might you use your own language—a language other than the English typically spoken in the undergraduate classroom? How would you react to other students using a language you didn't understand?

From Text to Field

1. As hooks moves from the origins of black English to the current "power of this speech," she insists that it is "absolutely essential that the revolutionary power

of black vernacular speech not be lost in contemporary culture" (par. 6). Write an essay that explores the current relationship between black vernacular speech and mainstream culture. Consider ways in which black English has been appropriated by or adopted by that culture. In what ways does black English influence mainstream culture? Does it wield power or provoke resistance? Does it get "lost in contemporary culture"?

2. In commenting on rap music, hooks warns that "one of the risks of this attempt at cultural translation is that it will trivialize black vernacular speech" (par. 7). As you reread this passage, think about this "risk" in terms of the larger concerns that drive the essay. In a brief essay, explore and respond to her concerns about rap music. What actions and attitudes is she referring to? Do you agree with her point of view? How do you respond to rappers and rap music, especially the words? What kinds of attitudes toward rap music and black rappers have you encountered in other people?

3. Although Ebonics—a term for African American language or black English vernacular—has been recognized by language scholars as a legitimate language or dialect, its use, especially in the public school system, remains controversial. If you have not directly encountered this controversy in the schools you have attended, you have probably heard the public debate. Similar debates surround any form of bilingual education. In light of hooks's argument, write an essay in which you argue for or against drawing on languages other than standard English in either the public school or undergraduate classroom. If you have encountered this in your own school system, you may wish to incorporate that experience.

4. Near the end of the essay, hooks makes the following appeal: "I suggest that we may learn from spaces of silence as well as spaces of speech, that in the patient act of listening to another tongue we may subvert that culture of capitalist frenzy and consumption that demands all desire must be satisfied immediately, or we may disrupt that cultural imperialism that suggests one is worthy of being heard only if one speaks in standard English" (par. 10). Write an essay in which you translate this passage into more concrete terms by interpreting her meaning, responding to that meaning, and offering a course of action. What actions, attitudes, and experiences is she calling into question? What, more specifically, is she asking her audience to do? Do you agree with her? If so, how would you carry out her vision? If not, what counter or alternative vision would you offer, and to what end?

5. In her closing paragraph, hooks claims that "[t]o heal the splitting of mind and body, we marginalized and oppressed people attempt to recover ourselves and our experiences in language" (par. 12). Consider the extent to which you have felt "marginalized" or "oppressed," even in a limited way or

in an isolated incident, as an outsider whose sense of self was somehow lost, diminished, or silenced. Write an essay in which you explore the use of language to "recover" yourself. Consider how hooks uses language in her essay to capture the lived experience of people whose experiences were discounted or hidden.

Where Is the Classroom?

Charles Bazerman

We tend to think of "genre" as a form of writing, such as a business proposal, a newspaper editorial, or a novel or poem. Yet the outer or surface form of language only begins to explain the power of genre in language and in our lives. Classrooms, you may be surprised to learn, can also be thought of as genres. Charles Bazerman, along with other rhetoricians, conceives of genre in light of an "activity system"—ways of acting and using language that are based on the challenges or demands of a recurrent situation. Such activities can then often become regularized and controlled by institutions. As you know through your own experience, classrooms as situations occur again and again, and the language practices that go on inside of classrooms have themselves become conventional and typified. With this "activity theory" in mind, we can begin to appreciate Bazerman's claim that "the classroom is always invented, always constructed, always a matter of genre." Classrooms are themselves genres in that they represent typified rhetorical actions in a recurrent situation. The shape of the classroom also emerges from the genres we bring into it, genres that capture institutional and departmental expectations as well as the experience and perspectives of teachers and students.

As professor of English and education at the University of California, Santa Barbara, Bazerman has gained prominence through his work in rhetoric, especially the rhetoric of science and technology. His book *Shaping Written Knowledge: The Genre and Activity of the Experimental Article in Science* (1988) won wide recognition, including awards from the American Medical Writers' Association and the National Council of Teachers of English. His textbooks include *Involved: Writing for College, Writing for Yourself* (1997) and *The Informed Writer* (1995), now in its fifth edition. His recent book, *The Languages of Edison's Light* (1999), examines the rhetorical and representational work that made Edison's incandescent light a social reality.

Whatever subject we teach, it is easy—too easy—to imagine that the classroom is simply the place where we transmit our subject to students. So then the job of the teacher—who is already presumed competent in the subject—is to figure out how to package and present the information to the students and how to structure assignments and activities so that students gain mastery of the subject matter and skills rapidly and deeply. All the rest of the universe, in which this moment hangs suspended, as the Earth in Milton's cosmos, is taken as a given not to be troubled over—unless one were a social critic who saw in the classroom the consequences and/or reproduction of those inequities, irrationalities, or cruelties that haunt our entire socioeconomic-political arrangements.

Even with the great experimentation in the teaching of writing during the last two decades, the givenness of the classroom is still taken for granted. Much of the work in our field has been to make explicit and consensually validated those aspects of the writing competence which we as literate people know as a practical matter, and to add to that new practical insights. Other parts of the professional work have been to develop and test new methods and materials for transmitting that competence. On the other hand, our insights into the competence and into ways of reorganizing the classroom in order to share that competence with students, very early upset our traditional notions of what can or should happen in this standard modular unit of the classroom. The centrality to writing of the students' processes, motives, and messages removed the teacher from the lectern and handed important aspects of authority over to the students—no matter which of the many varieties of writing pedagogy one pursued.

Once this first move in the disruption of the traditional classroom order was taken, it was not surprising (in the usual hyperbole of social movements) that many took this as a fully radical commitment. The traditional classroom, which we had to readjust for our needs, became the oppressor of all education and individual growth. We wanted to reinvent the university on our model. And some very useful achievements have indeed been gained on this front, although overall they have been much more modest (and much more integrated into the continuing practices of other disciplines) than our field's visionary gleam had hoped for.

Whatever effects process and empowerment pedagogies have had on the classroom, what we have learned about writing should make us consider more fundamentally the social-psychological-political-intellectual location of the classroom. We have always known that writing was a social act, but in recent years we have begun to examine more energetically the implications of that for anatomizing the social location, dynamics, and activity of each instance of writing. We have started to see how the classroom is a particular scene of writing—neither an innately natural nor an innately artificial scene;

neither necessarily an oppressive nor necessarily a liberating scene; just a scene of writing. The classroom is not even one particular fixed scene, but many scenes—the scenes as we make them from our own particular circumstances and desires. Each of those scenes sets in motion expectancies of role and behavior as well as possibilities for statement and action. Each of those scenes suggest genres of communication, genres of ways of being in that setting.

So the issue is no longer what is right or wrong in the classroom so that it must therefore be reinvented, but rather that the classroom is always invented, always constructed, always a matter of genre; therefore, no matter what choices we make, we are always better off to be aware of the materials out of which it is constructed and the spaces for communication created in the design. Then we can know our options, possibilities, and responsibilities as well as the compelling forces that we may be foolish to resist. Architecture must know its landscapes, even if it wants to call attention to its own difference.

The writing classroom is a complex forum. First it is encased in institutional beliefs that we will put students in proper shape for other teachers and will preserve the school from damaging embarrassment as we send our products out into the world. These imperatives are realized in requirements that mandate our courses and bring students unwillingly, but usually compliantly, into our domain. These beliefs are the source of our budget and our jobs, as much as we may rebel against an implied crudeness of understanding of writing that seems mandated by the bureaucracy and finances of public educational institutions. These institutional dynamics are realized through genres of testing and standards, curriculum guidelines and goals, policies and record keeping. There are genres that flow from the surrounding institutions into the classroom to regulate it; there are genres within the classroom that carry out the mandate of the regulation; and there are genres that flow out from the classroom that represent the work and competence of teacher and student, thereby holding them accountable to institutional expectations.

It is our choice whether these definitions of the classroom and the genres which act out these definitions are wholeheartedly accepted, wholeheartedly resisted, compromised with, or sublated into some fuller understanding of our tasks. Whichever choice we make we must consider the prices and responsibilities of our institutional places. Classrooms and hours and available (or unavailable) equipment are perhaps the most concrete manifestation of institutional shaping of the classroom, but we must also keep in mind such union issues as pay, workload, and status that shape the teacher's professional role, commitment, and life circumstances—all of which define limits to the teacher's involvement in the classroom and institution. All these concrete architectural features of the educational landscape are in turn influenced by institutional evaluation of the results of the classroom activity, as revealed in the genres of reporting and accountability that represent the results of the classroom to the wider world.

The institutional framework is given a constraining interpretation by the department's definition in the sequence, levels, and goals of courses, perhaps reinforced by syllabi, textbook lists, and departmental exams as well as by its hiring and course assignment policies. Departments create their own regulatory and coordinating genres. They then enact within various degrees of freedom, enforcement, and evasion the lives defined by those documents and utterances. Individual teachers comprise the department and have some say in setting the constraints, but the political process usually makes the result quite different from any one teacher's direct perception of what the class ought to be. On the other hand, teachers of various seniority and/or independence of spirit can expand the bounds of these departmental interpretations as far as local administrative oversight or negligence allows. Nonetheless, concerns for our own students' ability to proceed smoothly through the departmental offerings and the university maze, as well as a spirit of cooperation with our colleagues in the educational enterprise, may rein in our individual gallops after our own perceived ideal forms.

The next level, the one most professional discussions are aimed at, is the teacher's imaginative construct of the meaning of the course, which the teacher then realizes in a structure of relationships, activities, and materials that create the opportunities for the students' experience in the course. The teacher's construction of what is appropriate to the course also frames the teacher's response to the students' responses to the classroom. Given the usual definition of our professional task as increasing students' competence in written language, one would at first imagine that the teacher's imaginative construct would be built on that goal. However, accepting that definition in itself implies cooperation with various perceived social structures, and may become a point of contention for a number of teachers. Further, there may be a great range of ideas as to what comprises competence in written language and how one attains it.

The classroom is always invented, always constructed.

Most curriculum debates center on such issues as whether competence consists of mastery of the code, particular styles of personal communication, familiarity with self-discovery or other inventional procedures, self-conscious use of revision and editing procedures, rhetorical awareness of audience, or familiarity with selected genres. This professional debate carried out in the genres of professional journals, personal credos, and coffee-room discussion itself provides a frame for each teacher's conceptualizing of the classroom. How the teacher then conceives the classroom will influence the genres within which the teacher communicates to the students, the genres of materials and readings the teacher will bring into the classroom, and the written and spoken genres the teacher will elicit and welcome from the students.

The teacher's role in defining the dynamic of the classroom is realized not just through intellectual commitments and conscious choices, but also through the personal history that shapes the personality and competences and attitudes of the person who walks in front of the classroom. The teacher's history of participation in different situations and developing skill in and affinity towards those genres through which that participation is realized, prepares and predisposes the teacher to act in ways that have already proved personally successful. What competences the teacher has most to offer, what interactional skills the teacher can draw on, what habitual persona and behavior and reactional styles the teacher enacts—these all produce classroom environments and events almost beyond the control of conscious thought, although they may all be open to reflection and change.

Then there are the students' definitions of the situation and of themselves within the situation. Their understanding of where they are headed, where they are coming from, and how much they may bring their historical selves and desires into the classroom shape what the students make of the classroom and of the demands and opportunities presented to them by the teacher. Who do they perceive themselves to be and what are their prior experiences of writing? In what specific ways is the learning of writing rewarding or aversive to them? What are their motivations for being in college and how do these motives translate into their writing attitude in the classroom? What futures do they imagine for themselves and what college curricula stand between them and their goals? Where does writing enter into their actual academic and career goals as well as their imagined paths? How do they perceive teachers and or classmates as potential audiences for their communications? What subjects are compelling for them to communicate about and what are alienating? What underlying needs do they have which may be channeled through their writing? Many other psychological, social, economic, industrial, experiential, behavioral, self-presentational, and even spiritual issues enter into what these complex individuals bring with them into the classroom, what they expect of writing, and how they respond to the curious communicative world the classroom offers them. From the perspective of genre, the students' histories provide the genres that they carry with them into the classroom, their perception of how those forms of communicative participation may or may not be revealed in the classroom and with what encoding and transformation, and how they respond to the generic expectations the teacher builds into the dynamics of the classroom.

It is within the students, of course, that the learning occurs, but it is within the teacher, who sits at the juncture of forces above and below and sideways, that the learning situations are framed. It is in the intersection of all the forces that the classroom occurs. Teachers may try to simplify radically the forces through one or another pedagogical theory or commitment, very often some formal textualized reduction, requiring student enactment of well-defined genres, clearly distinct from the genres that come from outside the classroom. Students will often play along with reductionist strategies of classroom organization because of their own priorities and habits in dealing with bureaucratic institutions. Some simply want to get along institutionally and have learned how. Others perceive that learning grammar or spelling or the five-paragraph essay will serve them well. Others, however, may get lost because the reduction eliminates some important element that might link them more closely into the dynamics of written communication. In some cases formal textualized reduction is a useful and valid and successful thing to do.

On the other hand, teachers may attempt to bring a wider array of forces to play, even though every class is necessarily a reduction—an elimination of unrealized alternatives and underlying dynamics not attended to. Teachers can attempt to let in more of the students' past, future, current reality, or imaginative and emotional privacies. Teachers can look more to institutional and social forms that surround the students' lives and in which they participate; classroom work may be built around the genres of the workplace, journalism, the media, or political participation. Teachers may make much of the dyadic relationship between teacher/student, author/audience, master/apprentice, calling upon both the students' prior experience and interior life; intimate genres of journal, dialogue, personal narrative, and contemplation are given prominence. Or the teacher may constitute the entire class as a sociocommunitive microcosm, perhaps relying on genres of argument, suggesting either seminar room or public debate. Or the teacher may seek to place the students in direct contact with larger networks of communication, writing articles for the local newspaper, proposals for the reformation of campus life, or reports for their current employers.

Since writing is no single thing, but is the textual realization of a wide range of human interactions, one cannot say a priori that any particular path is the one proper path to writing, or that any particular genre ought to be practiced in the writing class. Writing will occur in a great variety of situations. The teacher has wide authority to attempt to select and rearrange the various forces around the classroom to create the character of the particular forum that the class will become, but then the classroom becomes the result of the forces that come to play within the forum. Thus the determination of how to teach writing is a matter of social-ethical choice, but the actual events of the classroom and the learning are dynamic products of interaction beyond any individual's control.

As I mentally review the many writing courses I have taught, the frame-   15
work I have just proposed helps me make sense of the eclecticism which not

only makes every class session a heterogeneous experience, but accounts for the great differences in the ways in which I have approached one course or group of students versus another course or group. Through a seat-of-the-pants estimate of the needs and possibilities and goals of each circumstance, I have located each course differently, enacting my teaching in different genres, bringing in different genres for student consideration, and presenting through assignment genres, differing communicative opportunities and challenges for students to realize their presence in the classroom forum. Within the complex multidimensional matrix of writing, I have tried to find different placements for the classroom, so that the unfolding drama of each term will take us all in the classroom to places we are satisfied with. Each term is a strange interactional journey, which my choices may frame—with bad choices leading to sterile landscapes and more fortunate choices tapping into important and vital communicative dynamics for this class at this time. But once the dynamics begin to unfold, the best I can do is watch where they are taking us, so that I can improvise most appropriately and creatively to allow these dynamics to fulfill themselves. Only then will the deepest and most useful practice of writing emerge.

Working with the Text

1. The term *genre* is key to Charles Bazerman's analysis of the writing classroom. In a brief essay, analyze how Bazerman uses the notion of genre to answer the question, "Where is the classroom?" In what ways is the classroom recurrent as a situation? What typified actions result from that recurrent situation? How are those actions influenced by the histories of classroom writing that teachers and students bring with them? In what ways is the title that Bazerman chose for the essay a tip-off that the classroom is not just one physical spot?

2. Within Bazerman's framework, the teacher "sits at the juncture" of the forces that determine the "learning situations" for students (par. 12). Within this framework, students themselves bring many of those forces into play. Write an essay in which you use Bazerman's framework to explore what he would consider to be a productive relationship between student and teacher. How is this relationship affected by the ways in which you as a student sit at the juncture of different forces, including not only the teacher but also your parents, the institution, and the world of work beyond the university?

3. Institutional or departmental forces that influence the structure of a writing course are often invisible to students. In a brief essay, reflect on the institutional/departmental forces that are beyond a teacher's control. Study those forces, as noted by Bazerman, and, from your own experience, consider what effect they might have on the shape and nature of the course.

From Text to Field

1. Select any one of the forces noted by Bazerman, and write a brief essay in which you imagine in greater detail the effect it might have on the course and classroom teaching.

2. Starting with the sentence "Then there are the students' definitions of the situation and of themselves within the situation" (par. 11), Bazerman devotes an extensive paragraph to the factors students contribute to the shaping of a writing course. Based on the statements and questions in this paragraph—up to the sentence that ends, "how they respond to the curious communicative world the classroom offers them"—write a personal essay in which you provide a profile of yourself as a writing student.

3. In his discussion of the forces students bring with them, Bazerman notes, "From the perspective of genre, the students' histories provide the genres that they carry with them into the classroom . . ." (par. 11). In an essay, identify the genres you carry into the classroom and analyze how those genres influence your expectations for a writing course. What elements from your histories in other classrooms—assignments, kinds of writing produced, approaches to learning, the relationships among students and teacher—do you expect to find in the writing classroom? What genres of writing do you bring from your personal life? How do they affect how you respond to the genres required in a classroom? What genres do you expect to be required of you in the workplace after college, and how do those expectations shape what you are looking for in a writing course?

4. In the paragraph that begins, "On the other hand, teachers may attempt to bring a wider array of forces to play" (par. 13), Bazerman suggests the range of choices left to the teacher in structuring a writing course. Using this paragraph as a prompt, construct your ideal writing course. Explain the reasoning behind your choices.

5. Based on the syllabus, your knowledge of your college's or university's writing requirement, and your experience in the classroom so far, write an essay in which you analyze your writing course. What specific forces have shaped which elements of the course? What choices has the teacher made, and why? What constraints must the teacher work with?

6. Bazerman's essay is written for other teachers. Write a companion piece addressed to other students just entering the university that translates Bazerman's argument into terms that will help them understand and enter into the undergraduate classroom.

INTO THE FIELD: Options for Writing Projects

1. What's in a Syllabus?

Sharon Rubin regards the course syllabus as an important vehicle for conveying the substance of the course to students. A number of the authors in Chapter 2, in particular Charles Bazerman, discuss the wide range of values and perspectives that teachers bring into the university classroom. To explore what a syllabus might be able to tell you about the values and perspectives of a course, write an analysis based on one of the following options.

- Choose a particular syllabus, or a set of syllabi, from your own or other recent university courses. Imagine you are a researcher from another planet who has stumbled upon this syllabus. Develop a description of this alien academic culture based on your interpretation of the syllabus. What inferences can you make about what is taught and why? How does a syllabus construct not just the course but also an image of its students? How does a syllabus position a student with respect to the course material, the professor, and peers?
- Identify a course that is taught by different professors within the same department or is shared and taught by different departments. Assuming that they do not use one required generic syllabus, contrast how the course is taught on the basis of the syllabus produced by each professor. What can you infer about the values and perspectives of each teacher? How does each teacher regard students and the learning process?
- Through a department secretary or a professor who has been in the department for a number of years, find a syllabus or syllabi from earlier decades. For example, for an American history or introduction to psychology course, compare syllabi from the 1950s, the 1970s, and today. What texts and other materials were included? What modes of learning—such as lectures, discussion, research papers, field projects—were being used? What were the primary texts? What were the secondary, critical texts? How was learning tested and evaluated? Based on the evidence, what can you infer about trends in interpretation or theory and/or in attitudes toward teaching?

2. Angels on a Pin

The fact that Alexander Calandra's barometer story has been so widely circulated for several decades indicates that his critique of teaching continues to strike an important chord. To understand Calandra's critique more fully, do some detective work, keeping in mind that he won a prestigious teaching award from the American Association of Physics Teachers. Research the teaching methods mentioned in the final paragraph of "Angels on a Pin"—the "scientific method," the "new mathematics," and scholasticism. Find out more about the medieval argument over how many angels could stand on the head of a pin. What educational philosophies might lie behind Calandra's dislike of "pedantry"? What do these external sources add to your understanding of Calandra's critique of teaching? What approach does he advocate instead? As part of your analysis, you might consider why the final paragraph was added to the version published for a more general audience.

3. **Technology and the Teaching of Science**

Alexander Calandra's critique of science education was made just as the space race of the 1960s was heating up, a time when technologies such as the computer and the Internet had yet to have an impact on the classroom. Given the growing use of new technologies in science education, such as computer simulations and interactive computer software, does Calandra's critique of science education still hold? Draw on your own experience in college science classes or in science classes in senior high school. One option for this project would be to write an update of Calandra's essay for the new millennium. Another option would be to explore what developments have occurred in science education in the last few years and to consider whether they would meet with Calandra's approval.

4. **The General-Education Curriculum**

Gerald Graff complains that in the typical undergraduate curriculum, courses have little connection to one another. In other words, the college curriculum is often an à la carte menu or a cafeteria. The criticism might apply most directly to the set of general education requirements that most colleges and universities expect students to fulfill during their first years of higher education. Familiarize yourself with the "gen.-ed." requirements on your campus, and with documents (catalogs, Web sites, advisement materials) that might explain or justify those requirements. Write an essay in which you identify and explore the educational assumptions and philosophy that might lie behind those requirements. Ask your instructor or advisor if the general-education requirements have changed on your campus during the last several decades. If so, what controversies or shifts in educational philosophy might have prompted the change? Likewise, ask whether your campus is currently rethinking its requirements. If so, what problems or dissatisfactions seem to be motivating the discussion, and what educational vision lies behind any proposed changes?

5. **Curricular Linkages**

In an effort to forge connections between otherwise discrete courses and educational experiences, many colleges and universities have instituted programs that seek to build links between both courses and the students who take them. Explore what programs your campus has in place, choose one, and evaluate its effectiveness in creating more cohesion both in the curriculum and in students' educational experience.

Here are just some of the kinds of programs that might be present on your campus. You may be able to uncover interesting programs not mentioned that also try to create linkages between otherwise separate course experiences.

- programs that link a set of courses or a group of students together so that a group of students take courses together
- residential academic programs, which offer courses in or through the dorms in ways that connect academics with residential life
- honors programs that might offer a curricular program and a sense of community that might link students' efforts in various courses
- bridge programs that seek to help minority or first-generation students adjust to what might be an unfamiliar academic culture
- programs that ask all entering students to read the same book over the summer, which might then inform discussion in a variety of classes
- freshman seminars that offer small-class experiences, often on interdisciplinary topics

6. Ebonics and Students' Right to Their Own Language

In her essay, bell hooks refers to the thwarted "longing to speak in tongues other than standard English" as "repression," repression that is "political." Her argument brings the past into the present. Today, the politics of language is a critical issue in the American educational system, from elementary schools through undergraduate and graduate education. Two professional organizations have taken strong stances on this issue, the National Council of Teachers of English (NCTE) and the Conference on College Composition and Communication (CCCC). Check the following Web sites to review their positions:

- "Statement on Ebonics," NCTE Positions and Guidelines, http://www.ncte .org/about/over/positions/level/gen/107644.htm
- "Students' Right to Their Own Language," CCCC Position Statements, http://www.ncte.org/about/over/positions/category/div/114918.htm

Drawing on these two position statements, choose one of the following projects.

- Based on your own background or research into an Ebonics or a bilingual program you identify, describe a program that successfully embodies the principles of the CCCC and the NCTE. Conversely, describe a program that falls short of those principles. As part of your description, analyze how the elements of the program work. What are the results for students? What is the perspective of the teachers and the administration? How does the public view the program?

- The NCTE "Statement on Ebonics" notes that "[n]ews media reports and commentaries regarding the recent Ebonics controversy have been, for the most part, incomplete, uninformed, and in some cases, purposefully distorted." Identify reports and commentaries in the mass media that reflect negatively on the use of Ebonics in the public school system. Compare the media reports to the analysis you find through professional organizations such as NCTE or CCCC. If possible, interview an expert on Ebonics or on bilingual education. What are the differences between the perspectives of the media and the language and education professionals? How do you account for those differences?

- As you think through the position statements, note your own questions about the uses of languages other than "standard English" in educational programs. Pursue answers to your key questions through research or interviews. Consider your own experience. On the basis of your reading of the professional position statements as well as your research and experience, write a position statement or a persuasive essay in which you argue for or against the use of languages other than "standard English." As an alternative writing project, develop your own recommendations for how those languages can be most effectively used in educational programs.

7. Classroom Spaces

This project asks you to consider classrooms closely, in very concrete terms. Choose a classroom in which you have a course, or several classrooms in which you have courses from different disciplines. Write a report in which you attend closely to the connection between classroom spaces and teaching.

Here are some questions to get you started: How is the classroom designed? How are the seats located, and what kind of interaction or rearrangement do the seats permit? How is "power" situated in the classroom? What are the material conditions of the classroom (blackboard, AV equipment, computer and Internet access), and how are they employed (or not employed)?

Using these questions as a point of departure, what does a particular classroom space imply about the teaching and learning that occurs there? What role, if any, does technology have in that classroom space, and in what ways does it support (or interfere with) the teaching and learning that occurs in that space? How would you reinvent the classroom space to better suit the objectives of the course? How might a classroom space reflect the particular goals or culture of a discipline? If your campus has remodeled or renovated classrooms recently, what advances or changes do you see over older or more traditional classrooms? Apart from newer chairs and better lighting, has there really been much change from older classrooms?

8. Writing the Writing Classroom

This project asks you to develop a set of "field notes" that you can then use to analyze how your writing classroom is constructed (both physically and through discourse). A good place to start is to attend closely to what happens in your writing class. How is space deployed and used? How do you interact with your teacher and with your peers? How is writing produced and consumed in and for the classroom? Based on these and a host of similar questions, develop an essay that "writes" the writing classroom. How and why does the writing classroom differ from other classrooms? How does the use of physical space, texts, conversation, and personal interaction contribute to that difference? Might there be the occasional incongruity or contradiction between the goals for the course and its institutional setting?

9. The Alternative Classroom

Although traditional classrooms continue to exert enormous influence on how you and others think of your college education, a number of alternatives to and extensions of that traditional classroom have now come into play. This project encourages you to explore an alternative classroom, if you have experienced one, and to consider what influence the traditional and the alternative classroom might have on each other. Does the traditional classroom continue to influence even the most alternative classes? And in what ways might an alternative classroom initiate new ways of thinking about traditional classrooms? In what ways do "traditional" and "alternative" classrooms presuppose one another?

The following is a modest and very incomplete list of alternative classroom experiences that you might find on your own campus.

- online classes
- distance education courses (televised)
- hybrid classes (some time spent online, some time spent in traditional classrooms)
- wired classrooms that extend the reach and resources of the traditional blackboard-and-chalk classroom
- fieldwork classes
- studio classes
- service-learning classes that use service as a means for reflection and learning

To this list one might also wish to add more traditional alternatives to the regular classroom, such as "recitation sections" attached to large lecture courses and "labs" that often accompany courses in the sciences.

Choose one such alternative classroom with which you are familiar, and explore the continuing shadow that is cast by traditional classrooms. Likewise, consider the many ways in which both teacher and learner have to refashion themselves in these new classroom environments. What might make these new environments more interesting, fun, challenging, or frustrating?

10. Discourse in the Classroom

When we think about how classrooms are constructed, we might first think of bricks and mortar, seats and blackboards. But classrooms are also constructed, perhaps most fundamentally constructed, through language. This project has you look at classrooms through the lens of discourse.

Your materials for this project can be found in the very concrete (and sometimes seemingly ordinary) uses of language in a particular classroom. It could be your very own writing classroom or any classes you are currently taking. Think about the texts you read and the texts you write. Think about the conversations and discussions you have in class and about what kind of turn taking occurs in those discussions. Think about who holds the floor and who might be silent (or silenced). What literacy practices and behaviors are in play—everything from the use of overheads and PowerPoint to your own note taking. In other words, think about the class period itself as a kind of text.

Based on your fieldwork over several class periods, write an essay about discourse in the classroom. You'll want to look beyond the immediate and obvious use of language (what is said about the subject matter) and focus on how things are said and how discourse is used in the classroom. In what ways is the classroom, and the course itself, a function of its language? What connection might there be between that language and your own or between that language and the language of a particular discipline or area of study? Are there instances in which the discourse of the classroom presents contradictions? In what ways is your college education not just about information on certain academic subjects but also about how to use language in the academy?

WRITING THE UNIVERSITY

As you enter the university and settle into the work of the academic term, it comes as little surprise that there is plenty of writing done there. You are writing several essays or term papers for some of your courses and surely more in a writing course. Even those courses that do not require much writing in a formal sense will still expect you to write for exams and short assignments, to take notes, and to use writing in a wide range of what are called literacy practices or literate behaviors. So pervasive is writing at the university that we often use it as a measure to describe our lives: I have three papers to write in the next two weeks.

Faculty, as you might imagine, also find their lives saturated with writing. Apart from research activities that find their way into books and articles, administrative activities of one kind or another are carried out through e-mail, memos, and reports. So central is writing to a faculty member's life that the phrase "publish or perish" has become cliché. Yet we might tweak that phrase just a bit. It need not refer exclusively to a faculty member's fate come time for tenure and promotion. It also reminds us that, unless committed to the page, the best of ideas, about research or about the college or university itself, can also disappear. Writing does more than happen at a college or university. Writing is a way of sustaining the institution itself.

The title for this unit hints at this central role for writing. Every day, faculty and, yes, students themselves are writing the university. True, the influence of any one piece of writing cannot be detected, and change at the university often seems glacial in its pace. But through our words, we create—and change—the place.

Because writing, both as process and as product, shapes the essential nature of a college or university, it is hardly surprising that words provide the gate of entry to this community. As you enter the classroom, you surely are trying to write and speak in ways that identify you as a college student. Writing marks us—indicating whether we have become the experts we hope to be or the novices that all of us, in one respect or another, will surely remain. How and what we read, and how we use language in our teaching and learning, also speak volumes about how we conceive of our college or university experience. Far from being the solid, ivy-covered entities we might assume they are, colleges and universities are in some sense continually up for grabs. In our writing and reading, we always return to the question "What are universities for?"

The six readings in this unit help us reflect on the many different ways that we write the university. No immutable text with a fixed meaning, the university is always being inscribed, just as it is being read in different ways.

C. H. Knoblauch reminds us that *literacy* is a complex term, implying much more than a set of objective skills. Indeed, the various meanings of the term are driven by the ideological dispositions of those who advocate one kind of literacy or another.

David Bartholomae writes of the challenges of the first-year college student, for whom writing and language necessarily become a way of demonstrating — or carrying off the bluff — that you do in fact fit in.

Joseph Williams and Gregory G. Colomb reflect on the differences between novice and expert writing. How do we move from one to the other? They take issue with the usual metaphor, often described as an upward curve of "growth," and suggest as an alternative that we think in terms of a different metaphor — that of the outsider entering a new community.

Katha Pollitt reframes the debate about which books should be required reading and thus part of the "canon" of great works that are thought to define our education. Instead of asking "what books we want others to read," she prefers to ask "why we read books ourselves."

Distrustful of an education that simply deposits or banks information in our heads, Paulo Freire proposes a different sort of educational process, a problem-posing process, and along with it a different relationship between teacher and student.

Behind these readings lies that tough but inevitable question, "What are universities for?" Louis Menand tackles that question head-on, prompting us to explore the relationship between universities and our larger society.

Reflecting on Prior Knowledge

1. The writing and reading you did in high school and the writing and reading you now do in college carry with them certain assumptions about why literacy is important. What values or purposes lie behind your literate activities?

2. In a journal entry, recall a time when you were new to an activity but were not entirely sure of its rules or processes. How did you feel, and how did you try to learn that activity and fit in with those who did it often?

3. All of us are, to some degree or another, experts at some things and sheer novices at others. Reflect on what kind of expertise does or doesn't transfer

from one activity or domain to another. Working with a partner, draw up a list of characteristics that distinguish experts from novices.

4. The terms *required* and *enjoyable* seem to be poles apart when it comes to the books we read. In a journal entry, reflect on why this is the case. What are the agendas or reasons that distinguish the two kinds of reading? When and why might you have enjoyed required reading?

5. Although it may be tempting to assume that all teachers "dispense" knowledge that students then "store," surely you have had one or two teachers who broke that stereotype. Why was your relationship different with that teacher, and how did teaching and learning take place?

6. Working in a group, develop a list of why you and others have decided to go to college. Are there items on that list that might become more or less important under certain conditions or to various groups of people? Would this be the same list that your parents or someone of their generation might have drawn up?

Literacy and the Politics
of Education

C. H. Knoblauch

Students are often not aware that their education has been shaped by heated debates over the definition of *literacy*. What does it mean to be literate? How do we identify and teach those who are considered to be illiterate? Since C. H. Knoblauch published "Literacy and the Politics of Education" in 1990, in a collection of papers from the Modern Language Association's 1988 Right to Literacy Conference, educators as well as those being educated have increasingly challenged the politics of literacy in terms of the questions Knoblauch raised. With any given approach to literacy, whose values, interests, position, or power will be preserved or promoted, and at whose expense?

A frequent contributor to academic journals and conferences, Knoblauch has taught at Brown University, Columbia University, New York University, and the State University of New York at Albany. His books include *Functional Writing* (1978), *The Process of Writing: Discovery and Control* (1982) with A. D. Van Nostrand, and *Critical Teaching and the Idea of Literacy* (1993) with Lil Brannon. Knoblauch and Brannon are most widely known for *Rhetorical Traditions and the Teaching of Writing* (1984), which served for many as a standard text for graduate studies in the teaching of writing.

Literacy is one of those mischievous concepts, like virtuousness and craftsmanship, that appear to denote capacities but that actually convey value judgments. It is rightly viewed, Linda Brodkey has noted, "as a social trope" and its sundry definitions "as cultural Rorschachs" (47). The labels *literate* and *illiterate* almost always imply more than a degree or deficiency of skill. They are, grossly or subtly, sociocultural judgments laden with approbation, disapproval, or pity about the character and place, the worthiness and prospects, of persons and groups. A revealing exercise would be to catalog the definitions of literacy that lie explicit or implicit in the pages of this collection, definitions that motivate judgments, political no less than scholarly, about which people belong in literate and illiterate categories; the numbers in each group; why and in what ways literacy is important; what should be done for or about those who are not literate or are less literate than others; and who has the power to say so. It would be quickly apparent that there is no uniformity of view, since the values that surround reading and writing abilities differ from argument to argument. Instead, there are competing views, responsive to the agendas of those who characterize the ideal. Invariably, definitions of literacy are also rationalizations of its importance. Furthermore, they are invariably offered by the literate, constituting, therefore, implicit rationalizations of the importance of literate people, who are powerful (the reasoning goes) because they are literate and, as such, deserving of power.

The concept of literacy is embedded, then, in the ideological dispositions of those who use the concept, those who profit from it, and those who have the standing and motivation to enforce it as a social requirement. It is obviously not a cultural value in all times and places; when Sequoya brought his syllabic writing system to the Cherokee, their first inclination was to put him to death for dabbling in an evil magic. The majority of the world's languages have lacked alphabets, though they have nonetheless articulated rich oral traditions in societies that have also produced many other varieties of cultural achievement. To be sure, there is ready agreement, at least among the literate, about the necessity of literacy in the so-called modern world; this agreement is reinforced by explanations that typically imply a more developed mode of existence among literate people. I. J. Gelb has written, for instance: "As language distinguishes man from animal, so writing distinguishes civilized man from barbarian," going on to point out that "an illiterate person cannot expect to participate successfully in human progress, and what is true of individuals is also true of any group of individuals, social strata, or ethnic units" (221–22). This argument offers a common and pernicious half-truth, representing the importance of literacy, which is unquestionable, in absolutist and ethnocentric terms.

However, if literacy today is perceived as a compelling value, the reason lies not in such self-interested justifications but in its continuing association with forms of social reality that depend on its primacy. During the Middle Ages, clerks were trained to read and write so that they could keep accounts for landowners, merchants, and government officials. Bureaucratic documentation was not conceived so that people could acquire literacy. Christian missionaries in nineteenth-century Africa spread literacy so that people could read the Bible; they did not teach the Bible so that the illiterate could become readers and writers. There is no question that literacy is necessary to survival and success in the contemporary world—a world where the literate claim authority to set the terms of survival and success, a world that reading and writing abilities have significantly shaped in the first place. But it is important to regard that necessity in the context of political conditions that account for it, or else we sacrifice the humanizing understanding that life can be otherwise than the way we happen to know it and that people who are measured positively by the yardstick of literacy enjoy their privileges because of their power to choose and apply that instrument on their own behalf, not because of their point of development or other innate worthiness. Possessing that understanding, educators in particular but other citizens as well may advance their agendas for literacy with somewhat less likelihood of being blinded by the light of their own benevolence to the imperial designs that may lurk in the midst of their compassion.

In the United States today, several arguments about the nature and importance of literacy vie for power in political and educational life. Sketching the more popular arguments may remind us of the extent to which definitions of the concept incorporate the social agendas of the definers, serving the needs of the nonliterate only through the mediation of someone's vision of the way the world should be. Literacy never stands alone in these perspectives as a neutral denoting of skills; it is always literacy for something—for professional competence in a technological world, for civic responsibility and the preservation of heritage, for personal growth and self-fulfillment, for social and political change. The struggle of any one definition to dominate the others entails no merely casual or arbitrary choice of values, nor does it allow for a conflating of alternatives in some grand compromise or list of cumulative benefits. At stake are fundamentally different perceptions of social reality; the nature of language and discourse; the importance of culture, history, and tradition; the functions of schools, as well as other commitments, few of which are regarded as negotiable. At the same time, since no definition achieves transcendent authority, their dialectical interaction offers a context of choices within which continually changing educational and other social policies find their justification. The process of choosing is visible every day, for better and worse, in legislative assemblies, television talk shows, newspaper editorials, and classrooms throughout the country.

The most familiar literacy argument comes from the functionalist per-   5 spective, with its appealingly pragmatic emphasis on readying people for the necessities of daily life—writing checks, reading sets of instructions— as well as for the professional tasks of a complex technological society. Language abilities in this view are often represented by the metaphors of information theory: Language is a code that enables the sending of messages and the processing of information. The concern of a functionalist perspective is the efficient transmission of useful messages in a value-neutral medium. Basic-skill and technical-writing programs in schools, many on-the-job training programs in business and industry, and the training programs of the United States military—all typically find their rationalization in the argument for functional literacy, in each case presuming that the ultimate value of language lies in its utilitarian capacity to pass information back and forth for economic or other material gain.

The functionalist argument has the advantage of tying literacy to concrete needs, appearing to promise socioeconomic benefit to anyone who can achieve the appropriate minimal competency. But it has a more hidden advantage as well, at least from the standpoint of those whose literacy is more than minimal· It safeguards the socioeconomic status quo. Whatever the rhetoric of its advocates concerning the "self-determined objectives" (Hunter and Harman 7) of people seeking to acquire skills, functionalism serves the world as it is, inviting outsiders to enter that world on the terms of its insiders by fitting themselves to roles that they are superficially free to choose but that have been prepared as a range of acceptable alternatives.

> **Literacy is one of those mischievous concepts that appear to denote capacities but that actually convey value judgments.**

Soldiers will know how to repair an MX missile by reading the field manual but will not question the use of such weapons because of their reading of anti-militarist philosophers; clerks will be able to fill out and file their order forms but will not therefore be qualified for positions in higher management. Functionalist arguments presume that a given social order is right simply because it exists, and their advocates are content to recommend the training of persons to take narrowly beneficial places in that society. The rhetoric of technological progressivism is often leavened with a mixture of fear and patriotism (as in A *Nation at Risk*) in order to defend a social program that maintains managerial classes—whose members are always more than just functionally literate—in their customary places while outfitting workers with the minimal reading and writing skills needed for usefulness to the modern information economy.

Cultural literacy offers another common argument about the importance of reading and writing, one frequently mounted by traditionalist educators but sustained in populist versions as well, especially among people who feel insecure about their own standing and their future prospects when confronted by the volatile mix of ethnic heritages and socioeconomic interests that make up contemporary American life. The argument for cultural literacy moves beyond a mechanist conception of basic skills and toward an affirmation of supposedly stable and timeless cultural values inscribed in the verbal memory—in particular, the canonical literature of Western European socie-ty. Its reasoning is that true literacy entails more than technical proficiency, a minimal ability to make one's way in the world; that literacy also includes an awareness of cultural heritage, a capacity for higher-order thinking, even some aesthetic discernment—faculties not automatically available to the encoders and decoders of the functionalist perspective. Language is no mere tool in this view but is, rather, a repository of cultural values and to that extent a source of social cohesion. To guard the vitality of the language, the advocates of cultural literacy say, citizens must learn to speak and write deco-rously, as well as functionally, and must also read great books, where the cul-ture is enshrined. In some popular versions of cultural literacy, English is regarded as the only truly American language and is, therefore, the appro-priate medium of commerce and government. The economic self-interest that pervades the functionalist perspective frequently gives way here to jin-goistic protectionism; cultural literacy advocates presume that the salvation of some set of favored cultural norms or language practices lies necessarily in the marginalizing or even extinction of others.

The argument for cultural literacy often presents itself within a myth of the fall from grace: Language and, by extension, culture once enjoyed an Edenlike existence but are currently degenerating because of internal decay and sundry forces of barbarism. People no longer read, write, or think with the strength of insight of which they were once capable. They no longer remember and, therefore, no longer venerate. The age of high culture has passed; minds and characters have been weakened by television or rock music or the 1960s. The reasons vary, but the message is clear: Unless her-itage is protected, the former purity of language reconstituted, the past life of art and philosophy retrieved, we risk imminent cultural decay. However extravagant such predictions appear to unbelievers, there is no mistaking the melancholy energy of contemporary proponents of cultural literacy or, if we are to judge from the recent best-seller lists, the number of solemn citizens—anxious perhaps about recent influxes of Mexicans, Vietnamese, and other aliens—who take their warnings to heart.

Arguments for cultural and functional literacy plainly dominate the American imagination at the moment and for obvious reasons. They articulate the needs, hopes, anxieties, and frustrations of the conservative temper. They reveal in different ways the means of using an ideal of literacy to preserve and advance the world as it is, a world in which the interests of traditionally privi-leged groups dominate the interests of the traditionally less privileged. Schools reflect such conservatism to the extent that they view themselves as agencies for preserving established institutions and values, not to mention the hierar-chical requirements of the American economy. But still other arguments, if not quite so popular, reflect the priorities and the agendas of liberal and even radical ideologies struggling to project their altered visions of social reality, seeking their own power over others under the banner of literacy. The liberal argument, for instance, emphasizes literacy for personal growth, finding voice in the process-writing movement in American high schools or in the various practices of personalized learning. The liberal argument has been successful, up to a point, in schools because it borrows from long-hallowed American myths of expressive freedom and boundless individual opportunity, romantic values to which schools are obliged to pay at least lip service even when otherwise promoting more authoritarian curricula.

The assumption of a literacy-for-personal-growth argument is that language   10 expresses the power of the individual imagination, so that nurturing a person's reading and writing abilities enables the development of that power, thereby promoting the progress of society through the progress of the individual learner. The political agenda behind this liberalism tends to be educational and other social change; its concern for personal learning draws attention to school practices that supposedly thwart the needs of individual students or that disenfranchise some groups of students in the interest of maintaining the values of the status quo. The kinds of change that the personal-growth argument recommends are, on the whole, socially tolerable because they are moderate in character: Let students read enjoyable novels, instead of basal reader selections; let young women and young Hispanics find images of themselves in schoolwork, not just images of white males. Using the rhetoric of moral sincerity, the personal-growth argument speaks compassionately on behalf of the disadvantaged. Meanwhile, it avoids, for the most part, the suggestion of any fundamental restructuring of institutions, believing that the essential generosity and fair-mindedness of American citizens will accommodate some liberalization of outmoded curricula and an improved quality of life for the less privileged as long as fundamental political and economic interests are not jeopardized. Frequently, Americans do hear such appeals, though always in the context of an implicit agreement that nothing important is going to change. Accordingly, advocates of expressive writing, personalized reading programs, whole-language curricula, and open classrooms have been permitted to carry out their educational programs, with politicians and school officials quick to realize the ultimate gain in administrative control that comes from allowing such modest symbols of self-determination to release built-up pressures of dissatisfaction.

A fourth argument, substantially to the left of the personal-growth advocates, is one for what Henry Giroux, among others, calls critical literacy (226). Critical literacy is a radical perspective whose adherents, notably Paulo Freire, have been influential primarily in the third world, especially Latin America. Strongly influenced by Marxist philosophical premises, critical literacy is not a welcome perspective in this country, and it finds voice currently in only a few academic enclaves, where it exists more as a facsimile of oppositional culture than as a practice, and in an even smaller number of community-based literacy projects, which are typically concerned with adult learners. Its agenda is to identify reading and writing abilities with a critical consciousness of the social conditions in which people find themselves, recognizing the extent to which language practices objectify and rationalize these conditions and the extent to which people with authority to name the world dominate others whose voices they have been able to suppress. Literacy, therefore, constitutes a means to power, a way to seek political enfranchisement—not with the naive expectation that merely being literate is sufficient to change the distribution of prerogatives but with the belief that the ability to speak alone enables entrance to the arena in which power is contested. At stake, from this point of view, is, in principle, the eventual reconstituting of the class structure of American life, specifically a change of those capitalist economic practices that assist the dominance of particular groups.

For that reason, if for no other, such a view of literacy will remain suspect as a theoretical enterprise and will be considered dangerous, perhaps to the point of illegality, in proportion to its American adherents' attempts to implement it practically in schools and elsewhere. The scholarly Right has signaled this institutional hostility in aggressive attacks on Jonathan Kozol's *Illiterate America*, the most popular American rendering of critical-literacy arguments, for its supposedly inaccurate statistics about illiteracy and in calculatedly patronizing Kozol's enthusiasm for radical change. Meanwhile, although critical literacy is trendy in some academic circles, those who commend it also draw their wages from the capitalist economy it is designed to challenge. Whether its advocates will take Kozol's risks in bringing so volatile a practice into community schools is open to doubt. Whether something important would change if they did take the risks is also doubtful. Whether, if successful, they would still approve a world in which their own privileges were withheld may be more doubtful still. In any case, one can hardly imagine NCTE° or the MLA,° let alone the Department of Education, formally sanctioning such a fundamental assault on their own institutional perquisites.

Definitions of literacy could be multiplied far beyond these popular arguments. But enumerating others would only belabor my point, which is that no definition tells, with ontological or objective reliability, what literacy is; definitions only tell what some person or group—motivated by political

NCTE: National Council of Teachers of English.

MLA: Modern Language Association.

commitments—wants or needs literacy to be. What makes any such perspective powerful is the ability of its adherents to make it invisible or, at least, transparent—a window on the world, revealing simple and stable truths—so that the only problem still needing to be addressed is one of implementation: how best to make the world—other people—conform to that prevailing vision. At the same time, what makes any ideology visible as such and, therefore, properly limited in its power to compel unconscious assent is critical scrutiny, the only safeguard people have if they are to be free of the designs of others. To the extent that literacy advocates of one stripe or another remain unconscious of or too comfortable with those designs, their offerings of skills constitute a form of colonizing, a benign but no less mischievous paternalism that rationalizes the control of others by representing it as a means of liberation. To the extent that the nonliterate allow themselves to be objects of someone else's "kindness," they will find no power in literacy, however it is defined, but only altered terms of dispossession. When, for instance, the memberships of U.S. English and English First, totaling around half a million citizens, argue for compulsory English, they may well intend the enfranchisement of those whose lack of English-language abilities has depressed their economic opportunities. But they also intend the extinction of cultural values inscribed in languages other than their own and held to be worthwhile by people different from themselves. In this or any other position on literacy, its advocates, no less than its intended beneficiaries, need to hear—for all our sakes—a critique of whatever assumptions and beliefs are fueling their passionate benevolence.

Works Cited

Brodkey, Linda. "Tropics of Literacy." *Journal of Education* 168 (1986):47–54.
Commission on Excellence in Education. *A Nation at Risk: The Imperative for Educational Reform.* Washington: GPO, 1983.
Gelb, I. J. *A Study of Writing.* Chicago: U of Chicago P, 1963.
Giroux, Henry A. *Theory and Resistance in Education: A Pedagogy for the Opposition.* South Hadley: Bergin, 1983.
Hunter, Carman St. John, and David Harman. *Adult Literacy in the United States.* New York: McGraw, 1979.
Kozol, Jonathan. *Illiterate America.* New York: Anchor, 1985.

Working with the Text

1. Offer a summary of the four types of literacy that C. H. Knoblauch examines, and place them on a spectrum from most conservative to most liberal. Can you think of a fifth type of literacy? If so, where might it fall on the spectrum you have laid out?

2. According to Knoblauch, all positions on literacy must be examined in order to expose the social and cultural agendas of those who promote them. Among the positions he examines, the liberal and the critical literacy arguments both challenge the status quo by centering on the identity of the student, but they still have competing agendas. To explore the significance of differences in positions on literacy, write a brief essay in which you analyze and compare the liberal and critical literacy agendas. How is *literacy* defined? How might it be achieved? Who would benefit? What, exactly, would the benefit be? Why does Knoblauch consider critical literacy to be more radical and threatening than the liberal idea of literacy for personal growth?

3. The values behind functional and cultural literacy still drive curriculum for both public school and higher education. In a brief essay, respond to Knoblauch's charge that these two approaches to literacy "preserve and advance the world as it is, a world in which the interests of traditionally privileged groups dominate the interests of the traditionally less privileged" (par. 9).

4. In effect, Knoblauch urges anyone who has a stake in literacy—which includes all of us—to enter into "a critique of whatever assumptions and beliefs" are driving any given position on literacy. Choose one literacy argument from the essay or from your own experience as a student. With Knoblauch's argument in mind, write a brief critique of that position. What perspective do you represent? Are you an "advocate" or one of "its intended beneficiaries"? What interests you or concerns you about this position on literacy? What "assumptions and beliefs" do you want to expose or promote, and why?

From Text to Field

1. Although some educational institutions are committed to one approach to literacy, most institutions incorporate more than one into their curriculum. Drawing on Knoblauch's descriptions as well as your own awareness of the objectives of your schools, write an essay in which you describe the position or positions on literacy behind your high school and undergraduate education. Does a particular teacher or teaching technique embody the aims and agendas of that approach to literacy?

2. Students often object to or challenge the approaches to literacy they encounter in school. In an essay, describe the literacy or combination of literacies you want for yourself. What do you want to learn through your formal education? Why? How can the literacy you envision for yourself be promoted or furthered outside of formal education?

3. Knoblauch delineates positions on literacy that in many ways are mutually exclusive. If the values and interests behind different literacies compete to the

extent that Knoblauch suggests, how should educational institutions arrive at a definition of literacy? In an essay, propose a process for deciding. Who would be involved in the process? What steps would be taken? Upon what basis would the final decision be made? What allows most institutions to avoid defining literacy in an explicit way?

Inventing the University

David Bartholomae

In the university classroom, you may feel as if you are expected to sound like an expert when you write. Through years of experience as a writing teacher, David Bartholomae has come to recognize that the missteps of inexperienced writers are the result of their efforts to speak authoritatively in a new and foreign language. As a writer new to the material, you must "invent the university," meaning you must not only make your way into new terminology, but you must also move step by step into unfamiliar, specialized ways of thinking, arguing, and establishing authority. Bartholomae suggests that the heart of the problem—and the challenge for teachers—is that students may not be equipped to imagine and conform to the goals of a reader who is an expert.

As professor and chair of the English department at the University of Pittsburgh, David Bartholomae has written widely on composition theory and instruction. A former chair of the Conference on College Composition and Communication, Bartholomae is currently coeditor of the Pittsburgh Series on Composition, Literacy, and Culture. His collection *Writing on the Margins: Essays on Composition and Teaching* (2005) won the Shaughnessey Award from the Modern Language Association. The essay "Inventing the University" first appeared in *When a Writer Can't Write* (1985), edited by Mike Rose. The excerpt from "Inventing the University" that follows is the first of four sections in that essay.

Education may well be, as of right, the instrument whereby every individual, in a society like our own, can gain access to any kind of discourse. But we well know that in its distribution, in what it permits and in what it prevents, it follows the well-trodden battle-lines of social conflict. Every educational system is a political means of maintaining or of modifying the appropriation of discourse, with the knowledge and the powers it carries with it.

— FOUCAULT, *The Discourse on Language*

. . . the text is the form of the social relationships made visible, palpable, material.

— BERNSTEIN, *Codes, Modalities and the Process of Cultural Reproduction: A Model*

Every time a student sits down to write for us, he has to invent the university for the occasion—invent the university, that is, or a branch of it, like history or anthropology or economics or English. The student has to learn to speak our language, to speak as we do, to try on the peculiar ways of knowing, selecting, evaluating, reporting, concluding, and arguing that define the discourse of our community. Or perhaps I should say the *various* discourses of our community, since it is in the nature of a liberal-arts education that a student, after the first year or two, must learn to try on a variety of voices and interpretive schemes—to write, for example, as a literary critic one day and as an experimental psychologist the next; to work within fields where the rules governing the presentation of examples or the development of an argument are both distinct and, even to a professional mysterious.

The student has to appropriate (or be appropriated by) a specialized discourse, and he has to do this as though he were easily and comfortably one with his audience, as though he were a member of the academy or a historian or an anthropologist or an economist; he has to invent the university by assembling and mimicking its language while finding some compromise between idiosyncracy, a personal history, on the one hand, and the requirements of convention, the history of a discipline, on the other. He must learn to speak our language. Or he must dare to speak it or to carry off the bluff, since speaking and writing will most certainly be required long before the skill is "learned." And this, understandably, causes problems.

Let me look quickly at an example. Here is an essay written by a college freshman.

In the past time I thought that an incident was creative was when I had to make a clay model of the earth, but not of the classical or your everyday model of the earth which consists of the two cores, the mantle and the crust. I thought of these things in a dimension of which it would be unique, but easy to comprehend. Of course, your materials to work with were basic and limited at the same time, but thought help to put this limit into a right attitude or frame of mind to work with the clay.

In the beginning of the clay model, I had to research and learn the different dimensions of the earth (in magnitude, quantity, state of matter, etc.). After this, I learned how to put this into the clay and come up with something different than any other person in my class at the time. In my opinion, color coordination and shape was the key to my creativity of the clay model of the earth.

Creativity is the venture of the mind at work with the mechanics relay to the limbs from the cranium, which stores and triggers this action. It can be a burst of energy released at a precise time a thought is being transmitted. This can cause a frenzy of the human body, but it depends on the characteristics of the individual and how they can relay the message clearly enough through mechanics of the body to us as an observer. Then we must determine if it is creative or a learned process varied by the individuals thought process. Creativity is indeed a tool which has to exist, or our world will not succeed into the future and progress like it should.

I am continually impressed by the patience and goodwill of our students. This student was writing a placement essay during freshman orientation. (The problem set to him was: "Describe a time when you did something you felt to be creative. Then, on the basis of the incident you have described, go on to draw some general conclusions about 'creativity.'") He knew that university faculty would be reading and evaluating his essay, and so he wrote for them.

In some ways it is a remarkable performance. He is trying on the discourse   5
even though he doesn't have the knowledge that would make the discourse more than a routine, a set of conventional rituals and gestures. And he is doing this, I think,

Every time a student sits down to write for us, he has to invent the university for the occasion.

even though he *knows* he doesn't have the knowledge that would make the discourse more than a routine. He defines himself as a researcher working systematically, and not as a kid in a high school class: "I thought of these things in a dimension of . . ."; "I had to research and learn the different dimensions of the earth (in magnitude, quantity, state of matter, etc.)." He moves quickly into a specialized language (his approximation of our jargon) and draws both a general, textbook-like conclusion — "Creativity is the venture of the mind at work . . ." — and a resounding peroration — "Creativity is indeed a tool which has to exist, or our world will not succeed into the future and progress like it should." The writer has even picked up the rhythm of our prose with that last "indeed" and with the qualifications and the parenthetical expressions of the opening paragraphs. And through it all he speaks with an impressive air of authority.

There is an elaborate but, I will argue, a necessary and enabling fiction at work here as the student dramatizes his experience in a "setting"—the setting required by the discourse—where he can speak to us as a companion, a fellow researcher. As I read the essay, there is only one moment when the fiction is broken, when we are addressed differently. The student says, "Of course, your materials to work with were basic and limited at the same time, but thought help to put this limit into a right attitude or frame of mind to work with the clay." At this point, I think, we become students and he the teacher giving us a lesson (as in, "You take your pencil in your right hand and put your paper in front of you"). This is, however, one of the most characteristic slips of basic writers. (I use the term *basic writers* to refer to university students traditionally placed in remedial composition courses.) It is very hard for them to take on the role—the voice, the persona—of an authority whose authority is rooted in scholarship, analysis, or research. They slip, then, into a more immediately available and realizable voice of authority, the voice of a teacher giving a lesson or the voice of a parent lecturing at the dinner table. They offer advice or homilies rather than "academic" conclusions. There is a similar break in the final paragraph, where the conclusion that pushes for a definition ("Creativity is the venture of the mind at work with the mechanics relay to the limbs from the cranium") is replaced by a conclusion that speaks in the voice of an elder ("Creativity is indeed a tool which has to exist, or our world will not succeed into the future and progress like it should").

It is not uncommon, then, to find such breaks in the concluding sections of essays written by basic writers. Here is the concluding section of an essay written by a student about his work as a mechanic. He had been asked to generalize about work after reviewing an on-the-job experience or incident that "stuck in his mind" as somehow significant.

> How could two repairmen miss a leak? Lack of pride? No incentive? Lazy?
> I don't know.

At this point the writer is in a perfect position to speculate, to move from the problem to an analysis of the problem. Here is how the paragraph continues, however (and notice the change in pronoun reference).

> From this point on, I take *my* time, do it right, and don't let customers get under *your* skin. If they have a complaint, tell them to call your boss and he'll be more than glad to handle it. Most important, worry about yourself, and keep a clear eye on everyone, for there's always someone trying to take advantage of you, anytime and anyplace. (Emphasis added)

We get neither a technical discussion nor an "academic" discussion but a Lesson on Life.[1] This is the language he uses to address the general question, "How could two repairmen miss a leak?" The other brand of conclusion, the more academic one, would have required him to speak of his experience in our terms; it would, that is, have required a special vocabulary, a special system of presentation, and an interpretive scheme (or a set of commonplaces) he could have used to identify and talk about the mystery of human error. The writer certainly had access to the range of acceptable commonplaces for such an explanation: "lack of pride," "no incentive," "lazy." Each commonplace would dictate its own set of phrases, examples, and conclusions; and we, his teachers, would know how to write out each argument, just as we know how to write out more specialized arguments of our own. A "commonplace," then, is a culturally or institutionally authorized concept or statement that carries with it its own necessary elaboration. We all use commonplaces to orient ourselves in the world; they provide points of reference and a set of "prearticulated" explanations that are readily available to organize and interpret experience. The phrase "lack of pride" carries with it its own account of the repairman's error, just as at another point in time a reference to "original sin" would have provided an explanation, or just as in certain university classrooms a reference to "alienation" would enable writers to continue and complete the discussion. While there is a way in which these terms are interchangeable, they are not all permissible: A student in a composition class would most likely be turned away from a discussion of original sin. Commonplaces are the "controlling ideas" of our composition textbooks, textbooks that not only insist on a set form for expository writing but a set view of public life.[2]

When the writer says, "I don't know," then, he is not saying that he has nothing to say. He is saying that he is not in a position to carry on this discussion. And so we are addressed as apprentices rather than as teachers or scholars. In order to speak as a person of status or privilege, the writer can either speak to us in our terms—in the privileged language of university discourse—or, in default (or in defiance) of that, he can speak to us as though we were children, offering us the wisdom of experience.

I think it is possible to say that the language of the "Clay Model" paper has come *through* the writer and not from the writer. The writer has located himself (more precisely, he has located the self that is represented by the "I" on the page) in a context that is finally beyond him, not his own and not available to his immediate procedures for inventing and arranging text. I would not, that is, call this essay an example of "writer-based" prose. I would not say that it is egocentric or that it represents the "interior monologue or a writer thinking and talking to himself" (Flower, 1981, p. 63). It is, rather, the record of a writer who has lost himself in the discourse of his readers. There is a context beyond the intended reader that is not the world but a way of talking about the world, a way of talking that determines the use of examples, the possible conclusions, acceptable commonplaces, and key words for an essay on the construction of a clay model of the earth. This writer has entered the discourse without successfully approximating it.

Linda Flower (1981) has argued that the difficulty inexperienced writers   10
have with writing can be understood as a difficulty in negotiating the transition
between "writer-based" and "reader-based" prose. Expert writers, in other words,
can better imagine how a reader will respond to a text and can transform or
restructure what they have to say around a goal shared with a reader. Teaching
students to revise for readers, then, will better prepare them to write initially
with a reader in mind. The success of this pedagogy depends on the degree to
which a writer can imagine and conform to a reader's goals. The difficulty of
this act of imagination and the burden of such conformity are so much at the
heart of the problem that a teacher must pause and take stock before offering
revision as a solution. A student like the one who wrote the "Clay Model" paper
is not so much trapped in a private language as he is shut out from one of the
privileged languages of public life, a language he is aware of but cannot control.

Notes

1. David Olson (1981) has made a similar observation about school-related problems of language learning in younger children. Here is his conclusion: "Hence,
depending upon whether children assumed language was primarily suitable for making assertions and conjectures or primarily for making direct or indirect commands,
they will either find school texts easy or difficult" (p. 107).

2. For Aristotle, there were both general and specific commonplaces. A speaker,
says Aristotle, has a "stock of arguments to which he may turn for a particular need."

> If he knows the *topoi* (regions, places, lines, or argument)—and a skilled speaker
> will know them—he will know where to find what he wants for a special case. The
> general topics, or *common*places, are regions containing arguments that are com-
> mon to all branches of knowledge.. . . But there are also special topics (regions,
> places, *loci*) in which one looks for arguments appertaining to particular branches
> of knowledge, special sciences, such as ethics or politics. (1932, pp. 154–55)

And, he says, "the topics or places, then, may be indifferently thought of as in the
science that is concerned, or in the mind of the speaker." But the question of location is "indifferent" *only* if the mind of the speaker is in line with set opinion, general assumption. For the speaker (or writer) who is not situated so comfortably in the
privileged public realm, this is indeed not an indifferent matter at all. If he does not
have the commonplace at hand, he will not, in Aristotle's terms, know where to go
at all.

References

Aristotle. (1932). *The Rhetoric of Aristotle* (L. Cooper, Trans.). Englewood Cliffs,
    NJ: Prentice-Hall.
Flower, L. S. (1981). Revising writer-based prose. *Journal of Basic Writing* 3, 62–74.
Olson, D. R. (1981). Writing: The divorce of the author from the text. In B. M. Kroll
    and R. J. Vann (Eds.), *Exploring speaking-writing relationships: Connections and
    contrasts.* Urbana, IL: National Council of Teachers of English.

Working with the Text

1. Although universities have been in existence for many centuries, the language of the university, its way of proceeding, is not a given. The purposes and structures of universities must themselves be invented and reinvented. David Bartholomae asserts that students, too, must "invent the university" as they enter this community, drawing on their own growing problem-solving skills. As you reread the essay, note the particular processes this involves for the student. Based on your understanding of these processes, write a short essay in which you analyze Bartholomae's use of the word *invent* to describe what the student has to do. Why would he use the term *invent*, rather than simply *learn* (a term he also uses)? Why is "assembling and mimicking [the university's] language" a matter of invention? What exactly is the student inventing?

2. In analyzing the "Clay Model" paper, Bartholomae decides that the paper "has come *through* the writer and not from the writer" (par. 9). Drawing on Bartholomae's argument, write a brief statement in which you explore what he means by this.

3. Bartholomae argues that students "invent the university by assembling and mimicking its language" (par. 2). Reflect on your own writing process or on a specific writing assignment that was especially challenging or difficult. As you reread the essay, highlight terms that seem to be the specialized language of Bartholomae's field. Write a brief essay in which you analyze your own writing process or the specific assignment, by mimicking Bartholomae's analysis of "Clay Model."

From Text to Field

1. Reread the passage in which Bartholomae discusses the use of "commonplaces" as a set of "'prearticulated' explanations that are readily available to organize and interpret experience" (par. 7). Choose a commonplace from a language that you use comfortably, such as a term used in a particular field, specialty, or working community. Write an essay in which you explain to an outsider how the commonplace is used and in what ways it offers a culturally or institutionally authorized means to orient us in that world.

2. As a student, in what ways have you "invented the university"? Focus on a particular class or on a discipline or field you have begun to enter. Using Bartholomae's selection as a prompt, write an essay in which you describe and reflect on the process you used to invent for yourself that segment of the university.

3. In the closing paragraph of this section of Bartholomae's essay, he challenges writing teachers to "pause and take stock" of the difficulty students face in imagining an audience for their academic writing (par. 10). In an essay, discuss the challenges you face as you try to imagine the audience that you write for in a particular class (perhaps even your writing class) or in a discipline or field you plan to enter.

4. Bartholomae's essay has been criticized in some quarters as expecting students to mimic already institutionalized ways of writing. What are the creative opportunities, but also the considerable risks, of college writing that does not seek to invent (yet again) the university? Draw on your own experiences of negotiating this tension—a tension between adhering to yet departing from existing norms or expectations.

Two Metaphors for Learning
and The Novice Writer

Joseph Williams and
Gregory G. Colomb

How often have you felt like a novice, able to manage only the simplest, most concrete thinking in a new subject area? How often have you admired the complex, abstract, articulate thinking of an expert? It might encourage you to know that studies have shown that even experts tend to think and write at the novice level once they leave their area of expertise. In light of these studies, Joseph Williams and Gregory G. Colomb propose that we think of learning to write in a particular field not as an upward curve of growth but in terms of a novice trying to join a community of experts, a metaphor that leaves room for acquiring the "extensive, structured knowledge" necessary for expert writing.

Williams and Colomb collaborate frequently on books and essays that explore style, argument, research, and the teaching of writing. With Wayne Booth, they have produced *The Craft of Research* (2003) and *The Craft of Argument* (2003). Joseph Williams is well known for his book *Style: Ten Lessons in Clarity and Grace* (2005). Williams is professor of English, the humanities, and linguistics in the Department of English Language and Literature at the University of Chicago. Gregory G. Colomb is professor of English at the University of Virginia.

Two Metaphors for Learning

PROGRESS AS LINEAR MOVEMENT. Metaphors influence not only how we think about experience, but how we deal with it. We speak of anger, for example, with images of liquids boiling inside sealed containers: "I was so boiling mad that I blew my lid. After I let off steam, though, I felt better" (Johnson, 1987). Had circumstances been different, our culture might have adopted the metaphor of the machine: "I was so racing mad that I was already running too high for my specs, so I knew I had to lower my rpms or burn out my bearings. After I cooled the system down, I operated better." Under our presiding metaphorical frame, we often encourage—or at least condone—the expression of anger because we consider its "release" therapeutic; under another metaphorical system, we might consider the expression of anger damaging because it could lead to systemic breakdown.

The metaphors we use to describe learning, particularly skills such as reading, writing, and thinking, are metaphors of natural development and growth. When we develop normally, we grow "up." As we grow "up," we also "progress" left to right along a time scale (controlled by the tacit metaphor of reaching a "goal"). So we visually graph development from low to high and progress from a starting point on the lower left to a goal on the upper right. We picture normal growth as a curve (or stair step, if we think growth has stages), from lower left to higher right. We typically combine this growth metaphor with construction metaphors: We have to "lay a solid foundation" and then "reinforce" what we learn so that we both "maintain" what we have learned and "build" on it toward mastery.

These metaphors of linear development and building up come so naturally to us that we become particularly receptive to theories of learning expressible through them. So it is not surprising that administrators and teachers, particularly those who teach "generic" skills such as reading, writing, and thinking, should be attracted to the work of developmentalists such as Jean Piaget (Inhelder and Piaget, 1958), William Perry (1968), Lawrence Kohlberg (1984), and others whose models of development would seem to impose order on the more puzzling patterns of student behavior.

For Piaget, developing children move from concrete operational thinking to formal operational thinking, not smoothly, but in ways that let us account for their early cognitive limitations not by IQ or diligence, but by a qualitative structure of mind. Young children are not yet able to manipulate the abstractions derived from sets of sets; they are not able to juggle multiple hypotheticals, think probabilistically, etc. To put it crudely, younger children are incapable of thinking abstractly, a cognitive constraint Piagetians explain not by intelligence or cultural background, but by genetic epistemology.

Perry found a roughly similar pattern of development in the social/academic development of Harvard undergraduates: In their academic careers, students often appeared in his office at a stage he calls "dualistic"—the stage at which students simply want to know who the authorities are and what they know. When students "progress," they move to what he called the "multiple/relative" stage, that stage where students believe that since there are no final authorities and no final answers, then "everyone's opinion must be equally good." Perry claimed that the dualist stage regularly precedes the multiple/relative stage, and that these are followed by stages in which the student is increasingly able to handle ambiguities, to appreciate the legitimacy of different conclusions drawn from different premises, to understand the importance of the process of reasoning as opposed to its outcome, etc.

Kohlberg laid out a sequence of moral reasoning that begins at the stage of preconventional moral reasoning involving immediate, concrete approval and disapproval; then moves up to conventional moral reasoning governed by socially established values and peer pressure; and culminates in postconventional moral reasoning, that stage where the mature moral reasoner comes to recognize that local systems in particular societies rest not on rules that govern, but on universal moral principles that guide. Again, this is movement from the concrete to the abstract.

All three of these models describe a pattern of cognitive growth that begins with the immediate, concrete, rule-governed here and now, and that develops to more abstract, hypothetical forms of reasoning guided by principles. To be sure, these models differ profoundly, in ways our reductive description ignores. But to put it in a way that is not deceptively reductive, they describe a movement from relatively "lower-level" concreteness to relatively "higher-order" abstraction.

Like all models that reflect tacit metaphors, however, these models have consequences. One is that "regression" is bad. A student who does not continue to perform at a level "reached" earlier has "fallen back" to a "lower" level of performance. And whoever taught the student at that "lower level" — teaching writing is a paradigm case — did not do the job right. The student failed to learn the "bas(e)ics."

It is a metaphoric scheme that motivates us to abuse those who taught our students before they reach us. In the case of writing, teachers of first-year college students criticize the high schools; teachers of upperclass students criticize teachers of first-year composition; teachers in professional and graduate schools criticize the colleges; and professional organizations such as law firms and businesses criticize the whole educational system. A skill such as writing, the story goes, should follow a model of steady, linear development from lower-left to upper-right. When our students do not write as we expect, we feel empowered by our metaphors to decide that our predecessors must have failed to raise them to the level we think they should have achieved. A related consequence is that entire curricula are constructed to "raise" the student to achieve objectifiable levels of performance. If students are identifiably dualists when they enter the system, they should be measurably closer to being multiple relativists at the end of the first semester. That kind of thinking produces a system of testing that reductively categorizes students according to their cognitive/moral/social/academic development.

But the most problematical consequences come when we rely on these [10] linear models to make policy decisions about education. Such decisions may be costly, because evidence suggests that these models may not entirely comport with reality. The evidence comes from three directions. First, some reports increasingly suggest that children who test at the concrete operational level of thinking can be induced to behave in ways that characterize formal operational thinking (Bryant, 1983). By manipulating the form of the test and particularly the kind of knowledge that the child controls about the materials of the test, one can "move" a concrete-operational-thinking child to a formal operational level of thinking.

A second line of evidence comes from an opposite direction. A number of researchers have asserted that up to half of first-year college students are still concrete operational thinkers, this long after Piaget's model would have had them move "up" to formal operational thinking (Dunlop and Fazio, 1976; Tomlinson-Keasey, 1972). And when the American Accounting Association studied a group of upper-class and graduate students, up to half were judged to be either concrete operational thinkers or in transition from concrete to formal operational thinking (Shute, 1979). Is it plausible that large numbers of graduate students think in ways generically similar to ten-year-olds? Possible, perhaps, but put together these two lines of evidence—young children can be taught to think in formal operational terms, and graduate students can seem to think in concrete operational terms—and a more likely hypothesis suggests itself. Perhaps what counts in "higher-level" cognitive processing is not only those abstract and generic operations, but also knowledge, experience, control over specific content (see Glaser, 1984). "Concrete" behavior may in fact indicate thin categories of knowledge, not some intrinsic quality of mind.

This hypothesis is encouraged by a third line of evidence emerging from research into expert versus novice thinking. Most of the research into this matter involves what is called in cognitive psychology "well-structured" problems, problems that have a single right answer and a relatively clear-cut algorithm for getting there (Larkin, McDermott, Simon, and Simon, 1980; Chi, Feltovitch, and Glaser, 1981). Experts and novices solve well-structured problems in different ways. Most relevant is that novices (not "lower-level" thinkers, please note) are characterized by relatively concrete thinking, while experts tend to be characterized by more abstract thinking. For example, a novice problem solver in physics might look at a problem containing a picture of a spring and assume that the problem belongs to the category of "spring problems" and begin to think about what she knows about springs. The expert looks at the problem and categorizes the problem not on the basis of its most concrete, physically present feature, but by the abstract character of its intellectual content.

Still more interesting is the line of research into "ill-formed" problems, problems for which there is no obviously "correct" answer, much less obviously correct algorithms for a solution. Voss and others (1985) put the following problem to four groups of subjects: If you were in charge, how would you solve the problems of agriculture in the Soviet Union? The problem solvers were grouped as follows:

1. Novice/low-knowledge: students taking a first course in Soviet affairs
2. Novice/high-knowledge: graduate students in Soviet affairs
3. Expert/low-knowledge: senior chemistry professors
4. Expert/high-knowledge: senior faculty in Soviet affairs

The high-knowledge experts differed from the novices in three ways: (a) the high-knowledge experts spent more time decomposing the problem, defining the problem space, explaining why the problem was complex; (b) where the novices would propose solutions at a relatively concrete level—more fertilizer, better roads, better farm machinery, etc.—the high-knowledge experts began at a "higher," more abstract level—with the system, infrastructure, or history; (c) the novices constructed relatively shorter chains of arguments, moving from point to point without developing any one of them extensively. However, once the high-knowledge experts introduced a topic, they stayed with it, developing a chain of reasoning based on that argument.

The most salient outcome is that of the low-knowledge experts, the chemistry professors. They behaved in ways similar to the low-knowledge novices. This outcome suggests that while there may be some generic quality of expert thinking that characterizes all experts *in their field*, its deployment is crucially linked both to the amount of knowledge one controls about the matter in question, and to the complexity of the structure of that knowledge. Confronting a problem in an unfamiliar area, experts in an alien field seem to behave in ways similar to generic novices.

It seems, then, that extensive, structured knowledge counts for much in good thinking. Some suggest everything. Indeed, it may count for much in development in general. If formal thinking can be induced in a young child by providing substantial experience with the problem materials, if a dualist becomes a relativist once he or she accumulates multiple points of view and sees that all of them are at best intrinsically tentative, if a preconventional moral reasoner becomes a conventional reasoner when that person becomes part of a larger community and understands the shared and therefore abstract values of the community, then the notion of intellectual growth as biological or cognitive epistemology with its own teleology becomes an open question. And so does the model of learning represented by linear movement on a steady or staggered lower-left, upper-right curve.

PROGRESS AS JOINING THE COMMUNITY. Another—and perhaps more productive—metaphor for growth is the equally familiar one of an "outsider" trying to "get into" a community, a metaphor that models the movement of a learner situated outside a bounded field, who then "enters" the field and so "joins" the community by acting like its members. (This metaphor does not place any single community at the upper right of the chart as an ultimate goal.) To join a disciplinary community is, in part, to master a body of knowledge. But that knowledge does not exist "out there," independent of those who control it, just waiting to be acquired. Knowledge belongs to groups of people who have some shared stake in exploring, preserving, and expanding it. The outsider must acquire knowledge from insiders, usually through some form of an apprenticeship. Perhaps we should not, but we draw institutional boundaries around knowledge by locating it in communities defined by experts and by those novices who are trying to learn what experts know. We call those communities by different names—subjects, fields, areas, majors, departments, disciplines. They often overlap, and they consist of subcommunities that also overlap. That these names cut up the pie so differently only reflects the unruliness of communities.

Whatever we call these fields and however we define them, the knowledge they bound is colored by the values, conventions, and styles of the communities that make that knowledge the object of their interest. While the novice is committed to mastering the knowledge that the community thinks is important, the novice is equally committed to acquiring the *ways* of thinking that characterize that community, the tone of voice that identifies one member to another, the required silences whose violation instantly identifies the outsider. However true it is that Shakespeare is a famous writer who wrote many plays, it is usually inappropriate for those trying to join the ranks of literary experts to express that sentiment, either in writing or in speech.

We want to use this metaphor to redescribe the concrete operational thinker or the dualist or the preconventional moral reasoner as a novice standing outside a knowledge community. Of course, our metaphor has its own consequences, particularly in regard to the central interest of this volume—projects that seek to extend writing "across the curriculum." But we believe that the consequences of our description do more justice to—and do more to help—the novice learner.

The Novice Writer

Those new to a knowledge community often exhibit some characteristic patterns of learning behavior, patterns that teachers can learn to anticipate. First, we should expect from novices behavior that is relatively "concrete" (*not* "lower-level"). A moment of reflection suggests why. Abstraction is at   20 least partially based on the number and variety of instances of a category. By definition, a novice's knowledge is simultaneously very thin and relatively unstructured, with categories defined by as few as a single instance. The student of architecture who knows only classical forms has a very thin category of "architectural style." From the point of view of someone who also knows romanesque, gothic, baroque, modern, etc., that less knowledgeable student's problem-solving behavior would seem concrete operational indeed.

In regard to writing, we can predict a number of "concrete," "immature" forms of behavior: mapping the particular (concrete) language of the assignment into the opening paragraph of the paper; mapping any hint of organization in the assignment onto the paper itself; close-

The novice is committed to acquiring the *ways* of thinking that characterize that community.

ly following the sequence of events or topics in an assigned text; and in particular, summarizing rather than analyzing. Novices will tend to say those things that are ordinarily left unsaid by insiders, things that can be left unsaid just because they are shared. Novices will also seize on those features of the "voice" that seem most markedly to characterize the discourse of the field. In a field as stylistically marked as the law, for example, new students typically seize on the *heretofore*'s and *whereas*'s because they are among the most concretely obvious signals of legal language, the language of the tribe.

Second, this "concrete" behavior may be compounded by a predictable deterioration of performance in skills mastered earlier. Someone trying to enter a new community of discourse must bring under control a new body of knowledge, new ways of thinking, new ways of writing and speaking. So it is entirely predictable that some skills already mastered will deteriorate, often by default reliance on the most concrete forms of behavior.

Concrete, novice behavior appears in those aspects of writing that depend on the ability to analyze and synthesize. Here the consequences can be especially damaging because this failing is so often perceived as a sign that the learner cannot think. Because it is so important to our pedagogy, we will examine this behavior at more length and at three different levels: (1) professional school writing, (2) advanced upper-class undergraduate writing, and (3) first-year undergraduate writing. (We might have included professional writing by new attorneys.)

We begin with the mixed professional/academic setting of law school because we want to emphasize that "novice" behavior is not limited to the young and untalented—the effort to join a discourse community invites it even at very high levels of professional writing. Nor are inappropriate judgments of novice behavior limited to teachers of the young: Even at "higher" levels, learners write in ways that can by the old, linear metaphor be described as "low-level," "immature," "unskilled," etc., but that we prefer to describe as the predictable response of the novice, independent of any level of development.

WRITING BY FIRST-YEAR LAW STUDENTS. Most schools of law require a first-year 25 legal-writing course, but most of those courses do not teach legal writing. They teach research, citation forms, some aspects of legal thinking. This is especially so at the most selective law schools. They understandably assume that students who had A− and B+ averages in college are not merely competent, but proficient writers. And yet in their first weeks and months of law school, many of those writers display the very forms of behavior that characterize writers in their first year of college.

Let us describe a paper given to us by a legal-writing instructor as an example of the work of a student who had not learned how to write well, a paper written by a law student in his fourth week. . . . This student attends one of the country's most selective law schools, has graduated from a prestigious college near the top of his class, and has produced laudatory letters of recommendation, high LSAT scores, and an articulate application essay. The assignment was to analyze how a jurist used precedent while deciding whether a person can be convicted of second-degree murder if that person was coerced into participating in a crime in which another participant commits murder in the first degree.

The faculty person teaching in the legal-writing program was led by a linear conception of development to decide that this writer had never learned to write well. But the essay paradigmatically illustrates the behavior of a novice trying to deal with a new field. First, it precisely tracks the sequence of the jurist's text rather than abstracting from the text the principles of law that the jurist followed. Second, each of the student's middle, supposedly analytical paragraphs (see excerpts) corresponds to one section of the decision and precisely tracks the sequence of its section. It is not surprising, therefore, that the instructor considered this "mere summary." Third, although the conclusion begins to address the abstractions that the jurist considered, it merely lists them in the order in which they appeared in the original text and in the essay. Finally and most importantly, the middle, analytical paragraphs do not (with a few exceptions) specifically state the key analytical terms of the conclusion, terms first announced only at the end of the paper, where the writer seemed to discover them.

Like so many novice performances, this paper replicates the act of discovery. The writer structured the paper on the narrative of his thinking, discovering the abstract terms of analysis only at the end, where he summarizes them in a list. On the one hand, this might be treated merely as an example of "writer-based prose" (Flower, 1979). But "writer-based prose" is not necessarily a sign of generic "novice writer," as Flower seemed at that time to suggest. It may reflect the concrete behavior of a very experienced writer who is a novice in the field.

The signs of concrete, novice behavior are also evident in the style of that essay. This peculiarly awkward sentence presents the jurist's thinking in the writer's own words:

> The final step in Lord Morris's **preparation** to introduce the precedents is his **consideration** of the idea of **conviction** despite the **presence** of duress and then immediate **pardon** for that crime as an unnecessary step which is in fact injurious for it creates the stigma of the criminal on a potentially blameless (or at least not criminal) individual.

Pervasive nominalization characterizes bad legal writing in particular and bad academic writing in general. But as we noted above, it also characterizes a kind of stylistic breakdown typical of mature writers trying to wrestle with difficult concepts. The student might have written

> Before he **introduces** the precedents, Lord Morris **considers** a final issue: If a court first **convicts** a defendant who acted under duress and then immediately **pardons** that defendant, has the court taken an unnecessary step, a step that may even injure the defendant by stigmatizing him as criminal when he may be blameless?

This is a complex "if-then" question, involving two conditionals ("if a court convicts . . . and then pardons"), one of which contains an embedded conditional ("a defendant who acted under duress"), followed by a conclusion ("taken an unnecessary step") that itself becomes a cause ("may even injure the defendant") of a complex consequence ("by stigmatizing him as criminal when he may be blameless"). It is not surprising that a novice in legal reasoning should suffer a stylistic breakdown in the face of complex conditions and consequences. But note that his confused tangle of nominalizations is akin to an equally ponderous but professionally deliberate legal style:

> Because the individualized assessment of the appropriateness of the death penalty is a moral inquiry into the culpability of the defendant, and not an emotional response to the mitigating evidence, I agree with the Court that an instruction informing the jury that they "must not be swayed by mere sentiment, conjecture, sympathy, passion, prejudice, public opinion or public feeling" does not by itself violate the Eighth and Fourteenth Amendments to the United States Constitution. (Sandra Day O'Connor, concurring, *California v. Albert Greenwood Brown, Jr.*)

As turgid as this is, it is not the turgidity of a novice unfamiliar with legal thinking. One of the great ironies of modern prose is that the turgid professional, most deeply socialized into the language of a profession, and the awkward novice can seem to have so much in common.

A related, though less turgid novice response is to concretize in the text too much of the writer's thinking process. In the following example, a new law student as academically distinguished as the previous one tries to adopt the voice of a judge. But in doing so he uses metadiscourse to raise to a level of textual concreteness the machinery of thinking and reasoning—"the main point supporting my point of view," etc.—that experts usually suppress. At the same time, this student raises to the same level of textual concreteness certain substantive matters that any expert would leave unsaid, such as the obvious assertion that a plaintiff must produce evidence against a defendant. (In this passage, we have boldfaced the metadiscourse and italicized the statements that anyone socialized into the world of the law would be unlikely to make.) ³⁰

> **It is my opinion that** *the ruling of the lower court concerning the case of* Haslem v. Lockwood **should be upheld, thereby denying** *the appeal of the plaintiff.* **The main point supporting my point of view** *on this case* **concerns** *the tenet of our court system which holds that in order to win his case, the plaintiff must prove that he was somehow wronged by the defendant. The burden of proof rests on the plaintiff. He must show enough evidence to convince the court that he is in the right.* **However, in this case, I do not believe that** *the plaintiff has satisfied this requirement. In order to prove that the defendant owes him recompense for the six loads of manure,* he must first show that he was the legal owner of those loads, and then show that the defendant removed the manure for his own use [the paper goes on for several more paragraphs].

A more professional (i.e., socialized, i.e., "expert") version would be, "Plaintiff has failed to show that he was the legal owner of the loads and that the defendant removed the manure for his own use. The court affirms *Haslem v. Lockwood.*"

In both cases, the instructors took these as examples of bad writing and unskilled writers. In our terms, they are examples of novices trying to express themselves in a field that largely baffles them, and displaying the signs of novice behavior—concreteness, saying what can be left unsaid, and occasional breakdowns in stylistic performance in the direction of the most visible and concrete features of the "voice" that characterizes the prose of a field.

These examples illustrate forms of writing familiar to every teacher of freshman composition: summary rather than analysis, thinking out loud, a conclusion discovered at the end, evident stylistic infelicity, etc. In neither case could we assert that the writers were in some general sense immature or unintelligent. And yet they display the generic shortcomings of novice, "concrete" writers.

WRITING BY UPPER-CLASS STUDENTS. As they move into a discipline, undergraduates face many of the conceptual difficulties faced by new professional students. The next example comes from a paper by a third-year student taking a course in Western civilization, a good student who had written excellent papers in his first-year humanities course, but who had had no preparation in historical thinking. By the concluding paragraph of his paper, he at last reached a point worth making:

> The Popes, Urban II and Gregory VII, used the concept of the Crusades as a means to achieve a form of unity important to them during their pontificate. During Urban's pontificate, he could establish his authority, fight the devil (Muslims), and control fighting amongst the Europeans and direct those energies elsewhere. Gregory VII wishes to achieve unification between the Roman Church and the Greek Orthodox Church. . . . Therefore the Crusade was not just a fight against the Muslims to recapture the Holy Land and to save God's faith, but it was an effort to save the Church and Europe from the dissensions which were tearing it apart.

This paper was given a C+ because it was considered "disorganized," "largely summary," etc. Why? Because all of the first five and most of the next five paragraphs offered only a close summary of the assigned texts, so that the central concept of the conclusion—the Crusades achieving Christian unity—did not begin to emerge until about the tenth paragraph. The introduction was wholly summary and pointless:

> During the eleventh through thirteenth centuries, the Roman Catholic Church initiated several Crusades against the Muslims in the Holy Lands. The Pope would usually instigate and call for armament and support for this endeavor. Pope Urban II started the first Crusade in 1096. His predecessor, Gregory VII, had also petitioned to get support for a crusade in 1074 but did not succeed in launching his Crusade. There are written statements from these Popes concerning the Crusades. Pope Urban II in "Speech at the Council of Clermont" in the year 1095 calls for a Crusade and Pope Gregory VII in a Letter to King Henry IV during the year 1074 also proposes a Crusade.

This is the writing of a student gripped by novice concreteness. Since he does not control the information from the sources well enough to hold it whole in his mind as he thinks through its implications, he predictably summarizes the source, closely following the structure of its text. Once the material is concretized in the form of a linear summary, he is able to draw from it some inferences that qualify as analysis.

WRITING BY FIRST-YEAR STUDENTS. By this point it is almost redundant to offer   35
a typical first-year student paper that might illustrate these same features. Let us briefly look at one from a student with a VSAT well over 600. He was in his third week of college and writing about two speeches in Thucydides' history of the Peloponnesian war, a subject wholly strange to him. This was the assignment:

In the second chapter of his history, Thucydides presents two speakers asking Athens for help against the other. As we know Thucydides wrote these speeches to represent what "probably would have been said." Compare and contrast the way Thucydides had the Corcyrans and Corinthians rhetorically appeal to the Athenians in different ways.

And here are some indicative excerpts from the paper:

A Comparison of the Corcyran and Corinthian Speeches

The Corcyran and Corinthian speeches in Thucydides's *The Peloponnesian War* differ in several ways. The most important way that the two speeches differ is in the particular appeals each side gives to support its arguments. I will first discuss the Corcyran speech and then the Corinthian speech in order to show what we can learn from these differences.

The Corcyrans first apologize. . . . Then they give three reasons why the Athenians should help them and join in an alliance. They say that . . . Then they predict that . . . They say that . . . Finally, they emphasize that . . .

The Corinthians start out by attacking the Corcyrans. . . .

The Athenians decide to join with the Corcyrans against the Corinthians because they are sure that there is going to be a war between them soon and that they would have a good ally with the Corcyrans. The speeches are different in that the Corcyrans had the better argument because they understood the Athenians better than the Corinthians since the Athenians were very practical and self-interested at this time. Therefore, the Corcyran speech was a more clever appeal.

We need not dwell on the obvious here: Like the novice problem solver who thinks that a concrete picture of a spring in the problem statement means the problem is a spring-type problem, the student here takes the concrete language of the problem statement—the assignment—and maps it directly into the opening paragraph. The writer takes the sequence of the speeches from the assignment and from the text. In each section, he marches through each speech in summary fashion, at the end discovering his conclusion. While the style of the paper is competent, the organization and thought reflect the student's "concrete" thinking, which is to say, his inexperience in thinking about matters of this kind.

In three cases (new law student, upper-class student new to a field, new college student) we see the same generic pattern—the tyranny of the concrete and the breakdown of control over skills mastered earlier. If our narrative is plausible, the upward curve of growth is at best misleading. While there must certainly be development of some kind, it is not the kind of development that can be graphed like height and weight. A metaphor more insightful and useful than the upward curve is that of the outsider trying to get in, that of the novice trying to join a community of experts, an experience that happens to our best students many times over.

References

Bryant, Peter. "Piaget's Struggle and the Struggle about Piaget." In *Jean Piaget: An Interdisciplinary Critique*, edited by Sohan Modgil, Celia Modgil, and Geoffrey Brown. London: Routledge & Kegan Paul, 1983.

Chi, M. P. Feltovitch, and R. Glaser. "Categorization and Representation of Physics Problems by Experts and Novices." *Cognitive Science* 5 (1981): 121–52.

Colomb, Gregory G., and Joseph M. Williams. "Perceiving Structure in Professional Prose." In *Writing in Non-Academic Settings* edited by Lee Odell and Dixie Goswami. New York: Guilford, 1986.

Colomb, Gregory G., and Mark Turner. "Computers, Literary Theory, and Theory of Meaning." In *Critical Projections: The Future of Literary Theory*, edited by Ralph Cohen. London: Methuen, 1988.

Dunlop, D., and F. Fazio. "Piagetian Theory and Abstract Preferences of College Science Students." *Journal of College Science Teaching* (May 1976): 297–300.

Flower, Linda. "Writer Based Prose: A Cognitive Basis for Problems in Writing." *College English* 41 (September 1979), 19–37.

Glaser, Robert. "Education and Thinking: The Role of Knowledge." *American Psychologist* 39 (1984): 93–104.

Inhelder, B., and Jean Piaget. *The Growth of Logical Thinking from Childhood to Adolescence*. New York: Basic Books, 1958.

Johnson, Mark. *The Body in the Mind: The Bodily Basis of Meaning, Reasoning and Imagination*. Chicago: University of Chicago Press, 1987.

Kohlberg, Lawrence. *The Psychology of Moral Development*. Vol. 2. New York: Harper & Row, 1984.

Larkin, J., J. McDermott, D. Simon, and H. Simon. "Expert and Novice Performance in Solving Physics Problems." *Science* 208 (1980): 1, 335–42.

Perry, William G., Jr. *Forms of Intellectual and Ethical Development in the College Years*. New York: Holt, Rinehart & Winston, 1968.

Shute, George E. *Accounting Students and Abstract Reasoning: An Exploratory Study*. Sarasota, FL: American Accounting Association, 1979.

Tomlinson-Keasey, C. "Formal Operations in Females Aged 11 to 54 Years of Age." *Developmental Psychologist* 6 (1972): 364.

Toulmin, Stephen, R. Rieke, and A. Janik. *An Introduction to Reasoning*. New York: Macmillan, 1979.

Voss, James, T. Green, T. Post, and B. Penner. "Problem-solving Skill in the Social Sciences." *The Psychology of Learning and Motivation* 17 (1985): 165–213.

Working with the Text

1. Joseph Williams and Gregory G. Colomb use the term *novice* rather than *lower-level thinker* to designate writers who have not yet mastered the language and the structured knowledge of a given learning community. As a salient example, Williams and Colomb point to the chemistry professor who has as much trouble handling a question about Soviet agriculture as do undergraduate students. Review this example (pars. 13–15). Why is it central to the case the authors are making?

2. Williams and Colomb develop their hypothesis by focusing on the "concrete" behaviors (par. 21) of novice writers. In a brief essay, identify those behaviors and reflect on why a novice writer would exhibit them. Draw on your own prior or current experience as a novice writer.

3. Williams and Colomb assert that the metaphor of an outsider trying to join a community is "more insightful and useful" (par. 37) than the metaphor of growth that is more commonly used to describe the process of learning to write. In what ways is the growth metaphor misleading? What does the outsider metaphor contribute to our understanding of the novice writer's situation that the growth metaphor does not? Write an essay in which you imagine the effect of each metaphor on a novice writer in one particular setting. What would the writer be expected to do? How would the teacher respond to the writer's work? What would the writer be thinking and feeling?

From Text to Field

1. In questioning the linear "growth" metaphor, Williams and Colomb voice their concern that "the most problematical consequences come when we rely on these linear models to make policy decisions about education" (par. 10). Consider your own experience in and knowledge of the American education system, from elementary schools through college and on to professional or graduate schools. Write an essay in which you suggest changes to the system, or to one level of the system, that would help it shift from the metaphor of linear growth to the metaphor of an outsider trying to join a community.

2. Williams and Colomb point out that within communities—defined by subjects, fields, departments, disciplines—"the knowledge they bound is colored by the values, conventions, and styles of the communities that make that knowledge the object of their interest" (par. 18). In an essay, analyze the values and styles that color the knowledge of a community you have entered, or are entering, or a community you have observed as an outsider. This community can be academic, civic, professional, or involve any area of expertise, such as music, sports, use of the Internet, or skateboarding.

3. Reflect on your experience as a novice writer. Do you recognize in yourself any of the behaviors that Williams and Colomb describe? In what respects might the metaphors of growth or entering a community apply to your experiences? In a personal essay, reflect on your own learning process as a novice writing for a "knowledge" community. What do you find discouraging—or comforting—in your experiences and in the metaphors used to describe them?

Why We Read: Canon to the Right of Me

Katha Pollitt

Katha Pollitt takes on the continuing debate over the literary canon—the list of books we are expected to read to be considered educated. At issue is not only the value of a book but also, more importantly, the criteria and perspectives that drive the judgment of value. *Why* should we read certain books? To what end? If books are to teach us about our culture—itself a debatable assumption—as members of a highly diverse culture we have to ask, whose culture? For Pollitt, the debate leads to the question of why we read the books we have chosen for ourselves and those that have been chosen for us.

Pollitt's perspective is informed by her education at Harvard University and the Columbia School of the Arts, as well as her experience teaching poetry at Barnard College and at the 92nd Street Y in New York City. As a widely published poet, she has received several grants, fellowships, and awards. As an essayist, Pollitt has won wide recognition for the incisiveness and wit of her social criticism. She has been contributing to the *Nation* since 1980 and has written essays for a number of high-profile publications, including the *New Yorker,* the *Atlantic,* the *New York Times, Harper's,* the *New Republic, Mother Jones,* and *Ms.* She has also been a guest on national television and radio programs. Her essays have been collected in *Reasonable Creatures: Essays on Women and Feminism* (1994) and, most recently, in *Subject to Debate: Sense and Dissents on Women, Politics, and Culture* (2001). "Why We Read: Canon to the Right of Me. . ." won the National Magazine award for essays and criticism.

For the past couple of years we've all been witness to a furious debate about the literary canon. What books should be assigned to students? What books should critics discuss? What books should the rest of us read, and who are "we" anyway? Like everyone else, I've given these questions some thought, and when an invitation came my way, I leaped to produce my own manifesto. But to my surprise, when I sat down to write — in order to discover, as E. M. Forster once said, what I really think — I found that I agreed with all sides in the debate at once.

Take the conservatives. Now, this rather dour collection of scholars and diatribists — Allan Bloom, Hilton Kramer, John Silber, and so on — are not a particularly appealing group of people. They are arrogant, they are rude, they are gloomy, they do not suffer fools gladly, and everywhere they look, fools are what they see. All good reasons not to elect them to public office, as the voters of Massachusetts recently decided. But what is so terrible, really, about what they are saying? I too believe that some books are more profound, more complex, more essential to an understanding of our culture than others; I too am appalled to think of students graduating from college not having read Homer, Plato, Virgil, Milton, Tolstoy — all writers, dead white Western men though they be, whose works have meant a great deal to me. As a teacher of literature and of writing, I too have seen at firsthand how ill-educated many students are, and how little aware they are of this important fact about themselves. Last year I taught a graduate seminar in the writing of poetry. None of my students had read more than a smattering of poems by anyone, male or female, published more than ten years ago. Robert Lowell was as far outside their frame of reference as Alexander Pope. When I gently suggested to one student that it might benefit her to read some poetry if she planned to spend her life writing it, she told me that yes, she knew she should read more but when she encountered a really good poem it only made her depressed. That contemporary writing has a history which it profits us to know in some depth, that we ourselves were not born yesterday, seems too obvious even to argue.

But ah, say the liberals, the canon exalted by the conservatives is itself an artifact of history. Sure, some books are more rewarding than others, but why can't we change our minds about which books those are? The canon itself was not always as we know it today: Until the 1920s, *Moby-Dick* was shelved with the boys' adventure stories. If T. S. Eliot could single-handedly dethrone the Romantic poets in favor of the neglected Metaphysicals and place John Webster alongside Shakespeare, why can't we dip into the sea of stories and fish out Edith Wharton or Virginia Woolf? And this position too makes a great deal of sense to me. After all, alongside the many good reasons for a book to end up on the required-reading shelf are some rather suspect reasons for its exclusion: because it was written by a woman and therefore presumed to be too slight; because it was written by a black person and therefore presumed to be too unsophisticated or to reflect too special a case. By all means, say the liberals, let's have great books and a shared culture. But let's make sure that all the different kinds of greatness are represented and that the culture we share reflects the true range of human experience.

If we leave the broadening of the canon up to the conservatives, this will never happen, because to them change only means defeat. Look at the recent fuss over the latest edition of the Great Books series published by Encyclopedia Britannica, headed by that old snake-oil salesman Mortimer Adler. Four women have now been added to the series: Virginia Woolf, Willa Cather, Jane Austen, and George Eliot. That's nice, I suppose, but really! Jane Austen has been a certified Great Writer for a hundred years! Lionel Trilling said so! There's something truly absurd about the conservatives earnestly sitting in judgment on the illustrious dead, as though up in Writers' Heaven Jane and George and Willa and Virginia were breathlessly waiting to hear if they'd finally made it into the club, while Henry Fielding, newly dropped from the list, howls in outer darkness and the Brontës, presumably, stamp their feet in frustration and hope for better luck in twenty years, when *Jane Eyre* and *Wuthering Heights* will suddenly turn out to have qualities of greatness never before detected in their pages. It's like Poets' Corner at Manhattan's Cathedral of St. John the Divine, where mortal men—and a woman or two—of letters actually vote on which immortals to honor with a plaque, a process no doubt complete with electoral campaigns, compromise candidates, and all the rest of the underside of the literary life. "No, I'm sorry, I just can't vote for Whitman. I'm a Washington Irving man myself."

Well, a liberal is not a very exciting thing to be, as *Nation* readers know, ⁵ and so we have the radicals, who attack the concepts of "greatness," "shared," "culture" and "lists." (I'm overlooking here the ultraradicals, who attack the "privileging" of "texts," as they insist on calling books, and think one might as well spend one's college years deconstructing *Leave It to Beaver.*) Who is to say, ask the radicals, what is a great book? What's so terrific about complexity, ambiguity, historical centrality, and high seriousness? If *The Color Purple*, say, gets students thinking about their own experience, maybe they ought to read it and forget about —— and here you can fill in the name of whatever classic work you yourself found dry and tedious and never got around to finishing. For the radicals the notion of a shared culture is a lie, because it means presenting as universally meaningful and politically neutral books that reflect the interests and experiences and values of privileged white men at the expense of those of others—women, blacks, Latinos, Asians, the working class, whoever. Why not scrap the one-list-for-everyone idea and let people connect with books that are written by people like themselves about people like themselves? It will be a more accurate reflection of a multifaceted and conflict-ridden society, and will do wonders for everyone's self-esteem, except, of course, living white men—but they have too much self-esteem already.

Now, I have to say that I dislike the radicals' vision intensely. How foolish to argue that Chekhov has nothing to say to a black woman — or, for that matter, myself — merely because he is Russian, long dead, a man. The notion that one reads to increase one's self-esteem sounds to me like more snake oil. Literature is not an aerobics class or a session at the therapist's. But then I think of myself as a child, leafing through anthologies of poetry for the names of women. I never would have admitted that I needed a role model, even if that awful term had existed back in the prehistory of which I speak, but why was I so excited to find a female name, even when, as was often the case, it was attached to a poem of no interest to me whatsoever? Anna Lactitia Barbauld, author of "Life! I know not what thou art / But know that thou and I must part!"; Lady Anne Lindsay, writer of languid ballads in incomprehensible Scots dialect; and the other minor female poets included by chivalrous Sir Arthur Quiller-Couch in the old *Oxford Book of English Verse:* I have to admit it, just by their presence in that august volume they did something for me. And although it had nothing to do with reading or writing, it was an important thing they did.

> Why is everyone so hot under the collar about what to put on the required-reading shelf?

Now, what are we to make of this spluttering debate, in which charges of imperialism are met by equally passionate accusations of vandalism, in which each side hates the others, and yet each one seems to have its share of reason? Perhaps what we have here is one of those debates in which the opposing sides, unbeknownst to themselves, share a myopia that will turn out to be the most telling feature of the whole discussion: a debate, for instance, like that of our Founding Fathers over the nature of the franchise. Think of all the energy and passion spent pondering the question of property qualifications or direct versus legislative elections while all along, unmentioned and unimagined, was the fact — to us so central — that women and slaves were never considered for any kind of vote.

Something is being overlooked: the state of reading, and books, and literature in our country at this time. Why, ask yourself, is everyone so hot under the collar about what to put on the required-reading shelf? It is because while we have been arguing so fiercely about which books make the best medicine, the patient has been slipping deeper and deeper into a coma.

Let us imagine a country in which reading is a popular voluntary activity. There, parents read books for their own edification and pleasure, and are seen by their children at this silent and mysterious pastime. These parents also read to their children, give them books for presents, talk to them about books and underwrite, with their taxes, a public library system that is open all day, every day. In school — where an attractive library is invariably to be found — the children study certain books together but also have an active reading life of their own. Years later it may even be hard for them to remember if they read *Jane Eyre* at home and Judy Blume in class, or the other way around. In college young people continue to be assigned certain books, but far more important are the books they discover for themselves—browsing in the library, in bookstores, on the shelves of friends, one book leading to another, back and forth in history and across languages and cultures. After graduation they continue to read, and in the fullness of time produce a new generation of readers. Oh happy land! I wish we all lived there.

In that other country of real readers—voluntary, active, self-determined   10 readers—a debate like the current one over the canon would not be taking place. Or if it did, it would be as a kind of parlor game: What books would *you* take to a desert island? Everyone would know that the top-ten list was merely a tiny fraction of the books one would read in a lifetime. It would not seem racist or sexist or hopelessly hidebound to put Hawthorne on the syllabus and not Toni Morrison. It would be more like putting oatmeal and hot noodles on the breakfast menu—a choice part arbitrary, part a nod to the national past, part, dare one say it, a kind of reverse affirmative action: School might frankly be the place where one read the books that are a little off-putting, that have gone a little cold, that you might pass over because they do not address, in reader-friendly contemporary fashion, the issues most immediately at stake in modern life, but that, with a little study, turn out to have a great deal to say. Being on the list wouldn't mean so much. It might even add to a writer's cachet *not* to be on the list, to be in one way or another too heady, too daring, too exciting to be ground up into institutional fodder for teenagers. Generations of high school kids have been turned off to George Eliot by being forced to read *Silas Marner* at a tender age. One can imagine a whole new readership for her if grown-ups were left to approach *Middlemarch* and *Daniel Deronda* with open minds, at their leisure.

Of course, they rarely do. In America today the assumption underlying the canon debate is that the books on the list are the only books that are going to be read, and if the list is dropped no books are going to be read. Becoming a textbook is a book's only chance; all sides take that for granted. And so all agree not to mention certain things that they themselves, as highly educated people and, one assumes, devoted readers, know perfectly well. For example, that if you read only twenty-five, or fifty, or a hundred books, you can't understand them, however well chosen they are. And that if you don't have an independent reading life—and very few students do—you won't *like* reading the books on the list and will forget them the minute you finish them. And that books have, or should have, lives beyond the syllabus—thus, the totally misguided attempt to put current literature in the classroom. How strange to think that people need professorial help to read John Updike or Alice Walker, writers people actually do read for fun. But all sides agree, if it isn't taught, it doesn't count.

Let's look at the canon question from another angle. Instead of asking what books we want others to read, let's ask why we read books ourselves. I think the canon debaters are being a little disingenuous here, are suppressing, in the interest of their own agendas, their personal experience of reading. Sure, we read to understand our American culture and history, and we also read to recover neglected masterpieces, and to learn more about the accomplishments of our subgroup and thereby, as I've admitted about myself, increase our self-esteem. But what about reading for the aesthetic pleasures of language, form, image? What about reading to learn something new, to have a vicarious adventure, to follow the workings of an interesting, if possibly skewed, narrow and ill-tempered mind? What about reading for the story? For an expanded sense of sheer human variety? There are a thousand reasons why a book might have a claim on our time and attention other than its canonization. I once infuriated an acquaintance by asserting that Trollope, although in many ways a lesser writer than Dickens, possessed some wonderful qualities Dickens lacked: a more realistic view of women, a more skeptical view of good intentions, a subtler sense of humor, a drier vision of life which I myself found congenial. You'd think I'd advocated throwing Dickens out and replacing him with a toaster. Because Dickens is a certified Great Writer, and Trollope is not.

Am I saying anything different from what Randall Jarrell said in his great 1953 essay "The Age of Criticism"? Not really, so I'll quote him. Speaking of the literary gatherings of the era, Jarrell wrote:

> If, at such parties, you wanted to talk about *Ulysses* or *The Castle* or *The Brothers Karamazov* or *The Great Gatsby* or Graham Greene's last novel—Important books—you were at the right place. (Though you weren't so well off if you wanted to talk about *Remembrance of Things Past*. Important, but too long.) But if you wanted to talk about Turgenev's novelettes, or *The House of the Dead*, or *Lavengro*, or *Life on the Mississippi*, or *The Old Wives' Tale*, or *The Golovlyov Family*, or Cunningham-Grahame's stories, or Saint-Simon's memoirs, or *Lost Illusions*, or *The Beggar's Opera*, or *Eugen Onegin*, or *Little Dorrit*, or the *Burnt Njal Saga*, or *Persuasion*, or *The Inspector-General*, or *Oblomov*, or *Peer Gynt*, or *Far from the Madding Crowd*, or *Out of Africa*, or the *Parallel Lives*, or *A Dreary Story*, or *Debits and Credits*, or *Arabia Deserta*, or *Elective Affinities*, or *Schweik*, or—any of a thousand good or interesting but Unimportant books, you couldn't expect a very ready knowledge or sympathy from most of the readers there. They had looked at the big sights, the current sights, hard, with guides and glasses; and those walks in the

country, over unfrequented or thrice-familiar territory, all alone—those walks from which most of the joy and good of reading come—were walks that they hadn't gone on very often.

I suspect that most canon debaters have taken those solitary rambles, if only out of boredom—how many times, after all, can you reread the *Aeneid*, or *Mrs. Dalloway*, or *Cotton Comes to Harlem* (to pick one book from each column)? But those walks don't count, because of another assumption all sides hold in common, which is that the purpose of reading is none of the many varied and delicious satisfactions I've mentioned; it's medicinal. The chief end of reading is to produce a desirable kind of person and a desirable kind of society. A respectful, high-minded citizen of a unified society for the conservatives, an up-to-date and flexible sort for the liberals, a subgroup-identified, robustly confident one for the radicals. How pragmatic, how moralistic, how American! The culture debaters turn out to share a secret suspicion of culture itself, as well as the antipornographer's belief that there is a simple, one-to-one correlation between books and behavior. Read the conservatives' list and produce a nation of sexists and racists—or a nation of philosopher kings. Read the liberals' list and produce a nation of spineless relativists—or a nation of open-minded world citizens. Read the radicals' list and produce a nation of psychobabblers and ancestor-worshipers—or a nation of stalwart proud-to-be-me pluralists.

But is there any list of a few dozen books that can have such a magical effect, for good or for ill? Of course not. It's like arguing that a perfectly nutritional breakfast cereal is enough food for the whole day. And so the canon debate is really an argument about what books to cram down the resistant throats of a resentful captive populace of students; and the trick is never to mention the fact that, in such circumstances, one book is as good, or as bad, as another. Because, as the debaters know from their own experience as readers, books are not pills that produce health when ingested in measured doses. Books do not shape character in any simple way—if, indeed, they do so at all—or the most literate would be the most virtuous instead of just the ordinary run of humanity with larger vocabularies. Books cannot mold a common national purpose when, in fact, people are honestly divided about what kind of country they want—and are divided, moreover, for very good and practical reasons, as they always have been.

For these burly and energetic purposes, books are all but useless. The way [15] books affect us is an altogether more subtle, delicate, wayward, and individual, not to say private, affair. And that reading is being made to bear such an inappropriate and simplistic burden speaks to the poverty both of culture and of frank political discussion in our time.

On his deathbed, Dr. Johnson°—once canonical, now more admired than read—is supposed to have said to a friend who was energetically rearranging his bedclothes, "Thank you, this will do all that a pillow can do." One might say that the canon debaters are all asking of their handful of chosen books that they do a great deal more than any handful of books can do.

Working with the Text

1. Katha Pollitt is known for her skill and style as an essayist. As you reread the essay, notice the structure of her argument. Write a brief analysis of her strategy. Why does she start with characterizing the debate? What does her summary, and the particular points she makes within it, allow her to do in the rest of the essay? In what ways has she succeeded in reframing the debate?

2. Pollitt makes the assumption that reading contributes to an understanding of our culture. Write a brief essay in which you analyze and elaborate on her view of the relationship between books and culture. What does it mean to understand culture? Whose culture is, or should be, at issue, and why? What role do books play in either entering into or challenging culture? What about our culture does Pollitt think our reading should reflect?

3. Pollitt's position on the canon debate is reflected in the tone of her writing. In a brief essay, describe the tone she uses and explore the effect it creates. What attitude does it project? How does it contribute to her argument? The article, adapted from Pollitt's participation in a panel discussion for the Columbia University Center for American Culture Studies, was published in the *Nation*. From the article, infer the intended audience. Why would she choose this tone for a panel discussion on culture studies? Why would the *Nation* choose to publish the article?

From Text to Field

1. Pollitt writes, "School might frankly be the place where one read the books that are a little off-putting, that have gone a little cold, that you might pass over because they do not address, in reader-friendly contemporary fashion, the issues most immediately at stake in modern life, but that, with a little study, turn out to have a great deal to say" (par. 10). Does this capture your experience of assigned reading in school? Using this passage as a guide, write

---

Dr. Johnson: Samuel Johnson (1709–1789), are of England's greatest literary figures who worked as a poet, essayist, biographer, and lexicographer.

a personal essay in which you reflect on your response to literature that is required reading. How do you respond to the reading itself? What is your attitude toward the fact that it is considered to be an essential or required part of your education? As an alternative, write a personal essay that re-creates your experience with one particular book that was required reading.

2. The debate over the canon leads Pollitt to consider the reasons we read. In an essay, explore your own reasons for reading or for not reading. What do you read voluntarily? What draws you to that kind of reading? What role does reading play in your life? If you don't read willingly, why don't you?

3. Consider the reading list for one of the literature classes you have taken or are taking, in either high school or college. Based on the reading list as well as the syllabus, lectures, discussions, and other materials for the course, write an essay in which you analyze your teacher's implicit position on the debate over the canon. What criteria does your teacher use for selecting required reading? What does the teacher regard as the purpose for reading? How does the teacher view the relationship between books and understanding our culture?

4. Pollitt does not address other media—such as television, film, and the Internet—that reflect or influence our culture. Write an essay in which you explore the ways in which these other media have affected how we read. You may choose to write a personal essay about the effect certain media have had on your reading, a cultural critique that analyzes contemporary attitudes and behaviors, or a combination of both.

The "Banking" Concept
of Education

Paulo Freire

Most of us have had learning experiences driven by what Paulo Freire calls the "banking" concept of education—the teacher, as the authority, "deposits" knowledge into students. Freire (pronounced "Fr-air-ah") believes that learning should instead be driven by inquiry involving dialogue between teachers and students, in which teachers become students and students become teachers. To submit to the "banking" concept, says Freire, is to capitulate to those in power, who control learning in order to maintain the status quo. Freire proposes displacing "banking" with "problem-posing" education, a process of seeing reality in terms of our relationship to the world. It is through this process that students are liberated, by "becoming more fully human."

Freire's approach to education was deeply influenced by his work with adults living in the impoverished urban and rural areas of Brazil. A native of Brazil, Freire was drawn to education after university studies in law, philosophy, and the psychology of language. In addition to reading extensively in education, he absorbed the writings of Marx as well as Catholic intellectuals. Working through government and university organizations, he developed a "pedagogy of the oppressed," for the purpose of giving marginalized people the power to shape their own lives. His approach encouraged political action during a time when competing reform movements in Brazil challenged those in positions of military and economic power. The effectiveness, and consequent threat, of Freire's work led to his exile from Brazil after a 1964 military coup.

Exile gave Freire the opportunity to continue developing and spreading the practice of his pedagogy, first in Chile, then as a teacher and fellow at Harvard University, and eventually through the World Council of Churches in Geneva, Switzerland. After sixteen years in exile, Freire returned to Brazil as a faculty member at the University of São Paulo. In his capacity as minister of education for the city of São Paulo, he later led in the reform of Brazil's schools.

Worldwide, Freire is regarded as one of the central figures in educational philosophy and practice. His books include *Education as the Practice of Freedom* (1967); *Pedagogy of the Oppressed* (1970), the source of the following selection; *Education for Critical Consciousness* (1973); and *The Politics of Education* (1985). Freire died in 1997 at the age of seventy-five.

A careful analysis of the teacher-student relationship at any level, inside or outside the school, reveals its fundamentally *narrative* character. This relationship involves a narrating Subject (the teacher) and patient, listening objects (the students). The contents, whether values or empirical dimensions of reality, tend in the process of being narrated to become lifeless and petrified. Education is suffering from narration sickness.

The teacher talks about reality as if it were motionless, static, compartmentalized, and predictable. Or else he expounds on a topic completely alien to the existential experience of the students. His task is to "fill" the students with the contents of his narration — contents which are detached from reality, disconnected from the totality that engendered them and could give them significance. Words are emptied of their concreteness and become a hollow, alienated, and alienating verbosity.

The outstanding characteristic of this narrative education, then, is the sonority of words, not their transforming power. "Four times four is sixteen; the capital of Pará is Belém." The student records, memorizes, and repeats these phrases without perceiving what four times four really means, or realizing the true significance of "capital" in the affirmation "the capital of Pará is Belém," that is, what Belém means for Pará and what Pará means for Brazil.

Narration (with the teacher as narrator) leads the students to memorize mechanically the narrated content. Worse yet, it turns them into "containers," into "receptacles" to be "filled" by the teacher. The more completely she fills the receptacles, the better a teacher she is. The more meekly the receptacles permit themselves to be filled, the better students they are.

Education thus becomes an act of depositing, in which the students are the depositories and the teacher is the depositor. Instead of communicating, the teacher issues communiqués and makes deposits which the students patiently receive, memorize, and repeat. This is the "banking" concept of education, in which the scope of action allowed to the students extends only as far as receiving, filing, and storing the deposits. They do, it is true, have the opportunity to become collectors or catalogers of the things they store. But in the last analysis, it is the people themselves who are filed away through the lack of creativity, transformation, and knowledge in this (at best) mis-guided system. For apart from inquiry, apart from the praxis, individuals cannot be truly human. Knowledge emerges only through invention and reinvention, through the restless, impatient, continuing, hopeful inquiry human beings pursue in the world, with the world, and with each other.

In the banking concept of education, knowledge is a gift bestowed by those who consider themselves knowledgeable upon those whom they consider to know nothing. Projecting an absolute ignorance onto others, a characteristic of the ideology of oppression, negates education and knowledge as processes of inquiry. The teacher presents himself to his students as their necessary opposite; by considering their ignorance absolute, he justifies his own existence. The students, alienated like the slave in the Hegelian dialectic,° accept their ignorance as justifying the teacher's existence—but, unlike the slave, they never discover that they educate the teacher.

The raison d'être° of libertarian education, on the other hand, lies in its drive towards reconciliation. Education must begin with the solution of the teacher-student contradiction, by reconciling the poles of the contradiction so that both are simultaneously teachers *and* students.

This solution is not (nor can it be) found in the banking concept. On the contrary, banking education maintains and even stimulates the contradiction through the following attitudes and practices, which mirror oppressive society as a whole:

a. the teacher teaches and the students are taught;
b. the teacher knows everything and the students know nothing;
c. the teacher thinks and the students are thought about;
d. the teacher talks and the students listen—meekly;
e. the teacher disciplines and the students are disciplined;
f. the teacher chooses and enforces his choice, and the students comply;
g. the teacher acts and the students have the illusion of acting through the action of the teacher;
h. the teacher chooses the program content, and the students (who were not consulted) adapt to it;
i. the teacher confuses the authority of knowledge with his or her own professional authority, which she and he sets in opposition to the freedom of the students;
j. the teacher is the Subject of the learning process, while the pupils are mere objects.

Hegelian dialectic: The dynamic model of nature and mind offered by German philosopher Georg Wilhelm Friedrich Hegel (1770–1831), where a thesis comes into tension with an antithesis leading to new or further synthesis).

raison d'être: Reason for being.

It is not surprising that the banking concept of education regards men as adaptable, manageable beings. The more students work at storing the deposits entrusted to them, the less they develop the critical consciousness which would result from their intervention in the world as transformers of that world. The more completely they accept the passive role imposed on them, the more they tend simply to adapt to the world as it is and to the fragmented view of reality deposited in them.

The capability of banking education to minimize or annul the students' creative power and to stimulate their credulity serves the interests of the oppressors, who care neither to have the world revealed nor to see it transformed. The oppressors use their "humanitarianism" to preserve a profitable situation. Thus they react almost instinctively against any experiment in education which stimulates the critical faculties and is not content with a partial view of reality but always seeks out the ties which link one point to another and one problem to another.   10

Indeed, the interests of the oppressors lie in "changing the consciousness of the oppressed, not the situation which oppresses them"[1] for the more the oppressed can be led to adapt to that situation, the more easily they can be dominated. To achieve this end, the oppressors use the banking concept of education in conjunction with a paternalistic social action apparatus, within which the oppressed receive the euphemistic title of "welfare recipients." They are treated as individual cases, as marginal persons who deviate from the general configuration of a "good, organized, and just" society. The oppressed are regarded as the pathology of the healthy society, which must therefore adjust these "incompetent and lazy" folk to its own patterns by changing their mentality. These marginals need to be "integrated," "incorporated" into the healthy society that they have "forsaken."

The truth is, however, that the oppressed are not "marginals," are not people living "outside" society. They have always been "inside"—inside the structure which made them "beings for others." The solution is not to "integrate" them into the structure of oppression, but to transform that structure so that they can become "beings for themselves." Such transformation, of course, would undermine the oppressors' purposes; hence their utilization of the banking concept of education to avoid the threat of student *conscientização.*°

The banking approach to adult education, for example, will never propose to students that they critically consider reality. It will deal instead with such vital questions as whether Roger gave green grass to the goat, and insist upon the importance of learning that, on the contrary, Roger gave green

---

conscientização: The ability to perceive social, political, and economic contradictions, and to act against the oppressive elements of reality.

grass to the rabbit. The "humanism" of the banking approach masks the effort to turn women and men into automatons—the very negation of their ontological vocation to be more fully human.

Those who use the banking approach, knowingly or unknowingly (for there are innumerable well-intentioned bank-clerk teachers who do not realize that they are serving only to dehumanize), fail to perceive that the deposits themselves contain contradictions about reality. But, sooner or later, these contradictions may lead formerly passive students to turn against their domestication and the attempt to domesticate reality. They may discover through existential experience that their present way of life is irreconcilable with their vocation to become fully human. They may perceive through their relations with reality that reality is really a *process*, undergoing constant transformation. If men and women are searchers and their ontological vocation is humanization, sooner or later they may perceive the contradiction in which banking education seeks to maintain them, and then engage themselves in the struggle for their liberation.

But the humanist, revolutionary educator cannot wait for this possibility to materialize. From the outset, her efforts must coincide with those of the students to engage in critical thinking and the quest for mutual humanization. His efforts must be imbued with a profound trust in people and their creative power. To achieve this, they must be partners of the students in their relations with them. 15

The banking concept does not admit to such partnership—and necessarily so. To resolve the teacher-student contradiction, to exchange the role of depositor, prescriber, domesticator, for the role of student among students would be to undermine the power of oppression and serve the cause of liberation.

Implicit in the banking concept is the assumption of a dichotomy between human beings and the world: a person is merely *in* the world, not *with* the world or with others; the individual is spectator, not re-creator. In this view, the person is not a conscious being (*corpo consciente*); he or she is rather the possessor of *a* consciousness: an empty "mind" passively open to the reception of deposits of reality from the world outside. For example, my desk, my books, my coffee cup, all the objects before me—as bits of the world which surrounds me—would be "inside" me, exactly as I am inside my study right now. This view makes no distinction between being accessible to consciousness and entering consciousness. The distinction, however, is essential: The objects which surround me are simply accessible to my consciousness, not located within it. I am aware of them, but they are not inside me.

It follows logically from the banking notion of consciousness that the educator's role is to regulate the way the world "enters into" the students. The teacher's task is to organize a process which already occurs spontaneously, to "fill" the students by making deposits of information which he or she considers to constitute true knowledge.[2] And since people "receive" the world as passive entities, education should make them more passive still, and adapt them to the world. The educated individual is the adapted person, because she or he is better "fit" for the world. Translated into practice, this concept is well suited to the purposes of the oppressors, whose tranquility rests on how well people fit the world the oppressors have created, and how little they question it.

The more completely the majority adapt to the purposes which the dominant minority prescribe for them (thereby depriving them of the right to their own purposes), the more easily the minority can continue to prescribe. The theory and practice of banking education serve this end quite efficiently. Verbalistic lessons, reading requirements,[3] the methods for evaluating "knowledge," the distance between the teacher and the taught, the criteria for promotion: Everything in this ready-to-wear approach serves to obviate thinking.

The bank-clerk educator does not realize that there is no true security in his hypertrophied role, that one must seek to live *with* others in solidarity. One cannot impose oneself, nor even merely, coexist with one's students. Solidarity requires true communication, and the concept by which such an educator is guided fears and proscribes communication. 20

Yet only through communication can human life hold meaning. The teacher's thinking is authenticated only by the authenticity of the students' thinking. The teacher cannot think for her students, nor can she impose her thought on them. Authentic thinking, thinking that is concerned about *reality*, does not take place in ivory-tower isolation, but only in communication. If it is true that thought has meaning only when generated by action upon the world, the subordination of students to teachers becomes impossible.

Because banking education begins with a false understanding of men and women as objects, it cannot promote the development of what Fromm calls "biophily," but instead produces its opposite: "necrophily."

> While life is characterized by growth in a structured, functional manner, the necrophilous person loves all that does not grow, all that is mechanical. The necrophilous person is driven by the desire to transform the organic into the inorganic, to approach life mechanically, as if all living persons were things. . . . Memory, rather than experience; having, rather than being, is what counts. The necrophilous person can relate to an object — a flower or a person — only if he possesses it; hence a threat to his possession is a threat to himself; if he loses possession he loses contact with the world. . . . He loves control, and in the act of controlling he kills life.[4]

Oppression — overwhelming control — is necrophilic; it is nourished by love of death, not life. The banking concept of education, which serves the interests of oppression, is also necrophilic. Based on a mechanistic, static, naturalistic, spatialized view of consciousness, it transforms students into receiving objects. It attempts to control thinking and action, leads women and men to adjust to the world, and inhibits their creative power.

When their efforts to act responsibly are frustrated, when they find themselves unable to use their faculties, people suffer. "This suffering due to impotence is rooted in the very fact that the human equilibrium has been disturbed."[5] But the inability to act which causes people's anguish also causes them to reject their impotence, by attempting

> . . . to restore [their] capacity to act. But can [they], and how? One way is to submit to and identify with a person or group having power. By this symbolic participation in another person's life, [men have] the illusion of acting, when in reality [they] only submit to and become part of those who act.[6]

Populist manifestations perhaps best exemplify this type of behavior by the oppressed, who, by identifying with charismatic leaders, come to feel that they themselves are active and effective. The rebellion they express as they emerge in the historical process is motivated by that desire to act effectively. The dominant elites consider the remedy to be more domination and repression, carried out in the name of freedom, order, and social peace (that is, the peace of the elites). Thus they can condemn—logically, from their point of view—"the violence of a strike by workers and [can] call upon the state in the same breath to use violence in putting down the strike."[7]

Education as the exercise of domination stimulates the credulity of students, with the ideological intent (often not perceived by educators) of indoctrinating them to adapt to the world of oppression. This accusation is not made in the naive hope that the dominant elites will thereby simply abandon the practice. Its objective is to call the attention of true humanists to the fact that they cannot use banking educational methods in the pursuit of liberation, for they would only negate that very pursuit. Nor may a revolutionary society inherit these methods from an oppressor society. The revolutionary society which practices banking education is either misguided or mistrusting of people. In either event, it is threatened by the specter of reaction.

Unfortunately, those who espouse the cause of liberation are themselves surrounded and influenced by the climate which generates the banking concept, and often do not perceive its true significance or its dehumanizing power. Paradoxically, then, they utilize this same instrument of alienation in what they consider an effort to liberate. Indeed, some "revolutionaries" brand as "innocents," "dreamers," or even "reactionaries" those who would challenge this educational practice. But one does not liberate people by alienating them. Authentic liberation—the process of humanization—is not another deposit to be made in men. Liberation is a praxis: the action and reflection of men and women upon their world in order to transform it. Those truly committed to the cause of liberation can accept neither the mechanistic concept of consciousness as an empty vessel to be filled, nor the use of banking methods of domination (propaganda, slogans—deposits) in the name of liberation.

Those truly committed to liberation must reject the banking concept in its entirety, adopting instead a concept of women and men as conscious beings, and consciousness as consciousness intent upon the world. They must abandon the educational goal of deposit-making and replace it with the posing of the problems of human beings in their relations with the world. "Problem-posing" education, responding to the essence of consciousness—*intentionality*—rejects communiqués and embodies communications. It epitomizes the special characteristic of consciousness: being *conscious of*, not only as intent on objects but as turned in upon itself in a Jasperian° "split"—consciousness as consciousness *of* consciousness.

Education is suffering from narration sickness.

Liberating education consists in acts of cognition, not transferrals of information. It is a learning situation in which the cognizable object (far from being the end of the cognitive act) intermediates the cognitive actors— teacher on the one hand and students on the other. Accordingly, the practice of problem-posing education entails at the outset that the teacher-student contradiction be resolved. Dialogical relations—indispensable to the capacity of cognitive actors to cooperate in perceiving the same cognizable object—are otherwise impossible.

Indeed, problem-posing education, which breaks with the vertical patterns characteristic of banking education, can fulfill its function as the practice of freedom only if it can overcome the above contradiction. Through dialogue, the teacher-of-the-students and the students-of-the-teacher cease to exist and a new term emerges: teacher-student with students-teachers. The teacher is no longer merely the-one-who-teaches, but one who is himself taught in dialogue with the students, who in turn while being taught also teach. They become jointly responsible for a process in which all grow. In this process, arguments based on "authority" are no longer valid; in order to function, authority must be *on the side of* freedom, not *against* it. Here, no one teaches another, nor is anyone self-taught. People teach each other, mediated by the world, by the cognizable objects which in banking education are "owned" by the teacher.

The banking concept (with its tendency to dichotomize everything) distinguishes two stages in the action of the educator. During the first, he

---

Jasperian: Karl Jaspers (1883–1969), a German psychiatrist and philosopher who had a strong influence on modern theology, psychiatry, and philosophy.

cognizes a cognizable object while he prepares his lessons in his study or his laboratory; during the second, he expounds to his students about that object. The students are not called upon to know, but to memorize the contents narrated by the teacher. Nor do the students practice any act of cognition, since the object towards which that act should be directed is the property of the teacher rather than a medium evoking the critical reflection of both teacher and students. Hence in the name of the "preservation of culture and knowledge" we have a system which achieves neither true knowledge nor true culture.

The problem-posing method does not dichotomize the activity of the teacher-student: She is not "cognitive" at one point and "narrative" at another. She is always "cognitive," whether preparing a project or engaging in dialogue with the students. He does not regard cognizable objects as his private property, but as the object of reflection by himself and the students. In this way, the problem-posing educator constantly re-forms his reflections in the reflection of the students. The students—longer docile listeners—are now critical coinvestigators in dialogue with the teacher. The teacher presents the material to the students for their consideration, and reconsiders her earlier considerations as the students express their own. The role of the problem-posing educator is to create, together with the students, the conditions under which knowledge at the level of the *doxa* is superseded by true knowledge, at the level of the *logos*.

Whereas banking education anesthetizes and inhibits creative power, problem-posing education involves a constant unveiling of reality. The former attempts to maintain the *submersion* of consciousness; the latter strives for the *emergence* of consciousness and *critical intervention* in reality.

Students, as they are increasingly posed with problems relating to themselves in the world and with the world, will feel increasingly challenged and obliged to respond to that challenge. Because they apprehend the challenge as interrelated to other problems within a total context, not as a theoretical question, the resulting comprehension tends to be increasingly critical and thus constantly less alienated. Their response to the challenge evokes new challenges, followed by new understandings; and gradually the students come to regard themselves as committed.

Education as the practice of freedom—as opposed to education as the practice of domination—denies that man is abstract, isolated, independent, and unattached to the world; it also denies that the world exists as a reality apart from people. Authentic reflection considers neither abstract man nor the world without people, but people in their relations with the world. In these relations consciousness and world are simultaneous: Consciousness neither precedes the world nor follows it.

La conscience et le monde sont donnés d'un même coup: extérieur par essence à la conscience, le monde est, par essence relatif à elle.[8]

In one of our culture circles in Chile, the group was discussing (based on a codification) the anthropological concept of culture. In the midst of the discussion, a peasant who by banking standards was completely ignorant said: "Now I see that without man there is no world." When the educator responded: "Let's say, for the sake of argument, that all the men on earth were to die, but that the earth itself remained, together with trees, birds, animals, rivers, seas, the stars . . . wouldn't all this be a world?" "Oh no," the peasant replied emphatically. "There would be no one to say: 'This is a world.'"

The peasant wished to express the idea that there would be lacking the consciousness of the world which necessarily implies the world of consciousness. *I* cannot exist without a *non-I*. In turn, the *not-I* depends on that existence. The world which brings consciousness into existence becomes the world *of* that consciousness. Hence, the previously cited affirmation of Sartre: "*La conscience et le monde sont donnés d'un même coup.*"

As women and men, simultaneously reflecting on themselves and on the world, increase the scope of their perception, they begin to direct their observations towards previously inconspicuous phenomena:

> In perception properly so-called, as an explicit awareness [*Gewahren*], I am turned towards the object, to the paper, for instance. I apprehend it as being this here and now. The apprehension is a singling out, every object having a background in experience. Around and about the paper lie books, pencils, inkwell, and so forth, and these in a certain sense are also "perceived," perceptually there, in the "field of intuition"; but whilst I was turned towards the paper there was no turning in their direction, nor any apprehending of them, not even in a secondary sense. They appeared and yet were not singled out, were not posited on their own account. Every perception of a thing has such a zone of background intuitions or background awareness, if "intuiting" already includes the state of being turned towards, and this also is a "conscious experience," or more briefly a "consciousness of" all indeed that in point of fact lies in the co-perceived objective background.[9]

That which had existed objectively but had not been perceived in its deeper implications (if indeed it was perceived at all) begins to "stand out," assuming the character of a problem and therefore of challenge. Thus, men and women begin to single out elements from their "background awarenesses" and to reflect upon them. These elements are now objects of their consideration, and, as such, objects of their action and cognition.

In problem-posing education, people develop their power to perceive critically *the way they exist* in the world *with which* and *in which* they find themselves; they come to see the world not as a static reality, but as a reality in process, in transformation. Although the dialectical relations of women and men with the world exist independently of how these relations are perceived (or whether or not they are perceived at all), it is also true that the form of action they adopt is to a large extent a function of how they perceive themselves in the world. Hence, the teacher-student and the students-teachers reflect simultaneously on themselves and the world without dichotomizing this reflection from action, and thus establish an authentic form of thought and action.

Once again, the two educational concepts and practices under analysis come into conflict. Banking education (for obvious reasons) attempts, by mythicizing reality, to conceal certain facts which explain the way human beings exist in the world; problem-posing education sets itself the task of demythologizing. Banking education resists dialogue; problem-posing education regards dialogue as indispensable to the act of cognition which unveils reality. Banking education treats students as objects of assistance; problem-posing education makes them critical thinkers. Banking education inhibits creativity and domesticates (although it cannot completely destroy) the *intentionality* of consciousness by isolating consciousness from the world, thereby denying people their ontological and historical vocation of becoming more fully human. Problem-posing education bases itself on creativity and stimulates true reflection and action upon reality; thereby responding to the vocation of persons as beings who are authentic only when engaged in inquiry and creative transformation. In sum: Banking theory and practice, as immobilizing and fixating forces, fail to acknowledge men and women as historical beings; problem-posing theory and practice take the people's historicity as their starting point.

Problem-posing education affirms men and women as beings in the process of *becoming*—as unfinished, uncompleted beings in and with a likewise unfinished reality. Indeed, in contrast to other animals who are unfinished, but not historical, people know themselves to be unfinished; they are aware of their incompletion. In this incompletion and this awareness lie the very roots of education as an exclusively human manifestation. The unfinished character of human beings and the transformational character of reality necessitate that education be an ongoing activity.   40

Education is thus constantly remade in the praxis. In order to *be*, it must *become*. Its "duration" (in the Bergsonian° meaning of the word) is found in the interplay of the opposites *permanence* and *change*. The banking method emphasizes permanence and becomes reactionary; problem-posing education—which accepts neither a "well-behaved" present nor a predetermined future—roots itself in the dynamic present and becomes revolutionary.

Bergsonian: Henri-Louis Bergson (1859–1941), a French philosopher influential in the first half of the twentieth century.

Problem-posing education is revolutionary futurity. Hence, it is prophetic (and, as such, hopeful). Hence, it corresponds to the historical nature of humankind. Hence, it affirms women and men as beings who transcend themselves, who move forward and look ahead, for whom immobility represents a fatal threat, for whom looking at the past must only be a means of understanding more clearly what and who they are so that they can more wisely build the future. Hence, it identifies with the movement which engages people as beings aware of their incompletion—a historical movement which has its point of departure, its Subjects and its objective.

The point of departure of the movement lies in the people themselves. But since people do not exist apart from the world, apart from reality, the movement must begin with the human-world relationship. Accordingly, the point of departure must always be with men and women in the "here and now," which constitutes the situation within which they are submerged, from which they emerge, and in which they intervene. Only by starting from this situation—which determines their perception of it—can they begin to move. To do this authentically they must perceive their state not as fated and unalterable, but merely as limiting—and therefore challenging.

Whereas the banking method directly or indirectly reinforces men's fatalistic perception of their situation, the problem-posing method presents this very situation to them as a problem. As the situation becomes the object of their cognition, the naive or magical perception which produced their fatalism gives way to perception which is able to perceive itself even as it perceives reality, and can thus be critically objective about that reality.

A deepened consciousness of their situation leads people to apprehend 45 that situation as a historical reality susceptible of transformation. Resignation gives way to the drive for transformation and inquiry, over which men feel themselves to be in control. If people, as historical beings necessarily engaged with other people in a movement of inquiry, did not control that movement, it would be (and is) a violation of their humanity. Any situation in which some individuals prevent others from engaging in the process of inquiry is one of violence. The means used are not important; to alienate human beings from their own decision-making is to change them into objects.

This movement of inquiry must be directed towards humanization—the people's historical vocation. The pursuit of full humanity, however, cannot be carried out in isolation or individualism, but only in fellowship and solidarity; therefore it cannot unfold in the antagonistic relations between oppressors and oppressed. No one can be authentically human while he prevents others from being so. Attempting *to be more* human, individualistically, leads to *having more*, egotistically, a form of dehumanization. Not that it is not fundamental *to have* in order *to be* human. Precisely because it *is* necessary, some men's *having* must not be allowed to constitute an obstacle to others' *having*, must not consolidate the power of the former to crush the latter.

Problem-posing education, as a humanist and liberating praxis, posits as fundamental that the people subjected to domination must fight for their emancipation. To that end, it enables teachers and students to become Subjects of the educational process by overcoming authoritarianism and an alienating intellectualism; it also enables people to overcome their false perception of reality. The world—no longer something to be described with deceptive words—becomes the object of that transforming action by men and women which results in their humanization.

Problem-posing education does not and cannot serve the interests of the oppressor. No oppressive order could permit the oppressed to begin to question: Why? While only a revolutionary society can carry out this education in systematic terms, the revolutionary leaders need not take full power before they can employ the method. In the revolutionary process, the leaders cannot utilize the banking method as an interim measure, justified on grounds of expediency, with the intention of *later* behaving in a genuinely revolutionary fashion. They must be revolutionary—that is to say, dialogical—from the outset.

Notes

1. Simone de Beauvoir, *La pensée de droite, aujourd'hui* (Paris); ST, *El pensamiento político de la derecha* (Buenos Aires, 1963), p. 34.

2. This concept corresponds to what Sartre calls the "digestive" or "nutritive" concept of education, in which knowledge is "fed" by the teacher to the students to "fill them out." See Jean-Paul Sartre, "Une idée fundamentale de la phénomenologie de Husserl: L'intentionalité," *Situations* I (Paris, 1947).

3. For example, some professors specify in their reading lists that a book should be read from pages 10 to 15—and do this to "help" their students!

4. Eric Fromm, *The Heart of Man* (New York, 1966), p. 41.

5. Ibid., p. 31.

6. Ibid.

7. Reinhold Niebuhr, *Moral Man and Immoral Society* (New York, 1960), p. 130.

8. Sartre, op. cit., p. 32. [The passage is obscure but could be read as "Consciousness and the world are given simultaneously: The outside world as it enters consciousness is relative to our ways of perceiving it." —Editor's note]

9. Edmund Husserl, *Ideas—General Introduction to Pure Phenomenology* (London, 1969), pp. 105–06.

Working with the Text

1. Paulo Freire opens his argument with a description of what he calls the "banking" concept of education, in which "the students are the depositories and the

teacher is the depositor" (par. 5). He uses related metaphors to describe students as "containers" or "receptacles" to be "filled" by the teacher. Write a brief essay in which you use specific examples from your own education to illustrate your understanding of what Freire means by the "banking" concept.

2. As you reread the essay, think about the ways in which Freire constructs his image of the student. In a brief essay, compare the student who is a "container" to the student who is a "problem-poser." What is their relationship to the teacher? How do they gather knowledge? Who do they become as the result of how they are educated?

3. Freire argues that the "capability of banking education to minimize or annul the students' creative power and to stimulate their credulity serves the interests of the oppressors, who care neither to have the world revealed nor to see it transformed" (par. 10). Based on what Freire sees as the effects of both banking education and problem-posing education, write a brief essay that teases out the meaning of this assertion. In what ways does banking education minimize creative power and stimulate credulity? In what ways does problem-posing education reveal and transform the world?

From Text to Field

1. In his description of problem-posing education, Freire emphasizes communication, intentionality, action, and becoming fully human. Identify passages in which he is most specific about what teachers and students do in the problem-posing process. In an essay, recall a time when you experienced some aspect of the process Freire describes. As you re-create the experience, capture not only what was said and done but also your awareness that you were seeing something new, making connections to what Freire calls your own "situation" or being moved to action. Alternatively, have you ever been in a class that seemed to be based on processes similar to Freire's problem-posing method but that did not challenge you to a commitment to learning and exploring? In an essay, describe the experience, using Freire's selection to help you analyze what was missing or what was not working.

2. Students will not necessarily, or will not always, respond to problem-posing education in the ways Freire describes. In a short essay, analyze why a student might prefer banking education or might sometimes find it more useful. Consider, in those cases, whether the student risks becoming the "adapted man" Freire warns against. Might the role or value of problem-posing education differ according to the discipline or the subject studied? Might there be a place for the "banking" concept in our educational system? Why or why not?

3. In describing the "problem-posing method," Freire says that "[t]he teacher presents the material to the students for their consideration, and reconsiders his earlier considerations as the students express their own" (par. 33). In Freire's sense of the word, "consider" his essay from the vantage point of your own experience and knowledge. In a letter, or in an imagined dramatic dialogue with Freire, respond to one of his concepts or assertions. Based on your understanding of his method, pose a problem that invites a response from him. Keep in mind that you, the student, are also the teacher, and that Freire, the teacher, is also the student.

What Are Universities For?

Louis Menand

Why are you pursuing a college education? What do universities regard as their mission? What does the American public expect higher education to contribute to the making of individuals as well as citizens? Louis Menand's question—"What are universities for?"—emerged as a national issue in 1987, when Allan Bloom, a professor of social thought at the University of Chicago, published the best-selling *The Closing of the American Mind.* Widely read outside as well as inside the academy, Bloom's book is an indictment of what he regards as the abandonment of Western culture—with principle, tradition, and depth of soul being displaced by relativism and the politicization of the humanities. Menand contends that Bloom's assessment, along with the debate it sparked, misses the mark because it fails to consider how students actually regard their college education and how, in historical and social terms, the university has become "too many things to too many people." In Menand's view, the university must face its limitations as a social force and "restrict itself to the business of imparting some knowledge to the people who need it."

Menand brings to the debate his own teaching experience at Princeton, Columbia, and the University of Virginia. He is currently professor of English at the Graduate Center of the City University of New York. A prolific and highly respected social critic, Menand is a contributing editor for the *New York Review of Books* and a staff writer at the *New Yorker.* He most recently published *The Metaphysical Club* (2001), a study of the rise of American pragmatism that explores the cultural contexts that shaped the work of William James, John Dewey, and others. Highly regarded, this book has won many awards, among them the Pulitzer Prize.

Several times in the last few years I have taught a course called Introduction to Poetry. The class was always overenrolled; I usually spent the beginning of the first few meetings turning students away. Its popularity had nothing to do with me—I was one of many instructors, teaching one of many sections, and all the sections were overenrolled. Introduction to Poetry was popular because it happened to satisfy three requirements: It was a prerequisite for English department courses; it could be used as the final installment in a sequence of composition courses all students had to take; and, as a "humanities" elective, it satisfied a college-wide distribution requirement.

There are 18,000 students at my school, which is one campus of a public university. Most of them are pursuing careers in fields remote from literature; many know English only as a second language. These students approach a course on poetry with the same sense of dread with which most English majors might approach an advanced course in statistics. Other students, though, are eager to take an English course—not because they hope to acquire an appreciation of poetry, but because they believe it will enhance their communications skills and help them get into law school. And there are a few students who want to become English majors because English literature is their primary academic interest.

All of these types of students have turned up in every section of Introduction to Poetry, so I found myself trying to teach some of my students how to write a grammatical sentence, to introduce others to the academic study of literature, and to give the rest of them—though most were essentially unacquainted with serious literary culture—exposure to the best that has been thought and said in the world. For the majority of the students, of course (as they were not shy about making me aware), the principal object was to secure the passing grade needed to fulfill whatever requirement happened to apply in their case. You could walk away from a session of Introduction to Poetry feeling that whatever the current public debate over the university was about—"political correctness," deconstruction, "multiculturalism," the canon—what you had just spent the last hour or so doing had very little to do with it. Ideology was about as remote a presence in an Introduction to Poetry classroom as leather bindings.

In all the uproar over the academy—which entered the mainstream of public debate in 1987 with Allan Bloom's best-selling *The Closing of the American Mind*, and which has produced, more recently, Roger Kimball's *Tenured Radicals*, Dinesh D'Souza's *Illiberal Education* (also a best seller), cover stories in almost every news and opinion magazine of note, and even some observations in a commencement address last spring by President Bush—no one has bothered to ask what practical effect the so-called politicization of the humanities has actually had on the undergraduate mind. Seventy-four percent of the nation's freshman class last year described themselves, in a poll conducted by the American Council on Education, as politically middle-of-the-road or conservative. When they were asked why they chose to attend college, the most popular answer, picked by 78 percent, was to "get a better job" followed by to "make more money" (73 percent). Asked to name an objective they considered "essential or very important," 74 percent chose "being very well-off financially"; second place went to "raising a family," named by 70 percent (an answer almost equally popular among male and female students).

There is no evidence I know of to suggest that in four years spent trying to   5
win the grades and recommendations needed for jobs or for admission to graduate or professional school, these students become radicalized, or are in any way deflected from the social mainstream, by the few humanities courses they are required to take. Students enrolled in Introduction to Poetry would learn just as much about poetry from a professor who thought Milton was a sexist as they would from one who didn't—which is to say, in either case, that they would have had to read and talk for a few hours about a writer of whom they would otherwise remain essentially ignorant. The professor's political slant, if it can be ferreted out, makes a difference to most students only insofar as it might determine the kind of questions likely to turn up on an exam. The effect the course might have on those students' good opinion of Milton—or of any other poet they are likely to be required to read—is a microscopic influence, rapidly diminishing to zero as college recedes behind them, on their ultimate sense of things.

The educational ethos is different at a selective, residential, private college. There students are likely to be better primed to become personally engaged with the course material; they are also likely to feel the loss of income higher education represents less acutely, which enables them to enter into the spirit of their instruction with their eyes a little less fixed on the bottom line. Students at elite colleges identify much more strongly with their professors: They want to argue the nuances and to pick up the insights. But in the end the practical impact is much the same. Anyone who has taught literature at such a school knows the phenomenon: The brightest students happily learn the most advanced styles of contemporary critical theory, with all of their radical political implications, and then they apply, with equal good cheer, to business school. Whatever subversiveness they have ingested has mostly served to give them a kind of superior intellectual sophistication that they are right to feel is not in the least bit incompatible with professional success on Wall Street or Madison Avenue.

Academic thought may have been heading left in the last ten years or so, in other words, but college students themselves have been heading straight into the mainstream. Even comfortably middle-class students feel an economic imperative almost unknown to middle-class students of twenty years ago. When I was a freshman, in 1969, I didn't have a thought in my head about how I was eventually going to support myself. I suppose I imagined that I would just hitchhike around the country with my guitar (which I didn't know how to play) reciting my poetry (which I didn't know how to write).

In the 1990s, though, young people in the middle class are perfectly alive to the fact that they go to college because they have to; young people not in the middle class continue to go to college for the reason they always have, which is to get into the middle class. It seems to me that there is every good reason to challenge these students for a semester or two to think with a little balanced skepticism about the conventional wisdom of the society they are so anxious to join. But whether they're being taught skepticism or not, literature classes are the last places students are likely to be getting their values. Madonna has done more to affect the way young people think about sexuality than all the academic gender theorists put together. Perhaps D'Souza should write a book about her.

It's easier, of course, to attack Catharine Stimpson, the former dean of graduate school at Rutgers and former president of the Modern Language Association, who has become one of the point persons in the defense of new academic trends. Stimpson doesn't appear on MTV, so there isn't a tidal wave of popular sentiment to overcome before one can take her to task. But the lack of a mass following ought to be a clue to the extent of Stimpson's, or any other academic's, real influence on the culture at large. A group of literature professors calling themselves Teachers for a Democratic Culture has come together this fall to launch a counteroffensive against the attack on "political correctness." I suspect that it's a little late in the day for a counteroffensive: The center on this issue has already been grabbed. But one of the arguments this new group wants to make is that the whole situation has been exaggerated. I think it's a just complaint.

It isn't hard to guess the motives behind the controversy in its present melo-   10
dramatic mode. It is always tempting to blame bad conditions on bad ideas, and it must seem to conservatives that since liberal and leftist thinking has been driven out of nearly every other part of American life, the pitiful remnant of left-wing ideology that has taken refuge in university literature departments must be the reason social problems so disobligingly persist. It is the good fortune of conservatives that this is a view that meets exactly the belief of some of the professors being attacked, which is that they are in possession of the one ground—the humanities curriculum of American colleges—on which real social change might be accomplished. The American media, for their rather inflammatory part, are always happy to find an occasion not to appear too liberal, and the excesses of "political correctness" are the perfect thing to get noisily to the right of. The whole controversy is marvelously apt in a country that no longer shows any interest in publicly funded social programs; for whichever political faction wins control of the undergraduate reading list, no taxpayer dollars will have been spent.

This doesn't mean that there's not a crisis. But the issue is not whether (in the words of some of the demonstrators against Stanford's core curriculum a few years ago) Western culture's got to go. Western culture, whether it's in good odor at the Modern Language Association these days or not, we're stuck with. The real issue concerns the role of higher education in American life. Too many people are fighting over how much T. S. Eliot versus how much Alice Walker young minds ought to be exposed to, and not enough people are asking why undergraduate English courses should be bearing the load of this debate in the first place. What is it we are expecting colleges to do that makes the particular mix of the reading lists in literature courses seem to spell the difference between—well, between culture and anarchy?

Matthew Arnold is, indeed, the name most frequently associated with the traditional idea of liberal arts education that the new wave of "politicization" in the academy is supposed to be wrecking. But the liberal arts component of higher education belongs to what is in some ways the least salient of the university's social functions. In fact, the Arnoldian program of using humanistic studies as a means of moral instruction, far from being the most venerable of the university's activities, entered the modern university almost as an afterthought.

The modern university in America is defined by two features, both of which date from the late nineteenth century: the existence of an elective curriculum for undergraduates and the existence of a graduate school, which trains the people who teach the undergraduates. The elective system was not designed to disseminate culture. When Charles William Eliot instituted the first elective system, at Harvard in 1883, his idea was to allow college students to "track" themselves in the direction of their future careers—not to acquire a common culture, but to specialize according to individual needs. Eliot believed that college ought to play a vocational role, to serve a frankly utilitarian function. His faith in the real-world utility of academic studies was great enough, in fact, to allow him, in 1901, to praise the assembled scholars of the Modern Language Association, virtually all of whom were philologists, by telling them that their work enjoyed "a vital connection with the industrial and commercial activities of the day."

At the same time, Eliot saw the need to provide specialists to train college students, and in 1890 he established the Harvard Graduate School of Arts and Sciences, modeled on the first research institution in the country, Johns Hopkins (founded in 1876). The principal function of the graduate school is the production of teachers, whom it certifies with the doctoral degree, to staff the modern college; but it also produces scholarly research, and the research ideal is expressly nonutilitarian. The researcher cannot be influenced by what the world will find profitable: The goal is knowledge for its own sake, without regard for "the industrial and commercial activities of the day."

So there was already in the modern university, as Eliot and the other 15 late-nineteenth-century pioneers of higher education helped to create it, a contradiction between what professors do, which is to follow their research interests, and what their students do, which is to prepare for careers outside the academy—to pursue "education for experience," as Eliot called it. There is no reason, of course, as William James complained in 1903 in an essay called "The Ph.D. Octopus," why the possession of a doctorate, earned by scholarship, should serve as a credential for teaching undergraduates; yet these separate functions were made to complement each other, and by the end of the nineteenth century the ideals of research and of vocational training had achieved such an ascendancy in American universities that a reaction against them occurred on behalf of what was called, by many of its champions, "liberal culture." This reaction is the origin of the idea that college is the place of future social leaders to be exposed to, in Arnold's phrase, "the study of perfection." The liberal arts "tradition" that the new scholarship is accused of trashing, in other words, is not even a century old.

The "true aim of culture," wrote Hiram Corson, the chairman of the Cornell English department and a proponent of "liberal culture," in 1894, is "to induce soul states or conditions, soul attitudes, to attune the inward forces to the idealized forms of nature and of human life produced by art, and not to make the head a cockloft for storing away the trumpery of barren knowledge." This ideal is both anti-utilitarian and antiresearch, and the reaction on its behalf was successful enough to lead, in 1909, to Eliot's replacement as president of Harvard by A. Lawrence Lowell—a member of the faculty who, many years before, had opposed the institution of the elective system. Thus emerged the third mission of the modern academy: the liberalization, through exposure to art, literature, and philosophy, of the undergraduate mind.

Although no school was ever purely one type or another, universities before 1910 could be distinguished according to their leading educational ideals: Harvard was utilitarian, for example; Johns Hopkins, Clark, and Chicago were research institutions. Schools like Princeton and Yale tended to resist both these trends. But after 1910 (as Laurence Veysey explains in *The Emergence of the American University*) there was a shift. Educators stopped arguing about ideals; the various versions of what properly constituted higher education were no longer regarded as conflicting. The university learned to accommodate divergent views of its purpose, and the goal of the people who administered universities became not the defense of an educational philosophy but the prosperity of the institution. And the prosperity of the institution depended on its being, to as great an extent as it found possible, all things to all people.

This is how a pedagogical portmanteau like Introduction to Poetry could come into being—a single course on a specific subject expected to serve, all at the same time, a utilitarian function (by training students how to read and write), a research function (by preparing future English majors for the scholarly study of literature), and a liberal arts function (by exposing students to the leavening influence of high culture).

Even at schools where there is no actual Introduction to Poetry course, the overall effect of the undergraduate curriculum is the same. Students in the humanities are expected to major in a field—French, say, or religion—that will provide them with a lot of knowledge most of which will be useful only in the unlikely event they decide to enter graduate school and become professors themselves. At the same time, they are required to fulfill "distribution" requirements designed to expose them to smatterings of learning in every major area—with the vague idea that this contributes to something approximating genuine well-roundedness, and thus serves a "liberalizing" function. And there is the expectation, now almost universal, that beyond college lies professional school, for which some practical training will be useful.

It's possible to argue that these three educational functions—scholarly, 20 vocational, and liberalizing—are only three ways of looking at the same thing, which is the exposure to knowledge. For higher

The university is unequipped to deal with conflicts that cannot be treated simply as conflicts of ideas.

education in any field certainly can serve, simultaneously, all three purposes: pure speculation, practical application, and general enlightenment. Even so, there needs to be a consensus that these benefits are worth pursuing, and that the traditional structure of the university provides the best means of doing so, in order for the system to work effectively. Three recent developments, none of them having to do explicitly with politics—illiberal or not—seem to me to have undermined this consensus.

The first is the major demographic change in the undergraduate population over the last twenty years, a change that reflects both a significant increase in the proportion of people who attend college (from 1970 to 1988, the percentage of Americans who had completed four years of college doubled) and a significant increase on most campuses in the proportion of students who are not white or not male. This means that the average college class is not the relatively homogeneous group, culturally and socioeconomically speaking, it once was: The level of preparation among students differs more widely, and their interests and assumptions differ as well.

Since the whole idea of liberal arts education is to use literature and philosophy as a way of learning how to value one's interests and assumptions, it is (or it ought to be) obviously absurd to insist that books that served this function when the audience was predominantly made up of young middle-class white men can serve the same function now that the audience is more diverse. When Columbia College admitted women for the first time, in 1983, it was suddenly realized by the faculty that the reading list for Humanities A, the famous great books course required of all students, had never included a book by a woman. Though for years it had been advertised as representing the best that the educated person needed to know, the list was changed: Sappho and Jane Austen became great writers. It took some fancy rhetoric to explain why this adjustment didn't amount to a confession that "the great books" is really just a grand name for "the books that will expose students to ideas we want them at the moment to be talking about." And that is part of the problem; for since so much has been emotionally (and, I think, mistakenly) invested in the traditional great books curriculum, changes can't happen without resentment and reaction.

The second development putting pressure on traditional educational ideals is the spread of critical theory as a kind of interdisciplinary currency in university humanities departments. For contemporary critical theory—in particular post-structuralist theories, emphasizing the indeterminacy of meaning, and ideological theories, emphasizing the social construction of values—rejects precisely the belief on which the professional apparatus of the university (graduate exams, dissertation defenses, tenure review, publication in refereed journals, and so forth) depends: the belief that the pursuit of knowledge is a disinterested activity whose results can be evaluated objectively by other trained specialists in one's field. "What's really going on" in the production of knowledge is now regarded, by these new theoretical lights, as not a disinterested enterprise at all but an effort to make the views of a particular class of people prevail.

This rejection of the positivistic model of knowledge production has helped to turn the system of professional rewards, always an arena for academic politics, into an arena for real-world politics as well. Critical theorists whose work attacks the traditional premises of scholarship are invited into humanities departments for the good marketing reason that their work is where the action is today: Every graduate program wants a prominent profile. But the system whose principles those professors teach one another to regard with skepticism remains, except that it has been thoroughly corrupted. It is now regarded as legitimate by some professors to argue that the absence of a political intention or multicultural focus in another professor's work constitutes a prima facie disqualification for professional advancement. And why not, if all scholarship is at bottom political anyway?

Finally, there has been a change in the role of college in the preparation 25 of young people for careers outside the academy. Although the number of bachelor's degrees awarded each year has been increasing steadily—by 28 percent between 1970 and 1989—the number of professional degrees has been increasing at a much greater rate. The material value of a BA is a function of supply: The greater the number of people who have one, the less a BA is worth in the marketplace. Particularly for students interested in "being very well-off financially" (74 percent, according to the American Council of Education survey), it has now become imperative not to stop with the BA but to proceed to professional school; and the number of MBAs awarded between 1970 and 1989 therefore increased by 239 percent, the number of MDs by 88 percent, the number of law degrees by 143 percent. Increases in advanced degrees in architecture, engineering, and a number of other nonacademic professional fields were similarly dramatic.

This wave of professionalism has transformed the experience of college. The academic demands on undergraduates are in a sense now more real, since good grades are essential for getting over the hurdle to the next degree program; but the content is somehow less real, since most students now perceive that the education that matters to them will take place after college is finished. This helps to explain the phenomenon of the undergraduate whiz in Foucauldian analysis who goes merrily on to a career in corporate finance.

These various challenges to the established design of higher education present difficulties that have little to do with politics. Perhaps the university will find a way to muddle through them, but muddling alone is not likely to be very effective. For it is not only a philosophical idea about education that is being thrown into doubt by these recent developments. It is also the institutional structure of the university itself.

I happen to think, for example—and without putting any political valuation on the judgment—that contemporary theoretical skepticism about the positivistic nature of "knowledge" in fields like literature is perfectly justified. It is absurd to treat literary criticism as a species of scientific inquiry; the professional system of rewards in the humanistic disciplines is essentially bogus and leads mostly to intellectual conformity, predictable "demonstrations" of theoretical points, and a panicky desire to please one's elders and superiors. But what university is about to tear down the bureaucratic system of professional advancement in the humanities? How would departments administer themselves without the fiction that they were engaged in the production of real knowledge about real specialities?

Similarly, the undergraduate major seems to me an institution that is at best pedagogically inefficient (why should students going on to law school have to pass a course of what amounts to preprofessional training for graduate school in English or some other academic discipline?) and at worst a contributor to the perpetuation of a fundamentally arbitrary definition of knowledge. The modern academic discipline is only as old as the modern university: Before the 1800s, no one imagined that history, political science, economics, anthropology, and sociology constituted distant areas of study, each with its own theoretical and methodological traditions. Nor was it imagined by most people that "literature" was a discriminable area of human endeavor that must be talked about exclusively in literary-critical (as opposed to sociological or ethical or theological) terms.

But these distinctions have become institutionalized in the form of aca- 30 demic departments; the people who work in those departments have professionalized themselves to keep out "unqualified" practitioners; and the professions run the fields, monopolizing both instruction and scholarship. It seems to me that a college student today might want, in four years, to acquire knowledge about American culture, about American politics and law, and about capitalism. What a student who bothers to seek out knowledge in these areas is likely to get are courses introducing him or her to the academic specialities of American studies, political science, and economics. Though there is no reason why every undergraduate should not receive it, a practical introduction to the law or to business must usually wait until law school or business school, since that is where the specialists are. Because there are no instructors who are not certified members of an academic discipline, there is very little genuinely general education going on in American colleges.

These problems are severe enough, but they don't explain completely why the university is in such a bad way right now. Questions about educational philosophy must eventually have educational answers; the contemporary university, though, has reached beyond the purview of education, and it has thereby become entangled in problems it lacks the means to resolve. Universities can decide the things people ought to know, and they can decide how those things should be taught. But universities cannot arbitrate disputes about democracy and social justice, or govern the manner in which people relate socially to one another, or police attitudes; and that is what they are being asked to do today.

To some extent this overreaching is the fault of the society as a whole, which is happy to turn over to educators problems it lacks the will (and, it believes, the means) to address politically. It is easier to integrate a reading list, or even a dormitory, than it is to integrate a suburban neighborhood. But to some extent it is the consequence of the university's own indiscriminate appetite, whose history begins in the 1960s.

The contention that the current problems in the academy are the natural outcome of sixties radicalism is common to many of the recent attacks on higher education—it can be found in Bloom's, Kimball's, and D'Souza's books. I think the claim is basically false, and that (as Camille Paglia argued in a long diatribe on the subject last spring in the journal *Arion*) the humorless ethos of the politically correct humanities department could not be more antithetical to the spirit of the 1960s. Even the most callow radicalism of that era has nothing to do with the sort of doctrinaire political attitudes critics of the contemporary academy complain about. Are the people who are so eager to censor "fighting words" on campus today the same people who went around in 1968 calling anyone wearing a uniform or a necktie a "pig"? If they are the same people, they've left their radicalism behind.

There is one thing, however, that the present situation does owe to the 1960s, and that is the belief that the university is a miniature reproduction of the society as a whole. That idea dominates, for example, the Port Huron Statement, the manifesto of the New Left drafted by Tom Hayden and endorsed by the Students for a Democratic Society in 1962. But it is not only a leftist idea; for the postwar university has always been eager to incorporate every new intellectual and cultural development that has come its way.

The university is, in fact, expressly designed to do this: It can accommo-   35
date almost any interest by creating a new course, a new program, a new studies center. It has managed, for instance, to institutionalize activities like painting and creative writing, not traditionally thought to require academic preparation, by devising MFA programs—which, in turn, provide a place on university faculties for practicing painters and writers. When new scholarly movements emerged—Third World Studies, Women's Studies—the university was quick to establish research centers and institutes to house them. Degrees are now offered in almost everything. There are few intellectual activities left that do not have an academic incarnation.

The problems begin when this process of absorption extends beyond the intellectual realm. In the late 1960s, serious attention began to be paid by university administrators to the quality of campus life. This, too, was in part a response to student protest: Everyone agreed, for example, that one of the lessons of the crisis that led to the shutdown of Columbia in 1968 was that the college had to become less like a corporation and more like a community. But it was also natural that, as higher education became accessible to (and desired by) a greater variety of people in the postwar boom years, the university would evolve in this direction of its own accord.

This development of the university as a social microcosm has been guided in most places by the view (which originated with the students themselves) that there should be available within the walls of the academy the full range of experiences available (or ideally available) outside. The initial breakthrough was a purely middle-class phenomenon: the liberalization of parietal restrictions. (In the late 1960s, to give an idea of the magnitude of the change that has taken place, a student at Barnard, a sophisticated school in a sophisticated city, was expelled for sharing an apartment with her boyfriend *off campus*.) The eventual abandonment of regulations governing relations between the sexes was followed by the sexual integration of many traditionally single-sex schools (Princeton, Yale, Dartmouth, Vassar), and by the recruitment of ethnic minorities in the interest (among other things) of social diversity on campus.

This enormous and successful engulfment of intellectual and social variety, coming on top of the shocks to the system's *academic* identity, is what has given the university its present headache. The university has become, at last, too many things to too many people. It now reproduces all the conflicts of the culture at large; but it reproduces them, as it were, in vitro. For unlike the society it simulates, the university is unequipped, both administratively and philosophically, to deal with conflicts that cannot be treated simply as conflicts of ideas. It has the machinery needed to arbitrate the sorts of disagreements that arise naturally in the pursuit of the university's traditional educational goals; but it is not designed to arbitrate among antagonistic interest groups, or to discover ways of correcting inequities and attitudes that persist in the society as a whole.

The reason is that the university is required, by its accommodationist philosophy, to give equal protection to every idea and point of view anyone chooses to express. This is, of course, an indispensable principle of intellectual freedom. But when the issue is political, when it involves the distribution of power, accommodationism fails. For power is a zero-sum game. In the real world, interest groups vie against one another for resources in the knowledge that one group gains by taking from other groups. Political and legal institutions exist to mediate these struggles.

In the university, though, no one has ever needed to cede ground to someone else, since conflict has always been avoided by expanding the playing field. But this strategy doesn't work when the stakes are not simply intellectual. As long as the activities of the Gay Student Alliance and the Bible Study Group remain merely academic, they can coexist. Once those groups become versions of their real-world counterparts—once they become actively political—there is no way to keep both of them happy. But who in the university wants to have to choose between them? In the nonacademic world, pluralism means a continual struggle over the distribution of a single pie. In the academic world (and the Democratic Party), it means trying to give every group a pie of its own.

Yet somehow it is expected that, once they are relocated to a campus, differences that have proved intractable elsewhere will be overcome, both in the classroom and in the student union. This insistence, on the part of academics and nonacademics alike, on making higher education the site for political and social disputes of all types, and on regarding the improvement of social relations and the mediation of political differences as one of higher education's proper functions, has produced ridiculous distortions. Thus we have a debate, for example, in which the economic rights of women are argued about in terms of reading lists for introductory literature courses—as

40

though devoting fewer class hours to male authors might be counted a blow against discrimination in the workplace. And outside the classroom, in the dorms and the dean's office, the university has managed to become a laboratory for the study and cure of social problems like date rape.

There are as well the notorious speech codes and disciplinary procedures aimed at enforcing campus "civility." These are mostly the results of hasty attempts to jury-rig disciplinary systems whose need had not been felt until it became commonly assumed that how students addressed one another was a matter college administrators ought to be concerned about. That the president of the university should have become the leading figure and spokesperson in the incident in which a Brown undergraduate was expelled for drunkenly shouting insults at no one in particular is an indication not only that the university doesn't know how seriously it is supposed to be taking these sorts of "problems" but that it has no appropriate administrative apparatus for dealing with them either.

And there is, to take a final example, the notion—much less prevalent than the critics of political correctness claim, but present nonetheless—that the undergraduate curriculum should include courses whose purpose is, in effect, to cheerlead for civil and sexual rights. There is no doubt that many civil and sexual rights remain to be secured in this country; there is no doubt that scandalous inequities persist unattended to. But English professors are not experts on these matters. They are taught how to identify tropes, not how to eliminate racist attitudes. To turn their courses into classes on (say) Post-Colonial Literature with the idea of addressing with some degree of insight the problem of ethnocentrism is to ask someone equipped to catch butterflies to trap an elephant.

This is done, usually, by pretending the butterfly is an elephant—by loading up a poem with so much ideological baggage that it can pass for an instrument of oppression. Poems won't bear the weight; most works of literature are designed to deflect exactly this kind of attention and to confute efforts to assign them specific political force. If literature is taught honestly from an ideological perspective—if what a book seems to say about the relations of power among people is made the focus of classroom discussion—students are just being led around the mulberry bush. It's not that the spirit of great literature is being dishonored, for literature can surely be talked about ideologically; it's that a false impression is being created among students that unhappiness whose amelioration lies in real-world political actions is being meaningfully addressed by classroom debates about the representation of the Other in the work of Herman Melville.

Professors should not be regarded as the people in possession of the "correct" views on subjects of public concern. But the idea that they ought to be   45 has become an illusion shared by academics and their critics alike. When George Will wrote last spring in *Newsweek* that the task faced by Secretary of Defense Dick Cheney was less urgent than the one confronting his wife, Lynne, who is the director of the National Endowment for the Humanities, he sounded clearly the note of hysteria that has come to dominate debate about higher education in America. Mrs. Cheney, Will suggested, "is secretary of domestic defense. The foreign adversaries her husband, Dick, must keep at bay are less dangerous, in the long run, than the domestic forces with which she must deal. Those forces are fighting against the conservation of the common culture that is the nation's social cement."

This is witch-hunt talk; but it repeats an error found in less partisan writing as well, which is that the care of "the common culture" is the responsibility of college professors. Professors are people trained to *study* culture, not to *conserve* it (whatever that would mean). Their purview is limited by the kind of work, always highly specialized and narrowly defined, professionals in their disciplines have traditionally done. It is no favor to these people to regard them as the guardians of our culture or as experts on ministering to its self-inflicted wounds. Nor is it a favor to the culture to hand it over to academics for its nourishment and protection.

Social and political controversies have swamped the academy for two reasons: because universities, unwilling to define their mission in specific terms and eager to accommodate everything that comes along, could not find a rationale for keeping those controversies at bay; and because there has been so little serious intellectual debate in the rest of American society in the last ten years. There have been no real ideas argued in American politics, for instance, since Ronald Reagan showed that ideas were overrated. And intellectual journalism has become dominated by position-taking—the point-counterpoint syndrome, which permits just two points of view to every prepackaged "issue."

It is almost certain that one of the effects of the public scrutiny of what professors do will be to turn the academy into another bastion of intellectual predictability. I'm not sure that hasn't happened already. But if not, the only way to prevent it is for the university to renounce the role of model community and arbiter of social disputes that it has assumed, to ignore the impulse to regulate attitudes and expressions that are the epiphenomena of problems far outside the college walls, to stop trying to set up academic housing for every intellectual and political interest group that comes along, and to restrict itself to the business of imparting some knowledge to the people who need it.

Working with the Text

1. Louis Menand's essay addresses what he considers to be a crisis in university education. In his argument, he assumes his audience has a certain amount of familiarity with the debate, a familiarity you might not share. As you reread the essay, what can you infer about the nature of the crisis? Based on your reading of Menand's argument, write a brief essay in which you provide a snapshot or distillation of the crisis to an audience of your peers—students with a level of familiarity similar to yours. What prompted the debate? What are the key issues? What is at stake, for university students as well as for American culture?

2. According to Menand, one of the recent developments that have undermined reaching consensus on university education has been "the major demographic change in the undergraduate population over the last twenty years" (par. 21). Choose one specific aspect of demographic change (socioeconomic status, access to education, gender, ethnic diversity, etc.) to analyze this assertion in more detail, adding your own observations and reasoning to Menand's. For example, how would such a shift in demographics influence codes of conduct or the attempt to "discover ways of correcting inequities and attitudes that persist in the society as a whole" (par. 38) or the trend toward more students going on to professional schools?

3. In the final sentence, Menand answers the question he poses in the essay's title by asserting that the university must "restrict itself to the business of imparting some knowledge to the people who need it." In a brief essay, respond to this assertion by first analyzing what Menand means by "some knowledge" and "the people who need it." According to Menand, who needs to know what? Why do they "need" to know it? Do you agree with him? Why or why not? Is Menand's assertion realistic or desirable? What might universities or citizens lose if Menand were to have his way?

4. In large part, Menand argues for what universities should be by arguing against what he believes they have become. As you reread the essay, note Menand's objections to particular roles now taken on by universities. In a brief essay, address one of those objections. Do you agree with him? Why or why not?

From Text to Field

1. As a point of departure for his argument, Menand notes the results of a poll conducted by the American Council on Education that asked students why they chose to attend college. Menand also describes student attitudes that he has encountered as an educator. With these and other passages in mind, write a personal essay that reveals your own reasons for pursuing an undergraduate degree. What "knowledge" do you think you "need," and to what end? Do you

expect certain courses to have a lasting influence or "a microscopic influence, rapidly diminishing to zero as college recedes" on your "ultimate sense of things" (par. 5)?

2. Menand criticizes "the notion . . . that the undergraduate curriculum should include courses whose purpose is, in effect, to cheerlead for civil and sexual rights" (par. 43). In a brief essay, analyze a course you are taking or have taken that has or seems to have cheerleading for rights as one of its purposes. What form does the advocacy for civil and sexual rights take? How large a part of the course is it? Is the advocacy effective? Do you think this is a legitimate purpose for a course? How realistic is it to avoid advocacy of any kind?

3. Commenting on where students get their values, Menand says, "Madonna has done more to affect the way young people think about sexuality than all the academic gender theorists put together" (par. 8). In a personal essay that reflects on your own values or in a cultural critique that examines the values of your peers or a particular group of your peers, identify the sources— outside of your family—of those values. Be specific about personalities, ideas, the medium (such as music, film, discussion groups, lectures, books), and style. What engages and moves you? How do values take root? What authority do the sources carry? As an alternative essay, reflect on one source—one artist, author, teacher, or group—that has been especially powerful in shaping your values or those of your peers.

INTO THE FIELD: Options for Writing Projects

1. **Agendas for Literacy**

   From elementary, high school, and college courses to community programs for recent immigrants and nonnative speakers, your community is the site for various literacy efforts. Choose one program—academic or community based—and examine how this program approaches its interest in literacy. What is its explicit or implied mission statement? How might various pedagogical tools (books, materials, etc.) reflect a choice in how literacy is defined? Does the funding source for the program suggest an interest in one approach over another? How does the program define the needs of its target audience? What other stakeholders are involved in the program's efforts?

   Drawing on your research and fieldwork, write a profile of the literacy program that reflects how it situates its definitions of *literacy* among other contending definitions.

2. **Writing the Writing Requirement**

   Based on interviews and available documents such as your college catalog or Web pages, analyze the writing program or writing requirement in your institution. What are its stated purposes? How is it structured, and why? What course options are available? What is the rationale behind the range (or lack of range) of options, and what assumptions about student growth and learning lie behind their sequencing? Based on your analysis, develop a flyer or pamphlet for incoming students in which you speak as one student to another, acting as a peer advisor, about what to expect from and how to navigate the writing program and the writing classroom. Use a style that will readily appeal to other students. Feel free to use humor as you try to help these new students feel comfortable in this new course.

3. **Exploring Your Writing Archive**

   Unearth examples of your writing from some years ago. Look to your parents as (unofficial) archivists, for they often keep copies of your work from elementary or middle school, even high school. As you reflect on your writing from years past, consider what struggles or challenges you had as a writer at that time. What virtues or strengths do you see in your old writing that you would like to regain, if at a more sophisticated level? Based on your close reading of a sample or two, choose one of the following for your writing project:

   - Offer an analysis of your writing and how it reflects your attempts to succeed at a task that is now quite familiar to you but was at the time new and foreign. What distinguishes your writing as that of a novice? As you look back at that writing and compare it to your current work, what specific details might help you explain your development as a writer?

- Offer a memoir of yourself as a writer, using the writing you have chosen as its centerpiece or touchstone. How does this seemingly isolated and discrete piece of writing provide a window on your life, both then and now?

4. Reviewing the Transition to College-Level Learning

Locate several books, articles and book chapters, or pamphlets that were written as guides to making the transition into college-level learning. To what extent does the material reflect learning theories as discussed in the readings by Williams and Colomb and by Freire? What alternatives to those theories does the material present, if only implicitly? Feel free to draw on other learning theorists. (You might, for example, be interested in exploring the work of William Perry and his scheme of multiple stages of intellectual development.) Write an analysis or a review of the guide material you have found in light of your reading and your own experience. You may wish to interview classmates or work together as an editorial or review team. How helpful are such guides? To what extent can they prepare you well for the transition to college-level learning? How valid are generalizations about "college-level learning"? What might make those generalizations difficult to offer?

5. The Expert as Novice

Have you ever found yourself in a situation where your expertise in one area offered little help as you moved to a slightly different area? Write an extended personal narrative using one of the options offered below.

- Choose an area in which you clearly have some expertise (such as music, sports, or art), and then reflect on the challenges you might face when trying your hand in a related area or activity at which you are a novice. Why might you easily become frustrated? What might happen—to your learning process, self-image, or confidence—when processes that are second nature in your field of expertise become conscious, concrete, rule-governed, and step by step in the new activity?
- By senior year in high school, you had become an expert in the system of secondary education. Now, as an undergraduate, you are more of a novice. Reflect on what has—and hasn't—changed for you. As you encounter college-level learning and knowledge making, how have your thinking and study habits changed in terms of your ability to master the subject matter, articulate questions, and solve the problems that are posed? Has anything other than the level or amount of knowledge changed? In what ways have expectations changed? Has anyone ever made explicit what those new expectations are? If not, why not?

6. Reading Fashions and Curricular Politics

When you enroll in a course for just one term, your sense of the syllabus can easily become limited to those few weeks during which you are engaged with the material. But beyond the artificial boundaries of any one term, courses and their reading lists evolve, often in response to reading fashions, the latest pedagogical trend, or curricular politics. Each of the options listed below can help you place your current work in a broader perspective.

- Find one particular course that has been part of the curriculum on your campus for twenty years or more. Based on a review of reading lists and syllabi, catalog course descriptions, and interviews with those faculty or department secretaries who carry around with them some "institutional memory," compare the course in the past to the course as it is currently taught. What inferences can you make about the changes? What hasn't changed?
- Every department has an array of required and elective courses. Choosing one department, consult the current edition of your college catalog for course descriptions and compare it to a catalog from twenty or forty or eighty years ago. (Your campus library or library archive should have a complete run of catalogs from the founding of your institution.) Which new courses have been added, which have disappeared, and which simply seem to endure? What might these changes tell you about which books are being read, and for what purposes? How has the department evolved over time? What might those changes tell you about the evolving mission of the department or your college or about the pressures and expectations that society might place on your institution?
- Propose a new course or a new reading list for an existing course. (Most campuses have a required form for such proposals, and you might find it interesting to try your hand at filling it out.) What decisions did you encounter in proposing that new course or reading list? How would you justify your choices? What are the prevailing interests and concerns of faculty and administrators who would have to approve your proposal?

7. Public Reading Habits

When Katha Pollitt turns her attention to required-reading lists and the currently accepted canon of "Important Books," she urges us not to forget why we read books ourselves. In that spirit, and using her essay as an invitation, check out the reading habits of your community as reflected by your local public library and bookstores. What's hot, and what is in demand? What local interests, concerns, or preferences might be reflected in library circulation statistics or bookstore sales figures? How might your community compare to others in your state or with more national indicators, such as the best-seller lists compiled by the *New York Times* and other publications? You may find it very helpful to interview a local librarian or library administrator.

Alternatively, you may wish to explore one of several national book clubs, such as Oprah Winfrey's. Such clubs have a long history in our society, and some communities even have local chapters. What do their reading lists look like, and how have they changed over the years? What influence might such clubs have in guiding the reading tastes of the public (or in confirming existing tastes)? What special satisfactions or enjoyments might be found in being a member of such a club?

8. What's Off the List: Reading Lists and Censorship

Our preoccupation with required-reading lists and the changing fortunes of various writers may hide from view the darker side of reading lists. Some books are not "on the list" because they have been censored by one of several local or national groups or because the threat of such censorship is very real. You may be surprised to learn that a number of well-known books—both classic and contemporary—have been the subjects of censorship campaigns, among them *The Adventures of Huckleberry Finn* by Mark Twain, *The Diary of a Young Girl* by Anne Frank, *The Catcher in the Rye* by J. D. Salinger, *Nineteen Eighty-four* by George Orwell, and the several books in the Harry Potter series. For your fieldwork project, consider one of the options below. You may find the following Web site to be a helpful point of departure for your fieldwork: http://www.ncte.org/about/over/positions/category/cens. This Web site has links to other national and international organizations concerned with censorship issues.

- Choose a book you know well that has been the subject of censorship battles. After you become familiar with the concerns that prompted calls for censorship, draw on your knowledge of the book to write an essay that evaluates the censorship debate and places it in historical context or the context of prevailing community attitudes.
- Contact the middle school or high school that you attended and interview an English teacher or the principal. Does he or she know of censorship issues that your school is currently experiencing or has experienced in the recent past? Contribute to that debate from the perspective of a former student who has now gone on to college. Alternatively, explore what selection procedures your middle school or high school has in place when determining what books will be read in the classroom. Do those procedures seem adequate or fair?

9. From Banking to Problem-Posing

Describe a course that you have taken that used what Paulo Freire refers to as the "banking concept" of education, and propose specific changes that would permit the course to emphasize to a greater degree a "problem-posing" approach. Focus in some detail on an activity, assignment, or other concrete aspect of the course. What are some of the challenges that both teachers and students might face in seeking to implement a problem-solving approach? What responsibilities do students have in making such an approach successful? Do certain kinds of courses, topics, or activities lend themselves more than others to this kind of reworking? What might be the risks in such a reworking, and what might be lost that you think is of value?

Alternatively, choose one of the many other readings in this book and write a teaching guide that would suggest how to work with that selection in a Freirian manner. How would you orchestrate the discussion, and what might you emphasize? What kind of writing assignment would suit a Freirian approach, and how might a Freirian-inspired instructor comment on that essay? Do you think students would respond positively to your approach? If not, why? What adjustments would your teaching and writing suggestions require of both teachers and students? Can you anticipate ways in which your suggestions might not work as you intend them to?

10. The Banking System

When reading Paulo Freire it is tempting to connect what he says to particular teachers or courses you have had. Yet for the banking approach to education to have such a strong grip on our society, more must be involved than just stories about particular people or courses, be they good or bad. This fieldwork project has you look beyond the particulars to the larger system of education that tends to reinforce the banking approach. What institutional practices support the banking concept? Referring to your secondary education or to your current experiences in college, discuss particular institutional practices and what influence they have. Those practices might include assessment and testing, transcripts and credit hours, the use of textbooks, prerequisites and the sequencing of courses, and the role of credentials. What positive role might some of these institutional practices have? Could a Freirian-inspired approach to education do without such institutional practices, or how might it change them?

11. Menand Comes to Campus

Louis Menand asserts that "universities cannot arbitrate disputes about democracy and social justice, or govern the manner in which people relate socially to one another, or police attitudes; and that is what they are being asked to do today" (par. 31). Identify a policy, practice, or program in your institution that Menand might say is aimed at taking on this kind of responsibility. Write an analysis of that policy, practice, or program. Why was it instituted? What debates surrounded its establishment? Who are its advocates and critics, and what are their positions? How effective is it in accomplishing its purpose? What is your view of its validity as a function of your particular institution?

12. A 1960s Retrospective

In discussing the changing role of higher education in our society, Louis Menand points to the 1960s and early 1970s as a watershed, a turning point in how universities conceived of their social and educational mission and in how society viewed universities. Here are two options for fieldwork projects that invite you to revisit that era.

- Interview one person, or ideally several people, who went to college during the 1960s and early 1970s. What was their firsthand experience? What do they remember of the incidents and developments discussed by Menand? What did they see as the purpose of their own university education? How do they describe their experience of being on a college campus during those years? If possible, include the perspective of someone who taught on a university level during those years. Offer the results of your interviews as a brief oral history or memoir.
- Explore the history of your college or university during the '60s and early '70s. In the context of broader historical events, what specific changes occurred on campus during that time or, if later, may be attributed to the new attitudes that this period fostered? In short, what is the legacy of this period on your campus? Was this period a watershed for your institution? For this fieldwork project, consider interviews with older faculty, back issues of campus newspapers, and published histories of your college or university (in print or online). You may wish to offer the results of your fieldwork as one chapter in such a history.

13. Student Attitudes and Educational Plans

How you "write the university" depends in good measure on your attitudes and educational plans. According to Louis Menand, these attitudes and plans have a profound effect on the changing role of colleges and universities in our society. With your classmates, you might explore why you and others are attending college and what your attitudes might be on a range of educational and career issues. How do your own attitudes square with Menand's portrayal of them?

To lend some national context to your discussions, you may wish to consult the Web site of the Higher Education Research Institute (HERI) at the UCLA Graduate School of Education and Information Studies (GSEIS): http://www.gseis.ucla.edu/heri/heri.html. For some forty years, the institute has conducted a comprehensive assessment survey of the attitudes and education plans of entering college students. For recent results and survey instruments,

consult http://www.gseis.ucla.edu/heri/cirp.html. More recently, the institute has begun to survey students about their experiences during freshman
year. Results of the latest "Your First College Year" survey can be found at
http://www.gseis.ucla.edu/heri/yfcy/. To what extent do you see your attitudes and plans captured in these surveys? Do you feel that your campus
reflects these national results, or is your college community distinctive in one
or more respects?

14. The Educational Mission of Your Campus

When Louis Menand speaks of the relationship between colleges and society
and tries to answer the question "What are universities for?" he speaks in the
most generic ways about higher education. Yet as you may know, there are
important differences between fields of study and between types of institutions (public and private, community colleges, regional four-year institutions,
flagship state institutions, elite or marquee institutions, etc.). Drawing on the
characteristics of your own institution, offer a response to Menand that takes
into account the kind of college or university you attend or the kind of degree
program in which you are enrolled.

Alternatively, offer an analysis of your institution's mission statement and
what it might suggest about the particular relationship with society that your
campus seeks to foster. Typically, such mission statements can be found in the
catalog or on your college or university Web site. You may find it helpful to
compare your school's mission statement with those of similar institutions
("peers," as it were) and with institutions that are quite different. Keep in mind
that such mission statements are lofty expressions of an ideal or a goal. To
what extent does your college or university follow through on that statement?
Consider offering suggestions for refining or revising that mission statement
and a rationale for making those suggestions.

3

Persuading Each Other

FRAMES OF REFERENCE

So much information, so little time. If you view your role as a student in the university as something akin to a sponge, soaking up facts, you can easily become overwhelmed and bewildered. Some college courses, alas, encourage that approach, with tests that put a premium on sheer recall of facts. And yet, just because tests may have familiarized you with a binge-regurgitate-forget cycle, the process is no less overwhelming. After all, there is no end to information, and all of it seems to make sense, at least on its own terms.

The key to orienting yourself when you are knee-deep in information is to ask what those "terms" are. As you have already noted, or will quickly learn, debates in the university often hinge on the propensity to define or—what is more often the case—work with terms that come laden with hidden assumptions and unexamined baggage. Understanding and evaluating what the terms of the discussion are can help you make sense of the academic and civic conversations that swirl around you, conversations to which you are now contributing.

Yet our impulse to define, or more broadly, our need to call on or accept any number of terms, can also blind us. We see things in certain ways and forget that other perspectives are possible or are already in play. Kenneth Burke, one of the most prominent and interesting rhetoricians and philosophers of language in the twentieth century, put it this way. "Even if any given terminology is a reflection of reality, by its very nature as a terminology it must be a selection of reality; and to this extent it must function also as a deflection of reality." Our terms function as the glasses on our noses, filtering, shaping, and coloring what and how we see. Terms offer a frame of reference, all too often unacknowledged and unexamined. Indeed, we would do well to think of terms as "filters," which let certain glimpses of the world appear but also withhold others. Kenneth Burke himself termed the screens—"terministic screens."

In much of your university work, it becomes tempting to think that you are working with reality, or at least reflections of reality. For this reason, Burke offers a healthy reminder that the terms we use can also select and deflect reality. But Burke even pushes his case further: "Not only does the nature of our terms affect the nature of our observations, in the sense that the terms direct the attention to one field rather than to another. Also many of the 'observations' are but implications of the particular terminology in terms of which the observations are made." What we see depends on what and how we name. To a writer, someone who trades in words and terms, this conundrum becomes both important and fascinating.

The several readings in this chapter ask us to take a step back from our studies, from the information we use and consume, to ask broader questions about the frames of reference that orient our work. Collectively, the readings help us ask how it is that (to quote Burke once again) "one's terms jump to conclusions." Theodore Roszak cautions us not to become too enamored with data, lest we forget that *the mind thinks with ideas, not with information.* Christopher Lasch challenges us to rethink the relationship between information and public debate. Playing off of our usual associations of science with facts and test tubes, George Orwell also urges us to think of science as a "rational, skeptical, experimental habit of mind." Roger Schank invites us to consider how underlying explanation patterns, or "story skeletons" as he calls them, influence how we perceive and interpret events, and even shape our memory and identity. George Lakoff and Mark Johnson round out the readings by exploring how we not only use metaphors to express what we think but also that those metaphors actually shape our thinking.

Reflecting on Prior Knowledge

1. In a journal entry, recall your experiences with what might be called "information overload." How do you respond to this overload? Does acquiring more information help you think? At what point does additional information make thinking more difficult, and why?

2. Reflect on your experiences with debate. How did you use and search for information? What new information, or the need for information, became evident in the process of debate?

3. In many of your prior courses, whether in college or in high school, you were working on two fronts at once: learning the material in the course ("what" is covered in that field of study) even as you were learning the methods of working in that field ("how" things are done in that field). Working in a small group of your peers, discuss the competing demands of learning both content and method.

4. Consider a scenario drawn from your own experience in which different people knew the same basic facts of a situation, yet developed very different stories to explain that situation to themselves and to others. In a journal entry,

examine how the stories we tell reflect our purposes and our audiences. How might those stories also affect how we recall past events or interpret future events?

5. Working as a team, develop a list of everyday phrases and expressions that we use to communicate, often unconsciously, larger ways of thinking. For example, "time is money" and "living on borrowed time" might suggest ways in which our culture thinks about time and about assigning value. Why do you suppose common, everyday expressions are often our best window on these otherwise hidden or unexamined ways of thinking?

Of Ideas and Data

Theodore Roszak

The proliferation of information made possible by computer technology can lead us to believe that more facts will result in better ideas. Theodore Roszak contends that technology enthusiasts—especially those who stand to gain from it—actively promote this stance, one that he insists is both intellectually and morally damaging.

The following essay is an excerpt from Roszak's book *The Cult of Information: The Folklore of Computers and the True Art of Thinking* (1986), which examines our fascination with information and the distortions such a fascination can bring to our pursuit of ideas. He writes, "Is our capacity to think creatively being undermined by the very 'information' that is supposed to help us? Is information processing being confused with science or even beginning to replace thought? And are we in danger of blurring the distinction between what machines do when they process information and what minds do when they think?" From Roszak's perspective, if we undermine the deepest ways the human mind works, we will lose the source of our greatest ideas, from scientific theory to moral concepts such as justice.

A professor of history and director of the Ecopsychology Institute of California State University, Hayward, Roszak has gained national recognition as a social commentator. His 1969 book, *The Making of a Counterculture: Reflections on the Technocratic Society and Its Youthful Opposition,* is regarded as a key commentary on the 1960s. His writings include fiction, *The Memoirs of Elizabeth Frankenstein* (1995), as well as nonfiction, such as *Ecopsychology: Restoring the Earth, Healing the Mind* (1995), and *Where the Wasteland Ends* (1995). He has received a Guggenheim Fellowship and has been nominated twice for the National Book Award.

Ideas Come First

In raising these questions about the place of the computer in our schools, it is not my purpose to question the value of information in and of itself. For better or worse, our technological civilization needs its data the way the Romans needed their roads and the Egyptians of the Old Kingdom needed the Nile flood. To a significant degree, I share that need. As a writer and teacher, I must be part of the 5 to 10 percent of our society which has a steady professional appetite for reliable, up-to-date information. I have long since learned to value the services of a good reference library equipped with a well-connected computer.

Nor do I want to deny that the computer is a superior means of storing and retrieving data. There is nothing sacred about the typed or printed page when it comes to keeping records; if there is a faster way to find facts and manipulate them, we are lucky to have it. Just as the computer displaced the slide rule as a calculating device, it has every right to oust the archive, the filing cabinet, the reference book, if it can prove itself cheaper and more efficient.

But I do want to insist that information, even when it moves at the speed of light, is no more than it has ever been: discrete little bundles of fact, sometimes useful, sometimes trivial, and never the substance of thought. I offer this modest, common-sense notion of information in deliberate contradiction to the computer enthusiasts and information theorists who have suggested far more extravagant definitions. In the course of this chapter . . . , as this critique unfolds, it will be my purpose to challenge these ambitious efforts to extend the meaning of information to nearly global proportions. That project, I believe, can only end by distorting the natural order of intellectual priorities. And insofar as educators acquiesce in that distortion and agree to invest more of their limited resources in information technology, they may be undermining their students' ability to think significantly.

That is the great mischief done by the data merchants, the futurologists, and those in the schools who believe that computer literacy is the educational wave of the future: They lose sight of the paramount truth that *the mind thinks with ideas, not with information*. Information may helpfully illustrate or decorate an idea; it may, where it works under the guidance of a contrasting idea, help to call other ideas into question. But information does not create ideas; by itself it does not validate or invalidate them. An idea can only be generated, revised, or unseated by another idea. A culture survives by the power, plasticity, and fertility of its ideas. Ideas come first, because ideas define, contain, and eventually produce information. The principal task of education, therefore, is to teach young minds how to deal with ideas: how to evaluate them, extend them, adapt them to new uses. This can be done with the use of very little information, perhaps none at all. It certainly does not require data processing machinery of any kind. An excess of information may actually crowd out ideas, leaving the mind (young minds especially) distracted by sterile, disconnected facts, lost among shapeless heaps of data.

It may help at this point to take some time for fundamentals. 5

The relationship of ideas to information is what we call a *generalization.* Generalizing might be seen as the basic action of intelligence; it takes two forms. *First,* when confronted with a vast shapeless welter of facts (whether in the form of personal perceptions or secondhand reports), the mind seeks for a sensible, connecting pattern. *Second,* when confronted with very few facts, the mind seeks to create a pattern by enlarging upon the little it has and pointing it in the direction of a conclusion. The result in either case is some general statement which is not in the particulars, but has been imposed upon them by the imagination. Perhaps, after more facts are gathered, the pattern falls apart or yields to another, more convincing possibility. Learning to let go of an inadequate idea in favor of a better one is part of a good education in ideas.

Generalizations may take place at many levels. At the lowest level, they are formulated among many densely packed and obvious facts. These are cautious generalizations, perhaps even approaching the dull certainty of a truism. At another level, where the information grows thinner and more scattered, the facts less sharp and certain, we have riskier generalizations which take on the nature of a guess or hunch. In science, where hunches must be given formal rigor, this is where we find theories and hypotheses about the physical world, ideas that are on trial, awaiting more evidence to strengthen, modify, or subvert them. This is also the level at which we find the sort of hazardous generalizations we may regard as either brilliant insights or reckless prejudices, depending upon our critical response: sweeping statements perhaps asserted as unassailable truths, but based upon very few instances.

Generalizations exist, then, along a spectrum of information that stretches from abundance to near absence. As we pass along that spectrum, moving away from a secure surplus of facts, ideas tend to grow more unstable, therefore more daring, therefore more controversial. When I observe that women have been the homemakers and child minders in human society, I make a safe but uninteresting generalization that embraces a great many data about social systems past and present. But suppose I go on to say, "And whenever women leave the home and forsake their primary function as housewives, morals decline and society crumbles." Now I may be hard pressed to give more than a few questionable examples of the conclusion I offer. It is a risky generalization, a weak idea.

In Rorschach psychological testing, the subject is presented with a meaningless arrangement of blots or marks on a page. There may be many marks or there may be few, but in either case they suggest no sensible image. Then, after one has gazed at them for a while, the marks may suddenly take on a form which becomes absolutely clear. But where is this image? Not in the marks, obviously. The eye, searching for a sensible pattern, has projected it into the material; it has imposed a meaning upon the meaningless. Similarly in Gestalt psychology, one may be confronted with a specially contrived perceptual image: an ambiguous arrangement of marks which seems at first to be one thing but then shifts to become another. Which is the "true" image? The eye is free to choose between them, for they are both truly there. In both cases — the Rorschach blots and the Gestalt figure—the pattern is in the eye of the beholder; the sensory material simply elicits it. The relationship of ideas to facts is much like this. The facts are the scattered, possibly ambiguous marks; the mind orders them one way or another by conforming them to a pattern of its own invention. *Ideas are integrating patterns which satisfy the mind when it asks the question, What does this mean? What is this all about?*

Information is never the substance of thought.

But, of course, an answer that satisfies me may not satisfy you. We may see different patterns in the same collection of facts. And then we disagree and seek to persuade one another that one or the other of these patterns is superior, meaning that it does more justice to the facts at hand. The argument may focus on this fact or that, so that we will seem to be disagreeing about particular facts — as to whether they really *are* facts, or as to their relative importance. But even then, we are probably disagreeing about ideas. For as I shall suggest further on, facts are themselves the creations of ideas.

Those who would grant information a high intellectual priority often like to assume that facts, all by themselves, can jar and unseat ideas. But that is rarely the case, except perhaps in certain turbulent periods when the general idea of "being skeptical" and "questioning authority" is in the air and attaches itself to any dissenting, new item that comes along. Otherwise, in the absence of a well-formulated, intellectually attractive, new idea, it is remarkable how much in the way of dissonance and contradiction a dominant idea can absorb. There are classic cases of this even in the sciences. The Ptolemaic cosmology° that prevailed in ancient times and during the Middle Ages had been compromised by countless contradictory observations over many generations. Still, it was an internally coherent, intellectually pleasing idea; therefore, keen minds stood by the familiar old system. Where there seemed to be any conflict, they simply adjusted and elaborated the idea, or

10

Ptolemaic cosmology: A geocentric view of the universe formulated by the Greek-speaking geographer and astronomer Claudius Ptolemaeus (90–168 A.D.) that was widely accepted until it was superseded by the heliocentric solar system of Copernicus.

restructured the observations in order to make them fit. If observations could not be made to fit, they might be allowed to stand along the cultural sidelines as curiosities, exceptions, freaks of nature. It was not until a highly imaginative constellation of ideas about celestial and terrestrial dynamics, replete with new concepts of gravitation, inertia, momentum, and matter, was created that the old system was retired. Through the eighteenth and nineteenth centuries, similar strategies of adjustment were used to save other inherited scientific ideas in the fields of chemistry, geology, and biology. None of these gave way until whole new paradigms were invented to replace them, sometimes with relatively few facts initially to support them. The minds that clung to the old concepts were not necessarily being stubborn or benighted; they simply needed a better idea to take hold of.

No Ideas, No Information

From the viewpoint of the strict, doctrinaire empiricism which lingers on in the cult of information, the facts speak for themselves. Accumulate enough of them, and they will conveniently take the shape of knowledge. But how do we recognize a fact when we see one? Presumably, a fact is not a mental figment or an illusion; it is some small, compact particle of truth. But to collect such particles in the first place, we have to know what to look for. There has to be the idea of a fact.

The empiricists were right to believe that facts and ideas are significantly connected, but they inverted the relationship. *Ideas create information*, not the other way around. Every fact grows from an idea; it is the answer to a question we could not ask in the first place if an idea had not been invented which isolated some portion of the world, made it important, focused our attention, and stimulated inquiry.

Sometimes an idea becomes so commonplace, so much a part of the cultural consensus, that it sinks out of awareness, becoming an invisible thread in the fabric of thought. Then we ask and answer questions, collecting information without reflecting upon the underlying idea that makes this possible. The idea becomes as subliminal as the grammar that governs our language each time we speak.

Take an example. The time of day, the date. These are among the simplest, least ambiguous facts. We may be right or wrong about them, but we know they are subject to a straightforward true or false decision. It is either 2:15 PM in our time zone, or it is not. It is either March 10, or it is not. This is information at its most irreducible level.   15

Yet behind these simple facts, there lies an immensely rich idea: the idea of time as a regular and cyclical rhythm of the cosmos. Somewhere in the distant past, a human mind invented this elegant concept, perhaps out of some rhapsodic or poetic contemplation of the bewilderingly congested universe. That mind decided the seemingly shapeless flow of time can be ordered in circles, the circles can be divided into equal intervals, the intervals can be counted. From this insight, imposed by the imagination on the flux of experience, we derive the clock and the calendar, the minutes, days, months, seasons we can now deal with as simple facts.

Most of our master ideas about nature and human nature, logic and value eventually become so nearly subliminal that we rarely reflect upon them as human inventions, artifacts of the mind. We take them for granted as part of the cultural heritage. We live off the top of these ideas, harvesting facts from their surface. Similarly, historical facts exist as the outcroppings of buried interpretive or mythic insights which make sense of, give order to the jumbled folk memory of the past. We pick up a reference book or log on to a data base and ask for some simple information. When was the Declaration of Independence signed and who signed it? Facts. But behind those facts there lies a major cultural paradigm. We date the past (not all societies do) because we inherit a Judeo-Christian view of the world which tells us that the world was created in time and that it is getting somewhere in the process of history. We commemorate the names of people who "made history" because (along other lines) we inherit a dynamic, human-centered vision of life which convinces us that the efforts of people are important, and this leads us to believe that worthwhile things can be accomplished by human action.

When we ask for such simple points of historical information, all this stands behind the facts we get back as an answer. We ask and we answer the questions within encompassing ideas about history which have become as familiar to us as the air we breathe. But they are nonetheless human creations, each capable of being questioned, doubted, altered. The dramatic turning points in culture happen at just that point — where new idea rises up against old idea and judgment must be made.

What happens, then, when we blur the distinction between ideas and information and teach children that information processing is the basis of thought? Or when we set about building an "information economy" which spends more and more of its resources accumulating and processing facts? For one thing, we bury even deeper the substructures of ideas on which information stands, placing them further from critical reflection. For example, we begin to pay more attention to "economic indicators" — which are always convenient, simple-looking numbers — than to the assumptions about work, wealth, and well-being which underlie economic policy. Indeed, our orthodox economic science is awash in a flood of statistical figments that serve mainly to obfuscate basic questions of value, purpose, and justice. What contribution has the computer made to this situation? It has raised the flood level, pouring out misleading and distracting information from every government agency and corporate boardroom. But even more ironically, the hard focus on information which the computer encourages must in time have the effect of crowding out new ideas, which are the intellectual source that generates facts.

In the long run, no ideas, no information.   20

Working with the Text

1. Theodore Roszak wrote this essay out of concern that the amount and speed of information available through computers could distort our view of the relationship between facts and ideas. In a brief essay, explore his concern. What misguided frame of reference does he think we're developing? How does he think we might come to regard information, in the form of facts? What damage does he think this attitude toward information might do to our ability to work with ideas?

2. Roszak's central argument is that *"the mind thinks with ideas, not with information"* (par. 4). Write a short essay in which you respond to his argument by analyzing his description of how the mind works. What does he mean by the assertion, "Ideas come first, because ideas define, contain, and eventually produce information" (par. 4)? Exactly how does Roszak think ideas emerge? What role does he think information plays? Do you agree with him? How do you think ideas emerge? Based on your own experience and observations, what role do you think information plays?

3. Roszak questions our assumptions about the origin of facts themselves, asserting that "Every fact grows from an idea; it is the answer to a question we could not ask in the first place if an idea had not been invented which isolated some portion of the world, made it important, focused our attention, and stimulated inquiry" (par. 13). As you reread the essay, think through the examples he gives of "the substructures of ideas" which serve as the foundation for information we accept as fact—the day and date or certain historical facts. Write a brief essay in which you explore Roszak's idea by proposing and then analyzing another example, one not mentioned in the text. Offer an analysis of the hidden idea behind that fact, in much the same fashion that Roszak might.

From Text to Field

1. A large part of pursuing a college education is learning that, as Roszak says, facts are "human creations, each capable of being questioned, doubted, altered . . . new idea rises up against old idea and judgment must be made" (par. 18). With Roszak's essay in mind, write about your own experience of a new idea

rising up against an old idea in a way that challenged you to either rethink or reaffirm a belief or a point of view.

2. Roszak asks, "What happens, then, when we blur the distinction between ideas and information and teach children that information processing is the basis of thought?" (par. 19). His argument is based on the assumption that computer literacy in the schools is promoting just that. Were you taught, directly or implicitly, that "information processing is the basis of thought"? In a personal essay, describe the approach to computer literacy that you developed in the course of your elementary and secondary education. What kind of information did you learn to gather? What were you asked to do with it? How were you taught to regard computer-based research? What attitudes and assumptions about sources available through the Internet did you develop on your own?

3. As you consider Roszak's description of how ideas and thinking emerge, reflect on your own processes of thinking and developing ideas. How do new ideas or new understandings of ideas emerge for you? Write a description of your thought process, either tracing the way it tends to work in general or recalling a specific experience developing an idea as you were learning new material. Do you, or did you, experience "generalization," as Roszak describes it? Do you recognize what Roszak is describing when he states, "*Ideas are integrating patterns* which satisfy the mind when it asks the question, What does this mean? What is this all about?" (par. 9). Can you say that for you, "*the mind thinks with ideas, not with information*"? Or does information seem to come before ideas in your thought process? If so, why might that seem to be the case?

4. If you have an interest in computer science, you may wish to consider to what extent Roszak's views still hold true or might be modified, given current work in the area of artificial intelligence.

The Lost Art of Political Argument

Christopher Lasch

Although we are less likely to believe that the American press actually achieves objectivity than we were a few decades ago, we still tend to hold it up as an ideal. American historian Christopher Lasch not only dismisses any remaining faith we might have in the objectivity of the press, but he also debunks the ideal itself. He contends that the press should be a forum for open and heated political debate, which he believes is the only course to true democracy. In Lasch's view, we are informed citizens, not when we accumulate information passively and arbitrarily, but when we seek information for deciding a specific, immediate course of action. For Lasch, argument is the vehicle for finding sound information: "We do not know what we need to know until we ask the right questions, and we can identify the right questions only by subjecting our own ideas about the world to the test of public controversy."

A historian at the University of Rochester, Lasch gained respect across the political spectrum as a deeply informed and relentless critic of contemporary American culture. In books published between 1962 and 1995, he challenged what he considered to be ineffective as well as spiritually and morally shallow attempts—particularly by liberals, progressives, and materialists—to shape American society. His influential 1979 book, *The Culture of Narcissism,* was a best seller. The range of his critique is reflected in the titles of other books: *The American Liberals and the Russian Revolution* (1962), *The New Radicalism in America* (1965), *The Minimal Self* (1984), and *The True and Only Heaven: Progress and Its Critics* (1991). The selection offered here was first published as part of the essay "Journalism, Publicity, and the Lost Art of Political Argument" in the *Gannett Center Journal* (Spring 1990) and excerpted shortly thereafter in the September 1990 edition of *Harper's Magazine.* Christopher Lasch died in 1994.

Let us begin with a simple proposition: What democracy requires is public debate, not information. Of course it needs information too, but the kind of information it needs can be generated only by vigorous popular debate. We do not know what we need to know until we ask the right questions, and we can identify the right questions only by subjecting our own ideas about the world to the test of public controversy. Information, usually seen as the precondition of debate, is better understood as its by-product. When we get into arguments that focus and fully engage our attention, we become avid seekers of relevant information. Otherwise, we take in information passively — if we take it in at all.

From these considerations it follows that the job of the press is to encourage debate, not to supply the public with information. But as things now stand the press generates information in abundance, and nobody pays any attention. It is no secret that the public knows less about public affairs than it used to know. Millions of Americans cannot begin to tell you what is in the Bill of Rights, what Congress does, what the Constitution says about the powers of the presidency, how the party system emerged or how it operates. Ignorance of public affairs is commonly attributed to the failure of the public schools, and only secondarily to the failure of the press to inform. But since the public no longer participates in debates on national issues, it has no reason to be better informed. When debate becomes a lost art, information makes no impression.

Let us ask why debate has become a lost art. The answer may surprise: Debate began to decline around the turn of the century, when the press became more "responsible," more professional, more conscious of its civic obligations. In the early nineteenth century the press was fiercely partisan. Until the middle of the century papers were often financed by political parties. Even when they became more independent of parties they did not embrace the ideal of objectivity or neutrality. In 1841 Horace Greeley launched his *New York Tribune* with the announcement that it would be a "journal removed alike from servile partisanship on the one hand and from gagged, mincing neutrality on the other." Strong-minded editors like Greeley, James Gordon Bennett, E. L. Godkin, and Samuel Bowles did not attempt to conceal their own views or to impose a strict separation of news and editorial content. Their papers were journals of opinion in which the reader expected to find a definite point of view, together with unrelenting criticism of opposing points of view.

It is no accident that journalism of this kind flourished during the period from 1830 to 1900, when popular participation in politics was at its height. Eighty percent of the eligible voters typically went to the polls in presidential elections. (After 1900 the percentage began to decline sharply.) Torchlight parades, mass rallies, and gladiatorial contests of oratory made nineteenth-century politics an object of consuming popular interest.

In the midst of such politics, nineteenth-century journalism served as an extension of the town meeting. It created a public forum in which the issues of the day were hotly debated. Newspapers not only reported political controversies but participated in them, drawing in their readers as well. And print culture rested on the remnants of an oral tradition: Printed language was still shaped by the rhythms and requirements of the spoken word, in particular by the conventions of verbal argumentation. Print served to create a larger forum for the spoken word, not yet to displace or reshape it.

The "best men," as they liked to think of themselves, were never altogether happy with this state of affairs, and by the 1870s and 1880s their low opinion of politics had come to be widely shared by the educated classes. The scandals of the Gilded Age° gave party politics a bad name. Genteel reformers — "mugwumps," to their enemies — demanded a professionalization of politics, designed to free the civil service from party control and to replace political appointees with trained experts.

The drive to clean up politics gained momentum in the Progressive Era. Under the leadership of Theodore Roosevelt, Woodrow Wilson, Robert La Follette, and William Jennings Bryan, the Progressives preached efficiency, "good government," "bipartisanship," and the "scientific management" of public affairs, and declared **What democracy requires is public debate, not information.** war on "bossism." These reformers had little use for public debate. Most political questions were too complex, in their view, to be submitted to popular judgment. They liked to contrast the scientific expert with the orator — the latter a useless windbag whose rantings only confused the public mind.

Professionalism in politics meant professionalism in journalism. The connection between the two was spelled out by Walter Lippmann in the twenties, in a series of books that provided a founding charter for modern journalism — an elaborate rationale for a journalism guided by the new idea of professional objectivity. Lippmann held up standards by which the press is still judged.

In Lippmann's view, democracy did not require that people literally govern themselves. Questions of substance should be decided by knowledgeable administrators whose access to reliable information immunized them against

---

Gilded Age: A term first coined by Mark Twain to characterize the difference between a gilded and a golden age. It refers to a time of economic excess, materialism, and political corruption in the 1870s and 1880s.

the emotional "symbols" and "stereotypes" that dominated public debate. The public, according to Lippmann, was incompetent to govern itself and did not even care to do so.

At one time this may not have been the case, but now, in the "wide and   10 unpredictable environment" of the modern world, the old ideal of citizenship was obsolete. A complex industrial society required a government carried on by officials who would necessarily be guided — since any form of direct democracy was now impossible — by either public opinion or expert knowledge. Public opinion was unreliable because it could be united only by an appeal to slogans and "symbolic pictures." Lippmann's distrust of public opinion rested on the epistemological distinction between truth and mere opinion. Truth, as he conceived it, grew out of disinterested scientific inquiry; everything else was ideology. Public debate was at best a disagreeable necessity. Ideally, it would not take place at all; decisions would be based on scientific "standards of measurement" alone.

The role of the press, as Lippmann saw it, was to circulate information, not to encourage argument. The relationship between information and argument was antagonistic, not complementary. He did not take the position that argumentation was a necessary outcome of reliable information; on the contrary, his point was that information precluded argument, made argument unnecessary. Arguments were what took place in the absence of reliable information.

Lippmann had forgotten what he learned (or should have learned) from William James and John Dewey,° that our search for reliable information is itself guided by the questions that arise during arguments about a given course of action. It is only by subjecting our preferences and projects to the test of debate that we come to understand what we know and what we still need to learn. Until we have to defend our opinions in public, they remain opinions in Lippmann's pejorative sense — half-formed convictions based on random impressions and unexamined assumptions. It is the act of articulating and defending our views that lifts them out of the category of "opinions," gives them shape and definition, and makes it possible for others to recognize them as a description of their own experience as well. In short, we come to know our own minds only by explaining ourselves to others.

The attempt to bring others around to our own point of view carries the risk, of course, that we may adopt their point of view instead. We have to enter imaginatively into our opponents' arguments, if only for the purpose of refuting them, and we may end up being persuaded by those we sought to

---

William James and John Dewey: Philosopher and psychologist William James (1842–1910) argued that the question or problem being considered should determine the "truth" of the theory or approach being used. John Dewey (1859–1952) embraced this philosophy, "pragmatism," to reform American education in ways that incorporate experiential learning.

persuade. Argument is risky and unpredictable — and therefore educational. Most of us tend to think of it (as Lippmann thought of it) as a clash of rival dogmas, a shouting match in which neither side gives any ground. But arguments are not won by shouting down opponents. They are won by changing opponents' minds.

If we insist on argument as the essence of education, we will defend democracy not as the most efficient but as the most educational form of government — one that extends the circle of debate as widely as possible and thus forces all citizens to articulate their views, to put their views at risk, and to cultivate the virtues of eloquence, clarity of thought and expression, and sound judgment. From this point of view, the press has the potential to serve as the equivalent of the town meeting.

This is what Dewey argued, in effect — though not, unfortunately, very clearly — in *The Public and Its Problems* (1927), a book written in reply to Lippmann's disparaging studies of public opinion. Lippmann's distinction between truth and information rested on a "spectator theory of knowledge," as James W. Carey explains in his recently published book, *Communication as Culture*. As Lippmann understood these matters, knowledge is what we get when an observer, preferably a scientifically trained observer, provides us with a copy of reality that we can all recognize. Dewey, on the other hand, knew that even scientists argue among themselves. He held that the knowledge needed by any community — whether it is a community of scientific inquirers or a political community — emerges only from "dialogue" and "direct give and take."

It is significant, as Carey points out, that Dewey's analysis of communication stressed the ear rather than the eye. "Conversation," Dewey wrote, "has a vital import lacking in the fixed and frozen words of written speech. . . . The connections of the ear with vital and outgoing thought and emotion are immensely closer and more varied than those of the eye. Vision is spectator; hearing is a participator."

The proper role of the press is to extend the scope of debate by supplementing the spoken word with the written word. The written word is indeed a poor substitute for the spoken word; nevertheless, it can serve as an acceptable substitute as long as written speech takes spoken speech (and not, say, mathematics) as its model. According to Lippmann, the press was unreliable because it could never give us accurate representations of reality, only "symbolic pictures" and stereotypes. Dewey's analysis implied a more penetrating line of criticism. As Carey puts it, "The press, by seeing its role as that of informing the public, abandons its role as an agency for carrying on the conversation of our culture." Having embraced Lippmann's ideal of objectivity, the press no longer serves to cultivate "certain vital habits" in the community — "the ability to follow an argument, grasp the point of view of another, expand the boundaries of understanding, debate the alternative purposes that might be pursued."

The rise of the advertising and public-relations industries, side by side, helps to explain why the press abdicated its most important function — enlarging the public forum — at the same time that it became more "responsible." A responsible press, as opposed to a partisan or opinionated one, attracted the kind of readers advertisers were eager to reach: well-heeled readers, most of whom probably thought of themselves as independent voters. These readers wanted to be assured that they were reading all the news that was fit to print, not an editor's idiosyncratic and no doubt biased view of things. Responsibility came to be equated with the avoidance of controversy because advertisers were willing to pay for it. Some advertisers were also willing to pay for sensationalism, though on the whole they preferred a respectable readership to sheer numbers. What they clearly did not prefer was "opinion" — not because they were impressed with Lippmann's philosophical arguments but because opinionated reporting did not guarantee the right audience. No doubt they also hoped that an aura of objectivity, the hallmark of responsible journalism, would rub off on the advertisements that surrounded increasingly slender columns of print.

In a curious historical twist, advertising, publicity, and other forms of commercial persuasion themselves came to be disguised as information and, eventually, to substitute for open debate. "Hidden persuaders" (as Vance Packard called them) replaced the old-time editors, essayists, and orators who made no secret of their partisanship. And information and publicity became increasingly indistinguishable. Today, most of the "news" in our newspapers consists of items churned out by press agencies and public-relations offices and then regurgitated intact by the "objective" organs of journalism.

The decline of the partisan press and the rise of a new type of journalism professing rigorous standards of objectivity do not assure a steady supply of usable information. Unless information is generated by sustained public debate, most of it will be irrelevant at best, misleading and manipulative at worst. Increasingly, information is generated by those who wish to promote something or someone — a product, a cause, a political candidate or officeholder — without either arguing their case on its merits or explicitly advertising it as self-interested material. Much of the press, in its eagerness to inform the public, has become a conduit for the equivalent of junk mail. When words are used merely as instruments of publicity or propaganda, they lose their power to persuade. Soon they cease to mean anything at all. People lose the capacity to use language precisely and expressively, or even to distinguish one word from another. The spoken word models itself on the written word instead of the other way around, and ordinary speech begins to sound like the clotted jargon we see in print. Ordinary speech begins to sound like "information"—a disaster from which the English language may never recover.

Working with the Text

1. Christopher Lasch bases his insistence that the press serve as a forum for public debate on an analysis of key developments in the history of American journalism. In a brief essay, reflect on his reasons for using history to build his argument. Why are these particular historical developments relevant to our current expectations of the press? What do these developments tell us about the relationship between American journalism and democracy?

2. For Lasch, American journalism began to depart from its critical role in public debate in the Progressive Era, when the "'scientific management' of public affairs" became the order of the day. According to Lasch, the press became an instrument of the Progressives under the influence of writer Walter Lippmann, who held the view that the public "was incompetent to govern itself and did not even care to do so" (par. 9). As you reread the essay, study the reasoning behind the views of the Progressives and Lippmann, as well as Lasch's challenge to their positions on professionalism and objectivity. In a brief essay, take a position on whether the public is competent to govern itself and wishes to do so. Do you agree or disagree with the Progressives, Lippmann, or Lasch? Why?

3. Lasch takes exception to Lippmann's view that the "role of the press . . . was to circulate information, not to encourage argument" (par. 11). Lasch counters this view with that of William James and John Dewey, who claimed, according to Lasch, that "our search for reliable information is itself guided by the questions that arise during arguments about a given course of action" (par. 12). In a brief essay, reflect on what the position of James and Dewey would mean for journalism. What would the press have to do to support or promote our "search for reliable information"?

4. In the closing paragraph of the essay, Lasch warns, "When words are used merely as instruments of publicity or propaganda, they lose their power to persuade. Soon they cease to mean anything at all." In light of your own observations and experience as well as Lasch's argument, review the final paragraph to think through the deterioration he describes. In a brief essay, analyze his claim, starting with the first sentence. Why would the "decline of the partisan press and the rise of a new type of journalism professing rigorous standards of objectivity" lead people to "lose the capacity to use language precisely and expressively, or even to distinguish one word from another"?

From Text to Field

1. Lasch claims that political argument has become a lost art largely because the American press long ago relinquished its role in public debate. With Lasch's argument in mind, write an essay in which you present your view of the state of public debate in terms of its political influence and of the current role of the press in promoting that debate. Do you think political argument has become a lost art? Why or why not?

2. In concurring with the views of William James and John Dewey, Lasch insists that "it is only by subjecting our preferences and projects to the test of debate that we come to understand what we know and what we still need to learn" (par. 12). Write an essay in which you describe and reflect on your own experience of this.

3. Lasch argues that the public has long confused "commercial persuasion" with objective journalism. In a small discussion group, review Lasch's claim and brainstorm examples of types of journalism or specific press coverage that demonstrate this confusion. Write an essay in which you analyze one or more of the examples identified by your discussion group. Why do readers tend to accept your example(s) as objective journalism? Why do you think it is actually "commercial persuasion"?

4. In the spirit of a rebuttal to Lasch, identify a form of journalism that you think may well create a forum for public debate. What are the features of this form? How does it promote participation and debate? Are there any gatekeepers to this forum? How might technology create and shape this forum?

What Is Science?

George Orwell

"What Is Science?" was published in 1945 in the *Tribune*, a British socialist weekly, in the wake of World War II and the first use of the atomic bomb. The fact that scientists had developed weaponry of unprecedented power threw science into a new kind of spotlight, one that prompted horror as well as respect.

The power of nations, however it was derived, had long been a concern for Eric Arthur Blair, who wrote under the pen name George Orwell. A British citizen born in India and educated in England, he gained his first insight into political and social power as a middle-class student trying to find his way in the prestigious preparatory and secondary schools designed to groom upper-class children. Instead of pursuing a university education, Orwell took a position as a policeman in the Burma branch of the Indian Imperial Police, an experience that prompted him to write, "When the white man turns tyrant it is his own freedom that he destroys. He wears a mask, and his face grows to fit it."

Orwell's career as a writer, soldier, and political activist was marked by independence of thought in an era of mass political movements that spanned capitalism, socialism, communism, and fascism. His aim was economic and social justice, and although he identified most strongly with socialism, he was unsparing in his criticism of any ideology or movement that limited personal freedom or undermined family life. His two most enduring novels—*Animal Farm* (1945) and *Nineteen Eighty-four* (1949)—still stand as landmark critiques of the abuse of power. His essay "Politics and the English Language" is an often-anthologized discussion about how language can be misused in "defense of the indefensible."

Orwell's body of work includes seven novels and seventeen books of nonfiction, a number of which are collections of his essays. In 1950, he died of tuberculosis at the age of forty-six. Orwell's obituary, written by V. S. Pritchett, a prominent writer who was his contemporary, named Orwell "the wintry conscience of a generation."

In last week's *Tribune*, there was an interesting letter from Mr. J. Stewart Cook, in which he suggested that the best way of avoiding the danger of a "scientific hierarchy" would be to see to it that every member of the general public was, as far as possible, scientifically educated. At the same time, scientists should be brought out of their isolation and encouraged to take a greater part in politics and administration.

As a general statement, I think most of us would agree with this, but I notice that, as usual, Mr. Cook does not define science, and merely implies in passing that it means certain exact sciences whose experiments can be made under laboratory conditions. Thus, adult education tends "to neglect scientific studies in favor of literary, economic, and social subjects," economics and sociology not being regarded as branches of science, apparently. This point is of great importance. For the word *science* is at present used in at least two meanings, and the whole question of scientific education is obscured by the current tendency to dodge from one meaning to the other.

Science is generally taken as meaning either (a) the exact sciences, such as chemistry, physics, etc., or (b) a method of thought which obtains verifiable results by reasoning logically from observed fact.

If you ask any scientist, or indeed almost any educated person, "What is science?" you are likely to get an answer approximating to (b). In everyday life, however, both in speaking and in writing, when people say "science" they mean (a). Science means something that happens in a laboratory: the very word calls up a picture of graphs, test-tubes, balances, Bunsen burners, microscopes. A biologist, an astronomer, perhaps a psychologist or a mathematician, is described as a "man of science": No one would think of applying this term to a statesman, a poet, a journalist, or even a philosopher. And those who tell us that the young must be scientifically educated mean, almost invariably, that they should be taught more about radioactivity, or the stars, or the physiology of their own bodies, rather than that they should be taught to think more exactly.

This confusion of meaning, which is partly deliberate, has in it a great danger. Implied in the demand for more scientific education is the claim that if one has been scientifically trained one's approach to *all* subjects will be more intelligent than if one had had no such training. A scientist's political opinions, it is assumed, his opinions on sociological questions, on morals, on philosophy, perhaps even on the arts, will be more valuable than those of a layman. The world, in other words, would be a better place if the scientists were in control of it. But a "scientist," as we have just seen, means in practice a specialist in one of the exact sciences. It follows that a chemist or a physicist, as such, is politically more intelligent than a poet or a lawyer, as such. And, in fact, there are already millions of people who do believe this.

But is it really true that a "scientist," in this narrower sense, is any likelier than other people to approach nonscientific problems in an objective way? There is not much reason for thinking so. Take one simple test — the ability to withstand nationalism. It is often loosely said that "Science is international," but in practice the scientific workers of all countries line up behind their own governments with fewer scruples than are felt by the writers and the artists. The German scientific community, as a whole, made no resistance to Hitler. Hitler may have ruined the long-term prospects of German science, but there were still plenty of gifted men to do the necessary research on such things as synthetic oil, jet planes, rocket projectiles, and the atomic bomb. Without them the German war machine could never have been built up.

The word *science* is at present used in at least two meanings.

On the other hand, what happened to German literature when the Nazis came to power? I believe no exhaustive lists have been published, but I imagine that the number of German scientists — Jews apart — who voluntarily exiled themselves or were persecuted by the regime was much smaller than the number of writers and journalists. More sinister than this, a number of German scientists swallowed the monstrosity of "racial science." You can find some of the statements to which they set their names in Professor Brady's *The Spirit and Structure of German Fascism.*

But, in slightly different forms, it is the same picture everywhere. In England, a large proportion of our leading scientists accept the structure of capitalist society, as can be seen from the comparative freedom with which they are given knighthoods, baronetcies, and even peerages. Since Tennyson, no English writer worth reading — one might, perhaps, make an exception of Sir Max Beerbohm — has been given a title. And those English scientists who do not simply accept the status quo are frequently Communists, which means that, however intellectually scrupulous they may be in their own line of work, they are ready to be uncritical and even dishonest on certain subjects. The fact is that a mere training in one or more of the exact sciences, even combined with very high gifts, is no guarantee of a humane or sceptical outlook. The physicists of half a dozen great nations, all feverishly and secretly working away at the atomic bomb, are a demonstration of this.

But does all this mean that the general public should *not* be more scientifically educated? On the contrary! All it means is that scientific education for the masses will do little good, and probably a lot of harm, if it simply boils down to more physics, more chemistry, more biology, etc., to the detriment of literature and history. Its probable effect on the average human being would be to narrow the range of his thoughts and make him more than ever contemptuous of such knowledge as he did not possess: And his political reactions would probably be somewhat less intelligent than those of an illiterate peasant who retained a few historical memories and a fairly sound aesthetic sense.

Clearly, scientific education ought to mean the implanting of a rational, 10 sceptical, experimental habit of mind. It ought to mean acquiring a *method* — a method that can be used on any problem that one meets — and not simply piling up a lot of facts. Put it in those words, and the apologist of scientific education will usually agree. Press him further, ask him to particularize, and somehow it always turns out that scientific education means more attention to the exact sciences, in other words — more *facts*. The idea that science means a way of looking at the world, and not simply a body of knowledge, is in practice strongly resisted. I think sheer professional jealousy is part of the reason for this. For if science is simply a method or an attitude, so that anyone whose thought-processes are sufficiently rational can in some sense be described as a scientist — what then becomes of the enormous prestige now enjoyed by the chemist, the physicist, etc., and his claim to be somehow wiser than the rest of us?

A hundred years ago, Charles Kingsley described science as "making nasty smells in a laboratory." A year or two ago a young industrial chemist informed me, smugly, that he "could not see what was the use of poetry." So the pendulum swings to and fro, but it does not seem to me that one attitude is any better than the other. At the moment, science is on the upgrade, and so we hear, quite rightly, the claim that the masses should be scientifically educated: We do not hear, as we ought, the counterclaim that the scientists themselves would benefit by a little education. Just before writing this, I saw in an American magazine the statement that a number of British and American physicists refused from the start to do research on the atomic bomb, well knowing what use would be made of it. Here you have a group of sane men in the middle of a world of lunatics. And though no names were published, I think it would be a safe guess that all of them were people with some kind of general cultural background, some acquaintance with history or literature or the arts — in short, people whose interests were not, in the current sense of the word, purely scientific.

Working with the Text

1. In this essay, written in 1945, George Orwell contends that "the demand for more scientific education" implies that the world "would be a better place if the scientists were in control of it" (par. 5). He questions this assumption by examining the two different ways he believes his readers use the term *science*. In a brief essay, analyze his use of these two definitions of science. What does he conclude about the connection between scientific thinking and a better world? How do the two differing definitions of *science* contribute to his argument?

2. Orwell distinguishes between experiments themselves and an "experimental habit of mind" (par. 10). To further describe that habit of mind, Orwell speaks of acquiring a "method" (par. 10). In a brief essay, explore what Orwell means by the term *method*.

3. Orwell asserts that "a mere training in one or more of the exact sciences, even combined with very high gifts, is no guarantee of a humane or sceptical outlook" (par. 8). As evidence, he cites not only the behavior of scientists in Nazi Germany but also the affiliations of scientists in England and "half a dozen great nations" (par. 8). In a brief essay, analyze Orwell's critique of the thinking exhibited by these scientists. How does Orwell view the relationship between science and public policy?

4. Orwell warns against "more physics, more chemistry, more biology, etc., to the detriment of literature and history" (par. 9). Concluding his essay, he makes the "safe guess" that physicists who refused to do research on the atomic bomb "were people with some kind of general cultural background, some acquaintance with history or literature or the arts" (par. 11). With the entire selection in mind (note especially his remark about writers and journalists in Nazi Germany) and drawing on your own understanding of history, literature, and the arts, write a brief essay in which you reflect on Orwell's view of these areas of study. Why does Orwell believe that the arts and the humanities, as opposed to "exact science," contribute to our ability to see the world humanely? How does the historical context of the essay — just after the end of World War II and after the dropping of the atomic bomb — color his view of what it means to be humane?

From Text to Field

1. Orwell observes that for his contemporaries "scientific education means more attention to the exact sciences, in other words — more *facts*. The idea that science means a way of looking at the world, and not simply a body of knowledge, is in practice strongly resisted" (par. 10). Has this been your experience of science education? Using Orwell's two definitions of *science*, write a personal essay in which you describe the progression of your scientific education and the purposes you understood to be behind it. Was it an accumulation of facts or practice in a certain way of thinking? What effect has science had on your own habits of mind?

2. History, literature, and art as well as math and science are standard fare in the American elementary and secondary curriculum. Orwell would urge educators to pursue this combination of subjects for the purpose of instilling "a humane or sceptical outlook" (par. 8). Write an essay in which you reflect on the extent

to which your schooling has made you more skeptical—more willing to pose questions — or more humane. How have your studies in the arts and the humanities influenced your view of the world? How have your studies in math and science influenced your view? What relationship, if any, have you found between being skeptical and being humane?

3. Orwell's essay was written in the context of British society and in the aftermath of World War II, when advanced weaponry as well as the atomic bomb drew new attention and concern to the practice of science. Since then, we have seen science and technology move rapidly into new territory. In an essay, update and revise Orwell's argument to address a contemporary American context. Analyze what you consider to be the American view of science and scientists and their relation to the arts and humanities and to public policy. In what ways has science become part of our lives? How do we regard scientists and scientific advances? Do you think our view is healthy?

Story Skeletons and Story-Fitting

Roger C. Schank

"We are," as Roger C. Schank reminds us, "the stories we tell." And yet storytelling is hardly straightforward, a simple matter of recounting events.

According to Schank, the stories we tell follow—and may perhaps be determined by—basic patterns for explaining events to ourselves and to others. Stories, in short, provide a hidden set of lenses or filters that cause us to understand and relay the same facts or events in very different ways. Roger Schank suggests that our stories follow certain explanation patterns by uncovering what he calls the "skeleton stories" that underlie the particulars of our immediate story. We "enter a storytelling situation," says Schank, "wanting to tell a certain kind of story and only then worry about whether the facts fit onto the bones of the skeleton." What's more, as we repeat these stories and use the same skeletons for new stories, we influence what we remember, how we perceive, and even how we see ourselves.

The example that Schank uses to explore these ideas has to do with an international incident in 1988: A civilian Iranian airliner was shot down by a United States Navy warship while on patrol in the Persian Gulf. The incident resulted in the loss of 290 passengers and crew, and heightened tensions throughout the Middle East. Schank draws on published statements by various world leaders to reveal the story skeletons in play. Far from a commentary on a now distant historical event, Roger Schank's discussion draws our attention to the frames of reference that always guide how we interpret our world. We don't so much tell stories as fit them into underlying explanatory patterns.

Roger Schank is a leading researcher in artificial intelligence, learning theory, cognitive science, and the construction of virtual learning environments. He served as distinguished professor at Carnegie Mellon University, founded the Institute for Learning Sciences at Northwestern University, and directed Yale University's Artificial

Intelligence Project. His most recent contributions have been in the area of education, where he has explored the role of technology in learning. The selection offered here is from his book *Tell Me a Story: A New Look at Real and Artificial Memory* (1990).

SOME SKELETON STORIES

If we construct our own version of truth by reliance upon skeleton stories, two people can know exactly the same facts but construct a story that relays those facts in very different ways. Because they are using different story skeletons, their perspectives will vary. For example, a United States Navy warship shot down an Iranian airliner carrying 290 passengers on July 3, 1988. Let's look at some different stories that were constructed to explain this event. All the stories that follow are excerpts from various *New York Times* reports in the days following this incident.

> Mr. Reagan smiled and waved at tourists as he returned to the White House. But in speaking to reporters he remarked on what he had previously called "a terrible human tragedy. I won't minimize the tragedy," Mr. Reagan said. "We all know it was a tragedy. But we're talking about an incident in which a plane on radar was observed coming in the direction of a ship in combat and the plane began lowering its altitude. And so, I think it was an understandable accident to shoot and think that they were under attack from that plane," he said.

In this quotation from Ronald Reagan, the use of skeletons to create stories can be easily seen. Mr. Reagan has chosen a common skeleton: *understandable tragedy*. The skeleton looks something like this:

> Actor pursues justifiable goal.
> Actor selects reasonable plan to achieve goal.
> Plan involves selection of correct action.
> Action taken has unintended and unanticipated result.
> Result turns out to be undesirable.
> Innocent people are hurt by result.

In essence, what Mr. Reagan has done is to select this skeleton and to interpret the events of the shooting down of the airplane in terms of that skeleton. Had he been asked to tell the story of what happened, he would simply have had to fill in each line above with the actual event that matches it. As it is, he merely had to recognize that that skeleton was applicable and to use the phrases "terrible human tragedy" and "understandable accident," which are well-known referents to that skeleton.

Now let's look at some other comments on the event:

After expressing "profound regret" about the attack, Mrs. Thatcher said: "We understand that in the course of an engagement following an Iranian attack on the U.S. force, warnings were given to an unidentified aircraft. We fully accept the right of forces engaged in such hostilities to defend themselves."

Mrs. Thatcher has used a much more specific skeleton, namely the *justi- 5 fiability of self-defense*. This skeleton proceeds as follows:

> First actor pursues unjustifiable goal.
> First actor selects plan.
> Plan has intention of negative effect on second actor.
> Second actor is justified in selecting goal.
> Second actor selects justifiable plan.
> Plan causes action to take place which harms first actor.

Let's look at the other side of the political spectrum now:

Libya's official press agency called the downing "a horrible massacre perpetrated by the United States." It said the attack was "new proof of state terrorism practiced by the American administration" and it called Washington "insolent" for insisting that the decision to down the plane was an appropriate defensive measure.

Here, two different skeletons are invoked. The first is *state terrorism* and the second is *insolence*. The insolence skeleton is an amusing one to invoke, but we shall ignore it and concentrate on the terrorism skeleton:

> Actor chooses high-level goal.
> Country blocks high-level goal.
> Actor chooses secondary goal to harm citizens of country.
> Actor endangers or actually harms citizens of country.
> Actor expects blockage of high-level goal by country to go away.

"State terrorism" supposedly means that the actor is a country too. But "state terrorism" is not exactly a well-known story skeleton for an American. In fact, Arab leaders refer to this skeleton quite often and we can figure what it must mean and why Arab leaders used it to justify their own actions. Other people's story skeletons, ones that we have not heard before, are usually best understood by analogy to skeletons we already know.

Notice that the events under discussion fit as easily into the state terrorism skeleton as into the above two skeletons. The art of skeleton selection is exactly that — an art. No real objective reality exists here. One can see and tell about events in any way that one wants to. In each case, certain aspects of the story being transmitted are enhanced and certain elements are left out altogether.

The real problem in using skeletons this way is that the storytellers usually believe what they themselves are saying. Authors construct their own reality by finding the events that fit the skeleton convenient for them to believe. They enter a storytelling situation wanting to tell a certain kind of story and only then worrying about whether the facts fit onto the bones of the skeleton that they have previously chosen. This method has almost comic qualities to it when various interpretations of an event are so clearly interpretations independent of the event itself. For example, consider the following comment:

> A newspaper in Bahrain, *Akhbar Al Khalij*, said, "No doubt yesterday's painful tragedy was the result of Iran's insistence in continuing the Iran-Iraq war. The United States as a great power does not lack moral courage in admitting the mistake. This will help contain the effects of the incident."

The remarks above refer to two skeletons: the *justifiable bad effects of war* 10 *on the aggressor* and *moral courage*. Both of these skeletons could have been used to describe nearly any event in the Middle East that the newspaper wanted to comment upon.

The use of new events as fodder for invoking old skeletons is the stuff of which international political rhetoric is made. In the *Times* of the same period, we have another reference to how Reagan commented on a similar situation some years back:

> President Reagan, in a speech after the Korean plane was shot down after straying over Soviet airspace above Sakhalin Island, said: "Make no mistake about it, this attack was not just against ourselves or the Republic of Korea. This was the Soviet Union against the world and the moral precepts which guide human relations among people everywhere.
>
> "It was an act of barbarism," Mr. Reagan went on, "born of a society which wantonly disregards individual rights and the value of human life and seeks constantly to expand and dominate other nations."

While the Americans used the *barbarism* skeleton, where the Koreans were the victim and the Russians the actor, to describe the shooting down of the Korean airliner, the Russians, in describing the Korean Airlines attack, used the *military aggressor* skeleton, where the Koreans were the actor and the Russians the victim. This same discrepancy occurred in the Russian statement about the Iranian airliner:

> The Tass statement said the attack Sunday was the inevitable result of the extensive American military presence in the Persian Gulf.
>
> "The tragedy, responsibility for which is wholly with the American command, has been far from accidental," the agency said. "It has been, in effect, a direct corollary of United States actions over the past year to increase its military presence in the gulf."

It added: "The Soviet Union has repeatedly warned at different forums that the path of military actions cannot lead to a normalized situation. If the warnings had been heeded, the July 3 tragedy would not have occurred."

International politicians are not alone in telling stories by selecting their favorite skeletons and fitting the event to the skeletons. The candidates for president [in the 1988 race] also had something to say:

Mr. Jackson said there was "no evidence that the U.S. ship was under attack by that plane." But he added, "The issue is not just failed technology, but failed and vague policy for the region." Mr. Jackson argued that the United States should not be in the gulf unilaterally, but as part of a United Nations peacekeeping effort that would have as its prime goal a negotiated settlement of the Iran-Iraq war.

At a Fourth of July address at the Charlestown Navy Yard in Boston today, Mr. Dukakis described the incident as a "terrible accident," adding: "Clearly we have the right to defend our forces against imminent threats. And apparently, the shooting down of the airliner occurred over what appears to have been an unprovoked attack against our forces."

For Mr. Jackson, the appropriate skeletons were *bad technology causes errors*, and *vague policy causes problems*. Mr. Dukakis, on the other hand, looked suspiciously like Mr. Reagan, indicating that he was already acting presidential. Mr. Jackson had already realized that he was not going to be president at this point, but he was still campaigning to be taken seriously. Therefore, he was still raising issues. The Iran incident reminded him of two of his favorite issues, so he chose to see the Iranian airplane event in terms of those issues.

Last, we should look at the Iranian point of view. They, too, have their   15
favorite skeletons in terms of which they can look at this event. First, let us look at the remarks of an exiled Iranian official:

"It must be clear that much of the policies in Iran today are dictated by the internal struggle for power," said Abolhassan Bani-Sadr, the first president of Iran. Mr. Bani-Sadr, who spoke in an interview, lives in exile in Paris and opposes the current regime.

"In that sense," Mr. Bani-Sadr said, "this American act of aggression will increase pressure to steer away from conciliatory policies in favor of radicals inside Iran who want to crush all talk of compromise. I am sure the trend now will be toward more mobilization for more war, although it will get nowhere."

Mr. Bani-Sadr was trying to predict the future rather than retell an old story. Nevertheless, he still relied upon a skeleton to create his new story. The skeleton he chose was *fanatics find fuel to add to fire*. Now look at a comment from inside Iran:

Hojatolislam Rafsanjani, who is the commander of Iran's armed forces, warned today against a hasty response to the American action. In a speech reported by the Teheran radio, he told Parliament, "We should let this crime be known to everyone in the world and be discussed and studied."

The Speaker, who has emerged as Iran's most powerful figure after Ayatollah Khomeini, went on to say that the Americans might "want a clumsy move somewhere in the world so that they can take the propaganda pressure off America and transfer it somewhere else."

Hojatolislam Rafsanjani added that Iran retains the right of taking revenge, but that "the timing is up to us, not America." He called the downing of the airliner "an unprecedented disaster in contemporary history" and said it should be used by Iran to "expose the nature of America," statements indicating that for now the Speaker favors a measured response.

Here again, we have a story about the future. Two skeletons are invoked as possible candidates for the basis of this story. One, *force opponents into bad move*, refers to the intentions of the United States as seen by the Iranians and is really a part of a continuing story of conflict between the two countries. The second, *avoid revenge to show up opponent*, is more or less the other side of the same coin. In both cases, we have a kind of conscious admission by Mr. Rafsanjani that the real question is which story skeleton will be followed in the creation of the next set of events. The only problem with this assertion is that Mr. Rafsanjani naively seems to assume that some audience is waiting to see the next act in the play. A more accurate assumption is that, no matter what happens next, all the viewers of the play will retell the story according to skeletons that they have already selected; i.e., they will probably not be moved to reinterpret any new event in terms of some skeleton that they do not already have in mind.

Skeletons and Memory

Story skeletons can have an important effect on memory. Since we see the world according to the stories we tell, when we tell a story in a given way, we will be likely to remember the facts in terms of the story we have told. This effect on memory has an interesting offshoot. When we select a particular skeleton because we have no real choice from a political point of view, we, most likely, will begin to believe the story we find ourselves telling. Consider the following statement, for example:

Iran Air's senior Airbus instructor, Captain Ali Mahdaviani, ruled out the possibility of pilot error in the tragedy. He said it was possible that the airliner's captain, Mohsen Rezaian, failed to respond to signals from the American cruiser *Vincennes* because at that stage in the flight he was busy receiving air controller instructions off two radios and from four control towers, Bandar Abbas, Teheran, Dubai, and Qeshon Island in the gulf.

He insisted that the airliner would not have been outside the flight corridor and certainly would not have been descending, as early Pentagon reports said. He attributed the incident to a panicky reaction from the American cruiser, but did concede that the decision to fire the two surface-to-air missiles was made in difficult circumstances. "I think the decision to shoot down the plane was taken in very nervous conditions," he said.

And now consider an opposing statement:

"We have in this briefing all the facts that were made available to the captain when he made his decision," said Senator John Warner, a Virginia Republican and former Navy Secretary. "We are all of the same view, that he acted properly and professionally."

Senator Sam Nunn, the Georgia Democrat who is the chairman of the Armed Services Committee, agreed. "I find nothing to second-guess him on, based on his information," Mr. Nunn said.

He was quick to add, however, that the information that Captain Will C. Rogers 3rd, the commanding officer of the *Vincennes*, was working with might be contradicted by information on the computer tapes, which are believed to have recorded every action taken by the ship's operators, every bit of data picked up by its sensors, and every communication heard in the region during the encounter.

"It is an entirely different matter to second-guess a decision that had to be made in three or four minutes, to second-guess it over a two-week period," Mr. Nunn said, referring to the deadline for Navy investigators looking into the events.

Each of these statements is what might have been expected from the people who made them. Yet how were the memories of the spokesmen affected by the stories they told? In some sense, they told stories that they had to tell. Neither of these spokesmen was necessarily one hundred percent sure that the pilot and/or the captain weren't somewhat wrong in what they did. Situations are rarely that black-and-white. But having made a statement to support his man, each spokesman probably believed more in his man after defending him. 20

We choose to see the world according to a view that we find convenient.

One issue in story understanding, then, is to determine which story skeleton is the right one to choose. Moreover, this issue is important in storytelling and, therefore, in memory as well. We can see an event in so many different ways that we must understand how we decide which story skeleton is applicable. In politics, this decision is easy. Russians or Iranians don't have to debate about which skeleton to choose. Rather, they make choices on the basis of political positions adopted before any story is heard. But for individuals who must decide how to look at a given situation, the possibilities are much larger.

One of the oddities of story-based understanding is that people have difficulty making decisions if they know that they will have trouble constructing a coherent story to explain their decision. In a sense, people tell stories to themselves to see whether they are comfortable enough with telling them for a while. You need to believe your own story in order to tell it effectively. Thus, decision making often depends upon story construction.

A storyteller might be more accurately described as a story-fitter. Telling stories of our own lives, especially ones with high emotional impact, means attempting to fit events to a story that has already been told, a well-known story that others will easily understand. Story-fitting, then, is a kind of deceptive process, one that creates stories that are not always exactly true, that lie by omission. These lies, however, are not necessarily intentional.

A true story could be told but would take much more time. So time, in many ways, is the villain here. Your listener doesn't have hours to listen to your story, so you create a short version that looks more standard, that fits a well-known story skeleton. The problem with this solution, as we have seen, is that the teller himself begins to believe his story. In short, storytelling is a very powerful process. We remember our own stories. Stories replace the memory of events that actually took place. So when people tell the kinds of stories we have seen [here], they usually believe them.

Married couples often comment on a sequence from the Woody Allen movie *Annie Hall*. The sequence involves two scenes, where first the female lead and then the male lead discuss their sex life as a couple with their respective therapists. The woman complains that her boyfriend wants to have sex all the time — two or three times a week. The man complains that they almost never have sex together — only two or three times a week.

This movie scene expresses the essence of story construction. We take the facts and we interpret them in such a way as to create a story. In order to facilitate communication and to allow easy conversation, we use standard story skeletons that we share as a culture. The choice, however, of which skeleton to use is, in essence, a political choice. We choose to see the world according to a view that we find convenient, and we communicate by adopting standard points of view. The stories we tell communicate this view both to others and to ourselves. In the end, we become shaped by the skeletons we use.

Which of the *Annie Hall* characters is right? This question is, of course, absurd. Both characters are right, as are all the politicians quoted earlier. The skeletons we use indicate our point of view. Storytelling causes us to adopt a point of view. With this adoption comes a kind of self-definition, however. We are the stories we tell. We not only express our vision of the world, we also shape our memory by the stories we tell. As we come to rely upon certain skeletons to express what has happened to us, we become incapable of seeing the world in any other way. The skeletons we use cause specific episodes to conform to one another. The more a given skeleton is used, the more the stories it helps to form begin to cohere in memory. Consequently, we develop consistent, and rather inflexible, points of view.

Working with the Text

1. Review the various comments made by world leaders in response to the downing of the Iranian airliner, and compare the "skeleton stories" or explanation patterns that underlie each of those comments. In what ways do the various skeleton stories serve the purpose of its teller and the audience being addressed?

2. Roger Schank suggests that the stories we'd like to tell trump the events that the stories are based on: "Authors construct their own reality by finding the events that fit the skeleton convenient for them to believe" (par. 9). As you review the various stories told by world leaders, consider what are the facts that each has foregrounded and emphasized, and what are the facts that each has downplayed or avoided altogether. What argument do you think Schank is advancing, if only implicitly, about truth, reality, memory, and language?

3. Given Schank's discussion about how our stories or explanations adhere to underlying patterns that draw on predetermined beliefs, it is only fair to ask whether there might be a story skeleton or explanation pattern at work in Schank's own account. If so, what might that story skeleton be?

4. At the end of the selection excerpted here, Schank states that "we are the stories we tell." Write a brief essay that explores what you think Schank means by that statement. In particular, what is the connection between narrative or storytelling on the one hand, and belief, memory, and identity on the other?

From Text to Field

1. Many explanation patterns or "story skeletons" are predictable; they literally offer a stock of commonplaces to which writers and speakers turn, and which audiences have come to expect. The following situations invoke story skeletons around which more detailed explanations can be fashioned. For each, list the basic explanation patterns that writers would likely turn to when justifying decisions. Clarify who your audience might be: friend, parents, or professor. Compare your list with those developed by your classmates.

> Changing your major from business to English
> Taking a year off between high school and college
> Attending college out of state, far away from home
> Joining the Peace Corps

> Choosing a small college rather than a large university
> Joining a fraternity or sorority

2. Schank states that "the use of new events as fodder for invoking old skeletons is the stuff of which international political rhetoric is made." We might add that the same often holds true for domestic politics as well. Choose a particular issue or event that is likely to preoccupy the news media for several days. What explanation patterns or story skeletons are being invoked by various political parties or groups, and how are those skeletons linked to prior explanation patterns and belief systems or ideologies? In what ways might story skeletons both express and help create or maintain these belief systems?

3. Although seemingly far removed from high-profile international events like the downing of the Iranian airliner, events on your own campus are also explained and understood in light of certain patterns or story skeletons. Examine a recent issue or event on your campus in light of Schank's discussion of story skeletons and story-fitting. The issue might be a scandal in the athletic department, controversy surrounding a particular campus policy, concerns about student life, or tensions between the campus and the city. How is the situation explained by various stakeholders—students, faculty, administration, city residents—using their own particular stock of story skeletons?

Concepts We Live By

George Lakoff and Mark Johnson

A linguist and a philosopher joined forces to produce *Metaphors We Live By*, which introduced a theory of metaphor based on the deep structure of thought and behavior. George Lakoff and Mark Johnson saw metaphor not as a literary device or a matter of mere words but rather as evidence for a "conceptual system" that determines how we think, which in turn drives how we act. *Metaphors We Live By*, published in 1980, continues to influence the work of scholars in fields ranging from cognitive science to literary theory. "Concepts We Live By" is the book's first chapter.

George Lakoff—the linguist—is a professor at the University of California at Berkeley. He has taught at Harvard University and the University of Michigan and has worked with the Center for Advanced Study in the Behavioral Sciences at Stanford University. He continues to research metaphor in the context of human conceptual systems, with a special interest in metaphors for time, events, causation, emotions, morality, the self, and politics. His work in cognitive linguistics includes the neural theory of language. Among his publications are *Women, Fire and Dangerous Things* (1987), *More Than Cool Reason: A Field Guide to Poetic Metaphor* (1989), and *Moral Politics* (2nd ed., 2004).

The philosopher, Mark Johnson, is a professor at the University of Oregon. His current research, an extension of his earlier study of metaphor, focuses on the question of how structures of meaning grow out of bodily experience. His books include *Philosophical Perspectives on Metaphor* (2nd ed., 1981), *The Body in the Mind* (1987), and *Moral Imagination: Implications of Cognitive Science for Ethics* (1993).

In 1999, Lakoff and Johnson published another collaborative effort, *Philosophy in the Flesh: The Embodied Mind and Its Challenge to Western Thought*.

Metaphor is for most people a device of the poetic imagination and the rhetorical flourish — a matter of extraordinary rather than ordinary language. Moreover, metaphor is typically viewed as characteristic of language alone, a matter of words rather than thought or action. For this reason, most people think they can get along perfectly well without metaphor. We have found, on the contrary, that metaphor is pervasive in everyday life, not just in language but in thought and action. Our ordinary conceptual system, in terms of which we both think and act, is fundamentally metaphorical in nature.

The concepts that govern our thought are not just matters of the intellect. They also govern our everyday functioning, down to the most mundane details. Our concepts structure what we perceive, how we get around in the world, and how we relate to other people. Our conceptual system thus plays a central role in defining our everyday realities. If we are right in suggesting that our conceptual system is largely metaphorical, then the way we think, what we experience, and what we do every day is very much a matter of metaphor.

But our conceptual system is not something we are normally aware of. In most of the little things we do every day, we simply think and act more or less automatically along certain lines. Just what these lines are is by no means obvious. One way to find out is by looking at language. Since communication is based on the same conceptual system that we use in thinking and acting, language is an important source of evidence for what that system is like.

Primarily on the basis of linguistic evidence, we have found that most of our ordinary conceptual system is metaphorical in nature. And we have found a way to begin to identify in detail just what the metaphors are that structure how we perceive, how we think, and what we do.

To give some idea of what it could mean for a concept to be metaphorical 5 and for such a concept to structure an everyday activity, let us start with the concept ARGUMENT and the conceptual metaphor ARGUMENT IS WAR. This metaphor is reflected in our everyday language by a wide variety of expressions:

> ARGUMENT IS WAR
>
> Your claims are *indefensible*.
> He *attacked every weak point* in my argument.
> His criticisms were *right on target*.
> I *demolished* his argument.
> I've never *won* an argument with him.
> You disagree? Okay, *shoot!*
> If you use that *strategy*, he'll *wipe you out*.
> He *shot down* all of my arguments.

It is important to see that we don't just *talk* about arguments in terms of war. We can actually win or lose arguments. We see the person we are arguing with as an opponent. We attack his positions and we defend our own. We gain and lose ground. We plan and use strategies. If we find a position indefensible, we can abandon it and take a new line of attack. Many of the things we *do* in arguing are partially structured by the concept of war. Though there is no physical battle, there is a verbal battle, and the structure of an argument — attack, defense, counterattack, etc. — reflects this. It is in this sense that the ARGUMENT IS WAR metaphor is one that we live by in this culture; it structures the actions we perform in arguing.

Try to imagine a culture where arguments are not viewed in terms of war, where no one wins or loses, where there is no sense of attacking or defending, gaining or losing ground. Imagine a culture where an argument is viewed as a dance, the participants are seen as performers, and the goal is to perform in a balanced and aesthetically pleasing way. In such a culture, people would view arguments differently, experience **Our ordinary conceptual** them differently, carry them out differently, and talk **system, in terms of which** about them differently. But *we* would probably not **we both think and act, is** view them as arguing at all: They would simply be doing something different. It would seem strange **fundamentally metaphori-** even to call what they were doing "arguing." Perhaps **cal in nature.** the most neutral way of describing this difference between their culture and ours would be to say that we have a discourse form structured in terms of battle and they have one structured in terms of dance.

This is an example of what it means for a metaphorical concept, namely, ARGUMENT IS WAR, to structure (at least in part) what we do and how we understand what we are doing when we argue. *The essence of metaphor is understanding and experiencing one kind of thing in terms of another.* It is not that arguments are a subspecies of war. Arguments and wars are different kinds of things — verbal discourse and armed conflict — and the actions performed are different kinds of actions. But ARGUMENT is partially structured, understood, performed, and talked about in terms of WAR. The concept is metaphorically structured, the activity is metaphorically structured, and, consequently, the language is metaphorically structured.

Moreover, this is the *ordinary* way of having an argument and talking about one. The normal way for us to talk about attacking a position is to use the words "attack a position." Our conventional ways of talking about arguments presuppose a metaphor we are hardly ever conscious of. The metaphor is not merely in the words we use — it is in our very concept of an argument. The language of argument is not poetic, fanciful, or rhetorical; it is literal. We talk about arguments that way because we conceive of them that way—and we act according to the way we conceive of things.

The most important claim we have made so far is that metaphor is not just a matter of language, that is, of mere words. We shall argue that, on the contrary, human *thought processes* are largely metaphorical. This is what we mean when we say that the human conceptual system is metaphorically structured and defined. Metaphors as linguistic expressions are possible precisely because there are metaphors in a person's conceptual system. Therefore, whenever . . . we speak of metaphors, such as ARGUMENT IS WAR, it should be understood that *metaphor* means *metaphorical concept.* 10

Working with the Text

1. In the opening paragraph of their book, George Lakoff and Mark Johnson establish a concept of metaphor that they consider to be more accurate than the typical usage of the term:

   > . . . metaphor is typically viewed as characteristic of language alone, a matter of words rather than thought or action. . . . We have found, on the contrary, that metaphor is pervasive in everyday life, not just in language but in thought and action.

   Write a brief essay in which you analyze the authors' conception of the difference between regarding metaphor as words and recognizing metaphor as thought or action. Why is establishing this difference important to their argument? Why did they choose to open with this contrast, instead of simply presenting their concept of metaphor?

2. In developing their argument, Lakoff and Johnson state, "Our concepts structure what we perceive, how we get around in the world, and how we relate to other people." As you reread the essay, look closely at the war metaphors we use for argument, as well as the dance metaphors the authors imagine another culture using for argument. In a brief essay, expand on Lakoff and Johnson's insight. If we conceptualize argument as war, what does that say about "what we perceive" and "how we relate to other people" (par. 2)? What would the dance metaphor for argument suggest about the culture that used it?

3. To underscore its importance to their argument, the authors italicize the statement, *"The essence of metaphor is understanding and experiencing one kind of thing in terms of another"* (par. 8). Think through the paragraph in which it appears. In a brief essay, explore the significance of this statement. What questions does it raise about human behavior? Why do the authors include this point in the opening chapter of their book? What does it suggest about the direction their argument will take?

From Text to Field

1. Lakoff and Johnson close their first chapter of their book by noting, "Metaphors as linguistic expressions are possible precisely because there are metaphors in a person's conceptual system" (par. 10). Reflect on your own use of the "argument is war" metaphor or on any other commonly used metaphor that illustrates the authors' thesis. Write an essay in which you suggest the origin of this metaphor. Do you think it is entirely socially conditioned? If so, how might it have been introduced? Is it somehow innate? Why did this particular metaphor, rather than another, take hold?

2. To illustrate their thesis, the authors list a number of expressions we use within the "argument is war" metaphor (par. 5). Using this list as a model, produce a similar list for the imaginary culture that uses dance as their metaphor for argument. As an alternative, choose another metaphor (such as music or barn raising or kneading bread) that suggests argument to you. To choose a metaphor, you might begin by reflecting on what argument is for you (if it's not war) or what you would prefer it to be.

3. Once the authors introduce the difference between metaphor as words and metaphor as thought and action, they move into illustrating the central assertion of their book, which is that "human *thought processes* are largely metaphorical" (par. 10). *Metaphors We Live By* is frequently used as a source in undergraduate courses. Taking the position of a reviewer writing for a student publication, explain the central assertion to an undergraduate audience who hasn't yet read any portion of the book. What does it mean for thought processes — not just thoughts themselves — to be metaphorical? Do you agree with the authors' conception? How important do you think this concept is to someone pursuing a college education? How might it help anyone understand daily life?

INTO THE FIELD: Options for Writing Projects

1. From Data Back to Ideas

One threat of the "information economy," according to Theodore Roszak, is that "we bury even deeper the substructures of ideas on which information stands, placing them further from critical reflection. For example," he says, "we begin to pay more attention to 'economic indicators'— which are always convenient, simple-looking numbers — than to the assumptions about work, wealth, and well-being which underlie economic policy" (par. 19). To explore the validity of Roszak's concern, consider one of the following two options for your fieldwork:

- Become familiar with the economic indicators that are most commonly used in the mass media. Through interviews with experts, if possible, as well as your own reading of the mass media and other observations, identify what you consider to be the American assumptions about "work, wealth, and well-being" that drive our economic policy. Taking on the role of a social commentator, write a critique of the relationship between the information conveyed by economic indicators and the values you think should drive economic policy.

- As an alternative, choose another social concern (e.g., marriage, low-wage jobs, home ownership and homelessness, capital punishment) that tends to be defined by statistics or other "facts" that you think camouflage or distort the underlying ideas and issues. What "substructure of ideas" do the statistics tend to remove from critical reflection?

2. Public Debate and the Information It Requires

This field project invites you to examine in some detail one current public debate in light of Christopher Lasch's essay. Your purpose in this project is not to take a side in the debate but rather to examine what assumptions the debate makes about information and the deliberative process. How does the debate you are considering involve information and misinformation? How might the debate encourage more access to or better use of information? Given the debate you are exploring, are appeals to objectivity helpful or would a more engaged or partisan approach yield better information and a more satisfying outcome? What assumptions do you see operating concerning the very nature of debate or deliberation?

3. The Rationale for Science in General Education

George Orwell suggests that two rival definitions of science tend to complicate our discussion about science education. For this field project, consider how implicit definitions of science have shaped your educational experience. Here are some specific options:

- Contact the school district or districts where you attended elementary and secondary school for documents and possible interviews. What definitions of *science* are at work in the elementary and secondary curriculum—as suggested either by its stated objectives or its progression over several grade levels?
- At your college or university, find documents and, if possible, conduct interviews that help you understand how your institution articulates the science curriculum for general education and for one of the specializations (biology, chemistry, physics, etc.). Based on the evidence, analyze and argue for or against the American approach to science education. Start by creating a "blueprint" of what educators have intended your exposure to science to accomplish. What are the key objectives? To what extent are those objectives met?
- What are the stages of science education, and how do they build on each other? In what ways do elementary, secondary, undergraduate general education, and specialized science education differ from each other? What is your view of this approach? In what ways would you change it?

4. Content and Method

George Orwell observes that "scientific education ought to mean the implanting of a rational, sceptical, experimental habit of mind. It ought to mean acquiring a *method*—a method that can be used on any problem that one meets—and not simply piling up a lot of facts" (par. 10). For your fieldwork, explore Orwell's observation in one of the following two ways:

- What frame of reference does one or more of your courses this term seem to have? Does the course stress covering content and "piling up a lot of facts" or does it help you to acquire a method? Why might some courses succeed in doing both?
- Apply Orwell's insight to your prospective major. Review courses and major requirements in your chosen department in light of this distinction between coverage and method. What kind of balance does your department strike between coverage of content and the practice of method?

5. Story Skeletons in the Classroom

Roger Schank discusses story skeletons and story-fitting in light of international politics. Yet story skeletons or explanation patterns are at work in everyday settings as well. One such setting is the college classroom. This field project invites you to explore the explanation patterns that are invoked in the day-to-day interactions between faculty and students.

These interactions might have to do with assignments, course policies, office hours, and the like. Pay attention to both the story skeletons used by your professor and the story skeletons that lie behind student comments and questions. You may also wish to consider the story skeletons that lie behind how your professor treats the actual topics being taught. That is, in introducing new material or summarizing the relevance of material you have just covered, your professor may invoke a story skeleton appropriate for that pedagogical situation or teaching moment.

What do the use of these story skeletons by both faculty and students reveal about your classrooms? Can tensions in the classroom be traced to the use of different story skeletons by students and faculty? Does the presence of story skeletons make the classroom seem rather conventional, a genre of its own, or does the background presence of these story skeletons help highlight moments when faculty or students depart from expected roles and patterns?

6. Academic Research and the Logic of Storytelling

It is easy to assume that academic research is far removed from storytelling. Yet storytelling often plays a role in research articles, especially as authors position their own work in light of previous publications. Read some academic articles in a field of interest to you (one you know a bit about, or one that might be your prospective major). You might focus on the introduction to the article, in which prior research is often summarized. Does the way the research is reported tend to follow the logic of storytelling? Are there heroes and villains, so to speak? Are there protagonists and antagonists? What sets the story in motion? Is there conflict or misunderstanding or a faulty assumption? To what extent is this storytelling logic fairly clear, or hidden? What are the explanation patterns or story skeletons that might underlie how the author tells the particulars of his or her story? For example, is the story skeleton behind the article one of "filling a gap in the research" or is it "new data prompts us to review our assumptions"?

7. "Argument Is War"—across the University

Argument is integral to university studies and is typically the focus of college-level writing courses. Indeed, some might refer to the university as a "house of argument." For your fieldwork, consider one of the following two options:

- Recall your experience with argumentative writing, in this or other university writing courses you have taken. Consider ways in which the "argument is war" metaphor is at work in the argumentative writing you do or have done for such a course. Write an essay in which you reflect on the extent to which the war metaphor has helped or hindered your ability to write an effective argument.

- Consider to what extent various disciplines have slightly different expectations about what constitutes argument. Identify a metaphor that is widely used in your prospective discipline or field. Write an essay in which you analyze it according to the theory of metaphor proposed by George Lakoff and Mark Johnson. You might find such a metaphor by reviewing the texts and materials used in your courses, by listening to experts in the field and reading their publications, or by interviewing one or more of your professors. What does this metaphor say about your field and how its members construct their sense of the world?

8. Other Metaphors We Live By

Choose an everyday activity or behavior, other than argument, that is governed by a metaphor widely used in our culture. For ideas, set aside a day for being aware of what you do (eating, going to class, driving, working, socializing) and what you observe (the news, television, other people around you). The media can be a good source for cultural metaphor. Using George Lakoff and Mark Johnson's argument, analyze your metaphor as a basis for thought and action and as an example of "understanding and experiencing one kind of thing in terms of another."

ARGUING IN COMMUNITIES

This unit explores the proposition that arguments have habitats. The very notion might seem strange if we think of arguments only in abstract, logical terms, as specimens to be dissected. Arguments are conversations that take place in communities — and thus are inherently social. Arguments are situated, touching on and drawing their strength from our problems, desires, needs, and agendas. When we argue or deliberate, we do so *with* others, *within* a community. When we advance a claim, it is more than a claim that something is so; it is a claim on the belief of our audience, our community.

The word *community* comes from the Latin for "common" or "shared." Communities develop and maintain themselves through the activities and interests we share and through the ways our lives intersect with each other. That very intersection also helps us understand how communities overlap, how we live simultaneously in several communities. Communities have internal tensions and disagreements, and where they overlap with other communities these tensions can become more apparent. College is no different. The arguments made in classes and on campus are shaped by that habitat and by the more particular habitats of departments and disciplines.

Communities sustain themselves through language, an important link apparent in words themselves: *communication* coming from the same Latin root as *community*. This relationship is nowhere more important than in university communities, where language use (and its accompanying behaviors and rituals) becomes especially prominent. You may have come to college thinking you were going to study biology or sociology. But a lot of what you end up studying is how biologists and sociologists speak about their work. Little wonder, for you are initiated into communities in good part through the language you learn. Likewise, language can be a barrier or gatekeeping device to restrict people from communities. Communities can facilitate communication, but they can also erect barriers to communication and thus fragment the university community as much as draw it together.

This unit invites you to explore the habitats of argument in college and university settings. We can speak of these habitats as "discourse communities."

In some respects, these discourse communities can easily remain invisible —
that is, until we are identified as the outsider by not having mastered the
appropriate linguistic "secret handshake."

The several readings in this unit can help demystify this link between language and community in your own college experience. David Russell questions whether there really is such a thing as one "academic community" or
whether there are many smaller communities. In other words, is college but
a Tower of Babel, with many languages making mutual comprehension difficult, if not impossible? Wayne C. Booth isn't nearly so ready to concede the
point. His essay helps identify how it is that we can understand as much as
we do when we talk to people in other fields.

The language games and rituals that define discourse communities in college are perhaps best exposed through parody. And here there is no finer
example than Horace Miner's now-classic send-up of cultural anthropology,
"Body Ritual among the Nacirema."

Why is it that initiation into an academic discipline has much in common
with initiation into some secret cult? Robin Tolmach Lakoff helps reveal the
mysteries behind such initiation rites and why the elders of any academic
tribe prefer that newcomers not be told too much. As you might imagine, it
all has to do with mystique and power.

Discourse communities are often mapped and divided into particular
groups or areas, like the sciences, social sciences, and humanities. In the
final selection Jared Diamond has us take a second look at those distinctions
and cautions us not to trust them. What seems less rigorous, even intuitive,
may in fact turn out to be more complex than we think.

Reflecting on Prior Knowledge

1. Develop an inventory of the various communities, on campus and off, of which
   you are a part. Include not only geographically specific communities but also
   social, intellectual, recreational, political, and religious ones. How are these
   communities formed and supported through the use of language — often a
   language specific to that community? Describe some of the distinct communities to which you belong. What common bonds hold these communities
   together? Where is there agreement and disagreement? Do you act or use language differently in one community than in another? After you have developed some initial responses, meet in teams to compare them.

2. In one way or another, all of us have had to convince a group to accept us as
   a member. We work to gain acceptance in groups ranging from a circle of
   friends to larger communities based on social, recreational, political, professional, religious, or cultural interests. Recall two different situations in which

you worked to gain acceptance. In a journal entry, describe what you said and did, noting the different approaches required by each situation or group.

3. Nearly all communities have a "secret handshake"—not necessarily an actual handshake but some way (often through language) by which insiders recognize each other and by which the outsider is immediately identified as such. In a journal entry, recall the secret "language" handshakes you were privy to in high school and college, and some of the handshakes—and communities—that were not available to you.

4. Working in teams, develop a list of traits that characterize your college as a language community—a group with common purposes that uses language in particular ways. Share your work with the class. Next, consider the ways in which your current or prospective major is likewise a language community, one that might differ from the language community of other majors. How much overlap is there between these various communities?

5. In a journal entry, explore the ways in which the obligation to "make an argument" (something very different from just "having an argument") encourages us to think strategically about conversations in a community, about finding community based reasons, and about objections to a position that stem from that community. To what extent do most real, situated deliberations involve the problems, needs, and interests of a community?

Academic Discourse: Community or Communities?

David R. Russell

Students in university writing programs are often unaware that their course work has grown out of heated, ongoing debates about how writing should be taught. David R. Russell became a key voice in the debates with the publication of *Writing in the Academic Disciplines, 1870–1990* (1991), which explores the historical context for understanding why teaching writing on the university level presents so many challenges. In the following excerpt from his book, Russell identifies what he considers to be one of the core challenges, tying it to particular developments in the emergence of the modern university.

In Russell's view, the shift from the traditional liberal-arts education provided before 1870 to the modern focus on professional preparation fragmented the academic community, a development that complicated the task of initiating students into a "discourse community." Instead of working with a uniform approach to academic and professional writing, students—and their writing teachers—now contend with "competing discourse communities," each requiring a specialized approach to communication.

Through his research, Russell has become a central figure in the development of "writing across the curriculum" or "communication across the curriculum," a teaching approach that seeks to use writing as a tool for learning, even as it addresses the diverse composing and speaking demands of specialized academic and professional fields. Among Russell's current interests are genre theory and how various kinds of writing grow out of systems of activity in which authors and readers find themselves.

Russell, a professor of English at Iowa State University, teaches in the PhD program in rhetoric and professional communication in addition to teaching undergraduate courses in writing and rhetoric.

A prolific writer and frequent speaker, Russell also collaborates on program development and has edited several collections of essays on writing and writing instruction.

The complex origins of mass education in America made it difficult for academia to view learning to write as an initiation into a discourse community, a process of gradually coming to use language in a certain way to become accepted, "literate," or, as is often the case in modern American higher education, credentialed in some profession. Before the advent of the modern university in the 1870s, academia was indeed a single discourse community. Institutions of higher learning built an intellectual and social community by selecting students primarily on the basis of social class (less than 1 percent of the population was admitted), which guaranteed linguistic homogeneity, and by initiating them intellectually through a series of highly language-dependent methods—the traditional recitation, disputation, debate, and oral examination of the old liberal curriculum. Equally important, most students shared common values (Christian, often sectarian) with their teachers (primarily ministers). They pursued a uniform course of study and were then duly welcomed as full members of the nation's governing elite.[1]

The modern university changed all that. It provided the specialized knowledge that drove the new urban-industrial economy and a new class of specialized *professionals* (the term came into use during the period) who managed that economy, with its secular rationale and complex bureaucratic organization — what Burton J. Bledstein has aptly called "the culture of professionalism." Beginning with the land-grant colleges of the late nineteenth century and continuing with the rise of the modern university on the German model, the academic discourse community became fragmented. Numbers swelled, with enrollments tripling as a percentage of the population between 1900 and 1925 alone. Students from previously excluded social groups were admitted, destroying linguistic homogeneity. The new elective curriculum was introduced to prepare students for a host of emerging professional careers in the new industrial society. The elective curriculum compartmentalized knowledge and broke one relatively stable academic discourse community into many fluctuating ones. And the active, personal, language-dependent instructional methods of the old curriculum were replaced by passive, rather impersonal methods borrowed from Germany or, later, from scientific management: lecture, objective testing, and the like. Ultimately, the professional faculty who replaced the gentlemen scholars and divines of the old curriculum came to see secondary and undergraduate education as only one of several competing responsibilities (along with graduate teaching, research, and professional service). And the teaching of writing — initiating the neophytes into a discourse community — suffered accordingly.

Because it is tempting to recall academia's very different past and hope for a very different future, the term *academic community* has powerful spiritual and political connotations, but today academia is a *discourse* community only in a context so broad as to have little meaning in terms of shared linguistic forms, either for the advancement of knowledge (which now goes on in disciplinary communities and subcommunities) or for the initiation of new members (who are initiated into a specific community's discourse). Thus, to speak of the academic community as if its members shared a single set of linguistic conventions and traditions of inquiry is to make a categorical mistake. In the aggregate of all the tightly knit, turf-conscious disciplines and departments, each of its own discourse community, the modern university consists. Many have wished it otherwise.

The term *academic community* has powerful spiritual and political connotations.

Despite these profound changes, American educators have continued to think of the academic community as holding out a single compositional norm, which would speak intelligently about the multiform new knowledge to a "general reader." In their complaints about student writing, academics hark back nostalgically to a golden age of academic community where Johnny could both read and write the "plain English" that purists enshrine. But that golden age never existed in the modern university (and writing per se was not valued or even evaluated in the old college). As Daniel P. and Lauren B. Resnick have observed, "There is little to go back to in terms of pedagogical method, curriculum, or school organization. The old tried and true approaches, which nostalgia today prompts us to believe might solve current problems, were designed neither to achieve the literacy standards sought today nor to assure successful literacy for everyone . . . there is no simple past to which we can return."[2] Though academia held onto a generalized ideal of an academic community sharing a single advanced literacy, there was never any consensus in the modern university about the nature of that community or its language. Academic discourse, like academia itself, continued its drive toward increasing specialization. The university became an aggregate of competing discourse communities; it was not a single community. But the myth of a single academic discourse community — and a golden age of student writing — endured.

American academia today (and for the last hundred years or so) is a community primarily in a broad institutional sense, a collection of people going about a vast enterprise, in much the same way that we speak of the "business community" as a sector of national life. The academic disciplines are in one   5 sense united through their common missions: teaching, research, and service. But disciplines have been so diverse, so independent, and so bound up with professional communities outside academia that they require no common language or even shared values and methods within the university in order to pursue those missions. Those genres and conventions of writing that are shared by all academic disciplines are also shared by professional communities outside academia. And within academia, the conventions (and beyond them the assumptions and methodologies) of the various disciplines are characterized more by their differences than by their similarities. The various disciplines have grown to constitute the modern university through accretion, as Gerald Graff has forcefully argued, and through their relevance to concerns in the wider society, not through their logical relation to each other — so much so that "interdisciplinary" study is always a notable (and often suspect) exception.[3] Indeed, an academic is likely to have more linguistic common ground with a fellow professional in the corporate sector than with another academic in an unrelated field, except in regard to purely institutional matters (governance, academic freedom, teaching loads, etc.). As a leading sociologist of higher education, Burton Clark, puts it, academia is made up of "small worlds, different worlds."[4]

Notes

1. See Halloran, "Rhetoric" 249–56.
2. Daniel P. Resnick and Lauren B. Resnick, "The Nature of Literacy: An Historical Exploration," *Harvard Educational Review* 47 (1977): 385, qtd. in Rose 355. On the increasing and proliferating standards of literacy, see also Dell H. Hymes, "Foreword," in Wagner xi–xvii.
3. Gerald Graff, *Professing Literature* (Chicago: U of Chicago P, 1987) 6–15. See also theoretical discussions in *Interdisciplinary Relationships in the Social Sciences*, ed. Muzafer Sherif and Carolyn W. Sherif (Chicago: Aldine, 1969); and Stanley Fish, "Being Interdisciplinary Is So Very Hard To Do," *Profession* (1989): 15–22.
4. See Clark, *Academic Life* esp. chap. 5.

Works Cited

Clark, Burton R. *The Academic Life: Small Worlds, Different Worlds.* Princeton: Carnegie Foundation for the Advancement of Teaching, 1987.

Halloran, S. Michael. "Rhetoric in the American College Curriculum: The Decline of Public Discourse." *Pre/Text* 3 (1982): 245–69.

Rose, Mike. "The Language of Exclusion: Writing Instruction at the University." *College English* 47 (1985): 341–59.

Wagner, Daniel A., ed. *The Future of Literacy in a Changing World.* Oxford: Pergamon, 1987.

Working with the Text

1. In order to explore problems in the teaching and use of writing in various fields, David Russell analyzes changes in university education that took place after the 1870s. As you reread the essay, note the concerns he raises— explicitly or implicitly — as he examines particular historical developments. In a brief essay, analyze how he uses history to make his argument. Why is the historical dimension important to how he sees the current challenges facing teachers and students of writing within the university? What particular changes does he consider to be significant? What specific difficulties did those changes create?

2. Russell is recognized internationally for his work in writing across the curriculum, which involves teaching writing within the context of particular academic disciplines and using writing as a means to learn disciplinary material. When you reread this excerpt from his book, note his use of *community* and *discourse community* — terms that are central to current research on the teaching of writing. Based on this excerpt, write a brief essay in which you analyze his position on how writing should be taught on a university level. What can you infer about his position from the problem he poses in this essay? What can you infer from what he says about communities and discourse communities? Why are discourse communities important to teaching and learning and, more particularly, to your success as a writer?

3. Russell summarizes the shift from "the old liberal curriculum" to "the modern university" by pointing out that "the active, personal, language-dependent instructional methods of the old curriculum were replaced by passive, rather impersonal methods borrowed from Germany or, later, from scientific management: lecture, objective testing, and the like" (par. 2). Drawing on your own experience in the classroom (in all of your courses, not just writing courses), reflect on what constitutes active and passive learning. Based on Russell's argument, write a brief essay in which you analyze how the shift from active to passive teaching methods affected where and how writing is taught and the role of writing assignments in various disciplines. Look for passages, in addition to the one quoted above, that might directly or indirectly indicate Russell's view on the effects of this shift.

From Text to Field

1. At the end of this excerpt from Russell's book, he quotes Burton Clark's observation that academia is made up of "small worlds, different worlds" (par. 5). Given your own experience on campus, what different worlds can you identify? Consider both academic and nonacademic "worlds" as you think about this

question. What makes these worlds distinct? Are there any intersections between them? Are these worlds shaped and maintained by their use of language? In what ways are these small and different worlds on campus different from the various communities you belong to off campus, or might they have some commonalities? Write an essay in which you introduce one such small world on campus and reflect on your entry into that world.

2. Review Russell's essay to focus on what he has to say about "the culture of professionalism" (par. 2) and the effect it has had on the university system of education, particularly on the teaching of writing. Write an essay in which you take a position on the relationship between higher education and the professions and how you think that relationship should influence the teaching of writing. To what extent should higher education be focused on preparing students for the professions? What other purposes, if any, are there for pursuing a college education? What are the reasons behind your stance? Given what you think should be the goals of higher education, how should writing be taught?

3. This unit also includes an excerpt from an influential essay by Wayne C. Booth, "The Idea of a *University* — as Seen by a Rhetorician" (p. 332). Booth describes what he sees as the common rhetoric — shared language, values, and thinking processes—sed to communicate across highly specialized disciplines. Russell's argument implies that there is no single approach to writing that could prepare students to write within all of the academic or professional communities they might encounter. Do you agree with Booth or with Russell? Is there some common form of communication that cuts across specialized fields? Write an essay in which you respond to Russell's argument by drawing on your own experience with writing and writing courses.

The Idea of a *University* — as Seen by a Rhetorician

Wayne C. Booth

In 1987, Wayne C. Booth, a professor at the University of Chicago, was asked to address his colleagues as part of an annual lecture series dedicated to helping academic specialists understand each other's areas of research. Booth opened his address by questioning the ambitious goal of the annual lectures and coming to the conclusion that academics are "a pack of ignoramuses."

> [E]ven if we could create a university inhabited solely by geniuses, geniuses who, unlike most actual geniuses, were full of an infinite good-will toward, and determination to understand, one another's disciplines . . . we would find that under modern conditions of inquiry, conditions that we have no hope of changing fundamentally, none of them could come to an understanding of more than a fraction of what the others would take to be real knowledge.

In the spirit of the lecture series, Booth continued the address by examining the problem of understanding each other's work through the lens of his expertise in rhetoric. The excerpt that follows presents his solution — a recognition that academics use what he considers to be several valid forms of rhetoric to inform judgments they would otherwise be too "ignorant" to make. Through rhetoric, Booth explores the means for mutual understanding that might help a *uni*versity from splintering into a *multi*versity.

At the time this lecture was written, Booth was a Distinguished Service Professor at the University of Chicago. After retiring in 1992 at the age of seventy-one, he was the George M. Pullman Professor Emeritus of English and continued to be active as a researcher, writer, and lecturer. Booth died in 2005. The first of several landmark books he wrote, *The Rhetoric of Fiction,* published in 1961, is considered essential to the study of narrative theory and technique. *A Rhetoric of*

Irony (1974) explores how authors and readers participate in the complex interchange of ironic communication. *Modern Dogma and the Rhetoric of Assent* (1974) explores how speakers are able to change listeners' minds and when and why listeners should change their minds. More recently, Booth published several collections of his essays and lectures. Through the breadth and importance of his writings — ranging from literary criticism and rhetorical studies to examinations of pluralism and ethics — Booth has become a major influence both in and beyond his field.

I assume that many of you have long since wanted to protest against my picture. We all know that the islands are not in fact totally isolated, that somehow we have managed to invent communication systems. Though it may be true that on each island we speak a language not fully intelligible on any other, and though it may be true that some of the islands conduct active warfare against some of the others, and though some islands are in a state of civil war, the fact is that somehow we do manage to talk with one another and come to judgments that we are convinced are not *entirely* capricious. We write interdepartmental and even interdivisional memos, we indite letters of recommendation at breakneck speed and in appalling numbers, purporting to appraise the quality of colleagues whose work we don't know beans about. We appraise other scholars according to what we take to be high standards, even when we ourselves cannot state literally what the standards are. We pass judgment upon students in "related fields" and one another whenever promotion is at stake, and we seem not to suffer intolerable anxiety about our decisions. Even more shocking, in view of the plight I have described, we ask our deans and provosts and presidents to approve our judgments, and even grant the right to reverse them, implying that somehow *somebody* can be competent to judge work in *all* fields. Finally, we busy ourselves with a great deal of what we call "interdisciplinary work": degree-granting committees like Ideas and Methods, imperialistic fields like geography, anthropology, English, and rhetoric, conferences and workshops galore. None of us really thinks that *all* of these operations are totally fraudulent. We act *as if* our discussions and conferences and tenure decisions make *real* sense. Do they?

How do we actually work, as we run those of our affairs that depend on some kind of understanding different from the one I have applied so far? Do we work, as some say, only according to blind trust of friends and mistrust of enemies? Do we work according to guesses only? Are we, as some would claim, simply servants of money and power? In what sense, if any, do we employ a kind of reasoning and proof—knowledge and genuine understanding under any definition — that we might point to without shame?

After my informants of the past months have confessed their ignorance, I have asked them to tell me how they in fact operate when judging colleagues whose work they do not understand. All of them have said something like this — though never in this precise language: "We are by no means fraudulent, because we have available certain rational resources that your definition of understanding leaves out. We have learned to make use of our knowledge [one professor even called it 'wisdom'] about character and how to appraise character witnesses; we have learned how to read the signs of quality even in the fields where we cannot follow the proofs. We have learned how to determine whether a referee is trustworthy, and we have learned something about how to judge the quality of a candidate's thinking, just by the way he or she writes and speaks." They have not gone on to say, though I wish we could have shared this language: "You see, what all this means is that we are experienced both as practitioners and students of — rhetoric."

When I press them further with the question, "Do you make mistakes with this kind of thinking?" the answer is always "Yes, sometimes." But nobody I've talked with has claimed that the process depends on a trust that is utterly blind, totally a matter of nonrational power grabs or logrolling or back-scratching or moneygrubbing. Everyone, absolutely everyone, has played into this rhetorician's hands by claiming to employ a kind of thought that is not identical with what we do when proving conclusions in our frontline inquiry — and yet a kind that is still genuine thought.

Of course nobody has claimed that we offer our rhetorical proofs to each other and test them as well as we ought; indeed my main point today is that   5 we could all employ them better, and thus improve our quality as a *university, if* we all studied how such peculiar yet rational persuasion works. But even in our fallen condition, even as we in our imperfection now operate, we do not perform our personal and administrative judgments on indefensible, nonscholarly grounds; we perform those judgments on grounds that are considered nonscholarly only by those who think that all knowledge is of the kind yielded by frontline specialties, only by those who embrace uncritically the criterion for understanding, and thus of knowledge, with which I began. If knowledge is confined to what experts discover at the front line, and if understanding is confined to participation in full dialogue at the front line, then we operate ourselves without *knowing* what we do and without *understanding* each other. If we know and understand only what we can *prove* — with empirical observation, or with statistics, or with rigorous logical deduction — we will never *know* whether a colleague is worth listening to or promoting, unless we ourselves can follow his or her proofs, in detail, and then replicate them. All else is dubious, all else is guesswork, all else is blind faith.

But one thing we all know is that we know more than that criterion implies. Though unable to tell for ourselves whether the new mathematical proof is indeed new and indeed a proof, we learn how to consider, with the eye of nonspecialists, both the rhetoric of scholarship that we cannot hope fully to understand, and the rhetoric offered us *about* the scholar, the arguments offered by those who give us some reason to trust or mistrust their judgment as specialists.

We all thus implicitly aspire to mastery in three kinds of rhetoric, leading to three kinds of understanding, not just one. There are, first, the many and diverse rhetorics peculiar to each of our various front lines. Here each small group of experts relies on what Aristotle calls *special topics* of persuasion, the often tacit convictions that are shared by all within a discipline and that are therefore available in constructing arguments within the field: The assumption, say, that photographs of bubble chambers and their interpretations can somehow be relied on; or the conventional agreements about how to deal with normal curves and chi-squares, about the proper use of graphs, about what makes a **All three of these rhetorics** sound equation, or about how to do a sensitive report **are of course highly fallible.** of poetic scansion or a convincing analysis of sonata form in a symphony. Though these assumptions shift over time, we can at any given time rely on them without argument in their support, as we construct our arguments to our peers. I'll risk offending some of you by dubbing this frontline stuff and its workings "rhetoric-1." If calling it "hard proof" will make you happier, feel free, but I know that few specialists will want to claim that they or their successors will find themselves fifty years from now relying on the same tacit assumptions, leading to the same conclusions, that they share today.

A second kind that I call "general rhetoric," or "rhetoric-2," is what we share with members of every functioning organization or society—businesses, governments, clubs, families: the whole range of plausible or probable beliefs and modes of proof that make the world go round. Think of it as what even the most rigorous of scientists must rely on when testifying before a government committee. Here we rely on the *common*, or general topics: "More of any good thing is better than less of it—usually"; "It's wrong to lie, at least to friends and colleagues"; "Loyalty matters"; "Actions that usually produce bad consequences should be avoided." Obviously many of these are included in everyone's notion of "common sense": what *makes* sense in any argument.

Though the common topics are indispensable in every domain, they are especially prominent in our running of the university whenever we must appraise character. We all have a little storehouse of beliefs about character that we have to rely on, more or less efficiently, whenever we read a letter of recommendation, or predict the future behavior of a colleague in order to grant or deny tenure. Such common topics, "commonplaces," crop up in all public debate. "It is probable that someone who failed to carry through on her previous research plan will fail in this one; turn her down." "Ah, yes, but she was deep in the anguish of a divorce then, and she's changed a lot. I say give her the grant." "Well, but her strongest supporter is Professor Smiler, who has usually been wrong in his predictions that young colleagues are late bloomers. Why should we believe him in this case?" Or: "The truth is that Louise and Harry used to live together, and they had an angry breakup. I think — though we must say nothing of it in public — that we cannot trust his negative judgment on her scholarly ability."

Rhetoric-2 is thus the set of resources available in the functioning of all   10
organizations, not just of universities. Arbitragers and government officers function or fail to function, depending on whether the trust they yield to their CEOs and marine sergeants and colonels is justified. We in the university similarly succeed to the degree that our trust is granted when it should be, withheld when it should not be. The case with which rhetoric-2 can be abused accounts largely for why rhetoric has always had, and probably always *will* have, a bad press. Philosophers and moralists have often wished that it would just go away — but of course they express the wish for a purer world in the only language available to any of us when we press our wishes on the world: rhetorical argument.

There is, thirdly, a kind of rhetoric that is neither as special as the first nor as general as the second, a rhetoric relying on shared topics that are proper or special only to those within a university, but to all within that university, not to any one special group. We have no name for this peculiar stuff that we all to some degree share, but call it "the rhetoric of inquiry," or of "intellectual engagement"; "academy-rhetoric," or "rhetoric-3." We learn how to judge whether the arguments in fields beyond our full competence *somehow* track, whether the style of presentation *somehow* accords with standards we recognize. We learn to sense whether a colleague, even in a quite remote field, *seems* to have mastered the tricks of the trade — not just the trade of this or that kind of economist or philosopher, but the tricks of this whole trade, the trade of learning and teaching for the sake of learning and teaching. One often hears, in the Quadrangle Club, not just the contemptuous comments I have mentioned about fools and knaves but comments like this: "What a mind that man has." "What a pleasure to argue with that woman — she never misses a stroke." "He always seems to have just the right analogy to make his point." "Have you noticed how you always come away from a conversation with him having to think through the problem in a different way?"

All three of these rhetorics are of course highly fallible. Even our many versions of rhetoric-1 are notoriously unstable, as I have already implied, shifting in threatening ways from decade to decade and field to field. But the second and third rhetorics are much more obviously fallible, indeed staggeringly so. Tough-minded appraisal of characters and witnesses through close reading of letters of recommendation and reader's reports, close listening during telephone calls and hallway conversations, careful appraisal of past records of performance — these are all dangerously unreliable, partly because charlatans can so easily mimic the proper use of the topics. If this were not so, we would not have so many successful frauds in every field. The Piltdown hoaxers, the Cyril Burts, the Darsees,° the unqualified but practicing surgeons, the undiploma-ed lawyers — all the hoaxers of our world succeed as they do because they have mastered the surface conventions of all three rhetorics and through that mastery have collected or forged references testifying to high quality. We read about so many successes in this burgeoning field of pseudoscientific conning that we are in danger of forgetting the solid and indispensable base of merely probable inferences on which it rests. The breakdowns in the system result from, and depend on, a process — the practice of producing sound conclusions from rhetorical proofs — that by its very necessities opens the door to frauds. But this is not to say that we, their dupes, could not protect ourselves better if we would study rhetoric as hard as we study lab techniques, say, or formal logic.

Again and again I have been told by my informants that "it's not really very hard to tell competent work from incompetent, even if you know nothing about the details and cannot replicate the argument or experiment." And when I then ask, "How do you *do* that?" I am told — never in this language — that "I do it using rhetorics-2 and -3 — not the appraisal of frontline proofs but the careful judgment of both 'general rhetoric' and 'academy rhetoric.' One editor told me, "Even when I know little or nothing about a special field, I can tell just by the opening paragraphs whether a would-be contributor is at least competent." What does that mean, if not that he claims to judge the author's skill in rhetorical conventions shared with other fields: skill in saying what needs saying and in not saying what should not be said; skill in implying a scholarly ethos appropriate to the subject; skill in avoiding moves that give away the novice; and so on. Though the practice and appraisal of

---

The Piltdown hoaxers . . . the Darsees: The Piltdown hoax was an infamous case in which faked remains of an unknown form of early man were planted near Piltdown, England. Cyril Burt was a British psychologist accused of scientific fraud. John Darsee was a medical researcher found to have fabricated data for his research publications.

such skills is chancy, if we ruled them out we could not operate for a day without disaster. Most of our journals would have to be scrapped, most of our grants and awards would have to be eliminated, and the university would have to surrender to total balkanization or even tribal warfare, becoming not a *university* at all but a multiversity, a mere collection of research institutes warring for funds.

Working with the Text

1. Because Wayne C. Booth explores the inner workings of the university from his point of view as a rhetorician, his argument centers on the term *rhetoric*. As you reread the selection, consider how he uses the term. In a brief essay, define the term as Booth uses it in the context of his argument. What actions or mental processes does rhetoric involve? Why and how is it used? What connection does it have to understanding and judgment?

2. Booth presents rhetoric-2 as a "general rhetoric" that "we share with members of every functioning organization or society — businesses, governments, clubs, families: the whole range of plausible or probable beliefs and modes of proof that make the world go round" (par. 8). Study Booth's examples of these "commonplaces." In a brief response, add your own examples and explain why you think they are what Booth describes as "'common sense': what *makes* sense in any argument" (par. 8).

3. By Booth's definition, rhetoric-1 (the basic knowledge, assumptions, and principles of a particular academic specialization) and rhetoric-3 (shared topics and modes of inquiry within a community that spans diverse specializations) grow out of different kinds of specialized knowledge and experience. Write a brief essay in which you analyze the differences in specialization required by these two rhetorics. For instance, what is the difference between the "tacit convictions" of rhetoric-1 and the "intellectual engagement" of rhetoric-3?

4. According to Booth, all of us share in rhetoric-2, which is based on "common sense" — the principles, values, and ways of reasoning that "we share with members of every functioning organization or society" (par. 8). For Booth, this kind of rhetoric makes particular demands on trust. Reread the definition of rhetoric-2 as well as the passage in which Booth points out its fallibility. Write a brief essay in which you reflect on the role that trust plays in the reliability of rhetoric-2.

From Text to Field

1. Inside or outside of an educational setting, all of us have pursued interests or specializations that involve making judgments about our work or the work of other people. As part of this process, we have developed what Booth calls "the often tacit convictions that are shared by all" (par. 7) within a specialized area. Choose an area in which you have developed a certain amount of expertise, an area in which you talk about quality or performance with other people who share your interest. Using the examples Booth provides under the definition of rhetoric-1 as prompts, develop a guide to the "tacit convictions" you share with members of your group or area of expertise.

2. Booth introduces the three kinds of rhetoric to other academics in order to identify the "rational resources" they already use to understand each other and to challenge them to learn to use those resources more effectively. To help yourself absorb Booth's insights, study the three kinds of rhetoric from your point of view as a student. Although students do not yet have the knowledge and experience that academics bring to judgments of each other's work, students do have "rational resources" that they use to judge the quality of their teachers. In the form of a brochure or a brief guide for students entering the university, challenge them to improve their judgments by applying the three kinds of rhetoric. Your task will be to translate Booth's description of each kind of rhetoric into terms other students would readily understand when evaluating their professors as teachers.

3. In this excerpt from his talk, Booth is arguing for what he considers to be a valid approach for judging the performance of people whose work we do not have the expertise to understand. Consider his argument as it applies to situations both inside and outside of academic communities. Reflect on how his approach might affect you, if you were an expert being judged by nonexperts or a nonexpert being called upon to judge an expert. Write an essay in which you respond to Booth's argument, calling upon experiences in which you were either the judge or the judged.

4. Booth appears to be more optimistic than David Russell regarding the possibility of understanding one another's work in different disciplines. After reading the selection by Russell in this unit, write an essay in which you assess Booth's response to the fragmentation of community that Russell identifies. Draw on your experiences that seem to confirm or question the views of these two authors.

Body Ritual among the Nacirema

Horace Miner

This classic essay was first published in *American Anthropologist* in 1956. Since then, it has been widely read, making frequent appearances in anthologies and on reading lists developed for undergraduate courses in anthropology, sociology, and the humanities.

"Body Ritual among the Nacirema" offers writing students a rich source for exploring form and style. Based on the language and methodology of anthropologists conducting fieldwork, the essay demonstrates how a discipline constructs (and potentially limits) meaning through specialized terms, frames of reference, and forms of inquiry. It reveals both the power and pitfalls of working within a well-developed construct.

Horace Miner studied archaeology in Paris and Munich before working in anthropology as a museum curator at the University of Kentucky, as a graduate student at the University of Chicago, and as a professor of anthropology and sociology at the University of Michigan. He is known primarily for his study of the Nacirema, which grew out of an interest in using anthropological techniques to examine modern communities. Miner died in 1993, at the age of eighty-one.

The anthropologist has become so familiar with the diversity of ways in which different peoples behave in similar situations that he is not apt to be surprised by even the most exotic customs. In fact, if all of the logically possible combinations of behavior have not been found somewhere in the world, he is apt to suspect that they must be present in some yet undescribed tribe. This point has, in fact, been expressed with respect to clan organization by Murdock (1949: 71). In this light, the magical beliefs and practices of the Nacirema present such unusual aspects that it seems desirable to describe them as an example of the extremes to which human behavior can go.

Professor Linton first brought the ritual of the Nacirema to the attention of anthropologists twenty years ago (1936: 326), but the culture of this people is still very poorly understood. They are a North American group living in the territory between the Canadian Cree, the Yaqui and Tarahumare of Mexico, and the Carib and Arawak of the Antilles. Little is known of their origin, although tradition states that they came from the east. According to Nacirema mythology, their nation was originated by a culture hero, Notgnihsaw, who is otherwise known for two great feats of strength—the throwing of a piece of wampum across the river Pa-To-Mac and the chopping down of a cherry tree in which the Spirit of Truth resided.

Nacirema culture is characterized by a highly developed market economy which has evolved in a rich natural habitat. While much of the people's time is devoted to economic pursuits, a large part of these labors and a considerable portion of the day are spent in ritual activity. The focus of this activity is the human body, the appearance and health of which loom as a dominant concern in the ethos of the people. While such a concern is certainly not unusual, its ceremonial aspects and associated philosophy are unique.

The fundamental belief underlying the whole system appears to be that the human body is ugly and that its natural tendency is to debility and disease. Incarcerated in such a body, man's only hope is to avert these characteristics through the use of the powerful influences of ritual and ceremony. Every household has one or more shrines devoted to this purpose. The more powerful individuals in the society have several shrines in their houses and, in fact, the opulence of a house is often referred to in terms of the number of such ritual centers it possesses. Most houses are of wattle and daub construction, but the shrine rooms of the more wealthy are walled with stone. Poorer families imitate the rich by applying pottery plaques to their shrine walls.

While each family has at least one such shrine, the rituals associated with it are not family ceremonies but are private and secret. The rites are normally only discussed with children, and then only during the period when they are being initiated into these mysteries. I was able, however, to establish sufficient rapport with the natives to examine these shrines and to have the rituals described to me.

The focal point of the shrine is a box or chest which is built into the wall. In this chest are kept the many charms and magical potions without which no native believes he could live. These preparations are secured from a variety of specialized practitioners. The most powerful of these are the medicine men, whose assistance must be rewarded with substantial gifts. However, the medicine men do not provide the curative potions for their clients, but decide what the ingredients should be and then write them down in an ancient and secret language. This writing is understood only by the medicine men and the herbalists who, for another gift, provide the required charm.

The charm is not disposed of after it has served its purpose, but is placed in the charm-box of the household shrine. As these magical materials are specific for certain ills, and the real or imagined maladies of the people are many, the charm-box is usually full to overflowing. The magical packets are so numerous that people forget what their purposes were and fear to use them again. While the natives are very vague on this point, we can only assume that the idea in retaining all the old magical materials is that their presence in the charm-box, before which the body rituals are conducted, will in some way protect the worshipper.

Beneath the charm-box is a small font. Each day every member of the family, in succession, enters the shrine room, bows his head before the charm-box, mingles different sorts of holy water in the font, and proceeds with a brief rite of ablution. The holy waters are secured from the Water Temple of the community, where the priests conduct elaborate ceremonies to make the liquid ritually pure.

In the hierarchy of magical practitioners, and below the medicine men in prestige, are specialists whose designation is best translated "holy-mouth-men." The Nacirema have an almost pathological horror of and fascination with the mouth, the condition of which is believed to have a supernatural influence on all social relationships. Were it not for the rituals of the mouth, they believe that their teeth would fall out, their gums bleed, their jaws shrink, their friends desert them, and their lovers reject them. They also believe that a strong relationship exists between oral and moral characteristics. For example, there is a ritual ablution of the mouth for children which is supposed to improve their moral fiber.

The daily body ritual performed by everyone includes a mouth-rite. 10 Despite the fact that these people are so punctilious **The magical beliefs and** about care of the mouth, this rite involves a practice **practices of the Nacirema** which strikes the uninitiated stranger as revolting. It **present . . . unusual aspects.** was reported to me that the ritual consists of inserting a small bundle of hog hairs into the mouth, along with certain magical powders, and then moving the bundle in a highly formalized series of gestures.

In addition to the private mouth-rite, the people seek out a holy-mouth-man once or twice a year. These practitioners have an impressive set of paraphernalia, consisting of a variety of augers, awls, probes, and prods. The use of these objects in the exorcism of the evils of the mouth involves almost unbelievable ritual torture of the client. The holy-mouth-man opens the client's mouth and, using the above mentioned tools, enlarges any holes which decay may have created in the teeth. Magical materials are put into

these holes. If there are no naturally occurring holes in the teeth, large sections of one or more teeth are gouged out so that the supernatural substance
can be applied. In the client's view, the purpose of these ministrations is to
arrest decay and to draw friends. The extremely sacred and traditional character of the rite is evident in the fact that the natives return to the holy-
mouth-men year after year, despite the fact that their teeth continue to decay.

It is to be hoped that, when a thorough study of the Nacirema is made,
there will be careful inquiry into the personality structures of these people.
One has but to watch the gleam in the eye of a holy-mouth-man, as he jabs
an awl into an exposed nerve, to suspect that a certain amount of sadism is
involved. If this can be established, a very interesting pattern emerges, for
most of the population shows definite masochistic tendencies. It was to these
that Professor Linton referred in discussing a distinctive part of the daily body
ritual which is performed only by men. This part of the rite involves scraping and lacerating the surface of the face with a sharp instrument. Special
women's rites are performed only four times during each lunar month, but
what they lack in frequency is made up in barbarity. As part of this ceremony,
women bake their heads in small ovens for about an hour. The theoretically
interesting point is that what seems to be a preponderantly masochistic people
have developed sadistic specialists.

The medicine men have an imposing temple, or *latipso*, in every community of any size. The more elaborate ceremonies required to treat very sick
patients can only be performed at this temple. These ceremonies involve not
only the thaumaturge° but a permanent group of vestal maidens who move
sedately about the temple chambers in distinctive costume and headdress.

The *latipso* ceremonies are so harsh that it is phenomenal that a fair proportion of the really sick natives who enter the temple ever recover. Small
children whose indoctrination is still incomplete have been known to resist
attempts to take them to the temple because "that is where you go to die."
Despite this fact, sick adults are not only willing but eager to undergo the
protracted ritual purification, if they can afford to do so. No matter how ill
the supplicant or how grave the emergency, the guardians of many temples
will not admit a client if he cannot give a rich gift to the custodian. Even after
one has gained admission and survived the ceremonies, the guardians will
not permit the neophyte to leave until he makes still another gift.

The supplicant entering the Temple is first stripped of all his or her   15
clothes. In every-day life the Nacirema avoids exposure of his body and its
natural functions. Bathing and excretory acts are performed only in the
secrecy of the household shrine, where they are ritualized as part of the body-
rites. Psychological shock results from the fact that body secrecy is suddenly

---

thaumaturge: A worker of marvels or miracles.

lost upon entry into the *latipso*. A man, whose own wife has never seen him in an excretory act, suddenly finds himself naked and assisted by a vestal maiden while he performs his natural functions into a sacred vessel. This sort of ceremonial treatment is necessitated by the fact that the excreta are used by a diviner to ascertain the course and nature of the client's sickness. Female clients, on the other hand, find their naked bodies are subjected to the scrutiny, manipulation, and prodding of the medicine man.

Few supplicants in the temple are well enough to do anything but lie on their hard beds. The daily ceremonies, like the rites of the holy-mouth-men, involve discomfort and torture. With ritual precision, the vestals awaken their miserable charges each dawn and roll them about on their beds of pain while performing ablutions, in the formal movements of which the maidens are highly trained. At other times they insert magic wands in the supplicant's mouth or force him to eat substances which are supposed to be healing. From time to time the medicine men come to their clients and jab magically treated needles into their flesh. The fact that these temple ceremonies may not cure, and may even kill the neophyte, in no way decreases the people's faith in the medicine men.

There remains one other kind of practitioner, known as a "listener." This witch-doctor has the power to exorcise the devils that lodge in the heads of people who have been bewitched. The Nacirema believe that parents bewitch their own children. Mothers are particularly suspected of putting a curse on children while teaching them the secret body rituals. The counter-magic of the witch-doctor is unusual in its lack of ritual. The patient simply tells the "listener" all his troubles and fears, beginning with the earliest difficulties he can remember. The memory displayed by the Nacirema in these exorcism sessions is truly remarkable. It is not uncommon for the patient to bemoan the rejection he felt upon being weaned as a babe, and a few individuals even see their troubles going back to the traumatic effects of their own birth.

In conclusion, mention must be made of certain practices which have their base in native esthetics but which depend upon the pervasive aversion to the natural body and its functions. There are ritual fasts to make fat people thin and ceremonial feasts to make thin people fat. Still other rites are used to make women's breasts larger if they are small, and smaller if they are large. General dissatisfaction with breast shape is symbolized in the fact that the ideal form is virtually outside the range of human variation. A few women afflicted with almost inhuman hypermammary development are so idolized that they make a handsome living by simply going from village to village and permitting the natives to stare at them for a fee.

Reference has already been made to the fact that excretory functions are ritualized, routinized, and relegated to secrecy. Natural reproductive functions are similarly distorted. Intercourse is taboo as a topic and scheduled as an act. Efforts are made to avoid pregnancy by the use of magical materials or by limiting intercourse to certain phases of the moon. Conception is actually very infrequent. When pregnant, women dress so as to hide their condition. Parturition takes place in secret, without friends or relatives to assist, and the majority of women do not nurse their infants.

Our review of the ritual life of the Nacirema has certainly shown them to be magic-ridden people. It is hard to understand how they have managed to exist so long under the burdens which they have imposed upon themselves. But even such exotic customs as these take on real meaning when they are viewed with the insight provided by Malinowski when he wrote (1948: 70):

> Looking from far and above, from our high places of safety in the developed civilization, it is easy to see all the crudity and irrelevance of magic. But without its power and guidance early man could not have mastered his practical difficulties as he has done, nor could man have advanced to the higher stages of civilization.

References Cited

Linton, Ralph. (1936). *The Study of Man*. New York: D. Appleton Century Co.
Malinowski, Bronislaw. (1948). *Magic, Science, and Religion*. Glencoe: The Free Press.
Murdock, George P. (1949). *Social Structure*. New York: The Macmillan Co.

Working with the Text

1. "Body Ritual among the Nacirema" is frequently assigned in introductory anthropology and sociology courses to explore the basic methods and ways of thinking used in those fields. The fact that the essay is a parody only serves to underscore how professional language is used to construct meaning. As you reread Horace Miner's essay, highlight words and phrases that suggest how anthropologists and sociologists gather and interpret data. In a brief essay, analyze Miner's use (and parody) of the professional language. What is the anthropologist's vantage point? What is the anthropologist looking for? How does he or she collect and interpret data? Study the references to other anthropologists. What professional categories and concepts does the narrator use? Where in the research process is there a risk of misinterpretation?

2. The essay is written to make you think by making you laugh. Note the particular places in the essay that make you smile or laugh. Choose five or six of those passages. In a series of journal entries, explain what you found funny about each passage and what you learned from your response. What mental images did the passage conjure up? What does your response reveal about

your attitudes as well as those of the Nacirema and the anthropologist? What new insights did you gain?

3. In his anthropologist's report on the Nacirema, Miner sends up Americans at the same time he is sending up anthropologists. Write a brief essay in which you respond to Miner's view of how Americans regard their bodies. What is his view? What data does he use to support it? Do you agree with his interpretation of the data? Why or why not?

From Text to Field

1. Remember that Miner's essay was published in *American Anthropologist* in 1956. Review the specific "data" Miner uses to demonstrate an American obsession with the human body. Entering into a persona similar to Miner's anthropologist, write a "report" in which you update "Body Ritual among the Nacirema." Revisit the culture as it functions now and interpret the data you gather. What are the current body-related practices? In what ways is the cult of the human body the same as it was in the 1956 report? In what ways has it changed over the last half century? Does the current data confirm the 1956 analysis or have you arrived at a somewhat different interpretation?

2. The persona and methods of Miner's anthropologist can be applied to any aspect of human culture. Choose a set of practices—other than those examined by Miner—to interpret in your own anthropological "study." You might choose a different aspect of American culture, or you might examine the culture of another country where you have lived or traveled. You might choose an American subculture, such as residents of a geographical region or a group with a distinctive identity. Your own family or hometown could constitute a culture worth studying. For your "study," write either a parody or a serious analysis. Whichever approach you adopt, base your interpretation on solid data and accurate observation. Think of yourself as an anthropologist entering into uncharted territory and a foreign, exotic culture.

3. An effective way to learn new methods and ways of thinking is to send them up in a parody. To experiment with your own parody, choose one form of communication between teachers and students, either written or spoken, that is used in a field or discipline you are just beginning to study. You could write a parody of the very questions you are reading right now. Other possibilities include lab reports, the course syllabus, the objective or short-answer tests in one of your science classes, or faculty Web pages. Use Miner's essay as a model for identifying ways to mimic and exaggerate terms, structures, concepts, and attitudes.

The Grooves of Academe

Robin Tolmach Lakoff

What we now know as the university was first called "the groves of academe" by the ancient Roman poet Horace, who wrote in his *Epistles,* "seek for truth in the groves of academe." The phrase evokes images of strolling among the trees, cultivating the mind through study and debate. To capture the current realities of academic survival, Robin Lakoff changes "groves" to "grooves," suggesting "moves" that are part of being "in the groove." She surely also has in mind being "in a rut."

At the center of her argument is a belief that the mission of the university is the pursuit of truth and knowledge. Her question is this: If our mission is truth and knowledge, and if language, discourse, and communication are the means for pursuing that mission (which she believes they are), why is academic discourse so marked by obscure language and rituals of silence? Why don't departments and professors simply tell students directly how they might succeed? Instead, they presume that students will figure out the mysteries of initiation into the field all on their own.

Lakoff gained an insider's view of academia as a PhD candidate at Harvard University and as a professor of pragmatics and sociolinguistics at the University of California, Berkeley. Her insights are informed by her research into the relationships among language, identity, and power. These concerns are reflected in the titles of her books, among them *Language and Women's Place* (1975), *Face Value: The Politics of Beauty* (1984), *When Talk Is Not Cheap* (1985), and *Talking Power: The Politics of Language in Our Lives* (1990). *The Language War* (2000) examines the interplay between language and politics in the media treatment of high-profile events such as the murder trial of O. J. Simpson and the impeachment of President Clinton. "The Grooves of Academe" is an excerpt from *Talking Power.*

My department is at it again.

Every five years or so we go through it, only to undo our work, like Penelope,° with perfect regularity some five years later. We are fighting about revamping the department's graduate program: how many courses, and which, and in what order, are to be required for the PhD. It always turns out to be a long-drawn-out process, entailing almost as much internecine acrimony as our all-time favorite fighting issue — hiring of new colleagues. And the real conflicts, the things that fill a simple process with dissension, are never brought out into the light of day: They remain covert, while we debate superficialities.

The Curriculum Committee (and academics do love committees, almost as much as we love subcommittees! they allow us to postpone the inevitable moment of climax, the decision) has proposed a new course, to be required of all graduate students in their first semester of residence, for one unit (most courses are three or four), meeting for one and a half hours, once a week — a very small commitment.

Ordinarily, such small fish don't attract a great deal of discussion, pro or con. We reserve our verbal ammunition for the bigger stuff. But the proposed course is largely concerned with the underpinnings of the field, its ineffable mystique. It would cover, for instance, how to get articles published; how to write abstracts; where to look for bibliography; which journals are geared toward which subfields; the professional interests of the various faculty members of the department.

And more, and worse: how power is allocated in the field of linguistics; who has it, why, and how to get it. And why linguists are such a contentious group, why we can't listen to one another across theoretical boundaries, why scholarly arguments too often turn into personal vendettas.   5

Everyone agrees that, to receive a PhD in linguistics from the University of California at Berkeley, a student must demonstrate knowledge in a variety of topics: sounds and sound-systems; word-formation and lexical semantics; syntax and sentence-level semantics; processes of historical change; methodology of various types; the claims of competing theories; and, of course, much much more. All this is the explicit and overt knowledge of the field, our public culture, as it were — what we transmit openly to the young and expect them to demonstrate proof of mastering. But that knowledge alone, however broad and deep, does not a competent professional linguist make.

Penelope: The wife of Odysseus, who held suitors at bay throughout his twenty-year absence during the Trojan War. She promised to wed when she finished weaving a burial shroud, which she wove by day and unraveled by night.

To be one, you not only have to know facts, theories, and methods, you have to know how to be a linguist, how to play by the rules. You have to know how to cite sources and which sources to cite; how to talk and how to write, in terms of style; how to talk and how to write, in terms of which questions may legitimately be raised and which (apparently equally attractive) may not, and what constitutes an "answer." You have to know something about the history of the field, which in turn explains the politics of the field: who likes who and who hates who, who invites contributions from who in the volume who is editing, who is not invited (though working in the same area) and why. You must master the forms, in terms of length, topic, and style: the *abstract*, the *paper* (or *article*), the *monograph*, the *book*, in writing; the *talk*, the *job talk*, the *lecture*, the *panel contribution*, among oral forms. These requirements exist in all academic fields, but each field does them differently and values them differently. In determining tenurability, some departments rank a single book higher than several articles with about the same number of pages; others, the reverse. It's useful to know these things — in fact, often vital for survival in an increasingly competitive business. But no one will tell you this — certainly not spontaneously. Some students know how to pick up a lot of underground stuff by judicious looking and listening; others are sophisticated and brash enough to frame the questions and insist on answers from diffident mentors. But many are not, and it takes them years of agonizing in pretenure positions before they understand — too often, too late.

We would be scandalized at a department that refused to tell its students about sentence-construction or typological differences among languages. But we are, some of us, equally scandalized at a proposal to provide the second kind of information openly to all, in the guise of formal course work. When the Curriculum Committee had submitted its lengthy proposal, the first and bitterest fight erupted over this peripheral one-unit course: whether, as "nonintellectual subject matter" it should be taught at all.

We are, in fact, fighting about something much bigger than a proposed Linguistics-200 requirement, but no one says so: that would be vulgar. We are fighting about mystique. We are elders in the tribal sweathouse, discussing the rites of initiation the next generation is to undergo. We went through them once, that's how we achieved our present esteemed status. They must, too, in their turn. We all agree on that, and we also agree pretty much that there are certain explicit skills the youth must know before they are deemed ready to take their place in adult society. But someone has raised an unheard-of question: Should they be told the secrets — what happens during the ordeal, what is done and why it is done? It would make it easier for them; the suffering (which we all agree is essential) would make sense; it would be coherent, all the fasting, mutilation, deprivation. Why not enlighten them?

But the oldest of the elders demurs indignantly. Don't we understand *any-* 10
thing? The whole point is in the mystery. The very senselessness gives the
experience a special meaning, a curious depth, makes tribal membership of
greater value. If they have to figure it out themselves, by vague hints and
overheard whispers, through trial and error, with pain and suffering, they will
prize full membership, when it is conferred, all the more. The elders of the
tribe must keep its mysteries holy.

Any anthropologically sophisticated Westerner can understand that reasoning in a primitive tribe. But it's a little disconcerting to encounter ourselves at it — ourselves, not only sophisticated Westerners, but intellectuals to
boot and, more, intellectuals in an institution which claims as its territory the
pursuit of knowledge by reason alone. Mystique has a place, but it is not the
stuff of which scholarship is made. But reason alone cannot explain the pas-
sions of the argument over Linguistics 200.

Like any other institution, the university has a complex mission, only
some of which is supposed to be overtly visible, even to insiders. Therefore,
its power relations are complex, and its communications — to outsiders, and
to and among its members — are more often than not obscure and ambiguous. In fact, the discourse of academe seems (and not only to noninitiates)
especially designed for incomprehensibility. This is demonstrably true. But
many of its ambiguities and eccentricities are intentional and intrinsic to the
institution, not (as sometimes argued) mere side effects of the university's
main communicative purpose.

Truth in Language: Mission Impossible?

Every institution has a public mission, its reason for being, generally
couched in benign and even lofty language. The mission of psychotherapy is
change or *understanding;* of the law, *justice;* of the military, *protection* or
defense; of government, *order.* In this semantic of noble purpose, we can
define the university's mission as the production of *truth,* or *knowledge,* a virtuous enterprise if ever there was one. Unlike the others, it would seem to
have no dark side, no hidden risk to anyone. There would seem to be nothing to hide or dissemble.

But for all its virtuousness, the university is an institution, like the others. As
such, it must ensure its own survival and the enhancement of the status of itself
and its members. It must appear to the outside world, and to its own personnel,
as benevolent and useful: It must have something the outside world needs
enough to pay for, to support the institution and guarantee its survival. It must
be awesome, to convince others of its value; and more, it must seem *good.*

This is a lot to ask of anyone, individual or institution. It is hard to require 15
both love and respect, to retain power and yet radiate benevolence, to get

from outsiders scarce resources against strong competition — even more for an institution whose product is abstract, often inscrutable, of no immediate use. We can see why we have to support the government and the military (well, some of us can, some of the time); if we are in pain, we can justify giving money to the medical or psychotherapeutic establishments; if we are legally entangled, we appreciate the necessity of supporting the representatives of the law. But the university has to persuade society that knowledge per se is worthy of support.

Institutions, then, like individuals, have interests at stake; they must compete for resources. But at the same time, to succeed in getting their needs met, they must convince others of their benevolence and disinterestedness. We know what individuals do in such a quandary: They lie. Institutions are no different. Unless the lies become too outrageous or harmful, we mostly accept them. Watergate was intolerable, but Iran-Contragate was within bounds. We know Freud lied, or at least engaged in self-deception, about "infantile seduction," but psychoanalysis retains society's respect. The university, as an institution, can be expected to lie to protect its power and authority.

Cases are not hard to come by. For example, universities are known to reinvent their history when convenient. In 1964, the University of California at Berkeley was shaken by the Free Speech Movement. Popular among students, it was anathema to the administration and many of the faculty, who did everything they could to stamp it out **We are fighting about** and remove its ringleaders from influence. But life **mystique.** goes on, times change, and what was once a dire threat to institutional business as usual is seen nostalgically, twenty years later, as the shot heard' round the world, the opening statement of the sixties. It was *important*, it was *historic*, it put the university on the cultural map.

Therefore, in 1984, it seemed appropriate to the university administration — heirs to the men who had called armed deputies in to their rescue — to celebrate the twentieth anniversary of the Free Speech Movement with a plethora of university-sponsored activities stressing the movement's historic role and the university's participation therein. There were speeches by the powerful and influential, publications, retrospective photography shows, colloquia, everything that can be trotted out to say, This was history and we were a part of it — we made it happen. Lost in the hoopla is the fact that the university was involved, all right — against its will and as a force in opposition. The administration never (that I am aware of) said in so many words: We supported the FSM. But the inviting of celebrities, the holding of public festivities, said as much and, by saying it implicitly, said it more potently, as the message could not easily be contradicted. Nowadays we see the willful distortion of history as evil when it is done by a government or the media. Should it be viewed any differently as an act of the benevolent university?

In fact, it's more troubling. Since it is an institution, it might seem unfair to hold the university to a standard of truthfulness higher than we demand of others. But there is a reason we must. The success of an institution is linked to its efficacy in turning out a well-functioning product. Any institution-internal uncertainty about that product, any hesitation or self-contradiction in the institution, will vitiate the product and, ultimately, eviscerate the institution itself. It may live on (institutions are survivors), but its influence will be much diminished.

Imagine if the military proved unable to protect the people, or if a government allowed rioting to go on unchecked. Those institutions would become objects of ridicule, and be either overthrown or ineffectual, because they were not fulfilling their mission, not producing the goods that they were created and supported in order to produce. Even a partial falling off, a single instance of failure of mission, will weaken an institution's legitimacy, though it probably takes either an egregious example or repeated lesser abuses to actually bring it down.

To catch any institution in a lie is disconcerting, but seldom deeply damaging. The member who lied may be punished, and the institution close over the injury, essentially untouched. Its mission is not compromised. But the mission of the university *is* truth, or knowledge: So when the university lies, it is precisely as if the government dissolved in chaos. To lie is to contravene the mission of the university directly. Therefore, when the university lies (or rather, is lied for by its representatives), it necessarily contributes in a serious way to its loss of legitimacy as an institution.

Unlike other institutions, then, the university has discourse of a particular sort as its mission and its sole product. Some institutions use language just peripherally: The military gets its job done via the giving of orders; but it is weapons that actually do the job, and the job is not intrinsically communicative in nature. The courts and psychotherapy are somewhat different, in that they use particular forms of language specifically to create specific real-world situations; the choice of language influences their result, so that communicative efficacy is crucial for their members, more than in less linguistically oriented institutions.

But the university alone trades only in language, discourse, communication. The university's only acts are speech acts, in Austin's sense.° Truth and knowledge are linguistic entities, existing only through and in language. Only for the university is language an end in itself. Therefore (one might

---

speech acts . . . in Austin's sense: A concept in linguistics and the philosophy of language developed by J. L. Austin, the speech act describes how, when we use language to say something, we also *do* something — as when a minister says "I pronounce you husband and wife." Common examples of speech acts include voicing a request, giving an order, or making a promise.

argue) the members of the university ought to be especially skillful communicators, since that is all they have to offer, and that is solely how they achieve their effects.

Well, but. . . .

Surely the members of the university community produce a lot of language, in a lot of forms, oral and written, public and private, formal and informal. But by any stylistic standards, the university's prose is inelegant. Indeed, some would call it abysmal—turgid, pompous, inflated, impenetrable, closing off understanding rather than furthering it. The conventional view is that this is a by-product of our mission. We are here to educate and inform not to entertain. Therefore there is no need for the product to be delightful, amusing, or pleasurable. But "no need" does not begin to express the prevailing attitude toward stylistic amenity. Those who write relatively accessibly are often the recipients of barely veiled hostility, in the form of scholarly disdain: "Just a popular piece." The idea is, if more than three people can understand it, it can't be worth much. In fact, the distress clarity arouses is oddly reminiscent of the discomfiture, at the faculty meeting described earlier at the breaching of the mystique. It's not that there's no need to be intelligible. It's that there is a need not to. Our power, our authority, is intertwined with our ability to maintain secrets even as we seem to dispense them. We write and speak, but we do not communicate. That is our art.

Horizontal Communication

The university and its members must speak with many voices to fit their many functions—no easy task. First, the university as an institution communicates with the outside world, to show that it is doing a valuable job well. Most universities have public-relations offices to send out items to the media on the accomplishments of the university and its members: awards won, public works performed, research completed. It arranges interviews with the media—if a reporter needs a semanticist in a hurry, it will provide one. The university also puts out informational pamphlets: how to apply for admission, the availability of financial aid, and so on. There are publications produced by and about the university intended for the outside world, often alumni, to solicit financial contributions. In all of these contacts, the university presents itself as "the University," a faceless monolith rather than the assortment of diverse interests that it is.

Individuals within the university sometimes communicate, in their identities as university personnel, with the world at large or at least nonacademic institutions. They carry from the university, as part of the presuppositions underlying their discourse, the intellectual legitimacy that comes of being a member of that community: Expertise is implicitly, if not always legitimately, transferable. In these roles, members consult for industry and government, serve on the panels of government and private granting agencies, serve as expert witnesses in the courtroom. In these roles almost uniquely, professors are addressed and referred to as "Professor" and "Doctor." Within the university, these titles are dispensed with; their use is a mark of naivete, outsidership (and so is mostly reserved for undergraduates, who are neither members nor even potential members).

More often, and more significantly, members of the university community, especially faculty, communicate as individuals to individuals. Faculty status brings with it membership in several constituencies. First, one is a member of a discipline, a relatively egalitarian relationship. At the same time, one is a member of a department, entailing some hierarchical distinctions; and of one's university's cross-disciplinary community, entailing status distinctions of a different kind. A linguist keeps in contact with other linguists, through publication, professional society meetings, and other conferences, as well as letters and visits. We exchange letters of recommendation for our students and junior colleagues; we review one another's grant applications and submissions for publication.

Within disciplines, we develop special languages. Like any linguistic code, these play two roles. Toward the outside world, they are elitist: We know, you cannot understand, you may not enter. But for insiders they are a secret handshake. When I encounter my profession's terms of art in a piece of writing or a talk, I am obscurely comforted: I am at home among friends. True, "ethnomethodology" and "equi-noun-phrase deletion" are not the friends everyone would choose, but when I find them, I know I am welcome. An article submitted for publication in a professional journal may contain useful and significant information; but if it has been submitted (as occasionally happens) by someone outside the field who does not know the communicative conventions, the reviewer will immediately sense that something is amiss from the absence of the secret wink. In all probability the paper will be rejected. It isn't just that we are being snobbish (we are, of course); but over time we become attuned to our special form of discourse, and literally become unable to understand anything labeled "linguistics" that is not expressed as "linguistics" is supposed to be. The form must match the context, or understanding fails.

A significant part of a graduate student's education consists of learning this language. Part of becoming worthy of the PhD, the certificate of membership, is the demonstration that one knows and can use the language. 30

There are recognizable power ploys in academic discourse, often lost on outsiders. In intradisciplinary prose, the footnote is wielded as cavemen wielded clubs, a blunt but effective weapon. The footnote (nowadays, to save printing expenses, more often the end note) says: I know everything about this topic. I could go on forever. Maybe I will. In any case, don't think you can overwhelm me with obscure information. I said it first, here. I control the scholarship, I've read everything, *this is my turf.* The conscientious reader of academic prose must break concentration to read the footnote, another secret signal between writer and reader: We are serious professionals. This communication is not for entertainment. It is *supposed* to be obnoxious.[1]

How to Write Like a Professor

The written style of the university, too, has its own separate formats, each justified by function. This is especially true of intradisciplinary scholarly writing. A significant part of a student's training involves learning these procedures, learning how to sound right as well as how to make valid contributions. I spoke earlier of the relation between the traditional convoluted style of academia and the academic's need for signals of solidarity and acceptance by peers. But turgidity does not come naturally. It must be acquired by slow degrees. Deviation in any direction is punishable.

Neophytes must learn both correct surface form and deeper matters of style and content. They must, first and most obviously, learn how to juggle the technical terminology of their field: the secret handshake par excellence. They must learn what each special term means, who introduced it, and therefore its political significance. (While *scenario, frame,* and *schema* may, in discourse semantics and pragmatics, be mutually interchangeable, students who study with the scholars responsible for each term will use that term rather than the others in their own writing.) They will learn what ideas justify the postulation of special terminology: how revolutionary, how important they must be. They will read enough of the literature to know, when they have thought of an idea, whether a term already exists for it, to avoid duplication. They will also learn that creating a term, and offering it to the world, is an act of power best left to the established members of the field. It takes some gall for graduate students to propose terms for their own ideas; for an undergraduate to attempt this borders on the treasonable. And of course, to propose a term when one already exists exposes one to ridicule; and to misuse someone else's terminology, worse.

Undergraduates (and beginning graduate students) are not encouraged to play the same game as their betters. It does not become an undergraduate to sound like a professor. Moreover, since the undergraduate does not

---

[1]See what I mean? [Lakoff's note].

have sufficient experience or knowledge, the attempt is apt to be risible. As students progress through graduate school, they are expected to acquire academic style, a little in course papers, more in qualifying papers. But the usage must grow gradually, sparingly, avoiding the appearance of presumptuousness, the accusations of usurpation of territory that belongs to the elders. The pinnacle is reached with the dissertation, wherein a student demonstrates worthiness to become a full-fledged member of the society, having passed all the ordeals the elders have to provide. The dissertation shows not only that the student has mastered the knowledge of the field and its methods; not only that the student has something original to add to that store of knowledge; but that the student knows the rules, knows how to behave like a member of the culture. So the dissertation must be couched in the finest and most etiolated of academese, redolent of footnotes, stylistically impenetrable, bristling with jargon. Only thus can proper deportment be demonstrated.

Indeed, never again is it expected to this extent. For the next several years, through the assistant professorship and until tenure, caution is recommended: Style should be academic, though a little relaxation is permissible. The dissertation showed one could take direction: Now one must show an ability to be on one's own. Tenure decisions involve the assessment of "collegiality": practically speaking, that means, Do nothing that might offend the thinnest-skinned colleague. Only after the granting of tenure is it safe to abandon the style for something snappier; and even then, obloquy is a probable outcome. But tenure smiles at obloquy.

If academic style were merely the result of carelessness or unconcern for the graces, it would increase as its user advanced in the field, in a straight upward direction; and if undergraduates were capable of using the style, it would be deemed an unmixed sign of competence, not a little off-color. But we find instead the parabolic curve . . . [in Fig. 1], which suggests that the style is connected to notions of privilege and power. You are *allowed* to use academese when you have convinced the elders that you are a serious apprentice, no longer an outsider (who is not allowed knowledge of the mysteries). You *must* use academese to prove your worthiness of acceptance and your ability to submit to discipline. You *may* abandon academese, wholly or more likely in part, when you are the gatekeeper and need no longer worry about being excluded from the society.

Over the course of an academic career, writing gradually becomes more overtly territorial, assumes more power for its producer, by achieving more length and broader topical scope. Undergraduate and early graduate course papers are unseemly if they exceed twenty pages or so. They deal with small and concrete topics: no total solutions, no metatheoretical debate. Later, through qualifying papers and other predissertation work, length increases to

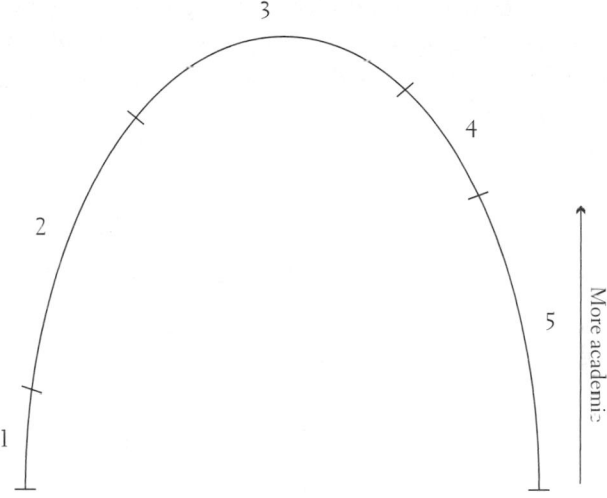

1. Undergraduates and beginning graduate students
2. Advanced graduate students
3. Students writing dissertations
4. Nontenured faculty
5. Tenured faculty

Figure 1. Privilege and Power in Academia

a maximum of fifty to one hundred pages, and topics become more abstract, more cutting-edge, and of broader scope, as the student demonstrates the desire to achieve full maturity and the ability to understand what the territorial battles are about. The dissertation stakes a claim. The writer takes a theoretical stance, either adapting a mentor's theory or inventing a modest theoretical innovation; applies it to a fairly broad swath of language; and tests it against the best that the field has to offer, engaging in conflict with established members of the group (but always respectfully). A dissertation is longer, too, around three hundred pages. Much more than that, though, or too grandiose a proposal, marks the writer as hubristic. The assistant professor is allowed a larger swath of territory. But because of the pressure to publish, the tendency is to stick to only mildly controversial topics that can be handled in a relatively short space, in a relatively short time. Later, with tenure, the sky's the limit—on length, breadth, and self-assurance, as well as interpersonal obnoxiousness.

The discourse style of academia turns out not to be solely a by-product of the knowledge factory. It is also the language of a society with complex and covert power and territorial assumptions, often in conflict with its express mission. As an institution, the university is relatively but not totally benign. As a society it is hierarchical and authoritarian, yet necessarily egalitarian and collaborative in its creation of a product. That it does so often produce products of value, that it protects its members from evaluation by the crass standards of the outside, make it an unusually benevolent institution. But that fact should not blind observers to its shortcomings, or cause them to overlook the ways in which those who have power in the university, as in any other institution, misuse it and abuse its weaker members.

Work Cited

Austin, J. L. *How To Do Things with Words.* Oxford: Clarendon Press, 1962.

Working with the Text

1. At the center of Robin Tolmach Lakoff's argument is the question of "mystique," especially as it relates to power. As you note Lakoff's use of the word, try to imagine how mystique plays itself out, from the point of view of those who are entering into the ritual as well as those who are creating it. Write an essay in which you analyze Lakoff's insight into the inner workings of academic mystique. What is that mystique? How is it created? How do initiates acquire mystique? What do those who create it hope to accomplish? What might be gained in the process, and what might be lost?

2. At one point Lakoff notes that "the university alone trades only in language, discourse, communication" (par. 23). What does Lakoff mean by that statement? Why might this place special responsibility on universities and pose special difficulties and hardships for students?

3. While acknowledging that the university is "an unusually benevolent institution" (par. 38) in producing products of value and in protecting its members from uninformed outsiders, Lakoff warns that observers must not "overlook the ways in which those who have power in the university . . . misuse it and abuse its weaker members" (par. 38). With this in mind, write a brief essay in which you elaborate on Lakoff's view of the contradiction between the university's pursuit of truth and knowledge and the questionable treatment of "its weaker members." Why would abuse of its weaker members call the university's mission into question? How might such abuse undermine the university's effectiveness in producing valuable products?

4. To illustrate how language and power play out in academia, Lakoff presents a figure of a parabolic curve that traces the uses of academic language over the course of a professor's career. Although Lakoff is addressing other academics, her insights could prove useful to undergraduates who are trying to understand how to work with their professors. Taking the position of a student helping to orient incoming students, offer an analysis of Lakoff's curve, with the

purpose of explaining why academics behave the way they do. Why do they use the language they use? What professional pressures might they be bringing into the classroom? How might these factors affect their teaching style, materials, and evaluation of student work?

From Text to Field

1. It is common for groups of people who share expertise, skill, or artistry to seek mystique in order to increase the power of their identity. Choose a group or shared identity you have either entered or observed that seeks to create mystique, along the lines described by Lakoff. The mystique might be sought through language, silence and secrecy, or ritual. The ritual might be formal (such as an initiation ceremony) or informal (a sequence of actions or words, whether part of the group's activity or part of the process of bringing in new members). In an essay, describe how the mystique surrounding this group identity is created. Include your perspective on whether these efforts actually increase the power of the identity. If you are part of the group you are describing, how does the mystique affect your image of yourself? If you are an outsider or observer, what is your attitude toward the group's mystique?

2. Lakoff claims that undergraduates are not encouraged to use academic style in their writing. Commenting wryly on the attitude of professors, Lakoff says, "It does not become an undergraduate to sound like a professor" (par. 34). Write a personal essay in which you reflect on your experience with academic language. Approach the essay as if you were writing your own "Grooves of Academe," from the point of view of an undergraduate. What is your response to the academic language that you encounter? To what extent do you try to use it? Do you think professors expect you to use it? Do you think they discourage you from using it? What kind of "game" do you feel you are expected to play to prove yourself as a student?

3. The mission of the university, according to Lakoff, is "the production of *truth,* or *knowledge*" (par. 13). Is this the mission you see for the university? As you reread the essay, take note of the high standards of truth Lakoff expects of an academic institution. Do you hold your college or university to the same high standards? Write an essay in which you set forth the mission of the university from your point of view as a student. What is the purpose of the university? What do you expect it to produce? What values should it embody? In what ways do you expect it to preserve its integrity as an institution? How are these purposes advanced or undermined by the language employed by the university?

Soft Sciences Are Often Harder than Hard Sciences

Jared Diamond

Why should we be concerned about "a dogfight among intellectuals," one in which a mathematician succeeds in blocking a highly regarded political scientist from membership in the National Academy of Sciences (NAS)? Jared Diamond, a member of the NAS, sees a threat in store for all of us if experts in the hard sciences continue to be ignorant of the rather different challenges in the so-called soft sciences, which include sociology, political science, and areas of psychology, as well as other fields. Diamond is convinced that soft science requires researchers to work harder to develop the controls necessary for testing their hypotheses. From Diamond's perspective, respect for their work — especially as it addresses human behavior — is critical to the survival of the human race.

A professor of physiology at the University of California, Los Angeles, School of Medicine, Diamond has pursued research that spans the hard and soft sciences. In 1999, he was awarded the National Medal of Science for his uncommon ability to write about important scientific issues for the public and for his groundbreaking research in applying Darwinian theory to the fields of human history, physiology, ecology, and conservation biology. Diamond's public writings include regular contributions to both *Nature* and *Discover* magazines. One of his major conservation efforts was to design a comprehensive nature-reserve system for Indonesian New Guinea. He is widely known for his Pulitzer Prize–winning book, *Guns, Germs, and Steel: The Fates of Human Societies* (1997), which examines 13,000 years of human development and behavior. Diamond's most recent book is *Collapse: How Societies Choose to Fail or Succeed* (2005).

In addition to his NAS membership, Diamond has been elected to the American Academy of Arts and Sciences and the American

Philosophical Society. He has also received the MacArthur Foundation Fellowship, known as the "genius grant."

The following essay was originally published in 1987, as an opinion piece in *Discover*.

> The overall correlation between frustration and instability [in 62 countries of the world] was 0.50.
>
> —SAMUEL HUNTINGTON, professor of government, Harvard

> This is utter nonsense. How does Huntington measure things like social frustration? Does he have a social-frustration meter? I object to the academy's certifying as science what are merely political opinions.
>
> — SERGE LANG, professor of mathematics, Yale

> What does it say about Lang's scientific standards that he would base his case on twenty-year-old gossip? . . . a bizarre vendetta . . . a madman . . .
>
> — Other scholars, commenting on Lang's attack

For those who love to watch a dogfight among intellectuals supposedly above such things, it's been a fine dogfight, well publicized in *Time* and elsewhere. In one corner, political scientist and coauthor of *The Crisis of Democracy*, Samuel Huntington. In the other corner, mathematician and author of *Diophantine Approximation on Abelian Varieties with Complex Multiplication*, Serge Lang. The issue: whether Huntington should be admitted, over Lang's opposition, to an academy of which Lang is a member. The score after two rounds: Lang 2, Huntington 0, with Huntington still out.

Lang vs. Huntington might seem like just another silly blood letting in the back alleys of academia, hardly worth anyone's attention. But this particular dogfight is an important one. Beneath the name calling, it has to do with a central question in science: Do the so-called soft sciences, like political science and psychology, really constitute science at all, and do they deserve to stand beside "hard sciences," like chemistry and physics?

The arena is the normally dignified and secretive National Academy of Sciences (NAS), an honor society of more than 1,500 leading American scientists drawn from almost every discipline. NAS's annual election of about sixty new members begins long before each year's spring meeting, with a multistage evaluation of every prospective candidate by members expert in the candidate's field. Challenges of candidates by the membership assembled at the annual meeting are rare, because candidates have already been so thoroughly scrutinized by the appropriate experts. In my eight years in NAS, I can recall only a couple of challenges before the Lang-Huntington episode, and not a word about those battles appeared in the press.

At first glance, Huntington's nomination in 1986 seemed a very unlikely one to be challenged. His credentials were impressive: president of the American Political Science Association; holder of a named professorship at Harvard; author of many widely read books, of which one, *American Politics: The Promise of Disharmony,* got an award from the Association of American Publishers as the best book in the social and behavioral sciences in 1981; and many other distinctions. His studies of developing countries, American politics, and civilian-military relationships received the highest marks from social and political scientists inside and outside NAS. Backers of Huntington's candidacy included NAS members whose qualifications to judge him were beyond question, like Nobel Prize–winning computer scientist and psychologist Herbert Simon.

If Huntington seemed unlikely to be challenged, Lang was an even more   5 unlikely person to do the challenging. He had been elected to the academy only a year before, and his own specialty of pure mathematics was as remote as possible from Huntington's specialty of comparative political development. However, as *Science* magazine described it, Lang had previously assumed for himself "the role of a sheriff of scholarship, leading a posse of academics on a hunt for error," especially in the political and social sciences. Disturbed by what he saw as the use of "pseudomathematics" by Huntington, Lang sent all NAS members several thick mailings attacking Huntington, enclosing photocopies of letters describing what scholar A said in response to scholar B's attack on scholar C, and asking members for money to help pay the postage and copying bills. Under NAS rules, a candidate challenged at an annual meeting is dropped unless his candidacy is sustained by two-thirds of the members present and voting. After bitter debates at both the 1986 and 1987 meetings, Huntington failed to achieve the necessary two-thirds support.

Much impassioned verbiage has to be stripped away from this debate to discern the underlying issue. Regrettably, a good deal of the verbiage had to do with politics. Huntington had done several things that are now anathema in U.S. academia: He received CIA support for some research; he did a study for the State Department in 1967 on political stability in South Vietnam; and he's said to have been an early supporter of the Vietnam War. None of this should have affected his candidacy. Election to NAS is supposed to be based solely on scholarly qualifications; political views are irrelevant. American academics are virtually unanimous in rushing to defend academic freedom whenever a university president or an outsider criticizes a scholar because of his politics. Lang vehemently denied that his opposition was motivated by Huntington's politics. Despite all those things, the question of Huntington's role with respect to Vietnam arose repeatedly in the NAS debates. Evidently, academic freedom means that outsiders can't raise the issue of a scholar's politics but other scholars can.

It's all the more surprising that Huntington's consulting for the CIA and other government agencies was an issue, when one recalls why NAS exists. Congress established the academy in 1863 to act as official adviser to the U.S. government on questions of science and technology. NAS in turn established the National Research Council (NRC), and NAS and NRC committees continue to provide reports about a wide range of matters, from nutrition to future army materials. As is clear from any day's newspaper, our government desperately needs professionally competent advice, particularly about unstable countries, which are one of Huntington's specialties. So Huntington's willingness to do exactly what NAS was founded to do — advise the government — was held against him by some NAS members. How much of a role his politics played in each member's vote will never be known, but I find it unfortunate that they played any role at all.

I accept, however, that a more decisive issue in the debates involved perceptions of the soft sciences — e.g., Lang's perception that Huntington used pseudomathematics. To understand the terms soft and hard science, just ask any educated person what science is. The answer you get will probably involve several stereotypes: Science is something done in a laboratory, possibly by people wearing white coats and holding test tubes; it involves making measurements with instruments, accurate to several decimal places; and it involves controlled, repeatable experiments in which you keep everything fixed except for one or a few things that you allow to vary. Areas of science that often conform well to these stereotypes include much of chemistry, physics, and molecular biology. These areas are given the flattering name of hard science, because they use the firm evidence that controlled experiments and highly accurate measurements can provide.

We often view hard science as the only type of science. But science (from the Latin *scientia*—knowledge) is something much more general, which isn't defined by decimal places and controlled experiments. It means the enterprise of explaining and predicting—gaining knowledge of—natural phenomena, by continually testing one's theories against empirical evidence. The world is full of phenomena that are intellectually challenging and important to understand, but that can't be measured to several decimal places in labs. They constitute much of ecology, evolution, and animal behavior; much of psychology and human behavior; and all the phenomena of human societies, including cultural anthropology, economics, history, and government.

These soft sciences, as they're pejoratively termed, are more difficult to study, for obvious reasons. A lion hunt or revolution in the third world doesn't fit inside a test tube. You can't start it and stop it whenever you choose. You can't control all the variables; perhaps you can't control *any* variable. You may even find it hard to decide what a variable is. You can still use empirical tests to gain knowledge, but the types of tests used in the

10

hard sciences must be modified. Such differences between the hard and soft sciences are regularly misunderstood by hard scientists, who tend to scorn soft sciences and reserve special contempt for the social sciences. Indeed, it was only in the early 1970s that NAS, confronted with the need to offer the government competent advice about social problems, began to admit social scientists at all. Huntington had the misfortune to become a touchstone of this widespread misunderstanding and contempt.

While I know neither Lang nor Huntington, the broader debate over soft versus hard science is one that has long fascinated me, because I'm among the minority of scientists who work in both areas. I began my career at the hard pole of chemistry and physics, then took my PhD in membrane physiology, at the hard end of biology. Today I divide my time equally between physiology and ecology, which lies at the soft end of biology. My wife, Marie Cohen, works in yet a softer field, clinical psychology. Hence I find myself forced every day to confront the differences between hard and soft science. Although I don't agree with some of Lang's conclusions, I feel he has correctly identified a key problem in soft science when he asks, "How does Huntington measure things like social frustration? Does he have a social-frustration meter?" Indeed, unless one has thought seriously about research in the social sciences, the idea that anyone could measure social frustration seems completely absurd.

The issue that Lang raises is central to any science, hard or soft. It may be termed the problem of how to "operationalize" a concept. (Normally I hate such neologistic jargon, but it's a suitable term in this case.) **We often view hard science as the only type of science.** To compare evidence with theory requires that you measure the ingredients of your theory. For ingredients like weight or speed it's clear what to measure, but what would you measure if you wanted to understand political instability? Somehow, you would have to design a series of actual operations that yield a suitable measurement — i.e., you must operationalize the ingredients of theory.

Scientists do this all the time, whether or not they think about it. I shall illustrate operationalizing with four examples from my and Marie's research, progressing from hard science to softer science.

Let's start with mathematics, often described as the queen of the sciences. I'd guess that mathematics arose long ago when two cave women couldn't operationalize their intuitive concept of "many." One cave woman said, "Let's pick this tree over here, because it has many bananas." The other cave woman argued, "No, let's pick that tree over there, because it has more bananas." Without a number system to operationalize their concept of "many," the two cave women could never prove to each other which tree offered better pickings.

There are still tribes today with number systems too rudimentary to settle the argument. For example, some Gimi villagers with whom I worked in   15

New Guinea have only two root numbers, *iya* = 1 and *rarido* = 2, which they combine to operationalize somewhat larger numbers: 4 = *rarido-rarido*, 7 = *rarido-rarido-rarido-iya*, etc. You can imagine what it would be like to hear two Gimi women arguing about whether to climb a tree with 27 bananas or one with 18 bananas.

Now let's move to chemistry, less queenly and more difficult to operationalize than mathematics but still a hard science. Ancient philosophers speculated about the ingredients of matter, but not until the eighteenth century did the first modern chemists figure out how to measure these ingredients. Analytical chemistry now proceeds by identifying some property of a substance of interest, or of a related substance into which the first can be converted. The property must be one that can be measured, like weight, or the light the substance absorbs, or the amount of neutralizing agent it consumes.

For example, when my colleagues and I were studying the physiology of hummingbirds, we knew that the little guys liked to drink sweet nectar, but we would have argued indefinitely about how sweet sweet was if we hadn't operationalized the concept by measuring sugar concentrations. The method we used was to treat a glucose solution with an enzyme that liberates hydrogen peroxide, which reacts (with the help of another enzyme) with another substance called dianisidine to make it turn brown, whereupon we measured the brown color's intensity with an instrument called a spectrophotometer. A pointer's deflection on the spectrophotometer dial let us read off a number that provided an operational definition of sweet. Chemists use that sort of indirect reasoning all the time, without anyone considering it absurd.

My next-to-last example is from ecology, one of the softer of the biological sciences, and certainly more difficult to operationalize than chemistry. As a bird watcher, I'm accustomed to finding more species of birds in a rain forest than in a marsh. I suspect intuitively that this has something to do with a marsh being a simply structured habitat, while a rain forest has a complex structure that includes shrubs, lianas, trees of all heights, and crowns of big trees. More complexity means more niches for different types of birds. But how do I operationalize the idea of habitat complexity, so that I can measure it and test my intuition?

Obviously, nothing I do will yield as exact an answer as in the case where I read sugar concentrations off a spectrophotometer dial. However, a pretty good approximation was devised by one of my teachers, the ecologist Robert MacArthur, who measured how far a board at a certain height above the ground had to be moved in a random direction away from an observer standing in the forest (or marsh) before it became half obscured by the foliage. That distance is inversely proportional to the density of the foliage at that height. By repeating the measurement at different heights. MacArthur could calculate how the foliage was distributed over various heights.

In a marsh all the foliage is concentrated within a few feet of the ground, [20] whereas in a rain forest it's spread fairly equally from the ground to the canopy. Thus the intuitive idea of habitat complexity is operationalized as what's called a foliage height diversity index, a single number. MacArthur's simple operationalization of these foliage differences among habitats, which at first seemed to resist having a number put on them, proved to explain a big part of the habitats' differences in numbers of bird species. It was a significant advance in ecology.

For the last example let's take one of the softest sciences, one that physicists love to deride: clinical psychology. Marie works with cancer patients and their families. Anyone with personal experience of cancer knows the terror that a diagnosis of cancer brings. Some doctors are more frank with their patients than others, and doctors appear to withhold more information from some patients than from others. Why?

Marie guessed that these differences might be related to differences in doctors' attitudes toward things like death, cancer, and medical treatment. But how on earth was she to operationalize and measure such attitudes, convert them to numbers, and test her guesses? I can imagine Lang sneering "Does she have a cancer-attitude meter?"

Part of Marie's solution was to use a questionnaire that other scientists had developed by extracting statements from sources like tape-recorded doctors' meetings and then asking other doctors to express their degree of agreement with each statement. It turned out that each doctor's responses tended to cluster in several groups, in such a way that his responses to one statement in a cluster were correlated with his responses to other statements in the same cluster. One cluster proved to consist of expressions of attitudes toward death, a second cluster consisted of expressions of attitudes toward treatment and diagnosis, and a third cluster consisted of statements about patients' ability to cope with cancer. The responses were then employed to define attitude scales, which were further validated in other ways, like testing the scales on doctors at different stages in their careers (hence likely to have different attitudes). By thus operationalizing doctors' attitudes, Marie discovered (among other things) that doctors most convinced about the value of early diagnosis and aggressive treatment of cancer are the ones most likely to be frank with their patients.

In short, all scientists, from mathematicians to social scientists, have to solve the task of operationalizing their intuitive concepts. The book by Huntington that provoked Lang's wrath discussed such operationalized concepts as economic well-being, political instability, and social and economic modernization. Physicists have to resort to very indirect (albeit accurate) operationalizing in order to "measure" electrons. But the task of operationalizing is inevitably more difficult and less exact in the soft sciences, because there are so many uncontrolled variables. In the four examples I've given, number of bananas and concentration of sugar can be measured to more decimal places than can habitat complexity and attitudes toward cancer.

Unfortunately, operationalizing lends itself to ridicule in the social sciences, 25 because the concepts being studied tend to be familiar ones that all of us fancy we're experts on. Anybody, scientist or no, feels entitled to spout forth on politics or psychology, and to heap scorn on what scholars in those fields write. In contrast, consider the opening sentences of Lang's paper *Diophantine Approximation on Abelian Varieties with Complex Multiplication:* "Let A be an abelian variety defined over a number field K. We suppose that A is embedded in projective space. Let A_K be the group of points on A rational over K." How many people feel entitled to ridicule these statements while touting their own opinions about abelian varieties?

No political scientist at NAS has challenged a mathematical candidate by asking "How does he measure things like 'many'? Does he have a many-meter?" Such questions would bring gales of laughter over the questioner's utter ignorance of mathematics. It seems to me that Lang's question "How does Huntington measure things like social frustration?" betrays an equal ignorance of how the social sciences make measurements.

The ingrained labels "soft science" and "hard science" could be replaced by hard (i.e., difficult) science and easy science, respectively. Ecology and psychology and the social sciences are much more difficult and, to some of us, intellectually more challenging than mathematics and chemistry. Even if NAS were just an honorary society, the intellectual challenge of the soft sciences would by itself make them central to NAS.

But NAS is more than an honorary society; it's a conduit for advice to our government. As to the relative importance of soft and hard science for humanity's future, there can be no comparison. It matters little whether we progress with understanding the diophantine approximation. Our survival depends on whether we progress with understanding how people behave, why some societies become frustrated, whether their governments tend to become unstable, and how political leaders make decisions like whether to press a red button. Our National Academy of Sciences will cut itself out of intellectually challenging areas of science, and out of the areas where NAS can provide the most needed scientific advice, if it continues to judge social scientists from a posture of ignorance.

Working with the Text

1. In addressing the controversy over whether to admit political scientist Samuel Huntington into the National Academy of Sciences (NAS), Jared Diamond, a member of the NAS, makes a point of explaining the origin and purposes of

the academy. As you reread the essay, note what Diamond chooses to say about the NAS. In a brief essay, analyze how he uses this information to make his case. Why does he include these particular points? How do they contribute to his argument?

2. Although Diamond is arguing an issue that can only be decided by members of the National Academy of Sciences (NAS), the essay was originally published as an opinion piece in *Discover*, a magazine primarily written for laypeople who have an interest in current scientific research. A regular contributor to *Discover*, Diamond chose to discuss this issue in its pages. Why would a physiology professor at UCLA Medical School and a member of the NAS choose to argue this issue publicly in *Discover*? What might he hope to accomplish? Why would *Discover* choose to publish it? Why might the audience of *Discover* read it? In a brief essay, reflect on the reasons for publishing this particular essay in this particular periodical.

3. The title of the essay captures Diamond's central assertion, which is that "soft sciences are often harder than hard sciences." He centers his argument around his own use of the term *operationalize*. Write a brief essay in which you examine the reasoning and structure of his argument by analyzing his use of this term. What does he mean by *operationalize*? Why would he choose the concept of "operationalizing" to argue this particular issue with an audience of scientists as well as of laypeople who have an interest in science? How does the sequencing of his examples contribute to his argument?

From Text to Field

1. "Soft Sciences Are Often Harder than Hard Sciences" ran as an opinion piece in *Discover* magazine, which is written for a lay audience. From your point of view as a student and layperson, write a response to Diamond's argument, as if you were submitting it to *Discover* for possible publication. Do you agree with his view of soft and hard sciences? Do you support Huntington or Lang in the controversy over admitting Huntington into the National Academy of Sciences? Take a position on at least one of the issues in Diamond's opinion piece, and present your reasons in essay form. Think in terms of what is at stake for you — as a student, a taxpayer, or someone with a special interest in the state of scientific research. If you plan to enter into a scientific field, consider addressing the issue from the perspective of someone who is looking into a professional future.

2. In our own reading as well as through our education system, all of us have been exposed to both soft and hard sciences. In a personal essay, compare your encounters with soft and hard science. You might choose to address them

broadly, drawing on examples from several books or courses, or you might choose to compare two books or two courses, one concerned with soft science and the other with hard science. How did these encounters compare in terms of difficulty—the amount of effort needed to understand and work with the material? Reflect on Diamond's assertion that "[o]ur survival depends on whether we progress with understanding how people behave" (par. 28)—in other words, our understanding of soft science. How does what you learned from soft science and from hard science compare in terms of preparing you to live in the "real world"?

3. Diamond points out that "all scientists, from mathematicians to social scientists, have to solve the task of operationalizing their intuitive concepts" (par. 24). Whether or not we are scientists, all of us have formed intuitive concepts based on observation and experience. In the course of our education, all of us have also been asked to think scientifically, in subjects ranging from psychology to chemistry or physics. Review Diamond's definition of *operationalizing* as well as his examples of intuitive concepts. Brainstorm for intuitive ideas of your own—theories based on human behavior or physical phenomena you have observed. In an essay, present your intuitive concept; then formulate ways in which you could operationalize that concept in order to test it.

INTO THE FIELD: Options for Writing Projects

1. Exploring Discourse Communities

According to David Russell's argument in "Academic Discourse: Community or Communities?" every discipline and profession creates and maintains its own discourse community. Here are two options for exploring discourse communities based on your interests and on your experience on campus:

- Through interviews and research, explore the discourse community of the discipline or field you are entering or considering, either as a major or as a profession. Analyze written documents that have been produced by members of that discourse community. What forms of writing does the community produce, for what purposes and what audiences, and how are those forms of writing related to concrete activities? What knowledge and critical-thinking skills are required? Develop a guide that might orient newcomers like yourself to this discourse community.
- Based on your own experience, write an essay in which you analyze the differences between the discourse in two fields, such as art history and political science. Pay special attention to the ways in which students experience the two discourse communities in terms of the classes taken, assignments completed, and assumptions present in the language of the field. Be sure to keep field notes about your experience, and draw, if possible, on interviews with students in both classes and with the instructors who teach them.

2. Academic Communities — Many or One?

As the essays by David Russell and Wayne C. Booth make clear, there is some discussion about whether the academic community is in fact one community or multiple communities. Clearly, the situation varies somewhat from campus to campus, as much depends on the size, mission of, and distinctive culture of the institution in question. This field project encourages you to particularize the various arguments about discourse communities to your campus. At least two options suggest themselves:

- Through interviews, Web sites, and informational materials, analyze what is being done in your institution to create dialogue among diverse discourse communities. These discourse communities may be academic in nature or they may involve student groups, or both. What are the goals of that dialogue? What mechanisms are used to encourage campus and disciplinary dialogue? How effective are they?
- Because the work of a writing program typically cuts across a number of discourse communities, such programs offer an interesting starting place to reflect on assumptions about discourse communities on your campus.

Given the general philosophy of the writing program, and its particular course offerings and course descriptions, analyze what you believe to be its assumptions about academic discourse. Where does the writing program on your campus lie on a spectrum that extends, at one end, from the notion that there is one generalized academic discourse to the other extreme, that writing can only be taught well when geared to writing in any one particular discipline? If you are studying at a four-year institution, how does curricular level affect the program's assumptions? That is, how different are the assumptions between first-year courses and courses taught for juniors and seniors? Through interviews, informational materials, and the published work of writing teachers in your institution, analyze how your writing program addresses the problem of multiple academic discourse communities.

3. The Rhetorics of Understanding Each Other's Fields

Although Wayne C. Booth is addressing his academic colleagues in his essay "The Idea of a *University*," the three kinds of rhetoric he describes can be found in other organizations, groups, and professions. Select a field of endeavor — such as music, athletics, or finance — that has a distinct identity and purpose but that also encompasses a number of areas of further specialization. You may choose a field in which you have experience or one that you are interested in exploring. Develop a project in which you investigate and describe how the three kinds of rhetoric would be applied in that field and its several areas of specialization. Write an essay in which you explore what permits — and prevents — understanding of each other's work in that field. Does the field you have chosen have its own "rhetoric-1" with its own "special topics"? Is there an equivalent, outside of the academy, for Booth's "rhetoric-3," which seems to be an important intermediary between very particular field-specific rhetorics and a much more generalized civic rhetoric available to all?

4. Parody of Your Own Discipline

Horace Miner could produce a parody such as "Body Ritual among the Nacirema" because, as a practicing anthropologist, he understood how the arguments in his field are structured. For a field or discipline you are entering or considering, locate two or three examples of the written arguments used among the experts. Identify the "moves" used in the arguments — how the central assertion is introduced, the kinds of language and common terminology that are used, the structure and progression of the argument, the evidence and reasoning. In the spirit of Horace Miner's send-up of cultural anthropology, write a parody of that form of argument in your chosen field, based on what you have learned so far about the discipline.

5. Parody of College Experience

Parody can represent an effective way to pursue an argument not by direct means, but by indirection. Horace Miner takes this approach when he examines the American obsession with bodies. By adopting the persona of an anthropologist, he is able to render the ordinary aspects of our lives as foreign and strange and thus make his point more effectively than might a straightforward argument.

For this field project, develop your own parody of one aspect of college or campus life. Using Miner's essay as a general model, offer an anthropologist's reflections on that one aspect. Among the many topics ripe for parody are the college admissions process, dorm life, sports, classroom behavior, and fraternities and sororities. Be sure your humor is grounded in close observation and extended reflection.

6. College 101

Robin Tolmach Lakoff opens her account of academic mystique, power, and privilege by describing the deliberations of a curriculum committee about a one-credit graduate course that would help students understand the "secret handshake" of their field. For your field project, consider what debates and arguments might surround the establishment of a similar course for first-year college students. Let's call it "College 101"—a course that would help orient new students to college academic life, such as how to study or how to use the library. Consider whether the need for such a course and reservations about offering it parallel the various arguments described by Lakoff regarding the graduate course. Depending on the situation on your campus, this project could take one of several forms:

- If your campus does not have such a course, you may wish to propose one. Consider using actual course-proposal forms employed by the curriculum committee on your campus. Alternatively, you may wish to offer a rationale for why such a course may not be appropriate for academic credit.
- If your campus does in fact offer such a course, evaluate its usefulness and the rationale for continuing or not continuing it. What controversies might have surrounded the course when it was first proposed?

7. Mapping and Divding the Disciplines: Hard, Soft, and in Between

As Jared Diamond makes clear in his essay, various academic fields take their places along a spectrum, from hard science (chemistry) to soft science (sociology), to the softer still (English, let's say). The point of Diamond's essay is to encourage us to rethink those categories. This field project has you venture forth on your campus to see how and in what way these distinctions matter to faculty and students.

In part as an administrative convenience, some universities divide departments in a large college like "Arts and Sciences" into science, social science, and arts and humanities divisions. Explore the rationale for which departments have found their way into which divisions. On your campus, is history in the humanities division or in the social-science division? Is psychology or geography in the science division or the social-science division? Anthropology is one rather eclectic discipline whose several subdisciplines can lay claim to belonging in any one of three areas. To support your inquiry, read departmental descriptions in the catalog and interview faculty in a department that interests you. Do you find tensions within certain fields? For example, do you find some faculty in the social sciences less than enthusiastic about the growing emphasis on "quantification" in their disciplines? Do these administrative divisions erect barriers to work between departments?

Your own course work can reflect these same divisions and struggles. For example, consider how your campus's general-education course requirements are carved up. If you need to take a certain number of credit hours in the social sciences, which departments offer which courses that satisfy that requirement? Is the rationale for that selection always clear? Do you find that categorizing fields in this way supports or hinders your broad education? How might such categorization hinder interdisciplinary work? Can you think of new or emerging fields that cut across the more traditional map of the disciplines?

4

Engagements

COLLABORATIONS

If asked to picture, in your mind, the image of a writer at work, you might easily conjure up a solitary figure working at a desk or sitting alone in front of a computer. Such an image is not entirely wrong so much as it is incomplete. Who among us hasn't spent some time (perhaps a good deal of time) working on a writing project while sitting alone at the keyboard? But such an image tends to discount just how collaborative the writing process is in many settings. Writing — and for that matter reading — is a social activity.

Our received image of the writer has its roots in the romantic notion of genius. The inspired individual, prompted by a creative muse, works alone in a dimly lit and poorly heated garret and finds from within the emotion and imagination to express great ideas. Oh, yes, did I mention that the writer is hungry and poor or that threadbare fingerless gloves keep this author's hands warm enough to allow for writing? And for good measure, we might throw in a romantic twist — perhaps a love that has been lost or a love that remains unrequited. You get the picture. Or rather, we've gotten this picture for some two hundred years. What's more, the image also suggests that good ideas come only to the creative, renegade mind and that those ideas are owned and capitalized on by the individual.

This romantic image of the writer is far removed from the realities of writing in most organizations and professional settings. We write when prompted by problems that affect not only ourselves but others as well. We discuss ideas with others, and those ideas evolve, often in a messy and unpredictable way. We produce drafts, often with others or at least aided by others. And we share those drafts with colleagues and friends, who help us anticipate the needs and interests of readers who will themselves respond to our words.

Even in the university setting, writing is far more social and collaborative than it often seems to be. Appearances can be deceiving. On one level, all that you may hear is the shuffle of paper as you silently hand in your essays and as they are later handed back. What's hidden is the din of voices just beyond the page or the tug and pull of ideas as they rub up against each other. Writing classes make such collaborative dynamics more visible and immediate. Peers not only help to shape the writing through feedback in workshops, but they also serve as readers who help the author orient the prose to the audience it must serve.

The Russian theorist of discourse Mikhail Bakhtin has observed that "language . . . lies on the borderline between oneself and the other. The word in language is half someone else's." Writing, too, is half someone else's, both in the collaboration that inevitably accompanies its creation, and in the presence and role of the reader, who collaborates in its reception.

This unit offers several voices that extend and enrich our notion of writing as a collaborative and social act — an act performed, not in the garret by that solitary creative genius, but in the marketplace and on the street, where ideas trade amidst a din of voices. By listening to the marginalia in books, Michael Parker helps us hear the voices that occur in the tug and pull of reading. Books, as it turns out, beckon us to talk back. Lisa Ede and Andrea Lunsford share the dynamics behind their several collaborative writing projects, encouraging us to rethink how we ourselves can be enriched by collaborations, through the written word, with other minds and hearts. Kenneth A. Bruffee explores how, through collaboration, we can learn from our knowledgeable peers. Highlighting the social processes by which we compose knowledge, Bruffee reminds us that "learning occurs among persons rather than between a person and things." Malcolm Gladwell offers the provocative notion that smart people may well be overrated, noting that organizations — and more generally collaborative activities—can make people smart. Thomas S. Kuhn likewise questions our preoccupation with the solitary, creative individual. As much as we may prize creative, divergent thinking, new advances in science and in other fields rest on our ability to work together to produce the convergent thinking out of which new insights emerge.

Reflecting on Prior Knowledge

1. In a journal entry, reflect on an experience in which you collaborated with other people in an activity that you normally pursue alone. What made this experience different, more valuable, or more difficult?

2. Working in groups, develop an inventory of various daily activities that require or invite collaboration or shared participation. Highlight those activities in which collaboration seems especially important or in which you feel enriched by the collaborative experience. Feel free to range widely, drawing on your nonacademic and personal lives.

3. Working in groups, develop a list of various factors that are essential to productive and enjoyable collaborative work, especially in writing. For example, you may find that your list includes such factors as trust, equal standing and equitable roles, ability to reflect on the collaboration, flexibility, and so on. Be

sure to brainstorm about factors that may not be immediately obvious. Draw on your own collaborative experiences, both positive and negative.

4. Although we may first think of collaboration as involving a group of people who share the same time and space, many activities can be highly collaborative even if the people participating do not occupy the same time and space. Develop and share a list of such activities. For example, writing letters and reading books seem to be highly private endeavors, yet clearly they have us talking to or engaging with others. In a journal entry, reflect on what makes these activities instances of collaboration.

5. In a small group, brainstorm a list of qualities that you think make a job candidate attractive to a potential employer. Be prepared to share your list with the entire class.

6. In a journal entry, reflect on the degree to which your prior educational experiences were private and highly individual or shared and essentially collaborative. In what ways are both dimensions important, although perhaps in different ways and for different purposes?

7. Americans have been known to have a penchant for individualism and divergent thinking, prizing creativity above nearly all other virtues. Working first in groups, develop a list of reasons why consensus is not only essential to some degree, but also highly productive. Drawing on the work of your group, in a journal entry reflect on the discussion you have had, integrating into your writing your personal experiences.

Talking Back to Books:
In Defense of Marginalia

Michael Parker

Michael Parker based his first novel, *Hello Down There* (1993), on the image of a hand reaching through a window to snatch the bag of morphine Parker's father regularly delivered from the drugstore. Parker wrote the novel to find out, through his own imagination, who the man might be.

The imagination that draws the writer Parker into seeing an entire life in one mysterious gesture also draws the reader Parker into engaging the marginal notes written in used books, as if he were in a running conversation with "a well-created fictional character." Whether marginalia suggests a student studying for a test, an armchair critic, or a reader with an attitude, Parker is fascinated by this urge to talk back to books, to record some form of personal conversation with the author.

Hello Down There was named a New York Times Notable Book. Parker has also published *The Geographical Cure* (1994), a collection of stories and novellas and winner of the 1994 Sir Walter Raleigh Award, and *Towns without Rivers* (2001), a novel. His latest novel is *If You Want Me to Stay* (2005). His fiction and nonfiction have appeared in journals such as the *Georgia Review, Idaho Review, Carolina Quarterly,* and the *Washington Post.* In 1996, *Granta Magazine* cited Parker as one of the best American fiction writers under forty, and in 2002 "Off Island," a story originally published in *Five Points,* won a Pushcart Award.

Michael Parker is a professor of English at the University of North Carolina—Greensboro, where he teaches graduate and undergraduate classes in fiction writing and contemporary literature.

If like me you spend hours foraging amongst the dank aisles of used bookstores because you can rarely afford the price of a trade paperback, and live in a place where the book business is cornered by chain stores whose selection reflects that week's best-seller list topped off with cat calendars and audio tapes of techno-thrillers; if like me you have happened upon treasures — Charles Olson's monograph of Melville, a battered but lovable copy of Frank O'Connor's *The Lonely Voice, Wide Sargasso Sea* in hardback — in stores which, to the untrained eye seem stocked with the usual excess of John O'Hara potboilers and Richard Henry Dana's *Two Years Before the Mast*; if after such finds you, like me, become convinced that more treasures lay hidden beneath the dust of disintegrating copies of *Ragtime*, then you have almost certainly brought home a book which contains in its margins the scribble-scribble of previous owners.

Marginalia comes with the territory, and it comes in categories. In my years of collecting second-hand books, I have identified three such categories. The first is peculiar but not exclusive to college towns and usually applies to books listed on syllabi. This type is meant to summarize; it reduces the subtleties of language and idea into a few words — one is preferable — which will help the student study for the test. Flipping through the *Aeneid* in the bookstore outside of Lynchburg, Virginia, I found the following written next to the line, "the news I heard was true, your death was I its cause?" "Aenas feels real sorry for what he had done to Dido." A few pages later, scrawled alongside the line "From under the tomb a gliding snake, seven huge circles, seven rolling coils," I found the penciled equation "Snake = Evil." A math major? Knocking out that liberal arts requirement? As for the idea, I've heard it somewhere before, though it always helps to write these things down.

Some marginalia is intentionally comic, but laughs are usually derived at the previous owner's expense. In keeping with the synoptic nature of note taking, student marginalia strives to hook the most literal developments of action, plot, or idea, and throw back all indigestible abstractions. Irony is rarely a keeper. Leafing through a copy of *Ulysses*, I read the following lines. "Watering cart: to provoke the rain. On earth as it is in heaven." The last line was underscored, the word "religious" clogging the margin. Somehow I doubt this line was meant to suggest that Leopold Bloom regularly attended Sunday school.

Of course marginalia is a harried act; astute, beautifully written commentary is not the objective. Although for years I seem to have blocked this fact from my mind, it turns out I was fairly active as a student marginaliast myself, and am guilty of some god-awful examples, some of which I discovered recently while leafing through an old copy of *King Lear*. I can only surmise that I was writing a paper — long forgotten and better that way — discussing the use of clothing as a metaphor in the play, for my copy is filled with examples which make the following seem smart. "Through tattered clothes small vices do appear; Robes and furred gowns hide all," says Lear in Act IV. Ever alert, I underscored the word "clothes" and wrote in the margin the word "clothes."

A step up from student marginalia is the more serious scribbling of arm- 5 chair (or for all I know, endowed-chair) critics. Since I have spent most of the past fifteen years in college towns, the timbre of marginalia found in my library tends to reflect the academy in all its various triumphs and failings. This type could qualify as annotation but for its slightly onanistic quality. In an early Saul Bellow novel I found these words in near indecipherable script on the inside flyleaf. "The meaning of the fact is Bellow's enduring concern. Is there a moral debt to be paid and by what means can it be paid? More than that, when is the debt actually discharged? . . . An early example of the advantages made available to morality through several decades of naturalistic fiction." Though I've long been curious as to what advantages naturalistic fiction availed to morality, I've never actually bothered to read the novel, its central themes (the meaning of the fact? the debt actually discharged?) having been summed up so nicely for me on the front flyleaf.

Marginalia does not make for speed-read or skim, which is only one of the reasons why detractors despise it in all forms. They say it distracts. They say it defaces books and that it is a moronic habit, the product of an inferior mind. They equate it with counting on fingers, with lips forming syllables while reading.

A retrograde strain in my sensibility leads me to defend most things in danger of extinction, and it seems to me that marginalia has suffered a falling off. I know how fashionable it has become to blame

The marginaliast . . . shapes everything from the quality of prose to the attention **indirectly your understand-** span of readers on the advent of word processors, yet it **ing of the idea at hand.** is a fact that these days many books are written entirely on screens; the scars and sutures of cross out and transposition evaporate at the touch of a key. Writers no longer care to see where they've been; the rich and decodeable battlefield upon which ideas take shape is no longer of interest. (It is no longer even a physical entity.) Something subliminal may be alerting readers: If the writer no longer bothers with us, why the hell should you, says margin to reader. Pens are capped and put away.

As for the third and final category, it can include both the student and the learned, and is defined more by attitude than intelligence or intent. My favorite example involves a bit of background. Back in 1982 I bought a copy of Schopenhauer's *The Art of Literature* from a used bookstore in Chapel Hill. Having just read *A Long Day's Journey into Night* and been struck by the scene in which Tyrone senior, admonishing Edwin for his literary tastes, consigns Schopenhauer (along with Voltaire, Rousseau, Neitzsche, and Ibsen) to a scrap heap of atheists, fools, and madmen, I was eager to try the great father of pessimism. Any writer one's father warns against is worth checking out, I reasoned. I must have flipped through the book before purchasing it and the few margin scrawls I noticed did not bother me, since they were only asking sixty-five cents.

On the first page of the first essay, I encountered the first of what would turn out to be numerous color fields of golfer's-slacks yellow which had somehow escaped my notice. (Underscoring does not to my mind qualify as marginalia unless it is accompanied by written commentary — a paltry distinction but a necessary one. Actually, I detest underscoring, and especially if rendered in day-glo lemon or lime.)

I was put off by the lurid highlight, yet I pushed on, intrigued by Schopenhauer's own attitude, the gleamings of recalcitrance which stood out amongst stock opinions on writing and writers. In his essay on style I encountered my first flourish of veritable marginalia. My predecessor had underscored the following line — "a man's style shows the formal nature of all his thoughts — the formal nature which can never change, be the subject or the character of his thoughts what it may . . ." — and written alongside, "No! No! No! How wrong!" Rather than irksome grammatical tic, these exclamation points seemed lightning bolts of vehemence. Already, on page 13, I understood Schopenhauer to be a formidable man to cross, and wasn't sure I'd venture to do so even considering the fact that he has been dead these 130 years. I began to feel that I was in the middle of something, and that something promised to be lively.

The next skirmish was a quiet one. "To find where the point lies is the problem of style, and the business of the critical faculty; for a word too much always defeats its purpose. This is what Voltaire means when he says that *the adjective is the enemy of the substantive.* [translator's italics] "But V. was one of greatest adjective abusers," responds my guide. It had been a while since I'd read *Candide*, but I seemed then to remember it as a bit of a pileup. I was impressed that my guide recognized the contradiction, even more impressed that he was on an initial basis with yet another of Tyrone senior's "atheists, fools, and madmen."

I came to Schopenhauer's chapter on the study of Latin, prepared for a berating, since I failed to learn even the simplest roots of the language despite the fact that my mother once earned her living by teaching it. I wasn't disappointed: Schopenhauer had unsheathed the exclamation points by the second paragraph. "If it should really come to this" [the abolition of Latin as the universal language of learned men] "then farewell, humanity! Farewell, noble taste and high thinking! The age of barbarism will return, in spite of railways, telegraphs, and balloons." I was ready to put in a call to the nearest classics department when my guide resurfaced. "Is it language or ideas that are important? Is the author insecure because he has spent time to learn the language and others have not? Does he feel thwarted?"

10

My guess is that only by expressions of joie de vivre did the granddaddy of gloom and doom feel thwarted, and the idea that Schopenhauer's bellicosity arises from insecurity strikes me now as pop psychology at its most tepid. Yet at the time I was searching for an ally, someone to help me rationalize my laziness and assert that erudition was possible without fluency in Latin and that, railways, telegraphs, and balloons notwithstanding, we are not all barbarians in this barbaric age.

Advantage: marginaliast.

The equanimity of my guide's last few exchanges was not to last, and the bullet-spray of departure was provoked by, to my mind, the most innocuous comment in the entire treatise. Discussing the practice of anonymity in literature and journalism, Schopenhauer suggests, rather mildly for him, that "every article should be accompanied by the name of its author; and the editor should be made strictly responsible for the accuracy of the signature." "You screaming socialist!" rants my guide in chicken scratch which suggests the surge of his blood pressure. "And how would you put this in motion? No doubt by government regulations. You idiot, don't you see what you are doing?"

While it is true that literary criticism is not Schopenhauer's forte (he is much better, I have since learned, in decrying the cracking of whips as "a genuine assassin of thought"), the man had a right to say what he thought without being labeled a socialist. Filled with doubt about my once trustworthy trailblazer, I scoured the book for clues. The only trace was rubber-stamped boldly across the front flyleaf: THE BOOK RACK, Trade 2 For 1; WINSTON-SALEM, N.C.

I checked the publication date: 1960, or years before the thaw of the Cold War. Though I had no idea when the book was bought, read, or written in, it seemed easy to blame my guide's outburst on the spirit of the times. With only a little less enthusiasm I plugged ahead. My guide was silent throughout the whole of Schopenhauer's essay on Reputation, which did not shy away from referring to the overwhelming idiocy of the masses as well as most writers, and in general was as in-your-face as any of the preceding essays. Did he agree? Did he not care much about literary reputations? Did he not even bother to read it? Though it is impossible to feel lost in an essay of Schopenhauer's—and anticipation of what mordant thing he'll say next spurs you onward—I felt a little disoriented, as if I was venturing out into a foreign city for the first time without an interpreter. Every time I turned the page I did a quick scan of the margin for signs of another conflagration.

And finally I found one: one word, in the manner of that first category, the student intent on extracting the essence, on summing up for later study. I did not allow myself to read the word. I entered slowly the underscored passage as if wading into frigid waters, giving myself time to become accustomed to the waves of sentences, savoring each for meaning and mood before they receded. Schopenhauer was complaining of the intellectual vacuity of the human race. "If anyone wishes for entertainment, such as will prevent him feeling solitary even when he is alone, let me recommend the company of dogs, whose moral and intellectual qualities may almost afford delight and gratification."

My fearless guide had circled "dogs," drawn a line out to the margin and in a primitive hand printed the word "SPIKE."

Well, now. What to think? I felt confident enough, after having gone 20 through the book with this person, to assume that he did not have a dog named Spike. His response showed a certain spunk — by dredging up one of the most generic of dog names and offering it unelaborated, in such stick-figure hand, he called attention to Schopenhauer's intellectual snobbishness with a certain subtle flair. Yet finally it seemed more desperate than humorous; it showed resignation, a flagging. I felt cheated. This is after all the screaming socialist you're up against, I felt like writing in the margin. Screaming socialists, like toddlers and students in survey courses, are not much on irony.

That the outcome was less than pyrotechnic has become over the years beside the point. Now, any time I come across mention of Schopenhauer I think of my experience with his *Art of Literature*, of how it was enlivened by the efforts of my ardent guide. His comments made the strident tone of the treatise even more strident, and more memorable. Personally I have nothing against socialists or even those socialists who scream, but the point is that it's not necessary to agree or disagree with this third stripe of marginaliast; like a well-created fictional character, their presence shapes indirectly your understanding of the idea at hand.

My purpose here is not to encourage the defacement of books or to suggest everyone should take pen to margin. Marginalia is not for everyone, though it tends to be practiced by all types of readers and thinkers. I would merely like to offer a gentle rebuff to those readers who see margins as sacrosanct, a demilitarized zone; to whom margins, with their white blanketed space, whisper "Don't tread on me." The marginaliast's is an art of accumulation, of yeas and nays accrued. When they say something stupid, you can choose to ignore or trounce. When they say something smart, something which mirrors your own incisive opinion, you pay attention. Yes, you say, I was just thinking the same thing myself. Only I got there first.

Working with the Text

1. Although Michael Parker's essay emphasizes the relationship between the writer and the reader of marginalia, the first phrase in his title is "Talking Back to Books." As you reread the essay, consider this phrase as it applies to both the marginaliast and the reader of marginalia. Write a brief essay in which you

reflect on what Parker means by "talking back to books." What does talking back to books involve, for both the marginaliast and the reader of marginalia? What can be gained by it?

2. As a practiced reader of the markings in used books, Parker has identified three categories of marginalia. He describes these categories primarily by offering examples. For his first category of marginalia, usually written by college students, he notes that it is "meant to summarize" (par. 2). For the other two categories, he provides no comparable definition. Based on analysis of the examples Parker offers, write a brief essay in which you define each category of marginalia. What kinds of comments do the marginaliasts make? What purposes do the comments serve? As you define the first category, think beyond Parker's note that it is "meant to summarize" by analyzing what the marginaliast is trying to capture and why.

3. In a paragraph that almost functions as an aside, Parker blames the invisible corrections made possible by word processors for what he views as a "falling off" of marginalia. Parker charges, "Something subliminal may be alerting readers: If the writer no longer bothers with us, why the hell should you, says margin to reader" (par. 7). As you reread the essay, consider this charge in light of Parker's larger argument in favor of marginalia. With Parker's phrase "says margin to reader" in mind, write a brief essay from the point of view of the margin. What relationship does the margin have to the writer? What changes when the writer replaces handwritten corrections with electronic ones? How might this change the relationship between the margin and the reader as well as the reader and the author of the text?

4. Parker devotes most of his essay to describing the marginalia he encountered in a used copy of Schopenhauer's *The Art of Literature.* At the end of the essay, Parker describes the effects of such an encounter: "[I]t's not necessary to agree or disagree with this third stripe of marginaliast; like a well-created fictional character, their presence shapes indirectly your understanding of the idea at hand" (par. 21). Write a brief essay in which you analyze the relationship that developed between Parker and the marginaliast. What does Parker's description of the encounter tell you about the personality of the "fictional character" that emerged from the marginalia? What does the encounter tell you about Parker himself? In what ways did the marginaliast shape Parker's understanding of Schopenhauer?

From Text to Field

1. Parker wrote "Talking Back to Books: In Defense of Marginalia" because he is well aware of what the detractors say: "They say it distracts. They say it defaces books and that it is a moronic habit, the product of an inferior mind" (par. 6).

In what respects is Parker's essay not just about talking back but is itself a response, or as the title suggests, a "defense"? Join this exchange. Write a short personal essay in which you describe your own response when you encounter marginalia. Do you welcome it or resent it? How does it affect your reading of the text? What kinds of thoughts do you have of the person who wrote it?

2. Behind the "well-created fictional character" that Parker finds in marginalia is a real person who talks back to books. When we write marginalia, we might not be conscious of the "fictional character" we may be creating for someone who reads it. In a short personal essay, analyze your own use of marginalia. If you are a marginaliast, what do you write and for what purpose? In what ways are you talking back to the book? What "character" or representation of yourself do you think you might be creating? If you never write in books, why not? If someone bought a used book of yours that has no marks in it, how might the new owner interpret this? Are there other characteristics of your used book — folded-down page corners, battered cover, food stains — that might provide some hint of who you are, as a person and as a reader? Are there other ways, outside of marking in a book, in which you talk back to it?

3. Parker's essay indicates that he is very conscious of his interaction with the marginalia. To practice this level of awareness, locate a used book that has a fair amount of marginalia. Write an analysis of that marginalia, which you have never before read or haven't read closely. Which of Parker's categories does it represent? What purpose did it seem to serve for the marginaliast? What does the marginaliast seem to be saying to the book? What "fictional character" is created by the marginalia? How did it influence your reading of the passage?

4. Work in pairs or small groups to analyze each other's marginalia. Each person might choose a short reading (perhaps one from this book) to "talk back to" in marginal notes. Then give the marked-up reading to a peer to analyze in light of the marginalia. Alternatively, the group might write marginal notes on Parker's essay to exchange and discuss as a way of interpreting the essay together.

Why Write . . . Together?

Lisa Ede and Andrea Lunsford

When Lisa Ede and Andrea Lunsford—professors of writing and rhetoric—cowrote "Why Write . . . Together?" (1983), they had already collaborated on two other articles. At the time, they acknowledged that their different styles, as both people and writers, created difficulties they didn't encounter when each of them wrote alone. Yet over the twenty years since their first round of collaborations, they have continued to work together on articles, books, conference presentations, and talks on campuses across the country.

Collaborative writing itself became a scholarly interest for both Ede and Lunsford, to the extent that they are considered to be among the foremost experts in the study and practice of collaboration, in professional as well as in academic writing. They were among the first in their field to recognize that university students are taught to write almost exclusively as individuals, even though most move into professions that require a substantial amount of coauthorship. As promoters of collaborative writing, Ede and Lunsford explore the situations in which two (or more) heads are better than one.

Lisa Ede is professor of English and director of the Center for Writing and Learning at Oregon State University. Andrea Lunsford taught at the University of British Columbia and then was for many years professor of English at Ohio State University. She is currently professor of English and director of the Program for Writing and Rhetoric at Stanford University. Among Ede and Lunsford's many collaborative projects, the most notable in this context is their detailed study of joint authorship in academic and professional worlds, *Singular Texts, Plural Authors: Perspectives on Collaborative Writing* (1990). The article presented here offers Lunsford and Ede's early — and prescient—thoughts on the role of collaboration; it was published in the January 1983 issue of *Rhetoric Review*.

It was 10:00 PM. We had just spent another twelve-hour day working on our paper. Lisa was settling into a chair with a hot toddy. Andrea was shoving off for a shower. We were grumpy, tired, full of self-pity; this was the third day we had worked at such a pace. Only one day remained before Lisa had to begin the eight-hour trek from Andrea's home in Vancouver to her own in Corvallis. We had to finish a draft of the paper, our first joint writing project, the next day.

All at once — we both remember it this way — Lisa sat upright and announced: "Andrea takes a shower every night; Lisa takes one every morning." Since the meaning of this toddy-stimulated statement was hardly self-evident, Lisa went on to explain that suddenly the significance of all our differences, of which this was just one example, seemed clear. How could two such opposite people ever hope to write a paper — together?

Warming to the silliness of the topic, we began to list all the ways we differ. Andrea showers every night; Lisa, every morning. Andrea drinks only iced tea, even at breakfast; Lisa drinks only the hottest of hot tea. Andrea hates milk and most dairy products; they form a staple of Lisa's diet. Andrea always wears her hair pulled back; Lisa gets a headache from even the thought of a single barrette. Andrea is a meticulous housekeeper; Lisa, so-so at best.

As the list of opposites grew, we felt a giddy sense of relief. No wonder the past few days had been so trying. Two such contrary, often downright cantankerous, people should have *expected* trouble. The struggle began to make sense: not just our personalities but our composing processes and, to a lesser degree, our styles, differed radically. After all, didn't Lisa love dashes, sprinkling them liberally through her prose, while Andrea seldom used them? Andrea preferred long paragraphs; Lisa's were usually shorter. Lisa wrote at a desk or (in a pinch) at a table; Andrea worked sitting cross-legged on the floor or on the bed. Andrea was a sprinter; she liked to write a draft straight through, as quickly as possible, revising and typing later. Lisa worked more slowly, dividing a paper into small sections, revising and typing as she went.

We decided that night that if we ever did complete our joint essay, we would someday explore the mystery — or the madness — of coauthorship. Since that time, we have coauthored two other articles and have several joint projects in mind. Thus, while we continue individual research efforts, our status as sometime coauthors seems assured. Somehow, despite the difficulties, we not only manage to write essays together, but actually like doing so. And, as we have worked together, the question that arose that night — how can two people with different interests, personalities, habits, and composing processes together write one essay? — has expanded into many questions. This article is a brief anecdotal response to some of those questions. In it, we wish to sketch the outlines of the process of coauthorship as we have come to understand it, to set forth the advantages and disadvantages we encountered, and to pose a series of questions which we hope will be explored in future research.

In our experience, coauthorship has meant the two of us creating one text — together. We discovered and thought through ideas together, talked through almost every section and draft of the papers together, and often wrote drafts by talking and then recording directly. Such is not always the case. Indeed, our use of the term is probably atypical. More typically, no doubt, two authors contribute separate sections, which are then put together. Only at that point do the coauthors revise the whole text, and even in revising authors may work separately. In this way, people can coauthor articles without ever being together or doing any writing together. This second form of coauthorship may best describe the kind of academic writing done by, say, a professor and a student, or the kind done by many researchers in science. It may also describe coauthorship in much professional and business writing. Yet a third concept covered by the blanket term *coauthorship* is that of group writing. It is not unusual, especially in business, for a number of people to contribute to a single text. The head of the writing division for an international mining corporation recently told us that as many as fifteen people contribute sections to their annual report. Subsequently, four or five of those people come together to revise the entire report, which generally goes through a dozen drafts.

We believe that important distinctions exist among these types of coauthorship and, indeed, that other types of coauthorship can be identified. Since our experience has been primarily of the first type, however — that of conceiving, drafting, and revising a text together — we will concentrate on that concept and will use the term *coauthorship* in this essay to refer to this type of writing together.

We are also here referring only to academic writing. The essays we have coauthored have all been addressed to those in our field, readers of *College Composition and Communication*, *College English*, and rhetoric journals. In that sense, we have gone into each project with a clear sense of audience, medium of publication, and purpose (although we could, of course, easily misjudge our audience or medium or alter our purposes). As with much academic writing, we began by working within only our own time constraints. But as so often is the case, this internal control soon gave way to external pressures. An invitation to speak at a conference was accepted; an article was solicited for a journal or committed to a book — and suddenly the external pressure to write on demand appeared. In this important regard, that of writing on demand, much academic writing may be closer to professional writing than we usually consider it to be. But in other ways, the genres vary markedly. As writers of an article for *Rhetoric Review*, for instance, we have a different kind of control over shape and substance than we would if we were writing an annual report for a mining company. As with the various types of coauthorship, we think these generic distinctions are important ones that need to be explored. While we hope to pursue these questions in the future, we are speaking here not of business or professional writing, but only of the academic genre with which we are all so familiar.

So what is this process of coauthoring an academic paper? We've drawn boxes and arrows, spirals and loops, but will offer no schematized representation of the process we have experienced. If you can imagine the words *talk . . . write . . . talk . . . read . . . talk . . . write . . . talk . . . read . . .* written in a large looping spiral — that comes closest to a description of the process as we know it. We wish especially to emphasize the frequency and proportion of *talking* in this process.

As we noted earlier, each of our projects grew out of a particular rhetori-   10 cal situation: We were constrained by a broad topic and by a medium of publication and an audience. Within those guidelines, our first and longest talks occurred. These early talks were characterized by a lot of foolishness (Why not claim that the concept of audience simply doesn't exist? or, How about writing a dialogue between Aristotle and Wittgenstein?), fantasy (What if we could visit Kenneth Burke for a month?), and unfocused rambling (Where do you suppose we've put our notes on those ten articles? What do you think is the best reading for *krisis*?)° In our first project, these talks helped us sound the depths of our topic and, most importantly, discover the enormity of what we did not know. Intensive periods of reading and research followed, as did more and more talking, trading of notes, and posing of yet more unanswered questions. All told, this first coauthored essay took us six months, during which we met four times for two- to four-day writing sessions. These sessions were pressure-filled, frustrating — and very exciting. For one of them, we met half-way between our homes, in Seattle, and worked for two-and-a-half days in a hotel room, distracted only by the person trying unsuccessfully to "tidy up" around the stacks of books, articles, and drafts, and by our husbands, who insisted on reporting on all the fun they were having while we worked. We estimate writing and talking time in these sessions to be almost equal, with more time given to writing in the last session and more to talk in the earlier ones. At the end of each session the process of talk . . . write . . . talk . . . read . . . talk . . . write . . . talk . . . read . . . left us tired but exhilarated. And in each case the process produced a draft, one we could take back home, work

---

krisis: A classical Greek term etymologically related to the verb *krinō,* "to pull apart or separate." The word *krisis* means an agreed-upon choice or judgment. Lunsford and Ede's choice of *krisis* as an example is interesting in that the coauthors themselves must make a choice or judgment about their reading of the term.

on, and talk about in our frequent phone calls. We have kept every draft, all our notes, and some protocols from each of our projects, but we do not wish to turn this into a full-blown case study of our admitted idiosyncrasies. Rather, we wish to turn to a brief discussion of how coauthoring altered our individual writing processes.

Most noticeable, as we have mentioned, was the much larger proportion of talking together about our research and writing. Papers written singly have never been completely silent affairs; we talk to others about our work or ask colleagues to read and discuss essays or drafts with us. But never had either of us (both prodigious talkers to begin with) ever talked so much or for so long while writing a paper. This talking, in fact, seemed to be a necessary part of coauthoring, one that made our writing more productive and efficient. Nor is this result surprising. Our "talks," after all, gave us the constant benefits of dialectic, the traditional counterpart of rhetoric.

> **We would . . . explore the mystery — or the madness — of coauthorship.**

Coauthorship effected a second, less pleasurable change in our ordinary writing processes. All academic writers are accustomed to the pressure of deadlines, but in single authorship these deadlines are more or less manageable. Coauthorship presented us with completely rigid time-schedules and hence with more pressure than either of us was used to working under: If we had only two-and-a-half days to work together, then we had to come up with a text at that very time. Or else.

We also noted shifts in our usual revision strategies. In the first place, neither of us was accustomed to having *talk* serve as the basis for a majority of the revisions we made. When writing alone, writers usually revise while or after reading. We found also that our individual revising strategies differed substantially: Lisa generally revises and types each section as it is drafted; Andrea favors long periods of staring into space during which she composes various alternative drafts in her head before beginning a long burst of writing. Editing strategies were equally affected. In the coauthored articles, we found ourselves attending much more closely to quotation format and footnote citations in our early drafts than we would ordinarily have done. We were concerned to get the citations exactly right, since our resources were split up between us and our two libraries. Going back to find a missing source would be much more difficult than usual.

These changes in revision strategies reflect, we believe, a change in the rhetorical situations coauthors work within; they must cooperate and collaborate at every turn. Coauthorship, then, demands flexibility and compromise, traits single writers can often eschew. For us, this changed situation meant giving up some of our cherished stylistic tics — like Lisa's dashes — or a favored revision strategy.

The spirit of cooperation and compromise necessary to coauthorship 15 helped us identify two additional ways in which our customary experience with writing was changed. As of this writing, we feel less ego involvement with the pieces we have coauthored than those we have written alone. Hence, we have a greater distance from the work. At this point, we cannot report whether coauthorship gives us more—or less — confidence in the written product. But the questions of confidence and of ego-involvement raise a number of issues, some of which we will address in the concluding section of this essay. Most importantly, we found that coauthoring led us to alter our normal problem-solving styles. In spite of the tendency to work on writing and revising a paper one small section at a time, Lisa's basic approach to problems is broad and synthetic; she ordinarily begins by casting a very wide net. Andrea, on the other hand, approaches problems analytically, narrowing and drawing out implications, searching for closure almost at once. Working as coauthors iden-tified this difference in approach for us, and led us to balance the two styles continually against one another. As a result, one often felt we were circling endlessly, spinning our wheels, while the other alternatively felt we were roar-ing hell-bent toward our conclusion.

Such changes obviously require significant accommodation and compro-mise, which can be seen as either advantages or disadvantages of coauthor-ship. Had we not finally decided on the former, we would not be writing this now. Many others, in similar situations and with similar interests, might choose differently. Indeed, some time in the future our own circumstances or any of a number of other internal or external changes could prompt us to decide that the advantages of coauthorship no longer outweigh the disad-vantages. Coauthorship, as we have pointed out, makes the whole process of writing more difficult in some ways. (Perhaps our worst moment occurred one afternoon in Seattle when Lisa revised the mid section of our first proj-ect three times — requiring Andrea to change the following pages, which she was working on at the time, substantially every time.) Those problems were offset for us, however, by the stimulation of working with someone who shares the same interests. Even more important to us was the strong sense that in some writing situations we were more likely to achieve a better under-standing, generate potentially richer and fresher ideas, and develop a stronger overall argument than we might have done working alone. (We specify "some writing situations" to emphasize that we chose the projects on which we collaborated carefully and for a number of particular reasons; as we have noted, we continued to work on independent research efforts dur-ing this period.)

We felt, in short, a kind of synergism when we worked together. This syn-ergism, the sense that by combining our efforts we could in some instances achieve more together than alone, carried us through some difficult times.

But other factors also played a role. Although we knew before we began writing together that we differed in our composing habits and stylistic preferences, we each shared a respect for the other's abilities. Also, each of us knew the other was a person on whom we could count, once committed, to complete a project no matter how much or how violently we differed. Finally, we *wanted* to work together, both because we are friends (who now can deduct the expenses for all the trips we would have taken anyway) and because we feel that collaboration and collegiality are ideals much discussed but little practiced in academic life.

Although we have gone into some detail about our relationship as coauthors, we have by no means given a full accounting of the ups and downs, ins and outs, arguments and counter-arguments involved in working together. (For a while we planned to include process footnotes such as [1]"Believe it or not, Andrea put this dash in here"; or [7]"At this point, Lisa *begged* to be able to type what we had written.") We hope in future research to investigate further the concepts and kinds of coauthorship and the implications coauthoring may hold for our field. In the meantime, we would very much like to hear from other coauthors about their experiences writing with others. Because Andrea lives in the land of lost mail, please write to Lisa. We hope shortly to begin a more formal gathering of data about coauthoring in various disciplines and professions. Even this brief exploration, however, has raised a number of questions which we believe need to be addressed.

(1) What specific features distinguish the processes of co- or group-authoring from those of single authorship? Are these features the same for the three types of coauthorship described above? Can these features of process be linked to any features of the resulting products? In short, how can we best *define* coauthorship?

(2) Is there a limit to how many people can write together? Are projects 20 such as the *Oxford English Dictionary*, Bible, *Short Title Catalogue*, elaborate computer programs, encyclopedias — all often involving more than 100 authors — examples of coauthorship? That is to say, what are the parameters of coauthorship?

(3) In what ways, if any, does co- or group-authorship affect the way we view the traditional rhetor-audience relationship?

(4) How does technology affect the processes of coauthoring? In our experience, writing together would have been much more difficult and much slower without the telephone, xerox, and self-correcting typewriter. Had we each had word processors at home and a computer link, what other differences might we have noted?

(5) What epistemological implications does coauthorship hold for traditional notions of creativity and originality? Our own strong sense that two

may create ideas that neither would have reached alone argues for the value of dialectic as invention.

(6) How might the ethics of coauthorship be examined and defined? We spoke earlier of noting less ego involvement in our coauthored pieces. Perhaps this factor is related to our sense of shared responsibility: If we are wrong, at least we are wrong together. But in cases of group authorship, where does the responsibility lie? Who stands behind the words of a report written by fifteen people? As group authorship becomes more and more the norm in some genres, such questions gather urgency.

(7) Is the emphasis on or weight of various cognitive and rhetorical 25 strategies different when coauthoring than when writing alone? As we noted, many of our customary revision strategies were altered by the process of coauthorship, and the rhetorical situation, which demanded collaboration and compromise, strongly affected our usual processes.

(8) Finally, we were led to think most seriously of the pedagogical implications of coauthorship. What do we know as a discipline about the advantages or disadvantages of having students participate in co- or group-writing? If advantages do exist, don't they in some ways contradict our profession's traditional insistence on students' working alone? And perhaps most importantly, do we have ways to teach students to adjust readily to co- or group-writing tasks?

Although this whimsical report of our experiences as coauthors is severely limited, perhaps serving best to raise questions, the issue of co- and group-authorship in general is not of limited or peripheral significance. As a rule, writers in the humanities have tended to ignore coauthorship, both in writing and in teaching, while colleagues in the sciences and the professions have long used it as a major mode. In view of this anomaly, the images of the lonely writer in a garret, or students hunched against the solitary ordeal of writing proficiency examinations, seem particularly inappropriate. We are, after all, most often responsible for teaching those who go into science and the professions how to write. And when we consider that these students are going into jobs already making use of rapidly developing computer technology, which holds such potential significance for coauthoring, the question for both writers and teachers may be not "Why write together?" but "Why NOT write together?"

Working with the Text

1. For the purposes of the article, Lisa Ede and Andrea Lunsford define *coauthorship* as "conceiving, drafting, and revising a text together" (par. 7). Although the collaborative process they describe is for writing within the field of humanities for an academic audience, many of the elements in their process could be

used by undergraduates coauthoring projects for humanities courses. Based on the article, write directions to be used by pairs of undergraduate writers preparing to coauthor a research project for a history, English, or other humanities class. How should they choose their project partner? What process or work sequence do you recommend? What options do they have for dividing and sharing the work? What attitudes and work habits do they need to bring to the process to make it work? Throughout, focus on the range of options that collaboration can present.

2. For Ede and Lunsford, one of the most essential features of collaboration is talking. "This talking, in fact, seemed to be a necessary part of coauthoring, one that made our writing more productive and efficient" (par. 11). In a brief essay, analyze what they mean by this claim. Why do they start with talking instead of with writing? In what ways does talking move their process forward? What do they accomplish through talking that they wouldn't accomplish through simply revising each other's writing? What work dynamic does talking produce for them?

3. In 2000, Ede and Lunsford were invited to present at a Modern Language Association forum on "Creative Collaboration: Alternatives to the Adversarial Academy." In "Why Write . . . Together?"—written seventeen years earlier—the authors stated that they work together in part "because we feel that collaboration and collegiality are ideals much discussed but little practiced in academic life" (par. 17). Based on evidence from the article, write a brief essay in which you reflect on what you have witnessed of the supposed adversarial dynamics of academic life, where "collaboration and collegiality" are "little practiced." Regard the article as the description of a process that is a distinct alternative to common practice among academics, especially in the humanities. What might cause such an adversarial atmosphere? What form might the conflict take? What might collaboration produce that cannot be accomplished by taking adversarial positions? Why is collaboration far more common in the sciences and more widespread in professional and workplace environments?

From Text to Field

1. Although "Why Write . . . Together?" describes collaboration in academic writing within the humanities, many elements in the process experienced by the authors can be found in any form of collaboration. Write an essay in which you reflect on a collaborative effort of your own that involved processes or dynamics similar to those described by Ede and Lunsford. You might have been involved in a collaborative effort such as a group project in a class, a music or drama production, a sport, a volunteer activity, or an activity for an organization.

How did the process unfold? What were the work dynamics among the group members? How was it different from pursuing the same activity as an individual? Did you consider it to be a success? Why or why not?

2. In a group of two or three students, cowrite a response to one of the questions in the "Working with the Text" section. Think of coauthorship as defined by Ede and Lunsford: "conceiving, drafting, and revising a text together" (par. 7). After you have completed your text, discuss your process with your cowriters. Review the article for ways to reflect on your process. What steps did you take? What difficulties did you encounter? How was working together on the text different from working alone? To what extent did you experience the "synergism" described by the authors? Be prepared to describe your process to the rest of the class.

3. Whether or not you have experience in collaborative writing, you probably have an opinion about whether or not you would pursue it, if given the choice. Write an essay in which you analyze your attitude toward coauthorship. In what situations, if any, would you choose to write collaboratively? If you would never choose to collaborate, why not? If you would choose to collaborate in certain situations, why do you think those situations would lend themselves to coauthoring? What conditions would have to exist for you to have confidence that the process would succeed?

4. Ede and Lunsford wrote "Why Write . . . Together?" before they had researched the collaborative process extensively. The questions at the end of the article, based on their early experience of working together, were a starting place for their later research. In a group of two or three, choose one of those questions. Based on the combined experience and judgment of the group members, collaboratively write an essay that offers an initial answer to the question. For each assertion you make, explain why you have come to that conclusion, using reasoning as well as evidence from your personal experience and observation.

The Art of Collaborative Learning: Making the Most of Knowledgeable Peers

Kenneth A. Bruffee

Most students pursue higher education as preparation for work in the "real world." As Kenneth A. Bruffee observes, the fact that the real world works primarily through collaboration has prompted teachers in colleges and universities to explore collaborative learning as a means for preparing students for professional life — and academic success. Studies indicate that not only do students learn the art of collaboration, they gain knowledge and judgment more quickly and effectively.

According to Bruffee, professional collaboration and collaborative learning work because knowledge itself is the result of our ongoing work with each other. In terms used by the social constructionists who have influenced Bruffee's thinking, knowledge is "socially constructed." For Bruffee, knowledge as a social construct means that "learning occurs among persons rather than between a person and things." This calls into question the authority we have traditionally assigned to some kinds of knowledge as being entirely objective and absolute and has us rethink the authority we traditionally grant to the teachers who convey that knowledge. Drawing on research in teaching and learning, Bruffee subscribes to the notion that learning "does not involve people's assimilation of knowledge, it involves people's assimilation into communities of knowledgeable peers" (par. 24).

Collaborative learning has been an area of specialization for Bruffee throughout his academic career. In addition to publishing articles and books — including *Collaborative Learning: Higher Education, Interdependence, and the Authority of Knowledge* (2nd ed., 1990) — he has led colloquia on collaborative learning, liberal education, and the authority of knowledge at a number of prominent colleges and universities. Bruffee is professor of English and director of the Scholars Program and the Honors Academy at Brooklyn College, City University of New York.

The essay reprinted here was originally published in 1987 in *Change*, a bimonthly magazine that focuses on contemporary issues in higher education. It was subsequently reprinted in 1994 in a special retrospective issue of *Change*. The author has kindly included a short bibliography that notes recent work on collaborative learning.

Late last spring, a colleague of mine at a university out West — I'll call him Jim — wrote and asked if I would read a manuscript of his. He felt he was finally ready for someone to take a close look at it.

Jim's an old friend. I dashed off a note saying of course I'd read it, with pleasure. At the beginning of June, which luckily for both of us was right at the end of exams, I got a weighty package in the mail – 279 pages plus notes. I read it, scribbled clouds of barely decipherable marginal notes, and drafted a six-page letter to Jim congratulating him on first-rate work, suggesting a few changes and mentioning one or two issues he might think through a bit further.

He phoned to thank me when he got the letter and asked some questions. We then spent an hour or so discussing these questions and supporting AT&T in the manner to which it has become accustomed.

Before the snow blows, I expect I shall see some of Jim's manuscript again. I doubt that he needs another reading, but I'm happy to do it if he wants me to. I learned a lot reading his book. We both learned something talking out the few stickier points in it. Anyway, I owe him one. He did the same for me five years ago, when I was thrashing about in the terminal throes of the book I was finishing. His name appeared prominently on my acknowledgments page; I suppose mine will appear prominently on his.

The experience I have just described is familiar to most readers of *Change*. To enjoy such an experience, you don't have to write a book. All you have to do is work with an intelligent, compatible committee on an interesting grant proposal or a new development plan for your college. You know how it can go. Joe gets an idea and sketches it out in a couple of pages. Mary says, hey, wait a minute — that makes me think of . . . . Then Fred says, but look, if we change this or add that. . . . In the end everyone, with a little help from his and her friends, exceeds what anyone could possibly have learned or accomplished alone.

If I'm right that this kind of experience is familiar, then no one reading this article is a stranger to collaborative learning, however strange the term may be. Jim and I are peers. When Jim asked me to read his work and I agreed, we became an autonomous collaborative learning group of two with the task of revising and developing the written product of one of its members.

The term "collaborative learning" has become increasingly familiar today because it is applied not only to voluntary associations such as my work with Jim, but also to teaching that tries to imitate that experience in college and university classrooms. Teachers of writing at institutions throughout the country are discovering that teaching students in a variety of ways to work productively on their writing demonstrably improves students' work.

And it is not just writing teachers who are interested. Clark Bouton and Russell Y. Clark's useful book, *Learning in Groups*, reports on the way collaborative learning is being applied in subjects from business management to medicine to math. And there is at least one physics lab manual in the country (at Montana State University) that presents an extended rationale of collaborative learning on its front cover.

Perhaps more to the point for some of us, at least one trenchant article exists that explains collaborative learning for the benefit of faculty and administrators who find themselves evaluating teachers. Harvey S. Wiener's "Collaborative Learning in the Classroom: A Guide to Evaluation" (*College English* 48) suggests ways to tell when teachers are using collaborative learning most effectively. It is also, therefore, a useful guide to, effective use of collaborative learning for teachers.

Admittedly, there is not much research to date on the effects of collaborative learning in college and university education. But recent work on its effect in primary and secondary schools is relevant. Surveys of research by David Johnson (*Psychological Bulletin* 89) and by Shlomo Sharan (*Review of Educational Research* 50) tend to support the experience of college and university instructors who have used collaborative learning. Students learn better through noncompetitive collaborative group work than in classrooms that are highly individualized and competitive. Robert E. Slavin's *Cooperative Learning* reports similar results.

Interest in collaborative learning in colleges and schools is motivated in part by these results. It is motivated also by the observation that the rest of the world now works collaboratively almost as a universal principle. Japanese "Theory-Z" quality circles on the factory floor aside, there is hardly a bank, legal firm, or industrial management team that strives — much less dares — to proceed in the old-fashioned individualistic manner. Physicians are increasingly collaborative, too, although they prefer to call it "consultation." At Harvard Medical School, 25 percent of each entering class currently studies in collaborative groups, bypassing systematic lecture courses almost entirely.

Interest in collaborative learning is motivated also by recent challenges to our understanding of what knowledge is. This challenge is being felt throughout the academic disciplines. That is, collaborative learning is related to the social constructionist views promulgated by, among others, the philosopher Richard Rorty (*Philosophy and the Mirror of Nature*) and the anthropologist Clifford Geertz. These writers say (as Geertz puts it in his recent book, *Local Knowledge*) that "the way we think now" differs in essential ways from the way we thought in the past. Social constructionists tend to assume that knowledge is a social construct and that, as the historian of science Thomas Kuhn has put it, all knowledge, including scientific knowledge, "is intrinsically the common property of a group or else nothing at all." (See Bruffee, "Social Construction, Language, and the Authority of Knowledge: A Bibliographical Essay," *College English*, vol. 48, December 1986, pp. 773–90.)

Collaborative learning is related to these conceptual changes by virtue of the fact that it assumes learning occurs among persons rather than between a person and things. It even turns out that some teachers who are using collaborative learning have found that social constructionist assumptions enhance their understanding of what they are trying to do and give them a better chance of doing it well.

So, although the term *collaborative learning* may be unfamiliar for some, collaborative learning itself is not new. Our understanding of its importance to higher education began in the late 1950s with Theodore Newcomb's work on peer-group influence among college students (*College Peer Groups, The American College*, ed. Nevitt Sanford) and with M. L. J. Abercrombie's research on educating medical students at University Hospital, University of London. Newcomb demonstrated that peer-group influence is a powerful but wasted resource in higher education. Abercrombie's book, *The Anatomy of Judgment*, showed medical students learning the key element in successful medical practice, diagnosis — that is, medical judgment — more quickly and accurately when they worked collaboratively in small groups than when they worked individually.

Abercrombie began her important study by observing the scene that most of us think is typical of medical education: the group of medical students with a teaching physician gathered around a ward bed to diagnose a patient. Then she made a slight but crucial change in the way that such a scene is usually played out. Instead of asking each individual medical student in the group to diagnose the patient on his or her own, Abercrombie asked the whole group to examine the patient together, discuss the case as a group, and arrive at a consensus — a single diagnosis agreed to by all. 15

When she did this, what she found was that students who learned diagnosis collaboratively in this way acquired better medical judgment faster than individual students working alone.

With the exception of small, recently instituted experimental programs at the medical schools of the University of New Mexico and Harvard University,

Abercrombie's conclusion has had little impact as yet on medical school faculties anywhere, in Britain or America. But when I read the book in 1972, a dozen years or so after it was published, her conclusion had an immediate and, I believe, positive impact on my thinking about university instruction and, eventually, on the role I see myself in as a classroom instructor.

The aspect of Abercrombie's book that I found most illuminating was her evidence that learning diagnostic judgment is not an individual process but a social one. Learning judgment, she saw, patently occurs on an axis drawn not between individuals and things, but among people. But in making this observation, she had to acknowledge that there is something wrong with our normal cognitive assumptions about the nature of knowledge. Cognitive assumptions, she says, disregard "the biological fact that [the human being] . . . is a social animal." "How [do] human relationships," that is, relations among persons, she asked, "influence the receipt of information about apparently nonpersonal events?"

In trying to answer this question, Abercrombie makes the brilliant observation that, in general, people learn judgment best in groups; she infers from this observation that we learn judgment well in groups because we tend to talk each other out of our unshared biases and presuppositions. And in passing, she drops an invaluable hint: The social process of learning judgment that she has observed seems to have something to do with language and with "interpretation."

These three principles underlie the practice of collaborative learning.   20 One thing that college and university instructors most hope to do through collaborative learning is increase their students' ability to exercise judgment within the teacher's field of expertise, whatever that field is.

But there is today another thing that instructors hope to do through collaborative learning. They hope to raise their students' level of social maturity as exercised in their intellectual lives. In doing so, instructors are trying to prepare their students for the "real world." They are preparing them to enter law, medicine, architecture, banking, engineering, research science — any field, in fact, that depends on effective interdependence and consultation for excellence.

This discovery that excellent undergraduate education also depends on effective interdependence and consultation awaited the work of William Perry. Perry's book, *Forms of Intellectual and Ethical Development in the College Years*, has made an indelible impression on the thinking of many college and university instructors, but not in every instance for the right reason. Like Abercrombie, Perry makes cognitive assumptions about the nature of knowledge, and most readers to date have found his developmental "scheme" of greatest interest.

Yet Perry himself is not entirely comfortable with the cognitive assumptions underlying his scheme. He has read Thomas Kuhn's *The Structure of Scientific Revolutions*, and he acknowledges that our current view that "knowledge is contextual and relative" is only the most recent phase in a tendency toward the assimilation of cultural diversity that needs for its fulfillment "a new social mind."

As a result, again like Abercrombie, Perry implies that the central educational issues today hinge on social relations, not on cognitive ones: relations among persons, not relations between persons and things. Learning as we must understand it today, he concludes, does not involve people's assimilation of knowledge, it involves people's assimilation into communities of knowledgeable peers. Liberal education today must be regarded as a process of leaving one community of knowledgeable peers and joining another.

Perry's discomfort with this conclusion when it comes to educational practice, however, suggests that he himself may never have quite recognized the full implications of his study. He denies that the creating of communities of knowledgeable peers among students is a legitimate part of rationally and consciously organized university education. He prefers to rely on "spontaneity" to organize knowledge communities among students. He politely dismisses as unprofessional attempts to foster communities among students by using "particular procedures or rituals." Students must independently manage their "identification with the college community" as they go about "divorcing themselves" from the communities they have left behind.

Fortunately, Perry quotes liberally from his raw material—statements made by a sizable number of informants among the Harvard College undergraduate body. And these undergraduates are not at all as ambivalent as Perry seems to be about regarding learning as a social process. Many of

Collaborative learning . . . assumes learning occurs among persons rather than between a person and things.

them see their undergraduate education quite explicitly as a difficult, perhaps even treacherous passage from one homogeneous community— the one they came from — to another homogeneous community — the college community of their student peers.

This "marrying into" the new community of students at college is clearly, as the students describe it, an informal, autonomous variety of collaborative learning that challenges students to define their individuality not as starkly and lonesomely independent, but as interdependent members of their new undergraduate community.

The more formal varieties of collaborative learning organized by instructors in classrooms imitate this informal type. And they imitate the "real world" interdependence and consultation that goes on in much business and professional work, including the work my friend Jim and I did together on his book and mine. In classroom collaborative learning, typically, students organized by the teacher into small groups discuss a topic proposed by the teacher with the purpose of arriving at consensus, much as Abercrombie's medical students practiced diagnosis on patients chosen by the teaching physician. Or students may edit each other's writing, or tutor each other, or develop and carry through assigned (or group-designed and teacher-approved) projects together.

But this classroom work, however collaborative, differs in striking ways from autonomous, "real world" interdependence. Classroom collaborative learning is inevitably no more than semiautonomous, because students don't usually organize their own groups or choose their own tasks, as Jim and I did. In most cases, teachers design and structure students' work for maximum learning as part of a course of study. And teachers evaluate the work when it is completed, comparing it with professional standards and the work other students have done, both currently and in the past.

Now, to be accurate to a fault, of course, Jim and I were not an absolutely   30 autonomous group either, any more than any interdependent consultative professional work is. Like most independently organized groups — such as political clubs, golf foursomes, and sand-lot baseball teams — he and I organized our working group on our own initiative for our own purposes, but we played the game, so to speak, by a set of rules we held in common with many other such groups.

The mores, conventions, values, and goals of our professional organization (in our case, the Modern Language Association), of that motley class of human beings called "university faculty," of promotion and tenure committees whose values are probably similar at Jim's college and mine, and so on — these large institutional communities determine to some extent what Jim and I did and said, how we did it and said it, and in point of fact, that we were doing it and saying it at all. Institutional motives and constraints always apply when people prepare themselves to take a hand in what is going on in the prevailing economic, legal, and educational world.

Formed within the immediate confines of a college's institutional structure, however, working groups in a collaborative learning classroom are clearly *semi*autonomous. Like the New York Yankees, a Boy Scout troop, or the United States Supreme Court, their collaboration is organized by a larger institutional community and with its sanction. Group members abide by the conventions, mores, values, and goals of that institution. The autonomy of classroom groups derives from the fact that once the tasks are set and the groups organized, instructors step back, leaving peers to work in groups or pairs to organize, govern, and pace their work by themselves and to negotiate its outcome.

That this partial autonomy is the key to the impact of collaborative learning is evident when we compare semiautonomous work with work that is entirely nonautonomous. The work of nonautonomous groups cannot reasonably be called collaborative learning at all. Like life in a Trappist monastery or an army platoon, in which activity is rigorously controlled, classroom group work is nonautonomous whenever instructors do not step back from the groups of working students, but rather "sit in" on them or "hover," predetermining the outcome of the work and maintaining the students' direct dependency on the teacher's presence, resources, and expertise.

Degree of autonomy is the key to collaborative learning because the issue that collaborative learning addresses is the way authority is distributed and experienced in college and university classrooms. It would be disingenuous to evade the fact that collaborative learning challenges our traditional view of the instructor's authority in a classroom and the way that authority is exercised.

This issue is much too complex to go into here. But perhaps we can get a provocative glimpse of the possible rewards that might accrue from pursuing it further if we take a brief look at the nature and source of the authority of knowledge in any autonomous working group. Return for a moment to my friend Jim and me at work together on his manuscript. What was the source of the authority exercised in that work? Where was it placed and how did it get there? Not to put too fine a point on it, where did I get the authority to comment on his writing? 35

The answer, of course, is that Jim and I together generated the authority in our group of two. And to occur at all in this way, that generation of authority required certain conditions. For starters, we like each other. We have read each other's stuff. We respect each other's intelligence. We have similar interests. We have worked together professionally in other circumstances. In short, we were *willing* to collaborate.

It was under these conditions that *Jim granted me* authority over his work by asking me to read it. The authority of my knowledge with regard to his manuscript originated primarily with him. I mean "primarily" here in the strongest possible sense. My authority began with his request, and the principal claim to the validity of my authority resulted from that request.

Furthermore, and equally important, when I responded positively, *I agreed to take on and assert* authority relative to him and his work. In that sense, the authority of my knowledge with regard to his manuscript originated primarily not only with his granting me the authority, but also with my accepting it, both, of course, in a context of friendliness and good grace.

Willingness to grant authority, willingness to take on and exercise authority, and a context of friendliness and good grace are the three ingredients essential to successful autonomous collaboration. If any of these three is missing or flags, collaboration fails. These three ingredients are essential also to successful semiautonomous collaboration, such as classroom collaborative learning.

But when instructors use semiautonomous groups in classes, the stark real- 40 ity is that willingness to grant authority, willingness to take it on and exercise it, and a context of friendliness and good grace are severely compromised. Classroom authority does not necessarily begin — as Jim's and mine began — with the participants' (that is, the students') willing consent to grant authority and exercise it. In a classroom, authority still begins in most cases with the representative or agent of the institution, the instructor. Furthermore, except in highly unusual classrooms, most students start the semester as relative strangers. They do not begin, as Jim and I did, as friends. It is not surprising that, as a result, in many classrooms students may at first be wary and not overly eager to collaborate.

That is, collaborative learning has to begin in most cases with an attempt to *reacculturate* students. Given most students' almost exclusively traditional experience of classroom authority, they have to learn, sometimes against considerable resistance, to grant authority to a peer ("What right has he got to . . . ?"), instead of the teacher. And students have to learn to take on the authority granted by a peer ("What right have I got to . . . ?"), and to exercise that authority responsibly and helpfully in the interest of a peer.

Skillfully organized, collaborative learning can itself reacculturate students in this way. Once the task is set and the groups organized, collaborative learning places students working in groups on their own to interpret the task and invent or adapt a language and means to get the work done. When the instructor is absent, the chain of hierarchical institutional authority is for the moment broken. Students are free to revert to the collaborative peership that they are quite used to exercising in other kinds of extracurricular activities from which faculty are usually absent.

Of course, students do not always exercise effective collaborative peership in classrooms, especially at first, because they have all so thoroughly internalized our long-prevailing academic prohibitions against it. And it need hardly be added that nonautonomous groups, in which the instructor insists on remaining in direct authority even after the task is set and the groups organized, cannot reacculturate students in these ways, because the chain of hierarchical institutional authority is never broken.

Because we usually identify the authority of knowledge in a classroom with the instructor's authority, the brief hiatus in the hierarchical chain of authority in the classroom that is at the heart of collaborative learning in the long run also challenges, willy-nilly, our traditional view of the nature and source of the knowledge itself. Collaborative learning tends, that is, to take its toll on the cognitive understanding of knowledge that most of us assume unquestioningly. Teachers and students alike may find themselves asking the sorts of questions Abercrombie asked. How can knowledge gained through a social process have a source that is not itself also social?

This is another aspect of collaborative learning too complex to go into here. But raising it momentarily gives us a hint about why collaborative learning may empower students to work more successfully beyond the confines of college or university classrooms. Collaborative learning calls on levels of ingenuity and inventiveness that many students never knew they had. And it teaches effective interdependence in an increasingly collaborative world that today requires greater flexibility and adaptability to change than ever before. 45

Bibliography

Brown, John Seely, and Paul Duguid. *The Social Life of Information*. Boston: Harvard Business School Press, 2000.

Bruffee, Kenneth A. *A Short Course in Writing: Composition, Collaborative Learning, and Constructive Reading* 5th ed. New York. Pearson Longman, 2006.

Cohen, Elizabeth G. *Designing Groupwork: Strategies for the Heterogeneous Classroom*. 2nd ed. New York: Teachers College, Columbia University Press, 1994.

Farrell, Michael P. *Collaborative Circles: Friendship Dynamics and Creative Work*. Chicago: University of Chicago Press, 2001.

Mazur, Eric. *Peer Instruction: A User's Manual*. Upper Saddle River, NJ: Prentice Hall, 1997.

Working with the Text

1. According to Kenneth A. Bruffee, his approach to collaborative learning assumes that "learning occurs among persons rather than between a person and things" (par. 13). Write a brief essay in which you reflect on this rather pithy statement, analyzing Bruffee's view of what knowledge is and how we acquire it. Point to examples in Bruffee's essay, and in your own experience, that might support this view.

2. Throughout the article, Bruffee is concerned not with the passive acquisition of knowledge but with "judgment." In a brief essay, explore what Bruffee means by judgment. Why might collaborative learning and assimilation into a community of knowledgeable peers be essential for the cultivation of judgment?

3. Bruffee champions collaborative learning as an approach that reflects the "real world" more accurately than traditional classroom teaching methods. Choose one or more of his examples of collaborative learning in various professional and work settings. In a brief essay, describe in more detail how you think collaborative learning would play itself out in a given setting. To prompt ideas on

ways collaborative learning might be used in a setting, refer to Bruffee's more general descriptions of how the process works.

From Text to Field

1. Forms of collaborative learning have now been used in elementary, secondary, and university classrooms for a number of years. Based on Bruffee's descriptions of collaborative learning, recall how it was used in one of your classrooms. In a personal essay, describe the experience, reflecting on how you responded to the approach and how it affected your learning process. If your experience with collaborative learning was positive, explore in some detail why that was the case. Do your reasons support or extend Bruffee's analysis? If your experience was less than positive (and, if so, you are not alone), explore why it did not support your learning process.

2. It is now widely accepted that students have different styles of learning. To what extent is collaborative learning one of several styles, or might it serve as a basis for all learning styles? When might some students not be well served by learning in groups? Are there learning tasks or disciplines in which collaborative learning is either particularly appropriate or, on occasion, inappropriate?

3. Bruffee observes that college and university teachers use collaborative learning for a number of reasons: to "increase their students' ability to exercise judgment within the teacher's field of expertise," to "raise their students' level of social maturity as exercised in their intellectual lives," and to prepare them to enter any field "that depends on effective interdependence and consultation for excellence" (pars. 20–21). In an essay, reflect on the extent to which collaborative learning as Bruffee describes it would prepare you for professional work in a field you are interested in entering or exploring. In what ways would collaborative learning help you enter that field? In what ways do you think other learning methods might be more effective? Be as specific as you can about the kinds of knowledge and skill required by the field.

4. In the latter part of the article, Bruffee raises issues that he says are too complex to address in the context of the article. One is the issue of classroom authority: "collaborative learning challenges our traditional view of the instructor's authority in a classroom and the way that authority is exercised" (par. 34). He raises this issue in the course of discussing the effects of different levels of autonomy for students doing group work. Another issue is the source of knowledge itself: "How can knowledge gained through a social process have a source that is not itself also social?" (par. 44). As you reread the article, consider these issues in light of your own experience and reasoning. Write an essay on one of these two questions, fleshing out views that Bruffee only touches on.

The Talent Myth:
Are Smart People Overrated?

Malcolm Gladwell

Business cultures are often influenced by, if not created by, the latest and hottest management theory. Malcolm Gladwell examines what he calls "the new orthodoxy of American management," which claims that competitiveness in today's economy hinges on hiring highly talented people and giving them free rein. Through the first half of 2001, one of the most enthusiastic — and, by most accounts, wildly successful — proponents of "the talent mind-set" was the corporate giant Enron. By 2002, Enron, along with its prestigious auditor, Arthur Andersen, were in shambles and its investment bankers were under investigation. Gladwell poses the question, "What if Enron failed not in spite of its talent mind-set but because of it?" We tend to think that smart people make organizations smart; Gladwell asks us to consider that an effective organization may well make people smart. In other words, the right kind of collaboration can trump individual talent.

Malcolm Gladwell has been a staff writer for the *New Yorker* since 1996 and wrote for the *Washington Post* from 1987 to 1996. The subtitles for his articles reflect his fascination with the many faces of our culture, from "The paradoxes of intelligence reform," "Big business and the myth of the lone investor," and "How far can airline safety go?" to "How caffeine created the modern world," "What does *Saturday Night Live* have in common with German philosophy?" and "The disposable diaper and the meaning of progress."

Building on his success at the *New Yorker*, Gladwell has recently published two well-received books. *The Tipping Point: How Little Things Can Make a Big Difference* (2002) explores the notion that ideas, products, messages, and behaviors can spread in much the same way that viruses do. That is, when even a few people start behaving differently, their preferences and ideas can spread outward until a "tipping point" is reached, one that can change the world. Drawing on research from a wide range of fields, *Blink: The Power of Thinking without Thinking* (2005) explores our "adaptive unconscious" that enables us to make snap — and often very perceptive and correct — judgments. The essay reprinted here was first published in the July 22, 2002, issue of the *New Yorker.*

Five years ago, several executives at McKinsey & Company, America's largest and most prestigious management-consulting firm, launched what they called the War for Talent. Thousands of questionnaires were sent to managers across the country. Eighteen companies were singled out for special attention, and the consultants spent up to three days at each firm, interviewing everyone from the CEO down to the human-resources staff. McKinsey wanted to document how the top-performing companies in America differed from other firms in the way they handle matters like hiring and promotion. But, as the consultants sifted through the piles of reports and questionnaires and interview transcripts, they grew convinced that the difference between winners and losers was more profound than they had realized. "We looked at one another and suddenly the light bulb blinked on," the three consultants who headed the project — Ed Michaels, Helen Handfield-Jones, and Beth Axelrod — write in their new book, also called *The War for Talent.* The very best companies, they concluded, had leaders who were obsessed with the talent issue. They recruited ceaselessly, finding and hiring as many top performers as possible. They singled out and segregated their stars, rewarding them disproportionately, and pushing them into ever more senior positions. "Bet on the natural athletes, the ones with the strongest intrinsic skills," the authors approvingly quote one senior General Electric executive as saying. "Don't be afraid to promote stars without specifically relevant experience, seemingly over their heads." Success in the modern economy, according to Michaels, Handfield-Jones, and Axelrod, requires "the talent mind-set": the "deep-seated belief that having better talent at all levels is how you outperform your competitors."

This "talent mind-set" is the new orthodoxy of American management. It is the intellectual justification for why such a high premium is placed on degrees from first-tier business schools, and why the compensation packages for top executives have become so lavish. In the modern corporation, the system is considered only as strong as its stars, and, in the past few years, this message has been preached by consultants and management gurus all over the world. None, however, have spread the word quite so ardently as McKinsey, and, of all its clients, one firm took the talent mind-set closest to heart. It was a company where McKinsey conducted twenty separate projects, where McKinsey's billings topped ten million dollars a year, where a McKinsey director regularly attended board meetings, and where the CEO himself was a former McKinsey partner. The company, of course, was Enron.

The Enron scandal is now almost a year old. The reputations of Jeffrey Skilling and Kenneth Lay, the company's two top executives, have been destroyed. Arthur Andersen, Enron's auditor, has been driven out of business, and now investigators have turned their attention to Enron's investment bankers. The one Enron partner that has escaped largely unscathed is McKinsey, which is odd, given that it essentially created the blueprint for the Enron culture. Enron was the ultimate "talent" company. When Skilling started the corporate division known as Enron Capital and Trade, in 1990, he "decided to bring in a steady stream of the very best college and MBA graduates he could find to stock the company with talent," Michaels, Handfield-Jones, and Axelrod tell us. During the nineties, Enron was bringing in 250 newly minted MBAs a year. "We had these things called Super Saturdays," one former Enron manager recalls. "I'd interview some of these guys who were fresh out of Harvard, and these kids could blow me out of the water. They knew things I'd never heard of." Once at Enron, the top performers were rewarded inordinately, and promoted without regard for seniority or experience. Enron was a star system. "The only thing that differentiates Enron from our competitors is our people, our talent," Lay, Enron's former chairman and CEO, told the McKinsey consultants when they came to the company's headquarters, in Houston. Or, as another senior Enron executive put it to Richard Foster, a McKinsey partner who celebrated Enron in his 2001 book, *Creative Destruction*, "We hire very smart people and we pay them more than they think they are worth."

The management of Enron, in other words, did exactly what the consultants at McKinsey said that companies ought to do in order to succeed in the modern economy. It hired and rewarded the very best and the very brightest—and it is now in bankruptcy. The reasons for its collapse are complex, needless to say. But what if Enron failed not in spite of its talent mind-set but because of it? What if smart people are overrated?

At the heart of the McKinsey vision is a process that the War for Talent advocates refer to as "differentiation and affirmation." Employers, they argue, need to sit down once or twice a year and hold a "candid, probing, no-holds-barred debate about each individual," sorting employees into A, B, and C groups. The As must be challenged and disproportionately rewarded. The Bs need to be encouraged and affirmed. The Cs need to shape up or be shipped out. Enron followed this advice almost to the letter, setting up internal Performance Review Committees. The members got together twice a year, and graded each person in their section on ten separate criteria, using a scale of one to five. The process was called "rank and yank." Those graded at the top of their unit received bonuses two-thirds higher than those in the next 30 percent; those who ranked at the bottom received no bonuses and no extra stock options — and in some cases were pushed out.

How should that ranking be done? Unfortunately, the McKinsey consultants spend very little time discussing the matter. One possibility is simply to hire and reward the smartest people. But the link between, say, IQ and job performance is distinctly underwhelming. On a scale where 0.1 or below means virtually no correlation and 0.7 or above implies a strong correlation (your height, for example, has a 0.7 correlation with your parents' height), the correlation between IQ and occupational success is between 0.2 and 0.3. "What IQ doesn't pick up is effectiveness at common-sense sorts of things, especially working with people," Richard Wagner, a psychologist at Florida State University, says. "In terms of how we evaluate schooling, everything is about working by yourself. If you work with someone else, it's called cheating. Once you get out in the real world, everything you do involves working with other people."

Wagner and Robert Sternberg, a psychologist at Yale University, have developed tests of this practical component, which they call "tacit knowledge." Tacit knowledge involves things like knowing how to manage yourself and others, and how to navigate complicated social situations. Here is a question from one of their tests:

> You have just been promoted to head of an important department in your organization. The previous head has been transferred to an equivalent position in a less important department. Your understanding of the reason for the move is that the performance of the department as a whole has been mediocre. There have not been any glaring deficiencies, just a perception of the department as so-so rather than very good. Your charge is to shape up the department. Results are expected quickly. Rate the quality of the following strategies for succeeding at your new position.
>
> a. Always delegate to the most junior person who can be trusted with the task.
> b. Give your superiors frequent progress reports.
> c. Announce a major reorganization of the department that includes getting rid of whomever you believe to be "dead wood."
> d. Concentrate more on your people than on the tasks to be done.
> e. Make people feel completely responsible for their work.

Wagner finds that how well people do on a test like this predicts how well they will do in the workplace: good managers pick (b) and (e); bad managers tend to pick (c). Yet there's no clear connection between such tacit knowledge and other forms of knowledge and experience. The process of assessing ability in the workplace is a lot messier than it appears.

An employer really wants to assess not potential but performance. Yet that's just as tricky. In *The War for Talent*, the authors talk about how the Royal Air Force used the A, B, and C ranking system for its pilots during the Battle of Britain. But ranking fighter pilots — for whom there are a limited and relatively objective set of performance criteria (enemy kills, for example, and the ability to get their formations safely home) — is a lot easier than assessing how the manager of a new unit is doing at, say, marketing or business development. And whom do you ask to rate the manager's performance? Studies show that there is very little correlation between how someone's peers rate him and how his boss rates him. The only rigorous way to assess performance, according to human-resources specialists, is to use criteria that are as specific as possible. Managers are supposed to take detailed notes on their employees throughout the year, in order to remove subjective personal reactions from the process of assessment. You can grade someone's performance only if you *know* their performance. And, in the freewheeling culture of Enron, this was all but impossible. People deemed "talented" were constantly being pushed into new jobs and given new challenges. Annual turnover from promotions was close to 20 percent. Lynda Clemmons, the so-called weather babe who started Enron's weather derivatives business, jumped, in seven quick years, from trader to associate to manager to director and, finally, to head of her own business unit. How do you evaluate someone's performance in a system where no one is in a job long enough to allow such evaluation?

The answer is that you end up doing performance evaluations that aren't 10 based on performance. Among the many glowing books about Enron written before its fall was the best seller *Leading the Revolution*, by the management consultant Gary Hamel, which tells the story of Lou Pai, who launched Enron's power-trading business. Pai's group began with a disaster: It lost tens of millions of dollars trying to sell electricity to residential consumers in newly deregulated markets. The problem, Hamel explains, is that the markets weren't truly deregulated: "The states that were opening their markets to competition were still setting rules designed to give their traditional utilities big advantages." It doesn't seem to have occurred to anyone that Pai ought to have looked into those rules more carefully before risking millions of dollars. He was promptly given the chance to build the commercial electricity-outsourcing business, where he ran up several more years of heavy losses before cashing out of Enron last year with $270 million. Because Pai had "talent," he was given new opportunities, and when he failed at those new opportunities he was given still more opportunities . . . because he had "talent." "At Enron, failure — even of the type that ends up on the front page of the *Wall Street Journal* — doesn't necessarily sink a career," Hamel writes, as if that were a good thing. Presumably, companies that want to encourage risk taking must be willing to tolerate mistakes. Yet if talent is defined as something separate from an employee's actual performance, what use is it, exactly?

What the War for Talent amounts to is an argument for indulging A employees, for fawning over them. "You need to do everything you can to keep them engaged and satisfied — even delighted," Michaels, Handfield-Jones, and Axelrod write. "Find out what they would most like to be doing, and shape their career and responsibilities in that direction. Solve any issues that might be pushing them out the door, such as a boss that frustrates them or travel demands that burden them." No company was better at this than Enron. In one oft-told story, Louise Kitchin, a twenty-nine-year-old gas trader in Europe, became convinced that the company ought to develop an online-trading business. She told her boss, and she began working in her spare time on the project, until she had 250 people throughout Enron helping her. After six months, Skilling was finally informed. "I was never asked for any capital," Skilling said later. "I was never asked for any people. They had already purchased the servers. They had already started ripping apart the building. They had started legal reviews in twenty-two countries by the time I heard about it." It was, Skilling went on approvingly, "exactly the kind of behavior that will continue to drive this company forward."

Kitchin's qualification for running EnronOnline, it should be pointed out, was not that she was good at it. It was that she wanted to do it, and Enron was a place where stars did whatever they wanted. "Fluid movement is absolutely necessary in our company. And the type of people we hire enforces that," Skilling told the team from McKinsey. "Not only does this system help the excitement level for each manager, it shapes Enron's business in the direction that its managers find most exciting." Here is Skilling again: "If lots of [employees] are flocking to a new business unit, that's a good sign that the opportunity is a good one. . . . If a business unit can't attract people very easily, that's a good sign that it's a business Enron shouldn't be in." You might expect a CEO to say that if a business unit can't attract *customers* very easily that's a good sign it's a business the company shouldn't be in. A company's business is supposed to be shaped in the direction that its managers find most *profitable*. But at Enron the needs of the customers and the shareholders were secondary to the needs of its stars.

A dozen years ago, the psychologists Robert Hogan, Robert Raskin, and Dan Fazzini wrote a brilliant essay called "The Dark Side of Charisma." It argued that flawed managers fall into three types. One is the High Likability Floater, who rises effortlessly in an organization because he never takes any difficult decisions or makes any enemies. Another is the Homme de Ressentiment, who seethes below the surface and plots against his enemies.

The most interesting of the three is the Narcissist, whose energy and self-confidence and charm lead him inexorably up the corporate ladder. Narcissists are terrible managers. They resist accepting suggestions, thinking it will make them appear weak, and they don't believe that others have anything useful to tell them. "Narcissists are biased to take more credit for success than is legitimate," Hogan and his coauthors write, and "biased to avoid acknowledging responsibility for their failures and shortcomings for the same reasons that they claim more success than is their due." Moreover:

> Narcissists typically make judgments with greater confidence than other people . . . and, because their judgments are rendered with such conviction, other people tend to believe them and the narcissists become disproportionately more influential in group situations. Finally, because of their self-confidence and strong need for recognition, narcissists tend to "self-nominate"; consequently, when a leadership gap appears in a group or organization, the narcissists rush to fill it.

Tyco Corporation and WorldCom were the Greedy Corporations; They were purely interested in short-term financial gain. Enron was the Narcissistic Corporation — a company that took more credit for success than was legitimate, that did not acknowledge responsibility for its failures, that shrewdly sold the rest of us on its genius, and that substituted self-nomination for disciplined management. At one point in *Leading the Revolution*, Hamel tracks down a senior Enron executive, and what he breathlessly recounts — the braggadocio, the self-satisfaction — could be an epitaph for the talent mind-set:

> "You cannot control the atoms within a nuclear fusion reaction," said Ken Rice when he was head of Enron Capital and Trade Resources (ECT), America's largest marketer of natural gas and largest buyer and seller of electricity. Adorned in a black T-shirt, blue jeans, and cowboy boots, Rice drew a box on an office whiteboard that pictured his business unit as a nuclear reactor. Little circles in the box represented its "contract originators," the gunslingers charged with doing deals and creating new businesses. Attached to each circle was an arrow. In Rice's diagram the arrows were pointing in all different directions. "We allow people to go in whichever direction that they want to go."

The distinction between the Greedy Corporation and the Narcissistic Corporation matters, because the way we conceive our attainments helps determine how we behave. Carol Dweck, a psychologist at Columbia University, has found that people generally hold one of two fairly firm beliefs about their intelligence: They consider it either a fixed trait or something that is malleable and can be developed over time. Five years ago, Dweck did a study at the University of Hong Kong, where all classes are conducted in

English. She and her colleagues approached a large group of social-sciences students, told them their English-proficiency scores, and asked them if they wanted to take a course to improve their language skills. One would expect all those who scored poorly to sign up for the remedial course. The University of Hong Kong is a demanding institution, and it is hard to do well in the social sciences without strong English skills. Curiously, however, only the ones who believed in malleable intelligence expressed interest in the class. The students who believed that their intelligence was a fixed trait were so concerned about appearing to be deficient that they preferred to stay home. "Students who hold a fixed view of their intelligence care so much about looking smart that they act dumb," Dweck writes, "for what could be dumber than giving up a chance to learn something that is essential for your own success?"

In a similar experiment, Dweck gave a class of preadolescent students a test filled with challenging problems. After they were finished, one group was praised for its effort and another group was praised for **The talent myth assumes** its intelligence. Those praised for their intelligence **that people make** were reluctant to tackle difficult tasks, and their per- **organizations smart.** formance on subsequent tests soon began to suffer. Then Dweck asked the children to write a letter to students at another school, describing their experience in the study. She discovered something remarkable: 40 percent of those students who were praised for their intelligence lied about how they had scored on the test, adjusting their grade upward. They weren't naturally deceptive people, and they weren't any less intelligent or self-confident than anyone else. They simply did what people do when they are immersed in an environment that celebrates them solely for their innate "talent." They begin to define themselves by that description, and when times get tough and that self-image is threatened they have difficulty with the consequences. They will not take the remedial course. They will not stand up to investors and the public and admit that they were wrong. They'd sooner lie.

The broader failing of McKinsey and its acolytes at Enron is their assumption that an organization's intelligence is simply a function of the intelligence of its employees. They believe in stars, because they don't believe in systems. In a way, that's understandable, because our lives are so obviously enriched by individual brilliance. Groups don't write great novels, and a committee didn't come up with the theory of relativity. But companies work by different rules. They don't just create; they execute and compete and coordinate the efforts of many different people, and the organizations that are most successful at that task are the ones where the system *is* the star.

There is a wonderful example of this in the story of the so-called Eastern Pearl Harbor, of the Second World War. During the first nine months of 1942, the United States Navy suffered a catastrophe. German U-boats, operating just off the Atlantic coast and in the Caribbean, were sinking our merchant ships almost at will. U-boat captains marvelled at their good fortune. "Before this sea of light, against this footlight glare of a carefree new world were passing the silhouettes of ships recognizable in every detail and sharp as the outlines in a sales catalog," one U-boat commander wrote. "All we had to do was press the button."

What made this such a puzzle is that, on the other side of the Atlantic, the British had much less trouble defending their ships against U-boat attacks. The British, furthermore, eagerly passed on to the Americans everything they knew about sonar and depth-charge throwers and the construction of destroyers. And still the Germans managed to paralyze America's coastal zones.

You can imagine what the consultants at McKinsey would have concluded: They would have said that the navy did not have a talent mind-set, that President Roosevelt needed to recruit and promote top performers into key positions in the Atlantic command. In fact, he had already done that. At the beginning of the war, he had pushed out the solid and unspectacular admiral Harold R. Stark as chief of naval operations and replaced him with the legendary Ernest Joseph King. "He was a supreme realist with the arrogance of genius," Ladislas Farago writes in *The Tenth Fleet*, a history of the navy's U-boat battles in the Second World War. "He had unbounded faith in himself, in his vast knowledge of naval matters, and in the soundness of his ideas. Unlike Stark, who tolerated incompetence all around him, King had no patience with fools."

The navy had plenty of talent at the top, in other words. What it didn't have was the right kind of organization. As Eliot A. Cohen, a scholar of military strategy at Johns Hopkins, writes in his brilliant book *Military Misfortunes in the Atlantic:*

> To wage the antisubmarine war well, analysts had to bring together fragments of information, direction-finding fixes, visual sightings, decrypts, and the "flaming datum" of a U-boat attack — for use by a commander to coordinate the efforts of warships, aircraft, and convoy commanders. Such synthesis had to occur in near "real time" — within hours, even minutes in some cases.

The British excelled at the task because they had a centralized operational system. The controllers moved the British ships around the Atlantic like chess pieces, in order to outsmart U-boat "wolf packs." By contrast, Admiral King believed strongly in a decentralized management structure: He held that managers should never tell their subordinates "'how' as well as what to 'do.'" In today's jargon, we would say he was a believer in "loose-tight" management, of the kind celebrated by the McKinsey consultants

Thomas J. Peters and Robert H. Waterman in their 1982 best seller, *In Search of Excellence*. But "loose-tight" doesn't help you find U-boats. Throughout most of 1942, the navy kept trying to act smart by relying on technical know-how, and stubbornly refused to take operational lessons from the British. The navy also lacked the organizational structure necessary to apply the technical knowledge it did have to the field. Only when the navy set up the Tenth Fleet — a single unit to coordinate all antisubmarine warfare in the Atlantic — did the situation change. In the year and a half before the Tenth Fleet was formed, in May of 1943, the navy sank thirty-six U-boats. In the six months afterward, it sank seventy-five. "The creation of the Tenth Fleet did *not* bring more talented individuals into the field of ASW" — antisubmarine warfare — "than had previous organizations," Cohen writes. "What Tenth Fleet did allow, by virtue of its organization and mandate, was for these individuals to become far more effective than previously." The talent myth assumes that people make organizations smart. More often than not, it's the other way around.

There is ample evidence of this principle among America's most successful companies. Southwest Airlines hires very few MBAs, pays its managers modestly, and gives raises according to seniority, not "rank and yank." Yet it is by far the most successful of all United States airlines, because it has created a vastly more efficient organization than its competitors have. At Southwest, the time it takes to get a plane that has just landed ready for takeoff — a key index of productivity — is, on average, twenty minutes, and requires a ground crew of four, and two people at the gate. (At United Airlines, by contrast, turnaround time is closer to thirty-five minutes, and requires a ground crew of twelve and three agents at the gate.)

In the case of the giant retailer Wal-Mart, one of the most critical periods in its history came in 1976, when Sam Walton "unretired," pushing out his handpicked successor, Ron Mayer. Mayer was just over forty. He was ambitious. He was charismatic. He was, in the words of one Walton biographer, "the boy-genius financial officer." But Walton was convinced that Mayer was, as people at McKinsey would say, "differentiating and affirming" in the corporate suite, in defiance of Wal-Mart's inclusive culture. Mayer left, and Wal-Mart survived. After all, Wal-Mart is an organization, not an all-star team. Walton brought in David Glass, late of the army and Southern Missouri State University, as CEO; the company is now ranked No. 1 on the Fortune 500 list.

Procter & Gamble doesn't have a star system, either. How could it? 25 Would the top MBA graduates of Harvard and Stanford move to Cincinnati to work on detergent when they could make three times as much reinventing the world in Houston? Procter & Gamble isn't glamorous. Its CEO is a lifer—a former navy officer who began his corporate career as an assistant brand manager for Joy dishwashing liquid—and, if Procter & Gamble's best played Enron's best at Trivial Pursuit, no doubt the team from Houston would win handily. But Procter & Gamble has dominated the consumer-products field for close to a century, because it has a carefully conceived managerial system, and a rigorous marketing methodology that has allowed it to win battles for brands like Crest and Tide decade after decade. In Procter & Gamble's navy, Admiral Stark would have stayed. But a cross-divisional management committee would have set the Tenth Fleet in place before the war ever started.

Among the most damning facts about Enron, in the end, was something its managers were proudest of. They had what, in McKinsey terminology, is called an "open market" for hiring. In the open-market system — McKinsey's assault on the very idea of a fixed organization—anyone could apply for any job that he or she wanted, and no manager was allowed to hold anyone back. Poaching was encouraged. When an Enron executive named Kevin Hannon started the company's global broadband unit, he launched what he called Project Quick Hire. A hundred top performers from around the company were invited to the Houston Hyatt to hear Hannon give his pitch. Recruiting booths were set up outside the meeting room. "Hannon had his fifty top performers for the broadband unit by the end of the week," Michaels, Handfield-Jones, and Axelrod write, "and his peers had fifty holes to fill." Nobody, not even the consultants who were paid to think about the Enron culture, seemed worried that those fifty holes might disrupt the functioning of the affected departments, that stability in a firm's existing businesses might be a good thing, that the self-fulfillment of Enron's star employees might possibly be in conflict with the best interests of the firm as a whole.

These are the sort of concerns that management consultants ought to raise. But Enron's management consultant was McKinsey, and McKinsey was as much a prisoner of the talent myth as its clients were. In 1998, Enron hired ten Wharton MBAs; that same year, McKinsey hired forty. In 1999, Enron hired twelve from Wharton; McKinsey hired sixty-one. The consultants at McKinsey were preaching at Enron what they believed about themselves. "When we would hire them, it wouldn't just be for a week," one former Enron manager recalls, of the brilliant young men and women from McKinsey who wandered the hallways at the company's headquarters. "It would be for two to four months. They were always around." They were there looking for people who had the talent to think outside the box. It never occurred to them that, if everyone had to think outside the box, maybe it was the box that needed fixing.

Working with the Text

1. At a pivotal point in his argument, Malcolm Gladwell claims that "The talent myth assumes that people make organizations smart. More often than not, it's the other way around" (par. 22). In light of Gladwell's contrast between failed "talent" ventures and successful "systems," write a brief essay in which you analyze his claim. What does Gladwell mean by *smart*? How is it possible for talented people to fail to make an organization smart? How can systems within organizations make people smart?

2. Gladwell points out that the management consulting firm McKinsey & Company "escaped largely unscathed . . . which is odd, given that it essentially created the blueprint for the Enron culture" (par. 3). In a brief essay, reflect on the differences between McKinsey and Enron that made it possible for McKinsey to continue working in the "talent mind-set." What did the "talent" at Enron do? What does the "talent" at McKinsey do? Why might the differences in their job descriptions create differences in how long they could think and work "outside the box"?

3. McKinsey advocates a process called "differentiation and affirmation" that drives a talent-centered work culture. Review this process, as well as how the "A, B, and C ranking system" was applied by the Royal Air Force in World War II. Based on your own observation and experience as well as Gladwell's critique, write a brief essay in which you argue for or against using such systems in the workplace.

4. To show how Enron applied the "talent mind-set," Gladwell tells the stories of a few of Enron's "stars." As you reread the article, review these stories in light of Gladwell's critique of the "talent myth." In a brief essay, provide a profile Enron might have used in hiring new staff. How do you think Enron defined *talent*? What signs or measures of talent do you think they were seeking?

From Text to Field

1. In his critique of the "talent myth," Gladwell touches on a number of approaches to management. Drawing on Gladwell's analysis as well as your own experience and observations, write an essay in which you advocate a management theory of your own.

2. In questioning the value of IQ scores to predict work performance, Gladwell notes the conclusion of Florida State University psychologist Richard Wagner: "In terms of how we evaluate schooling, everything is about working by yourself. If you work with someone else, it's called cheating. Once you get out in the real world, everything you do involves working with other people" (par. 6).

While students do spend a significant amount of time doing individual work, they also gain experience in working with groups—and being evaluated as a group—not only in the classroom but also in extracurricular activities. In a personal essay, reflect on the differences you have experienced between performing as an individual and performing as a member of a group. What skills do you use in each situation? Which skills are essential to performing well in each situation?

3. To illustrate the differences in skill required for performing individually and in groups, Gladwell includes a question from a test of "tacit knowledge," developed by psychologists Richard Wagner of Florida State University and Robert Sternberg of Yale University (par. 7). Based on your own responses to the question, write an essay in which you analyze your "tacit knowledge." Why would "good managers" pick *b* and *e*? Why would "bad managers" pick *c*? Which strategies would you choose, and why? What do your responses suggest about how you would perform as a manager? What strengths and weaknesses do your preferences in strategy suggest?

4. Gladwell notes three types of "flawed managers" identified by psychologists Robert Hogan, Robert Raskin, and Dan Fazzini: the High Likability Floater, the Homme de Ressentiment, and the Narcissist. Based on the definitions of each type, write a character sketch of someone you know or have known who is either already one of these types or who you predict will become one of these types of flawed manager.

The Essential Tension: Tradition and Innovation in Scientific Research

Thomas S. Kuhn

In 1959, the Third University of Utah Research Conference on the Identification of Scientific Talent invited Thomas S. Kuhn to address the issue of cultivating creative thinking in science students. The conference sought to encourage "divergent thinking"—the "flexibility and open-mindedness" to depart from conventional methods and theories. Somewhat to the surprise of conference participants, Kuhn made the case for "convergent thinking"—training in and commitment to accepted methods and theories—as the necessary precursor to the divergent thinking that produces scientific revolutions or any progress in the development of science. His study of the history of science helped him formulate the concept of "paradigms" and had convinced him that the very best scientists are capable of sustaining the "essential tension" between working rigorously within a paradigm and recognizing the evidence that will overturn that paradigm.

Kuhn's theory of scientific progress challenged assumptions about development and change, not only within the sciences but also in disciplines ranging from economics and sociology to history, philosophy, and the arts. Kuhn's most widely known and influential book is *The Structure of Scientific Revolutions* (1962), which examines the making and changing of knowledge in scientific communities. Required reading in a number of disciplines and now translated into some sixteen languages, this book explores how scientific knowledge is based not on objective reality alone but also on the contingent judgment of specific communities of knowers.

Shortly after earning his PhD in physics, Kuhn changed his focus to the history of science, which he taught first at Harvard University, then at the University of California at Berkeley, Princeton University, and the Massachusetts Institute of Technology (MIT). He held honorary degrees from institutions such as the University of Chicago, Columbia University, and the University of Athens. In 1982, he was awarded the George Sarton Medal in the History of Science. Thomas Kuhn died in 1996.

I am grateful for the invitation to participate in this important conference, and I interpret it as evidence that students of creativity themselves possess the sensitivity to divergent approaches that they seek to identify in others. But I am not altogether sanguine about the outcome of your experiment with me. As most of you already know, I am no psychologist, but rather an ex-physicist now working in the history of science. Probably my concern is no less with creativity than your own, but my goals, my techniques, and my sources of evidence are so very different from yours that I am far from sure how much we do, or even *should*, have to say to each other. These reservations imply no apology: Rather they hint at my central thesis. In the sciences, as I shall suggest below, it is often better to do one's best with the tools at hand than to pause for contemplation of divergent approaches.

If a person of my background and interests has anything relevant to suggest to this conference, it will not be about your central concerns, the creative personality and its early identification. But implicit in the numerous working papers distributed to participants in this conference is an image of the scientific process and of the scientist; that image almost certainly conditions many of the experiments you try as well as the conclusions you draw; and about it the physicist-historian may well have something to say. I shall restrict my attention to one aspect of this image—an aspect epitomized as follows in one of the working papers: The basic scientist "must lack prejudice to a degree where he can look at the most 'self-evident' facts or concepts without necessarily accepting them, and, conversely, allow his imagination to play with the most unlikely possibilities" (Selye, 1959). In the more technical language supplied by other working papers (Getzels and Jackson), this aspect of the image recurs as an emphasis upon "divergent thinking, . . . the freedom to go off in different directions, . . . rejecting the old solution and striking out in some new direction."

I do not at all doubt that this description of "divergent thinking" and the concomitant search for those able to do it are entirely proper. Some divergence characterizes all scientific work, and gigantic divergences lie at the core of the most significant episodes in scientific development. But both my own experience in scientific research and my reading of the history of sciences lead me to wonder whether flexibility and open-mindedness have not been too exclusively emphasized as the characteristics requisite for basic research. I shall therefore suggest below that something like "convergent thinking" is just as essential to scientific advance as is divergent. Since these two modes of thought are inevitably in conflict, it will follow that the ability to support a tension that can occasionally become almost unbearable is one of the prime requisites for the very best sort of scientific research.

I am elsewhere studying these points more historically, with emphasis on the importance to scientific development of "revolutions."[1] These are episodes — exemplified in their most extreme and readily recognized form by the advent of Copernicanism, Darwinism, or Einsteinianism—in which a scientific community abandons one time-honored way of regarding the world and of pursuing science in favor of some other, usually incompatible, approach to its discipline. I have argued in the draft that the historian constantly encounters many far smaller but structurally similar revolutionary episodes and that they are central to scientific advance. Contrary to a prevalent impression, most new discoveries and theories in the sciences are not merely additions to the existing stockpile of scientific knowledge. To assimilate them the scientist must usually rearrange the intellectual and manipulative equipment he has previously relied upon, discarding some elements of his prior belief and practice while finding new significances in and new relationships between many others. Because the old must be revalued and reordered when assimilating the new, discovery and invention in the sciences are usually intrinsically revolutionary. Therefore, they do demand just that flexibility and open-mindedness that characterize, or indeed define, the divergent thinker. Let us henceforth take for granted the need for these characteristics. Unless many scientists possessed them to a marked degree, there would be no scientific revolutions and very little scientific advance.

Yet flexibility is not enough, and what remains is not obviously compatible with it. Drawing from various fragments of a project still in progress, I must now emphasize that revolutions are but one of two complementary aspects of scientific advance. Almost none of the research undertaken by even the greatest scientists is designed to be revolutionary, and very little of it has any such effect. On the contrary, normal research, even the best of it, is a highly convergent activity based firmly upon a settled consensus acquired from scientific education and reinforced by subsequent life in the profession. Typically, to be sure, this convergent or consensus-bound research ultimately results in revolution. Then, traditional techniques and beliefs are abandoned and replaced by new ones. But revolutionary shifts of a scientific tradition are relatively rare, and extended periods of convergent research are the necessary preliminary to them. As I shall indicate below, only investigations firmly rooted in the contemporary scientific tradition are likely to break that tradition and give rise to a new one. That is why I speak of an "essential tension" implicit in scientific research. To do his job the scientist must undertake a complex set of intellectual and manipulative commitments. Yet his claim to fame, if he has the talent and good luck to gain one, may finally rest upon his ability to abandon this net of commitments in favor of another of his own invention. Very often the successful scientist must simultaneously display the characteristics of the traditionalist and of the iconoclast.[2]

The multiple historical examples upon which any full documentation of these points must depend are prohibited by the time limitations of the conference. But another approach will introduce you to at least part of what I have in mind — an examination of the nature of education in the natural sciences. One of the working papers for this conference (Getzels and Jackson) quotes Guilford's very apt description of scientific education as follows: "[It] has emphasized abilities in the areas of convergent thinking and evaluation, often at the expense of development in the area of divergent thinking. We have attempted to teach students how to arrive at 'correct' answers that our civilization has taught us are correct. . . . Outside the arts [and I should include most of the social sciences] we have generally discouraged the development of divergent-thinking abilities, unintentionally." That characterization seems to me eminently just, but I wonder whether it is equally just to deplore the product that results. Without defending plain bad teaching, and granting that in this country the trend to convergent thinking in all education may have proceeded entirely too far, we may nevertheless recognize that a rigorous training in convergent thought has been intrinsic to the sciences almost from their origin. I suggest that they could not have achieved their present state or status without it.

Let me try briefly to epitomize the nature of education in the natural sciences, ignoring the many significant yet minor differences between the various sciences and between the approaches of different educational institutions. The single most striking feature of this education is that, to an extent totally unknown in other creative fields, it is conducted entirely through textbooks. Typically, undergraduate *and* graduate students of chemistry, physics, astronomy, geology, or biology acquire the substance of their fields from books written especially for students. Until they are ready, or very nearly ready, to commence work on their own dissertations, they are neither asked to attempt trial research projects nor exposed to the immediate products of research done by others, that is, to the professional communications that scientists write for each other. There are no collections of "readings" in the natural sciences. Nor are science students encouraged to read the historical classics of their fields — works in which they might discover other ways of regarding the problems discussed in their textbooks, but in which they would also meet problems, concepts, and standards of solution that their future professions have long since discarded and replaced.

In contrast, the various textbooks that the student does encounter display different subject matters, rather than, as in many of the social sciences, exemplifying different approaches to a single problem field. Even books that compete for adoption in a single course differ mainly in level and in pedagogic detail, not in substance or conceptual structure. Last, but most important of all, is the characteristic technique of textbook presentation. Except in their occasional introductions, science textbooks do not describe the sorts of problems that the professional may be asked to solve and the variety of techniques available for their solution. Rather, these books exhibit concrete problem solutions that the profession has come to accept as paradigms, and they then ask the student, either with a pencil and paper or in the laboratory, to solve for himself problems very closely related in both method and substance to those through which the textbook or the accompanying lecture has led him. Nothing could be better calculated to produce "mental sets" or *Einstellungen*. Only in their most elementary courses do other academic fields offer as much as a partial parallel.

Even the most faintly liberal educational theory must view this pedagogic technique as anathema. Students, we would all agree, must begin by learning a good deal of what is already known, but we also insist that education give them vastly more. They must, we say, learn to recognize and evaluate problems to which no unequivocal solution has yet been given; they must be supplied with an arsenal of techniques for approaching these future problems; and they must learn to judge the relevance of these techniques and to evaluate the possibly partial solutions which they can provide. In many respects these attitudes toward education seem to me entirely right, and yet we must recognize two things about them. First, education in the natural sciences seems to have been totally unaffected by their existence. It remains a dogmatic initiation in a preestablished tradition that the student is not equipped to evaluate. Second, at least in the period when it was followed by a term in an apprenticeship relation, this technique of exclusive exposure to a rigid tradition has been immensely productive of the most consequential sorts of innovations.

I shall shortly inquire about the pattern of scientific practice that grows out 10 of this educational initiation and will then attempt to say why that pattern proves quite so successful. But first, a historical excursion will reinforce what has just been said and prepare the way for what is to follow. I should like to suggest that the various fields of natural science have not always been characterized by rigid education in exclusive paradigms, but that each of them acquired something like that technique at precisely the point when the field began to make rapid and systematic progress. If one asks about the origin of our contemporary knowledge of chemical composition, of earthquakes, of biological reproduction, of motion through space, or of any other subject matter known to the natural sciences, one immediately encounters a characteristic pattern that I shall here illustrate with a single example.

Today, physics textbooks tell us that light exhibits some properties of a wave and some of a particle: Both textbook problems and research problems are designed accordingly. But both this view and these textbooks are products of an early twentieth-century revolution. (One characteristic of scientific revolutions is that they call for the rewriting of science textbooks.) For more than half a century before 1900, the books employed in scientific education had been equally unequivocal in stating that light was wave motion. Under those circumstances scientists worked on somewhat different problems and often embraced rather different sorts of solutions to them. The nineteenth-century textbook tradition does not, however, mark the beginning of our subject matter. Throughout the eighteenth century and into the early nineteenth, Newton's *Opticks* and the other books from which men learned science taught almost all students that light was particles, and research guided by this tradition was again different from that which succeeded it. Ignoring a variety of subsidiary changes within these three successive traditions, we may therefore say that our views derive historically from Newton's views by way of two revolutions in optical thought, each of which replaced one tradition of convergent research with another. If we make appropriate allowances for changes in the locus and materials of scientific education, we may say that each of these three traditions was embodied in the sort of education by exposure to unequivocal paradigms that I briefly epitomized above. Since Newton, education and research in physical optics have normally been highly convergent.

The history of theories of light does not, however, begin with Newton. If we ask about knowledge in the field before his time, we encounter a significantly different pattern — a pattern still familiar in the arts and in some social sciences, but one which has largely disappeared in the natural sciences. From remote antiquity until the end of the seventeenth century there was no single set of paradigms for the study of physical optics. Instead, many men advanced a large number of different views about the nature of light. Some of these views **The successful scientist must simultaneously display the characteristics of the traditionalist and of the iconoclast.** found few adherents, but a number of them gave rise to continuing schools of optical thought. Although the historian can note the emergence of new points of view as well as changes in the relative popularity of older ones, there was never anything resembling consensus. As a result, a new man entering the field was inevitably exposed to a variety of conflicting viewpoints: He was forced to examine the evidence for each, and there always was good evidence. The fact that he made a choice and conducted himself accordingly could not entirely prevent his awareness of other possibilities. This earlier mode of education was obviously more suited to produce a scientist without prejudice, alert to novel phenomena, and flexible in his approach to his field. On the other hand, one can scarcely escape the impression that, during the period characterized by this more liberal educational practice, physical optics made very little progress.[3]

The preconsensus (we might here call it the divergent) phase in the development of physical optics is, I believe, duplicated in the history of all other scientific specialties, excepting only those that were born by the subdivision and recombination of preexisting disciplines. In some fields, like mathematics and astronomy, the first firm consensus is prehistoric. In others, like dynamics, geometric optics, and parts of physiology, the paradigms that produced a first consensus date from classical antiquity. Most other natural sciences, though their problems were often discussed in antiquity, did not achieve a first consensus until after the Renaissance. In physical optics, as we have seen, the first firm consensus dates only from the end of the seventeenth century; in electricity, chemistry, and the study of heat, it dates from the eighteenth; while in geology and the nontaxonomic parts of biology no very real consensus developed until after the first third of the nineteenth century. This century appears to be characterized by the emergence of a first consensus in parts of a few of the social sciences.

In all the fields named above, important work was done before the achievement of the maturity produced by consensus. Neither the nature nor the timing of the first consensus in these fields can be understood without a careful examination of both the intellectual and the manipulative techniques developed before the existence of unique paradigms. But the transition to maturity is not less significant because individuals practiced science before it occurred. On the contrary, history strongly suggests that, though one can practice science — as one does philosophy or art or political science — without a firm consensus, this more flexible practice will not produce the pattern of rapid consequential scientific advance to which recent centuries have accustomed us. In that pattern, development occurs from one consensus to another, and alternate approaches are not ordinarily in competition. Except under quite special conditions, the practitioner of a mature science does not pause to examine divergent modes of explanation or experimentation.

I shall shortly ask how this can be so — how a firm orientation toward an   15 apparently unique tradition can be compatible with the practice of the disciplines most noted for the persistent production of novel ideas and techniques. But it will help first to ask what the education that so successfully transmits such a tradition leaves to be done. What can a scientist working within a deeply rooted tradition and little trained in the perception of significant alternatives hope to do in his professional career? Once again limits of time force me to drastic simplification, but the following remarks will at least suggest a position that I am sure can be documented in detail.

In pure or basic science — that somewhat ephemeral category of research undertaken by men whose most immediate goal is to increase understanding rather than control of nature — the characteristic problems are almost always repetitions, with minor modifications, of problems that have been undertaken and partially resolved before. For example, much of the research undertaken within a scientific tradition is an attempt to adjust existing theory or existing observation in order to bring the two into closer and closer agreement. The constant examination of atomic and molecular spectra during the years since the birth of wave mechanics, together with the design of theoretical approximations for the prediction of complex spectra, provides one important instance of this typical sort of work. Another was provided by the remarks about the eighteenth-century development of Newtonian dynamics in the paper on measurement supplied to you in advance of the conference.[4] The attempt to make existing theory and observation conform more closely is not, of course, the only standard sort of research problem in the basic sciences. The development of chemical thermodynamics or the continuing attempts to unravel organic structure illustrate another type — the extension of existing theory to areas that it is expected to cover but in which it has never before been tried. In addition, to mention a third common sort of research problem, many scientists constantly collect the concrete data (e.g., atomic weights, nuclear moments) required for the application and extension of existing theory.

These are normal research projects in the basic sciences, and they illustrate the sorts of work on which all scientists, even the greatest, spend most of their professional lives and on which many spend all. Clearly their pursuit is neither intended nor likely to produce fundamental discoveries or revolutionary changes in scientific theory. Only if the validity of the contemporary scientific tradition is assumed do these problems make much theoretical or any practical sense. The man who suspected the existence of a totally new type of phenomenon or who had basic doubts about the validity of existing theory would not think problems so closely modeled on textbook paradigms worth undertaking. It follows that the man who does undertake a problem of this sort — and that means all scientists at most times — aims to elucidate the scientific tradition in which he was raised rather than to change it. Furthermore, the fascination of his work lies in the difficulties of elucidation rather than in any surprises that the work is likely to produce. Under normal conditions the research scientist is not an innovator but a solver of puzzles, and the puzzles upon which he concentrates are just those which he believes can be both stated and solved within the existing scientific tradition.

Yet — and this is the point — the ultimate effect of this tradition-bound work has invariably been to change the tradition. Again and again the continuing attempt to elucidate a currently received tradition has at last produced one of those shifts in fundamental theory, in problem field, and in scientific standards to which I previously referred as scientific revolutions. At least for the scientific community as a whole, work within a well-defined and deeply ingrained tradition seems more productive of tradition-shattering novelties than work in which no similarly convergent standards are involved. How can this be so? I think it is because no other sort of work is nearly so well suited to isolate for continuing and concentrated attention those loci of trouble or causes of crisis upon whose recognition the most fundamental advances in basic science depend.

As I have indicated in the first of my working papers, new theories and, to an increasing extent, novel discoveries in the mature sciences are not born de novo. On the contrary, they emerge from old theories and within a matrix of old beliefs about the phenomena that the world does *and does not* contain. Ordinarily such novelties are far too esoteric and recondite to be noted by the man without a great deal of scientific training. And even the man with considerable training can seldom afford simply to go out and look for them, let us say by exploring those areas in which existing data and theory have failed to produce understanding. Even in a mature science there are always far too many such areas, areas in which no existing paradigms seem obviously to apply and for whose exploration few tools and standards are available. More likely than not the scientist who ventured into them, relying merely upon his receptivity to new phenomena and his flexibility to new patterns of organization, would get nowhere at all. He would rather return his science to its preconsensus or natural history phase.

Instead, the practitioner of a mature science, from the beginning of his 20 doctoral research, continues to work in the regions for which the paradigms derived from his education and from the research of his contemporaries seem adequate. He tries, that is, to elucidate topographical detail on a map whose main outlines are available in advance, and he hopes — if he is wise enough to recognize the nature of his field — that he will some day undertake a problem in which the anticipated does *not* occur, a problem that goes wrong in ways suggestive of a fundamental weakness in the paradigm itself. In the mature sciences the prelude to much discovery and to all novel theory is not ignorance, but the recognition that something has gone wrong with existing knowledge and beliefs.

What I have said so far may indicate that it is sufficient for the productive scientist to adopt existing theory as a lightly held tentative hypothesis, employ it faute de mieux in order to get a start in his research, and then abandon it as soon as it leads him to a trouble spot, a point at which something has gone wrong. But though the ability to recognize trouble when confronted by it is surely a requisite for scientific advance, trouble must not be too easily recognized. The scientist requires a thoroughgoing commitment to the tradition with which, if he is fully successful, he will break. In part this commitment is demanded by the nature of the problems the scientist normally undertakes. These, as we have seen, are usually esoteric puzzles whose challenge lies less in the information disclosed by their solutions (all but its details are often known in advance) than in the difficulties of technique to be surmounted in providing any solution at all. Problems of this sort are undertaken only by men assured that there is a solution which ingenuity can disclose, and only current theory could possibly provide assurance of that sort. That theory alone gives meaning to most of the problems of normal research. To doubt it is often to doubt that the complex technical puzzles which constitute normal research have any solutions at all. Who, for example, would have developed the elaborate mathematical techniques required for the study of the effects of interplanetary attractions upon basic Keplerian orbits if he had not assumed that Newtonian dynamics, applied to the planets then known, would explain the last details of astronomical observation? But without that assurance, how would Neptune have been discovered and the list of planets changed?

In addition, there are pressing practical reasons for commitment. Every research problem confronts the scientist with anomalies whose sources he cannot quite identify. His theories and observations never quite agree; successive observations never yield quite the same results; his experiments have both theoretical and phenomenological by-products which it would take another research project to unravel. Each of these anomalies or incompletely understood phenomena could conceivably be the clue to a fundamental innovation in scientific theory or technique, but the man who pauses to examine them one by one never completes his first project. Reports of effective research repeatedly imply that all but the most striking and central discrepancies could be taken care of by current theory if only there were time to take them on. The men who make these reports find most discrepancies trivial or uninteresting, an evaluation that they can ordinarily base only upon their faith in current theory. Without that faith their work would be wasteful of time and talent.

Besides, lack of commitment too often results in the scientist's undertaking problems that he has little chance of solving. Pursuit of an anomaly is fruitful only if the anomaly is more than nontrivial. Having discovered it, the scientist's first efforts and those of his profession are to do what nuclear physicists are now doing. They strive to generalize the anomaly, to discover other and more revealing manifestations of the same effect, to give it structure by examining its complex interrelationships with phenomena they still feel they understand. Very few anomalies are susceptible to this sort of treatment. To be so they must be in explicit and unequivocal conflict with some structurally central tenet of current scientific belief. Therefore, their recognition and evaluation once again depend upon a firm commitment to the contemporary scientific tradition.

This central role of an elaborate and often esoteric tradition is what I have principally had in mind when speaking of the essential tension in scientific research. I do not doubt that the scientist must be, at least potentially, an innovator, that he must possess mental flexibility, and that he must be prepared to recognize troubles where they exist. That much of the popular stereotype is surely correct, and it is important accordingly to search for indices of the corresponding personality characteristics. But what is no part of our stereotype and what appears to need careful integration with it is the other face of this same coin. We are, I think, more likely fully to exploit our potential scientific talent if we recognize the extent to which the basic scientist must also be a firm traditionalist, or, if I am using your vocabulary at all correctly, a convergent thinker. Most important of all, we must seek to understand how these two superficially discordant modes of problem solving can be reconciled both within the individual and within the group.

Everything said above needs both elaboration and documentation. Very [25] likely some of it will change in the process. This paper is a report on work in progress. But, though I insist that much of it is tentative and all of it incomplete, I still hope that the paper has indicated why an educational system best described as an initiation into an unequivocal tradition should be thoroughly compatible with successful scientific work. And I hope, in addition, to have made plausible the historical thesis that no part of science has progressed very far or very rapidly before this convergent education and correspondingly convergent normal practice became possible. Finally, though it is beyond my competence to derive personality correlates from this view of scientific development, I hope to have made meaningful the view that the productive scientist must be a traditionalist who enjoys playing intricate games by preestablished rules in order to be a successful innovator who discovers new rules and new pieces with which to play them.

As first planned, my paper was to have ended at this point. But work on it, against the background supplied by the working papers distributed to conference participants, has suggested the need for a postscript. Let me therefore briefly try to eliminate a likely ground of misunderstanding and simultaneously suggest a problem that urgently needs a great deal of investigation.

Everything said above was intended to apply strictly only to basic science, an enterprise whose practitioners have ordinarily been relatively free to choose their own problems. Characteristically, as I have indicated, these problems have been selected in areas where paradigms were clearly applicable but where exciting puzzles remained about how to apply them and how to make nature conform to the results of the application. Clearly the inventor and applied scientist are not generally free to choose puzzles of this sort. The problems among which they may choose are likely to be largely determined by social, economic, or military circumstances external to the sciences. Often the decision to seek a cure for a virulent disease, a new source of household illumination, or an alloy able to withstand the intense heat of rocket engines must be made with little reference to the state of the relevant science. It is, I think, by no means clear that the personality characteristics requisite for preeminence in this more immediately practical sort of work are altogether the same as those required for a great achievement in basic science. History indicates that only a few individuals, most of whom worked in readily demarcated areas, have achieved eminence in both.

I am by no means clear where this suggestion leads us. The troublesome distinctions between basic research, applied research, and invention need far more investigation. Nevertheless, it seems likely, for example, that the applied scientist, to whose problems no scientific paradigm need be fully relevant, may profit by a far broader and less rigid education than that to which the pure scientist has characteristically been exposed. Certainly there are many episodes in the history of technology in which lack of more than the most rudimentary scientific education has proved to be an immense help. This group scarcely needs to be reminded that Edison's electric light was produced in the face of unanimous scientific opinion that the arc light could not be "subdivided," and there are many other episodes of this sort.

This must not suggest, however, that mere differences in education will transform the applied scientist into a basic scientist or vice versa. One could at least argue that Edison's personality, ideal for the inventor and perhaps also for the "oddball" in applied science, barred him from fundamental achievements in the basic sciences. He himself expressed great scorn for scientists and thought of them as wooly-headed people to be hired when needed. But this did not prevent his occasionally arriving at the most sweeping and irresponsible scientific theories of his own. (The pattern recurs in the early history of electrical technology: Both Tesla and Gramme advanced absurd cosmic schemes that they thought deserved to replace the current scientific knowledge of their day.) Episodes like this reinforce an impression that the personality requisites of the pure scientist and of the inventor may be quite different, perhaps with those of the applied scientist lying somewhere between.[5]

Is there a further conclusion to be drawn from all this? One speculative thought forces itself upon me. If I read the working papers correctly, they suggest that most of you are really in search of the *inventive* personality, a sort of person who does emphasize divergent thinking but whom the United States has already produced in abundance. In the process you may be ignoring certain of the essential requisites of the basic scientist, a rather different sort of person, to whose ranks America's contributions have as yet been notoriously sparse. Since most of you are, in fact, Americans, this correlation may not be entirely coincidental.

Notes

1. *The Structure of Scientific Revolutions* (Chicago, 1962).

2. Strictly speaking, it is the professional group rather than the individual scientist that must display both these characteristics simultaneously. In a fuller account of the ground covered in this paper that distinction between individual and group characteristics would be basic. Here I can only note that, though recognition of the distinction weakens the conflict or tension referred to above, it does not eliminate it. Within the group some individuals may be more traditionalistic, others more iconoclastic, and their contributions may differ accordingly. Yet education, institutional norms, and the nature of the job to be done will inevitably combine to insure that all group members will, to a greater or lesser extent, be pulled in both directions.

3. The history of physical optics before Newton has recently been well described by Vasco Ronchi in *Histoire de la lumière*, trans. J. Taton (Paris, 1956). His account does justice to the element I elaborate too little above. Many fundamental contributions to physical optics were made in the two millennia before Newton's work. Consensus is not prerequisite to a sort of progress in the natural sciences, any more than it is to progress in the social sciences or the arts. It is, however, prerequisite to the sort of progress that we now generally refer to when distinguishing the natural sciences from the arts and from most social sciences.

4. A revised version appeared in *Isis* 52 (1961): 161–93.

5. For the attitude of scientists toward the technical possibility of the incandescent light see Francis A. Jones, *Thomas Alva Edison* (New York, 1908), pp. 99–100, and Harold C. Passer, *The Electrical Manufacturers, 1875–1900* (Cambridge, Mass., 1953), pp. 82–83. For Edison's attitude toward scientists see Passer, ibid., pp. 180–81. For a sample of Edison's theorizing in realms otherwise subject to scientific treatments see Dagobert D. Runes, ed., *The Diary and Sundry Observations of Thomas Alva Edison* (New York, 1948), pp. 205–44, passim.

Working with the Text

1. Note that Thomas S. Kuhn speaks at some length early in his talk about his audience, the topic of the conference, and the interests and agendas of his listeners. Why and in what ways does Kuhn's awareness of his audience shape his remarks? How do these early comments give us clues about Kuhn's "rhetorical situation"?

2. Kuhn's talk turns on several key terms: *convergent, divergent, paradigm,* and *anomaly.* In a brief essay, clarify what these words mean and why they give us insight into scientific knowledge and innovation.

3. Early in his talk, Kuhn refers to two fairly common terms—*tradition* and *innovation*—and then proceeds to translate them into a pair of terms: *convergent* and *divergent.* What does Kuhn gain by this shift in terms? What

unhelpful assumptions or baggage might have come with the terms *tradition* and *innovation*?

4. In making a case for the importance of convergent thinking, Kuhn states that for much of a career, a scientist "aims to elucidate the scientific tradition in which he was raised rather than to change it" (par. 17). As you reread the essay, consider what is involved in "elucidating" a tradition. Based on your own experience in the science classroom as well as on Kuhn's argument, write a brief essay in which you interpret what Kuhn means by this statement. How does the scientist do this? What does it contribute to the development of science? Under what circumstances does this lead to change?

From Text to Field

1. Recalling Kuhn's definition of the term *paradigm*, consider what paradigms we use today in areas beyond basic science. How do these paradigms influence what we think and how we act?

2. Reflect on a time when, as part of a group, you experienced "rapid progress" as a result of "consensus," in the sense that Kuhn uses those terms. What was the consensus? How was it formed? What was the catalyst for "rapid progress"? What form did it take? What was the effect of the progress on the earlier consensus? In other words, how did the experience of progress change what you or the group had earlier held as a value or an assumption? Why might collaboration be especially important, even (or perhaps especially) for the divergent thinker?

3. Although Kuhn's theory has been applied to a number of other disciplines, in this early essay he makes a sharp distinction between the practice of science and the practice of other disciplines: "[H]istory strongly suggests that, though one can practice science—as one does philosophy or art or political science—without a firm consensus, this more flexible practice will not produce the pattern of rapid consequential scientific advance to which recent centuries have accustomed us" (par. 14). Write an essay in which you respond to Kuhn's assertion that consensus plays a more critical role in the progress of science than in the progress of other fields. If "firm consensus" is more critical to scientific advancement, why is this the case? How do the applied sciences, such as engineering, which often emphasize invention or innovation, fit into this tension between convergent and divergent thinking? Can philosophy or art or political science be practiced without firm consensus? What role does consensus play in these disciplines? Does the lack of firm consensus in these disciplines mean that they have advanced less rapidly than science? Why or why not?

INTO THE FIELD: Options for Writing Projects

1. Talking Back and Listening: Reading Revealed

It is easy, if not tempting, to construe reading as a passive process. Yet Michael Parker's essay alerts us to the tensions and back talk that are possible, and perhaps even desirable, in the process of reading. Reading thus becomes highly collaborative, hardly the one-way street it might seem to be.

This field project asks you to reflect on the process of reading the written page and responding to it. The marginalia that Parker discusses are only one aspect of this larger process. Often in college, you are asked to attend to the content that is on the page. Here we'll try something different, inviting you to attend to the reading process itself. You may wish to address some of the following issues in your field project:

- Explore ways of talking back that go beyond or are different from the physical marginalia in actual books. What role might a "double-entry notebook" have, one in which you record quotes in one column and your responses in another? Do you engage in unrecorded dialogues or debates with an author? What options for talking back are offered or encouraged in your various classes?
- When might it be okay, or even preferable, to listen attentively to the author, rather than responding right away? In what ways do different kinds of texts in different disciplines change the dynamic of your reading process?
- How do the various purposes for and types of reading (skimming, test preparation, critical reading, etc.) influence your reading habits? Have you become habituated to one kind of reading? How do you shift gears? How has nonacademic pleasure reading influenced your approach to reading in college?
- Reading is in one sense a very private affair. In what ways and for what purposes might reading groups play an especially valuable role?
- How have technology and online resources changed your role as a reader? Do you find it enjoyable or annoying to read "on the screen"? Does the availability of online texts and resources affect your willingness to engage hard-copy texts and books?
- How do you handle the rhythms of reading during a longer project? When is sympathetic reading, or "reading with the grain," particularly useful? And when is it important to become skeptical and read "against the grain"?

For this project, be sure to attend carefully to your reading process. Consider keeping a journal or log in which you record your habits as a reader.

2. Collaborative Constructions

When you enter a classroom, you enter an arena that is already, to some degree, constructed for you and that even structures, to some degree, your identity. Different styles of teaching and particular classroom settings encourage you to adopt a particular role as a student in that class. This field project invites you to reflect on how your role as a student and as a reader is guided and on how your interaction and collaboration with other students is constructed. You may reflect on any of your college classes, including your writing class. Here are several options for you to pursue:

- Consider the manner in which texts and textbooks construct your role as a reader. In what ways is your response to the readings guided? How are you expected to behave as a reader? And how are you expected to collaborate with fellow students in the process of learning course material?
- The physical classroom setting can go a long way in determining what options you and your instructor have for collaborative activities. Think about the material conditions that either encourage or inhibit collaboration: Can chairs and tables be moved? Can you arrange the room in ways that depart from the usual lecture configuration (rows of chairs, with the professor up front)? Does the use of technology encourage or undermine potential collaboration?
- What indications can you glean from the syllabus about the role of collaboration in your classroom? How or to what extent is collaboration with fellow classmates part of the normal rhythm of classroom activities? In what ways might tradition and the history of teaching in that discipline affect how collaboration is or isn't enacted in your classroom?

3. Group Work: An Insider's Perspective

Lisa Ede and Andrea Lunsford offer in their essay a detailed analysis of their own collaborative process. This field project invites you to contribute an analysis of your own experience in collaborative writing or in a group project, whether it occurred in college or in high school. Offer a detailed account of your experience, an evaluation of its success or failure, and recommendations about how the experience might be improved in the future. Remember, a collaborative experience doesn't have to be completely successful and enjoyable for you to derive benefit and insight from it. Here are some issues you may wish to address:

- How and by whom is your role determined in the collaborative undertaking? What latitude do you have to negotiate your roles?
- What guidance has your instructor offered in advance about the dynamics of collaborative work? Are you thrown together in a group and expected to discover

effective means for collaboration? Or has the collaboration been charted out in advance, with particular expectations about roles and procedures?

- How has the collaborative nature of your work affected assessment? Will individual contributions to the collaborative project be taken into account (and should they)? In what ways were individual contributions and responsibilities unevenly distributed? Can such responsibilities always be fairly divided?
- Occasionally you will find in your midst a "slacker," someone who doesn't shoulder his or her responsibilities as a group member or collaborative partner. How have you or other members of your group handled the situation? To what extent, if any, is the instructor expected to intervene?
- Some conscientious students find themselves in a situation such that they carry more than their fair share of the burden in a collaborative undertaking. If you have found yourself in that situation, how have you handled it? To what extent has that extra burden on you shaped your perception about the nature and value of collaborative work?

4. Niches for Collaboration

Our desire and need for social interaction in the process of education is so strong that collaborative activities may take place even when they are not explicitly sanctioned or authorized. Indeed, collaboration often thrives in those niches where it becomes self-organizing and not in some sense "official." This field project invites you to explore collaboration in your courses and on your campus that occurs "under the radar." Your job is to go "undercover," seek out collaborative work that occurs outside of formal classroom time, and analyze what role it plays in student learning and in the development of a learning community.

Here are some tips on where to find these collaborative niches and on what questions you might pose:

- What ways do students in a course find to interact with each other outside of the classroom? What kinds of conversations occur before and after class? Do students trade phone numbers, or is there a class e-mail list? Do some students form study groups on their own initiative?
- What kinds of collaboration occur in the dorms or in off-campus housing? In what ways is collaboration different, or richer, when conducted in pajamas over a bowl of popcorn?
- What are some of the different venues for collaboration? Does collaboration take place in the library, the computer lab, the campus or dorm cafeteria, the nearby coffeehouse, the rec center, online?
- Do any of your courses encourage collaboration outside of class? In what ways could or does your campus facilitate collaboration outside of class?
- What are the barriers to or fears concerning collaboration? To what extent does the specter of plagiarism or cheating haunt collaborative work?

- Why might the social dimension of collaboration — getting to know each other as fellow students and as friends — play an important part in the success of academic purposes for collaboration?
- What would you change — on campus or in a particular course — to encourage collaboration?

5. Workplace Collaborations

Investigate and report on the role of collaborative activities, especially as they pertain to writing, in the profession you have chosen for yourself. If you currently have a job, even part-time, you may wish to explore collaboration in that workplace. Your investigations can include "ethnographic field notes" (close observations of ongoing daily activities), an analysis of typical documents, and interviews. The following tips and questions might help you launch your exploration:

- Find a company or an organization in your community that offers a local resource for your investigations into your future profession.
- Conduct an "environmental scan" of the profession, or an organization in that profession, to determine where and how collaboration might take place. How does collaboration figure into the daily work of people in that organization?
- You may wish to focus on the life cycle of a major project in that organization. How does collaboration enter into the development of the project and its final presentation in written form? What is the interplay of writing and speaking, and virtual and physical meetings, as modes through which collaboration takes place?
- Who "owns" the material? What is the role of "boilerplate" or generic prewritten material? What issues of intellectual property or plagiarism arise in the writing activities of this profession or organization?
- In what ways does the "culture" of the organization or profession encourage collaborative work? What rewards or incentives support collaborative work?
- How does collaboration in this profession or workplace differ from collaboration on campus and in classrooms?
- If you are in a major that is in some sense preprofessional (business, engineering, nursing, etc.), to what extent does your present academic training help prepare you for the collaborative environment that is part of the workplace reality you will face in the future?

6. Collaboration in Your Academic Discipline

This field project invites you to explore attitudes toward collaboration in your academic major. You may find that these attitudes vary considerably, depending on whether your major is in the humanities, the social sciences, or the sciences.

A good barometer of these attitudes can be found in how professors in your field carry out and publish their work. Choose the top three academic journals in your field (an instructor in your major or a reference librarian can help you identify those journals). Scan the tables of contents of those journals from one year to determine how many of the articles are coauthored or have multiple authors. You may wish to compare notes with other classmates who are majoring in different fields. What does your inventory suggest about collaboration in your field?

You may wish to augment your study by conducting several interviews with professors or by scanning faculty Web sites. What can you gather about the role of collaboration in the development and funding of research in your field? How do faculty interact with their colleagues— on campus or across the country —as they carry on their professional activities?

A further resource in your fieldwork may initially strike you as somewhat odd: the acknowledgments section in the prefatory material of published work, especially books. Yes, you'll find loving tributes to the supportive spouse, apologies to the children who have lost time with the parent, and perhaps even mention of the household pet. But beyond these more personal expressions of gratitude are debts to colleagues and reviewers. An author's acknowledgment of these personal and intellectual debts can give you a good behind-the-scenes look at collaboration in your field.

7. An Insider's Guide to the Collaborative Classroom

Throughout his article, Kenneth A. Bruffee argues for particular characteristics of collaborative learning that his research and teaching experience have convinced him will lead to the most effective classroom practice. From the point of a student, write instructions for college-level teachers who are planning to experiment with collaborative learning in their classrooms. Draw from your experience as a student as well as from Bruffee's argument. In your instructions, include suggestions for introducing collaborative learning to students, setting up work groups, determining how and to what extent the teacher will interact with the groups, and evaluating group work.

As an alternative project, draw on your experience as well as Bruffee's argument to compose a manual or pamphlet for incoming freshmen to prepare them for what Bruffee describes as the process of "assimilation into communities of knowledgeable peers." Given your own experience on campus, how might you be able to help incoming students find their way into learning communities or discover ways of collaborating with one another? Address why entry into such collaborative communities can benefit their personal and academic lives, what the process involves, how they should regard it, and how they can make it work for them.

8. The Talent Myth—On Campus and Beyond

Malcolm Gladwell challenges our received notions about the importance of talent and asks us to reconsider just how important collaboration in organizations may be. This field project invites you to consider his proposition in light of organizations you know well. One such organization is your college or university itself. Another organization may be a current or prior workplace. Here are three project options for your consideration:

- Explore what Gladwell terms "the talent myth" in light of your own classes and course work. To what extent do your professors look for native individual talent, or do they also prize collaborative skills? Are you just waiting for a professor to come up to you and say, "You've got talent, kid!" or are you concerned that your skills in collaboration and group work may hide the talent you feel you possess? As you work your way through college and prepare for professional life, do you believe the talent expected of you in college and the talent expected of you in the workplace are different? As a student, how do you deal with this discrepancy or negotiate the difference?
- Your campus is a complex organization. This field project invites you to consider how it handles "individual talent." Chances are, you'll find some tensions around that question. In many respects, individual talent is prized in university settings, with some professors acting as if they were free agents. Nevertheless, research labs and whole departments—indeed the campus itself—need to function well as groups. Through interviews with faculty and staff, consider the climate on your campus or in your major department with regard to the role of individual talent in an organization.
- A third option for this field project invites you to consider an organization for which you have worked. Through interviews with coworkers and with owners and managers, assess the respective roles of individual talent and organizational collaboration. How well does Gladwell's argument apply to that particular work setting? What influence does the type of work the company performs have in your assessment? How does seniority or the level of employment factor into your assessment?

9. Handling the Tension: Received Wisdom and New Ideas

Thomas S. Kuhn presented his talk on "The Essential Tension" to suggest that it is not enough to encourage creative, divergent thinking in its own right. Divergent thinking needs to be grounded in and held in tension with convergent thinking—thinking that honors the traditions, practices, and received wisdom of a field.

Although Kuhn speaks of this "essential tension" in light of advanced scientific research, that tension can also exist in your own studies as an undergraduate.

On the one hand, you are expected to master concepts and techniques that have long been established by others. Yet on the other hand, you are also expected to offer (in some fields more than in others) your own fresh insights and new ideas. This "essential tension" can become an "essential quandary" and can lead to more than a few headaches. How can you be expected to learn, master, and demonstrate knowledge of received wisdom and also offer serious, new ideas?

This field project provides an opportunity to explore and understand that tension in your own course of study. Because the tension presents itself differently in different areas of study, place your own experience in one of several ways:

- If you are intending to major in the sciences, write an introduction, from your perspective as a student, to the "essential tension" in scientific work for undergraduates considering a career in that field. How does the ratio of convergent and divergent thinking appear during the undergraduate years? How might the emphasis on convergent thinking explain a whole range of undergraduate experiences, from the lecture style of teaching, to the replication of classic experiments in the lab, to the role of science textbooks?
- If you are intending to major in the humanities, write an explanation of this "essential tension" for undergraduates who may be a bit puzzled or threatened by the demand that they offer fresh, original ideas. Given the classes you have taken or are now taking, how do you handle this tension? Why might the ratio of convergent to divergent thinking differ in the humanities? To what extent is there a commonly agreed-upon set of theories, practices, and techniques in any of the humanities fields? As you try to offer new, fresh ideas, how do you establish your authority as someone who knows the received wisdom in that field?
- If you are planning to major in one of the "applied" fields, such as engineering, business, or studio arts, write an introduction to the "essential tension" as it presents itself in your field. In what ways does the tension between convergent and divergent thinking present itself a bit differently in applied fields? In what ways does the need to be "inventive" or to apply knowledge in very specific, concrete circumstances present different challenges from those experienced by majors in the sciences or the humanities?

For this field project, draw on your experience in the classroom or with particular assignments. Use this project as an opportunity to explore how the "essential tension" between convergent and divergent thinking might apply to a field or area of expertise you are familiar with or would like to pursue.

10. Textbooks, Convergence, and Collaboration

Early in his lecture on "The Essential Tension," Thomas S. Kuhn points to textbooks in the sciences as offering a revealing glimpse of convergent thinking in action. Not only do students immerse themselves in textbooks until well into their graduate education, those textbooks themselves provide a distillation of agreed-upon knowledge. In this sense, divergent thinking and textbooks can hardly be thought to go together. Nevertheless, not all fields are quite as insistent on convergent thinking as the sciences, and the role of textbooks in nonscientific fields departs from what Kuhn had in mind.

This field project invites you to examine textbooks and other classroom instructional materials as a way of gaining insight into how they establish and pass on a discipline's particular approach to the tension between convergent and divergent thinking. Consider the varied purposes of textbooks in different disciplines and how those textbooks are deployed in different ways in the classroom. Although some textbooks might be thought of as providing definitive knowledge, others may be thought of as providing resources for engagement with course materials. As you conduct your fieldwork, pay special attention to new kinds of classroom materials, often electronic in nature. How do new advances in software, such as Individualized diagnostic testing, interactive tutorials, or customized applications, affect your assessment of textbooks and teaching materials in your field?

You may also want to take your field project in a slightly different direction by examining the relationship between textbooks and collaborative learning. In what ways do the textbooks you use in your various classes support or hinder collaboration? In what ways might an emphasis on convergent thinking lead, oddly enough, to some fairly private learning experiences? On the other hand, why might some very collaborative group learning activities lead to some very divergent insights or outcomes?

BORDER CROSSINGS

Borders mark boundaries. They demarcate what lies on our side of the world, what is ours or near and familiar to us, even as they mark off what lies beyond us and, thus, what we count as foreign and strange. Borders separate zones of comfort and arenas of influence. Through the borders we encounter — or erect — we find ourselves at home or abroad.

Geopolitical borders, those boundaries that separate countries, are only one of many kinds of borders. There are others, and those with the most influence tend not to be marked with a fence or appear on maps. Given the many borders we encounter and sometimes cross in our daily lives and interactions with each other, we live simultaneously in many lands, even as many realms lie beyond our ken.

Day in and day out, we come upon many opportunities to cross borders. But college offers a special opportunity to do so. In ways that are more explicit and insistent, college asks us to cross borders we may not have contemplated and, thus, to cross into lands—intellectual and cultural — that we owe it to ourselves to know. With each border crossing, we hear and learn new voices and come to discover new resources and depth in our own.

This unit invites you to cross borders by offering you a chance to reflect on how words, language, and verbal representations operate in those social spaces where cultures meet. In these borderlands, we come to be more aware of the implicit rules that govern our conversations and how various games are played. We likewise are given opportunities we might not otherwise have to reflect on how we represent other cultures and how those representations offer a sometimes unflattering portrait of ourselves. We learn about borders with an eye to how power is often unequally distributed and to the role of conflict even within seemingly coherent communities. And we learn above all about many voices and the challenges we face in trying to find, if not our own voice, at least those several voices that speak authentically to our own experiences and the needs of others.

The three readings included in this unit provide both invitations and provocations. What they share is an interest in the life of words at the various borders we encounter. Nancy Masterson Sakamoto offers a glimpse of the unspoken rules that govern conversations in different cultures. Learning the language—any language, even academese — is not enough, nor is it even sufficient to know, in some abstract sense, what the rules are. We need to learn how to play the conversational game in any particular culture. Inviting us with her as she tours and reflects on several museums, Jane Tompkins has us look behind the exhibit cases to ponder how we represent other cultures and how our museums represent us. Her essay has the unsettling effect of having us wonder which side of the exhibit case we are on. By coining the term *contact zone*, Mary Louise Pratt gives us the means to interpret and enter those "social spaces where cultures meet, clash, and grapple with each other." The social spaces she considers include the baseball-card world of preteens, the Spanish conquest of the Andean peoples, and a controversial new course at Stanford University.

Reflecting on Prior Knowledge

1. Most of us have experienced awkward moments when speaking to people from other cultures. The difficulties we — and surely they — experienced cannot always be attributed to weak vocabulary or an imperfect mastery of verb tenses. Working in groups, develop a set of reasons why conversations may be hard to carry on between peoples of difficult cultures. What do we assume about our conversations that may not always be shared by others?

2. In a journal entry, recall a visit to a museum where the lives and histories of other cultures were represented. What did you expect from the museum? What would you imagine the response to be from a member of that culture? In what ways might museums offer insights not just into different cultures, but also into your own?

3. Recall an experience when, as a member of a group, you met, clashed, or grappled with a group that had more power or influence. In a journal entry, reflect on that encounter and on the role of language in that encounter. What rhetorical and linguistic resources did you — and they — have at hand?

4. In some respects, entering the college or university community is like trying to enter a different (and seemingly odd or exotic) culture. Working in groups, consider what challenges you have encountered while trying to pass yourself off as a native. In what ways do you continue to straddle several cultures or communities?

5. While tackling writing assignments in college, you encounter a good many voices as you read and research. In a journal entry, reflect on how you handle these voices and how you decide which voice you will adopt in your own writing.

Conversational Ballgames

Nancy Masterson Sakamoto

She knew the right Japanese words and phrases, but Nancy Masterson Sakamoto couldn't enter a conversation with her husband's Japanese family and friends without unsettling them. She taught English to Japanese students but couldn't get them to converse like English speakers. She decided to find out why and discovered two very different conversational ballgames.

"Conversational Ballgames" was first published in 1982 in *Polite Fictions: Why Japanese and Americans Seem Rude to Each Other,* which Sakamoto coauthored with a Japanese colleague, Reiko Naotsuka. The essay has since been widely anthologized, recognized in particular for the game analogies that capture the complex use of language in social settings marked by the meeting of different cultures. In an increasingly multicultural society, and as travel permits us to cross cultural borders ever more frequently, her brief essay stands as a welcome reminder that we need to be aware of the implicit rules of our own culture, even as we strive to learn the different rules that govern other cultures. We might also bear in mind that college can be its own rather odd culture, and learning how to play the academic ballgame, in conversation and in writing, may seem every bit as difficult as learning how to interact in a foreign language.

Born in Los Angeles, Nancy Masterson Sakamoto straddled two cultures in her professional and personal life. Living in Japan with her Japanese husband, she was for many years a teacher of English and a teacher trainer. Coauthor of *Mutual Understanding of Different Cultures* (1981), Sakamoto served as professor of American Studies at Shitennoji Gakuen University and at Hawaii Institute, as well as at the University of Hawaii.

After I was married and had lived in Japan for a while, my Japanese gradually improved to the point where I could take part in simple conversations with my husband and his friends and family. And I began to notice that often, when I joined in, the others would look startled, and the conversational topic would come to a halt. After this happened several times, it became clear to me that I was doing something wrong. But for a long time, I didn't know what it was.

Finally, after listening carefully to many Japanese conversations, I discovered what my problem was. Even though I was speaking Japanese, I was handling the conversation in a Western way.

Japanese-style conversations develop quite differently from Western-style conversations. And the difference isn't only in the languages. I realized that just as I kept trying to hold Western-style conversations even when I was speaking Japanese, so my English students kept trying to hold Japanese-style conversations even when they were speaking English. We were unconsciously playing entirely different conversational ballgames.

A Western-style conversation between two people is like a game of tennis. If I introduce a topic, a conversational ball, I expect you to hit it back. If you agree with me, I don't expect you simply to agree and do nothing more. I expect you to add something — a reason for agreeing, another example, or an elaboration to carry the idea further. But I don't expect you always to agree. I am just as happy if you question me, or challenge me, or completely disagree with me. Whether you agree or disagree, your response will return the ball to me.

And then it is my turn again. I don't serve a new ball from my original starting line. I hit your ball back again from where it has bounced. I carry your idea further, or answer your questions or objections, or challenge or question you. And so the ball goes back and forth, with each of us doing our best to give it a new twist, an original spin, or a powerful smash. 5

And the more vigorous the action, the more interesting and exciting the game. Of course, if one of us gets angry, it spoils the conversation, just as it spoils a tennis game. But getting excited is not at all the same as getting angry. After all, we are not trying to hit each other. We are trying to hit the ball. So long as we attack only each other's opinions, and do not attack each other personally, we don't expect anyone to get hurt. A good conversation is supposed to be interesting and exciting.

If there are more than two people in the conversation, then it is like doubles in tennis, or like volleyball. There's no waiting in line. Whoever is nearest and quickest hits the ball, and if you step back, someone else will hit it. No one stops the game to give you a turn. You're responsible for taking your own turn.

But whether it's two players or a group, everyone does his best to keep the ball going, and no one person has the ball for very long.

A Japanese-style conversation, however, is not at all like tennis or volley-ball. It's like bowling. You wait for your turn. And you always know your place in line. It depends on such things as whether you are older or younger, a close friend or a relative stranger to the previous speaker, in a senior or junior position, and so on.

When your turn comes, you step up to the starting line with your bowling 10 ball, and carefully bowl it. Everyone else stands back and watches politely, murmuring encouragement. Everyone waits until the ball has reached the end of the alley, and watches to see if it knocks down all the pins, or only some of them, or none of them. There is a pause, while everyone registers your score.

Then, after everyone is sure that you have completely finished your turn, the next person in line steps up to the same starting line, with a different ball. He doesn't return your ball, **Everyone is trying to bowl** and he does not begin from where your ball stopped. **with a volleyball.** There is no back and forth at all. All the balls run par-allel. And there is always a suitable pause between turns. There is no rush, no excitement, no scramble for the ball.

No wonder everyone looked startled when I took part in Japanese conver-sations. I paid no attention to whose turn it was, and kept snatching the ball halfway down the alley and throwing it back at the bowler. Of course the con-versation died. I was playing the wrong game.

This explains why it is almost impossible to get a Western-style conversa-tion or discussion going with English students in Japan. I used to think that the problem was their lack of English language ability. But I finally came to realize that the biggest problem is that they, too, are playing the wrong game.

Whenever I serve a volleyball, everyone just stands back and watches it fall, with occasional murmurs of encouragement. No one hits it back. Everyone waits until I call on someone to take a turn. And when that person speaks, he doesn't hit my ball back. He serves a new ball. Again, everyone just watches it fall.

So I call on someone else. This person does not refer to what the previous 15 speaker has said. He also serves a new ball. Nobody seems to have paid any attention to what anyone else has said. Everyone begins again from the same starting line, and all the balls run parallel. There is never any back and forth. Everyone is trying to bowl with a volleyball.

And if I try a simpler conversation, with only two of us, then the other per-son tries to bowl with my tennis ball. No wonder foreign English teachers in Japan get discouraged.

Now that you know about the difference in the conversational ballgames, you may think that all your troubles are over. But if you have been trained all your life to play one game, it is no simple matter to switch to another, even if you know the rules. Knowing the rules is not at all the same thing as play-ing the game.

Even now, during a conversation in Japanese I will notice a startled reac-tion, and belatedly realize that once again I have rudely interrupted by instinctively trying to hit back the other person's bowling ball. It is no easi-er for me to "just listen" during a conversation, than it is for my Japanese students to "just relax" when speaking with foreigners. Now I can truly sym-pathize with how hard they must find it to try to carry on a Western-style conversation.

If I have not yet learned to do conversational bowling in Japanese, at least I have figured out one thing that puzzled me for a long time. After his first trip to America, my husband complained that Americans asked him so many questions and made him talk so much at the dinner table that he never had a chance to eat. When I asked him why he couldn't talk and eat at the same time, he said that Japanese do not customarily think that dinner, especially on fairly formal occasions, is a suitable time for extended conversation.

Since Westerners think that conversation is an indispensable part of dining, and indeed would consider it impolite not to converse with one's dinner part-ner, I found this Japanese custom rather strange. Still, I could accept it as a cultural difference even though I didn't really understand it. But when my husband added, in explanation, that Japanese consider it extremely rude to talk with one's mouth full, I got confused. Talking with one's mouth full is certainly not an American custom. We think it very rude, too. Yet we still manage to talk a lot and eat at the same time. How do we do it? 20

For a long time, I couldn't explain it, and it bothered me. But after I dis-covered the conversational ballgames, I finally found the answer. Of course! In a Western-style conversation, you hit the ball, and while someone else is hitting it back, you take a bite, chew, and swallow. Then you hit the ball again, and then eat some more. The more people there are in the conversa-tion, the more chances you have to eat. But even with only two of you talk-ing, you still have plenty of chances to eat.

Maybe that's why polite conversation at the dinner table has never been a traditional part of Japanese etiquette. Your turn to talk would last so long without interruption that you'd never get a chance to eat.

Working with the Text

1. Nancy Masterson Sakamoto uses sports analogies to capture the differences between Western and Japanese conversations. While her article is primarily descriptive, she is pinpointing behaviors that suggest deep cultural differences in the *purpose* of conversation. In a brief essay, analyze the purpose of each style of conversation. From the analogies, what can you infer about how each

culture views relationships? In what ways does each culture expect conversation to define or advance relationships? What cultural values do you think are at play?

2. Sakamoto gained insight into these "conversational ballgames" through her attempts as a Westerner to converse with Japanese people and as an English teacher to engage her Japanese students in conversation. With her essay as a guide, use conversation to explore the difficulties she faced. With a group of other students in the class, imagine that you are preparing for a cultural-exchange trip to Japan. Choose a topic that will give you a substantial amount of conversational material. First, converse in your usual style. After ending the conversation, discuss the extent to which you used the Western "tennis" style described by Sakamoto. Using the same topic, try to converse in the Japanese "bowling" style she describes. Discuss the difficulties as well as any new avenues created by the style. Consider why it might be difficult to mimic the tacit or deeply ingrained conversational rules of a different culture. Individually, reflect on your experience in a brief essay.

3. As we encounter other cultures, we tend to judge, reject, or borrow what is unfamiliar or intriguing to us; at the same time, we come to see our own culture in a new light. As you reread Sakamoto's essay, be aware of your own response to the cultural differences she describes. In a brief essay, note what you consider to be the advantages and disadvantages of each conversational style in building personal relationships and in making decisions in professional situations.

4. Sakamoto frequently uses analogies to support her analysis. An analogy offers an extended comparison between two ideas, objects, or processes, for the purpose of explaining something unfamiliar or foreign by referring to something more familiar. What analogies does Sakamoto use in this brief essay, and do they serve her purpose?

From Text to Field

1. Although cultural differences come in many forms, Sakamoto focuses on conversation, the point of personal contact. Most of us have met someone whose first language is not English, or we have learned a new spoken language. Many of us have traveled abroad. In an essay, recall an experience of conversing with someone whose first language was not English. You might have spoken together in English or in the other person's first language. With Sakamoto's essay as an example, use analogies to explore the differences in conversational style. Find sports analogies other than tennis or bowling, or look for analogies in other fields, such as music, dance, or some form of craftsmanship.

2. Personal interaction with people from other cultures can change our perception of their culture, making it more understandable or more mysterious, more

attractive or more suspicious. In a brief essay, reflect on such an encounter of your own. How did you regard the culture before the encounter? How did your perception of the culture change? What was it about the personal interaction that created the change?

3. Even those who share English as a first language can confuse, unnerve, or offend each other with their different conversational styles. Conversations with your parents probably work under very different rules than talks with your friends. You may be disoriented by the conversation style of a roommate from another part of the country or from another race, ethnic group, or economic level. Approaching a college professor may require a style you never had to know in approaching a high school teacher. Membership in a new group might involve learning not only a new vocabulary but also a new game for initiating or entering conversations. Identify a situation that required or is requiring you to learn or teach a new game for conversing with someone who speaks English as a first language. Write a short guide in which you describe the two clashing styles and advise the reader on how to adjust to the new game.

4. In her analysis of conversational rules, Sakamoto focuses in large part on how we "take turns" in conversation and on continuity or changes in topic. Yet there are many other cultural rules that inform our conversations. These include how physical space and gesture guide our interactions. Write a brief essay in which you reflect on the role of such things as personal space, gesture, and eye contact. Alternatively, you may wish to pay close attention to certain key moments in the course of a conversation, such as greetings or introductions and leave-takings.

5. As you take courses in different departments on campus, you may find that members of particular disciplines, each with their own kind of "culture," have distinctive ways of carrying on conversations, whether spoken or in print. Choose a discipline you are interested in, perhaps your prospective major, and try to articulate what might be the conversation rules that govern how the academic game is played in that field.

A Visit to the Museum

Jane Tompkins

Jane Tompkins is aware of her surroundings. As a teacher, author, lecturer, and workshop leader, she brings a holistic perspective to issues of teaching and learning in higher education. For her, this includes attention to the physical environment. Tompkins has also made a career of seeing into the self, not only in terms of cultivating individual identity, but also in terms of understanding other selves. In addition to literary theory, her work has spanned personal criticism, the opening of the American canon, popular culture, and women's writing.

In "A Visit to the Museum," first published in the *Georgia Review,* Tompkins's interests merge. Identity, self-examination, education, and the physical elements of culture come into play as she questions the American fascination with Indians. She touches on a range of issues that have to do with how we represent other cultures — and ourselves. How can non-Indians know Native Americans? How can museums reveal them? What, in the first place, should museums be about?

Tompkins was for many years professor of English at Duke University. She is currently professor of English and education at the University of Illinois at Chicago. In addition to books on reader-response criticism and the cultural work of American fiction, Tompkins has authored the widely acclaimed *A Life in School: What a Teacher Learned* (1996) and *West of Everything: The Inner Life of Westerns* (1992).

On impulse, during a recent trip across the country, I turned off the interstate at Oklahoma City to follow the signs to the National Cowboy Hall of Fame. I had taken to visiting museums lately, not only because I was interested in their contents, but also because I wanted to see how the contents had been selected, with what aim and what results. I knew that anthropologists and cultural historians had been writing about the politics of museums, and I shared their concerns, but I was interested too in the kinds of experience one has in a museum: The feelings and thoughts they arouse, the physical sensations they provide. I had started to reflect, in particular, on how museums devoted to the American West educated people to see the country's past in a certain way.

As befits a museum that celebrates the grandeur of the West, everything in the National Cowboy Hall of Fame is on a large scale. A long colonnade leads to the broad entranceway; the lobby is open and inviting. An attractive older woman greeted me after I had paid admission, handed me a brochure, and asked if I had any questions. All this opulence and graciousness made me feel well launched, if a little guilty. I had gone in prepared to analyze and find fault (a previous experience at a Western museum had alerted me to the bloodthirsty, conquistador character of some commemorations of the West), but the generosity and sophistication of this environment disarmed me almost completely. So what if the paintings showed stereotyped Indian chiefs and idealized cowboys; so what if the Indian art was displayed as if it were in an apartment featured by *Architectural Digest*; I was lulled by the soothing colors, the luminous spaces, the hushed admiration of the visitors, and the excellent air-conditioning. Even the enormous hall devoted to busts of the museum's donors wasn't enough to mar the experience.

Exiting along the stone path that curves across a pond dotted by fountains, I found it impossible to cavil. It no longer mattered if a hundred pictures of rodeo stars, shown next to a hundred saddles and a hundred lassos, had been boring (never mind that it celebrated an American tradition of cruelty to animals). The museum itself had been beautiful, comfortable, and serene. I had enjoyed looking at the contemporary paintings; the portraits of western movie stars were a particular treat for me — and so was the John Wayne alcove, which offered a video full of wonderful clips from his films and a display of his collection of Chinese art and Western Americana. The hour had been a pleasure — exactly right as a respite from the long, hot drive between Amarillo and Tulsa.

This benign episode made me wonder. If I, a professional critic blooded for the kill, had come away from the Cowboy Hall of Fame grateful for the pleasant interlude, maybe museum-going wasn't the serious business I had long considered it. Maybe it was more like going to the ballpark and eating a hot dog than attending a lecture or reading a book. Maybe, on the model of TV news programs like *60 Minutes* and *20/20*, it was information as entertainment. The product was no longer "culture" in the standard sense but a total experience — gorgeous gift shop, great snack bar, fantastic lighting, terrific videos — all of these making up the package. I had to admit that I liked visiting a really luxurious rest room, browsing through expensive art books, looking at some curious paintings, and listening to the splash of fountains. Under these conditions, questions of cultural indoctrination – of racism, male-worship, and ethnocentrism — just couldn't get any purchase in my brain. I felt refreshed.

In the history of my experiences with museums this one was uncharacter- 5 istically mild. I have an indelible memory of the children's lunchroom in the Museum of Natural History in New York: the little, olive-drab lockers where we deposited our brown paper bags reeking of bananas and mayonnaise, cheese, and oranges and bologna. The huge dinosaurs made of bones, the great canoe filled with terrifying warriors, the dioramas of Indians in their villages — these are among the most vivid impressions of my childhood. From a later period, I remember the Museum of the Works of the Duomo in Florence — an austere, light-filled space, all stone and air — with its Donatello statues of the prophets, radiating moral purpose.

These and other museums became for me touchstones, summarizing eras of experience, my cultural capital, homes away from home. I had a love affair once with the De Young Museum in Golden Gate Park in San Francisco. Its jade collection and fierce Chinese bronzes drew me again and again; it was a temple where I came to worship something I now cannot describe. Museums always seemed to me to hold the key to higher realms. They stood for knowledge, skill, treasure, and ungraspable values, things for which a person ought to strive. They were like secular churches where people could come to reverence what they loved— baseball, Thomas Jefferson, the French Impressionists — and their teaching had been influential in my life.

What museums didn't say, however, turned out to be more important than what they did. For I have recently learned that museums can teach one much amiss. Their power to distort history and to frustrate learning, as well as to inspire emulation, was brought home to me a few months ago when, on a sunny December afternoon, I made a visit to the Museum of the American Indian in New York.

After a half-hour delay on the 7th Avenue subway, I emerged blinking into the sunlight of Spanish Harlem, feeling unsure of myself. Should I be frightened? Everything looked seedy, normal, and unthreatening. Instead of feeling I was in a war zone, which was what people had led me to expect, it was more like having left the capital for the provinces. No downtown bustle and importance here, just old people pulling grocery carts. I made my way across Broadway to the sidewalk at 155th Street, the old-fashioned kind made of hexagonal pieces of stone, to where the museum stands. It occupies the left wing of a large gray building that surrounds three sides of a disused courtyard, most of which is shut off from the public by an iron fence. The whole thing looked as if it had been built a hundred years ago and then forgotten. And inside, the Museum of the American Indian also has the air of a place that hasn't changed in a long time. It's the lighting that contributes to this impression most. A dim light spreads itself evenly over everything, giving all the spaces and the objects in them an indescribable tinge of sickly yellow-gray, the color of old train-station lavatories and ancient public-school buildings.

For here, indeed, is the museum of one's childhood. Here were cases crammed with unfamiliar objects, glutting the eye and mind before one had even begun to look. The burden of so many things made me desperate for information, anything to stay mentally afloat. But in the Museum of the American Indian, aids to reflection are few. There's a mimeographed pamphlet available in the bookshop whose title sums up the situation nicely: "On Your Own with Great North American Indians." The information the museum does provide comes on placards, hand-lettered, a little shakily, in a vaguely gothic script, conveying an impression of old age all by themselves. The first one I read, propped in the corner of an overstuffed case, had two misspelled words, "enviornment" and "develope." Maybe it's just that I've been an English teacher all my life, but those misspelled words — and the thought of generations of schoolchildren reading them — filled me with despair and foreboding. These mistakes, along with the studied penmanship, prepared me for the prose, which had the character of labored student compositions: monotonous sentence structure, everything in the passive voice, no concrete details.

After a while, still reading to get my bearings, I began to notice a certain   10 turn these descriptions took. It often seemed that the clothing or decorative style or implement under discussion wasn't, in some subtle way, all that it could have been. What the case contained would be secondary to, or less important than, or not so brilliant as what had been produced by some other tribe, or in some other period, or at some different location. It was as if whoever had been responsible for the descriptions was unconsciously sabotaging an already doomed operation, unable to help himself. I felt rage mounting in me, and frustration. Why couldn't these objects have been displayed better, with imagination and flair, not to mention adequate lighting? Why couldn't the museum have provided lively, engaging accounts of the life these objects stood for? Why, for heaven's sake, couldn't they even get the *spelling* right? Why did they (whoever "they" were) have to be so *negative* about the things they had? And why, after all, was it the remains of the American Indians that were being treated in this shabby way? I had seen, two days before, Sienese paintings at the Metropolitan Museum of Art treated as holy treasures, magnificently offered for our veneration. Why were fourteenth-century Italians so much more important to us than the inhabitants of our own continent?

The sense of failure hit me strongest when I heard a metallic voice emanating from behind some cases on the first floor. Wending my way back I discovered the Indian Museum's excuse for a video: a box with some colored slides of Indian artifacts that changed every few seconds, while a voiceover recited facts about the museum. These, too, were tinged by the air of defeat. The museum displayed 11,000 items; *however*, these were only a fraction of the one million items it owned, which were stored in a warehouse in the Bronx. The man who had amassed the collection, George Gustav Heye, had established the museum early in the century; *however*, the opening was delayed by World War I. Why include this fact in a two-minute description?

There were other depressing features: On the walls of the dark stairwell hung small hand-colored pictures of, I think, Indian costumes: it was hard to tell because they were unidentified. Stylistically flat, amateurishly mounted, brightly colored, they seemed more appropriate for a kindergarten than for a major collection As I stood on the landing, deciding whether to look at the exhibit of contemporary Indian painting on my left, I heard someone urinating, long and heavy. I was standing outside the men's room. When I reflected on why I'd never had this experience before — hearing what I was hearing while staring into a roomful of paintings — I realized it was because in most museums the rest rooms are located at some distance from the exhibits.

Leaving the second floor, I went up to the third where, in a special exhibit of artifacts from Central America, the museum seemed to be putting its best foot forward. Here, what my colleague Marianna Torgovnick calls "the jewelry-store method" of display had been adopted with a vengeance. Small cases with dark interiors housed a small number of items, spotlit from unexpected angles. Each case was visually stunning, a striking composition in light and shade. But most of the objects were lit only on one side or not illuminated at all, and this, coupled with the scarcity of information, made it hard to know what you were looking at and harder to remember what you had seen.

Museums can teach one much amiss.

By this time I was so aggravated I couldn't look at anything without getting angry. I realized that if I were going to get something out of this visit I would have to change my frame of mind. I would have to stop imagining the way it should have been — lustrous marble, elegant spaces, brilliant illumination, sophisticated aids to comprehension — and start looking for what *was* there. So, determined to get what I had come for, some experience or insight to treasure, I went back downstairs and began to look at the cases again, carefully, state by state — Oklahoma, Nebraska, Kentucky. And little by little I began to notice that what was in them was much richer, more varied, and more beautiful than any collection of American Indian artifacts I had ever seen.

There was statuary: I hadn't known that North American Indians made statues, if you except the totem carvings of the Northwest. Yet here were

15

wooden figures of men and women, squat, square, austere, enigmatic, and powerful as any African carvings I had ever seen. There was an incredible variety of clothing, of different styles, in different materials, intricately and beautifully decorated. There were gorgeous cloaks, vests, leggings, shawls, headdresses, slippers, boots. Explosions of jewelry, amulets, necklaces, arm bands, leg bands. Every kind of implement, bowls, baskets, sieves, carving tools, weapons, pipes, cooking utensils, blankets, toys, carrying bags, dolls, masks, fetishes, drawings. And all of it made from so many kinds of skins, furs, hides, bones, teeth, claws, horns, stones, woods, clays, and grasses.

One reads about the intense spiritual lives of the North American Indians, but their physical existence, it is always implied, was nasty, brutish, and short. The display cases in the Museum of the American Indian contradict these notions. What came through to me in a way it never had before was the richness of the material lives of these peoples, the reality of the Indians' contact with things. Things they had held in their hands, things they had protected and adorned their bodies with, things they had used, things they had simply seen. The beauty, stylistic coherence, workmanship, and utility of the objects in each case, and the way they fit together into a kind of whole made me think, involuntarily, the word *culture*. I knew of course that North American Indians had a culture, or rather, individual cultures. All "peoples" had "cultures," no matter how technologically unlike our culture theirs may have been. I had known this, but until now, I had known it only as a piety of cultural relativism, not as an immediate experience. *That* was what the Museum of the American Indian gave me. The immediate visual and tactile experience, the sensory evidence, abundant, amassed, incontrovertible, of the textural life-world of Native American people.

But this was not just an impression of material shapes. For as the objects of a given tribe reflected those of others stylistically, the labor that went into them, the knowledge and skill, the time and care, the consistency with which motifs were repeated, and the talismanic power that certain objects obviously possessed, combined to hint at what must have been the density and force of the cultural stories that gave the objects meaning. And yet their stillness now, cheek by cheek with one another, under glass where they had lain for so many years, was the stillness of death. Testaments of life, of the vibrancy, cohesion, and viability of a particular way of life, now they were testaments of extinction.

It was odd. Something about the way the objects were displayed — too many, too close together, not really explained, in depressing surroundings — or something in the objects themselves, or something in me, allowed them to speak in a way they had never spoken to me before. I didn't know what to feel. The objects had given me a glimpse of an independent life, glorious and untouchable, an integrity of action and being that had existed once in

Oklahoma, in Kentucky, and perhaps existed somewhere still, on another plane, like music. That was cause for celebration. But at the same time and all around me was evidence of failure — whose failure was hard to say — the museum's failure to honor what it possessed, the failure of the society that had produced Spanish Harlem, the failure of the nation that had destroyed the civilizations whose remnants it now half-heartedly preserved?

Museums are halls of fame, meant to honor those whose works they preserve, not to superintend their slide into oblivion. In our culture — and who, exactly, were "we"? — honor meant space, light, opulence, being up-to-date; it meant pride of place, prominence, visibility. The Museum of the American Indian had been accorded none of these. The feelings of secondariness and disappointment I had felt creeping into even the most impersonal information did not come out of nowhere: They were a response to neglect. I felt neglected myself as I stood there, and at the same time, responsible. I looked at the meager offerings of the gift shop and went home.

Three days later I came back to learn more about the museum (it was my [20] last day in New York), and to verify some of the observations I had made. It was Friday of the week after Christmas and New York was full of tourists; I had twice fought my way through crowds at the Met. But the Indian Museum seemed even more deserted than it had before. It was only early afternoon, and a weekday, but on reaching the entrance I found a pair of great brass doors — depicting, in bas-relief, scenes from American Indian life — swung tightly shut. There was no sign telling when the Museum would be open or when it would be closed, only the doors, and from their surface, staring back at me, indecipherable, some patches of brilliant white graffiti.

I wasn't surprised. The day before I had imagined the museum staff working in crowded back rooms, ill lit, with old oak desks (or if you were lower in the pecking order, old metal ones), ancient filing cabinets, partitions made of wood or pebbled glass, linoleum floors, and vintage watercoolers. The people who staffed the museum, I thought as I stood by the closed doors, probably didn't want to work. They were too demoralized. They would jump at a holiday, I thought. But of course this couldn't be the real reason the museum was closed. The real reason, as someone suggested later, was probably that there wasn't enough money to keep it open. Not enough to pay the heat and electricity. Still, it came to the same thing: No one had cared enough.

There was a certain logic in this. The main traditions of this country grow out of Europe. The masters of fourteenth-century Sienese painting currently being honored at the Met had been Christian and urban, they had spoken an Indo-European language, they had the alphabet, the printing press, gunpowder, the stirrup; their institutions, their technology, their worldviews were the grandfathers of ours. Some of their kinsmen would "discover" this continent a century or so later. Culturally, they were more "American" than the Iroquois and the Chippewa, so it made sense that we should honor their works.

But there was another logic which spoke more plainly still. The line that led from the European "discovery" of the continent led also to the near extinction of Native Americans and to the massive destruction of animals, even of entire species. It led to cancer, unbreathable air, dead lakes, dying forests, toxic-waste dumps, chemical disasters, and the possible annihilation of all living creatures through nuclear war. There was a connection, I thought, between these dusty trophies and the dying continent. Whatever ferocities the Indian peoples might have practiced, their traditions had a reverence for the whole web of creation that could have served us as a model for understanding the planet we inhabited, that could have helped us to live less destructively.

Books I had read about the native peoples of North America — *Black Elk Speaks*, Paula Gunn Allen's *The Sacred Hoop*, Calvin Martin's *Keepers of the Game*, Anthony F. C. Wallace's *The Death and Rebirth of the Seneca*, James Axtell's *The European and the Indian*, Vine Deloria's *God Is Red* — these books and others had taught me that Indians did not behave as if the human species were infinitely more important and valuable than all other species, or even more important than plants and stones, rivers and mountains. A person could become a wolf or an owl without loss of status. The instrumental relationship people of "our" culture have to the material world, treating nonhuman existents as if they had no value except their utility for us, allowed for a dazzling manipulation of the external environment. But the price seemed to be a loss of mutuality. If you treat a person as a slave, naturally that person will hate you. If you treat things as if they have no intrinsic worth, they will turn against you, too.

I had scarcely any right to these speculations, knowing so little about   25 Indian cultures. But I couldn't help thinking that the neglect of their treasures, and what that neglect stood for in terms of our ignorance, was correlated with the dungeon of the subway I had ridden, the trash I had seen on Broadway, and the graffiti glaring back from the doors. The subway that had gotten me to the museum and the airplane that had brought me to New York and that I was about to board again in a few hours belonged to the same machinery that had made these items into relics. I saw that, being a creature of modern technology, my coming to the museum on a subway, reading some placards, and then going home in an airplane guaranteed that I would never know what the objects in the museum meant in any thoroughgoing, tangible sense. And it occurred to me that the way to find out about them would not be to read more books about Indians.

Studying had its place, but studying was what *we* did — collecting, in the process, so many dry bones. (I subsequently learned that there were tens of thousands of Indian skeletons being held in American museums for purposes of "study.") Studying was part of the machinery, which is to say, of the instrumentalism that destroyed the environment that had made Indian life possible. Study was what had motivated collections such as this. Later on, I read about the controversy surrounding the Museum of the American Indian— where it should be housed, who should control it, who should pay, how much — and discovered that the founder, George Gustav Heye, had cared nothing for the public, nothing for what Native Americans themselves felt about his disposition of their treasures, but only for "solving the great mystery of the origin of the prehistoric races of the Western Hemisphere." I wanted to distance myself from this way of relating to the objects in the cases, I wanted to see the world as the people who made the objects saw it, I wanted to get into their bodies and feel what they had felt, and I saw that to do this, it would be necessary to live differently.

What would have to happen was this: A rattle in one of the cases would have to begin to shake, a headdress start to tremble, an amulet to levitate and hurtle through the glass and into my hand. I would have to walk onto a reservation somewhere and start living without books or TV. I would have to get to the other plane. It didn't matter that the Museum of the American Indian was on 155th Street instead of further downtown. It didn't matter that the lighting was dim. A better address and glitzier surroundings wouldn't have made the difference, as far as learning was concerned. In fact, the opulent, high pressure, visually exciting, marble-and-mirrors display I'd imagined as an alternative to the museum's dinginess might have been the worst thing of all. Such an exhibition would have sent me home satisfied, having created the illusion of "being there." The dim light and dull paint let me know I wasn't anywhere but in an underfunded, dispirited, bureaucratic institution. Maybe that was why the objects spoke. It was the contrast that had allowed them to appear.

So my visit was a success after all. The museum had done its work. I had received my instruction.

Or so I thought — until I sent this description of my museum visit to my friend Annette Kolodny, who had recently become Dean of Humanities at the University of Arizona in Tucson. Her reply was hard to take, like some good medicines that in the end will make you better. For though deeply appreciative of the essay, she begged me to consider the following:

> . . . The awakening you describe . . . leaves you open to charges of "romanticizing" the Indian yourself. For example: Except for a small enclave of rabid traditionalists on a very few reservations, you would have great difficulty "walking onto a reservation somewhere and starting to live without books or TV." TV is ubiquitous on the reservations. Books less so.

The essay also has an insistently nostalgic tone which assumes the "vanishing Red Man" motif. In fact, Native Americans continue to have and practice a viable, meaningful culture; some of the native people I have come to know here would bridle at your suggestion that all is vanished; or that the adaptations made to the modern world (and to white conquest) are somehow inauthentic. For many native people, the white tendency nowadays to sing the praises of the Indian as having lived in harmony with nature is a species of white self-delusion. Whites make the Indian the new pastoral locus; but whites don't do a damned thing to help reverse the appalling statistics of infant mortality or TB on the reservations. What I'm saying, Jane, is that you need to monitor the essay to make certain you're not inadvertently singing another hymn to some version of the Noble Savage (in harmony with nature, freed of the constraints of modern society, unfettered by the complications of technology, etc.). The rugs now being woven by Navajo, Hopi, etc. — but which don't sell to the tourists — show reservation scenes, representationally, with broken-down cars behind a shack, in the front yard of a hogan, and various animals scattered around. Tourists don't buy these rugs, of course, because the rugs are true; and we still want our Indians living in some kind of pure rural splendor. No place in the image for abandoned cars.

I love what you're trying to do and say in that essay. Just try to read it as a Pascua Yaqui living on a reservation in the middle of Tucson, where whites repeatedly come to "watch" the seasonal dances but never stay to help teach the children or provide medicine for the ill. And imagine the Yaqui's seething resentment of those whites who believe that, because they attend the public dances, they "know" or "understand" or have experienced something authentic about Yaqui culture. And also imagine the rage of some other native person who *knows* that contained within the walls of that museum are precious religious artifacts belonging to the tribe, indeed, without which the tribe can no longer prosper. That Indian doesn't want a better museum to display the artifacts; s/he wants the thing(s) returned to the tribe!

Everything Annette had said rang true. I knew that white people like me used Indian culture as a way of dreaming about what their own culture couldn't give them while ignoring the present realities of Native American life, behaving as if there weren't any Indians any more or as if those who survived were somehow less real than those who had lived in the seventeenth century. I had even written, in an essay published three years ago: "The relationship most non-Indians have to the people who first populated this continent . . . [is] characterized by narcissistic fantasies of freedom and adventure, of a life lived closer to nature and to spirit than the life we lead now. . . . The American Indian Movement in the early seventies couldn't get people to pay attention to what was happening to Indians who were alive in the present, so powerful was this country's infatuation with people who wore loincloths, lived in tepees, and roamed the plains and forests long ago." Knowing this, why had I fallen into the trap? For it was true that I had been "romanticizing" for my own purposes.

It was worse than that. I had recently read an entire book manuscript by Marianna Torgovnick, *Gone Primitive*, about the way modern anthropologists, art critics, novelists, psychologists, explorers, and ordinary citizens use primitive peoples as the site for elaborating their dreams — of power, sexual conquest, racial superiority, belonging. How had I forgotten all this? And finally: Was my dream of another life — away from TV and airplanes and worry over spelling mistakes — just an ignorant fantasy? Or did it represent some legitimate impulse to deepen and intensify my contact with the world, to get closer to reality, and to myself? 30

I don't have an answer to such questions, but they, in turn, raise others that are worth considering. It is one thing to think and write in the abstract about the politics of museums. It is another to make a visit: to take the subway uptown on Christmas vacation, or to turn off the highway on a cross-country trip and walk into a real place, have real sensations, react to spaces, lighting, information (or the lack thereof); to see actual objects — feathers, bones, paintings; and then to browse in a gift shop, have a cup of coffee, sit down to rest your feet.

Something about the immediacy of the experience makes museum-going not the purely intellectual encounter it becomes when one is writing professional criticism about it. The real-life context of a visit—time pressures, physical needs, the desire to be lifted out of oneself momentarily—push other considerations aside. In the event, one tries to get some enjoyment out of what is there, and to learn something from it, no matter how inadequately presented or overproduced the exhibits may be. For one does feel educated, however minimally, by the information that typically accompanies a Native American artifact displayed in a glass case; one learns what it was made from and how, what it was used for, and by what kind of person. The trouble is, the placards never say how, and by what right, this particular object got to the museum, who took it away from whom, under what circumstances, and for what reason. Museum information provides a kind of false contextualization. One learns more than enough about decorative styles and methods of production, but nothing about the historical and political conditions that put the objects there — nothing that would interrupt one's dream of another life.

Could there be an Indian museum that represented the totality of Native American experience to which people would want to come on their vacations? Should such a museum provoke utopian desires as well as a sense of tragedy and the need for present help?

I once visited a small museum in Cherokee, North Carolina — the "Cyclorama" — that was controlled by Indians themselves. It was modest: a few dioramas that told the story of the Trail of Tears, a few artifacts exhibited so that you could really see how they had been used, and a sound-and-light show (made of practically nothing) that dramatized the Cherokees' loss of territory and the diminution of their numbers over the years.

The visit took little more than a half hour (my husband was waiting for me in the parking lot). Everything in the place looked homemade and more than a little worn. But this museum had achieved its purpose fully: It had taught me some things about the Cherokee Nation in a straightforward and consistently interesting way. Whoever had put it together had brought to it two elements that most such enterprises lack: a sense of what works and what doesn't when it comes to educating the public — and the Cherokee point of view.

I learned recently that museum curators are beginning to respond to critiques of their policies and practices. Stanford University and the University of Minnesota are returning their entire collections to local tribes, and the Smithsonian itself has agreed to return burial artifacts and skeletal remains, on request, to contemporary tribes that can prove with "reasonable certainty" that the objects in question belong to them. Signs, perhaps, that museums of the future may be differently conceived and organized. I hope so. The Cherokee museum suggests to me that what will be needed, however, is not a great deal of money, nor a great deal of space, nor a lot of high-tech video equipment, nor even hundreds of objects to put on display, but rather — in the case of Indian museums — the Native American perspective and some good pedagogical sense.

One month ago, it was announced that the long and bitter controversy over where to house the extensive collection of the Museum of the American Indian had at long last been resolved, and that, ironically, it was to be given the last available space on the Mall in Washington. At one time, I would have been overjoyed at the news. Now, I am not so sure.

Working with the Text

1. As you read "A Visit to the Museum," it quickly becomes apparent that the focus of the essay is on the Museum of the American Indian. Why, then, does Jane Tompkins open the essay with an account of her visit to the Cowboy Hall of Fame? What rhetorical purpose does this opening have? In what ways might it provide historical and cultural context for the entire essay?

2. As a cultural critic, Tompkins examines the effects of specific, concrete elements of American culture. To draw the reader into her response to the National Cowboy Hall of Fame and the Museum of the American Indian,

Tompkins uses sensory detail—color, shape, light, movement—to describe the exhibits and their surroundings. Review the essay, focusing on just the sensory detail. Imagine yourself in both museums. Using Tompkins's essay as a model, write your reflections on the significance and meaning of the design of each museum.

3. The structure of this essay is built on successive stages, each of which marks a change in thinking. What changes of mind does Tompkins record? Why has she adopted this structure as a rhetorical strategy?

4. Tompkins's critique of the Museum of the American Indian takes an unexpected turn when she sends the description of her visit to her colleague Annette Kolodny, the dean of humanities at the University of Arizona. Kolodny tells her that "[t]he awakening you describe . . . leaves you open to charges of 'romanticizing' the Indian yourself" (par. 29). Consider Tompkins's view of Indian culture in the description she sent to Kolodny, Kolodny's critique of the description, and Tompkins's reflections on Kolodny's critique. Does the succession of reflections and critiques invalidate—or enrich—prior views? What does Tompkins achieve by including the critique of her essay? Write an essay in which you respond to their views of Indian culture and how non-Indians have represented it, as if Tompkins had sent the entire essay to you to critique.

From Text to Field

1. Work with a group of students in your class to design or plan the elements of a museum of Native American culture. Include a rationale for the design or plan. What should the purpose of a museum be? How should Native American culture be represented? Who should be involved in the planning process? Why? If visitors to your museum are to achieve a more informed understanding of American Indian culture, what should they do besides visit museums?

2. Since the publication of Tompkins's essay, the National Museum of the American Indian (part of the Smithsonian Institution) has opened a new facility on the National Mall in Washington, D.C. Based on Web sites ‹nmai.si.edu›, published reviews of the new space, or perhaps a personal visit, offer a comparison of the two museums. How does the new museum fare, given the concerns that Tompkins offers in her essay?

3. Recall a visit to a particular museum, or head off to visit a museum, notebook in hand. It could be a museum representing another culture, another time in history, natural history, science, or some specialized field. Write an autobiographical essay in which you reflect on and perhaps critique the museum. What did the surroundings and exhibits suggest about the attitude of the exhibitors toward their subject? What current cultural attitudes were reflected in the surroundings? In what ways did it educate you or influence your perception of the

culture, history, or field represented in the museum? In what ways might the museum romanticize its subject or inaccurately position the objects it has on display in cultural terms?

4. Tompkins's essay raises questions about the non-Indian view of Native Americans. Write an essay in which you reflect on your own view. What image do you have of Native Americans? What is your perspective on their place in our cultural history? What are the sources—in popular culture and in your own childhood—of these images and perspectives?

5. Write a plan for a museum representing a culture or field of specialty you know well. The possibilities range from an ethnic group or a time in history to an area of expertise such as music, sports, or science. What would you display? How would you display it? What kind of building would you house it in? What image and purpose would determine its design?

Arts of the Contact Zone

Mary Louise Pratt

In the early seventeenth century, after the fall of the Inca Empire to the Spanish, an Andean sends a thousand pages, written in a mix of his native language and Spanish, to King Philip III of Spain — an attempt to reveal the effects of conquest on the Andean people. In the early 1980s, an American schoolboy hands in an essay, full of misspellings, that proposes an "inventchin" — "a shot that would put every thing you learn at school in your brain." Later that decade, students at Stanford University confront their own and each other's identities in a course that explores "multiple cultural histories." All of them have entered the "contact zone."

Mary Louise Pratt developed the concept of "contact zones" as a way of examining interactions between people from clashing cultures. Pratt offers this term as a way to refer to "social spaces where cultures meet, clash, and grapple with each other, often in contexts of highly asymmetrical relations of power." She found that when the people of one culture are subordinated, they wield particular "arts" to challenge the image imposed on them by those in power.

As a scholar in Spanish and Portuguese as well as comparative literature, Mary Louise Pratt brings both historical and multicultural perspectives to her writing and teaching. A professor at Stanford University, Pratt works in areas that span Latin American women's studies, literature, and cultural theory; postcolonial criticism and theory; discourse and ideology; and travel literature. Her books include *Toward a Speech Act Theory of Literary Discourse* (1977); *Linguistics for Students of Literature* (coauthored with Elizabeth Closs Traugott, 1980); *Amor Brujo: The Images and Culture of Love in the Andes* (1990); and *Imperial Eyes: Travel Writing and Transculturation* (1992).

> "Arts of the Contact Zone" was first delivered as a keynote address at the second Modern Language Association Literacy Conference, held in Pittsburgh in 1990.

Whenever the subject of literacy comes up, what often pops first into my mind is a conversation I overheard eight years ago between my son Sam and his best friend, Willie, aged six and seven, respectively: "Why don't you trade me Many Trails for Carl Yats . . . Yesits . . . Ya-strum-scrum." "That's not how you say it, dummy, it's Carl Yes . . . Yes . . . oh, I don't know." Sam and Willie had just discovered baseball cards. Many Trails was their decoding, with the help of first-grade English phonics, of the name Manny Trillo. The name they were quite rightly stumped on was Carl Yastremski. That was the first time I remembered seeing them put their incipient literacy to their own use, and I was of course thrilled.

Sam and Willie learned a lot about phonics that year by trying to decipher surnames on baseball cards, and a lot about cities, states, heights, weights, places of birth, stages of life. In the years that followed, I watched Sam apply his arithmetic skills to working out batting averages and subtracting retirement years from rookie years; I watched him develop senses of patterning and order by arranging and rearranging his cards for hours on end, and aesthetic judgment by comparing different photos, different series, layouts, and color schemes. American geography and history took shape in his mind through baseball cards. Much of his social life revolved around trading them, and he learned about exchange, fairness, trust, the importance of processes as opposed to results, what it means to get cheated, taken advantage of, even robbed. Baseball cards were the medium of his economic life too. Nowhere better to learn the power and arbitrariness of money, the absolute divorce between use value and exchange value, notions of long- and short-term investment, the possibility of personal values that are independent of market values.

Baseball cards meant baseball card shows, where there was much to be learned about adult worlds as well. And baseball cards opened the door to baseball books, shelves and shelves of encyclopedias, magazines, histories, biographies, novels, books of jokes, anecdotes, cartoons, even poems. Sam learned the history of American racism and the struggle against it through baseball; he saw the Depression and two world wars from behind home plate. He learned the meaning of commodified labor, what it means for one's body and talents to be owned and dispensed by another. He knows something about Japan, Taiwan, Cuba, and Central America and how men and boys do things there. Through the history and experience of baseball stadiums he thought about architecture, light, wind, topography, meteorology, the dynamics of public space. He learned the meaning of expertise, of knowing about something well enough that you can start a conversation with a stranger and feel sure of holding your own. Even with an adult— especially with an adult. Throughout his preadolescent years, baseball history was Sam's luminous point of contact with grown-ups, his lifeline to caring. And, of course, all this time he was also playing baseball, struggling his way through the stages of the local Little League system, lucky enough to be a pretty good player, loving the game and coming to know deeply his strengths and weaknesses.

Literacy began for Sam with the newly pronounceable names on the picture cards and brought him what has been easily the broadest, most varied, most enduring, and most integrated experience of his thirteen-year life. Like many parents, I was delighted to see schooling give Sam the tools with which to find and open all these doors. At the same time I found it unforgivable that schooling itself gave him nothing remotely as meaningful to do, let alone anything that would actually take him beyond the referential, masculinist ethos of baseball and its lore.

However, I was not invited here to speak as a parent, nor as an expert on literacy. I was asked to speak as an MLA [Modern Language Association] member working in the elite academy. In that capacity my contribution is undoubtedly supposed to be abstract, irrelevant, and anchored outside the real world. I wouldn't dream of disappointing anyone. I propose immediately to head back several centuries to a text that has a few points in common with baseball cards and raises thoughts about what Tony Sarmiento, in his comments to the conference, called new visions of literacy. In 1908 a Peruvianist named Richard Pietschmann was exploring in the Danish Royal Archive in Copenhagen and came across a manuscript. It was dated in the city of Cuzco in Peru, in the year 1613, some forty years after the final fall of the Inca Empire to the Spanish and signed with an unmistakably Andean indigenous name: Felipe Guaman Poma de Ayala. Written in a mixture of Quechua and ungrammatical, expressive Spanish, the manuscript was a letter addressed by an unknown but apparently literate Andean to King Philip III of Spain. What stunned Pietschmann was that the letter was twelve hundred pages long. There were almost eight hundred pages of written text and four hundred of captioned line drawings. It was titled *The First New Chronicle and Good Government.* No one knew (or knows) how the manuscript got to the library in Copenhagen or how long it had been there. No one, it appeared, had ever bothered to read it or figured out how. Quechua was not thought of as a written language in 1908, nor Andean culture as a literate culture.

Pietschmann prepared a paper on his find, which he presented in London in 1912, a year after the rediscovery of Machu Picchu by Hiram

Bingham. Reception, by an international congress of Americanists, was apparently confused. It took twenty-five years for a facsimile edition of the work to appear in Paris. It was not till the late 1970s, as positivist reading habits gave way to interpretive studies and colonial elitisms to postcolonial pluralisms, that Western scholars found ways of reading Guaman Poma's *New Chronicle and Good Government* as the extraordinary intercultural tour de force that it was. The letter got there, only 350 years too late, a miracle and a terrible tragedy.

I propose to say a few more words about this erstwhile unreadable text, in order to lay out some thoughts about writing and literacy in what I like to call the *contact zones*. I use this term to refer to social spaces where cultures meet, clash, and grapple with each other, often in contexts of highly asymmetrical relations of power, such as colonialism, slavery, or their aftermaths as they are lived out in many parts of the world today. Eventually I will use the term to reconsider the models of community that many of us rely on in teaching and theorizing and that are under challenge today. But first a little more about Guaman Poma's giant letter to Philip III.

Insofar as anything is known about him at all, Guaman Poma exemplified the sociocultural complexities produced by conquest and empire. He was an indigenous Andean who claimed noble Inca descent and who had adopted (at least in some sense) Christianity. He may have worked in the Spanish colonial administration as an interpreter, scribe, or assistant to a Spanish tax collector — as a mediator, in short. He says he learned to write from his half brother, a mestizo whose Spanish father had given him access to religious education.

Guaman Poma's letter to the king is written in two languages (Spanish and Quechua) and two parts. The first is called the *Nueva corónica*, "New Chronicle." The title is important. The chronicle of course was the main writing apparatus through which the Spanish presented their American conquests to themselves. It constituted one of the main official discourses. In writing a "new chronicle," Guaman Poma took over the official Spanish genre for his own ends. Those ends were, roughly, to construct a new picture of the world, a picture of a Christian world with Andean rather than European peoples at the center of it — Cuzco, not Jerusalem. In the *New Chronicle* Guaman Poma begins by rewriting the Christian history of the world from Adam and Eve (Fig. 1), incorporating the Amerindians into it as offspring of one of the sons of Noah. He identifies five ages of Christian history that he links in parallel with the five ages of canonical Andean history — separate but equal trajectories that diverge with Noah and reintersect not with Columbus but with Saint Bartholomew, claimed to have preceded Columbus in the Americas. In a couple of hundred pages, Guaman Poma constructs a veritable encyclopedia of Inca and pre-Inca history, customs, laws, social forms, public offices, and dynastic leaders. The depictions resemble European manners and customs description, but also reproduce the meticulous detail with which knowledge in Inca society was stored on *quipus*° and in the oral memories of elders.

Guaman Poma's *New Chronicle* is an instance of what I have proposed to call an *autoethnographic* text, by which I mean a text in which people undertake to describe themselves in ways that engage with representations others have made of them. Thus if ethnographic texts are those in which European metropolitan subjects represent to themselves their others (usually their conquered others), autoethnographic texts are representations that the so-defined others construct *in response to* or in dialogue with those texts. Autoethnographic texts are not, then, what are usually thought of as autochthonous forms of expression or self-representation (as the Andean *quipus* were). Rather they involve a selective collaboration with and appropriation of idioms of the metropolis or the conqueror. These are merged or infiltrated to varying degrees with indigenous idioms to create self-representations intended to intervene in metropolitan modes of understanding. Autoethnographic works are often addressed to both metropolitan audiences and the speaker's own community. Their reception is thus highly indeterminate. Such texts often constitute a marginalized group's point of entry into the dominant circuits of print culture. It is interesting to think, for example, of American slave autobiography in its autoethnographic dimensions, which in some respects distinguish it from Euramerican autobiographical tradition. The concept might help explain why some of the earliest published writing by Chicanas took the form of folkloric manners and customs sketches written in English and published in English-language newspapers or folklore magazines (see Treviño). Autoethnographic representation often involves concrete collaborations between people, as between literate ex-slaves and abolitionist intellectuals, or between Guaman Poma and the Inca elders who were his informants. Often, as in Guaman Poma, it involves more than one language. In recent decades autoethnography, critique, and resistance have reconnected with writing in a contemporary creation of the contact zone, the *testimonio*.

Guaman Poma's *New Chronicle* ends with a revisionist account of the Spanish conquest, which, he argues, should have been a peaceful encounter of equals with the potential for benefiting both, but for the mindless greed of the Spanish. He parodies Spanish history. Following contact with the Incas,

---

quipus: Recording devices consisting of colored threads with numeric and other values encoded by knots, used chiefly by administrators in the Inca Empire. Some quipus have up to 2,000 strands.

Figure 1. Adam and Eve.

he writes, "In all Castille, there was a great commotion. All day and at night in their dreams the Spaniards were saying, 'Yndias, yndias, oro, plata, oro, plata del Piru'" ("Indies, Indies, gold, silver, gold, silver from Peru") (Fig. 2). The Spanish, he writes, brought nothing of value to share with the Andeans, nothing "but armor and guns con la codicia de oro, plata oro y plata, yndias, a las Yndias, Piru" ("with the lust for gold, silver, gold and silver, Indies, the Indies, Peru") (372). I quote these words as an example of a conquered subject using the conqueror's language to construct a parodic, oppositional representation of the conqueror's own speech. Guaman Poma mirrors back to the Spanish (in their language, which is alien to him) an image of themselves that they often suppress and will therefore surely recognize. Such are the dynamics of language, writing, and representation in contact zones.

The second half of the epistle continues the critique. It is titled *Buen gobierno y justicia*, "Good Government and Justice," and combines a description of colonial society in the Andean region with a passionate denunciation of Spanish exploitation and abuse. (These, at the time he was writing, were

Figure 2. Conquista. Meeting of Spaniard and Inca. The Inca says in Quechua, "You eat this gold?" Spaniard replies in Spanish, "We eat this gold."

decimating the population of the Andes at a genocidal rate. In fact, the potential loss of the labor force became a main cause for reform of the system.) Guaman Poma's most implacable hostility is invoked by the clergy, followed by the dreaded *corregidores*, or colonial overseers (Fig. 3). He also praises good works, Christian habits, and just men where he finds them, and offers at length his views as to what constitutes "good government and justice." The Indies, he argues, should be administered through a collaboration of Inca and Spanish elites. The epistle ends with an imaginary question-and-answer session in which, in a reversal of hierarchy, the king is depicted asking Guaman Poma questions about how to reform the empire — a dialogue imagined across the many lines that divide the Andean scribe from the imperial monarch, and in which the subordinated subject single-handedly gives himself authority in the colonizer's language and verbal repertoire. In a way, it worked — this extraordinary text did get written — but in a way it did not, for the letter never reached its addressee.

Figure 3. Corregidor de minas. Catalog of Spanish abuses of indigenous labor force.

To grasp the import of Guaman Poma's project, one needs to keep in mind that the Incas had no system of writing. Their huge empire is said to be the only known instance of a full-blown bureaucratic state society built and administered without writing. Guaman Poma constructs his text by appropriating and adapting pieces of the representational repertoire of the invaders. He does not simply imitate or reproduce it; he selects and adapts it along Andean lines to express (bilingually, mind you) Andean interests and aspirations. Ethnographers have used the term *transculturation* to describe processes whereby members of subordinated or marginal groups select and invent from materials transmitted by a dominant or metropolitan culture. The term, originally coined by Cuban sociologist Fernando Ortiz in the 1940s, aimed to replace overly reductive concepts of acculturation and assimilation used to characterize culture under conquest. While subordinate peoples do not usually control what emanates from the dominant culture, they do determine to varying extents what gets absorbed into their own and what it gets used for. Transculturation, like autoethnography, is a phenomenon of the contact zone.

As scholars have realized only relatively recently, the transcultural character of Guaman Poma's text is intricately apparent in its visual as well as its written component. The genre of the four hundred line drawings is European — there seems to have been no tradition of representational drawing among the Incas — but in their execution they deploy specifically Andean systems of spatial symbolism that express Andean values and aspirations.[1]

In figure 1, for instance, Adam is depicted on the left-hand side below the sun, while Eve is on the right-hand side below the moon, and slightly lower than Adam. The two are divided by the diagonal of Adam's digging stick. In Andean spatial symbolism, the diagonal descending from the sun marks the basic line of power and authority dividing upper from lower, male from female, dominant from subordinate. In figure 2, the Inca appears in the same position as Adam, with the Spaniard opposite, and the two at the same height. In figure 3, depicting Spanish abuses of power, the symbolic pattern is reversed. The Spaniard is in a high position indicating dominance, but on the "wrong" (right-hand) side. The diagonals of his lance and that of the servant doing the flogging mark out a line of illegitimate, though real, power. The Andean figures continue to occupy the left-hand side of the picture, but clearly as victims. Guaman Poma wrote that the Spanish conquest had produced *"un mundo al reves,"* "a world in reverse."

In sum, Guaman Poma's text is truly a product of the contact zone. If one thinks of cultures, or literatures, as discrete, coherently structured, monolingual edifices, Guaman Poma's text, and indeed any autoethnographic work, appears anomalous or chaotic — as it apparently did to the European scholars Pietschmann spoke to in 1912. If one does not think of cultures this way, then Guaman Poma's text is simply heterogeneous, as the Andean region was itself and remains today. Such a text is heterogeneous on the reception end as well as the production end: It will read very differently to people in different positions in the contact zone. Because it deploys European and Andean systems of meaning making, the letter necessarily means differently to bilingual Spanish-Quechua speakers and to monolingual speakers in either language; the drawings mean differently to monocultural readers, Spanish or Andean, and to bicultural readers responding to the Andean symbolic structures embodied in European genres.

In the Andes in the early 1600s there existed a literate public with considerable intercultural competence and degrees of bilingualism. Unfortunately, such a community did not exist in the Spanish court with which Guaman Poma was trying to make contact. It is interesting to note

15

that in the same year Guaman Poma sent off his letter, a text by another Peruvian was adopted in official circles in Spain as the canonical Christian mediation between the Spanish conquest and Inca history. It was another huge encyclopedic work, titled the *Royal Commentaries of the Incas,* written, tellingly, by a mestizo, Inca Garcilaso de la Vega. Like the mestizo half brother who taught Guaman Poma to read and write, Inca Garcilaso was the son of an Inca princess and a Spanish official, and had lived in Spain since he was seventeen. Though he too spoke Quechua, his book is written in eloquent, standard Spanish, without illustrations. While Guaman Poma's life's work sat somewhere unread, the *Royal Commentaries* was edited and re-edited in Spain and the New World, a mediation that coded the Andean past and present in ways thought unthreatening to colonial hierarchy.[2] The textual hierarchy persists; the *Royal Commentaries* today remains a staple item on PhD reading lists in Spanish, while the *New Chronicle and Good Government,* despite the ready availability of several fine editions, is not. However, though Guaman Poma's text did not reach its destination, the transcultural currents of expression it exemplifies continued to evolve in the Andes, as they still do, less in writing than in storytelling, ritual, song, dance-drama, painting and sculpture, dress, textile art, forms of governance, religious belief, and many other vernacular art forms. All express the effects of long-term contact and intractable, unequal conflict.

Autoethnography, transculturation, critique, collaboration, bilingualism, mediation, parody, denunciation, imaginary dialogue, vernacular expression — these are some of the literate arts of the contact zone. Miscomprehension, incomprehension, dead letters, unread masterpieces, absolute heterogeneity of meaning — these are some of the perils of writing in the contact zone. They all live among us today in the transnationalized metropolis of the United States and are becoming more widely visible, more pressing, and, like Guaman Poma's text, more decipherable to those who once would have ignored them in defense of a stable, centered sense of knowledge and reality.

Contact and Community

The idea of the contact zone is intended in part to contrast with ideas of community that underlie much of the thinking about language, communication, and culture that gets done in the academy. A couple of years ago, thinking about the linguistic theories I knew, I tried to make sense of a utopian quality that often seemed to characterize social analyses of language by the academy. Languages were seen as living in "speech communities," and these tended to be theorized as discrete, self-defined, coherent entities, held together by a homogeneous competence or grammar shared identically and equally among all the members. This abstract idea of the speech community seemed to reflect, among other things, the utopian way modern nations conceive of themselves as what Benedict Anderson calls "imagined communities."[3] In a book of that title, Anderson observes that with the possible exception of what he calls "primordial villages," human communities exist as *imagined* entities in which people "will never know most of their fellow-members, meet them or even hear of them, yet in the mind of each lives the image of their communion." "Communities are distinguished," he goes on to say, "not by their falsity/genuineness, but by *the style in which they are imagined*" (15; emphasis mine). Anderson proposes three features that characterize the style in which the modern nation is imagined. First, it is imagined as *limited*, by "finite, if elastic, boundaries"; second, it is imagined as *sovereign*; and, third, it is imagined as *fraternal*, "a deep, horizontal comradeship" for which millions of people are prepared "not so much to kill as willingly to die" (15). As the image suggests, the nation-community is embodied metonymically in the finite, sovereign, fraternal figure of the citizen-soldier.

Anderson argues that European bourgeoisies were distinguished by their ability to "achieve solidarity on an essentially imagined basis" (74) on a scale far greater than that of elites of other times and places. Writing and literacy play a central role in this argument. Anderson maintains, as have others, that the main instrument that made bourgeois nation-building projects possible was print capitalism. The commercial circulation of books in the various European vernaculars, he argues, was what first created the invisible networks that would eventually constitute the literate elites and those they ruled as nations. (Estimates are that 180 million books were put into circulation in Europe between the years 1500 and 1600 alone.)

Now obviously this style of imagining of modern nations, as Anderson describes it, is strongly utopian, embodying values like equality, fraternity, liberty, which the societies often profess but systematically fail to realize. The prototype of the modern nation as imagined community was, it seemed to me, mirrored in ways people thought about language and the speech community. Many commentators have pointed out how modern views of language as code and competence assume a unified and homogeneous social world in which language exists as a shared patrimony—as a device, precisely, for imagining community. An image of a universally shared literacy is also part of the picture. The prototypical manifestation of language is generally taken to be the speech of individual adult native speakers face-to-face (as in Saussure's famous diagram) in monolingual, even monodialectal situations—in short, the most homogeneous case linguistically and socially. The same goes for written communication. Now one could certainly imagine a theory that assumed different things — that argued, for instance, that the most revealing speech situation for understanding language was one involving a gathering of people each of whom spoke two languages and understood a third and held only one language in common with any of the others. It depends on what workings of language you want to see or want to see first, on what you choose to define as normative.

In keeping with autonomous, fraternal models of community, analyses of language use commonly assume that principles of cooperation and shared understanding are normally in effect. Descriptions of interactions between people in conversation, classrooms, medical and bureaucratic settings, readily take it for granted that the situation is governed by a single set of rules or norms shared by all participants. The analysis focuses then on how those rules produce or fail to produce an orderly, coherent exchange. Models involving games and moves are often used to describe interactions. Despite whatever conflicts or systematic social differences might be in play, it is assumed that all participants are engaged in the same game and that the game is the same for all players. Often it is. But of course it often is not, as, for example, when speakers are from different classes or cultures, or one party is exercising authority and another is submitting to it or questioning it. Last year one of my children moved to a new elementary school that had more open classrooms and more flexible curricula than the conventional school he started out in. A few days into the term, we asked him what it was like at the new school. "Well," he said, "they're a lot nicer, and they have a lot less rules. But know *why* they're nicer?" "Why?" I asked. "So you'll obey all the rules they don't have," he replied. This is a very coherent analysis with considerable elegance and explanatory power, but probably not the one his teacher would have given.

Social spaces where cultures meet, clash, and grapple with each other.

When linguistic (or literate) interaction is described in terms of orderliness, games, moves, or scripts, usually only legitimate moves are actually named as part of the system, where legitimacy is defined from the point of view of the party in authority — regardless of what other parties might see themselves as doing. Teacher-pupil language, for example, tends to be described almost entirely from the point of view of the teacher and teaching, not from the point of view of pupils and pupiling (the word doesn't even exist, though the thing certainly does). If a classroom is analyzed as a social world unified and homogenized with respect to the teacher, whatever students do other than what the teacher specifies is invisible or anomalous to the analysis. This can be true in practice as well. On several occasions my fourth grader, the one busy obeying all the rules they didn't have, was given writing assignments that took the form of answering a series of questions to build up a paragraph. These questions often asked him to identify with the interests of those in power over him — parents, teachers, doctors, public authorities. He invariably sought ways to resist or subvert these assignments. One assignment, for instance, called for imagining "a helpful invention." The students were asked to write single-sentence responses to the following questions:

> What kind of invention would help you?
> How would it help you?
> Why would you need it?
> What would it look like?
> Would other people be able to use it also?
> What would be an invention to help your teacher?
> What would be an invention to help your parents?

Manuel's reply read as follows:

A grate adventchin

Some inventchins are GRATE!!!!!!!!!!! My inventchin would be a shot that would put every thing you learn at school in your brain. It would help me by letting me graduate right now!! I would need it because it would let me play with my friends, go on vacachin and, do fun a lot more. It would look like a regular shot. Ather peaple would use to. This inventchin would help my teacher parents get away from a lot of work. I think a shot like this would be GRATE!

Despite the spelling, the assignment received the usual star to indicate the task had been fulfilled in an acceptable way. No recognition was available, however, of the humor, the attempt to be critical or contestatory, to parody the structures of authority. On that score, Manuel's luck was only slightly better than Guaman Poma's. What is the place of unsolicited oppositional discourse, parody, resistance, critique in the imagined classroom community? Are teachers supposed to feel that their teaching has been most successful when they have eliminated such things and unified the social world, probably in their own image? Who wins when we do that? Who loses?

Such questions may be hypothetical, because in the United States in the 1990s, many teachers find themselves less and less able to do that even if they want to. The composition of the national collectivity is changing and so are the styles, as Anderson put it, in which it is being imagined. In the 1980s in many nation-states, imagined national syntheses that had retained hegemonic force began to dissolve. Internal social groups with histories and lifeways different from the official ones began insisting on those histories and lifeways *as part of their citizenship*, as the very mode of their membership in the national collectivity. In their dialogues with dominant institutions, many groups began asserting a rhetoric of belonging that made demands beyond those of representation and basic rights granted from above. In universities we started to hear, "I don't just want you to let me be here, I want to belong here; this institution should belong to me as much as it does to anyone else."

Institutions have responded with, among other things, rhetorics of diversity and multiculturalism whose import at this moment is up for grabs across the ideological spectrum.

These shifts are being lived out by everyone working in education today,   25 and everyone is challenged by them in one way or another. Those of us committed to educational democracy are particularly challenged as that notion finds itself besieged on the public agenda. Many of those who govern us display, openly, their interest in a quiescent, ignorant, manipulable electorate. Even as an ideal, the concept of an enlightened citizenry seems to have disappeared from the national imagination. A couple of years ago the university where I work went through an intense and wrenching debate over a narrowly defined Western-culture requirement that had been instituted there in 1980. It kept boiling down to a debate over the ideas of national patrimony, cultural citizenship, and imagined community. In the end, the requirement was transformed into a much more broadly defined course called Cultures, Ideas, Values.[4] In the context of the change, a new course was designed that centered on the Americas and the multiple cultural histories (including European ones) that have intersected here. As you can imagine, the course attracted a very diverse student body. The classroom functioned not like a homogeneous community or a horizontal alliance but like a contact zone. Every single text we read stood in specific historical relationships to the students in the class, but the range and variety of historical relationships in play were enormous. Everybody had a stake in nearly everything we read, but the range and kind of stakes varied widely.

It was the most exciting teaching we had ever done, and also the hardest. We were struck, for example, at how anomalous the formal lecture became in a contact zone (who can forget Atahuallpa throwing down the Bible because it would not speak to him?). The lecturer's traditional (imagined) task — unifying the world in the class's eyes by means of a monologue that rings equally coherent, revealing, and true for all, forging an ad hoc community, homogeneous with respect to one's own words — this task became not only impossible but anomalous and unimaginable. Instead, one had to work in the knowledge that whatever one said was going to be systematically received in radically heterogeneous ways that we were neither able nor entitled to prescribe.

The very nature of the course put ideas and identities on the line. All the students in the class had the experience, for example, of hearing their culture discussed and objectified in ways that horrified them; all the students saw their roots traced back to legacies of both glory and shame; all the students experienced face-to-face the ignorance and incomprehension, and occasionally the hostility, of others. In the absence of community values and the hope of synthesis, it was easy to forget the positives; the fact, for instance, that kinds of marginalization once taken for granted were gone. Virtually every student was having the experience of seeing the world described with him or her in it. Along with rage, incomprehension, and pain, there were exhilarating moments of wonder and revelation, mutual understanding, and new wisdom — the joys of the contact zone. The sufferings and revelations were, at different moments to be sure, experienced by every student. No one was excluded, and no one was safe.

The fact that no one was safe made all of us involved in the course appreciate the importance of what we came to call "safe houses." We used the term to refer to social and intellectual spaces where groups can constitute themselves as horizontal, homogeneous, sovereign communities with high degrees of trust, shared understandings, temporary protection from legacies of oppression. This is why, as we realized, multicultural curricula should not seek to replace ethnic or women's studies, for example. Where there are legacies of subordination, groups need places for healing and mutual recognition, safe houses in which to construct shared understandings, knowledges, claims on the world that they can then bring into the contact zone.

Meanwhile, our job in the Americas course remains to figure out how to make that crossroads the best site for learning that it can be. We are looking for the pedagogical arts of the contact zone. These will include, we are sure, exercises in storytelling and in identifying with the ideas, interests, histories, and attitudes of others; experiments in transculturation and collaborative work and in the arts of critique, parody, and comparison (including unseemly comparisons between elite and vernacular cultural forms); the redemption of the oral; ways for people to engage with suppressed aspects of history (including their own histories), ways to move *into and out of* rhetorics of authenticity; ground rules for communication across lines of difference and hierarchy that go beyond politeness but maintain mutual respect; a systematic approach to the all-important concept of *cultural mediation*. These arts were in play in every room at the extraordinary Pittsburgh conference on literacy. I learned a lot about them there, and I am thankful.

Works Cited

Adorno, Rolena. *Guaman Poma de Ayala: Writing and Resistance in Colonial Peru.* Austin: U of Texas P, 1986.

Anderson, Benedict. *Imagined Communities: Reflections on the Origins and Spread of Nationalism.* London: Verso, 1984.

Garcilaso de la Vega, El Inca. *Royal Commentaries of the Incas.* 1613. Austin: U of Texas P, 1966.

Guaman Poma de Ayala, Felipe. *El primer nueva corónica y buen gobierno.*
    Manuscript. Ed. John Murra and Rolena Adorno. Mexico: Siglo XXI, 1980.
Pratt, Mary Louise. "Linguistic Utopias." *The Linguistics of Writing.* Ed. Nigel
    Fabb et al. Manchester: Manchester UP, 1987. 48–66.
Trevño, Gloria. "Cultural Ambivalence in Early Chicano Prose Fiction." Diss.
    Stanford U, 1985.

Notes

1. For an introduction in English to these and other aspects of Guaman Poma's work, see Rolena Adorno. Adorno and Mercedes Lopez-Baralt pioneered the study of Andean symbolic systems in Guaman Poma.

2. It is far from clear that the *Royal Commentaries* was as benign as the Spanish seemed to assume. The book certainly played a role in maintaining the identity and aspirations of indigenous elites in the Andes. In the mid-eighteenth century, a new edition of the *Royal Commentaries* was suppressed by Spanish authorities because its preface included a prophecy by Sir Walter Raleigh that the English would invade Peru and restore the Inca monarchy.

3. The discussion of community here is summarized from my essay "Linguistic Utopias."

4. For information about this program and the contents of courses taught in it, write Program in Cultures, Ideas, Values (CIV), Stanford Univ., Stanford, CA 94305.

Working with the Text

1. Mary Louise Pratt's essay may at first seem to bring together at least three seemingly unrelated subjects: her son's interest in baseball cards, a seventeenth-century Peruvian text, and a new course at Stanford University. Yet with these diverse subjects, Pratt draws on her research, classroom experience, and personal life to question our assumptions about language and community. In a brief essay, explain Pratt's concept of a "contact zone" by identifying and analyzing the common thread that runs through the stories of the early seventeenth-century Andean writer Guaman Poma; students in Stanford University's Cultures, Ideas, and Values course; and Pratt's son.

2. In the context of defining the contact zone, Pratt introduces the term *autoethnographic* text — a text in which subordinated people "undertake to describe themselves in ways that engage with representations others have made of them" (par. 10). The "others" in her definition are people who dominate culture or have conquered another people. Review Pratt's descriptions of autoethnographic texts. Drawing on the concepts and examples she presents, write a brief essay in which you introduce autoethnography to your peers or to another group as a means for resisting authority or asserting identity.

3. Two key terms in Pratt's essay — *culture and community* — are often thought of in broad, positive, even warm and fuzzy ways. One of the many virtues of

Pratt's essay is that she encourages us to look for the tensions and ambiguities in these two terms. In a brief essay, reflect on Pratt's use of these terms. What received or traditional definitions are implied in her essay? In what ways does her term *contact zone* help us rethink these terms?

From Text to Field

1. When Pratt introduces her concept of contact zones, she presents them as places of conflict, "social spaces where cultures meet, clash, and grapple with each other, often in contexts of highly asymmetrical relations of power" (par. 7). When she applies the term to the classes in culture she teaches, she also refers to "exhilarating moments of wonder and revelation, mutual understanding, and new wisdom—the joys of the contact zone" (par. 27). In a personal essay, reflect on your experience within one or more contact zones. Was the contact zone primarily a place of conflict and domination? Did it produce mutual understanding? Were both conflict and understanding parts of the experience?

2. In discussing Benedict Anderson's concept of "imagined communities," Pratt describes the "nation-building" made possible through the "commercial circulation of books in the various European vernaculars," starting in the fifteenth and sixteenth century (par. 20). Based on Pratt's definition of "imagined communities," write an essay in which you identify media—especially commercial media—that promote nation-building or the development of imagined communities today. How do media bring people into an imagined community? What images or identities do the media create? How accurate do you think the images or identities are? In what ways might such communities be, to use Pratt's term, "linguistic utopias"?

3. In the final paragraph of Pratt's essay, she notes, "We are looking for the pedagogical arts of the contact zone" (par. 29). Drawing on the extensive list she provides, consider your own educational experiences in college. Do any of your courses or professors draw on "the pedagogical arts of the contact zone"? If so, in what ways and with what effectiveness? In not, in what ways could a particular course be reimagined so that it might draw on such arts?

4. In Pratt's view, teachers—especially those in higher education—can no longer assume that they are in a position to deliver knowledge that "rings equally coherent, revealing, and true for all" (par. 26). According to Pratt, movements that emerged in and after the 1980s began questioning the supposed homogeneity in American education:

> In their dialogues with dominant institutions, many groups began asserting a rhetoric of belonging that made demands beyond those of representation and basic rights granted from above. In universities we started

> to hear, "I don't just want you to let me be here, I want to belong here; this institution should belong to me as much as it does to anyone else." (par. 24)

In an essay, interpret this passage by providing examples from your own observation, experience, and awareness of the role of contact zones and conflict in communities and community building.

INTO THE FIELD: Options for Writing Projects

1. Conversation Partners

Nancy Masterson Sakamoto gleaned her insights into conversation patterns as they differ across cultures not from theory or cloistered research but from her daily interactions with Japanese friends, neighbors, and students. This field project invites you to extend and amplify Sakamoto's thoughts on cross-cultural conversation by joining such a conversation yourself with a foreign student on campus.

Most colleges and universities offer what is sometimes called a "conversation partners" program for foreign students on campus or for students for whom English is a second language. Such programs are often sponsored by an office of international education or by an English as a second language (ESL) program, typically housed in English or linguistics departments. A "conversation partners" program matches American students with foreign students so that they might meet about one hour per week to converse. Apart from helping the nonnative speaker develop fluency in English, you'll find yourself amply rewarded by learning about a foreign culture and gaining a new perspective on American culture. You'll be introduced to a potential new friend and to the foreign student's circle of friends.

This field project invites you to reflect on the conversational patterns you see occurring with your partner and on the delights and challenges of cross-cultural understanding. Your essay might focus as much on your own changing attitudes as on the foreign student's background. As you both cross borders to find common ground and mutual interests, how does your conversation grow and evolve? In what ways are you now able to see American culture through a new set of eyes?

2. Sharing Tables: The Cultures of Food

In the final section of Nancy Masterson Sakamoto's essay, she turns to the connection between conversation and eating food. Little wonder. Cuisine offers a wonderfully rich opportunity to explore foreign cultures and the regional cultures in our own country. Sharing a table with others sparks conviviality and conversation in ways not otherwise possible. Share food and drink, and you share an experience that connects you with people in ways that can sometimes transcend cultural barriers.

This field project invites you to share your table with others and in the process explore how cuisine can further cultural awareness. Here are just some of the many directions you might pursue:

- Share a charged memory from childhood that turns on a particular food dish or on the role of food in a special celebration or event.

- Investigate regional or ethnic cookbooks, cookbooks or recipes that have been handed down in your family, or old cookbooks that are themselves historical documents.
- Explore the role of food in civic events — be it the pie-baking contest at the local county fair or the large urban food festival.
- Reflect on the role of food in campus activities — be it in student organizations or in departmental events. Ask why the first law of drumming up attendance at meetings — "feed them and they will come" — has more to it than just the natural instinct for free munchies.
- Hold a potluck in your writing class, perhaps at a special evening meeting. You might use this event either as a kick-off for food-related projects or as a culminating event during which you and your classmates read from your essays. Think of your words, and those of others, as tasty morsels.
- Analyze the ways in which students share — or don't share — tables in your dorm or campus cafeteria. How does ethnic or cultural difference reflect itself in the cafeteria setting? In what ways does the cafeteria promote or undermine interactions among students and the ability to cultivate new friendships?
- Explore the underworld of student cooking in your dorm. It may not be entirely legal or sanctioned, but if experience rings true, students try to escape from the institutionalized world of the food service — be it through hotplates, microwaves, toaster ovens, or popcorn poppers.

3. Touring the Campus or Local Museum

The visits that Jane Tompkins made to the Cowboy Hall of Fame and the Museum of the American Indian might inspire you to explore museums and galleries on your campus or in your community. Armed with Tompkins's insights about the problems of representing others — and yourself — you are now in a position to cast a more critical eye on the various installations or exhibits that you will see. Here are just some of the places your museum tour might take you:

- Many campuses will have a heritage center that showcases the history of your college or university, often focusing on the accomplishments of alumni and the prowess of sports teams. In what ways does your campus represent itself to others? Who is the intended or anticipated audience, and what are their expectations and assumptions? What presence might academics have in the exhibits? If sports have a prominent place in the exhibits, what might that tell you about how our culture constructs the college experience or about the role of sports in your institution's sense of itself?
- Your campus or community may also have a natural history museum or a fine-arts gallery, with permanent collections and visiting exhibits. What

issues of cultural representation might arise in these venues? How do such exhibits project an image of the college or university for the community and the state? Consider interviewing the curators of the shows, seeking their views on the role of the museum and the often difficult issues of representation that can arise in exhibits.

- Your campus library and even some departments may present more modest exhibits, which can nevertheless offer fascinating case studies about how we represent others and how we represent ourselves.
- Consider planning (and even mounting) a modest exhibit about writing and writing instruction on your campus. What might you present in a hallway exhibit case or on the wall-mounted bulletin board? What is difficult to represent about the writing process? Who is your audience, and what expectations or attitudes might they carry with them to your exhibit? Considering that most exhibits are veiled arguments of one kind or another, what message or argument would you want to present? What is the role of text, graphic devices, and visual arguments in exhibit design? How do you plan to implement them?

4. Representations of Other Cultures in Popular Media

Although Jane Tompkins focuses on museums as important sites through which to study cultural representation, museums are by no means the only such sites, nor are they the most influential. This field project invites you to explore other sites where cultures are represented. Popular media, such as film and television, offer rich resources for such a study.

In addition to studying depictions of foreign cultures (e.g., the Disney film *Aladdin*), you might also wish to consider any one of many marginalized groups in American culture. In what ways does popular media stereotype such groups or cultures? What opportunities or risks might a film (or some other form of popular media) take to more genuinely address the challenges of cultural representation?

Your field project might take the form of an academic analysis or of a more popular journalistic piece, such as a review.

5. Contact Zones in Your Core Curriculum

As a teacher and scholar whose work challenges dominant cultures, Mary Louise Pratt brought her interest in contact zones to her involvement in broadening the Western-culture course requirement at Stanford University to include "multiple cultural histories." Reread her description of the dynamics of the new course so that you might consider discussions of curriculum on your own campus. This field project invites you to evaluate the core or general-education curriculum on your campus in light of the discussions in Pratt's essay and on the Stanford campus. Address the questions of how history and culture should be taught to undergraduates and what bearing Pratt's discussion of "contact zones" might have on those questions. Depending on the state of discussions on your campus, your field project could take one of several forms:

- If your campus does not have a required course or set of courses in the area of history and culture, argue for or against adopting the approach suggested by Pratt. Given the particular culture on your campus and the history of curricular discussions, what specific arguments on either side of the issue appear to be most relevant? Make a point of interviewing faculty for their views on the issue. Depending on your stance and on the audience you wish to address, your project might take the form of an essay, a substantive letter to an administrator, an opinion piece in the campus newspaper, or even a formal course proposal (using the required forms).
- If your institution already requires a course that comes close to meeting the spirit of Pratt's suggestion, offer an assessment of the course, with recommendations for retaining, improving, or transforming it. What concerns or controversies accompanied the proposal for the course, and to what degree do those same concerns and controversies still exist? Your project might take the form of an essay or a substantive letter to the faculty member who administers the course.
- Even if your campus does not have a course that meets the spirit of Pratt's discussion and there is little likelihood of such a course coming into existence, there are surely several courses already "on the books" that might lend themselves to some of her suggestions. What innovative "pedagogical arts of the contact zone" might be introduced into existing courses? Focus on one or two courses you have taken or are currently taking which might benefit from those pedagogical arts. You might find interviews with faculty currently teaching those courses to be especially helpful.

6. The Composition Classroom as Contact Zone

Because writing courses are usually taught in small classes, it may be tempting to assume that the sense of community that develops in the classroom over the course of a term is entirely unproblematic. After all, the instructor and students get to know each other in ways that are not possible in most courses, and they are working on some of the most intimate and revealing concerns — one's own writing and its inevitable link to one's identity. It would be hard to imagine a classroom community coming out of a composition course that did not emerge stronger, more cooperative, and more homogeneous — a discrete, self-defined, and coherent speech community. Yet for all of the positive ways in which a composition classroom can come together, it may still be far from the idealized or utopian speech community that we might imagine. Indeed, the classroom may resemble the sort of "contact zone" that Mary Louise Pratt discusses.

This field project invites you to attend closely to your composition class-room. Your goal is not to criticize per se but rather to speak frankly about the tensions and differences that can sometimes intersect in this contact zone. Composition classrooms emerge stronger when they acknowledge these issues and make productive use of them through what Pratt calls innovative "pedagogical arts of the contact zone." Your essay should contribute to an honest and healthy classroom.

Drawing on Pratt's definition of a "contact zone" early in her essay, and attending closely to her discussion of "contact and community" later in the piece, develop a set of questions you want to address in the context of your own composition classroom. In addition to uncovering some of the character-istics that may make the classroom a contact zone, you should also address the "pedagogical arts" that are being used or that could be used to make pro-ductive use of those characteristics. Remember that for all of the "rage, incom-prehension, and pain" that can occur in a contact zone, Pratt also stresses "exhilarating moments of wonder and revelation, mutual understanding, and new wisdom — the joys of the contact zone."

7. Mapping and Crossing Borders on Campus

When judged by the map you held in your hands during your first days on cam-pus, your college or university may seem to be one undifferentiated (if some-times vast) territory. The borders that you see may divide your campus from the nearby town, but once on campus you may see little in the way of internal boundaries — at first. After only a few weeks, you were surely far more aware of the different territories or regions on campus and the subtle barriers between them.

This field project invites you to map and discuss the internal borders on your campus. You'll want to note the tensions that may exist and how those tensions can take shape in concrete ways — often physical or geographic. In addition to describing those existing tensions, you may want to inquire into their causes and propose ways in which various members of your campus com-munity can cross those borders.

A good place to start your investigation is to look for contact zones, for those "seams" in what is otherwise the large fabric of your campus. You may find those seams (paraphrasing Mary Louise Pratt) in the social spaces where campus cultures meet and rub up against each other. Look to interactions between students and faculty, faculty and staff, administration and faculty, administration and parents, or between various student groups themselves.

You may also wish to explore what might be thought of as "disciplinary geographies" on your campus. Are the science departments clustered in one area? Are the professional schools (such as engineering, business, and law) located at the far end of campus? What of the boundaries between academic areas and dorm areas or between dorms and "fraternity or sorority row"? Who has the new buildings, and who is housed in the old? Where is the writing program located? (Chances are it is in a basement or in a "temporary building.") What key geographic landmarks seem to have a leading role in orienting people on campus? Is it the student union, the main administration building, or some tower or other landmark? In addition to your essay, you may wish to craft an interpretive map of campus, much as those early explorers developed when they were charting new territories.

8. The Freshman Year as a Borderland Experience

As you enter college, you must straddle the community from which you came and the new community of college. In the process, you must find a way of dealing with the voices of your home and heritage, even as you develop an academic voice. This field project encourages you to explore your experience in college as you find yourself at the borders between different cultures and their voices. In many respects the first year of college can be especially challenging—and rewarding—because of experiences "at the border."

In addition to taking a close look at your experiences, place them in a larger context by talking to other students, your resident advisor, and people on campus who are involved in the first-year experience. You may also wish to consult the growing research literature on experiences during the first year of college. As you plan and draft your essay, ask yourself how you wish to present yourself, and with what voice or voices. Use this essay as an opportunity to reflect on — or even experiment with— different voices.

5

(En)gendering Knowledge

SPEAKING OF GENDER

As a topic of casual conversation or academic interest, we may sometimes "speak of gender." The subject has grown in interest, and sometimes controversy, over the years. The women's movement has evolved, and some might even speak of past or present "gender wars." Indeed, our very notion of gender has grown more complex as we recognize how difficult it may be to make easy distinctions about what is male or female. Yet more may be at stake than simply the many things we may say or write "about" men and women. This chapter explores the notion that speaking and writing are themselves gendered. Gender can be voiced and silenced as well. That is, gender is more than one of many topics of conversation; it also influences our conversation and, no matter what the subject, our use of language to learn, know, and communicate. As we speak here of gender, we may find that speaking is itself gendered.

History teaches us that our speaking has always been gendered, but the prevalence of male power — patriarchal ideologies and institutions — made that gender influence all but invisible. Indeed, *feminist* originally meant the same thing as *feminine* — "of the female" and remained so through much of the nineteenth century. In the mid-to-late nineteenth century, the meaning of *feminist* began to shift, with efforts to improve the status of women lending the term what some saw as negative connotations.

In the nineteenth century, women who worked on behalf of other reform movements — agitating against slavery, alcohol abuse, and prostitution — prompted debate about whether women should even exercise a public voice in such matters. When activists worked more directly on behalf of women's rights, that debate only grew in intensity. Women had to struggle for a voice because they asserted their concerns publicly, beyond the home and the domestic realm, and in ways that were seen as selfish, even uppity. In a word, they were unwomanly.

Struggling to win a voice only raised a related question: how that voice might be found credible. Gender is an influential factor in rhetoric, as it is in personal identity. So much of the speaker's ethos or character and his or her persuasiveness are tied to the extent to which that individual embodies community values. With many rhetorical strategies — such as rational deliberation, refutation, and debate — linked to what were often perceived as masculine qualities, women needed to choose between or balance two options. They could adopt those traditional strategies or find a credible voice of their own, developing a feminist rhetoric built on qualities such as egalitarian cooperation and connection to the personal and the experiential. These rhetorical choices mirror a larger question: Should feminist arguments be based on equality or on sexual and gender difference? Both options continue to offer rhetorical resources in contemporary debates.

What has become clear in the last few years is that questions of gender speak to the very ways we use language to learn, know, and communicate. Our knowledge of gender has contributed to an awareness of the ways in which we engender knowledge.

The four essays in this unit offer complementary perspectives on speaking and writing as gendered activities. Well known for her research on the role of gender in workplace and in personal conversations, Deborah Tannen offers an essay on how male and female students use language differently in the classroom. Aware that verbal put-downs can offer salient examples of gender in language, Beverly Gross explores the history and current use of the word *bitch*, finding that what men fear most in women is power. Hermione Lee takes up the issue of power in language more directly as she questions the value of both utopian and confrontational uses of language in feminist discourse. For Lee, we find power in language by embracing its potential—a potential to transform not just the world but ourselves as well. Barbara Smith cautions us to consider ways in which some issues of gender and sexual orientation can be silenced. Drawing attention to the ways in which various kinds of oppression are intertwined, she notes that homophobia is rarely brought up, for it seems to be the one *ism* that progressive people still tolerate.

Reflecting on Prior Knowledge

1. In all the hours you have spent in classrooms, you have observed the ways in which students—including you—conduct themselves during class discussions. In a journal entry, reflect on whether you have noticed differences between the ways male and female students participate in discussions. If you have noticed differences, what are the primary ones? Why do you think these differences exist? If, in your experience, differences in classroom behavior do not fall along gender lines, what do you think does cause differences? In what ways, if any, is your own class participation influenced by gender?

2. Humans have a long history of pointing out differences in the ways females and males use language. We often talk about female and male ways of carrying on a conversation or about differences in the books and movies that tend to attract significantly more of one gender or the other. In preparation for a

class discussion, write down what you consider to be the typically female *and* typically male version of one of the following: conversations (make a point of listening to real ones before you start writing), types or titles of books, or types or titles of movies. When you share your notes in class, discuss the reasons for any differences you have observed, as well as the attitudes females and males might have toward the conversation or book or movie preferences of the opposite gender.

3. Stereotypes abound when it comes to gender, and they often come into play most clearly when someone offers a verbal put-down. In gender-segregated groups, develop a list of ways—or specific words—that are used when putting down men and putting down women. Share your group's lists with the entire class. In a follow-up journal entry, reflect on the role of language in gender identity and gender conflict.

4. Personal power is a common theme in American culture—in music, the mass media, popular writing, and academic writing. In a journal entry, reflect on your own power. In what ways do you express or experience it? Who challenges or tries to suppress it? How might it be suppressed, either through language or action?

5. In a journal entry, describe the man who had the greatest influence on how you regard men or the woman who had the greatest influence on how you regard women. What personal attributes led to your choice? Are those attributes usually shared by the same gender?

How Male and Female Students Use Language Differently

Deborah Tannen

As a linguist and writer, Deborah Tannen has encouraged millions of her readers to improve their relationships by becoming more aware of how they talk. Her insights transformed her own approach to teaching, as a result of her work on the international best seller *You Just Don't Understand: Women and Men in Conversation* (1990). As a professor, she discovered that differences in male and female conversational styles find their way into the classroom. As she notes in the following essay on gender in classroom conversations, published in the *Chronicle of Higher Education* in 1991, "treating people the same is not equal treatment if they are not the same."

University professor and professor of linguistics in the Department of Linguistics at Georgetown University, Tannen conducts research in the areas of sociolinguistics and discourse analysis and is widely known for her ability to speak to both academic and lay audiences. A prolific writer of numerous articles and nineteen books, Tannen has also held positions at Princeton and Stanford universities, lectured throughout the world, and appeared on programs ranging from CBS, ABC, and CNN news broadcasts to *The Oprah Winfrey Show* and *Larry King Live.*

Her 1994 book, *Talking from 9 to 5: Women and Men at Work,* was a *New York Times* business best seller and served as the basis for a training video. Her 1998 book, *The Argument Culture,* criticizes our tendency to resort to debate instead of dialogue. In 2001, she received the Books for a Better Life Award for *I Only Say This Because I Love You: Talking to Your Parents, Partner, Sibs, and Kids When You're All Adults* (2001).

When I researched and wrote my latest book, *You Just Don't Understand: Women and Men in Conversation,* the furthest thing from my mind was reevaluating my teaching strategies. But that has been one of the direct benefits of having written the book.

The primary focus of my linguistic research always has been the language of everyday conversation. One facet of this is conversational style: how different regional, ethnic, and class backgrounds, as well as age and gender, result in different ways of using language to communicate. *You Just Don't Understand* is about the conversational styles of women and men. As I gained more insight into typically male and female ways of using language, I began to suspect some of the causes of the troubling facts that women who go to single-sex schools do better in later life, and that when young women sit next to young men in classrooms, the males talk more. This is not to say that all men talk in class, nor that no women do. It is simply that a greater percentage of discussion time is taken by men's voices.

The research of sociologists and anthropologists such as Janet Lever, Marjorie Harness Goodwin, and Donna Eder has shown that girls and boys learn to use language differently in their sex-separate peer groups. Typically, a girl has a best friend with whom she sits and talks, frequently telling secrets. It's the telling of secrets, the fact and the way that they talk to each other, that makes them best friends. For boys, activities are central: Their best friends are the ones they do things with. Boys also tend to play in larger groups that are hierarchical. High-status boys give orders and push low-status boys around. So boys are expected to use language to seize center stage: by exhibiting their skill, displaying their knowledge, and challenging and resisting challenges.

These patterns have stunning implications for classroom interaction. Most faculty members assume that participating in class discussion is a necessary part of successful performance. Yet speaking in a classroom is more congenial to boys' language experience than to girls', since it entails putting oneself forward in front of a large group of people, many of whom are strangers and at least one of whom is sure to judge speakers' knowledge and intelligence by their verbal display.

Another aspect of many classrooms that makes them more hospitable to 5 most men than to most women is the use of debatelike formats as a learning tool. Our educational system, as Walter Ong argues persuasively in his book *Fighting for Life* (Cornell University Press, 1981), is fundamentally male in that the pursuit of knowledge is believed to be achieved by ritual opposition: public display followed by argument and challenge. Father Ong demonstrates that ritual opposition — what he calls "adversativeness" or "agonism" — is fundamental to the way most males approach almost any activity. (Consider, for example, the little boy who shows he likes a little girl by pulling her braids and shoving her.) But ritual opposition is antithetical to the way most females learn and like to interact. It is not that females don't fight, but that they don't fight for fun. They don't *ritualize* opposition.

Anthropologists working in widely disparate parts of the world have found contrasting verbal rituals for women and men. Women in completely unrelated cultures (for example, Greece and Bali) engage in ritual laments: spontaneously produced rhyming couplets that express their pain, for example, over the loss of loved ones. Men do not take part in laments. They have their own, very different verbal ritual: a contest, a war of words in which they vie with each other to devise clever insults.

When discussing these phenomena with a colleague, I commented that I see these two styles in American conversation: Many women bond by talking about troubles, and many men bond by exchanging playful insults and put-downs, and other sorts of verbal sparring. He exclaimed: "I never thought of this, but that's the way I teach: I have students read an article, and then I invite them to tear it apart. After we've torn it to shreds, we talk about how to build a better model."

This contrasts sharply with the way I teach: I open the discussion of readings by asking, "What did you find useful in this? What can we use in our own theory building and our own methods?" I note what I see as weaknesses in the author's approach, but I also point out that the writer's discipline and purposes might be different from ours. Finally, I offer personal anecdotes illustrating the phenomena under discussion and praise students' anecdotes as well as their critical acumen.

These different teaching styles must make our classrooms wildly different places and hospitable to different students. Male students are more likely to be comfortable attacking the readings and might find the inclusion of personal anecdotes irrelevant and "soft." Women are more likely to resist discussion they perceive as hostile, and, indeed, it is women in my classes who are most likely to offer personal anecdotes.

A colleague who read my book commented that he had always taken for ¹⁰ granted that the best way to deal with students' comments is to challenge them; this, he felt it was self-evident, sharpens their minds and helps them develop debating skills. But he had noticed that women were relatively silent in his classes, so he decided to try beginning discussion with relatively open-ended questions and letting comments go unchallenged. He found, to his amazement and satisfaction, that more women began to speak up.

Though some of the women in his class clearly liked this better, perhaps some of the men liked it less. One young man in my class wrote in a questionnaire about a history professor who gave students questions to think about and called on people to answer them: "He would then play devil's advocate . . . i.e., he debated us. . . . That class *really* sharpened me intellectually. . . . We as students do need to know how to defend ourselves." This young man valued the experience of being attacked and challenged publicly. Many, if not most, women would shrink from such "challenge," experiencing it as public humiliation.

A professor at Hamilton College told me of a young man who was upset because he felt his class presentation had been a failure. The professor was puzzled because he had observed that class members had listened attentively and agreed with the student's **One monolithic classroom-**observations. It turned out that it was this very agree-**participation structure is not** ment that the student interpreted as failure: since no **equal opportunity.** one had engaged his ideas by arguing with him, he felt they had found them unworthy of attention.

So one reason men speak in class more than women is that many of them find the "public" classroom setting more conducive to speaking, whereas most women are more comfortable speaking in private to a small group of people they know well. A second reason is that men are more likely to be comfortable with the debatelike form that discussion may take. Yet another reason is the different attitudes toward speaking in class that typify women and men.

Students who speak frequently in class, many of whom are men, assume that it is their job to think of contributions and try to get the floor to express them. But many women monitor their participation not only to get the floor but to avoid getting it. Women students in my class tell me that if they have spoken up once or twice, they hold back for the rest of the class because they don't want to dominate. If they have spoken a lot one week, they will remain silent the next. These different ethics of participation are, of course, unstated, so those who speak freely assume that those who remain silent have nothing to say, and those who are reining themselves in assume that the big talkers are selfish and hoggish.

When I looked around my classes, I could see these differing ethics and 15 habits at work. For example, my graduate class in analyzing conversation had twenty students, eleven women and nine men. Of the men, four were foreign students: two Japanese, one Chinese, and one Syrian. With the exception of the three Asian men, all the men spoke in class at least occasionally. The biggest talker in the class was a woman, but there were also five women who never spoke at all, only one of whom was Japanese. I decided to try something different.

I broke the class into small groups to discuss the issues raised in the readings and to analyze their own conversational transcripts. I devised three ways of dividing the students into groups: one by the degree program they were in, one by gender, and one by conversational style, as closely as I could guess it. This meant that when the class was grouped according to conversational style, I put Asian students together, fast talkers together, and quiet students together. The class split into groups six times during the semester, so they met in each grouping twice. I told students to regard the groups as examples of interactional data and to note the different ways they participated in the different groups. Toward the end of the term, I gave them a questionnaire asking about their class and group participation.

I could see plainly from my observation of the groups at work that women who never opened their mouths in class were talking away in the small groups. In fact, the Japanese woman commented that she found it particularly hard to contribute to the all-woman group she was in because "I was overwhelmed by how talkative the female students were in the female-only group." This is particularly revealing because it highlights that the same person who can be "oppressed" into silence in one context can become the talkative "oppressor" in another. No one's conversational style is absolute; everyone's style changes in response to the context and others' styles.

Some of the students (seven) said they preferred the same-gender groups; others preferred the same-style groups. In answer to the question "Would you have liked to speak in class more than you did?" six of the seven who said yes were women; the one man was Japanese. Most startlingly, this response did not come only from quiet women; it came from women who had indicated they had spoken in class never, rarely, sometimes, and often. Of the eleven students who said the amount they had spoken was fine, seven were men. Of the four women who checked "fine," two added qualifications indicating it wasn't completely fine: One wrote in "maybe more," and one wrote, "I have an urge to participate but often feel I should have something more interesting/relevant/wonderful/intelligent to say!!"

I counted my experiment a success. Everyone in the class found the small groups interesting, and no one indicated he or she would have preferred that the class not break into groups. Perhaps most instructive, however, was the fact that the experience of breaking into groups, and of talking about participation in class, raised everyone's awareness about classroom participation. After we had talked about it, some of the quietest women in the class made a few voluntary contributions, though sometimes I had to ensure their participation by interrupting the students who were exuberantly speaking out.

Americans are often proud that they discount the significance of cultural 20 differences: "We are all individuals," many people boast. Ignoring such issues as gender and ethnicity becomes a source of pride: "I treat everyone the same." But treating people the same is not equal treatment if they are not the same.

The classroom is a different environment for those who feel comfortable putting themselves forward in a group than it is for those who find the prospect of doing so chastening, or even terrifying. When a professor asks, "Are there any questions?" students who can formulate statements the fastest have the greatest opportunity to respond. Those who need significant time to do so have not really been given a chance at all, since by the time they are ready to speak, someone else has the floor.

In a class where some students speak out without raising hands, those who feel they must raise their hands and wait to be recognized do not have equal opportunity to speak. Telling them to feel free to jump in will not make them feel free; one's sense of timing, of one's rights and obligations in a classroom, are automatic, learned over years of interaction. They may be changed over time, with motivation and effort, but they cannot be changed on the spot. And everyone assumes his or her own way is best. When I asked my students how the class could be changed to make it easier for them to speak more, the most talkative woman said she would prefer it if no one had to raise hands, and a foreign student said he wished people would raise their hands and wait to be recognized.

My experience in this class has convinced me that small-group interaction should be part of any class that is not a small seminar. I also am convinced that having the students become observers of their own interaction is a crucial part of their education. Talking about ways of talking in class makes students aware that their ways of talking affect other students, that the motivations they impute to others may not truly reflect others' motives, and that the behaviors they assume to be self-evidently right are not universal norms.

The goal of complete equal opportunity in class may not be attainable, but realizing that one monolithic classroom participation structure is not equal opportunity is itself a powerful motivation to find more-diverse methods to serve diverse students — and every classroom is diverse.

Working with the Text

1. Deborah Tannen bases her approach to stimulating classroom discussions on what she describes as "typically male and female ways of using language." As you reread the article, consider her claims for how males and females learn to converse and how these disparate conversational styles affect their behavior in the classroom. In light of your own experience, write a brief essay in which you agree or disagree with Tannen's characterization of male and female styles of participation in class discussions.

2. Whether or not you agree with Tannen that styles of class participation are typically "male" or "female," you probably recognize the behaviors she

describes. Based on Tannen's descriptions as well as your own experience, write a brief essay in which you analyze the strengths and weaknesses of each style. In what contexts and for what purposes might each style be especially effective?

3. Based on observations of her students, Tannen claims that there is an unspoken "ethics of participation" behind decisions to speak or remain silent in class, which can result in misinterpretations of someone else's motives: "[T]hose who speak freely assume that those who remain silent have nothing to say, and those who are reining themselves in assume that the big talkers are selfish and hoggish" (par. 14). Drawing on Tannen's descriptions of typically male and female conversational styles, write a brief essay in which you analyze these conflicting ethical viewpoints. What is the reasoning behind them? Why would the reasoning be a matter of ethics?

4. In small groups, discuss your response to Tannen's description of how females and males develop their use of language or their conversational styles. Do you agree with her? Why or why not? As you discuss, observe your group's style of interaction, especially in terms of Tannen's argument. Write a brief essay analyzing the group's interaction, to share and discuss with the entire class.

From Text to Field

1. As you review Tannen's essay, reflect on your own style of participating in class discussion. In a personal essay, analyze your style. In what ways would Tannen regard your style as "female"? In what ways would she consider it "male"? Why do you participate in this way? What do you consider to be your "ethics of participation"? Describe any approaches you use that Tannen does not address in her essay.

2. Draw on Tannen's essay to analyze how you developed your particular conversational style. In what ways does it fit within or depart from Tannen's analysis of how females and males learn to use language? Looking back over your schooling, do any particular moments, classes, or teachers stand out in ways that you think may have shaped your current conversational style? In what ways has the development of your conversational style paralleled your growing sense of an "ethics of participation"?

3. Tannen's descriptions of typically male and female classroom behavior include teachers as well as students. Review her anecdotes comparing her own teaching style to the styles of male colleagues. In a personal essay, reflect on your experience working with female and male teachers. Did they use the typically female and male styles described by Tannen? What styles

did they use other than those Tannen describes? What style or styles were more hospitable to you, in terms of your ability to learn as well as to contribute to class discussions?

4. Based on Tannen's argument as well as your experience in the classroom, write an essay as if you were a teacher, articulating a teaching style or philosophy that you think would create the best learning environment for both female and male students. How would you approach classroom discussions? Why would you use this approach?

Bitch

Beverly Gross

Slang can provide some of the most powerful expressions of how men and women regard each other and themselves. Both abuse and endearment take the form of slang. As straightforward as the words can sound, they often camouflage or skew the meaning behind the emotion. Beverly Gross began exploring how the word *bitch* is used after a student in her course on Women Writers and Literary Tradition asked why critics so often referred to twentieth-century novelist Mary McCarthy as a "bitch." Why McCarthy? What did they mean?

Gross reaches back to the eighteenth century to trace the history of the word's meaning, from "the female of the dog" and "a lewd or sensual woman" through the nineteenth century, to "a malicious, unpleasant, selfish woman . . . who stops at nothing to reach her goal" in the twentieth century. Why this progression? And why, according to Gross, are there no equivalent terms for men?

An engaging meditation on language and gender, Gross's essay "Bitch" was published in 1994 in *Salmagundi,* a quarterly magazine devoted to the humanities and social sciences that publishes poetry, fiction, critical essays, and social analysis. A professor of English, Gross has taught at Northwestern University, Vassar College, and Queens College of the City University of New York. She is the coeditor of *The Shapes of Fiction: Open and Closed* (1970) and served as literary editor for *Nation* (1969–1970) and fiction editor for the *Chicago Review* (1962–1964). Her work has appeared in journals such as the *Antioch Review* and the *South Atlantic Quarterly.*

We were discussing Mary McCarthy's *The Group* in a course called Women Writers and Literary Tradition. McCarthy's biographer Carol Gelderman, I told the class, had been intrigued by how often critics called Mary McCarthy a bitch. I read a few citations. "Her novels are crammed with cerebration and bitchiness" (John Aldridge). "Her approach to writing [is] reflective of the modern American bitch" (Paul Schlueter). Why McCarthy? a student asked. Her unrelenting standards, I ventured, her tough-minded critical estimates — there was no self-censoring, appeasing Angel in the House of Mary McCarthy's brain. Her combativeness (her marital battles with Edmund Wilson became the stuff of academic legend). Maybe there were other factors. But the discussion opened up to the more inclusive issue of the word *bitch* itself. What effect does that appellation have on women? What effect might it have had on McCarthy? No one ever called Edmund Wilson a bitch. Do we excuse, even pay respect when a man is critical, combative, assertive? What is the male equivalent of the word bitch, I asked the class.

"Boss," said Sabrina Sims.

This was an evening class at a branch of the City University of New York. Most of the students are older adults trying to fit a college education into otherwise busy lives. Most of them have full-time jobs during the day. Sabrina Sims works on Wall Street, is a single mother raising a ten-year-old daughter, is black, and had to take an Incomplete in the course because she underwent a kidney transplant in December.

Her answer gave us all a good laugh. I haven't been able to get it out of my mind. I've been thinking about *bitch,* watching how it is used by writers and in conversation, and have explored its lexical history. "A name of reproach for a woman" is how Doctor Johnson's Dictionary dealt with the word in the eighteenth century, as though anticipating the great adaptability of this particular execration, a class of words that tends toward early obsolescence. Not *bitch,* however, which has been around for a millennium, outlasting a succession of definitions. Its longevity is perhaps attributable to its satisfying misogyny. Its meaning matters less than its power to denounce and subjugate. Francis Grose in *A Classical Dictionary of the Vulgar Tongue* (1785) considered *bitch* "the most offensive appellation that can be given to an English woman, even more provoking than that of whore." He offered as evidence "a low London woman's reply on being called a bitch" in the late-eighteenth century: "I may be a whore but can't be a bitch!" The meaning of *bitch* has changed over the centuries but it remains the word that comes immediately to the tongue, still "the most offensive appellation" the English language provides to hurl at a woman.

The *Oxford English Dictionary* records two main meanings for the noun 5 *bitch* up through the nineteenth century.

1. The female of the dog
2. Applied opprobriously to a woman; strictly a lewd or sensual woman. Not now in decent use.

It was not until the twentieth century that *bitch* acquired its opprobrious application in realms irrespective of sensuality. The Supplement to the *OED* (1972) adds:

2a: "In mod. use, esp. a malicious or treacherous woman."

Every current desk dictionary supplies some such meaning:

A spiteful, ill-tempered woman [*World Book Dictionary*]
A malicious, unpleasant, selfish woman, esp. one who stops at nothing to reach her goal. [*Random House Dictionary*]

But malice and treachery only begin to tell the story. The informal questionnaire that I administered to my students and a number of acquaintances elicited ample demonstration of the slippery adaptability of bitch as it might be used these days:

a conceited person, a snob
a self-absorbed woman
a complainer
a competitive woman
a woman who is annoying, pushy, possibly underhanded (in short, a man in a woman's body)
someone rich, thin, and free!

"A word used by men who are threatened by women" was one astute response. Threat lurks everywhere: for women the threat is in being called a bitch. "Someone whiny, threatening, crabby, pestering" is what one woman offered as her definition. "Everything I try hard not to be," she added, "though it seeps through." I offer as a preliminary conclusion that *bitch* means to men whatever they find threatening in a woman and it means to women whatever they particularly dislike about themselves. In either case the word functions as a misogynistic club. I will add that the woman who defined *bitch* as everything she tries hard not to be when asked to free associate about the word came up immediately with "mother." That woman happens to be my sister. We share the same mother, who was often whiny and crabby, though I would never have applied the word *bitch* to her, but then again, I don't consider whiny, crabby and pestering to be prominent among my own numerous flaws.

Dictionaries of slang are informative sources, in touch as they are with nascent language and the emotive coloration of words, especially words of abuse. A relatively restrained definition is offered by the only female lexicographer I consulted for whom *bitch* is "a nasty woman" or "a difficult task" (Anita Pearl, *Dictionary of Popular Slang*). The delineations of *bitch* by the male lexicographers abound with such cascading hostility that the compilers sometimes   10 seem to be reveling in their task. For example, Howard Wentworth and Stuart Berg Flexner in *Dictionary of American Slang*:

> A woman, usu., but not necessarily, a mean, selfish, malicious, deceiving, cruel, or promiscuous woman.

Eugene E. Landy's *The Underground Dictionary* (1971) offers:

> 1. Female who is mean, selfish, cruel, malicious, deceiving. a.k.a. cunt.
> 2. Female. See Female.

I looked up the entry for *Female* (Landy, by the way, provides no parallel entry for *Male*):

> beaver, bird, bitch, broad, bush, cat, chick, crack, cunt, douche, fish, fox, frail, garbage can, heffer, pussy, quail, ruca, scag, snatch, stallion, slave, sweet meat, tail, trick, tuna. See GIRLFRIEND; WIFE.

Richard A. Spear's *Slang and Euphemism* comments on the derivative adjective:

> bitchy 1. pertaining to a mood wherein one complains incessantly about anything. Although this applies to men or women, it is usually associated with women, especially when they are menstruating. Cf. DOG DAYS

Robert L. Chapman's definition in *Thesaurus of American Slang* starts off like a feminist analysis:

> bitch. 1 n. A woman one dislikes or disapproves of.

Followed, however, by a sobering string of synonyms: "broad, cunt, witch."

And then this most interesting note:

> Female equivalents of the contemptuous terms for men, listed in this book under *asshole*, are relatively rare. Contempt for females, in slang, stresses their putative sexual promiscuity and weakness rather than their moral vileness and general odiousness. Some terms under *asshole*, though, are increasingly used of women.

"See ball-buster." Chapman suggests under his second definition for *bitch* ("anything arduous or very disagreeable"). I looked up "ball-buster":

> n. Someone who saps or destroys masculinity.
> ball-whacker
> bitch
> nut-cruncher.

Some*thing* has become some*one*. The ball-buster is not a disagreeable thing but a disagreeable (disagreeing?) person. A female person. "A woman one dislikes or disapproves of." For someone so sensitive to the nuances of hostility and 15 verbal put-down, Chapman certainly takes a circuitous route to get to the underlying idea that no other dictionary even touches: *Bitch* means ball-buster.

What one learns from the dictionaries: there is no classifiable thing as a bitch, only a label produced by the act of name-calling. The person named is almost always a female. The name-calling refers to alleged faults of ill-temper, selfishness, malice, cruelty, spite, all of them faults in the realm of interpersonal relating — women's faults: It is hard to think of a put-down word encompassing these faults in a man. *Bastard* and even *son of a bitch* have bigger fish to fry. And an asshole is an asshole in and of himself. A bitch is a woman who makes the name-caller feel uncomfortable. Presumably that name-caller is a man whose ideas about how a woman should behave toward him are being violated.

What men primarily fear and despise in women is power.

"Women," wrote Virginia Woolf, "have served all these centuries as looking-glasses possessing the magic and delicious power of reflecting the figure of man at twice its natural size." The woman who withholds that mirror is a bitch. Bitchiness is the perversion of womanly sweetness, compliance, pleasantness, ego-building. (Male ego-building, of course, though that is a virtual tautology; women have egos but who builds them?) If a woman is not building ego she is busting balls.

Ball-buster? The word is a nice synecdoche (like asshole) with great powers of revelation. A ball-buster, one gathers, is a demanding bitch who insists on overexertion from a man to satisfy her sexual or material voraciousness. "The bitch is probably his wife." But balls also bust when a disagreeable woman undermines a guy's ego and "saps or destroys masculinity." The bitch could be his wife, but also his boss, Gloria Steinem, the woman at the post office, the woman who spurns his advances. The familiar Freudian delineation of the male-female nexus depicts male sexuality as requiring the admiration, submission, and subordination of the female. The ultimate threat of (and to) the back-talking woman is male impotence.

Bitch, the curse and concept, exists to insure male potency and female submissiveness. Men have deployed it to defend their power by attacking and neutralizing the upstart. *Bitch* is admonitory, like *whore*, like *dyke*. Borrowing something from both words, *bitch* is one of those verbal missiles with the power of shackling women's actions and impulses.

The metamorphosis of *bitch* from the context of sexuality (a carnal 20 woman, a promiscuous woman) to temperament (an angry woman, a malicious woman) to power (a domineering woman, a competitive woman) is a touchstone to the changing position of women through this century. As women have become more liberated, individually and collectively, the word has taken on connotations of aggressive, hostile, selfish. In the old days a bitch was a harlot; nowadays she is likely to be a woman who won't put out.

Female sensuality, even carnality, even infidelity, have been supplanted as what men primarily fear and despise in women. Judging by the contemporary colorations of the word *bitch*, what men primarily fear and despise in women is power.

Some anecdotes:

1. Barbara Bush's name-calling of Geraldine Ferraro during the 1984 presidential election: "I can't say it but it rhymes with 'rich.'"

How ladylike of the future First Lady to avoid uttering the unmentionable. The slur did its dirty work, particularly among those voters disturbed by the sudden elevation of a woman to such unprecedented political heights. In what possible sense did Barbara Bush mean that Geraldine Ferraro is a bitch? A loose woman? Hardly. A nasty woman? Not likely. A pushy woman? Almost certainly. The unspoken syllable was offered as a response to Ferraro's lofty ambitions, potential power, possibly her widespread support among feminists. Imagine a woman seeking to be vice president instead of vice husband.

The ascription of bitchery seems to have nothing to do with Ferraro's bearing and behavior. Certainly not the Ferraro who wrote about the event in her autobiography:

> Barbara Bush realized what a gaffe she had made. . . .
>
> "I just want to apologize to you for what I said," she told me over the phone while I was in the middle of another debate rehearsal. "I certainly didn't mean anything by it."
>
> "Don't worry about it," I said to her. "We all say things at times we don't mean. It's all right."
>
> "Oh," she said breathlessly. "You're such a lady."
>
> All I could think of when I hung up was: Thank God for my convent school training.

2. Lady Ashley at the end of *The Sun Also Rises*: "It makes one feel rather   25 good, deciding not to be a bitch." The context here is something like this: A bitch is a woman who ruins young heroic bullfighters. A woman who is propelled by her sexual drive, desires, and vanity. The fascination of Brett Ashley is that she lives and loves like a man: Her sexuality is unrepressed and she doesn't care much for monogamy. (Literary critics until the 1960s commonly called her a nymphomaniac.) She turns her male admirers into women— Mike becomes a self-destructive alcoholic, Robert a moony romantic, Pedro a sacrificial virgin, and Jake a frustrated eunuch. At her entrance in the novel she is surrounded by an entourage of twittering fairies. Lady Ashley is a bitch not because she is nasty, bossy, or ill-tempered (she has lovely manners and a terrific personality). And perhaps not even because of her freewheeling, strident sexuality. She is a bitch because she overturns the male/female nexus. What could be a more threatening infraction in a Hemingway novel?

2a. Speaking of Hemingway: After his falling out with Gertrude Stein who had made unflattering comments about his writing in *The Autobiography of Alice B. Toklas,* Hemingway dropped her off a copy of his newly published *Death in the Afternoon* with the handwritten inscription, "A bitch is a bitch is a bitch."

[Q.] Why was Gertrude Stein a bitch?

[A.] For no longer admiring Hemingway. A bitch is a woman who criticizes.

3. "Ladies and gentlemen. I don't believe Mrs. Helmsley is charged in the indictment with being a tough bitch" is how her defense lawyer Gerald A. Feffer addressed the jury in Leona Helmsley's trial for tax fraud and extortion. He acknowledged that she was "sometimes rude and abrasive," and that she "may have overcompensated for being a woman in a hard-edged men's business world." Recognizing the difficulty of defending what the New York *Post* called "the woman that everyone loves to hate," his tactic was to pre-empt the prosecution by getting there first with "tough bitch." He lost.

4. *Esquire* awarded a Dubious Achievement of 1990 to Victor Kiam, owner of the New England Patriots football team, for saying "he could never have called Boston *Herald* reporter Lisa Olson 'a classic bitch' because he doesn't use the word *classic.*" Some background on what had been one of that year's most discussed controversies: Olson aroused the ire of the Patriots for showing up in their locker room with the male reporters after a game. Members of the Patriots, as *Esquire* states, surrounded her, "thrusting their genitals in her face and daring her to touch them."

Why is Lisa Olson a bitch? For invading the male domain of sports reportage and the male territory of the locker room? For telling the world, instead of swallowing her degradation, pain, and anger? The club owner's use of "bitch" seems meant to conjure up the lurking idea of castrating female. Seen in that light the Patriots' act of "thrusting their genitals in her face" transforms an act of loutishness into a position of innocent vulnerability.

5. Bumper sticker observed on back of pickup truck:

30

Impeach Jane Fonda, American Traitor Bitch

The bumper sticker seemed relatively new and fresh. I observed it a full two decades after Jane Fonda's journey to North Vietnam which is the event that surely inspired this call to impeachment (from what? aerobics class?). *Bitch* here is an expletive. It originates in and sustains anger. Calling Jane Fonda a "traitor" sounds a bit dated in the 1990s, but adding "bitch" gives the accusation timelessness and does the job of rekindling old indignation.

6. Claude Brown's account in *Manchild in the Promised Land* of how he learned about women from a street-smart older friend:

Johnny was always telling us about bitches. To Johnny, every chick was a bitch. Even mothers were bitches. Of course there were some nice bitches, but they were still bitches. And a man had to be a dog in order to handle a bitch.

Johnny said once, "If a bitch ever tells you she's only got a penny to buy the baby some milk, take it. You take it, 'cause she's gon git some more. Bitches can always git some money." He really knew about bitches. Cats would say, "I saw your sister today, and she is a fine bitch." Nobody was offended by it. That's just the way things were. It was easy to see all women as bitches.

Bitch in black male street parlance seems closer to its original meaning of a female breeder—not a nasty woman and not a powerful woman, but the biological bearer of litters. The word is likely to be used in courting as well as in anger by males seeking the sexual favor of a female, and a black female addressed as bitch by an admirer is expected to feel not insulted but honored by the attention. (*Bitch* signifies something different when black women use it competitively about other black women.) But even as an endearment, from male to female, there is no mistaking the lurking contempt.

A *Dictionary of Afro-American Slang* compiled by Clarence Major (under the imprint of the leftist International Publishers) provides only that *bitch* in black parlance is "a mean, flaunting homosexual," entirely omitting any reference to its rampant use in black street language as the substitute word for woman. A puzzling omission. Perhaps the word is so taken for granted that its primary meaning is not even recognized as black vernacular.

Bitch, mama, motherfucker—how frequently motherhood figures in street language. Mothers are the object of insults when playing the dozens. The ubiquitous motherfucker simultaneously strikes out at one's immediate foe as well as the sanctity of motherhood. Mama, which Clarence Major defines as "a pretty black girl," is an endearment that a man might address to a sexy contemporary. "Hey mama" is tinged with a certain sweetness. "Hey bitch" has more of an edge, more likely to be addressed to a woman the man no longer needs to sweet-talk. It is hard to think of white males coming on by evoking motherhood or of white women going for it. A white male addressing a woman as bitch is not likely to be expecting a sexual reward. She will be a bitch behind her back and after the relationship is over or didn't happen.

The widespread use of *bitch* by black men talking to black women, its currency in courting, and its routine acceptance by women are suggestive of some powerful alienation in male-female relations and in black self-identity. Although there may be the possibility of ironic inversion, as in calling a loved one nigger, a black man calling a loved one bitch is expressing contempt for the object of his desire with the gratuitous fillip of associative contempt for the woman who gave him life. Bitch, like motherfucker, bespeaks something threatening to the male sense of himself, a furious counter to emasculation in a world where, as the young Claude Brown figured out, mothers have all 35 the power. It is not hard to see that the problem of black men is much more with white racism than it is with black women. Whatever the cause, however, the language sure doesn't benefit the women. Here is still one more saddening instance of the victim finding someone even more hapless to take things out on. (Does this process explain why Clarence Major's only reference for *bitch* is to the "mean, flaunting homosexual"?)

7. "Do you enjoy playing that role of castrating bitch" is a question put to Madonna by an interviewer for the *Advocate*. Madonna's answer: "I enjoy expressing myself. . . ."

A response to another question about the public's reaction to her movie *Truth or Dare*: "They already think I'm a cunt bitch, they already think I'm Attila the Hun. They already compare me to Adolf Hitler and Saddam Hussein."

Bitch has lost its power to muzzle Madonna. Unlike other female celebrities who have cringed from accusations of bitchiness (Joan Rivers, Imelda Marcos, Margaret Thatcher, Nancy Reagan), Madonna has made her fortune by exploiting criticism. Her career has skyrocketed with the media's charges of obscenity and sacrilege; she seems to embrace the *bitch* label with the same eager opportunism.

"I enjoy expressing myself" is not merely the explanation for why Madonna gets called bitch; "I enjoy expressing myself" is the key to defusing the power of *bitch* to fetter and subdue. Madonna has appropriated the word and turned the intended insult to her advantage. This act of appropriation, I predict, will embolden others with what consequences and effects it is impossible to foresee.

Working with the Text

1. Beverly Gross devotes the first half of her essay to exploring dictionary meanings of the word *bitch*, starting with Doctor Johnson's Dictionary in the eighteenth century: "A name of reproach for a woman." In a brief essay, analyze her use of these evolving dictionary definitions. What do the definitions tell us about the dictionary compilers and the eras in which they lived? What does this history tell us about how we use the word today? How does the history of the word contribute to Gross's argument? How would you summarize her argument?

2. In addition to studying dictionaries, Gross conducted an informal survey of her students and friends to explore contemporary meanings of *bitch*. She lists the following responses:

   a conceited person, a snob
   a self-absorbed woman

a complainer

a competitive woman

a woman who is annoying, pushy, possibly underhanded (in short, a man in a woman's body)

someone rich, thin, and free!

In a brief essay, reflect on how all of these meanings could come from the same word. What is the relationship among the meanings? What does this range of meaning suggest about current ideas of what it is to be a woman — both in terms of what we think women should be and what we think they actually are?

3. One of Gross's central claims is that there is no "put-down word" for men comparable to *bitch* for women. As you reread the essay, reflect not only on the contemporary meanings of the word but also on the effect Gross argues the word is intended to have on the woman being called a bitch. In particular, consider Gross's assertion that "*Bastard* and even *son of a bitch* have bigger fish to fry. And an asshole is an asshole in and of himself. A bitch is a woman who makes the name-caller feel uncomfortable" (par. 16). Write a brief essay in which you analyze put-downs used for men, comparing the effect they are intended to have on men to the effect *bitch* is intended to have on women. Do you agree with Gross that there is no comparable name for men? Why or why not? To what extent does *boss*, proposed by one of Gross's students, offer a comparable put-down?

4. Gross comes to the conclusion that "what men primarily fear and despise in women is power" (par. 20). Drawing on your experience as well as Gross's argument, write a brief essay in which you respond to this assertion. To what extent do you agree with Gross's conclusion? What is the basis for your position?

From Text to Field

1. The crux of Gross's argument is that the word *bitch* reflects a long history of misogyny — the hatred of women. Women, as well as men, can be misogynists. Based on your experience and knowledge of history, literature, psychology, and other relevant fields of study, write an essay in which you reflect on whether there has been a comparable history of hatred of men. If you think there has been such a history, what is the male equivalent of the word *misogyny?* If you cannot identify such a word, what term would you invent? What attitudes toward men are represented by the existing term or the term you would invent? If you think there has not been a history of some form of hating men, why do you think that has been the case? How does your knowledge of the women's movement fit into your view of this history?

2. To illustrate contemporary uses of *bitch*, Gross presents several anecdotes. Using the anecdotes and her commentary as a model, write an essay in which you present one or more anecdotes from your own experience or knowledge of celebrities or public figures. What circumstances surrounded the woman being called a bitch? What did the name-caller mean by the word? What is your view of the woman and the situation? How does gender figure into the use of the term? If a man is called a bitch, is it emasculating? Have you ever been called a "bitch"?

3. Toward the end of her essay, Gross notes an apparent exception to her analysis: the use of *bitch* in black male street parlance as a term of endearment. How does Gross integrate this example into her overall analysis? In what ways does the example serve her general argument about the fear of power — and powerlessness? Drawing on this example in the essay, consider other instances in which gendered terms, or other highly charged terms, have distinctive meanings within particular communities.

4. Gross uses Madonna to signal what may be a shift in our culture's take on bitches. Make a list of celebrities or public figures you think have used their designation as a bitch to their advantage. Discuss your list in a small group. On the basis of your discussion, write an essay in which you analyze either the actions of one of the "bitches" or what you see as a shift in how the term is being regarded and used.

Power: Women and the Word

Hermione Lee

We use the word *power* so often that its meaning becomes fragmented or blurred. Hermione Lee recognizes how susceptible *power* is to the context in which it is used. What is it? Who is wielding it? Who is gaining it and who is losing it? As Lee enters into the debate among feminists over the sources and uses of power, she examines in particular the feminist concern over the power of words themselves. If, as feminists claim, power is gained in large part through language, how can women use words to gain power?

In this essay, Lee reviews and critiques two very different approaches to "making over the language": a utopian impulse to reinvent the language for feminism and a confrontational impulse that turns the language of power against men. Lee finds both approaches to be problematic. Her essay was first published in *The State of the Language* (1980), edited by Leonard Michaels and Christopher Ricks, a collection of essays on the English language as a sensitive register of our ideas, feelings, politics, and manners.

As a biographer and critic, Lee has gained an international reputation among both academic and lay audiences for her keen analysis of writers. Her work includes books on Elizabeth Bowen, Phillip Roth, Willa Cather, and Virginia Woolf. *Virginia Woolf: A Biography* (1996) won an award from the British Academy and was a best seller in England as well as a *New York Times Book Review* Editor's Choice and a National Book Critics Circle Award finalist. Currently, she is writing a biography of Edith Wharton.

In England, where she is widely known as a broadcaster and commentator on the arts, Lee is the Goldsmiths' Professor of English Literature and fellow of New College, Oxford. In the United States, she has been a visiting fellow at Princeton University, Yale University, and the University of Indiana at Bloomington.

Power. Meanings: the ability to do something, to effect, to act upon. A faculty of body or mind. A force. Political or national strength. Authority or dominion over. Legal authority. A ruler, a state, a prerogative, a celestial body or influence. A body of armed men. The rate at which electrical energy is fed into a system. A measure of magnification. A large amount. Nuclear energy. Power drill, power house, power plant, power politics, black power, power of attorney. Examples: from kings, fathers, patriarchs, princes, bishops, armies, lawyers. (Exceptional cases: the daughter of Jove, Cleopatra.) Quotations: Absolute power corrupts absolutely, thine is the Kingdom, the Power and the Glory, happy men that have the power to die, the balance of power, Him the Almighty Power hurl'd headlong flaming, He that hath power to hurt and will do none, the awful shadow of some unseen power. Etymology: from Middle English *poër*, Old French *poer, poeir, pouoir. Pouoir* goes forward into Modern French *pouvoir*, and backwards to *podere*, from late vulgar Latin *potere*, from Latin *posse*, to be able. The present participle of *posse, potentem*, provides *potentia*, and hence Old French *potence.* Meaning: power, ability, strength, sexual power (male). From this comes *potency*, also potent, potentate, potential, and potentiality.[1]

No wonder, with this pedigree, that the word *power*, derived from the same root as *potency*, is used more often than any other word in feminist discourse to stand for male supremacy. That supremacy is frequently identified as linguistic: Naming is power. The word *power* belongs to those who are in power. It follows that the feminist use of the word is extremely ambivalent. *Power* names something which is resented and feared, but which is also desired and aspired to. It is a revealing word in current feminist discourse because it can take opposite meanings. Other key words do not require a context for their value to be expressed. *Creative*, or *pleasure*, or *freedom* is likely to mean well; *rape*, or *humiliation*, is bound to be bad. *Power* is bad when it is identified with male supremacy and the oppression of women, as in Andrea Dworkin's "it is through intercourse that men express and maintain their power and dominance over women," or Kate Millett's "both the courtly and the romantic versions of love are 'grants' which the male concedes out of his total power."[2] *Power* is good when it is identified with female creativity and potential.

In the good sense it is frequently associated with the use of language, as when Adrienne Rich asks women to consider "language as transforming power," or Mary Daly plays with language to release "the complex creative power" of women, or Toril Moi describes Kate Millett's rhetoric as "a powerful fist in the solar plexus of patriarchy."[3] A word that can mean both well and ill is a manipulable word. Adrienne Rich, in an essay called "Power and Danger," gives a feminist history of the word as used against women:

> Powerless, women have been seduced into confusing love with false power—
> the "power" of mother-love, the "power" of gentle influence, the "power" of
> nonviolence, the "power" of the meek who are to inherit the earth.[4]

Rich's scorn of a rhetoric which pretends that powerlessness can be a form of power is directed, of course, at male (and especially Christian) rhetoric. But strategic manipulations of the word are not a male prerogative. In the uses to which it is put in current feminist writing, two ways of making over the language can be discerned, the one utopian, the other confrontational. Both are intensely problematic.

If the language is to be reinvented for feminism, the word *power* presents a crucial challenge — and invitation. Can it be transformed, or must it be rejected? Any rewriting of women's history, as in this neutrally informative passage, has to center on the word:

> An understanding of the interdependence of the spheres reveals that women have wielded more power than has been apparent, and that aspects of women's lives which appear to be restrictive may actually be enabling. Women's history is concerned to see women, not as victims of oppression, as passive spectators of the drama of history, but as having an influence and a history of their own. . . . Historians of women broaden their conception of power to include subtler forms — informal, invisible, collective — recognizing that "the location of power" is "a tricky business."[5]

Here the word changes its value through a historical reinterpretation which makes powerlessness, after all, into a form of power. This would presumably not suit Adrienne Rich, who argues in "Power and Danger" that this is what women have always been told, and much good it has done us. Rich requires more than historical reconsideration. Like Virginia Woolf in *A Room of One's Own*, inviting women writers to make use of the special knowledge they have inherited from their mothers' history of exclusion and silence, Rich wants a history of powerlessness to issue in a distinctive language (essentially a language of poetry) which will

Strategic manipulations of the word [*power*] are not a male prerogative.

express "that instinct for true power, not domination, which poets like Barrett Browning, Dickinson, H.D., were asserting in their own very different ways and voices."[6] Rich's phrasing shows what a tricky business it is to give a utopian meaning to the word *power*. *Power* still has to go with *asserting* (though *asserting* is an inaccurate description of what Emily Dickinson and H.D. were doing). Yet *asserting* is contrasted, in a shaky opposition, with *domination*. And *power* itself has to be qualified by *true*, in order to distinguish it from the bad old "false power" (that is, powerlessness) offered to women by the male oppressors. We are presented, then, somewhat awkwardly, with a utopian idea of a language of "true power" which will assert but not dominate. What could such a language actually be?

Feminist revisions of language in the last decade, powerfully influenced 5 by Julia Kristeva's critique of Freud and Lacan, have insisted on a female language as the expression of *what has been repressed* in the male sentence.

Mary Jacobus defines *écriture féminine* as that which is "located in the gaps, the absences, the unsayable or unrepresentable of discourse and representation."[7] Female language is identified, in such now-legendary texts as Hélène Cixous's "Le Rire de la Méduse" (1975) and Luce Irigaray's "Ce sexe qui n'en est pas un" (1977), as a playful revealing of what has been hidden. Language as an eruption of female sexuality, or *jouissance*, can be a potent alternative discourse. This discourse is indebted to Kristeva's theory that the pre-Oedipal phase of childhood, in intimate connection with the mother, which precedes the "entry into signification and the symbolic order," can persist in "oral and instinctual aspects of language which punctuate, evade, or disrupt the symbolic order — in prosody, intonation, puns, verbal slips, even silences."[8] For Irigaray, this means that "woman would find herself on the side of everything in language that is multiple, duplicitous, unreliable"; her language is "a deranging power."[9]

Utopian polemicists for a female language repeatedly oppose its "deranging power" to the established power systems within which it must operate. So woman must be, and speak, "that which is neither power nor structure."[10] How can this be put into practice? Recommendations vary from the use of myth and fable, diaries and notebooks, gaps on the page, poetical prose and domestic imagery, to, at the most inept, "the vocabulary of menstruation, reproduction, or craft work."[11] More specific linguistic programs call for women to coin neologisms, break grammatical rules, and defamiliarize taken-for-granted parts of speech.

If this fabricated language is to express "that which is neither power nor structure," it has to be identified with negatives: amorphousness, evasiveness, splits, darkness, and depth. Here, for instance, a conscientious Americanized version of *écriture féminine* uses strategies of syntactical blurring, fragmentation, exclamation, rhythmic patterns, and an alternative vocabulary to ridicule the culture's mythical respect for male linguistic power:

> But that male body, how IT dominates the culture, the environment, the language. Since 3,000 BC in Sumeria, Tiamat's monsters again and again, and every myth an effort to keep the sun rising. Save the sun, everybody, from the watery deeps, the dark underneath it must go—Into— Every night into such dangers, such soft inchoate darkness, what will become of it, will it rise again will it will it rise again? The language of criticism: "lean, dry, terse, powerful, strong, spare, linear, focused, explosive," — god forbid it should be "limp"!! But — "soft, moist, blurred, padded, irregular, going around in circles," and other descriptions of *our* bodies — the very *abyss* of aesthetic judgment, danger, the wasteland for artists! That limp dick — an entire civilization based on it, help the sun rise, watch out for the dark underground, focus focus focus, keep it high, let it soar, let it transcend, let it aspire to Godhead ———.[12]

This kind of programmatic writing consigns women and their language, all over again (as they have traditionally been consigned by inspired "phallo-centric" writers such as Yeats, Whitman, and Lawrence) to the realms of "inchoate darkness," the unconscious, mothering, hysteria, and bab-ble. It is a version of female "powers" which has been emphatically challenged, very often as part of a debate between the Gallic school of psychoanalytical and linguistic feminists, and the Anglo-American school of Marxist/socialist/"materialist" feminists. The latter criticize the essentialist identification of the feminine with "absence, silence, incoherence, even madness" as "a mistaken strategy" which "abandons territory which can and ought to be defended against masculine imperialism: coherence, rationality, articulateness."[13]

A more socialized, functional attempt at fabricating a female language is currently being made by the American feminist theologian Mary Daly. In *Gyn/Ecology: The Metaethics of Radical Feminism* (1978) and *Pure Lust: Elemental Feminist Philosophy* (1984) she makes determined efforts at "wrenching back some word power."[14] The phrase refers to her title, *Gyn/Ecology,* which Daly says is meant to draw attention to the pollution spread by patriarchal myth and language. Daly's split words and coinages (dis-membering and re-membering, a-maze, man/ipulate, O-Zone, Hag-ocracy, the/rapist, Nag-Gnostics) belong to a self-conscious process of reeducating the users of the language by "targeting/humiliating the right objects."

> Gynocentric writing means risking. Since the language and style of patri-archal writing simply cannot contain or carry the energy of women's exor-cism and ecstasy, in this book I invent, dis-cover, re-member. At times I make up words (such as *gynaesthesia* for women's synaesthesia). Often I unmask deceptive words by dividing them and employing alternate mean-ings for prefixes (for example, *re-cover* actually says "cover again"). I also unmask their hidden reversals, often by using less known or "obsolete" meanings (for example, *glamour* as used to name a witch's power). Sometimes I simply invite the reader to listen to words in a different way (for example, *de-light*). When I play with words I do this attentively, deeply, paying attention to etymology, to varied dimensions of meaning, to deep Background meanings and subliminal associations.[15]

Daly subverts the word *power* by pluralizing it, proposing an opposition between "Elemental Powers of Be-ing" (female, naturally) and "patriarchal power." The strategy perfectly sums up the utopian feminist desire to reclaim all the "established" meanings of power (potency, control, activity, authority) and change their value:

> Women who are unveiling the Archimage, Realizing active potency, are unleashing Archaic powers. To be actively potent is to Realize/release that

which is most Dreadful to the impotent priests, the prurient patriarchs —
our participation in Be-ing. . . . It is predictable that priestly predators will
attempt to use fear-filled women as powers holding down Elemental
female powers.[16]

Daly's self-conscious, artificial wordplay, bent on reminding us that language is a construct which can therefore be de- and re-constructed according to different laws, is liable to disbelief or ridicule. Why? Partly because her
educative intention — to alert readers to the covert or suppressed potential in
their language and to make moribund usages or weakened meanings come
back to life — can look too much like willfulness or whimsicality. (Daly's passion for puns and coy alliterative pairings, and her solemnity about her own
playfulness, don't help.) But the problem is not just one of manner. This
extreme example of a utopian project to manufacture an alternative language
differs from comparable attempts of dialect or minority-language speakers to
free themselves from the superimposition of a dominant culture's "standard"
language.[17] The aim of such groups is to *write what they speak*: to challenge
the power of a mainstream, colonial literary tradition by the force of an oral
tradition. But no one speaks, or has ever spoken, a distinctive, alternative
female language. If it is to come into being, it must be an entirely fabricated,
artificial, written invention.

The danger — the "risking" — of a utopian, alternative female language   10
expressive of "woman's powers" is that it will be felt to fall short of, or evade,
the real world's balance of power. In which case, feminists have to find another
way of making their words potent.

The confrontational mode of female language mimics or mirrors the
enemy's use of the word *power.* Kristeva, in a section called "The terror of
power or the power of terrorism" in *Women's Time* (1979), analyzes the tendency of women struggling against the "power structure" to "make of the second sex a counter-society," "a counter-power which necessarily generates . . .
its essence as a simulacrum of the combated society or of power." This coun-
tersociety is as violent, as paranoid, and as power-hungry, as the system it
opposes. Hence, according to this argument, the large number of women in
terrorist groups.[18]

Monique Wittig demonstrates a linguistic version of terrorist "counter-
power," explaining her use, in *Les Guérillères*, of the pronoun *elles*:

> To succeed textually, I needed to adopt some very draconian measures,
> such as to eliminate . . . *he* or *they-he*. I had to provide a shock for the reader
> entering a text in which *elles* by its unique presence constitutes an assault,
> yes, even for female readers. . . . The adoption of a pronoun as my subject
> matter dictated the form of the book. Although the theme of the text was
> total war, led by *elles* on *ils*, in order for this new person to take effect,

two-thirds of the text had to be totally inhabited, haunted, by *elles*. Word by word, *elles* establishes itself as a sovereign subject [and] also imposed an epic form, where it is not only the complete subject of the world but its conqueror.[19]

Draconian measures, eliminate, shock, assault, dictated, total war, sovereign subject, imposed, epic, conqueror: The language of power is being not transformed, but turned against the enemy with a vengeance.

The most offensive of these counteroffensives is that of the American polemicist Andrea Dworkin, frequently referred to as a "powerful" voice in the women's movement, whose argument is that the sex act is an act of terrorism against women. There are no exceptions to this rule, since the world according to Dworkin is a constructed male-dominated system of social institutions, sexual practices, and economic relations in which women are silenced, exploited, and damaged. There is ("thus") an essential connection between the foul end — what Dworkin calls "the real shit" — of sexual relations (pornography, rape, wife-battering, incest, prostitution) and the sanctioned end (marriage, love, "so-called" normal intercourse). As much in the legal as in the illegal sphere, "intercourse is political dominance; power as power or power as pleasure." The conspiracy to believe that women like to be hurt is universal. Just as the law allows for unspeakable abuses of women in pornography, so it gives "protective legitimacy" to the ownership of women by men. *Ergo,* "marriage is a legal license to rape," "fucking is the means by which the male colonializes the female":

> Women are a degraded and terrorized people. Women are degraded and terrorized by men. Rape is terrorism. Wife-beating is terrorism. Medical butchering is terrorism. Sexual abuse in its hundred million forms is terrorism. . . . Women are an occupied people. . . . This fascist ideology of female inferiority is the preeminent ideology on this planet.

Dworkin thinks of, and uses, language as a weapon: "dirty words" and "antifeminist epithets" are the equivalent of physical attacks. "Women live defensively, not just against rape but against the language of the rapist." She provides the clearest and most extreme example in the feminist belief in language as power, since, in her argument, "power determines the meaning of language." It is, noticeably, her most used word, as in "Intercourse consistently expresses illegitimate power, unjust power, wrongful power."[20]

Dworkin's weapons, like those of Kristeva's "counter-society," are simulacrums of the enemy's. So her strategies—generalizations, diktats, exhortations—are those of dictatorship. The objects of her attack are, frequently, horrifyingly convincing. But her totalitarian refusal to allow exceptions ("Men love death"; "Women have to pretend to like men to survive"; "Relationships called love are based on exploitation") makes a desolating language which can only imitate what it opposes. In this language, the meaning of *power* cannot be transformed.

Must it be so? Toril Moi (arguing with Irigaray over the word *power*) writes   15 these heartening words:

> Women's relationship to power is not exclusively one of victimization. Feminism is not simply about rejecting power, but about transforming the existing power structures — and, in the process, transforming the very *concept* of power itself.[21]

How is the "very *concept*" of power to be transformed? We go back to the beginning again. There are no conclusions, only arguments. But it may be that through the arguments themselves, transformation begins to occur, and *power* takes on its most promising and least hurtful meaning, that of *potential*.

Notes

1. *Oxford English Dictionary*, *Collins English Dictionary*, *Oxford Dictionary of Quotations*.

2. Andrea Dworkin, *Right-Wing Women* (New York, 1983), p. 83; Kate Millett, *Sexual Politics* (1969; London, 1977), p. 37.

3. Adrienne Rich, *On Lies, Secrets, and Silences* (New York, 1979; London, 1980, p. 247); Mary Daly, *Gyn/Ecology: The Metaethics of Radical Feminism* (Boston, 1978; London, 1979), p. 79; Toril Moi, *Sexual/Textual Politics* (London, 1985), p. 26.

4. Rich, *On Lies, Secrets, and Silences*, p. 254.

5. Gayle Greene and Coppélia Kahn, eds., *Making a Difference: Feminist Literary Criticism* (London, 1985), p. 17.

6. Rich, *On Lies, Secrets, and Silences*, p. 257.

7. Mary Jacobus, *Reading Woman: Essays in Feminist Criticism* (New York and London, 1986), p. 109.

8. *Reading Woman*, p. 148.

9. *Reading Woman*, p. 65.

10. Josette Féral, "Antigone or *The Irony of the Tribe*," *Diacritics* 8 (1978): II, quoted by Elizabeth Meese, *Crossing the Double-Cross* (Chapel Hill, 1986), p. 112.

11. Maggie Humm, *Feminist Criticism* (Brighton, 1986), p. 8.

12. Frances Jaffer and Rachel Blau du Plessis, "For the Etruscans: The Debate over a Female Aesthetic," in *Feminist Literary Theory: A Reader*, ed. Mary Eagleton (Oxford, 1986), p. 228.

13. Terry Lovell, "Writing Like a Woman," in *Feminist Literary Theory*, p. 85.

14. Daly, *Gyn/Ecology*, p. 9.

15. Daly, *Gyn/Ecology*, p. 24.

16. Mary Daly, *Pure Lust: Elemental Feminist Philosophy* (London, 1984), pp. 188–89.

17. See the essays on "Identities," especially those by Geneva Smitherman and Monroe K. Spears, in *The State of the Language*, ed. Leonard Michaels and Christopher Ricks (Berkeley and Los Angeles, 1980).

18. Julia Kristeva, "Women's Time" (1979), trans. Alice Jardine and Harry Blake, in *The Kristeva Reader*, ed. Toril Moi (Oxford, 1986), pp. 201–3.

19. Monique Wittig, "The Mark of Gender," in *The Poetics of Gender*, ed. Nancy K. Miller (New York, 1986), p. 70.

20. Andrea Dworkin, *Intercourse* (1987; London, 1988), p. 197; *Letters from a War Zone* (London, 1988), p. 200; *Right-Wing Women*, p. 202; *Intercourse*, p. 201; *Right-Wing Women*, p. 84.

21. Toril Moi, *Sexual/Textual Politics*, p. 148.

Working with the Text

1. Hermione Lee's argument works from a central tenet of feminist thought: "Naming is power" (par. 2). She bases her analysis on the recognition that feminists "have insisted on a female language as the expression of *what has been repressed* in the male sentence" (par. 5). As you reread the essay, look for indications of what feminists might mean by these assertions. Drawing inferences from Lee's argument for an effective "female language," write a brief essay in which you analyze the source of her concern. What problem is she addressing? Why would the claim that naming "is power" lead to the need for a different language? What has been repressed?

2. After analyzing "utopian" and "confrontational" attempts to develop a distinctively female language, Lee concludes, "There are no conclusions, only arguments. But it may be that through the arguments themselves, transformation begins to occur, and *power* takes on its most promising and least hurtful meaning, that of *potential*" (par. 15). As an introduction to undergraduates who are not familiar with Lee's essay or with feminist arguments for a female language, distill the three approaches — utopian, confrontational, and power as potential — and translate them into terms you think your peers would understand.

3. As she builds her argument, Lee quotes from another source in almost every paragraph. In a brief essay, consider her reasons for incorporating so much material from the work of other writers. How does she use the sources? Who are they? What do they contribute to her argument? Why would Lee approach her argument in this way?

4. Lee concludes her essay with the following statement: "There are no conclusions, only arguments. But it may be that through the arguments themselves, transformation begins to occur, and *power* takes on its most promising and least hurtful meaning, that of *potential*." Write a brief essay in which you explain Lee's concluding statement. Does power as potential represent a distinct third alternative to the utopian and confrontational approaches she criticizes? Or does Lee believe that power as potential can only be realized

or developed by engaging—even criticizing—the utopian and confrontational approaches? Does Lee believe that those two approaches, even if misguided, are nevertheless important for us to consider if we are to discover in language the potential for transformation?

From Text to Field

1. Lee opens and closes her essay by offering her own concept of power. Although her argument draws on concepts of power developed by other writers, Lee's analysis of their thinking reveals her own perspective. In a personal essay, explore your concept of the male and female forms of power Lee examines. What is the power relationship between women and men? Who has power, and in what forms? What does it mean to have personal power? What does it mean to be empowered? In the spirit of the power in language that Lee advocates, focus on using your own voice, the language and tone that express who you are.

2. A central theme in feminist writing is an indictment of the ways in which the "dominant male culture" silences women. As you review Lee's essay, infer from her argument as well as the arguments of her sources how they think this silencing takes place. Write an essay in which you reflect on your experience of women being silenced by men or by a culture dominated by men. What does it mean to be silenced? As a woman, do you feel silenced? As a man, do you find that a male-dominated culture could silence women? Have you observed women being silenced? In what ways? Based on your own experience, do you think the feminist argument is valid?

3. Feminists argue that men suppress women because they fear the unleashing of female power. In an essay, argue for or against this view. As you develop your argument, consider the source of your perspective: what you have been taught, your own experience and observation, images from the media or from other forms of American culture, or other sources you identify. Do you think these sources are valid? Why or why not?

4. The writers Lee cites in developing her argument make a number of provocative claims. In an essay, reflect on your response to one of these writers. Which source would you want to read in full? Why? What attracts or provokes you? In what ways do you agree or disagree with the writer's claims, as Lee quotes or summarizes them in her essay? What in the writer's claims would you want to explore further?

Homophobia: Why Bring It Up?

Barbara Smith

Over the last decades, Barbara Smith's ideas, courage, and spirit have inspired social justice work. Smith is a black feminist writer and activist who has been at the forefront of discussions about race, gender, and sexuality. She consistently underscores the connections among ostensibly separate patterns of discrimination.

Smith cofounded the groundbreaking Combahee River Collective, a black feminist organizing group that became famous for its 1977 statement confronting racism in the gay movement and homophobia in the black community. Also in 1977, Smith wrote the influential essay "Toward a Black Feminist Criticism," which called for literary studies to directly address race and gender politics. She is cofounder and publisher of Kitchen Table: Women of Color Press, which has brought to wide attention a series of books and collected essays on race and gender.

Smith has written, coauthored, and coedited a number of books, among them *All the Women Are White, All the Blacks Are Men, but Some of Us Are Brave: Black Women's Studies* (1982), *Home Girls: A Black Feminist Anthology* (1983), and more recently *The Truth That Never Hurts: Writings on Race, Gender, and Freedom* (1998), a collection of her essays. Her articles and essays have appeared in a wide variety of publications, among them the *Nation* and the *New York Times Book Review*. Smith has lectured and served as writer in residence at numerous colleges and universities.

Originally published in 1990 in the *Interracial Books for Children Bulletin*, the essay included here takes as its occasion the brutal police beating of patrons at Blues, a gay, black, working-class bar. The widespread reluctance of newspapers to cover this incident and of civil rights groups to call for a response becomes for Smith further confirmation that homophobia is the one "ism" that otherwise progressive people tolerate.

In 1977 the Combahee River Collective, a Black feminist organization in Boston of which I was a member, wrote:

> The most general statement of our politics at the present time would be that we are actively committed to struggling against racial, sexual, heterosexual, and class oppression and see as our particular task the development of integrated analysis and practice based upon the fact that the major systems of oppression are interlocking. . . . We . . . often find it difficult to separate race from class from sex oppression because in our lives they are most often experienced simultaneously.[1]

Despite the logic and clarity of third world women's analysis of the simultaneity of oppression, people of all colors, progressive ones included, seem peculiarly reluctant to grasp these basic truths, especially when it comes to incorporating an active resistance to homophobia into their everyday lives. Homophobia is usually the last oppression to be mentioned, the last to be taken seriously, the last to go. But it is extremely serious, sometimes to the point of being fatal.

Consider that on the night of September 29, 1982, 20–30 New York City policemen rushed without warning into Blues, a Times Square bar. They harassed and severely beat the patrons, vandalized the premises, emptied the cash register, and left without making a single arrest. What motivated such brutal behavior? The answer is simple. The cops were inspired by three cherished tenets of our society: racism, classism, and homophobia: The bar's clientele is Black, working class, and gay. As the police cracked heads, they yelled racist and homophobic epithets familiar to every schoolchild. The attackers' hatred of both the queer and the colored, far from making them exceptional, put them squarely in the mainstream. If their actions were more extreme than most, their attitudes certainly were not.

The Blues bar happens to be across the street from the offices of the *New York Times*. The white, upper-middle-class, presumably heterosexual staff of the nation's premier newspaper regularly calls in complaints about the bar to the police. Not surprisingly, none of the New York daily papers, including the *Times*, bothered to report the incident. A coalition of third world and white lesbians and gay men organized a large protest demonstration soon after the attack occurred. Both moderate and militant civil rights and antiracist organizations were notably absent, and they have yet to express public outrage about a verifiable incident of police brutality, undoubtedly because the Black people involved were not straight.

Intertwining "Isms"

What happened at Blues perfectly illustrates the ways in which the major 5 "isms" *including* homophobia are intimately and violently intertwined. As a

Black woman, a lesbian, a feminist, and an activist, I have little difficulty seeing how the systems of oppression interconnect, if for no other reason than
that their meanings so frequently affect my life. During the 1970s and 1980s
political lesbians of color have often been the most
astute about the necessity for developing understand-   **Homophobia is usually the**
ings of the connections between oppressions. They   **last oppression to be men-**
have also opposed the building of hierarchies and chal-   **tioned. . . .**
lenged the "easy way out" of choosing a "primary
oppression" and downplaying those messy inconsistencies that occur whenever race, sex, class, and sexual identity actually mix. Ironically, for the forces
on the right, hating lesbians and gay men, people of color, Jews, and women
go hand in hand. *They* make connections between oppressions in the most
negative ways with horrifying results. Supposedly progressive people, on the
other hand, who oppose oppression on every other level, balk at acknowledging the societally sanctioned abuse of lesbians and gay men as a serious
problem. Their tacit attitude is "Homophobia, why bring it up?"

There are numerous reasons for otherwise sensitive people's reluctance to
confront homophobia in themselves and others. A major one is that people
are generally threatened about issues of sexuality, and for some the mere existence of homosexuals calls their sexuality/heterosexuality into question.
Unlike many other oppressed groups, homosexuals are not a group whose
identity is clear from birth. Through the process of coming out, a person
might indeed acquire this identity at any point in life. One way to protect
one's heterosexual credentials and privilege is to put down lesbians and gay
men at every turn, to make as large a gulf as possible between "we" and "they."

There are several misconceptions and attitudes which I find particularly
destructive because of the way they work to isolate the concerns of lesbians
and gay men:

1. Lesbian and gay male oppression is not as serious as other oppressions.
   It is not a political matter, but a private concern. The life-destroying
   impact of lost jobs, children, friendships, and family; the demoralizing
   toll of living in constant fear of being discovered by the wrong person
   which pervades all lesbians and gay men's lives whether closeted or out;
   and the actual physical violence and deaths that gay men and lesbians
   suffer at the hands of homophobes can be, if one subscribes to this myth,
   completely ignored.
2. "Gay" means gay white men with large discretionary incomes, period.
   Perceiving gay people in this way allows one to ignore that some of us
   are women *and* people of color *and* working class *and* poor *and* disabled
   and old. Thinking narrowly of gay people as white, middle class, and
   male, which is just what the establishment media want people to think,
   undermines consciousness of how identities and issues overlap. It is

essential, however, in making connections between homophobia and other oppressions, not to fall prey to the distorted reasoning that the justification for taking homophobia seriously is that it affects some groups who are "verifiably" oppressed, for example, people of color, women, or disabled people. Homophobia is in and of itself a verifiable oppression and in a heterosexist system, all nonheterosexuals are viewed as "deviants" and are oppressed.

3. Homosexuality is a white problem or even a "white disease." This attitude is much too prevalent among people of color. Individuals who are militantly opposed to racism in all its forms still find lesbianism and male homosexuality something to snicker about or, worse, to despise. Homophobic people of color are oppressive not just to white people, but to members of their own groups—at least 10 percent of their own groups.

4. Expressions of homophobia are legitimate and acceptable in contexts where other kinds of verbalized bigotry would be prohibited. Put-downs and jokes about "dykes" and "faggots" can be made without the slightest criticism in circles where "nigger" and "chink" jokes, for instance, would bring instant censure or even ostracism. One night of television viewing indicates how very acceptable public expressions of homophobia are.

How can such deeply entrenched attitudes and behavior be confronted and changed? Certainly gay and lesbian/feminist activism has made significant inroads since the late 1960s, both in the public sphere and upon the awareness of individuals. These movements have served a highly educational function, but they have not had nearly enough impact upon the educational system itself. Curriculum that focuses in a positive way upon issues of sexual identity, sexuality, and sexism is still rare, particularly in primary and secondary grades. Yet schools are virtual cauldrons of homophobic sentiment, as witnessed by everything from the graffiti in the bathrooms and the put-downs yelled on the playground, to the heterosexist bias of most texts and the firing of teachers on no other basis than that they are not heterosexual.

In the current political climate schools are constantly under hostile scrutiny from well-organized conservative forces. More than a little courage is required to challenge students' negative attitudes about what it means to be homosexual, female, third world, etc., but these attitudes *must* be challenged if pervasive taken-for-granted homophobia is ever to cease. I have found both in teaching and in speaking to a wide variety of audiences that making connections between oppressions is an excellent way to introduce the subjects of lesbian and gay male identity and homophobia, because it offers people a frame of reference to build upon. This is especially true if efforts have already been made in the classroom to teach about racism and sexism. It is factually inaccurate and strategically mistaken to present gay materials as if all gay people were white and male. Fortunately, there is an increasing body of work available, usually written by third world feminists, that provides an integrated approach to the intersection of a multiplicity of identities and issues.

Perhaps some readers are still wondering, "Homophobia, why bring it up?" One reason to bring it up is that at least 10 percent of your students will be or already are lesbians and gay males. Ten percent of your colleagues are as well. Homophobia may well be the last oppression to go, but it will go. It will go a lot faster if people who are opposed to *every* form of subjugation work in coalition to make it happen. 10

Note

1. The Combahee River Collective, "A Black Feminist Statement," in *All the Women Are White, All the Blacks Are Men, but Some of Us Are Brave: Black Women's Studies*, pp. 13, 16 (The Feminist Press), 1982.

Working with the Text

1. Barbara Smith describes the incident at the Blues bar early in her essay. Why did she include the details of a particular incident? Why did she place it where she did in the essay? Why is the location of the bar, in Times Square, especially relevant to Smith's point?

2. Smith notes that "[u]nlike many other oppressed groups, homosexuals are not a group whose identity is clear from birth" (par. 6). In what ways is this observation important as Smith comments on the intertwining of "isms"?

3. Smith titles her essay with a question. Offer a succinct summary of her response. In what ways does her title speak to the "silencing" of homophobia and its connection to other forms of oppression?

From Text to Field

1. Smith observes that "schools are virtual cauldrons of homophobic sentiment" (par. 8). Describe and reflect on incidents or experiences in your education that confirm or respond to Smith's characterization. Why does Smith focus on schools and schooling in her essay?

2. Smith notes four specific misconceptions or attitudes that she finds particularly destructive. Focusing on any one of the four, offer detailed, concrete instances of that misconception or attitude. Why is it destructive? Might there be a fifth misconception or attitude that merits inclusion in Smith's list? If so, what is it and why should it be included?

3. Either in your library or on the Internet, locate a copy of or an excerpt from the statement produced by the Combahee River Collective in 1977. What in the document might be tied to the history of its day? What endures and continues to be relevant? If you were to update this statement or offer one of your own, given more contemporary concerns, what would you focus on?

INTO THE FIELD: Options for Writing Projects

1. Logging the Classroom Conversation

The conversations you have in your college classrooms surely vary by subject matter, and their dynamics are constrained by the size of the class. A small seminar in the humanities will permit and encourage different conversational styles than a larger class in the sciences. Yet even within the same general context, conversational styles and patterns can vary, depending on the professor, the teaching philosophy employed, the gender composition of the class, and even the time of day.

This field project invites you to offer a fine-grained analysis of the conversational styles employed in one of your classes. Drawing on Deborah Tannen's discussion (p. 781) of gender in conversation and her own close observation of conversation in one of her classes, record in your notebook or diary the give-and-take of classroom talk. You may opt to choose your writing class for this study, in which case you may want to focus on the relationship between talk and the writing or revision process. You may also choose to work undercover in one of your other classes. (Whichever site you choose, be sure to respect the privacy of your classmates. For example, you may simply wish to identify speakers by number, rather than by name.)

As you log the conversation during one or several class periods, here are just a few of the many questions you may wish to consider: Who initiates the conversation? Who asks questions? How long do speakers hold the floor? Who speaks, and just as importantly, who doesn't tend to speak? How is turn taking handled? To what extent are there interruptions or overlaps in speaking? Are different styles of conversation evident based on the genders involved? How prevalent are challenges and counterarguments in the conversation? Are other speakers acknowledged or referred to, and if so how? How are shifts in topic handled? To what degree does the instructor orchestrate the conversation and its outcome? Does the physical environment of the classroom (e.g., how seats are arranged) have an effect on the conversation? To what extent do shadow conversations (e.g., whispered asides) occur during the primary conversation? Do you discern an educational philosophy or pedagogical approach that informs how and why the instructor has called upon conversation in this course?

As you offer your analysis, based on these observations, do you believe that "talking about ways of talking" has helped you understand the course and its classroom dynamics in a new or deeper way? Based on your analysis, what recommendations might you have for the instructor, the students, or both?

2. Gender, Conversation, and Group Dynamics

Small groups for discussion or other activities, often formed within a larger group setting, prove interesting test subjects by which to explore the role of gender in group dynamics. Some courses, such as your writing class, may make frequent use of small groups for peer feedback. Other courses may also use group work on occasion, and more than a few courses call for group or collaborative projects. Small groups, such as informal study groups, may also form outside of class and its more structured academic setting. Although academic discussion may be the overt purpose for the work of these groups, the dynamics that shape the group and its conversations are influenced by gender and conversational style. This field project invites you to explore the dynamics at work in a group in which you participate.

Many of the questions you may wish to ask about small groups parallel those in question 1 above that pertain to classroom conversation. Here are a few additional questions, many of which take into account the special dynamics of small groups. How does your group regulate itself? How is consensus achieved? If there seems to be a leader in the group, what kind of leadership style does he or she seem to present? How are roles assumed or assigned? How does the group encourage or respond to its less active members? How are conflicts or disagreements handled? What conversational style seems to predominate in your interactions with each other? What role does "off-task" conversation (e.g., what you did on Saturday night) have in developing trust and group solidarity? How do group members assume and grant authority and responsibility? Do gender and gender roles have a discernible effect on the group's dynamics?

As an alternative to this field project, you may wish to focus on a group outside of an explicitly academic setting, such as a group in your residence halls, a student group active on campus, or a group of citizens that is active in your community.

3. The Ethics of Conversational Participation

In her essay "How Male and Female Students Use Language Differently" (p. 496), Deborah Tannen briefly refers to what she terms an "ethics of participation" that can guide our role in conversations. This field project encourages you to flesh out what those ethics might be, either in your own life or in a particular classroom setting.

- In a substantive essay, explore your ethics for participation in conversation. How did you acquire those ethics? What educational or other experiences had a formative influence on those ethics? How do you see your ethics playing themselves out in real conversational contexts that often present dilemmas that cannot be addressed in easy ways? Have your participatory ethics conflicted with those of people who hold different ethics? How do such ethics vary given different contexts and perhaps different cultural backgrounds? How do your ethics of participation relate to your educational goals and to your views on learning and teaching? What influence do you think gender and gender roles might have on your ethics of participation?

- Explore the ethics of participation that are at work in a particular class you are taking. In what ways has your instructor articulated a conversational ethics for the class? How might that ethic be rooted in an education philosophy or a distinctive teaching style? To what extent might the ethics of participation or the class's conversational style be influenced by unspoken "rules" in that academic discipline or by a certain disciplinary "culture"? How does that ethic play itself out in actual classroom conversation? What learning outcomes seem to follow from or are posited by that ethic? Do you detect any dissonance or disconnect between the announced conversational ethic and the ethic as practiced in the classroom? What role does conversation, and its ethical and educational underpinnings, have in your attitude toward the class and toward your own learning? What place does conversation have in your distinctive learning style and gender role?

4. Academic Put-Downs: Language, Gender, and Power

In her meditation on the effect of calling someone a "bitch," Beverly Gross (p. 504) explores the intersection of language, gender, and power. This field project invites you to extend her investigation of "put-downs" by focusing on a distinctive type, as practiced in college classrooms and labs and during professors' office hours.

Your college or university campus would seem to be above the sort of street talk that Gross encounters when she explores the purposes toward which the appellation *bitch* is put. After all, isn't college supposed to be about tweed jackets and sherry hours, polite and learned conversation, and the life of the mind? Isn't college all about getting beyond high school behaviors? Although academic conversation is generally more polite, it can also be as ruthless and hurtful as conversations in other contexts. Indeed, part of what makes it so ruthless is that it masks itself with polite subtlety.

This field project is your opportunity to exact a measure of equally polite revenge. Surely all of us have been subjected to the hurtful academic put-down more than a few times. Sometimes the put-down comes from the instructor, but often it comes from a fellow classmate. It can take the form of exposing ignorance of something you supposedly should have known or of denigrating your abilities in a particular area. It might involve gender, as when a science or an engineering professor questions the interest or ability of a female student or when a male student feels put down in a women's studies class. Or the put-down might involve, as it often does, hierarchy and differences in power. (By the way, professors have raised academic put-downs to a high art by practicing among themselves.)

You might find it convenient and effective to organize the essay that comes out of this field project in the following way.

- First, describe the conversation or interaction in which the put-down occurred, including context that will help the reader of your essay understand the encounter.
- Next, analyze the details of the encounter. Here you might offer insights into the language strategies employed and what response, if any, you made. Why and in what ways do academic put-downs trade on people's facility (or lack of facility) with language and texts? How might gender and power have come into play? You also may wish to reflect on what response you would have liked to have made, given your current perspective on the situation.
- For the final section of your essay, generalize and extend your analysis. In what ways does the encounter you discuss reflect on academic culture (and its neuroses) or on the challenges you face when studying or majoring in a particular field?

5. Gender, in a Word

As identified and discussed by Beverly Gross (p. 504), the word *bitch* is certainly a term that captures many of the gender issues of our time. Yet that one word is by no means the only barometer of current or past attitudes. This field project encourages you to explore other words that might help us trace and understand our evolving discussions on gender.

How might you choose a particular word or term? Class discussion or brainstorming in small groups can provide a rich list of candidates. Dictionaries of slang, some of which Gross cites, are also good sources for terms that carry gender implications. Although terms of a sexual nature may be the first to spring to mind, don't overlook a whole host of terms that speak more generally of a male-oriented culture. The essay by Hermione Lee (p. 515), for example, turns to the word *power* to capture key issues — and problems — in feminist discourse.

You may find it highly instructive to review the etymology, or historical development, of your chosen word, as do both Gross and Lee. The *Oxford English Dictionary*, often referred to by its acronym *OED*, is the authoritative source on such matters. Your college library will have the multivolume print copy but may have online access to this reference work as well. Use other, more specialized dictionaries, such as dictionaries of slang, to supplement your work with the *OED*.

Once you have a solid grounding in the history of the word and a sense of its range of meanings, work collaboratively with others in your class to offer anecdotal evidence of its use and an analysis of how that particular term might offer insight into issues of gender.

6. Bathroom Graffiti: Tracing Gendered Conversation

Academic discussion of gender politics can often obscure the reality and influence that gendered conversation can have in our lives. One site where that conversation can be observed is the bathroom stall, a realm that is public in one sense, but also private and uncensored. Graffiti, and graffiti on graffiti, often reveal, in the most intimate ways, our obsession and fears about sexuality and gender orientation, our concerns about personal and group identity, and our worries about fitting in or standing out.

This field project invites you to explore a site that is in some sense taboo: graffiti in bathroom stalls and graffiti in other areas of campus. Your task is to observe the inscriptions not so much in their own terms, but as part of a conversation. Graffiti are written to mark or tag a site but also to make a statement and initiate a conversation. And those conversations may vary considerably between men and women.

This project calls for collaboration and a division of roles. Working in coed pairs or teams, divide up the field research so that men and women visit their respective bathrooms and other graffitied sites and then share notes with other members of the team. Working in this fashion, your team can gather and record data and then interpret and analyze it in ways that highlight differences in bathroom discourse. The goal throughout is to understand how issues of gender and sexuality are expressed in sites that are at once public yet also uncensored. (Caution: This project is not an invitation to add to graffiti. Moreover, because of the often explicit nature of graffiti texts, the project demands that all members of the team exercise good taste and discretion.)

Here are just a few questions to get you started: Based on the data that your team has gathered, do you see differences in the graffiti? Are men more competitive, with issues of power and performance often emerging as central? Do women express more cooperation and solidarity? How are members of the opposite sex portrayed? How do multiple responses to an initial item of graffiti suggest different ways in which conversation might unfold? Do graffiti vary according to location (the library, the dorm, the student center)? What do the graffiti tell us about our obsessions, desires, and fears?

7. Bias in Language

Because language is such a powerful instrument in the creation and reflection of our identities, the presence of bias in language has become a growing concern. Such bias can involve gender and has prompted greater awareness about how we might write in more gender-neutral or nonsexist ways. Bias also involves issues of race, ethnicity, and disability. This field project invites you to explore such bias and our responses to it.

For a brief but well-done introduction to bias in language, you should consult the Web site of the American Psychological Association (APA). This organization has developed the APA style manual for authors working in the social sciences, which offers an excellent introduction to the role of bias and to practical editorial remedies for addressing bias in language ‹apastyle.org›.

Your work can take one of several directions, depending on your interests and on the field site you wish to explore:

- You may wish to focus on one aspect of bias. Among the most common are gender bias, bias in race and ethnicity, and bias regarding disability.
- You should focus your work in one domain or field site, such as bias in the media or bias in the classroom.
- You may find it helpful to focus on one or more concrete instances of bias, as a way of grounding your work.
- In the course of your fieldwork, you might find it quite helpful to interview people who have experienced bias or those who have sought — as writers, teachers or community activists — to address and correct such bias.

Throughout, you may wish to consider whether bias in language is a reflection of the biases we have or whether it might also create or perpetuate those biases.

8. Gender Equity and Support on Your Campus

Your campus offers a compelling and multifaceted site in which to see issues of gender being played out. This field project offers several options for exploring gender equity and gender support on your campus, with respect to either students or faculty. Here are some avenues you may wish to pursue:

- Does your campus offer support for students majoring in a field in which women are underrepresented (engineering or some of the sciences, for example)? If so, how effective are those programs? If not, might such a program be helpful?
- What effect has Title IX (gender equity in sports) had on your campus? What steps did your campus take to come into compliance with Title IX? What problems might still persist for your campus to come into full compliance?
- What programs might your campus have for so-called nontraditional students, many of whom may be women with families? What issues for nontraditional students remain unaddressed on your campus?
- Are women faculty (especially in male-dominated fields) present in sufficient numbers? Are there special programs for the recruitment and retention of

women faculty? Do women faculty have their own support group? Are there discussions on your campus about salary inequities between male and female faculty?

As you inventory the state of discussion about gender or about programs that address gender issues on your campus, focus on one particular issue or problem as the nexus for further exploration.

9. Same-Sex Colleges

Early in her essay on how male and female students use language differently, Deborah Tannen (p. 496) offers a passing comment on the possible value of single-sex or same-sex schools and colleges. This field project offers you an opportunity to explore in far more detail the rationale for such institutions and how these institutions present themselves to prospective students and parents. Web sites for each college, and their comments on institutional mission and history, offer a valuable resource.

Although several elite East-coast colleges for women may immediately come to mind (among them Smith, Mount Holyoke, Wellesley, and Bryn Mawr), there are some seventy women's colleges in the United States. Consult the Women's College Coalition for a list of member institutions ‹womenscolleges.org›. Although many prominent men's colleges started accepting women students in the 1970s and are now fully coeducational (among them Amherst and Wesleyan), there remain a handful of men's colleges. For representative instances, you may wish to consult the Web sites of Hampden-Sydney College, Morehouse College, and Wabash College. Debates about single-sex or coed housing facilities may replicate some aspects of this larger debate.

As you explore the rationale for same-sex institutions, pay special attention to the role of language and of a common community. You may wish to compare the rationale to that of attending a religiously affiliated institution or historically black college or university.

As you explore this world of single-sex colleges and universities, reflect on the role that gender played in your decision about where to go to college. Although the vast majority of students have chosen to attend coeducational institutions, what role did a range of gender-related issues have in your decision? To what extent do gender-related issues have a role in your decision to major in a particular field?

10. Bringing up Homophobia

As we speak of gender and sexual orientation, it is important to note what is silent or silenced. In her essay, Barbara Smith (p. 525) makes the case that homophobia remains the one "ism" (among such concerns as racism or sexism) that otherwise progressive people will tolerate.

Drawing on one particular site, such as your campus or your hometown, explore the extent to which homophobia is silent or silenced. To what extent are the concerns of the queer community (e.g., gays, lesbians, bisexuals) given voice? How does that particular community respond to other concerns of social justice, such as racism or sexism? Develop a substantive essay in which you particularize and test Smith's observations, given one local community.

MINDING GENDER

Our minds are in many respects a theater of memory. Rarely if ever do we encounter something or someone in fresh, unencumbered ways. Those encounters are invariably filtered through the images we carry in our minds. This is especially true of experiences concerning or influenced by gender.

Our "images in mind" about gender roles and expectations, about what it means to be a man or a woman, filter and help construct our experience. Yet those very images in mind can also be — and indeed should be — the subject of reflection and self-awareness. If we remain unaware of those images, we know little about their influence and know even less about the alternative images we might develop for ourselves over time. This unit considers those images, looking *at* them rather than through them.

Most of us will clearly grant that our "images in mind" about gender shape our personal lives and identities and, what is more, our social interactions. Our parents and our family life surely have enormous influence on how we think of ourselves. That influence can start at the earliest of ages and continues, in various forms, throughout our adolescent and adult lives. The advice we receive about being a boy or a girl, or a man or woman, shapes our self-image and, in turn, the advice we give to others. Sometimes that advice will prompt us to challenge expected gender roles and refashion or experiment with received identities.

It only follows that the very personal images we carry in our minds shape our social interactions. How we behave in social and public settings — in the classroom and the dorm, in the workplace and on the street — is in good measure shaped by the images that we see in our theater of the mind. Indeed, that internal theater guides how we perceive the advantages and liabilities of both genders and influences how we might respond to the so-called gender wars of the last decades. Yet even as we begin to appreciate the social expression of our internal images, we also find that social conventions of behavior have likewise had a hand in shaping them. Social roles and constraints become internalized and help form our sense of who we are.

If the gender images we carry in our minds shape our personal lives and social interactions, they can likewise influence endeavors that may seem far more objective and impersonal. Scientific research lies at the far end of that spectrum, yet here too the influence of gender may be more telling than we might think. We presume that such research is untainted from bias, yet the history of science teaches us that bias—here, gender bias—can at times influence the conclusions drawn from data and the data themselves. The same can hold true for the ways in which scientific research is communicated. The language we employ and the metaphors we call upon can carry hidden freight and unexamined implications. Our "images in mind" regarding gender—our assumptions and dispositions—can profoundly influence the supposedly impartial observation of phenomena. Even scientific work, it seems, remains rooted in human culture.

The four essays in this unit offer different yet complementary perspectives on the theater of the mind—one in which images of gender hold surprising sway. Caribbean-born author Jamaica Kincaid explores in her short, evocative story "Girl" how images of being a girl and a woman are shaped by culture and are passed on from mother to daughter. Scott Russell Sanders likewise places the issue of gender identity in social and interpersonal contexts as he traces the role of men back to "the men we carry in our minds." The eminent scientist and science writer Stephen Jay Gould offers an excursion into the history of science devoted to brain size and intelligence. In the process, he reminds us that research interests and scientific conclusions can remain rooted in human culture and gender assumptions. Emily Martin explores the ways in which dominant or accepted metaphors about male-female roles make their way into serious scientific study and helps us appreciate that cultural assumptions can shape how scientists interpret and describe what they observe.

Reflecting on Prior Knowledge

1. The "images in mind" that we hold regarding gender affect how and what we know. In a journal entry, reflect on the origins or sources of what you know about gender. When, where, and from whom did you learn about gender—about being a boy or girl, man or woman? Have recent experiences reinforced or challenged your "images in mind"?

2. Cultural critics and political commentators have on occasion talked about the "gender wars." Implied by this term, to be sure, are the struggles faced by women as they work toward equality and equity. Yet the term also points to the challenges experienced by men as they adapt to evolving expectations and roles. Above all, the term suggests that these struggles and challenges have pitted woman against man. In a journal entry, or through a classroom activity where you pair up with another student, reflect on the term *gender wars*. Does

the term capture your experience or the experiences of your mother or father? What, if anything, might be misleading about the term? If you have struggled, in what ways, and how might those ways be misunderstood by others?

3. All of us have misjudged matters, and this can often be the case when it comes to gender and sexual orientation. Not only might we misjudge others, but we might also misjudge ourselves. In a journal entry, reflect on an image you held in mind about yourself or others that needed or invited correction or further consideration. How or why might your confidence in certain assumptions be misplaced? What have you learned or how have you grown through that experience and others like it?

4. The stories we tell, and the accounts we give of our world, often reflect in their very language and metaphors the gendered perspectives that we carry with us. In a journal entry, or perhaps in a brief story, offer two or more versions of a conversation, an encounter, or an event, each one guided by a different sense of gender and sexual identity. I think of this invitation as an opportunity to create your own *Rashomon* based on issues of gender—*Rashomon* (1950) being a famous movie by Japanese filmmaker Akira Kurosawa in which different versions of the same event are told by several individuals.

Girl

Jamaica Kincaid

Born Elaine Potter Richardson in 1949, Jamaica Kincaid adopted this pen name when she began writing for the *New Yorker* magazine, becoming a regular contributor for nearly twenty years (1976–1995) with her "Talk of the Town" column. But behind this name change lies a quest for self and a journey from home.

Kincaid was born in St. John's, Antigua, which was then a British colony in the Caribbean. Her mother's family members were landed peasants and her father a carpenter and cabinetmaker. Precocious and an early reader, Jamaica fled her island home and family at seventeen. Arriving in New York, she worked as an au pair and a receptionist, studied photography, and attended college before her writing caught the attention of editors at the *New Yorker*. She now lives in Vermont with her husband, son, and daughter.

Kincaid's experience as an exile and her troubled relationship with her mother inform much of her writing. Her tight, lyrical prose captures the conflicted emotions of that mother-daughter relationship and of her connection to, yet distance from, her homeland. In addition to her magazine writing, Kincaid has published many books, among them *Annie John* (1985), her story of growing up and leaving home; *A Small Place* (1988), an angry account of colonization; *Lucy* (1990), the story of an au pair in a family whose happiness unravels; and *Autobiography of My Mother* (1994).

"Girl" was first published in the *New Yorker* and then anthologized in Kincaid's collection of stories *At the Bottom of the River* (2000), which focuses on the childhood and coming of age of a Caribbean girl.

Wash the white clothes on Monday and put them on the stone heap; wash the color clothes on Tuesday and put them on the clothesline to dry; don't walk barehead in the hot sun; cook pumpkin fritters in very hot sweet oil; soak your little cloths right after you take them off; when buying cotton to make yourself a nice blouse, be sure that it doesn't have gum on it, because that way it won't hold up well after a wash; soak salt fish overnight before you cook it; is it true that you sing benna in Sunday school?; always eat your food in such a way that it won't turn someone else's stomach; on Sundays try to walk like a lady and not like the slut you are so bent on becoming; don't sing benna in Sunday school; you mustn't speak to wharf-rat boys, not even to give directions; don't eat fruits on the street — flies will follow you; *but I don't sing benna on Sundays at all and never in Sunday school*; this is how to sew on a button; this is how to make a buttonhole for the button you have just sewed on; this is how to hem a dress when you see the hem coming down and so to prevent yourself from looking like the slut I know you are so bent on becoming; this is how you iron your father's khaki shirt so that it doesn't have a crease; this is how you iron your father's khaki pants so that they don't have a crease; this is how you grow okra — far from the house, because okra tree harbors red ants; when you are growing dasheen, make sure it gets plenty of **This way they won't recognize immediately the slut I have warned you against becoming.** water or else it makes your throat itch when you are eating it; this is how you sweep a corner; this is how you sweep a whole house; this is how you sweep a yard; this is how you smile to someone you don't like too much; this is how you smile to someone you don't like at all; this is how you smile to someone you like completely; this is how you set a table for tea; this is how you set a table for dinner; this is how you set a table for dinner with an important guest; this is how you set a table for lunch; this is how you set a table for breakfast; this is how to behave in the presence of men who don't know you very well, and this way they won't recognize immediately the slut I have warned you against becoming; be sure to wash every day, even if it is with your own spit; don't squat down to play marbles — you are not a boy, you know; don't pick people's flowers — you might catch something; don't throw stones at blackbirds, because it might not be a blackbird at all; this is how to make a bread pudding; this is how to make doukona; this is how to make pepper pot; this is how to make a good medicine for a cold; this is how to make a good medicine to throw away a child before it even becomes a child; this is how to catch a fish; this is how to throw back a fish you don't like, and that way something bad won't fall on you; this is how to bully a man; this is how a man bullies you; this is how to love a man, and if this doesn't work there are other ways, and if they don't work don't feel too bad about giving up; this is how to spit up in the air if you feel like it, and this is how to move quick so that it doesn't fall on you; this is how to make ends meet; always squeeze bread to make sure it's fresh; *but what if the baker won't let me feel* *the bread?*; you mean to say that after all you are really going to be the kind of woman who the baker won't let near the bread?

Working with the Text

1. The two italicized lines in the story clarify that there are two speakers involved in this encounter. Who is the main speaker, and who is speaking in italics? How would you describe the interaction between the two speakers?

2. Jamaica Kincaid's story is cast as one very long sentence. Why do you think she made this choice? What effect does this form have on you, and how might it underscore the point she wishes to make or the effect she wishes to create?

3. How would you describe this "girl," and what attitude does the speaker have about her? What can you discern about the attitude of the girl? What identity does the speaker encourage her to adopt?

From Text to Field

1. Study the advice given to the "girl" for what it implies about the cultural context in which she is growing up. What can you infer about Antigua's society? How valuable or effective might the advice be as the girl comes to terms with the island's traditional social hierarchies?

2. In offering a cascade of advice—presumably parental advice—this brief lyrical story places you, the reader, in a familiar position. You too have received a cascade of advice about what to do and how to act. Using Kincaid's story as a loose model, write your own version, titled "Boy" or "Girl," in which you capture the kind of advice you have been offered, given your own cultural and historical context.

3. Writers are used to receiving—and giving—advice. Write your own version of Kincaid's story in which you portray someone giving advice to a young writer. The speaker could be a teacher or a fellow student. What advice about writing might matter to the speaker, and what would the reader or listener wish to hear? What role might grammatical correctness or certain conventions in writing play in the advice? How might the advice capture the complex relationships between the writing process and the final product of that process? What connection might the advice forge between the demands of writing for an audience and the concerns about the writer's own identity?

The Men We Carry in Our Minds

Scott Russell Sanders

Scott Russell Sanders is a widely published author of essays, short stories, novels, and children's books. He has won numerous awards for his writing, and his essays have been selected four times for inclusion in the annual *Best American Essays*. His writings are frequently reprinted in anthologies, including *The Norton Reader* and *The Art of the Essay*. He has received fellowships from institutions such as the National Endowment for the Arts and the Guggenheim Foundation. With a PhD from Cambridge University, Sanders is a professor of English at Indiana University, where he has won that institution's highest teaching award and has earned the rank of distinguished professor.

These are not the credentials usually expected of someone who grew up in what Sanders calls "the back roads of Tennessee and Ohio." A scholarship to Brown University gave him opportunities that few of his childhood friends ever even imagined for themselves.

Although education enabled Sanders to become a distinguished writer, his life and writing are haunted by the world he grew up in. In the following essay, "The Men We Carry in Our Minds," Sanders reveals memories that set him apart from men who, as many women insist, carry the guilt for "having kept all the joys and privileges of the earth for themselves."

"The Men We Carry in Our Minds," originally published in *Milkweed Chronicle* (1984), was included in Sanders's essay collection *Paradise of Bombs* (1987), which won the Associated Writing Programs Award in Creative Nonfiction in 1987. Sanders's collections of essays also include *Secrets of the Universe: Scenes from the Journey Home* (1991), *Writing from the Center* (1995), *Hunting for Hope: A Father's Journey* (1998), and *The Force of Spirit* (2000).

"This must be a hard time for women," I say to my friend Anneke. "They have so many paths to choose from, and so many voices calling them."

"I think it's a lot harder for men," she replies.

"How do you figure that?"

"The women I know feel excited, innocent, like crusaders in a just cause. The men I know are eaten up with guilt."

We are sitting at the kitchen table drinking sassafras tea, our hands 5 wrapped around the mugs because this April morning is cool and drizzly. "Like a Dutch morning," Anneke told me earlier. She is Dutch herself, a writer and midwife and peacemaker, with the round face and sad eyes of a woman in a Vermeer painting who might be waiting for the rain to stop, for a door to open. She leans over to sniff a sprig of lilac, pale lavender, that rises from a vase of cobalt blue.

"Women feel such pressure to be everything, do everything," I say. "Career, kids, art, politics. Have their babies and get back to the office a week later. It's as if they're trying to overcome a million years' worth of evolution in one lifetime."

"But we help one another. We don't try to lumber on alone, like so many wounded grizzly bears, the way men do." Anneke sips her tea. I gave her the mug with owls on it, for wisdom. "And we have this deep-down sense that we're in the *right*—we've been held back, passed over, used—while men feel they're in the wrong. Men are the ones who've been discredited, who have to search their souls."

I search my soul. I discover guilty feelings aplenty—toward the poor, the Vietnamese, Native Americans, the whales, an endless list of debts—a guilt in each case that is as bright and unambiguous as a neon sign. But toward women I feel something more confused, a snarl of shame, envy, wary tenderness, and amazement. This muddle troubles me. To hide my unease I say, "You're right, it's tough being a man these days."

"Don't laugh." Anneke frowns at me, mournful-eyed, through the sassafras steam. "I wouldn't be a man for anything. It's much easier being the victim. All the victim has to do is break free. The persecutor has to live with his past."

How deep is that past? I find myself wondering after Anneke has left. How 10 much of an inheritance do I have to throw off? Is it just the beliefs I breathed in as a child? Do I have to scour memory back through father and grandfather? Through St. Paul? Beyond Stonehenge and into the twilit caves? I'm convinced the past we must contend with is deeper even than speech. When I think back on my childhood, on how I learned to see men and women, I have a sense of ancient, dizzying depths. The back roads of Tennessee and Ohio where I grew up were probably closer, in their sexual patterns, to the campsites of Stone Age hunters than to the genderless cities of the future into which we are rushing.

The first men, besides my father, I remember seeing were black convicts and white guards, in the cottonfield across the road from our farm on the outskirts of Memphis. I must have been three or four. The prisoners wore dingy gray-and-black zebra suits, heavy as canvas, sodden with sweat. Hatless, stooped, they chopped weeds in the fierce heat, row after row, breathing the acrid dust of boll-weevil poison. The overseers wore dazzling white shirts and broad shadowy hats. The oiled barrels of their shotguns flashed in the sunlight. Their faces in memory are utterly blank. Of course those men, white and black, have become for me an emblem of racial hatred. But they have also come to stand for the twin poles of my early vision of manhood — the brute toiling animal and the boss.

When I was a boy, the men I knew labored with their bodies. They were marginal farmers, just scraping by, or welders, steelworkers, carpenters; they swept floors, dug ditches, mined coal, or drove trucks, their forearms ropy with muscle; they trained horses, stoked furnaces, built tires, stood on assembly lines wrestling parts onto cars and refrigerators. They got up before light, worked all day long whatever the weather, and when they came home at night they looked as though somebody had been whipping them. In the evenings and on weekends they worked on their own places, tilling gardens that were lumpy with clay, fixing broken-down cars, hammering on houses that were always too drafty, too leaky, too small.

The bodies of the men I knew were twisted and maimed in ways visible and invisible. The nails of their hands were black and split, the hands tattooed with scars. Some had lost fingers. Heavy lifting had given many of them finicky backs and guts weak from hernias. Racing against conveyor belts had given them ulcers. Their ankles and knees ached from years of standing on concrete. Anyone who had worked for long around machines was hard of hearing. They squinted, and the skin of their faces was creased like the leather of old work gloves. There were times, studying them, when I dreaded growing up. Most of them coughed, from dust or cigarettes, and most of them drank cheap wine or whiskey, so their eyes looked bloodshot and bruised. The fathers of my friends always seemed older than the mothers. Men wore out sooner. Only women lived into old age.

I was baffled. What privileges? What joys?

As a boy I also knew another sort of men, who did not sweat and break down like mules. They were soldiers, and so far as I could tell they scarcely worked at all. During my early school years we lived on a military base, an arsenal in Ohio, and every day I saw GIs in the guardshacks, on the stoops of barracks, at the wheels of olive drab Chevrolets. The chief fact of their lives was boredom. Long after I left the arsenal I came to recognize the sour smell the soldiers gave off as that of souls in limbo. They were all waiting — for wars, for transfers, for leaves, for promotions, for the end of their hitch — like so many braves waiting for the hunt to begin. Unlike the warriors of older tribes, however, they would have no say about when the battle would start or how it would be waged. Their waiting was broken only when they practiced for war. They fired guns at targets, drove tanks across the churned-up fields of the military reservation, set off bombs in the wrecks of old fighter planes. I knew this was all play. But I also felt certain that when the hour for killing arrived, they would kill. When the real shooting started, many of them would die. This was what soldiers were *for*, just as a hammer was for driving nails.

Warriors and toilers: Those seemed, in my boyhood vision, to be the chief 15 destinies for men. They weren't the only destinies, as I learned from having a few male teachers, from reading books, and from watching television. But the men on television— the politicians, the astronauts, the generals, the savvy lawyers, the philosophical doctors, the bosses who gave orders to both soldiers and laborers —seemed as remote and unreal to me as the figures in tapestries. I could no more imagine growing up to become one of these cool, potent creatures than I could imagine becoming a prince.

A nearer and more hopeful example was that of my father, who had escaped from a red-dirt farm to a tire factory, and from the assembly line to the front office. Eventually he dressed in a white shirt and tie. He carried himself as if he had been born to work with his mind. But his body, remembering the earlier years of slogging work, began to give out on him in his fifties, and it quit on him entirely before he turned sixty-five. Even such a partial escape from man's fate as he had accomplished did not seem possible for most of the boys I knew. They joined the army, stood in line for jobs in the smoky plants, helped build highways. They were bound to work as their fathers had worked, killing themselves or preparing to kill others.

A scholarship enabled me not only to attend college, a rare enough feat in my circle, but even to study in a university meant for the children of the rich. Here I met for the first time young men who had assumed from birth that they would lead lives of comfort and power. And for the first time I met women who told me that men were guilty of having kept all the joys and privileges of the earth for themselves. I was baffled. What privileges? What joys? I thought about the maimed, dismal lives of most of the men back home. What had they stolen from their wives and daughters? The right to go five days a week, twelve months a year, for thirty or forty years to a steel mill or a coal mine? The right to drop bombs and die in war? The right to feel every leak in the roof, every gap in the fence, every cough in the engine, as a wound they must mend? The right to feel, when the lay-off comes or the plant shuts down, not only afraid but ashamed?

I was slow to understand the deep grievances of women. This was because, as a boy, I had envied them. Before college, the only people I had ever known who were interested in art or music or literature, the only ones who read books, the only ones who ever seemed to enjoy a sense of ease and grace were the mothers and daughters. Like the menfolk, they fretted about money, they scrimped and made-do. But, when the pay stopped coming in, they were not the ones who had failed. Nor did they have to go to war, and that seemed to me a blessed fact. By comparison with the narrow, ironclad days of fathers, there was an expansiveness, I thought, in the days of mothers. They went to see neighbors, to shop in town, to run errands at school, at the library, at church. No doubt, had I looked harder at their lives, I would have envied them less. It was not my fate to become a woman, so it was easier for me to see the graces. Few of them held jobs outside the home, and those who did filled thankless roles as clerks and waitresses. I didn't see, then, what a prison a house could be, since houses seemed to me brighter, handsomer places than any factory. I did not realize — because such things were never spoken of — how often women suffered from men's bullying. I did learn about the wretchedness of abandoned wives, single mothers, widows; but I also learned about the wretchedness of lone men. Even then I could see how exhausting it was for a mother to cater all day to the needs of young children. But if I had been asked, as a boy, to choose between tending a baby and tending a machine, I think I would have chosen the baby. (Having now tended both, I know I would choose the baby.)

So I was baffled when the women at college accused me and my sex of having cornered the world's pleasures. I think something like my bafflement has been felt by other boys (and by girls as well) who grew up in dirt-poor farm country, in mining country, in black ghettos, in Hispanic barrios, in the shadows of factories, in third world nations — any place where the fate of men is as grim and bleak as the fate of women. Toilers and warriors. I realize now how ancient these identities are, how deep the tug they exert on men, the undertow of a thousand generations. The miseries I saw, as a boy, in the lives of nearly all men I continue to see in the lives of many — the body-breaking toil, the tedium, the call to be tough, the humiliating powerlessness, the battle for a living and for territory.

When the women I met at college thought about the joys and privileges 20 of men, they did not carry in their minds the sort of men I had known in my childhood. They thought of their fathers, who were bankers, physicians, architects, stockbrokers, the big wheels of the big cities. These fathers rode the train to work or drove cars that cost more than any of my childhood houses. They were attended from morning to night by female helpers, wives and nurses and secretaries. They were never laid off, never short of cash at month's end, never lined up for welfare. These fathers made decisions that mattered. They ran the world.

The daughters of such men wanted to share in this power, this glory. So did I. They yearned for a say over their future, for jobs worthy of their abilities, for the right to live at peace, unmolested, whole. Yes, I thought, yes yes. The difference between me and these daughters was that they saw me, because of my sex, as destined from birth to become like their fathers, and therefore as an enemy to their desires. But I knew better. I wasn't an enemy, in fact or in feeling. I was an ally. If I had known, then, how to tell them so, would they have believed me? Would they now?

Working with the Text

1. In the story that opens the essay, Scott Russell Sanders's friend Anneke tells him, "The men I know are eaten up with guilt" (par. 4). In the soul-searching this comment prompts for Sanders, he finds that instead of guilt toward women he feels "something more confused, a snarl of shame, envy, wary tenderness, and amazement" (par. 8). With the title in mind, reread the essay for insight into the difference between the guilt felt by the men Anneke knows and the more confused emotions felt by Sanders. In a brief essay, reflect on this difference. Given the men in their minds, why might Anneke's friends feel guilty, while Sanders feels other emotions?

2. Sanders's descriptions of men tend to focus on their bodies and their jobs. Write a brief essay in which you reflect on the role these descriptions play in Sanders's exploration of "the joys and privileges of men" (par. 20). Why does Sanders introduce men in terms of their jobs? Why does he place so much emphasis on their bodies? What effects do these aspects of men's lives have on his own identity? What effect does this identity have on the women who live with and around men, and on the men's attitudes toward these women?

3. Sanders confronts one of the most significant social issues of our time—the roles and competing rights of men and women—by drawing on his personal experience. While the essay centers on the men—and women—in his own mind, his title refers to the men in *our* minds. In a brief essay, analyze the significance of this approach to his argument. Why would Sanders search for the people in his own mind to address a social issue? Why would he shift the emphasis, in his title, to include the minds of his readers? In what ways does basing the essay on personal experience strengthen the argument? In what ways does it weaken the argument?

4. Sanders closes the essay by claiming that he was an ally, not an enemy, to the women he knew in college who regarded men as "an enemy to their desires." He asks, "If I had known, then, how to tell them so, would they have believed me? Would they now?" (par. 21). In a brief essay, answer this question from your

point of view. Do you believe that Sanders is an ally of women? In what ways do you think he truly identifies with them? In what ways do you think he fails to speak to their concerns? As an alternative assignment, write a brief essay in which you reflect on Sanders's reasons for ending the essay with these questions. Why would he doubt that women would believe him?

From Text to Field

1. When Sanders went to college, he found that his peers regarded the roles and identities of men and women very differently than he did because they had grown up in very different worlds. In a personal essay, respond to Sanders's story by telling your own. Who are the men in your mind? How do they regard and treat the women in your mind? How does your story of men and women compare to the story of someone you have met who grew up in different circumstances? What bearing do you think these differences have on your view of the roles and identities of men and women?

2. Sanders's friend Anneke believes that men feel guilty toward women. Sanders says that he feels "shame, envy, wary tenderness, and amazement" (par. 8), but not guilt. Write an essay in which you explore your beliefs and feelings about how men regard women. If you are a man, what feelings do you have toward women? Why? How do you think women regard you? If you are a woman, how do you think men regard you? Why? How do you feel about the attitude you believe men have toward you?

3. As Sanders searches for the roots of his feelings toward women, he asks, "How much of an inheritance do I have to throw off?" (par. 10). As he draws the essay to a close, he observes, "I realize now how ancient these identities are, how deep the tug they exert on men, the undertow of a thousand generations" (par. 19). Although he points out that the history of "toilers and warriors" is ancient, he makes only general references to that history. In an essay, draw on your knowledge and awareness of history to seek out the roots of your view of men. What ancient roles do the men in your mind play? What were the origins of these roles, and how have they developed over time? Think of the essay as a brief history, driven by your own interpretations and commentary.

Women's Brains

Stephen Jay Gould

Late in the nineteenth century, scientists went to great lengths to determine whether women's brains were smaller than the brains of men. Interpretations of the early data claimed that women's brains were significantly smaller. Later data, corrected for factors that influence brain size, indicated that the difference in size was significantly less than earlier thought, or that there was no difference, or that women's brains were actually larger.

In the following essay, Stephen Jay Gould examines the data not only for accuracy but also for the social significance that can be found in the range of interpretations. As a prominent evolutionary theorist and writer — internationally recognized by lay audiences as well as academics — Gould influenced both scientific inquiry and public opinion. He spoke out against biological determinism and often emphasized in his writings that while scientists pursue objective data, their research interests and scientific conclusions are invariably rooted in human culture.

"Women's Brains" was originally published in a collection of essays, *The Panda's Thumb: More Reflections in Natural History* (1980), which won a National Book Award and an American Library Association Notable Book citation. A version of the essay appeared in *The Mismeasure of Man* (1981)—a winner of awards from the National Book Critics Circle and the American Educational Research Association as well as a nominee for the American Book Award in science — which challenged scientific attempts, through IQ testing, to develop objective measures of human intelligence.

When Gould died in 2002 at the age of sixty, he was professor of zoology at Harvard University. He was among the first to receive the MacArthur Foundation Prize Fellowship, informally known as the "genius grant." Throughout his career, he received awards and widespread praise for his engaged and engaging writing as well as for his scientific achievement.

In the prelude to *Middlemarch*, George Eliot lamented the unfulfilled lives of talented women:

> Some have felt that these blundering lives are due to the inconvenient indefiniteness with which the Supreme Power has fashioned the natures of women: If there were one level of feminine incompetence as strict as the ability to count three and no more, the social lot of women might be treated with scientific certitude.

Eliot goes on to discount the idea of innate limitation, but while she wrote in 1872, the leaders of European anthropometry were trying to measure "with scientific certitude" the inferiority of women. Anthropometry, or measurement of the human body, is not so fashionable a field these days, but it dominated the human sciences for much of the nineteenth century and remained popular until intelligence testing replaced skull measurement as a favored device for making invidious comparisons among races, classes, and sexes. Craniometry, or measurement of the skull, commanded the most attention and respect. Its unquestioned leader, Paul Broca (1824–80), professor of clinical surgery at the Faculty of Medicine in Paris, gathered a school of disciples and imitators around himself. Their work, so meticulous and apparently irrefutable, exerted great influence and won high esteem as a jewel of nineteenth-century science.

Broca's work seemed particularly invulnerable to refutation. Had he not measured with the most scrupulous care and accuracy? (Indeed, he had. I have the greatest respect for Broca's meticulous procedure. His numbers are sound. But science is an inferential exercise, not a catalog of facts. Numbers, by themselves, specify nothing. All depends upon what you do with them.) Broca depicted himself as an apostle of objectivity, a man who bowed before facts and cast aside superstition and sentimentality. He declared that "there is no faith, however respectable, no interest, however legitimate, which must not accommodate itself to the progress of human knowledge and bend before truth." Women, like it or not, had smaller brains than men and, therefore, could not equal them in intelligence. This fact, Broca argued, may reinforce a common prejudice in male society, but it is also a scientific truth. L. Manouvrier, a black sheep in Broca's fold, rejected the inferiority of women and wrote with feeling about the burden imposed upon them by Broca's numbers:

> Women displayed their talents and their diplomas. They also invoked philosophical authorities. But they were opposed by *numbers* unknown to Condorcet or to John Stuart Mill. These numbers fell upon poor women like a sledge hammer, and they were accompanied by commentaries and sarcasms more ferocious than the most misogynist imprecations of certain church fathers. The theologians had asked if women had a soul. Several

centuries later, some scientists were ready to refuse them a human intelligence.

Broca's argument rested upon two sets of data: the larger brains of men in modern societies, and a supposed increase in male superiority through time. His most extensive data came from autopsies performed personally in four Parisian hospitals. For 292 male brains, he calculated an average weight of 1,325 grams; 140 female brains averaged 1,144 grams for a difference of 181 grams, or 14 percent of the male weight. Broca understood, of course, that part of this difference could be attributed to the greater height of males. Yet he made no attempt to measure the effect of size alone and actually stated that it cannot account for the entire difference because we know, a priori, that women are not as intelligent as men (a premise that the data were supposed to test, not rest upon):

> We might ask if the small size of the female brain depends exclusively upon the small size of her body. Tiedemann has proposed this explanation. But we must not forget that women are, on the average, a little less intelligent than men, a difference which we should not exaggerate but which is, nonetheless, real. We are therefore permitted to suppose that the relatively small size of the female brain depends in part upon her physical inferiority and in part upon her intellectual inferiority.

In 1873, the year after Eliot published *Middlemarch*, Broca measured the   5 cranial capacities of prehistoric skulls from L'Homme Mort cave. Here he found a difference of only 99.5 cubic centimeters between males and females, while modern populations range from 129.5 to 220.7. Topinard, Broca's chief disciple, explained the increasing discrepancy through time as a result of differing evolutionary pressures upon dominant men and passive women:

> The man who fights for two or more in the struggle for existence, who has all the responsibility and the cares of tomorrow, who is constantly active in combating the environment and human rivals, needs more brain than the woman whom he must protect and nourish, the sedentary woman, lacking any interior occupations, whose role is to raise children, love, and be passive.

In 1879, Gustave Le Bon, chief misogynist of Broca's school, used these data to publish what must be the most vicious attack upon women in modern scientific literature (no one can top Aristotle). I do not claim his views were representative of Broca's school, but they were published in France's most respected anthropological journal. Le Bon concluded:

> In the most intelligent races, as among the Parisians, there are a large number of women whose brains are closer in size to those of gorillas than to the

most developed male brains. This inferiority is so obvious that no one can contest it for a moment; only its degree is worth discussion. All psychologists who have studied the intelligence of women, as well as poets and novelists, recognize today that they represent the most inferior forms of human evolution and that they are closer to children and savages than to an adult, civilized man. They excel in fickleness, inconstancy, absence of thought and logic, and incapacity to reason. Without doubt there exist some distinguished women, very superior to the average man, but they are as exceptional as the birth of any monstrosity, as, for example, of a gorilla with two heads; consequently, we may neglect them entirely.

Nor did Le Bon shrink from the social implications of his views. He was horrified by the proposal of some American reformers to grant women higher education on the same basis as men:

> A desire to give them the same education, and, as a consequence, to propose the same goals for them, is a dangerous chimera. . . . The day when, misunderstanding the inferior occupations which nature has given her, women leave the home and take part in our battles; on this day a social revolution will begin, and everything that maintains the sacred ties of the family will disappear.

Sound familiar?[1]

I have reexamined Broca's data, the basis for all this derivative pronouncement, and I find his numbers sound but his interpretation ill-founded, to say the least. The data supporting his claim for increased difference through time can be easily dismissed. Broca based his contention on the samples from L'Homme Mort alone — only seven male and six female skulls in all. Never have so little data yielded such far ranging conclusions.

In 1888, Topinard published Broca's more extensive data on the Parisian hospitals. Since Broca recorded height and age as well as brain size, we may use modern statistics to remove their effect. Brain weight decreases with age, and Broca's women were, on average, considerably older than his men. Brain weight increases with height, and his average man was almost half a foot taller than his average woman. I used multiple regression, a technique that allowed me to assess simultaneously the influence of height and age upon brain size. In an analysis of the data for women, I found that, at average male height and age, a woman's brain would weigh 1,212 grams. Correction for height and age reduces Broca's measured difference of 181 grams by more than a third, to 113 grams.

---

[1]When I wrote this essay, I assumed that Le Bon was a marginal, if colorful, figure. I have since learned that he was a leading scientist, one of the founders of social psychology, and best known for a seminal study on crowd behavior, still cited today (*La psychologie des foules*, 1895), and for his work on unconscious motivation.

I don't know what to make of this remaining difference because I cannot   10
assess other factors known to influence brain size in a major way. Cause of
death has an important effect: degenerative disease often entails a substantial
diminution of brain size. (This effect is separate from the decrease attributed
to age alone.) Eugene Schreider, also working with Broca's data, found that
men killed in accidents had brains weighing, on average, 60 grams more
than men dying of infectious diseases. The best modern data I can find (from
American hospitals) records a full 100-gram difference between death by
degenerative arteriosclerosis and by violence or accident. Since so many of
Broca's subjects were very elderly women, we may assume that lengthy
degenerative disease was more common among them than among the men.

More importantly, modern students of brain size still have not agreed on
a proper measure for eliminating the powerful effect of body size. Height is
partly adequate, but men and women of the same height do not share the
same body build. Weight is even worse than height, because most of its variation reflects nutrition rather than intrinsic size — fat versus skinny exerts little influence upon the brain. Manouvrier took up this subject in the 1880s
and argued that muscular mass and force should be used. He tried to measure this elusive property in various ways and found a marked difference in
favor of men, even in men and women of the same height. When he corrected for what he called "sexual mass," women actually came out slightly
ahead in brain size.

Thus, the corrected 113-gram difference is surely too large; the true figure
is probably close to zero and may as well favor women as men. And 113
grams, by the way, is exactly the average difference
Women, like it or not, had between a 5 foot 4 inch and a 6 foot 4 inch male in
smaller brains than men. Broca's data. We would not (especially us short folks)
want to ascribe greater intelligence to tall men. In
short, who knows what to do with Broca's data? They certainly don't permit
any confident claim that men have bigger brains than women.

To appreciate the social role of Broca and his school, we must recognize
that his statements about the brains of women do not reflect an isolated prejudice toward a single disadvantaged group. They must be weighed in the
context of a general theory that supported contemporary social distinctions
as biologically ordained. Women, blacks, and poor people suffered the same
disparagement, but women bore the brunt of Broca's argument because he
had easier access to data on women's brains. Women were singularly deni-
grated but they also stood as surrogates for other disenfranchised groups. As
one of Broca's disciples wrote in 1881: "Men of the black races have a brain
scarcely heavier than that of white women." This juxtaposition extended
into many other realms of anthropological argument, particularly to claims
that, anatomically and emotionally, both women and blacks were like white

children — and that white children, by the theory of recapitulation, represented an ancestral (primitive) adult stage of human evolution. I do not regard as empty rhetoric the claim that women's battles are for all of us.

Maria Montessori did not confine her activities to educational reform for young children. She lectured on anthropology for several years at the University of Rome, and wrote an influential book entitled *Pedagogical Anthropology* (English edition, 1913). Montessori was no egalitarian. She supported most of Broca's work and the theory of innate criminality proposed by her compatriot Cesare Lombroso. She measured the circumference of children's heads in her schools and inferred that the best prospects had bigger brains. But she had no use for Broca's conclusions about women. She discussed Manouvrier's work at length and made much of his tentative claim that women, after proper correction of the data, had slightly larger brains than men. Women, she concluded, were intellectually superior, but men had prevailed heretofore by dint of physical force. Since technology has abolished force as an instrument of power, the era of women may soon be upon us: "In such an epoch there will really be superior human beings, there will really be men strong in morality and in sentiment. Perhaps in this way the reign of women is approaching, when the enigma of her anthropological superiority will be deciphered. Woman was always the custodian of human sentiment, morality, and honor."

This represents one possible antidote to "scientific" claims for the constitutional inferiority of certain groups. One may affirm the validity of biological distinctions but argue that the data have been misinterpreted by prejudiced men with a stake in the outcome, and that disadvantaged groups are truly superior. In recent years, Elaine Morgan has followed this strategy in her *Descent of Woman*, a speculative reconstruction of human prehistory from the woman's point of view — and as farcical as more famous tall tales by and for men. ⟨15⟩

I prefer another strategy. Montessori and Morgan followed Broca's philosophy to reach a more congenial conclusion. I would rather label the whole enterprise of setting a biological value upon groups for what it is: irrelevant and highly injurious. George Eliot well appreciated the special tragedy that biological labeling imposed upon members of disadvantaged groups. She expressed it for people like herself — women of extraordinary talent. I would apply it more widely — not only to those whose dreams are flouted but also to those who never realize that they may dream — but I cannot match her prose. In conclusion, then, the rest of Eliot's prelude to *Middlemarch*:

> The limits of variation are really much wider than anyone would imagine from the sameness of women's coiffure and the favorite love stories in prose and verse. Here and there a cygnet is reared uneasily among the ducklings in the brown pond, and never finds the living stream in fellowship with its own oary-footed kind. Here and there is born a Saint Theresa, foundress of

nothing, whose loving heartbeats and sobs after an unattained goodness tremble off and are dispersed among hindrances instead of centering in some long-recognizable deed.

Working with the Text

1. Stephen Jay Gould opens and closes the essay with quotations from the prelude to *Middlemarch*, a novel published in 1872 by George Eliot, the pen name for novelist Mary Ann Evans. Gould also notes that the craniometry scientist Paul Broca gathered data from prehistoric skulls in the year after Eliot published *Middlemarch*. The novel is set in a small English country town in the 1830s and explores the prevailing morals and conventions of that time. As you reread the essay, look for connections between Gould's argument and his references to *Middlemarch*. In a brief essay, analyze Gould's reasons for including these references. Even if you have not read the novel, you can infer its central theme from the prelude excerpts. Consider not only the plight of the protagonist implied in these excerpts but also the fact that Evans took the pen name of a man.

2. The scientists whose data Gould examines published their findings a century before he wrote the essay. Write a brief essay in which you explore whether and in what way the work of these scientists might hold significance today. If the findings have been largely discredited, why does Gould pay attention to that work? What can we learn from Gould about the role of social attitude in the interpretation of supposedly objective data?

3. Gould devotes most of the essay to analyzing how data on brain size was gathered, interpreted, and corrected for factors influencing brain size, only to come to the conclusion that "the whole enterprise of setting a biological value upon groups" is "irrelevant and highly injurious" (par. 16). In a brief essay, analyze the progression of Gould's argument. Why would he work to determine the validity of this series of scientific developments in order to dismiss scientific inquiry into biological factors in intelligence as "irrelevant"? Consider, in particular, the attention he gives to "corrected" data. In what way does Gould's essay offer an intriguing look at our obsession with numbers and quantification, especially when it comes to discussions about intelligence?

4. Gould's essay on nineteenth-century studies of brain size was incorporated into a book, *The Mismeasure of Man*, in which Gould challenges IQ testing. Drawing on "Women's Brains," write an essay in which you analyze Gould's reasons for believing that "setting a biological value upon groups" is "highly injurious" (par. 16). In what ways does Gould's essay raise larger questions about

intelligence (What do we mean by "smart"?) and objective assessment (How do we "measure" it?)?

From Text to Field

1. Gould captures the perspective of nineteenth-century scientists by quoting directly from their writings. Choose one or more of the following passages: "The man who fights for two or more in the struggle for existence . . ." (Topinard, par. 5), "In the most intelligent races, as among the Parisians . . ." (Gustave Le Bon, par. 6), or "A desire to give them the same education . . ." (Le Bon, par. 7). In an essay, write a response to the passage or passages, as if you were writing directly to the scientist Gould is quoting.

2. Relatively recent efforts by feminists and by scientists sympathetic to women have generated a number of approaches to comparing the characteristics and abilities of men and women. Each of us holds a personal view of the differences, or lack of difference, between the sexes. In a personal essay, present your view of gender identity. You may find it helpful to focus your essay on a specific trait. Is that trait biologically based or socially determined? From your perspective, does that trait suggest one way that one gender is superior to the other? Look beyond commonly discussed general traits (e.g., physical strength) to uncover more specific, and perhaps telling, concerns. Select a specific point of comparison that can be addressed well within the length of an essay.

3. In the essay, Gould points out, "To appreciate the social role of Broca and his school, we must recognize that his statements about the brains of women do not reflect an isolated prejudice toward a single disadvantaged group" (par. 13). He ends the same paragraph with the assertion, "I do not regard as empty rhetoric the claim that women's battles are for all of us." After reflecting on the entire paragraph, write an essay in which you interpret the final sentence in terms of your own education, observations, and experience. In what ways have you seen that "women's battles are for all of us"?

4. To most twenty-first-century ears, the nineteenth-century studies of brain size and comparisons between women and gorillas or children are outrageous, even comic. Many of us would agree with Gould that "setting a biological value upon groups" is "irrelevant." As a send-up of nineteenth-century attitudes (many of which still influence us), write a parody of the scientific pursuits of that era in which you claim—in our century—the superiority or inferiority of one gender based on a biological or physical characteristic (other than brain size) that you consider to be irrelevant.

The Egg and the Sperm: How Science Has Constructed a Romance Based on Stereotypical Male-Female Roles

Emily Martin

We tend to view science as being objective, driven by impartial observation of phenomena and interpretation of data. When Emily Martin studies scientific practices through the lens of an anthropologist, she sees the cultural assumptions that influence how scientists interpret and describe what they observe. In the essay that follows, she scrutinizes biological research on one of the deepest, most enduring mysteries of human existence — the relationship between egg and sperm. How much of what scientists see is biological phenomena, and how much is romance?

"The Egg and the Sperm," originally published in *Signs: Journal of Women in Culture and Society* in 1991, has been widely reprinted in journals and anthologies throughout the United States and abroad. The essay is drawn from research presented in Martin's influential 1987 book, *The Woman in the Body: A Cultural Analysis of Reproduction*, which was published in a second edition (1992) as well as a third (2001).

Martin is a professor of anthropology at New York University. In addition to gender and science, Martin's research interests include medicine, money and other measures of value, and the ethnography of work. Her published works often interpret culture in terms of how the human body — especially a woman's body — is regarded and described.

> The theory of the human body is always a part of a world-picture. . . . The theory of the human body is always a part of a *fantasy*.
> — JAMES HILLMAN, *The Myth of Analysis*[1]

As an anthropologist, I am intrigued by the possibility that culture shapes how biological scientists describe what they discover about the natural world. If this were so, we would be learning about more than the natural world in high school biology class; we would be learning about cultural beliefs and practices as if they were part of nature. In the course of my research I realized that the picture of egg and sperm drawn in popular as well as scientific accounts of reproductive biology relies on stereotypes central to our cultural definitions of male and female. The stereotypes imply not only that female biological processes are less worthy than their male counterparts but also that women are less worthy than men. Part of my goal in writing this article is to shine a bright light on the gender stereotypes hidden within the scientific language of biology. Exposed in such a light, I hope they will lose much of their power to harm us.

Egg and Sperm: A Scientific Fairy Tale

At a fundamental level, all major scientific textbooks depict male and female reproductive organs as systems for the production of valuable substances, such as eggs and sperm.[2] In the case of women, the monthly cycle is described as being designed to produce eggs and prepare a suitable place for them to be fertilized and grown — all to the end of making babies. But the enthusiasm ends there. By extolling the female cycle as a productive enterprise, menstruation must necessarily be viewed as a failure. Medical texts describe menstruation as the "debris" of the uterine lining, the result of necrosis, or death of tissue. The descriptions imply that a system has gone awry, making products of no use, not to specification, unsalable, wasted, scrap. An illustration in a widely used medical text shows menstruation as a chaotic disintegration of form, complementing the many texts that describe it as "ceasing," "dying," "losing," "denuding," "expelling."[3]

Male reproductive physiology is evaluated quite differently. One of the texts that sees menstruation as failed production employs a sort of breathless prose when it describes the maturation of sperm: "The mechanisms which guide the remarkable cellular transformation from spermatid to mature sperm remain uncertain. . . . Perhaps the most amazing characteristic of spermatogenesis is its sheer magnitude: The normal human male may manufacture several hundred million sperm per day."[4] In the classic text *Medical Physiology*, edited by Vernon Mountcastle, the male/female, productive/destructive comparison is more explicit: "Whereas the female *sheds* only a single gamete each month, the seminiferous tubules *produce* hundreds of millions of sperm each day" (emphasis mine).[5] The female author of another text marvels at the length of the microscopic seminiferous tubules, which, if uncoiled and placed end to end, "would span almost one-third of a mile!" She writes, "In an adult male these structures produce millions of sperm cells each day." Later she asks, "How is this feat accomplished?"[6] None of these texts expresses such intense enthusiasm for any female processes. It is surely no accident that the "remarkable" process of making sperm involves precisely what, in the medical view, menstruation does not: production of something deemed valuable.[7]

One could argue that menstruation and spermatogenesis are not analogous processes and, therefore, should not be expected to elicit the same kind of response. The proper female analogy to spermatogenesis, biologically, is ovulation. Yet ovulation does not merit enthusiasm in these texts either. Textbook descriptions stress that all of the ovarian follicles containing ova are already present at birth. Far from being *produced*, as sperm are, they merely sit on the shelf, slowly degenerating and aging like overstocked inventory: "At birth, normal human ovaries contain an estimated one million follicles [each], and no new ones appear after birth. Thus, in marked contrast to the male, the newborn female already has all the germ cells she will ever have. Only a few, perhaps 400, are destined to reach full maturity during her active productive life. All the others degenerate at some point in their development so that few, if any, remain by the time she reaches menopause at approximately 50 years of age."[8] Note the "marked contrast" that this description sets up between male and female: the male, who continuously produces fresh germ cells, and the female, who has stockpiled germ cells by birth and is faced with their degeneration.

Nor are the female organs spared such vivid descriptions. One scientist 5 writes in a newspaper article that a woman's ovaries become old and worn out from ripening eggs every month, even though the woman herself is still relatively young: "When you look through a laparoscope . . . at an ovary that has been through hundreds of cycles, even in a superbly healthy American female, you see a scarred, battered organ."[9]

To avoid the negative connotations that some people associate with the female reproductive system, scientists could begin to describe male and female processes as homologous. They might credit females with "producing" mature ova one at a time, as they're needed each month, and describe males as having to face problems of degenerating germ cells. This degeneration would occur throughout life among spermatogonia, the undifferentiated germ cells in the testes that are the long-lived, dormant precursors of sperm.

But the texts have an almost dogged insistence on casting female processes in a negative light. The texts celebrate sperm production because it is continuous from puberty to senescence, while they portray egg production as inferior because it is finished at birth. This makes the female seem unproductive, but some texts will also insist that it is she who is wasteful.[10] In a section heading for *Molecular Biology of the Cell*, a best-selling text, we are told

that "Oogenesis is wasteful." The text goes on to emphasize that of the seven million oogonia, or egg germ cells, in the female embryo, most degenerate in the ovary. Of those that do go on to become oocytes, or eggs, many also degenerate, so that at birth only two million eggs remain in the ovaries. Degeneration continues throughout a woman's life: By puberty 300,000 eggs remain, and only a few are present by menopause. "During the forty or so years of a woman's reproductive life, only 400 to 500 eggs will have been released," the authors write. "All the rest will have degenerated. It is still a mystery why so many eggs are formed only to die in the ovaries."[11]

The real mystery is why the male's vast production of sperm is not seen as wasteful.[12] Assuming that a man "produces" 100 million (10^8) sperm per day (a conservative estimate) during an average reproductive life of sixty years, he would produce well over two trillion sperm in his lifetime. Assuming that a woman "ripens" one egg per lunar month, or thirteen per year, over the course of her forty-year reproductive life, she would total five hundred eggs in her lifetime. But the word "waste" implies an excess, too much produced. Assuming two or three offspring, for every baby a woman produces, she wastes only around two hundred eggs. For every baby a man produces, he wastes more than one trillion (10^{12}) sperm.

How is it that positive images are denied to the bodies of women? A look at language — in this case, scientific language — provides the first clue. Take the egg and the sperm.[13] It is remarkable how "femininely" the egg behaves and how "masculinely" the sperm.[14] The egg is seen as large and passive.[15] It does not *move* or *journey*, but passively "is transported," "is swept,"[16] or even "drifts"[17] along the fallopian tube. In utter contrast, sperm are small, "streamlined,"[18] and invariably active. They "deliver" their genes to the egg, "activate the developmental program of the egg,"[19] and have a "velocity" that is often remarked upon.[20] Their tails are "strong" and efficiently powered.[21] Together with the forces of ejaculation, they can "propel the semen into the deepest recesses of the vagina."[22] For this they need "energy," "fuel,"[23] so that with a "whiplashlike motion and strong lurches"[24] they can "burrow through the egg coat"[25] and "penetrate" it.[26]

At its extreme, the age-old relationship of the egg and the sperm takes on   10 a royal or religious patina. The egg coat, its protective barrier, is sometimes called its "vestments," a term usually reserved for sacred, religious dress. The egg is said to have a "corona,"[27] a crown, and to be accompanied by "attendant cells."[28] It is holy, set apart and above, the queen to the sperm's king. The egg is also passive, which means it must depend on sperm for rescue. Gerald Schatten and Helen Schatten liken the egg's role to that of Sleeping Beauty: "a dormant bride awaiting her mate's magic kiss, which instills the spirit that brings her to life."[29] Sperm, by contrast, have a "mission,"[30] which is to "move through the female genital tract in quest of the ovum."[31] One

popular account has it that the sperm carry out a "perilous journey" into the "warm darkness," where some fall away "exhausted." "Survivors" "assault" the egg, the successful candidates "surrounding the prize."[32] Part of the urgency of this journey, in more scientific terms, is that "once released from the supportive environment of the ovary, an egg will die within hours unless rescued by a sperm."[33] The wording stresses the fragility and dependency of the egg, even though the same text acknowledges elsewhere that sperm also live for only a few hours.[34]

In 1948, in a book remarkable for its early insights into these matters, Ruth Herschberger argued that female reproductive organs are seen as biologically interdependent, while male organs are viewed as autonomous, operating independently and in isolation:

> At present the functional is stressed only in connection with women: It is in them that ovaries, tubes, uterus, and vagina have endless interdependence. In the male, reproduction would seem to involve "organs" only.
>
> Yet the sperm, just as much as the egg, is dependent on a great many related processes. There are secretions which mitigate the urine in the urethra before ejaculation, to protect the sperm. There is the reflex shutting off of the bladder connection, the provision of prostatic secretions, and various types of muscular propulsion. The sperm is no more independent of its milieu than the egg, and yet from a wish that it were, biologists have lent their support to the notion that the human female, beginning with the egg, is congenitally more dependent than the male.[35]

Bringing out another aspect of the sperm's autonomy, an article in the journal *Cell* has the sperm making an "existential decision" to penetrate the egg: "Sperm are cells with a limited behavioral repertoire, one that is directed toward fertilizing eggs. To execute the decision to abandon the haploid state, sperm swim to an egg and there acquire the ability to effect membrane fusion."[36] Is this a corporate manager's version of the sperm's activities — "executing decisions" while fraught with dismay over difficult options that bring with them very high risk?

There is another way that sperm, despite their small size, can be made to loom in importance over the egg. In a collection of scientific papers, an electron micrograph of an enormous egg and tiny sperm is titled "A Portrait of the Sperm."[37] This is a little like showing a photo of a dog and calling it a picture of the fleas. Granted, microscopic sperm are harder to photograph than eggs, which are just large enough to see with the naked eye. But surely the use of the term *portrait*, a word associated with the powerful and wealthy, is significant. Eggs have only micrographs or pictures, not portraits.

One depiction of sperm as weak and timid, instead of strong and powerful — the only such representation in Western civilization, so far as I know — occurs in Woody Allen's movie *Everything You Always Wanted to Know*

About Sex**But Were Afraid to Ask. Allen, playing the part of an apprehensive sperm inside a man's testicles, is scared of the man's approaching orgasm. He is reluctant to launch himself into the darkness, afraid of contraceptive devices, afraid of winding up on the ceiling if the man masturbates.

The more common picture — egg as damsel in distress, shielded only by her sacred garments; sperm as heroic warrior to the rescue — cannot be proved to be dictated by the biology of these events. While the "facts" of biology may not *always* be constructed in cultural terms, I would argue that in this case they are. The degree of metaphorical content in these descriptions, the extent to which differences between egg and sperm are emphasized, and the parallels between cultural stereotypes of male and female behavior and the character of egg and sperm all point to this conclusion.

New Research, Old Imagery

As new understandings of egg and sperm emerge, textbook gender imagery is being revised. But the new research, far from escaping the stereotypical representations of egg and sperm, simply replicates elements of textbook gender imagery in a different form. The persistence of this imagery calls to mind what Ludwik Fleck termed "the self-contained" nature of scientific thought. As he described it, "the interaction between what is already known, what remains to be learned, and those who are to apprehend it, go to ensure harmony within the system. But at the same time they also preserve the harmony of illusions, which is quite secure within the confines of a given thought style."[38] We need to understand the way in which the cultural content in scientific descriptions changes as biological discoveries unfold, and whether that cultural content is solidly entrenched or easily changed.

In all of the texts quoted above, sperm are described as penetrating the egg, and specific substances on a sperm's head are described as binding to the egg. Recently, this description of events was rewritten in a biophysics lab at Johns Hopkins University — transforming the egg from the passive to the active party.[39]

Prior to this research, it was thought that the zona, the inner vestments of the egg, formed an impenetrable barrier. Sperm overcame the barrier by mechanically burrowing through, thrashing their tails and slowly working their way along. Later research showed that the sperm released digestive enzymes that chemically broke down the zona; thus, scientists presumed that the sperm used mechanical *and* chemical means to get through to the egg.

In this recent investigation, the researchers began to ask questions about the mechanical force of the sperm's tail. (The lab's goal was to develop a contraceptive that worked topically on sperm.) They discovered, to their great surprise, that the forward thrust of sperm is extremely weak, which contradicts the assumption that sperm are forceful penetrators.[40] Rather than thrusting forward, the sperm's head was now seen to move mostly back and forth. The sideways motion of the sperm's tail makes the head move sideways with a force that is ten times stronger than its forward movement. So even if the overall force of the sperm were strong enough to mechanically break the zona, most of its force would be directed sideways rather than forward. In fact, its strongest tendency, by tenfold, is to escape by attempting to pry itself off the egg. Sperm, then, must be exceptionally efficient at *escaping* from any cell surface they contact. And the surface of the egg must be designed to trap the sperm and prevent their escape. Otherwise, few if any sperm would reach the egg.

The researchers at Johns Hopkins concluded that the sperm and egg stick together because of adhesive molecules on the surfaces of each. The egg traps the sperm and adheres to it so tightly that the sperm's head is forced to lie flat against the surface of the zona, a little bit, they told me, "like Br'er Rabbit getting more and more stuck to tar baby the more he wriggles." The trapped sperm continues to wiggle ineffectually side to side. The mechanical force of its tail is so weak that a sperm cannot break even one chemical bond. This is where the digestive enzymes released by the sperm come in. If they start to soften the zona just at the tip of the sperm and the sides remain stuck, then the weak, flailing sperm can get oriented in the right direction and make it through the zona — provided that its bonds to the zona dissolve as it moves in.

Although this new version of the saga of the egg and the sperm broke through cultural expectations, the researchers who made the discovery continued to write papers and abstracts as if the sperm were the active party who attacks, binds, penetrates, and enters the egg. The only difference was that sperm were now seen as performing these actions weakly.[41] Not until August 1987, more than three years after the findings described above, did these researchers reconceptualize the process to give the egg a more active role. They began to describe the zona as an aggressive sperm catcher, covered with adhesive molecules that can capture a sperm with a single bond and clasp it to the zona's surface.[42] In the words of their published account: "The innermost vestment, the *zona pellucida*, is a glyco-protein shell, which captures and tethers the sperm before they penetrate it. . . . The sperm is captured at the initial contact between the sperm tip and the *zona*. . . . Since the thrust [of the sperm] is much smaller than the force needed to break a single affinity bond, the first bond made upon the tip-first meeting of the sperm and *zona* can result in the capture of the sperm."[43]

Experiments in another lab reveal similar patterns of data interpretation. Gerald Schatten and Helen Schatten set out to show that, contrary to conventional wisdom, the "egg is not merely a large, yolk-filled sphere into which the sperm burrows to endow new life. Rather, recent research suggests the almost heretical view that sperm and egg are mutually active partners."[44] This sounds like a departure from the stereotypical textbook view, but further reading reveals Schatten and Schatten's conformity to the aggressive-sperm metaphor. They describe how "the sperm and egg first touch when, from the tip of the sperm's triangular head, a long, thin filament shoots out and harpoons the egg." Then we learn that "remarkably, the harpoon is not so much fired as assembled at great speed, molecule by molecule, from a pool of protein stored in a specialized region called the acrosome. The filament may grow as much as twenty times longer than the sperm head itself before its tip reaches the egg and sticks."[45] Why not call this "making a bridge" or "throwing out a line" rather than firing a harpoon? Harpoons pierce prey and injure or kill them, while this filament only sticks. And why not focus, as the Hopkins lab did, on the stickiness of the egg, rather than the stickiness of the sperm?[46] Later in the article, the Schattens replicate the common view of the sperm's perilous journey into the warm darkness of the vagina, this time for the purpose of explaining its journey into the egg itself: "[The sperm] still has an arduous journey ahead. It must penetrate farther into the egg's huge sphere of cytoplasm and somehow locate the nucleus, so that the two cells' chromosomes can fuse. The sperm dives down into the cytoplasm, its tail beating. But it is soon interrupted by the sudden and swift migration of the egg nucleus, which rushes toward the sperm with a velocity triple that of the movement of chromosomes during cell division, crossing the entire egg in about a minute."[47]

Like Schatten and Schatten and the biophysicists at Johns Hopkins, another researcher has recently made discoveries that seem to point to a more interactive view of the relationship of egg and sperm. This work, which Paul Wassarman conducted on the sperm and eggs of mice, focuses on identifying the specific molecules in the egg coat (the zona pellucida) that are involved in egg-sperm interaction. At first glance, his descriptions seem to fit the model of an egalitarian relationship. Male and female gametes "recognize one another," and "interactions . . . take place between sperm and egg."[48] But the article in *Scientific American* in which those descriptions appear begins with a vignette that presages the dominant motif of their presentation: "It has been more than a century since Hermann Fol, a Swiss zoologist, peered into his microscope and became the first person to see a sperm penetrate an egg, fertilize it, and form the first cell of a new embryo."[49] This portrayal of the sperm as the active party — the one that *penetrates* and *fertilizes* the egg and *produces* the embryo — is not cited as an example of an earlier, now outmoded view. In fact, the author reiterates the point later in the article: "Many sperm can bind to and penetrate the zona pellucida, or outer coat, of an unfertilized mouse egg,

One clear feminist challenge is to wake up sleeping metaphors in science.

but only one sperm will eventually fuse with the thin plasma membrane surrounding the egg proper (*inner sphere*), fertilizing the egg and giving rise to a new embryo."[50]

The imagery of sperm as aggressor is particularly startling in this case: The main discovery being reported is isolation of a particular molecule *on the egg coat* that plays an important role in fertilization! Wassarman's choice of language sustains the picture. He calls the molecule that has been isolated, ZP3, a "sperm receptor." By allocating the passive, waiting role to the egg, Wassarman can continue to describe the sperm as the actor, the one that makes it all happen: "The basic process begins when many sperm first attach loosely and then bind tenaciously to receptors on the surface of the egg's thick outer coat, the zona pellucida. Each sperm, which has a large number of egg-binding proteins on its surface, binds to many sperm receptors on the egg. More specifically, a site on each of the egg-binding proteins fits a complementary site on a sperm receptor, much as a key fits a lock."[51] With the sperm designated as the "key" and the egg the "lock," it is obvious which one acts and which one is acted upon. Could this imagery not be reversed, letting the sperm (the lock) wait until the egg produces the key? Or could we speak of two halves of a locket matching, and regard the matching itself as the action that initiates the fertilization?

It is as if Wassarman were determined to make the egg the receiving partner. Usually in biological research, the *protein* member of the pair of binding molecules is called the receptor, and physically it has a pocket in it rather like a lock. As the diagrams that illustrate Wassarman's article show, the molecules on the sperm are proteins and have "pockets." The small, mobile molecules that fit into these pockets are called ligands. As shown in the diagrams, ZP3 on the egg is a polymer of "keys"; many small knobs stick out. Typically, molecules on the sperm would be called receptors and molecules on the egg would be called ligands. But Wassarman chose to name ZP3 on the egg the receptor and to create a new term, "the egg-binding protein," for the molecule on the sperm that otherwise would have been called the receptor.[52]

Wassarman does credit the egg coat with having more functions than those of a sperm receptor. While he notes that "the zona pellucida has at times been viewed by investigators as a nuisance, a barrier to sperm and hence an impediment to fertilization," his new research reveals that the egg coat "serves as a sophisticated biological security system that screens incoming sperm, selects only those compatible with fertilization and development, prepares sperm for fusion with the egg and later protects the resulting embryo from polyspermy [a lethal condition caused by fusion of more than one sperm with a single egg]."[53] Although this description gives the egg an active role, that role is drawn in stereotypically feminine terms. The egg *selects* an appropriate mate, *prepares* him for fusion, and then *protects* the resulting offspring from harm. This is courtship and mating behavior as seen through the eyes of a sociobiologist: woman as the hard-to-get prize, who, following union with the chosen one, becomes woman as servant and mother.

And Wassarman does not quit there. In a review article for *Science*, he outlines the "chronology of fertilization."[54] Near the end of the article are two subject headings. One is "Sperm Penetration," in which Wassarman describes how the chemical dissolving of the zona pellucida combines with the "substantial propulsive force generated by sperm." The next heading is "Sperm-Egg Fusion." This section details what happens inside the zona after a sperm "penetrates" it. Sperm "can make contact with, adhere to, and fuse with (that is, fertilize) an egg."[55] Wassarman's word choice, again, is astonishingly skewed in favor of the sperm's activity, for in the next breath he says that sperm *lose* all motility upon fusion with the egg's surface. In mouse and sea urchin eggs, the sperm enters at the *egg's* volition, according to Wassarman's description: "Once fused with egg plasma membrane [the surface of the egg], how does a sperm enter the egg? The surface of both mouse and sea urchin eggs is covered with thousands of plasma membrane-bound projections, called microvilli [tiny "hairs"]. Evidence in sea urchins suggests that, after membrane fusion, a group of elongated microvilli cluster tightly around and interdigitate over the sperm head. As these microvilli are resorbed, the sperm is drawn into the egg. Therefore, sperm motility, which ceases at the time of fusion in both sea urchins and mice, is not required for sperm entry."[56] The section called "Sperm Penetration" more logically would be followed by a section called "The Egg Envelops," rather than "Sperm-Egg Fusion." This would give a parallel—and more accurate— sense that both the egg and the sperm initiate action.

Another way that Wassarman makes less of the egg's activity is by describing components of the egg but referring to the sperm as a whole entity. Deborah Gordon has described such an approach as "atomism" ("the part is independent of and primordial to the whole") and identified it as one of the "tenacious assumptions" of Western science and medicine.[57] Wassarman employs atomism to his advantage. When he refers to processes going on within sperm, he consistently returns to descriptions that remind us from whence these activities came: They are part of sperm that penetrate an egg or generate propulsive force. When he refers to processes going on within eggs, he stops there. As a result, any active role he grants them appears to be assigned to the parts of the egg, and not to the egg itself. In the quote above, it is the microvilli that actively cluster around the sperm. In another example, "the driving force for engulfment of a fused sperm comes from a region of cytoplasm just beneath an egg's plasma membrane."[58]

Social Implications: Thinking Beyond

All three of these revisionist accounts of egg and sperm cannot seem to escape the hierarchical imagery of older accounts. Even though each new account gives the egg a larger and more active role, taken together they bring into play another cultural stereotype: woman as a dangerous and aggressive threat. In the Johns Hopkins lab's revised model, the egg ends up as the female aggressor who "captures and tethers" the sperm with her sticky zona, rather like a spider lying in wait in her web.[59] The Schatten lab has the egg's nucleus "interrupt" the sperm's dive with a "sudden and swift" rush by which she "clasps the sperm and guides its nucleus to the center."[60] Wassarman's description of the surface of the egg "covered with thousands of plasma membrane-bound projections, called microvilli" that reach out and clasp the sperm adds to the spiderlike imagery.[61]

These images grant the egg an active role but at the cost of appearing disturbingly aggressive. Images of woman as dangerous and aggressive, the femme fatale who victimizes men, are widespread in Western literature and culture.[62] More specific is the connection of spider imagery with the idea of an engulfing, devouring mother.[63] New data did not lead scientists to eliminate gender stereotypes in their descriptions of egg and sperm. Instead, scientists simply began to describe egg and sperm in different, but no less damaging, terms.

Can we envision a less stereotypical view? Biology itself provides another model that could be applied to the egg and the sperm. The cybernetic model — with its feedback loops, flexible adaptation to change, coordination of the parts within a whole, evolution over time, and changing response to the environment — is common in genetics, endocrinology, and ecology and has a growing influence in medicine in general.[64] This model has the potential to shift our imagery from the negative, in which the female reproductive system is castigated both for not producing eggs after birth and for producing (and thus wasting) too many eggs overall, to something more positive. The female reproductive system could be seen as responding to the environment (pregnancy or menopause), adjusting to monthly changes (menstruation), and flexibly changing from reproductivity after puberty to nonreproductivity later in life. The sperm and egg's interaction could also be described in cybernetic terms. J. F. Hartman's research in reproductive biology demonstrated fifteen years ago that if an egg is killed by being pricked with a needle, live sperm cannot get through the zona.[65] Clearly, this evidence shows that the egg and sperm *do* interact on more mutual terms, making biology's refusal to portray them that way all the more disturbing.

We would do well to be aware, however, that cybernetic imagery is hardly neutral. In the past, cybernetic models have played an important part in the imposition of social control. These models inherently provide a way of thinking about a "field" of interacting components. Once the field can be seen, it can become the object of new forms of knowledge, which in turn can allow new forms of social control to be exerted over the components of the field. During the 1950s, for example, medicine began to recognize the psychosocial *environment* of the patient: the patient's family and its psychodynamics. Professions such as social work began to focus on this new environment, and the resulting knowledge became one way to further control the patient. Patients began to be seen not as isolated, individual bodies, but as psychosocial entities located in an "ecological" system: Management of "the patient's psychology was a new entrée to patient control."[66]

The models that biologists use to describe their data can have important social effects. During the nineteenth century, the social and natural sciences strongly influenced each other: The social ideas of Malthus about how to avoid the natural increase of the poor inspired Darwin's *Origin of Species*.[67] Once the *Origin* stood as a description of the natural world, complete with competition and market struggles, it could be reimported into social science as social Darwinism, in order to justify the social order of the time. What we are seeing now is similar: the importation of cultural ideas about passive females and heroic males into the "personalities" of gametes. This amounts to the "implanting of social imagery on representations of nature so as to lay a firm basis for reimporting exactly that same imagery as natural explanations of social phenomena."[68]

Further research would show us exactly what social effects are being wrought from the biological imagery of egg and sperm. At the very least, the imagery keeps alive some of the hoariest old stereotypes about weak damsels in distress and their strong male rescuers. That these stereotypes are now being written in at the level of the *cell* constitutes a powerful move to make them seem so natural as to be beyond alteration.

The stereotypical imagery might also encourage people to imagine that 35 what results from the interaction of egg and sperm — a fertilized egg — is the result of deliberate "human" action at the cellular level. Whatever the intentions of the human couple, in this microscopic "culture" a cellular "bride" (or femme fatale) and a cellular "groom" (her victim) make a cellular baby. Rosalind Petchesky points out that through visual representations such as sonograms, we are given *"images* of younger and younger, and tinier and tinier, fetuses being 'saved.'" This leads to "the point of visibility being 'pushed back' *indefinitely*."[69] Endowing egg and sperm with intentional action, a key aspect of personhood in our culture, lays the foundation for the point of viability being pushed back to the moment of fertilization. This will likely lead to greater acceptance of technological developments and new forms of scrutiny and manipulation, for the benefit of these inner "persons": court-ordered restrictions on a pregnant woman's activities in order to protect her fetus, fetal surgery, amniocentesis, and rescinding of abortion rights, to name but a few examples.[70]

Even if we succeed in substituting more egalitarian, interactive metaphors to describe the activities of egg and sperm, and manage to avoid the pitfalls of cybernetic models, we would still be guilty of endowing cellular entities with personhood. More crucial, then, than what *kinds* of personalities we bestow on cells is the very fact that we are doing it at all. This process could ultimately have the most disturbing social consequences.

One clear feminist challenge is to wake up sleeping metaphors in science, particularly those involved in descriptions of the egg and the sperm. Although the literary convention is to call such metaphors "dead," they are not so much dead as sleeping, hidden within the scientific content of texts — and all the more powerful for it.[71] Waking up such metaphors, by becoming aware of when we are projecting cultural imagery onto what we study, will improve our ability to investigate and understand nature. Waking up such metaphors, by becoming aware of their implications, will rob them of their power to naturalize our social conventions about gender.

Notes

Portions of this article were presented as the 1987 Becker Lecture, Cornell University. I am grateful for the many suggestions and ideas I received on this occasion. For especially pertinent help with my arguments and data I thank Richard Cone, Kevin Whaley, Sharon Stephens, Barbara Duden, Susanne Kuechler, Lorna Rhodes, and Scott Gilbert. The article was strengthened and clarified by the comments of the anonymous *Signs* reviewers as well as the superb editorial skills of Amy Gage.

1. James Hillman, *The Myth of Analysis* (Evanston, Ill.: Northwestern University Press, 1972), 220.

2. The textbooks I consulted are the main ones used in classes for undergraduate premedical students or medical students (or those held on reserve in the library for these classes) during the past few years at Johns Hopkins University. These texts are widely used at other universities in the country as well.

3. Arthur C. Guyton, *Physiology of the Human Body*, 6th ed. (Philadelphia: Saunders College Publishing, 1984), 624.

4. Arthur J. Vander, James H. Sherman, and Dorothy S. Luciano, *Human Physiology: The Mechanisms of Body Function*, 3d ed. (New York: McGraw Hill, 1980), 483–84.

5. Vernon B. Mountcastle, *Medical Physiology*, 14th ed. (London: Mosby, 1980), 2:1624.

6. Eldra Pearl Solomon, *Human Anatomy and Physiology* (New York: CBS College Publishing, 1983), 678.

7. For elaboration, see Emily Martin, *The Woman in the Body: A Cultural Analysis of Reproduction* (Boston: Beacon, 1987), 27–53.

8. Vander, Sherman, and Luciano, 568.

9. Melvin Konner, "Childbearing and Age," *New York Times Magazine* (December 27, 1987), 22–23, esp. 22.

10. I have found but one exception to the opinion that the female is wasteful: "Smallpox being the nasty disease it is, one might expect nature to have designed antibody molecules with combining sites that specifically recognize the epitopes on smallpox virus. Nature differs from technology, however: It thinks nothing of wastefulness. (For example, rather than improving the chance that a spermatozoon will meet an egg cell, nature finds it easier to produce millions of spermatozoa.)" (Niels Kaj Jerne, "The Immune System," *Scientific American* 229, no. 1 [July 1973]: 53). Thanks to a *Signs* reviewer for bringing this reference to my attention.

11. Bruce Alberts et al., *Molecular Biology of the Cell* (New York: Garland, 1983), 795.

12. In her essay "Have Only Men Evolved?" (in *Discovering Reality: Feminist Perspectives on Epistemology, Metaphysics, Methodology, and Philosophy of Science,* ed. Sandra Harding and Merrill B. Hintikka [Dordrecht: Reidel, 1983], 45–69, esp. 60–61), Ruth Hubbard points out that sociobiologists have said the female invests more energy than the male in the production of her large gametes, claiming that this explains why the female provides parental care. Hubbard questions whether it "really takes more 'energy' to generate the one or relatively few eggs than the large excess of sperms required to achieve fertilization." For further critique of how the greater size of eggs is interpreted in sociobiology, see Donna Haraway, "Investment Strategies for the Evolving Portfolio of Primate Females," in *Body/Politics,* ed. Mary Jacobus, Evelyn Fox Keller, and Sally Shuttleworth (New York: Routledge, 1990), 155–56.

13. The sources I used for this article provide compelling information on interactions among sperm. Lack of space prevents me from taking up this theme here, but the elements include competition, hierarchy, and sacrifice. For a newspaper report, see Malcolm W. Browne, "Some Thoughts on Self Sacrifice," *New York Times* (July 5, 1988), C6. For a literary rendition, see John Barth, "Night-Sea Journey," in his *Lost in the Funhouse* (Garden City, NY: Doubleday, 1968), 3–13.

14. See Carol Delaney, "The Meaning of Paternity and the Virgin Birth Debate," *Man* 21, no. 3 (September 1986): 494–513. She discusses the difference between this scientific view that women contribute genetic material to the fetus and the claim of long-standing Western folk theories that the origin and identity of the fetus comes from the male, as in the metaphor of planting a seed in soil.

15. For a suggested direct link between human behavior and purportedly passive eggs and active sperm, see Erik H. Erikson, "Inner and Outer Space: Reflections on Womanhood," *Daedalus* 93, no. 2 (Spring 1964): 582–606, esp. 591.

16. Guyton (n. 3 above), 619; and Mountcastle (n. 5 above), 1609.

17. Jonathan Miller and David Pelham, *The Facts of Life* (New York: Viking Penguin, 1984), 5.

18. Alberts et al., 796.

19. Ibid., 796.

20. See, e.g., William F. Ganong, *Review of Medical Physiology,* 7th ed. (Los Altos, Calif. Lange Medical Publications, 1975), 322.

21. Alberts et al. (n. 11 above), 796.

22. Guyton, 615.

23. Solomon (n. 6 above), 683.

24. Vander, Sherman, and Luciano (n. 4 above), 4th ed. (1985), 580.

25. Alberts et al., 796.

26. All biology texts quoted above use the word *penetrate*.

27. Solomon, 700.

28. A. Beldecos et al., "The Importance of Feminist Critique for Contemporary Cell Biology," *Hypatia* 3, no. 1 (Spring 1988): 61–76.

29. Gerald Schatten and Helen Schatten, "The Energetic Egg," *Medical World News* 23 (January 23, 1984): 51–53, esp. 51.

30. Alberts et al., 796.

31. Guyton (n. 3 above), 613.

32. Miller and Pelham (n. 17 above), 7.

33. Alberts et al. (n. 11 above), 804.

34. Ibid., 801.

35. Ruth Herschberger, *Adam's Rib* (New York: Pelligrini & Cudaby, 1948), esp. 84. I am indebted to Ruth Hubbard for telling me about Herschberger's work, although at a point when this paper was already in draft form.

36. Bennett M. Shapiro. "The Existential Decision of a Sperm," *Cell* 49, no. 3 (May 1987): 293–94, esp. 293.

37. Lennart Nilsson, "A Portrait of the Sperm," in *The Functional Anatomy of the Spermatozoan*, ed. Bjorn A. Afzelius (New York: Pergamon, 1975), 79–82.

38. Ludwik Fleck, *Genesis and Development of a Scientific Fact*, ed. Thaddeus J. Trenn and Robert K. Merton (Chicago: University of Chicago Press, 1979), 38.

39. Jay M. Baltz carried out the research I describe when he was a graduate student in the Thomas C. Jenkins Department of Biophysics at Johns Hopkins University.

40. Far less is known about the physiology of sperm than comparable female substances, which some feminists claim is no accident. Greater scientific scrutiny of female reproduction has long enabled the burden of birth control to be placed on women. In this case, the researchers' discovery did not depend on development of any new technology. The experiments made use of glass pipettes, a manometer, and a simple microscope, all of which have been available for more than one hundred years.

41. Jay Baltz and Richard A. Cone, "What Force Is Needed to Tether a Sperm?" (abstract for Society for the Study of Reproduction, 1985), and "Flagellar Torque on the Head Determines the Force Needed to Tether a Sperm" (abstract for Biophysical Society, 1986).

42. Jay M. Baltz, David F. Katz, and Richard A. Cone, "The Mechanics of the Sperm-Egg Interaction at the Zona Pellucida," *Biophysical Journal* 54, no. 4 (October 1988): 643–54. Lab members were somewhat familiar with work on metaphors in the biology of female reproduction. Richard Cone, who runs the lab, is my husband, and he talked with them about my earlier research on the subject from time to time. Even though my current research focuses on biological imagery and I heard about the lab's work from my husband every day, I myself did not recognize the role of imagery in the sperm research until many weeks after the period of research and writing I describe. Therefore, I assume that any awareness the lab members may have had about how underlying metaphor might be guiding this particular research was fairly inchoate.

43. Ibid., 643, 650.

44. Schatten and Schatten (n. 29 above), 51.

45. Ibid., 52.

46. Surprisingly, in an article intended for a general audience, the authors do not point out that these are sea urchin sperm and note that human sperm do not shoot out filaments at all.

47. Schatten and Schatten, 53.

48. Paul M. Wassarman, "Fertilization in Mammals," *Scientific American* 259, no. 6 (December 1988): 78–84, esp. 78, 84.

49. Ibid., 78.

50. Ibid., 79.

51. Ibid., 78.

52. Since receptor molecules are relatively *immotile* and the ligands that bind to them relatively *motile*, one might imagine the egg being called the receptor and the sperm the ligand. But the molecules in question on egg and sperm are immotile molecules. It is the sperm as a *cell* that has motility, and the egg as a cell that has relative immotility.

53. Wassarman, 78–79.

54. Paul M. Wassarman, "The Biology and Chemistry of Fertilization," *Science* 235, no. 4788 (January 30, 1987): 553–60, esp. 554.

55. Ibid., 557.

56. Ibid., 557–58. This finding throws into question Schatten and Schatten's description (n. 29 above) of the sperm, its tail beating, diving down into the egg.

57. Deborah R. Gordon, "Tenacious Assumptions in Western Medicine," in *Biomedicine Examined,* ed. Margaret Lock and Deborah Gordon (Dordrecht: Kluwer, 1988), 19–56, esp. 26.

58. Wassarman, "The Biology and Chemistry of Fertilization," 558.

59. Baltz, Katz, and Cone (n. 42 above), 643, 650.

60. Schatten and Schatten, 53.

61. Wassarman, "The Biology and Chemistry of Fertilization," 557.

62. Mary Ellman, *Thinking about Women* (New York: Harcourt Brace Jovanovich, 1968), 140; Nina Auerbach, *Woman and the Demon* (Cambridge, Mass.: Harvard University Press, 1982), esp. 186.

63. Kenneth Alan Adams, "Arachnophobia: Love American Style," *Journal of Psychoanalytic Anthropology* 4, no. 2 (1981): 157–97.

64. William Ray Arney and Bernard Bergen, *Medicine and the Management of Living* (Chicago: University of Chicago Press, 1984).

65. J. F. Hartman, R. B. Gwatkin, and C. F. Hutchison, "Early Contact Interactions between Mammalian Gametes *In Vitro,*" *Proceedings of the National Academy of Sciences* (U.S.) 69, no. 10 (1972): 2767–69.

66. Arney and Bergen, 68.

67. Ruth Hubbard, "Have Only Men Evolved?" (n. 12 above), 51–52.

68. David Harvey, personal communication, November 1989.

69. Rosalind Petchesky, "Fetal Images: The Power of Visual Culture in the Politics of Reproduction," *Feminist Studies* 13, no. 2 (Summer 1987): 263–92, esp. 272.

70. Rita Arditti, Renate Klein, and Shelley Minden, *Test-Tube Women* (London: Pandora, 1984); Ellen Goodman, "Whose Right to Life?" *Baltimore Sun* (November 17, 1987); Tamar Lewin, "Courts Acting to Force Care of the Unborn," *New York*

Times (November 23, 1987), A1 and B10; Susan Irwin and Brigitte Jordan, "Knowledge, Practice, and Power: Court Ordered Cesarean Sections," *Medical Anthropology Quarterly* 1, no. 3 (September 1987): 319–34.
    71. Thanks to Elizabeth Fee and David Spain, who in February 1989 and April 1989, respectively, made points related to this.

Working with the Text

1. On a first reading of Emily Martin's essay, it is possible to become overwhelmed by the various scientific descriptions of reproductive processes. To help you discern the argumentative strategy at work in the essay, take a step back from the details of the text to consider the overall shape and structure of the article. Where does Martin start? How does she move through her evidence? Consider the role of subheadings in guiding the reader. Why does Martin start with the fairy tale and only then consider more recent research? Does that new research still bear traces of the fairy tale? In a brief essay, describe the strategy behind the organization of the article.

2. Martin's essay focuses on the metaphorical language scientists use to describe the phenomena they are observing. She notes in particular the verbs and verb forms that create metaphorical images. As you reread the essay, highlight descriptions of scientific observation that seem to you to be objective data, free of metaphor. In a brief essay, create a summary of the research that conveys the progression of what you consider to be the objective findings, omitting images and metaphors that depict the egg and the sperm as adult women and men or other creatures or objects. Exchange your essay with one or more of your classmates. Mark any language in your classmates' essays that seems to carry images or metaphors. Discuss your findings with the class. Were you able to omit metaphorical language? If so, what language did you use instead? How did you choose it? If not, what images and metaphors crept into your writing without you realizing it?

3. Although gender stereotypes can be found in virtually every discipline or profession, Martin focuses on those perpetuated by scientists, particularly those who publish textbooks. Write a brief essay in which you explore Martin's reasons for pursuing this line of inquiry. Why is she concerned about gender stereotypes in reproductive research? What influence does she seem to think science and medicine have on our culture? What is the significance of finding so many gender stereotypes in textbooks?

From Text to Field

1. Martin opens the essay by announcing, "As an anthropologist, I am intrigued by the possibility that culture shapes how biological scientists describe what they discover about the natural world" (par. 1). The presumption behind Martin's comment is that the realm of science is based exclusively on objective fact and that scientists should remain untouched by matters of culture and language. Based on Martin's insights as well as your understanding of how scientists— and human beings—work and think, write an essay in which you reflect further on why and how scientists are influenced by culture and by language.

2. In her opening paragraph, as Martin raises the possibility that scientists are influenced by the culture they live in, she points out, "If this were so, we would be learning about more than the natural world in high school biology class; we would be learning about cultural beliefs and practices as if they were part of nature." In high school, you were required to take one or more science courses, very likely a biology course. In a personal essay, reflect on the extent to which the science you learned was influenced by images and assumptions from American or even world culture. Did you receive them as if they were "part of nature"? Consider, in particular, whether changes in social attitudes toward gender and ethnicity were reflected in how science was presented to you.

3. Martin moves through her critique of gender stereotyping to the conclusion that projecting human behavior onto the egg and sperm is ill conceived and dangerous. As she brings her argument to a close, she asserts, "More crucial, then, than what *kinds* of personalities we bestow on cells is the very fact that we are doing it at all" (par. 36). In an essay, respond to this premise. If the biological relationship between the egg and sperm determines whether and how a new human being is created, do you think that it is unreasonable to treat that relationship as a reflection of — or a precursor to—stereotypically male and female characteristics? Why or why not? You might consider why Martin argues that recent biological research shows a more mutual relationship between the sperm and egg than is reflected in the language that traditionally describes it. Why does Martin only then turn to the argument that assigning any personality at all is highly questionable?

INTO THE FIELD: Options for Writing Projects

1. Family Ties: A Memoir

The "images in mind" that we have of gender—our own and that of others—can have their origins in our parents and in the parenting we received. In our mother or father we find embodied our first memories of gender roles and the source of influence and advice on our own roles. We also find in their roles confirmation of, or perhaps resistance to, broader social conventions about gender. The effect of our parents lingers on, long after we become more independent. The essays by Jamaica Kincaid (p. 542) and Scott Russell Sanders (p. 545) both address that effect.

This field project invites you to recall, honor, or resist the profound gender influences that family ties exert. Drawing on your own lived experience, and perhaps on some readings (both in and beyond this collection), write a memoir on gender identities, and through that memoir reflect on the images those gender identities have left in your mind. A memoir does more than simply tell a story from the past. It also reflects on that story, unraveling what it means in light of current self-knowledge. Whereas stories unfold and move forward, a memoir provides a retrospective glance, a chance to make sense of an incident given further experience. The term literally means "memory," and thus memoir has as much to do with an image in the mind as with any actual event.

You may find that focusing on one particular episode may afford a greater chance for reflection than an attempt to tell the "whole story." Moreover, because of the premium placed on reflection in a memoir, feel free to draw in other sources and material as you make sense of your experience. You will also find yourself shuttling back and forth between an experience you recall and your present reflections on its meaning and relevance.

As an alternative field project, you may wish to focus your memoir on the role of a friend or mentor who, through their own embodied experience, influenced your gender identity.

2. A Word of Advice

When you arrived as a new student on campus, you were surely inundated with advice of all sorts—from parents, from school administrators, from residence-hall advisors, and from fellow students. This field project invites you to make sense of that advice and of assumptions about gender identity that lie just behind that advice.

Jamaica Kincaid's "Girl" (p. 542) offers an engaging if somewhat distinctive model for offering advice. Consider imitating Kincaid's piece, but with a focus on the advice offered about going to and arriving at college. Be sure to draw on the distinctive features of your campus and the particularities of your background and cultural context. What does it mean to be a man or woman on your campus? What does it mean to explore gender at a time when you are shaping and reshaping your identity?

Accompany the advice with a separate essay that reflects on that advice and the decisions you made about focus and voice. What roles and identities did you assign to the speaker or narrator of the first piece and to its listener or reader? What was conventional in your advice, and what was perhaps intentionally radical or unexpected? How did you handle the urge to resist or question advice? What did you learn about yourself and your early experiences on campus as you wrote this project?

3. A Dialogue on Gender

Scott Russell Sanders (p. 545) opens his essay on gender in terms of a dialogue between himself and his friend Anneke. Their conversation about men and women, and in turn about envy, shame, guilt, and confusion, becomes the setting in which Sanders then interrogates his own memories and pursues his own reflections. In Sanders's essay on different perspectives, dialogue, or perhaps more accurately the desire for dialogue and trust, becomes the guiding structural device.

For this field project, Sanders's essay offers an invitation to create your own extended dialogue about the complex questions of gender identity. Your dialogue can be explicit, much as the text of a drama assigns different speaking roles, or it can take shape in your prose through your juxtaposition of different perspectives. Likewise, the dialogue can be between a man and a woman, between several men and women, between a group of women or a group of men, or for that matter between the contending voices in one person's head. Your dialogue might also capture *how* men and women might speak of gender.

4. Engendering Knowledge through Play

What we know about the world and what we know about ourselves are often profoundly shaped not just through formal schooling but through informal play. This field project invites you to explore a particular facet of the world of play. Here are just some of the possibilities you may wish to consider:

- Offer a detailed analysis of the informal games that children create during their play. What roles are assumed, and how are rules negotiated? What expectations govern improvised play? In what ways does such play follow or at times resist conventional gender roles?
- Consider in some detail one of the classic toys or games that has shaped gender identities for an entire generation of children. The Barbie and Ken dolls and GI Joe are among the more obvious examples. You may wish to focus on a toy or game that is somewhat less well known, but nevertheless influential.

- Visit a local toy store and consider the ways in which toys and games are marketed. Walk the aisles and note packaging and promotion. Media representations of play, whether on television or on the Internet, might also serve as an engaging focus for your work.
- In recent years, there has been considerable interest in gender-neutral games and toys or in activities that may even actively resist stereotypical gender roles. Evaluate this movement and some representative toys or activities. Alternatively, consider the ways in which the world of play can also be a world of hurt. Offer a close analysis of the ways in which gender identity can be used as a weapon during play.
- Some children's games explicitly call on language as part of the activity. The songs and rhymes sung during jumping rope are but one example. What do those songs say about the game and its cultural context and about the participants themselves?
- Offer a detailed analysis of one toy or game that actively wishes to reshape gender perceptions. Consider, for example, the American Girls Collection americangirl.com/agcn/. It offers a series of dolls from various periods in American history, accompanied by books about the lives of girls in that period. Does that collection have more to do with contemporary perceptions of self than with historical reality, or can it accomplish both ends?

5. Media Constructions of Gender Identity

If contemporary media have a powerful influence on the construction of gender identities, that influence is felt in particular films, television shows, advertisements, and media campaigns. Resisting sweeping generalization, this field project has you study in some detail one specific text or instance of gender construction. In what ways does your particular instance reinforce stereotypical gender identities and our responses to them, or in what ways might your particular instance resist or subvert gender expectations? The results of your field project might take the form of an academic paper, a review in the media or entertainment section of a newspaper or magazine, or perhaps a series of pages in a critic's notebook.

6. Gendered Histories of Your Field

As a student majoring in a particular field, your first preoccupation might be to learn its disciplinary content. Yet that content can be influenced by the field's sense of its own history and the way it may be discovering and reclaiming the role of women in that field. From literature departments to science departments, previously neglected women in the field are now being celebrated as path breakers.

This field project invites you to profile one such leader whose accomplishments are only now being appreciated and to analyze how that person might be affecting your education and your own initiation into your field. You may wish to consult a professor in your major or an instructor in one of your courses for suggestions on which figure might be an appropriate choice to study. A search in your campus library can also uncover rich resources. Conduct a Library of Congress subject-heading search for "Women in [your field]." To locate helpful compilations of resources in reference books, do a word search using the search string "women and biography and encyclopedia" or "women and biography and dictionary." But even as you unearth biographical information, bear in mind that this field project should go well beyond recounting a life. Your focus should be on assessing the impact of that figure on your own education in your major.

7. Gendering the Curriculum and the Classroom

Our collective conversations on gender over the last several decades have had an impact on the curricula you now study and on the classrooms in which you now learn. This field project invites you to explore what that impact has been in your major or in a field that holds some interest for you.

Historical perspective on your curriculum may help highlight the changes that have occurred. Consider engaging in a bit of archival work by consulting your college's course catalog from forty or even eighty years ago (contact a reference librarian to help you locate these resources). By comparing those historical documents with today's curriculum, you will find that in many fields new courses have appeared, as have whole new subfields, such as women's literature in the English department or gender studies in the sociology department. In fact, whole new majors or departments might have appeared, such as women's studies.

If your field leaves little explicit room for gender in the curriculum (such as in an engineering or a science major), consider the ways that your field has considered gender in the teaching and learning of its subject or in its efforts to attract women professors and students. You may also wish to consider how traditionally female-gendered fields, such as nursing, are now attracting males.

8. Gender and Campus Climate

This field project invites you to take the temperature, so to speak, of your campus with regard to its attitudes toward gender. What climate does your campus offer for heterosexual women and men and the queer communities (gay, lesbian, bisexual)? What tensions or controversial concerns might be a subject of campus conversation? In what ways might your campus reflect broader social conventions, or in what ways might your campus actively seek to question some of those conventions? To explore these and other questions, you may find it helpful to contact one of several campus groups concerned with gender issues or to interview a professor or staff member who has taken a leading role in campus discussions.

Based on your fieldwork, consider writing a proposal for action on behalf of a campus group or writing a profile of your campus with respect to gender climate for a magazine or college guidebook.

As an alternative, you may wish to delve into the history of your college or university to explore how questions of gender might have influenced it. For example, an episode in the early history of the University of Colorado at Boulder captures just how strong conventional gender roles were. When Mary Rippon was invited to join the faculty in 1878, she became one of the first female professors at any public university in the country. Popular and esteemed both on campus and in the community, she nevertheless led a very secret and separate life. She married one of her students and had a daughter, yet she hid her family life for decades for fear of losing her job. Only well after her death did her private life emerge. Consider writing a profile of an influential figure in the history of your campus, analyzing how that figure either embodied gender norms of the time or successfully challenged them.

9. Science and Gender/Cultural/Political Bias

It is both easy and convenient to work under the assumption that the sciences are immune to the sorts of bias that can affect other disciplines. But if the essays by Stephen Jay Gould (p. 552) and Emily Martin (p. 560) are any indication, such biases can indeed influence fields that most would consider to be data driven and objective. This field project invites you to consider such bias by engaging in one of three kinds of fieldwork:

- Report on and consider the implications of a current or historical case of bias in science that involved one of the following factors: race, nationality, age, sexual orientation, religion, values and beliefs, political leanings, and vested interests and financial support.
- One way to learn how to recognize and understand bias in scientific studies is to propose a fraudulent or biased study yourself. Think of this field project as a kind of explicit satire. Write a proposal for a fictional scientific study in which you consciously embed an element of bias, whether it is in data collection or in the hidden assumptions that guide your work. Consider how you can nevertheless give your study the veneer of respectability so that others may not immediately recognize how bias operates in your work. Analyze how the bias in your study might affect the results of your work and its reception.
- One particular kind of bias has to do with political leanings and their effect on the funding, use, and dissemination of scientific studies and the role of

those studies in setting public policy. For this field project, choose one scientific concern (e.g., water quality) that you are already interested in. Your task is to analyze how and to what extent political interests may have a role in how hard science is used to craft public policy. Although it may be tempting to disparage the influence of political groups with whom you disagree, do not discount the influence of groups you are sympathetic to. For an initial orientation to possible scientific issues you might focus on, consult Web sites hosted by organizations that track the role of science in public affairs. One such organization is the Union of Concerned Scientists ucsusa.org/.

10. Gender, Intelligence, and Intellectual Development

The "images in mind" that we carry with us about gender can easily influence how we regard intelligence and intellectual development. This field project offers you three different avenues for exploring the influence of gender in your learning environment.

- If you are interested in or majoring in a field that has traditionally been dominated by one gender (e.g., engineering, nursing), explore the influence of gender bias and stereotyping on teaching and learning in that field. You may wish to contact or interview someone in a support group, organization, or office that seeks to help students overcome those barriers, such as a group supporting women in engineering.
- In your precollegiate educational experiences, did you find that one gender was favored or discriminated against, perhaps in one particular sphere of activity (e.g., sports, reading, math)? Offer an educational memoir that reflects on the challenges of growing up as a boy or a girl in your school system and how you may have had to challenge assumptions about your intellectual development and interests.
- Many parents, teachers, and students hold that girls or boys may be better at something or learn that thing more easily or more quickly (at least at the outset). Drawing on educational and psychological research, consider to what extent there may or may not be any truth to such claims. Given what you have learned, how would you improve learning environments or teaching techniques? How might your own learning have been affected by such perceptions or improved by the changes you suggest?

6

Learning Technology

VIRTUAL COMMUNITIES

Technology has a powerful grip on our society. That grip extends well beyond the various electronic gizmos that may capture our immediate attention. Technologies represent ways of designing our world, of lending one kind of order, among many possible orders, to our endeavors and our relationships. Thus, even as we focus our attention on mastering the use of the latest gizmo, that gizmo can be thought of as "using" us. For all of our focus on "learning technology," on knowing how to work something, we too easily forget that technology also influences how we learn about and encounter the world.

This chapter explores this second, less obvious meaning: Technologies are ways of learning, of mastering and being mastered. It may be tempting to think of technology as an ally, or even as a boon, but it is also a contested site of social and educational struggle. In these pages, we set aside our habitual concern with becoming competent users of technology, as we consider how technology shapes us and how we can become more conscious of and savvy about that technology.

This unit focuses on how communities, because of digital technologies such as the Internet, now have a virtual dimension to them. Some communities may be almost entirely virtual. We no longer need to be together physically in order to think of ourselves as a community. Our colleagues can be across the ocean, not just down the hall. With the advent of online education, students taking the same course you are may be hundreds of miles away. Thus, by loosening the strictures of space and time, technology is reworking our relations with each other. Although we tend to think of virtual communities as offering new communities or additional kinds of communities, one of the strongest influences that technology has is to augment and expand those local communities that already have a place in our lives.

Of the local communities that have a place in your life, perhaps the most pervasive and influential is school. Certainly, your experiences from kindergarten through twelfth grade were as much about the community you were a part of as what you learned from books in that community. New technologies offer the prospect of decoupling learning from the traditional community of the school. Yet even as we may celebrate and take advantage of that possibility, we also become more aware of the value of physical community in the learning process.

The learning process occurs, then, not just *through* technology but also *about* technology. Given the latest developments in cyberspace, literacy (traditionally, the ability to read and write) has itself acquired a new dimension. No longer is it sufficient to be computer literate — that is, to know how to work computers. We must now be literate about computers, in the broadest sense. We must know how computers work to shape our lives and how we can shape our own lives through technology more consciously.

One key aspect of our new literacy about cyberspace is our willingness to question the assumption that new technologies arrive unencumbered with old baggage. Even though the latest technologies may push the envelope of what we think is possible, trailing behind them are issues — questions of gender and communication style, for example — that endure, no matter what the technology. If we are to take a self-reflective and activist approach to "learning technologies" (in the double meaning of that phrase), we need to assess not only the new prospects that technology opens up but also the enduring questions that technology continues to have us ask.

The three readings in this unit invite you to explore how technology is asking us to learn afresh about community, learning, literacy, and gender. Each of the readings takes up a particular challenge.

Nancy Hass explores how Facebook.com is more than a benign tool for social networking; it raises concerns that shed light on "the changing nature of public and private identity." Media critic Neil Postman challenges the utopian dream that technology can deliver education anytime and anywhere, reminding us that there are reasons why gathering together in a classroom is still valid. Challenging the notion that computer-mediated communication is more gender neutral and democratic, Susan Herring reminds us that new technologies can carry with them familiar baggage. Together, these three readings emphasize that our success in dealing with all that is new in technology might best be measured by how we deal, through that technology, with issues that are all too familiar.

Reflecting on Prior Knowledge

1. All of us live in communities or find ourselves, more accurately, in a variety of overlapping communities. But not all communities are now built and maintained exclusively through face-to-face contact in a geographically specific place. Some communities have virtual or electronic components, and some even exist largely, if not solely, as virtual entities with no physical location. In a journal entry, explore your acquaintance with virtual communities. What might draw you to them? What qualities might you miss in such communities?

2. Describe a project for school or college that was based on extensive use of the computer and that was either a very effective or very disappointing learning experience. How did you use the computer for the project? In what ways did technology contribute to or obstruct the process?

3. In a journal entry, reflect on what you think computer technology contributes, or could contribute, to education. How do you think it should be used? In what ways might such technology be misused? Used well, how does it enhance learning?

4. Recall school or college projects based on research. Some you may have conducted primarily through books, while others may have employed some form of computer technology. In a journal entry, compare the effectiveness of the approaches. What, if any, differences did you find in the type and quality of material? In your sense of discovery? In the level of thinking you were prompted to do? In the quality of your writing?

5. Working in small groups and drawing on your own experience, discuss whether communication using computer technology can help us overcome gender differences or whether such technology only heightens or perpetuates those differences.

6. In a journal entry, recall an experience in which something you were trying to communicate was misconstrued or ignored. What were you trying to convey? How was it received and interpreted? Why do you think your audience responded in this way?

In Your Facebook.com

Nancy Hass

How many times have you logged on to Facebook during the last week? Or during the last 24 hours? If national statistics are any indication, three-quarters of Facebook users log on every day, and average users check their sites six times a day. Popular on college campuses, the site is among the top ten most visited on the Internet.

What accounts for Facebook's popularity, and what can Facebook tell us about how college students present themselves, or at any rate about how they would like to be seen? For Nancy Hass, writing in the *New York Times* on January 8, 2006, Facebook sheds light on the "changing nature of public and private identity." Hass acknowledges the powerful potential of Facebook as a community-building tool, a tool that draws on current interest in social networks. Yet Hass also notes the concerns that have developed amid Facebook's growing popularity. Questions about privacy and propriety abound, even as many students relish the role-playing opportunities and social connections that Facebook offers. As Facebook continues to evolve, and students accommodate their own use of the site to the particulars of their situation and interests, this much remains clear: Facebook has become far more than a digital version of the old hard copy facebooks that were meant as a way for students to get to know each other. Facebook has implicated itself into the very fabric of college life.

Nancy Hass is a freelance journalist living in the New York area. She teaches journalism at New York University and has written on culture, education, fashion, and the media for such publications as the *New York Times*, *New York Magazine*, *Elle*, *Newsweek*, and *The Economist*.

As far as Kyle Stoneman is concerned, the campus police were the ones who started the Facebook wars. "We were just being, well, college students, and they used it against us," says Mr. Stoneman, a senior at George Washington

University in Washington. He is convinced that the campus security force got wind of a party he and some buddies were planning last year by monitoring Facebook.com, the phenomenally popular college networking site. The officers waited till the shindig was in full swing, Mr. Stoneman grouses, then shut it down on discovering underage drinking.

Mr. Stoneman and his friends decided to fight back. Their weapon of choice? Facebook, of course.

Once again they used the site, which is visited by more than 80 percent of the student body, to chat up a beer blast. But this time, when the campus police showed up, they found 40 students and a table of cake and cookies, all decorated with the word *beer*. "We even set up a cake-pong table," a twist on the beer-pong drinking game, he says. "The look on the faces of the cops was priceless." As the coup de grâce, he posted photographs of the party on Facebook, including a portrait of one nonplussed officer.

A university spokesman, Tracy Schario, insists that noise complaints, not nosing around Facebook, led the police to both parties. But, she says, "it's sort of an inevitability that if a party is talked about on the site, word of it will reach the enforcement people, who then have no choice but to investigate." In fact, two campus police officers and the chief's assistant are among the fourteen thousand Facebook members at George Washington.

The stunt could be read as a sign that Facebook has become more than a way for young people to stay in touch. Started in 2004 by Harvard students who wanted to animate the black-and-white thumbnail photos of freshman directories, the site is the ninth most visited on the Internet, according to Nielsen/Net Ratings, and is used by nearly five million college students. Facebook is available at most of the country's four-year colleges, and many two-year colleges, too.

Because of its popularity, though, the site has become a flashpoint for debates about free speech, privacy, and whether the Internet should be a tool for surveillance. It has also raised concerns from parents, administrators, and even students about online "addiction." "There are people on this campus who are totally obsessed with it, who check their profile five, six, twenty times a day," says Ingrid Gallagher, a sophomore at the University of Michigan. "But I think that more and more people are realizing that it also has a dark side."

Her estimates are not far off. Nearly three-quarters of Facebook users sign on at least once every twenty-four hours, and the average users sign on six times a day, says Chris Hughes, a spokesman for the site.

Using it is simple: Students create online profiles, which they can stock with personal details like sexual preferences, favorite movies, and phone contact numbers, with links to photo albums and diaries. The details listed are by no means reliable; it's common, under "personal relationships," to list a spouse as a joke (as does Mr. Stoneman). Like most networking sites, Facebook enables users to compile lists of friends whose names and photos are displayed, and to post public comments on other people's profiles.

One of the most attractive features to many students is that they can track down friends from high school at other colleges. Users can also join or form groups with names that run from the prosaic ("Campus Republicans") to the prurient ("We Need to Have Sex in Widener Before We Graduate") and the dadaesque ("I Am Fond of Biscuits and Scones"). Unlike general networking sites like Friendster and myspace.com, which let anyone join, Facebook and xuqa.com, which was started last year by a student at Williams, are confined to the insular world of the campus, which Internet experts say is the key to their success. Last fall, Facebook opened a parallel site for high school students. To sign up, a high school student has to be referred by a college student who is a Facebook user.

Facebook's charms are obvious even to administrators. "It's a fantastic tool   10 for building community," says Anita Farrington-

Facebook illuminates the Brathwaite, assistant dean for freshmen at New York

changing nature of public University. "In a school like ours that doesn't have an

and private identity. enclosed campus, it really gives people a way to find each other and connect." Harvard's president, Lawrence H. Summers, gave kudos to Facebook in the opening lines of his address to freshmen in September, saying he had been browsing the site to get to know everyone.

But concerns have flourished with Facebook's popularity. Despite safeguards placed on access—only those with valid university e-mail addresses, ending in *edu*, can register as users, and students can bar specific people from viewing their profiles—administrators and parents worry about cyberstalking.

Robin Raskin, a technology consultant whose three children are in college and use Facebook, says students should be cautious about putting personal information on the site. "There's something about all that ivy climbing up those walls that makes kids feel they're safe, but anybody can get in there who wants to," Ms. Raskin says.

It's not just parents who are uneasy.

"Every girl I know has had some sort of weird experience," says Shanna Andus, a freshman at the University of California, Berkeley. "Someone gets on a 'friend list' of one of your friends and starts to contact you. They met you at a party or checked out your picture online or went to high school with someone you barely know. It's just a little creepy."

Some colleges have taken action: In October, the University of New   15 Mexico banned access to Facebook on its campus system, citing numerous concerns, including student privacy. Campus officials say they will restore the service for this semester. Mr. Hughes, the Facebook spokesman, says that when the site could not be accessed via the university's networks, half the users continued to sign on through outside networks.

Mr. Hughes defends the site's privacy safeguards, insisting that it rarely receives reports of stalking or other harassment, and that complaints usually require only a readjustment of a user's privacy settings and a warning message sent to the person accused of inappropriate behavior.

But parents and administrators have another worry: that potential employers are wangling themselves e-mail addresses ending with *edu*—perhaps someone in the office was given one by his alma mater or has signed up for an extension course at a college with Facebook access—so that they can vet job applicants. Administrators at both NYU and Brandeis say on-campus employers use the site for just that purpose. Aware that many students post pictures and descriptions of their X-rated, booze-soaked exploits, administrators at Tufts and Texas Christian University began offering seminars in Facebook propriety last year.

Students themselves seem split on the issue of Facebook exposure: Some are outraged that their youthful indiscretions may be used against them; others seem resigned to privacy being a fantasy in the age of the Internet. In a case that was reported in the *Boston Globe* last year and that many students cite as a cautionary tale, a Brandeis student included her "appreciation of the festive greens" in her profile, a not-so-subtle allusion to marijuana that got to her parents and became the buzz at her grandmother's retirement home.

"The way I look at it is that in the future with the growing nature of information transparency, having embarrassing pictures out there will be the norm," says Mr. Stoneman, a political communications major who has a job lined up with a consulting firm that specializes in online campaign fundraising. "Sure, five years down the line it might hurt me, but ten or fifteen years, I don't think it will matter."

But, as Mr. Stoneman's beer party hoax suggests, he and his peers may not 20 be as sanguine about how some colleges are using Facebook to police the student body or at least influence it. As part of freshman orientation at Rollins College in Florida, student coordinators will create Facebook groups for campus organizations like the Rollins Outdoor Club.

"We cannot deny the impact of Facebook, but we believe that it's the responsibility of the institution to find ways to create the most positive communities," says Roger Casey, dean of faculty. "These communities can be positive or negative."

Other colleges are even more aggressive. A student at Fisher College in Boston was expelled last year for his online criticism of a campus security officer. Officials at the University of California, Santa Barbara, said they would discipline students living on campus who posted information or photographs on their profiles that involved illegal activity like underage drinking. At North Carolina State, residential advisers, the upperclassmen who oversee dorm life, wrote up fifteen students seen consuming alcohol in photos on Facebook; it caused an uproar and resulted in a town-hall-style meeting.

Campus officials are not the only ones trawling for miscreants: The Secret Service investigated a student at the University of Oklahoma who posted a comment on Facebook about assassinating the president.

Ms. Farrington-Brathwaite acknowledges that the privacy issues presented by Facebook create challenges for administrators, even at liberal institutions like NYU, which she says has not used the site to patrol student behavior. While several hundred professors and deans across the country have added their own profiles as a way to reach out to students—a development that, arguably, has lowered Facebook's cool quotient—she does not plan to do so. "I wouldn't want to come upon something that I felt was inappropriate," she says, "so I just choose not to get involved."

But Ms. Farrington-Brathwaite encourages resident advisers to come to her if they spot a Facebook cry for help, like an allusion to suicide. NYU has experienced a spate of student suicides in recent years. "Still, it's a difficult balancing act, preserving student privacy and freedom, yet not sticking our head in the sand," she says. 25

With the abundance of groups that treat almost everything with irreverence, Facebook has also inflamed racial conflicts. At Indiana University and the University of Virginia, two Facebook groups recently caused fracases by poking fun at Asian students, who make up a large part of their student bodies. Students created dueling groups, and Asian organizations made the conflict a cause célèbre.

Mr. Hughes says the site does not censor content but tries to deal directly with offensive or inflammatory postings if there are complaints. At both campuses, students removed the groups of their own accord after administrators brought complaints to their attention. "We see Facebook as a land mine," says Daisy Rodriguez, assistant dean of students at the University of Virginia, "but we understand we have no authority over it. So our policy is to meet with students who may post things that people find offensive and talk about the issues and consequences. Then we hope for the best."

Mr. Stoneman of George Washington considers such an attitude enlightened—and realistic. "Facebook is part of an evolving dialogue," he says. "One of the things that's most fascinating about it is how it illuminates the changing nature of public and private identity. This is new ground on every level. What people in positions of power have to realize is that people my age have a completely different attitude about what is fair game."

Working with the Text

1. Nancy Hass opens her article on Facebook.com with a four-paragraph story about an incident at George Washington University. What is the function of that story as the opening to the article? How does the story open up a range of issues that Hass explores regarding Facebook?

2. In an article that is otherwise preoccupied with the issues and conflicts that Facebook.com has opened up on college campuses, Hass quotes an administrator as saying that Facebook offers "a fantastic tool for building community" (par. 10). Drawing on the article, and your own acquaintance with Facebook, explain this reference to community building. What are social networks, and how can a virtual tool like Facebook help establish and maintain them?

3. Hass notes that some universities are now offering seminars in Facebook propriety. What is meant by the term *propriety*? What is or isn't proper in an environment like Facebook? Can propriety be seen as a general or universal standard, or can it only be judged in light of a specific situation or context? Can something that is improper in some circumstances be proper or acceptable in others? What bearing does the digital or virtual environment of Facebook have on the question of propriety?

4. Hass concludes her article with a quote that Facebook "illuminates the changing nature of public and private identity." Explain the quote more fully. Why might this quote be a fitting conclusion to the article and the various issues that it discusses?

From Text to Field

1. Drawing on the article by Hass and your own experience with Facebook.com, assess Facebook as a tool for community building. How do real and artificial or virtual communities coexist, or do they sometimes conflict or work at cross purposes? How does the "group" function work on Facebook, and what role does it have in the formation and maintenance of groups? What are the possibilities and limits of community building through Facebook?

2. Given the frequency with which Facebook users are reported to log on to their site, or the sites of friends (often multiple times each day), discuss the attraction of Facebook, and possible "addiction" to Facebook. As you interview users that you know, also be sure to interview those who do not use Facebook or who only log on sporadically.

3. How does Facebook encourage you to define "friendship"? Among the functions available on a Facebook site is the opportunity to ask to be someone's friend, or to accept others as your friend. Facebook also allows you to "poke"

someone else on Facebook. How do Facebook users treat or perceive these functions? Does Facebook further friendships in a social network, or does it trivialize friendship?

4. Given the popularity of Facebook as students' preferred means of contact and interaction, it is perhaps understandable that professors are interested in tapping this resource for their teaching and their communication with students. How do you and other students feel about this use of Facebook? Do you welcome it? Or do you feel it intrudes on and changes the nature of Facebook communications?

5. Nearly every user of Facebook has his or her own Facebook "story," some notable consequence of using the site, whether positive or negative. What is your story? Does your story support some of the points made in the article by Hass, or does your story offer a different perspective?

Virtual Students, Digital Classroom

Neil Postman

Will technology eventually replace schools? Will access to the Internet as well as other computer-based sources of information transform our attitudes toward knowledge? What will we want to learn, and how will high-tech learning influence the ways we think? In the following article from the *Nation*, adapted from his 1996 book, *The End of Education: Redefining the Value of School*, Neil Postman addresses these questions, observing that the deeper issue about all of our technologies is "not how to use them but how they use *us.*"

As an educator internationally recognized for his writings on the media, Postman was especially concerned about the effects of technology on learning and civic life. His own classroom experience as well as his research convinced him that teachers and school environments contribute to our social and psychological health in ways that can never be duplicated by any form of technology. Postman warned that we too easily idolize technology, embracing its allure and convenience without reflecting on what its real goals and long-term effects might be.

A prolific writer who attracted a wide readership by fearlessly debunking fashionable trends, Postman authored nearly twenty books. He is perhaps best known for his 1985 book, *Amusing Ourselves to Death: Public Discourse in the Age of Show Business*, in which he criticizes the television industry for treating the world's most serious issues as entertainment. Postman was also particularly troubled by how the media shaped children's lives, a concern expressed in *The Disappearance of Childhood* (1982). Other notable books include *Teaching as a Subversive Activity* (1969, with Charles Weingartner), *Technopoly: The Surrender of Culture to Technology* (1992), and *Building a Bridge to the 18th Century: How the Past Can Improve Our*

Future (1999). A member of the *Nation's* editorial board, Postman published articles in periodicals ranging from the *New York Times Magazine*, the *Atlantic*, and *Harper's* to *Time* magazine and the *Harvard Education Review*.

A faculty member at New York University for forty-four years, Postman founded its program in media ecology and was for many years chair of the Department of Culture and Communication. His interest in education extended to his own classroom, where his work was honored with several teaching awards. Postman died in October 2003.

If one has a trusting relationship with one's students (let us say, graduate students), it is not altogether gauche to ask them if they believe in God (with a capital G). I have done this three or four times and most students say they do. Their answer is preliminary to the next question: If someone you love were desperately ill, and you had to choose between praying to God for his or her recovery or administering an antibiotic (as prescribed by a competent physician), which would you choose?

Most say the question is silly since the alternatives are not mutually exclusive. Of course. But suppose they were — which would you choose? God helps those who help themselves, some say in choosing the antibiotic, therefore getting the best of two possible belief systems. But if pushed to the wall (e.g., God does not always help those who help themselves; God helps those who pray and who believe), most choose the antibiotic, after noting that the question is asinine and proves nothing. Of course, the question was not asked, in the first place, to prove anything but to begin a discussion of the nature of belief. And I do not fail to inform the students, by the way, that there has recently emerged evidence of a "scientific" nature that when sick people are prayed for they do better than those who aren't.

As the discussion proceeds, important distinctions are made among the different meanings of "belief," but at some point it becomes far from asinine to speak of the god of Technology — in the sense that people believe technology works, that they rely on it, that it makes promises, that they are bereft when denied access to it, that they are delighted when they are in its presence, that for most people it works in mysterious ways, that they condemn people who speak against it, that they stand in awe of it, and that, in the "born again" mode, they will alter their lifestyles, their schedules, their habits and their relationships to accommodate it. If this be not a form of religious belief, what is?

In all strands of American cultural life, you can find so many examples of technological adoration that it is possible to write a book about it. And I would if it had not already been done so well. But nowhere do you find more enthusiasm for the god of Technology than among educators. In fact, there are those, like Lewis Perelman, who argue (for example, in his book, *School's Out*) that modern information technologies have rendered schools entirely irrelevant since there is now much more information available outside the classroom than inside it. This is by no means considered an outlandish idea. Dr. Diane Ravitch, former Assistant Secretary of Education, envisions, with considerable relish, the challenge that technology presents to the tradition that "children (and adults) should be educated in a specific place, for a certain number of hours, and a certain number of days during the week and year." In other words, that children should be educated in school. Imagining the possibilities of an information superhighway offering perhaps a thousand channels, Dr. Ravitch assures us that:

> in this new world of pedagogical plenty, children and adults will be able to dial up a program on their home television to learn whatever they want to know, at their own convenience. If Little Eva cannot sleep, she can learn algebra instead. At her home-learning station, she will tune in to a series of interesting problems that are presented in an interactive medium, much like video games. . . .
>
> Young John may decide that he wants to learn the history of modern Japan, which he can do by dialing up the greatest authorities and teachers on the subject, who will not only use dazzling graphs and illustrations, but will narrate a historical video that excites his curiosity and imagination.

In this vision there is, it seems to me, a confident and typical sense of unreality. Little Eva can't sleep, so she decides to learn a little algebra? Where does Little Eva come from? Mars? If not, it is more likely she will tune in to a good movie. Young John decides that he wants to learn the history of modern Japan? How did young John come to this point? How is it that he never visited a library up to now? Or is it that he, too, couldn't sleep and decided that a little modern Japanese history was just what he needed? 5

What Ravitch is talking about here is not a new technology but a new species of child, one who, in any case, no one has seen up to now. Of course, new technologies do make new kinds of people, which leads to a second objection to Ravitch's conception of the future. There is a kind of forthright determinism about the imagined world described in it. The technology is here or will be; we must use it because it is there; we will become the kind of people the technology requires us to be, and whether we like it or not, we will remake our institutions to accommodate technology. All of this must happen because it is good for us, but in any case, we have no choice. This point of view is present in very nearly every statement about the future relationship of learning to technology. And, as in Ravitch's scenario, there is always a cheery, gee-whiz tone to the prophecies. Here is one produced by the National Academy of Sciences, written by Hugh McIntosh.

School for children of the information age will be vastly different than it was for mom and dad.

Interested in biology? Design your own life forms with computer simulation.

Having trouble with a science project? Teleconference about it with a research scientist.

Bored with the real world? Go into a virtual physics lab and rewrite the laws of gravity.

These are the kinds of hands-on learning experiences schools could be providing right now. The technologies that make them possible are already here, and today's youngsters, regardless of economic status, know how to use them. They spend hours with them every week—not in the classroom, but in their own homes and in video-game centers at every shopping mall.

It is always interesting to attend to the examples of learning, and the motivations that ignite them, in the songs of love that technophiles perform for us. It is, for example, not easy to imagine research scientists all over the world teleconferencing with thousands of students who are having difficulty with their science projects. I can't help thinking that most research scientists would put a stop to this rather quickly. But I find it especially revealing that in the scenario above we have an example of a technological solution to a psychological problem that would seem to be exceedingly serious. We are presented with a student who is "bored with the real world." What does it mean to say someone is bored with the real world, especially one so young? Can a journey into virtual reality cure such a problem? And if it can, will our troubled youngster want to return to the real world? Confronted with a student who is bored with the real world, I don't think we can solve the problem so easily by making available a virtual-reality physics lab.

The role that new technology should play in schools or anywhere else is something that needs to be discussed without the hyperactive fantasies of cheerleaders. In particular, the computer and its associated technologies are awesome additions to a culture, and are quite capable of altering the psychic, not to mention the sleeping, habits of our young. But like all important technologies of the past, they are Faustian bargains,° giving and taking away, sometimes in equal measure, sometimes more in one way than the other. It is strange—indeed, shocking — that with the twenty-first century so close, we can still talk of new technologies as if they were unmixed blessings — gifts, as it were, from the gods. Don't we all know what the combustion engine has done for us and against us? What television is doing for us and against us? At the very least, what we need to discuss about Little Eva, Young John, and McIntosh's trio is what they will lose, and what we will lose, if they enter a

---

Faustian bargains: Faust is the protagonist of a popular German folktale that concerns his pact with the devil.

world in which computer technology is their chief source of motivation, authority, and, apparently, psychological sustenance. Will they become, as Joseph Weizenbaum warns, more impressed by calculation than human judgment? Will speed of response become, more than ever, a defining quality of intelligence? If, indeed, the idea of a school will be dramatically altered, what kinds of learning will be neglected, perhaps made impossible? Is virtual reality a new form of therapy? If it is, what are its dangers?

These are serious matters, and they need to be discussed by those who know something about children from the planet Earth, and whose vision of children's needs, and the needs of society, go beyond thinking of school mainly as a place for the convenient distribution of information. Schools are not now and have never been largely about getting information to children. That has been on the schools' agenda, of course, but has always been way down on the list. For technological utopians, the computer vaults information access to the top. This reshuffling of priorities comes at a most inopportune time. The goal of giving people greater access to more information faster, more conveniently and in more diverse forms was the main technological thrust of the nineteenth century. Some folks haven't noticed it but that problem was largely solved, so that for almost a hundred years there has been more information available to the young outside the school than inside. That fact did not make the schools obsolete, nor does it now make them obsolete. Yes, it is true that Little Eva, the insomniac from Mars, could turn on an algebra lesson, thanks to the computer, in the wee hours of the morning. She could also, if she wished, read a book or magazine, watch television, turn on the radio or listen to music. All of this she could have done before the computer. The computer does not solve any problem she has but does exacerbate one. For Little Eva's problem is not how to get access to a well-structured algebra lesson but what to do with all the information available to her during the day, as well as during sleepless nights. Perhaps this is why she couldn't sleep in the first place. Little Eva, like the rest of us, is overwhelmed by information. She lives in a culture that has 260,000 billboards, 17,000 newspapers, 12,000 periodicals, 27,000 video outlets for renting tapes, 400 million television sets, and well over 500 million radios, not including those in automobiles. There are 40,000 new book titles published every year, and each day 41 million photographs are taken. And thanks to the computer, more than 60 billion pieces of advertising junk come into our mailboxes every year. Everything from telegraphy and photography in the nineteenth century to the silicon chip in the twentieth has amplified the din of information intruding on Little Eva's consciousness. From millions of sources all over the globe, through every possible channel and medium—

> **Nowhere do you find more enthusiasm for the god of Technology than among the educator.**

light waves, air waves, ticker tape, computer banks, telephone wires, television cables, satellites, and printing presses—information pours in. Behind it in every imaginable form of storage—on paper, on video, on audiotape, on disks, film, and silicon chips—is an even greater volume of information waiting to be retrieved. In the face of this we might ask, What can schools do for Little Eva besides making still more information available? If there is nothing, then new technologies will indeed make schools obsolete. But in fact, there is plenty.

One thing that comes to mind is that schools can provide her with a seri- 10
ous form of technology education. Something quite different from instruction in using computers to process information, which, it strikes me, is a trivial thing to do, for two reasons. In the first place, approximately 35 million people have already learned how to use computers without the benefit of school instruction. If the schools do nothing, most of the population will know how to use computers in the next ten years, just as most of the population learns how to drive a car without school instruction. In the second place, what we needed to know about cars — as we need to know about computers, television, and other important technologies — is not how to use them but how they use *us*. In the case of cars, what we needed to think about in the early twentieth century was not how to drive them but what they would do to our air, our landscape, our social relations, our family life, and our cities. Suppose in 1946 we had started to address similar questions about television: What will be its effects on our political institutions, our psychic habits, our children, our religious conceptions, our economy? Would we be better positioned today to control TV's massive assault on American culture? I am talking here about making technology itself an object of inquiry so that Little Eva and Young John are more interested in asking questions about the computer than getting answers from it.

I am not arguing against using computers in school. I am arguing against our sleepwalking attitudes toward it, against allowing it to distract us from important things, against making a god of it. This is what Theodore Roszak warned against in *The Cult of Information*: "Like all cults," he wrote, "this one also has the intention of enlisting mindless allegiance and acquiescence. People who have no clear idea of what they mean by information or why they should want so much of it are nonetheless prepared to believe that we live in an information age, which makes every computer around us what the relics of the True Cross were in the age of faith: emblems of salvation." To this, I would add the sage observation of Alan Kay of Apple Computer. Kay is widely associated with the invention of the personal computer, and certainly has an interest in schools using them. Nonetheless, he has repeatedly said that any problems the schools cannot solve without computers, they cannot solve with them. What are some of those problems? There is, for example, the traditional task of teaching children how to behave in groups. One might even say that schools have never been essentially about individualized learning. It is true, of course, that groups do not learn, individuals do. But the idea of a school is that individuals must learn in a setting in which individual needs are subordinated to group interests. Unlike other media of mass communication, which celebrate individual response and are experienced in private, the classroom is intended to tame the ego, to connect the individual with others, to demonstrate the value and necessity of group cohesion. At present, most scenarios describing the uses of computers have children solving problems alone; Little Eva, Young John, and the others are doing just that. The presence of other children may, indeed, be an annoyance.

Like the printing press before it, the computer has a powerful bias toward amplifying personal autonomy and individual problem solving. That is why educators must guard against computer technology's undermining some of the important reasons for having the young assemble (to quote Ravitch) "in a specific place, for a certain number of hours, and a certain number of days during the week and year."

Although Ravitch is not exactly against what she calls "state schools," she imagines them as something of a relic of a pretechnological age. She believes that the new technologies will offer all children equal access to information. Conjuring up a hypothetical Little Mary who is presumably from a poorer home than Little Eva, Ravitch imagines that Mary will have the same opportunities as Eva "to learn any subject, and to learn it from the same master teachers as children in the richest neighborhood." For all of its liberalizing spirit, this scenario makes some important omissions. One is that though new technologies may be a solution to the learning of "subjects," they work against the learning of what are called "social values," including an understanding of democratic processes. If one reads the first chapter of Robert Fulghum's *All I Really Need to Know I Learned in Kindergarten*, one will find an elegant summary of a few things Ravitch's scenario has left out. They include learning the following lessons: Share everything, play fair, don't hit people, put things back where you found them, clean up your own mess, wash your hands before you eat, and, of course, flush. The only thing wrong with Fulghum's book is that no one has learned all these things at kindergarten's end. We have ample evidence that it takes many years of teaching these values in school before they have been accepted and internalized. That is why it won't do for children to learn in "settings of their own choosing." That is also why schools require children to be in a certain place at a certain time and to follow certain rules, like raising their hands when they wish to speak, not talking when others are talking, not chewing gum, not leaving until the bell rings, exhibiting patience toward slower learners, etc. This process is called making civilized people. The god of Technology does not appear interested in this function of schools. At least, it does not come up much when technology's virtues are enumerated.

The god of Technology may also have a trick or two up its sleeve about something else. It is often asserted that new technologies will equalize learning opportunities for the rich and poor. It is devoutly to be wished for, but I doubt it will happen. In the first place, it is generally understood by those who have studied the history of technology that technological change always produces winners and losers. There are many reasons for this, among them economic differences. Even in the case of the automobile, which is a commodity most people can buy (although not all), there are wide differences between the rich and poor in the quality of what is available to them. It would be quite astonishing if computer technology equalized all learning opportunities, irrespective of economic differences. One may be delighted that Little Eva's parents could afford the technology and software to make it possible for her to learn algebra at midnight. But Little Mary's parents may not be able to, may not even know such things are available. And if we say that the school could make the technology available to Little Mary (at least during the day), there may be something else Little Mary is lacking.

It turns out, for example, that Little Mary may be having sleepless nights   15
as frequently as Little Eva but not because she wants to get a leg up on her algebra. Maybe because she doesn't know who her father is, or, if she does, where he is. Maybe we can understand why McIntosh's kid is bored with the real world. Or is the child confused about it? Or terrified? Are there educators who seriously believe that these problems can be addressed by new technologies?

I do not say, of course, that schools can solve the problems of poverty, alienation, and family disintegration, but schools can *respond* to them. And they can do this because there are people in them, because these people are concerned with more than algebra lessons or modern Japanese history, and because these people can identify not only one's level of competence in math but one's level of rage and confusion and depression. I am talking here about children as they really come to us, not children who are invented to show us how computers may enrich their lives. Of course, I suppose it is possible that there are children who, waking at night, want to study algebra or who are so interested in their world that they yearn to know about Japan. If there be such children, and one hopes there are, they do not require expensive computers to satisfy their hunger for learning. They are on their way, with or without computers. Unless, of course, they do not care about others or have no friends, or little respect for democracy or are filled with suspicion about those who are not like them. When we have machines that know how to do something about these problems, that is the time to rid ourselves of the expensive burden of schools or to reduce the function of teachers to "coaches" in the uses of machines (as Ravitch envisions). Until then, we must be more modest about this god of Technology and certainly not pin our hopes on it.

We must also, I suppose, be empathetic toward those who search with good intentions for technological panaceas. I am a teacher myself and know how hard it is to contribute to the making of a civilized person. Can we blame those who want to find an easy way, through the agency of technology? Perhaps not. After all, it is an old quest. As early as 1918, H. L. Mencken° (although completely devoid of empathy) wrote, "There is no sure-cure so idiotic that some superintendent of schools will not swallow it. The aim seems to be to reduce the whole teaching process to a sort of automatic reaction, to discover some master formula that will not only take the place of competence and resourcefulness in the teacher but that will also create an artificial receptivity in the child."

Mencken was not necessarily speaking of technological panaceas but he may well have been. In the early 1920s a teacher wrote the following poem:

Mr. Edison says
That the radio will supplant the teacher.
Already one may learn languages by means of Victrola records.
The moving picture will visualize
What the radio fails to get across.
Teachers will be relegated to the backwoods,
With fire-horses,
And long-haired women;
Or, perhaps shown in museums.
Education will become a matter
Of pressing the button.
Perhaps I can get a position at the switchboard.

I do not go as far back as the radio and Victrola, but I am old enough to remember when 16-millimeter film was to be the sure-cure. Then closed-circuit television. Then 8-millimeter film. Then teacher-proof textbooks. Now computers.

I know a false god when I see one.   20

Working with the Text

1. In arguing for his view of education, Neil Postman pits what he considers to be the limitations of technology against the "process" of "making civilized people." In a brief essay, argue for or against Postman's stance. Do you agree with

---

H. L. Mencken: Henry Louis Mencken (1880–1956) was a journalist, satirist, and social critic often regarded as one of the most influential writers in the early twentieth century.

his assessment of technology-based learning? Do you think schools do, or should, focus on the kinds of socialization he promotes? Why or why not?

2. Postman opens his essay by asserting that in our culture technology has become a god. He refers to the godlike nature of technology throughout the essay, ending with the assertion, "I know a false god when I see one" (par. 20). Review the first four paragraphs of the essay. In a small group, debate the questions Postman poses to his students. Drawing on your debate, write a brief essay in which you reflect on Postman's use of *god* in making his argument. How does it contribute to the argument? Why does he place so much emphasis on it? Do you agree that we treat technology as a god?

3. When Postman asserts that what we need to know about technologies is "not how to use them but how they use *us*" (par. 10), he is referring to cars and television as well as computers. Throughout the essay, he draws on history to make his argument. In a brief essay, analyze his comparisons of computers to earlier technologies. What characteristics does Postman claim that the technologies have in common? What does he want us to learn from our culture's attitudes toward earlier technologies? What does he mean by the phrase, "how they use *us*"?

From Text to Field

1. In his essay, Postman examines technology-based education through the lenses of educators and administrators. In a personal essay, examine your experience of and relationship to technology as a tool for learning. Possible approaches to your essay include the following:

   - Compare how you have used technology for completing school assignments to how you have used it for pursuing subject matter you have chosen for yourself.
   - Compare your experience of learning through technology to learning through traditional teaching methods.
   - Compare your use of technology in a school setting to your use of it outside of school.

2. Throughout the essay, Postman challenges the descriptions of "Little Eva" and "Young John" envisioned by Dr. Diane Ravitch, former assistant secretary of education. When Little Eva cannot sleep, she goes to her computer to learn algebra. Young John takes it upon himself to learn the history of modern Japan by "dialing up the greatest authorities and teachers on the subject" (par. 4). Based on your observations of real school-age people — and awareness of your own behaviors — write your own "Little Eva" or "Young John" scenario.

3. Postman claims that "[s]chools are not now and have never been largely about getting information to children" (par. 9). With Postman's analysis of schools in mind, write a personal essay in which you explore what your own experience of school has been "largely about."

4. Referring to the fictional characters Little Eva and Young John in the scenarios posed by proponents of technology-based learning, Postman insists that "[a]t the very least, what we need to discuss . . . is what they will lose, and what we will lose, if they enter a world in which computer technology is their chief source of motivation, authority, and, apparently, psychological sustenance" (par. 8). In a small group, discuss this question. Based on your discussion, develop a brief presentation for the entire class in which you postulate "what we will lose" or in which, rebutting Postman, you clarify what we will gain that offsets such losses

Bringing Familiar Baggage to the New Frontier: Gender Differences in Computer-Mediated Communication

Susan Herring

When network technology ushered in online discussion groups, enthusiasts regarded computer-mediated communication (CMC) as highly democratic. The claim was that everyone could participate as equals, without regard to social standing, race, or gender. Susan Herring was among the first to observe that gender differences in styles of CMC actually tended to extend the gender inequalities found off-line. Based on online surveys as well as her study of a number of computer-mediated discussion lists, Herring concluded that differences in communication style were driven by differences in values. She found that males and females typically held conflicting views of what constitutes a productive online discussion.

Herring is a professor of information science and linguistics at Indiana University, where she is a fellow at the Center for Social Informatics and at the Center for Research on Learning and Technology. Her recent research has focused on media and technology and their influence on the evolution of language, with an emphasis on issues related to gender. Among her numerous publications are *Computer-Mediated Conversation* (2004) and *Computer-Mediated ommunication: Linguistic, Social, and Cross-Cultural Perspectives* (1996). She has also edited several special issues of leading journals, the most recent being *The Multilingual Internet: Language, Culture, and Communication in Instant Messaging, E-mail, and Chat*, a special 2003 issue of the *Journal of Computer-Mediated*

Communication. Herring's essay was originally delivered as a speech in June 1994 at a meeting of the American Library Association, as part of a panel entitled "Making the Net*Work*."

Introduction

Although research on computer-mediated communication (CMC) dates back to the early days of computer network technology in the 1970s, researchers have only recently begun to take the gender of users into account.[1] This is perhaps not surprising considering that men have traditionally dominated the technology and have comprised the majority of users of computer networks since their inception, but the result is that most of what has been written about CMC incorporates a very one-sided perspective. However, recent research has been uncovering some eye-opening differences in the ways men and women interact "online," and it is these differences that I will address here.

My basic claim has two parts: first, that women and men have recognizably different styles in posting electronic messages to the Internet, contrary to claims that CMC neutralizes distinctions of gender, and second, that women and men have different communication ethics — that is, they value different kinds of online interactions as appropriate and desirable. I illustrate these differences — and some of the problems that arise because of them — with specific reference to the phenomenon of "flaming."

Background

Since 1991 I've been lurking (or what I prefer to call "carrying out ethnographic observation") on various computer-mediated discussion lists, downloading electronic conversations and analyzing the communicative behaviors of participants. I became interested in gender shortly after subscribing to my first discussion list, LINGUIST-L, an academic forum for professional linguists. Within the first month after I began receiving messages, a conflict arose on the list (what I would later learn to call a "flame war") in which the two major theoretical camps within the field became polarized around an issue of central interest. My curiosity was piqued by the fact that very few women were contributing to this important professional event; they seemed to be sitting on the sidelines while men were airing their opinions and getting all the attention. In an attempt to understand the women's silence, I made up an anonymous survey which I sent to LINGUIST-L asking subscribers what they thought of the discussion and, if they hadn't contributed, why not.

Initial Observations

The number one reason given by both men and women for not contributing to the LINGUIST discussion was "intimidation"—as one respondent commented, participants were "ripping each other's lungs out." Interestingly, however, men and women responded differently to feeling intimidated. Men seemed to accept such behavior as a normal feature of academic life, making comments to the effect that "Actually, the barbs and arrows were entertaining, because of course they weren't aimed at me." In contrast, many women responded with profound aversion. As one woman put it: "That is precisely the kind of human interaction I committedly avoid. . . . I am dismayed that human beings treat each other this way. It makes the world a dangerous place to be. I dislike such people and I want to give them WIDE berth."

When I analyzed the messages in the thread itself, another gender difference emerged, this time relating to the linguistic structure and rhetoric of the messages. A daunting 68 percent of the messages posted by men made use of an adversarial style in which the poster distanced himself from, criticized, and/or ridiculed other participants, often while promoting his own importance. The few women who participated in the discussion, in contrast, displayed features of attenuation—hedging, apologizing, asking questions rather than making assertions—and a personal orientation, revealing thoughts and feelings and interacting with and supporting others.

It wasn't long before I was noticing a similar pattern in other discussions and on other lists. Wherever I went on mixed-sex lists, men seemed to be doing most of the talking and attracting most of the attention to themselves, although not all lists were as adversarial as LINGUIST. I started to hear stories about and witness men taking over and dominating discussions even of women-centered topics on women-centered lists.[2] In contrast, on the few occasions when I observed women attempting to gain an equal hearing on male-dominated lists, they were ignored, trivialized, or criticized by men for their tone or the inappropriateness of their topic.[3] It wasn't until I started looking at lists devoted to women's issues, and to traditionally "feminized" disciplines such as women's studies, teaching English as a second language, and librarianship, that I found women holding forth in an amount consistent with their numerical presence on the list. I also found different interactional norms: little or no flaming, and cooperative, polite exchanges.

Different Styles

As a result of these findings, I propose that women and men have different characteristic online styles. By characteristic styles, I do not mean that all or even the majority of users of each sex exhibit the behaviors of each style, but rather that the styles are recognizably—even stereotypically—gendered. The male style is characterized by adversariality: put-downs, strong, often contentious assertions, lengthy and/or frequent postings, self-promotion, and sarcasm. Below are two examples, one from an academic list (LINGUIST) and the other from a nonacademic list (POLITICS).[4]

> 1. [Jean Linguiste's] proposals towards a more transparent morphology in French are exactly what he calls them: a farce. Nobody could ever take them seriously — unless we want to look as well at pairs such as *pe`re - me`re*, *coq - poule* and defigure the French language in the process.

[strong assertions ("exactly," "nobody"), put-downs ("JL's proposals are a farce"; implied: "JL wants to defigure the French language")]

> 2. >yes, they did . . . This is why we must be allowed to remain armed
> . . .
> >who is going to help us if our government becomes a tyranny?
> >no one will.

oh yes we *must* remain armed. anyone see day one last night abt charlestown where everyone/s so scared of informing on murderers the cops have given up? where the reply to any offense is a public killing? knowing you/re not gonna be caught cause everyone/s to afraid to be a witness?

yeah, right, twerp.

> — [RON) "THE WISE"—

what a joke.

[sarcasm, name calling, personal insults]

The second example would be characterized as a "flame" by most readers because of its personally offensive nature.

Less exclusively male-gendered but still characteristic of male postings is an authoritative, self-confident stance whereby men are more likely than women to represent themselves as experts, e.g., in answering queries for information. The following example is from NOTIS-L.

> 3. The NUGM Planning meeting was canceled before all of this came up. It has nothing to do with it. The plans were simply proceeding along so well that there was no need to hold the meeting. That is my understanding from talking to NOTIS staff just last week.

[authoritative tone, strong assertions ("nothing," "simply," "just")]

The female-gendered style, in contrast, has two aspects which typically co-occur: supportiveness and attentuation. "Supportiveness" is characterized by expressions of appreciation, thanking, and community-building activities that make other participants feel accepted and welcome. "Attenuation" includes hedging and expressing doubt, apologizing, asking questions, and contributing ideas in the form of suggestions. The following examples from a nonacademic list (WOMEN) and an academic list (TESL-L) illustrate each aspect:

4. >[AILEEN],
    >
    >I just wanted to let you know that I have really enjoyed all
    >your posts about Women's herstory. They have been
    >extremely informative and I've learned alot about the
    >women's movement. Thank you!
    >
    >—[ERIKA]

    DITTO!!!! They are wonderful!

    Did anyone else catch the first part of a Century of Women? I really enjoyed it. Of course, I didn't agree with everything they said. . . . but it was really informative.
    [ROBERTA]~~~~~~~~~~~~~~~~~~~~~~~~~~~~~~

    [appreciates, thanks, agrees, appeals to group]

5   [. . .] I hope this makes sense. This is kind of what I had in mind when I realized I couldn't give a real definitive answer. Of course, maybe I'm just getting into the nuances of the language when it would be easier to just give the simple answer. Any response?

    [hedges, expresses doubt, appeals to group]

The female style takes into consideration what the sociologist Erving   10
Goffman called the "face" wants of the addressee — specifically, the desire of the addressee to feel ratified and liked (e.g., by expressions of appreciation) and her desire not to be imposed upon (e.g., by absolute assertions that don't allow for alternative views). The male style, in contrast, confronts and threatens the addressee's "face" in the process of engaging him in agonistic debate.

Although these styles represent in some sense the extremes of gendered behavior, they have symbolic significance above and beyond their frequency of use. For example, other users regularly infer the gender of message posters on the basis of features of these styles, especially when the self-identified gender of a poster is open to question. Consider the following cases, the first involving a male posting as a female, the second a suspected female posting as a male:

i. A male subscriber on SWIP-L (Society for Women in Philosophy list) posted a message disagreeing with the general consensus that discourse on SWIP-L should be nonagonistic, commenting, "There's nothing like a healthy denunciation by one's colleagues every once in a while to get one's blood flowing, and spur one to greater subtlety and exactness of thought." He signed his message with a female pseudonym, however, causing another (female) subscriber to comment later, "I must confess to looking for the name of the male who wrote the posting that [Suzi] sent originally and was surprised to find a female name at the end of it." The female subscriber had (accurately) inferred that anyone actively advocating "denunciation by one's colleagues" was probably male.

ii. At a time when one male subscriber had been posting frequent messages to the WOMEN list, another subscriber professing to be a man posted a message inquiring what the list's policy was towards men participating on the list, admitting, "I sometimes feel guilty for taking up bandwidth." The message, in addition to showing consideration for the concerns of others on the list, was very attenuated in style and explicitly appreciative of the list: "I really enjoy this list (actually, it's the best one I'm on)." This prompted another (female) subscriber to respond, "Now that you've posed the question . . . how's one to know you're not a woman posing this question as a man?" Her suspicion indicates that on some level she recognized that anyone posting a message expressing appreciation and consideration for the desires of others was likely to be female.

The existence of gendered styles has important implications, needless to say, for popular claims that CMC is anonymous, "gender blind," and hence inherently democratic. If our online communicative style reveals our gender, then gender differences, along with their social consequences, are likely to persist on computer-mediated networks.[5]

Entire lists can be gendered in their style as well. It is tacitly expected that members of the nondominant gender will adapt their posting style in the direction of the style of the dominant gender. Thus men on women's special interest lists tend to attenuate their assertions and shorten their messages, and women, especially on male-dominated lists such as LINGUIST and PAGLIA-L, can be contentious and adversarial. Arguably, they must adapt in order to participate appropriately in keeping with the norms of the local list culture. Most members of the nondominant gender on any given list, however, end up style mixing, that is, taking on some attributes of the dominant style while preserving features of their native style — for example, with men often preserving a critical stance and women a supportive one at the macromessage level. This suggests that gendered communication styles are deeply rooted — not surprising, since they are learned early in life — and that some features are more resistant to conscious reflection and modification than others.

Different Communication Ethics

The second part of this essay concerns the value systems that underlie and are used to rationalize communicative behavior on the Net. In particular, I focus on the phenomenon of flaming, which has been variously defined as "the expression of strong negative emotion," use of "derogatory, obscene, or inappropriate language," and "personal insults." A popular explanation advanced by CMC researchers[6] is that flaming is a by-product of the medium itself — the decontextualized and anonymous nature of CMC leads to "disinhibition in users and a tendency to forget that there is an actual human being at the receiving end of one's emotional outbursts. However, until recently CMC research has largely overlooked gender as a possible influence on behavior, and the simple fact of the matter is that it is virtually only men who flame. If the medium makes men more likely to flame, it should have a similar effect on women, yet if anything the opposite appears to be the case. An adequate explanation of flaming must therefore take gender into account.

Women and men constitute different discourse communities in cyberspace.

Why do men flame? The explanation, I suggest, is that women and men have different communication ethics, and flaming is compatible with male ethical ideals. I stumbled upon this realization recently as a result of a survey I conducted on politeness on the Internet. I originally hypothesized that the differences in the extremes of male and female behavior online — in particular, the tendency for women to be considerate of the "face" needs of others while men threaten others' "face" — could be explained if it turned out that women and men have different notions of what constitutes appropriate behavior. In other words, as a woman I might think adversarial behavior is rude, but men who behave adversarially might think otherwise. Conversely, men might be put off by the supportive and attenuated behaviors of women.

In the survey, I asked subscribers from eight Internet discussion lists to rank their like or dislike for 30 different online behaviors, including "flaming," "expressing thanks and appreciation," and "overly tentative messages," on a scale of 1 (like) to 5 (dislike). The survey also asked several open-ended questions, including most importantly: "What behaviors bother you most on the Net?" [15]

My initial hypothesis turned out to be both correct and incorrect. It was incorrect in that I found no support whatsoever for the idea that men's and women's value systems are somehow reversed. Both men and women said they liked expressions of appreciation (avg. score of 2), were neutral about tentative messages (avg. about 3), and disliked flaming (although women expressed a stronger dislike than men, giving it a score of 4.3 as compared with only 3.9 for men). This makes male flaming behavior all the more puzzling. Should we conclude, then, that men who flame are deliberately trying to be rude?

The answers to the open-ended questions suggest a different explanation. These answers reveal a gender contrast in values that involves politeness but cannot be described in terms of politeness alone. It seems women place a high value on consideration for the wants and needs of others, as expressed in the following comment by a female Net user:

> If we take responsibility for developing our own sensitivities to others and controlling our actions to minimize damage—we will each be doing [good deeds] for the whole world constantly.

Men, in contrast, assign greater value to freedom from censorship (many advocate absolute free speech), forthright and open expression, and agonistic debate as a means to advance the pursuit of knowledge. Historically, the value on absolute freedom of speech reflects the civil libertarian leanings of the computing professionals who originally designed the Net and have contributed much of the utopian discourse surrounding it; the value on agonistic debate is rooted in the Western (male) philosophical tradition.

These ideals are stirringly evoked in the following quote from R. Hauben (1993) praising the virtues of the Usenet system, on which 95 percent of the contributors are estimated to be male:

> The achievement of Usenet News demonstrates the importance of facilitating the development of uncensored speech and communication—there is debate and discussion — one person influences another — people build on each other's strengths and interests, differences, etc.

One might think that uncensored speech if abused could cause problems, but M. Hauben (1993) explains that there is a democratic way of handling this eventuality:

> When people feel someone is abusing the nature of Usenet News, they let the offender know through e-mail. In this manner . . . people fight to keep it a resource that is helpful to society as a whole.

In daily life on the Internet, however, the ideal of "people fight[ing] to keep [the Net] a resource that is helpful to society as a whole" often translates into violent action. Consider, for example, the response of a male survey respondent to the question: "What behaviors bother you most on the Net?" (typos are in the original):

> As much as I am irritated by [incompetent posters], I don't want imposed rules. I would prefer to "out" such a person and let some public minded citizen fire bomb his house to imposing rules on the Net. Letter bombing a annoying individual's feed is usually preferable to building a formal heirarchy of Net cops.

Another Net vigilante responds graphically as follows:

> I'd have to say commercial shit. Whenever someone advertises some damn get-rich-quick scheme and plasters it all over the Net by crossposting it to

every newsgroup, I reach for my "gatling gun mailer crasher" and fire away at the source address.

These responses not only evoke an ideal of freedom from external author- 20 ity, they provide an explicit justification for flaming — as a form of self-appointed regulation of the social order, a rough-and-ready form of justice on the virtual frontier. Thus a framework of values is constructed within which flaming and other aggressive behaviors can be interpreted in a favorable (even prosocial) light. This is not to say that all or even most men who flame have the good of Net society at heart, but rather that the behavior is in principle justifiable for men (and hence tolerable) in ways that it is not for most women.

Netiquette

Further evidence that flaming is tolerated and justified within a system of male values comes from the content of written rules of network etiquette, or "netiquette," such as are available on many public FTP sites and in introductory messages to new members of some discussion lists. I analyzed the content of netiquette rules from six lists, along with those found in the guidelines for Usenet and in the print publication *Towards an Ethics and Etiquette for Electronic Mail*, by Norman Shapiro and Robert Anderson (1985). What do netiquette rules have to say about flaming?

The answer is: remarkably little, given that it is one of the most visible and frequently complained about "negatives" cited about the Internet. One might even say there is a striking *lack* of proscription against flaming, except on a few women-owned and women-oriented lists. And in the rare instances where flaming is mentioned, it is implicitly authorized. Thus the guidelines for new subscribers to the POLITICS list prohibit "flames of a personal nature," and Shapiro and Anderson advise, "Do not insult or criticize third parties without giving them a chance to respond." While on the surface appearing to oppose flaming, these statements in fact implicitly authorize "flames other than of a personal nature" (for example, of someone's ideas or values) and "insulting or criticizing third parties" (provided you give them a chance to respond!). Normative statements such as these are compatible with male values and male adversarial style; the intimidating rhetoric on LINGUIST and many other lists is not a violation of Net etiquette according to these rules.[7] Yet these are behaviors that female survey respondents say intimidate them and drive them away from lists and newsgroups. Can the Internet community afford to tolerate behaviors that intimidate and silence women? This is a question that urgently needs to be raised and discussed Net wide.

Conclusions

To sum up, I have argued that women and men constitute different discourse communities in cyberspace — different cultures, if you will — with differing communicative norms and practices. However, these cultures are not "separate but equal," as recent popular writing on gender differences in communication has claimed. Rather, the norms and practices of masculine Net culture, codified in netiquette rules, conflict with those of the female culture in ways that render cyberspace — or at least many "neighborhoods" in cyberspace — inhospitable to women. The result is an imbalance whereby men control a disproportionate share of the communication that takes place via computer networks.

This imbalance must be redressed if computer-mediated communication is ever to live up to its much-touted democratic potential. Fortunately, there are ways in which women can promote their concerns and influence the discourse of the Net;[8] I will mention three here. First and foremost is to participate, for example in women-centered lists. Such lists provide supportive fora for women online and are frequently models of cooperative discourse whose norms can spread if subscribers participate in other lists as well. But separatism has its disadvantages, among them the risk of ghettoization. Women must not let themselves be driven by flame throwers away from mainstream, mixed-sex fora, but rather should also actively seek to gain influence there, individually and collectively, especially in fora where metadiscourse about the Net itself takes place.

The second way to promote women's interests Netwide is to educate   25
online communities about the rhetorical strategies used in intimidating others, and to call people on their behavior and its consequences when they use such strategies.[9] This is already happening on some women-centered lists such as WMST-L and SWIP-L— aware of the tendency for a single man or group of men to dominate discussions, female subscribers call attention to this behavior as soon as they realize it is happening; interestingly, it is happening less and less often on these lists. Group awareness is a powerful force for change, and it can be raised in mixed-sex fora as well.

Finally, women need to contribute in any way they can to the process that leads to the encoding of netiquette rules. They need to instigate and participate persuasively in discussions about what constitutes appropriate and inappropriate behavior online — seeking to define in concrete terms what constitutes "flaming," for instance, since women and men are likely to have different ideas about this. They must be alert to opportunities (or make their own opportunities) to write out guidelines for suggested list protocol (or modifications to list protocol if guidelines already exist) and post them for discussion. No greater power exists than the power to define values, and the structure of the

Internet— especially now, while it is still evolving and seeking its ultimate definition —provides a unique opportunity for individual users to influence the normative process.

Indeed, it may be vital that we do so if women's online communication styles are to be valued along with those of men, and if we are to insure women the right to settle on the virtual frontier on their own — rather than on male-defined —terms.

Notes

This essay was originally delivered as a speech to the American Library Association as part of a panel entitled "Making the Net*Work*: Is there a Z39.50 in gender communication?", Miami, June 27, 1994. Copyright rests with the author.

1. A notable exception to this generalization is the work of Sherry Turkle in the 1980s on how women and men relate to computers.

2. For an extreme example of this phenomenon that took place on the soc.feminism Usenet newsgroup, see Sutton (1994).

3. Herring, Johnson, and DiBenedetto (1992, in press).

4. All names mentioned in the messages are pseudonyms.

5. This problem is discussed in Herring (1993a).

6. For example, Kiesler et al. (1984), Kim and Raja (1990), and Shapiro and Anderson (1985).

7. The discussion of politeness and communication ethics here is an abbreviated version of that presented in Herring (In press a, In press b).

8. For other practical suggestions on how to promote gender equality in networking, see Kramarae and Taylor (1993).

9. Cases where this was done, both successfully and unsuccessfully, are described in Herring, Johnson & DiBenedetto (In press).

References

Hauben, Michael. 1993. "The social forces behind the development of Usenet News." Electronic document. (FTP weber.ucsd.edu, directory/pub/usenet.hist)

Hauben, Ronda. 1993. "The evolution of Usenet News: The poor man's ARPANET." Electronic document. (FTP weber.ucsd.edu, directory/pub/usenet.hist)

Herring, Susan. 1992. "Gender and participation in computer-mediated linguistic discourse." Washington, DC: ERIC Clearinghouse on Languages and Linguistics, document no. ED345552.

Herring, Susan. 1993a. "Gender and democracy in computer-mediated communication." *Electronic Journal of Communication* 3(2), special issue on Computer-Mediated Communication, T. Benson, ed. Reprinted in R. Kling (ed.), *Computerization and Controversy*, 2nd ed. New York: Academic (In press).

Herring, Susan. 1993b. "Men's language: A study of the discourse of the Linguist list." In A. Crochetihre, J. -C. Boulanger, and C. Ouellon (eds.), *Les Langues Menacies: Actes du XVe Congres International des Linguistes*, Vol. 3. Quebec: Les Presses de I'Université Laval, 347–350.

Herring, Susan. In press a. "Politeness in computer culture: Why women thank and men flame." In M. Bucholtz, A. Liang, and L. Sutton (eds.), *Communicating In, Through, and Across Cultures: Proceedings of the Third Berkeley Women and Language Conference*. Berkeley Women and Language Group.

Herring, Susan. In press b. "Posting in a different voice: Gender and ethics in computer-mediated communication." In C. Ess (ed.), *Philosophical Perspectives on Computer-Mediated Communication*. Albany: SUNY Press.

Herring, Susan. In press c. "Two variants of an electronic message schema." In S. Herring (ed.), *Computer-Mediated Communication: Linguistic, social, and cross-cultural perspectives*. Amsterdam/Philadelphia: John Benjamins.

Herring, Susan, Deborah Johnson, and Tamra DiBenedetto. 1992. "Participation in electronic discourse in a 'feminist' field." In M. Bucholtz, K. Hall, and B. Moonwomon, eds., *Locating Power: Proceedings of the Second Berkeley Women and Language Conference*. Berkeley Women and Language Group.

Herring, Susan, Deborah Johnson, and Tamra DiBenedetto. In press d. "'This discussion is going too far!' Male resistance to female participation on the Internet." In M. Bucholtz and K. Hall, eds., *Gender Articulated: Language and the Socially-Constructed Self*. New York: Routledge.

Kiesler, Sara, Jane Seigel, and Timothy W. McGuire. 1984. "Social psychological aspects of computer-mediated communication." *American Psychologist*, 39, 1123–34.

Kim, Min-Sun, and Narayan S. Raja. 1990. "Verbal aggression and self-disclosure on computer bulletin boards." ERIC document (ED334620).

Kramarae, Cheris, and H. Jeanie Taylor. 1993. "Women and men on electronic networks: A conversation or a monologue?" In Taylor, Kramarae, and Ebben, eds., *Women, Information Technology and Scholarship*, 52–61. Urbana, IL: Center for Advanced Study.

Rheingold, Howard. 1993. *The Virtual Community: Homesteading on the Electronic Frontier*. Reading, MA: Addison-Wesley.

Seabrook, John. 1994. "My first flame." *The New Yorker*, June 6, 1994, 70–79.

Shapiro, Norman Z., and Robert H. Anderson. 1985. *Toward an Ethics and Etiquette for Electronic Mail*. The Rand Corporation.

Sutton, Laurel. 1994. "Using USENET: Gender, power, and silencing in electronic discourse." *Proceedings of the 20th Annual Meeting of the Berkeley Linguistics Society* (BLS-20). Berkeley: Berkeley Linguistics Society, Inc.

Turkle, Sherry. 1984. *The Second Self: Computers and the Human Spirit*. London: Granada.

Working with the Text

1. In the "Conclusions" section of her article, Susan Herring implies that the female style of computer-mediated communication (CMC) is preferable to the male style. Write a brief essay in which you analyze her position, arguing for or against it. What characteristics of the female style does she value? What characteristics of the male style does she think should be changed? Why? Do you agree with her? Why or why not?

2. Herring calls into question what she refers to as the "popular claims that CMC is anonymous, 'gender blind,' and hence inherently democratic" (par. 11). Based on your inferences from, as well as direct assertions in, the essay, analyze her argument. What about CMC does she consider to be undemocratic? What does her position on equality in communication reveal about her values?

3. To examine male and female styles in CMC, Herring analyzes messages she has found on online discussion lists. To test the currency of her analysis, find an online discussion list. Based on Herring's descriptions of gender differences in CMC, analyze the messages, using her examples as models. Develop your analysis into a brief paper. Prepare to share your findings with the entire class.

From Text to Field

1. By the time you enter college, many of you have participated in online discussions or chat rooms. With Herring's analysis of gender styles in mind, write a personal essay in which you describe your experience with computer-mediated communication (CMC). Have you noticed or have you yourself used some of the discourse features that Herring mentions in her article? If you have not participated in an online discussion, interview someone who has, first explaining Herring's arguments as a point of reference.

2. Review Herring's "Netiquette" section as well as her "Conclusions," where she discusses the need for protocols (etiquette and behavior guidelines) for computer-mediated communication. In a small group, draft a list protocol for a discussion group, then post it for discussion by sending it via e-mail or other electronic means to one other small group from the class. Individually, write a list protocol based on those online discussions. How would such a protocol differ from a protocol for effective in-class discussions? What makes communication that is not face-to-face more challenging to understand, maintain, and regulate?

3. After arguing that male styles of computer-mediated communication can exclude women, Herring raises the question, "Can the Internet community afford to tolerate behaviors that intimidate and silence women?" (par. 22). With Herring's descriptions of gender styles in mind, write an essay in which you answer this question from your own perspective.

4. In calling upon women to "promote their concerns and influence the discourse of the Net," Herring observes that "[no] greater power exists than the power to define values" (par. 26). In an essay, apply this statement to a situation from your own experience involving communication—online or off-line—in which you were either subject to someone else's values regarding acceptable styles of communication or able to participate in defining those values.

INTO THE FIELD: Options for Writing Projects

1. Facebook Culture on Your Campus

Although Facebook is widely used at colleges and universities across the country, each institution has what might be called its own "Facebook culture." For this field project, describe and assess the Facebook culture on your campus. Has that culture evolved over time, perhaps in response to concerns or incidents? What administrative policies (if any) are in place, and how does the administration view Facebook? Feel free to draw on national discussions about Facebook, but be sure to ground your assessment in the specifics of Facebook use on your particular campus.

2. Local Community Networks

When we consider community building through virtual means, we might easily think of worldwide communities or far-flung, but like-minded, people brought together by technology. But technology can also extend and augment the bond of local communities that already have some face-to-face social networking in place. This project invites you to explore one particular local community network. Such a network can function as part of local government; a civic or public interest group; a school or other local educational institution; a religious, arts, or recreational group; or most any other kind of citizen-based community information system.

For your own fieldwork, choose an online civic network that is functioning in your hometown or in the town where you now go to college, ideally a network in which you are already involved or in which you might have an interest. Your task is to evaluate the effectiveness of this online network in fostering stronger community.

You may wish to consider how such a network contributes to the presence of a public space for that group, how it might encourage discussion and deliberation in ways not possible by face-to-face meetings alone, and how such a civic network both relies on and contributes to social capital (that is, the trust and reciprocity needed to maintain community). How does the civic network you have chosen encourage deliberation on shared issues, expand participation, and develop local culture, pride, and community ownership? You may also wish to analyze why a particular civic network may fall short of those goals, despite the best of intentions.

As you conduct your fieldwork, you may wish to do more than navigate and analyze a Web site or electronic discussion list. Consider interviewing some of the key leaders in that civic network to learn more about the history of the group, its mission, and its reasons for developing an online presence of its members. You may even wish to query members on that very network about its effectiveness and its role in their lives and the life of their community. This project may have the added bonus of encouraging you to become more active in one or more networks in your community.

3. Bowling Alone

This field project is by no means reserved just for bowling aficionados. Rather, this project asks you to consider how technology might be strengthening or weakening the bonds that hold us together. In other words, does technology really provide any kind of social "glue"?

In a 1995 article "Bowling Alone," and in a subsequent book by the same title, Robert D. Putnam claims that for the last twenty or thirty years civic engagement has been declining and with it "social capital." Putnam notes that while bowling itself has grown in popularity, participation in organized bowling leagues has fallen dramatically. Putnam uses this observation as the touchstone for a broader argument: We have become increasingly disconnected from family and friends, from neighbors and local communities, and from our democratic structures. The stock of our social capital — those qualities that make our connections with each other possible — has dramatically declined. Putnam himself notes that the jury is still out on the role of technology. Will the Internet reinforce existing social networks (much as the telephone has done), or will it substitute for them, in virtual and all too often solitary ways?

For this field project, draw on your experience as you assess the current state of civic engagement and social capital. Does your experience differ from the experiences of your parents and your grandparents? What do you do alone? What role do groups and social ties have in your life? Do you find yourself living alone even as you live next to others? Do minority groups experience a heightened degree of isolation and, consequently, appreciate even more opportunities to associate with members of their group? To what extent does college life mirror the trends that Putnam discerns, or is the college environment a special case? Given these general questions, what is the effect of technology on your responses?

As you pursue your fieldwork, consider focusing on one kind of activity or one specific group or opportunity for association. Or, you may wish to focus on college life itself, where dorms, classes, and the local party scene might offer a certain kind of "glue" yet also hide or mask an underlying social isolation. What role does technology play on your campus in overcoming that isolation or contributing to it?

4. Building Campus Community on the Net

It may be tempting to assume that a college campus offers a ready-made community. But like all communities, the one on your campus requires ongoing maintenance and attention if it is to stay vibrant and avoid the fragmentation and dissention that can so easily occur. But even as we cling to the representations of community that we find in college brochures and public-relations materials, we also sense that communities are never quite as homogeneous as they might appear. Most college campuses offer multiple communities, each overlapping to some degree. Tension among these communities is a given and may in fact be healthy and normal. In short, even as we might speak of "the campus community," the real nature of that community may be far more divided and contentious than we would like to admit.

In an effort to foster community and greater cohesion on campus, administrators, faculty, and student leaders often turn to technology. E-mail, Web sites, and other forms of electronic communication are seen as new vehicles for creating and maintaining civic, social, and intellectual communities on campus. To facilitate such interaction some colleges have launched so-called Web portals, which offer ways for students and others to receive and communicate information, often in a very customized fashion.

This field project invites you to explore and assess the role of technology in building community on your campus. This issue is a broad one, so be sure to focus your efforts on one dimension or case study. Here are just a few examples:

- Evaluate the effectiveness of campus e-mail messages in building community.
- What role does your campus Web site or Web portal play in fostering community?
- Does your major's department use technology to make you feel invited into that disciplinary community?
- What role did (or could) technology play in helping you join and feel welcome in the campus community, especially during the period from acceptance through your first semester?
- How do student groups make use of technology to organize themselves? Could a particular group make more effective use of technology?
- How might a particular dorm or housing unit use technology to support face-to-face contact?
- Does technology minimize or exaggerate real or potential conflicts within campus communities?

Depending on your focus or issue and the audience involved, your project could take the form of a personal essay, an analytic or argumentative report, or a proposal for action.

5. Seat Time

When Neil Postman (p. 597) defends the idea that students should be educated in school, he is responding to the prospect that technology might liberate us from an educational tradition that roots instruction in time and place. Your own educational career, in school and now in college, was surely shaped by the notion that you should be educated in a certain place or class-room, for a certain number of hours. So pervasive is this thinking that much of education is planned, budgeted, and assessed in terms of one metric: the student credit hour, which itself is a measure of how much time you spend in a seat taking a particular course. In so many ways, education is reduced to "seat time."

This field project invites you to explore how technology is asking us to reassess "seat time." There are good reasons why technology might liberate us from seat time, for it facilitates such approaches as self-paced learning and distance education. Yet, even as we avail ourselves of technology, face-to-face meeting and, yes, seat time, may prove valuable in ways that we might easily underestimate. As you weigh these positions, you may find it helpful to focus your efforts around one case or instance of technology at work in education. Here are just a few of the many ways that you might ground your work:

- Is there a class you have taken in which seat time was not used productively and in which technology might have been an effective tool to release you from the constraints of time and place? Assess the course and the teaching style, and consider the prospect of technology as a tool for teaching and learning.
- Conversely, is there a class you have taken in which seat time was enor-mously valuable and technology, even if used, would not have dissuaded you from attending and actively participating? Assess the course and the teaching style, and consider the value of gathering as a class in one place at the same time.
- Have you encountered an experience in which educational technology was used either successfully or poorly in an effort to transcend seat time, as in an online course? Where did the success or failure lie, and what lessons might you have taken away from the experience?
- Writing instruction can and has benefited enormously from recent tech-nologies, which have prompted the development of new teaching methods and fresh ways for delivering courses. Even so, contact with fellow writers and your audience, even face-to-face contact, remains particularly valuable. As a writer and as a student in a writing course, how do you weigh both the value of traditional seat time and the prospects of new technologies?

6. Digital Classrooms . . . and Those Who Are in Them

When Neil Postman (p. 597) discusses the promises of the digital classroom (false promises, he would add), he also focuses attention on the kind of stu-dent such technology presumes, or may well create. These twin interests are captured in the title of his essay: "Virtual Students, Digital Classroom."

This field project encourages you to examine not just the technology you experience in the classroom but also the ways in which the uses of that technology construct roles and identities for both students and faculty. For the site of your fieldwork, choose one particular course in which classroom technology or the use of technology in assignments had an important presence. Here are some questions you may wish to consider:

- What does the technology assume about you and your teacher, in terms of your roles, responsibilities, and learning or teaching styles?
- In what ways does the technology bring out or encourage capacities and talents that might otherwise have remained dormant?
- In what ways might that technology construct roles and identities for you and others that you find uncomfortable or unproductive?
- What recommendations do you have—for the instructor and for fellow students—about how best to maximize the advantages of the technology and minimize its negative or unfortunate consequences?
- If the course you have chosen is a writing course, what role did the technology play in constructing you as a writer or as a particular kind of writer? In what ways did the technology help or hinder you in constructing a sense of your audience?

To answer these and other questions, you will need to look beyond the sheer use of technology and inquire into the ways that technology uses us, instructor and student alike.

You can present your findings either through a personal essay about your experiences in the course, a report about teaching and learning in digital classrooms, or a set of recommendations to the instructor or the department chair. Consider how your writing and analysis will need to change as you accommodate a particular audience or pursue a specific purpose.

7. Cyber Assumptions

This field project asks you to uncover, analyze, and respond to the assumptions that your college makes about what it expects of its entering students when it comes to computer knowledge relevant to the classroom. Although some of this information can be found in admissions and orientation materials, much of your work will involve close analysis of those expectations as they play out in specific courses, online tutorials, and computer labs. Much of your fieldwork may involve, not texts, but conversations and interviews.

Because this topic offers several different paths of inquiry, you may wish to select from the following incomplete list of options:

- Are the assumptions the college has about your cyberliteracy largely correct, or have they misjudged you or other students (either by assuming too much or too little)? Do these assumptions become visible only when they prove to be inaccurate? What should your college assume about the computer skills and cyberawareness of its entering students?

- What does your college assume about your access to computers and the Internet? Are those assumptions accurate? Have you ever found yourself on the wrong side of the "digital divide," not having the equipment or access that teachers or other students assumed that you did? How did this digital divide affect your performance, your attitudes, and your sense of self?

- Does your college offer a computer-skills course or an introduction to college life or an introduction to the library that seeks to establish some baseline competence with information technology? If so, was that course helpful or unnecessary? If not, would such a course prove useful?

- When considering computer literacy, there is a strong tendency to focus on discrete computer skills and slight the need for a critical, self-reflective awareness of the social and ethical dimensions of computer technology. Do you find this to be the case on your campus or in a particular course?

8. Internet Activism

Not only has the Internet added new dimensions to how we think of building community, it has also changed the face of civic and political activism. These changes are certainly visible on the national political scene, yet important lessons can also be learned from the local scene.

This field project invites you to study a specific instance of Internet activism on campus or in your community. Whether the issue involves a campus issue, a matter of local politics, a concern in the local schools, or a focused special-interest cause, your project should analyze how the technology involved made an impact on that particular instance of advocacy. Among many possible aspects, you may wish to address how the issue was brought to the Internet, what role that speed and reach played in mobilizing members or interested parties, what impact the Internet presence had on the audience being lobbied, what Internet response was elicited from those disagreeing with the campaign, and what relationship that one instance of Internet activism had to the group's overall activities and mission. The questions you ask will be specific to the instance of Internet activism you are studying. In some cases, a preexisting group may have used the Internet for activist purposes; in other instances, a loose coalition of people might have formed and then dissolved, only coming together to address one pressing concern. You may also wish to offer recommendations on how the Internet activism might have been improved or how certain errors or missteps might have been avoided.

To study an instance of Internet activism, you will need to have access to the conversation, of course. But beyond the conversation itself, you might find it productive to interview key players in this instance of Internet activism, and ask them for their reflections on how that medium influenced their strategies and purposes.

9. Chats, Blogs, and IM

Susan Herring's analysis of gender differences in computer-mediated communication (p. 608) is based on data drawn from e-mail-based academic listserv discussion groups in the early and mid-1990s. Even as the "familiar baggage of gender differences" remains recognizable a decade or more later, the new technological frontier that Herring explores continues to expand. Widely available today are forms of computer-mediated communication — chat rooms, blogs, and instant messaging — that were only beginning to catch on when Herring wrote her article.

This field project invites you to explore one or more of the issues raised by Herring — gender styles, identity, communication ethics, and language change — in technological arenas not discussed by Herring. Chat rooms, with their online, real-time conversation and with their opportunities to play with identity, offer an engaging environment for analysis. Blogs — sorts of hybrid diary and guide sites that are both personal and public—have likewise emerged as a new form of electronic communication that deserves closer analysis. Likewise, instant messaging heightens the speed of exchanges and has introduced new shorthand into our language. In addition to examining your own use of such technology, pay attention, as does Herring, to the actual language and conversational dynamics. Close analysis of concrete examples can launch you into engaging fieldwork more effectively than sticking to broad generalizations can.

Feel free to explore technologies or applications not listed here. Who knows what lies over the horizon? Your fieldwork is important in that it will address the need to assess the use of the latest technologies in light of perennial issues.

10. Computer-Mediated Communication in the Writing Class

As computer technologies and electronic communication become ever more central to writing courses, their use and effectiveness should become the concern not just of instructors and researchers but also of students of writing themselves. This field project offers a chance to reflect on the impact of technology in your writing class and in writing instruction on your campus.

Given the many possible directions this project could take, you will find it useful to focus on one particular issue or concern. Here are just a few possibilities:

- What role does or could computer-mediated communication play in collaboration or jointly authored projects?

- What impact does computer technology have for peer editing and the revision process?
- What are the opportunities — and the pitfalls — of using computers as you develop your information literacy or research skills?
- What new opportunities for publication and dissemination do computers offer?
- How do computers affect the communication between teacher and student, and among students themselves?

MINDING THE MACHINE

As we learn to use and maximize the potential of computers and other digital tools, our focus is surely on the instrumental: how to get the software or hardware to work, and how to minimize our own errors. If something goes wrong, we tend to blame ourselves, confessing our general clumsiness with technology. This unit invites you to look beyond our efforts to use machines well. More is at stake, as the unit title "Minding the Machine" suggests.

In addition to working the machine, we must understand how the machine works to influence our larger lives, even our minds. What role do digital tools play in shaping society and personal relations? How do these tools mold daily behaviors and activities? To answer these and other questions, we must do more than use the machine; we must become aware of its reach and its capacity for using us. In short, we must "mind the machine."

One further reason why we should be mindful of the reach and influence of digital tools is that those tools affect our thinking and learning. Not only do we sometimes ascribe intelligence to the machines, but those machines also both assist and shape our own intelligence. Here we discover a further meaning in the title of this unit. We are "minding the machine" in the sense that these tools have a mind (or so it sometimes seems) and work to influence our own.

Given the wordplay in the unit title, we will explore several areas in which we are "minding the machine." The first concerns education. Computers and other tools are shaping the face of learning, from preschool to college. Computers, the World Wide Web, and other digital tools open up new opportunities for accessing information and for simulating and testing our ideas. The networked computer becomes an extension of our own networked mind. It becomes a tool for thinking, not just a tool to be used when we think.

One key aspect of these tools is their ability to link one application or Web site to another. Such links have a powerful influence on how we organize and navigate the world of knowledge. Whereas our knowledge was at one time logical, linear, and hierarchical, the tools now invite us to operate in a different fashion: knowledge appears associative, lateral, and wildly democratic. With a mere click, we can access most anything, and most anyone can try to claim our attention and elicit our belief. Learning tools that capitalize on this technology do more than provide information; they shape the very way we learn.

Because our new digital tools provide ways of integrating images with text, the way we make arguments has become visual, not just verbal. For evidence, we need look no further than the latest presentation software, such as PowerPoint. With its animations and its array of bulleted lists, PowerPoint lends clarity, force, and even an air of cockiness and certainty to the most complex arguments. Yet so pervasive has this tool become that we must ask whether PowerPoint now has a role in shaping how we argue. In presenting what's on our minds, it may also have a role in shaping them.

New technologies for writing may not only be shaping our minds but also our collective sense of identity. As print makes way for digital media, we find that we are becoming a network culture. This transformation is challenging everything from our assumptions about cultural unity to the ways in which we think about intellectual property.

The three readings in this unit pick up on these themes as they challenge us to reflect on how we "mind our machines." Sven Birkerts cautions us that the very tools we find so helpful and powerful may have effects beyond our imagining. They might influence how we organize and navigate the world of knowledge, and even how we attend to and learn from artifacts and texts. The next reading takes up a particular software tool that has become especially pervasive in our culture: PowerPoint. Here, Ian Parker explores how and why the software tool was developed, and its possible effect on how we present — and shape — our thoughts. Says one of its developers: "Oh Lord, what have we done?" For Jay David Bolter it is but one small step from arguing that writing and writing technologies shape our mind to arguing that such technologies also write our culture. Bolter explores the late age of print, where print technologies vie with new digital media, creating cultural tensions that we experience in our daily lives.

Reflecting on Prior Knowledge

1. All of us entered the digital age not in one dramatic moment but in a series of small steps, chiefly as we learned our way around computers. Meet in groups of two or three and discuss how you first became acquainted with digital tools for writing and researching. What are children, at home or in school, learning about reading, accessing, and writing texts in a digital age? What is common and different in your experiences? How are your experiences different from what your parents learned about texts? Write an account of your childhood exposure to these tools or describe how today's children are likely to encounter the digital age.

2. As we navigate and read digital texts and Web sites, it is commonplace to find a host of links to other sites and resources. But even as we become adept at clicking on those links, we may not pause to consider how they affect our thinking and learning. In a journal entry, reflect on your use of hyperlinks. What kind of learning does a hypertext link make possible? What kind of intellectual navigation and exploration does it privilege, and what kind does it discourage?

3. Imagine the following scenario: You enter a meeting room or a lecture hall and discover that the next hour will be dominated by a PowerPoint presentation. In a journal entry that you can then share with your class, give voice to what goes through your mind as people take their seats and the lights are dimmed. What prior experiences with PowerPoint have you had—either constructing or listening to presentations—and how have those experiences influenced your attitudes toward this presentation software?

4. Growing up in the early twenty-first century, you are a product of what is becoming a "network culture." Meet in small groups and discuss what it means to be or to have been a network kid. What kind of culture—and cultural conflicts—have new digital tools produced? How has this network culture influenced your relationship to the world and your relationships with each other? Record your comments and observations—both positive and negative—so that you can report back to the class as a whole.

Perseus Unbound

Sven Birkerts

In 1992, Perseus 1.0, an interactive database published on CD-ROM and videodisc, became the hottest new resource for the study of ancient Greek culture. The impressive capacity and flexibility of Perseus accelerated the ongoing debate over the use of computer technology in education. "Perseus Unbound" is an excerpt from Sven Birkerts's 1994 book, *The Gutenberg Elegies: The Fate of Reading in an Electronic Age*. Referring to Johann Gutenberg, the German printer often credited with inventing movable type and thereby spawning the widespread availability of books, *Elegies* questions the wisdom of indiscriminately replacing print media with high-speed access to a limitless reservoir of information. A now-classic discussion about computers in the late age of print, *Elegies* continues to provoke consideration and debate well after its publication.

The Gutenberg Elegies continues to draw Birkerts, a writer specializing in literature and culture, into a debate that intensifies as technology makes further inroads into not only education, but also into the information gathering and thinking habits of the entire culture. In addition to books and collections of essays on literary subjects ranging from Tolstoy to twentieth-century literature, Birkerts has written articles for publications such as the *New York Times Sunday Book Review,* the *New Republic, Esquire, Atlantic Monthly,* and *Village Voice.* He was awarded the Citation for Excellence in Reviewing by the National Book Critics Circle and has received Guggenheim and Lila Wallace fellowships. Birkerts has taught writing and literature at Harvard University, Emerson College, and Amherst College, and is currently a lecturer at Mount Holyoke College and a member of the core faculty of the Bennington Writing Seminars.

Like it or not, interactive video technologies have muscled their way into the formerly textbound precincts of education. The videodisc has mated with the microcomputer to produce a juggernaut: a flexible and encompassing teaching tool that threatens to overwhelm the linearity of print with an array of option-rich multimedia packages. And although we are only in the early stages of implementation — institutions are by nature conservative — an educational revolution seems inevitable.

Several years ago in *Harvard Magazine,* writer Craig Lambert sampled some of the innovative ways in which these technologies have already been applied at Harvard. Interactive video programs at the Law School allow students to view simulated police busts or actual courtroom procedures. With a tap of a digit they can freeze images, call up case citations, and quickly zero-in on the relevant fine points of precedent. Medical simulations, offering the immediacy of video images and instant access to the mountains of data necessary for diagnostic assessment, can have the student all but performing surgery. And language classes now allow the learner to make an end run around tedious drill repetitions and engage in protoconversations with video partners.

The hot news in the classics world, meanwhile, is Perseus 1.0, an interactive database developed and edited by Harvard associate professor Gregory Crane. Published on CD-ROM and videodisc, the program holds, according to its publicists, "the equivalent of twenty-five volumes of ancient Greek literature by ten authors (one million Greek words), roughly four thousand glosses in the online classical encyclopedia, and a 35,000-word online Greek lexicon." Also included are an enormous photographic database (six thousand images), a short video with narration, and "hundreds of descriptions and drawings of art and archeological objects." The package is affordable, too: Perseus software can be purchased for about $350. Plugged in, the student can call up a text, read it side by side with its translation, and analyze any word using the Liddell-Scott lexicon; he can read a thumbnail sketch on any mythic figure cited in the text, or call up images from an atlas, or zoom in on color Landsat photos;° he can even study a particular vase through innumerable angles of vantage. The dusty library stacks have never looked dustier.

Although skepticism abounds, most of it is institutional, bound up with established procedures and the proprietorship of scholarly bailiwicks. But there are grounds for other, more philosophic sorts of debate, and we can expect to see flare-ups of controversy for some time to come. For more than any other development in recent memory, these interactive technologies throw into relief the fundamental questions about knowledge and learning.

Landsat photos: Photographs of earth from satellites; the Landsat program has satellites in orbit that survey the earth's natural resources and monitor ecological changes.

Not only what are its ends, but what are its means? And how might the means be changing the ends?

From the threshold, I think, we need to distinguish between kinds of knowl- 5 edge and kinds of study. Pertinent here is German philosopher Wilhelm Dilthey's distinction between the natural sciences (*Naturwissenschaften*), which seek to explain physical events by subsuming them under causal laws, and the so-called sciences of culture (*Geisteswissenschaften*), which can only understand events in terms of the intentions and meanings that individuals attach to them.

To the former, it would seem, belong the areas of study more hospitable to the new video and computer procedures. Expanded databases and interactive programs can be viewed as tools, pure and simple. They give access to more information, foster cross-referentiality, and by reducing time and labor allow for greater focus on the essentials of a problem. Indeed, any discipline where knowledge is sought for its application rather than for itself could only profit from the implementation of these technologies. To the natural sciences one might add the fields of language study and law.

But there is a danger with these sexy new options — and the rapture with which believers speak warrants the adjective — that we will simply assume that their uses and potentials extend across the educational spectrum into realms where different kinds of knowledge, and hence learning, are at issue. The realms, that is, of *Geisteswissenschaften*, which have at their center the humanities.

In the humanities, knowledge is a means, yes, but it is a means less to instrumental application than to something more nebulous: understanding. We study history or literature or classics in order to compose and refine a narrative, or a set of narratives about what the human
Here are a few reservations world used to be like, about how the world came to be
worth pondering. as it is, and about what we have been — and are — like
as psychological or spiritual creatures. The data — the facts, connections, the texts themselves — matter insofar as they help us to deepen and extend that narrative. In these disciplines the *process* of study may be as vital to the understanding as are the materials studied.

Given the great excitement generated by Perseus, it is easy to imagine that in the near future a whole range of innovative electronic-based learning packages will be available and, in many places, in use. These will surely include the manifold variations on the electronic book. Special new software texts are already being developed to bring us into the world of, say, Shakespeare, not only glossing the literature, but bathing the user in multimedia supplements. The would-be historian will step into an environment rich in choices, be they visual detailing, explanatory graphs, or suggested connections and sideroads. And so on. Moreover, once the price is right, who will be the curmudgeons who would deny their students access to the state of the art?

Being a curmudgeon is a dirty job, but somebody has to do it. Someone 10 has to hoist the warning flags and raise some issues that the fast-track prose-lytizers might overlook. Here are a few reservations worth pondering.

1. Knowledge, certainly in the humanities, is not a straightforward matter of access, of conquest via the ingestion of data. Part of any essential under-standing of the world is that it is opaque, obdurate. To me, Wittgenstein's° famous axiom, "The world is everything that is the case," translates into a recognition of otherness. The past is as much about the disappearance of things through time as it is about the recovery of traces and the reconstruc-tion of vistas. Say what you will about books, they not only mark the back-ward trail, but they also encode this sense of obstacle, of otherness. The look of the printed page changes as we regress in time; under the orthographic changes are the changes in the language itself. Old-style textual research may feel like an unnecessarily slow burrowing, but it is itself an instruction: It confirms that time is a force as implacable as gravity.

Yet the multimedia packages would master this gravity. For opacity they substitute transparency, promoting the illusion of access. All that has been said, known, and done will yield to the dance of the fingertips on the ter-minal keys. Space becomes hyperspace, and time, hypertime (*hyper-* being the fashionable new prefix that invokes the nonlinear and nonsequential "space" made possible by computer technologies). One gathers the data of otherness, but through a medium which seems to level the feel — the truth — of that otherness. The field of knowledge is rendered as a lateral and synchronic enterprise susceptible to collage, not as a depth phenome-non. And if our media restructure our perceptions, as McLuhan° and oth-ers have argued, then we may start producing generations who know a great deal of "information" about the past but who have no purchase on pastness itself.

Described in this way, the effects of interactive programs on users sound a good deal like the symptoms of postmodernism. And indeed, this recent cultural aesthetic, distinguished by its flat, bright, and often affectless assem-blages of materials may be a consequence of a larger transformation of sen-sibility by information-processing technologies. After all, our arts do tend to mirror who we are and anticipate what we might be becoming. Changes of this magnitude are of course systemic, and their direction is not easily dic-tated. Whether the postmodern "vision" can be endorsed as a pedagogic plat-form, however, is another question.

Wittgenstein's: Ludwig Wittgensten (1889–1951), an Austrian philosopher interested in language, thought, the mind, and reality.
McLuhan: Herbert Marshall McLuhan (1911–1980), a Canadian communication theorist and one of the pioneers in the study of media ecology.

2. Humanistic knowledge, as I suggested earlier, differs from the more instrumental kinds of knowledge in that it ultimately seeks to fashion a comprehensible narrative. It is, in other words, about the creation and expansion of meaningful contexts. Interactive media technologies are, at least in one sense, anticontextual. They open the field to new widths, constantly expanding relevance and reference, and they equip their user with a powerful grazing tool. One moves at great rates across subject terrains, crossing borders that were once closely guarded. The multimedia approach tends ineluctably to multidisciplinarianism. The positive effect, of course, is the creation of new levels of connection and integration; more and more variables are brought into the equation.

But the danger should be obvious: The horizon, the limit that gave defi- 15
nition to the parts of the narrative, will disappear. The equation itself will become nonsensical through the accumulation of variables. The context will widen until it becomes, in effect, everything. On the model of Chaos science, wherein the butterfly flapping its wings in China is seen to affect the weather system over Oklahoma, all data will impinge upon all other data. The technology may be able to handle it, but will the user? Will our narratives—historical, literary, classical—be able to withstand the data explosion? If they cannot, then what will be the new face of understanding? Or will the knowledge of the world become, perforce, a map as large and intricate as the world itself?

3. We might question, too, whether there is not in learning as in physical science a principle of energy conservation. Does a gain in one area depend upon a loss in another? My guess would be that every lateral attainment is purchased with a sacrifice of depth. The student may, through a program on Shakespeare, learn an immense amount about Elizabethan politics, the construction of the Globe theater, the origins of certain plays in the writings of Plutarch, the etymology of key terms, and so on, but will this dazzled student find the concentration, the will, to live with the often burred and prickly language of the plays themselves? The play's the thing —but will it be? Wouldn't the sustained exposure to a souped-up cognitive collage not begin to affect the attention span, the ability if not willingness to sit with one text for extended periods, butting up against its cruxes, trying to excavate meaning from the original rhythms and syntax? The gurus of interaction love to say that the student learns best by doing, but let's not forget that *reading* a work is also a kind of doing.

4. As a final reservation, what about the long-term cognitive effects of these new processes of data absorption? Isn't it possible that more may be less, and that the neural networks have one speed for taking in—a speed that

can be increased—and quite another rate for retention? Again, it may be that our technologies will exceed us. They will make it not only possible but irresistible to consume data at what must strike people of the book as very high rates. But what then? What will happen as our neural systems, evolved through millennia to certain capacities, modify themselves to hold ever-expanding loads? Will we simply become smarter, able to hold and process more? Or do we have to reckon with some other gain/loss formula? One possible cognitive response— call it the "SAT cram-course model"— might be an expansion of the short-term memory banks and a correlative atrophying of long-term memory.

But here our technology may well assume a new role. Once it dawns on us, as it must, that our software will hold all the information we need at ready access, we may very well let it. That is, we may choose to become the technicians of our auxiliary brains, mastering not the information but the retrieval and referencing functions. At a certain point, then, we could become the evolutionary opposites of our forebears, who, lacking external technology, committed everything to memory. If this were to happen, what would be the status of knowing, of being educated? The leader of the electronic tribe would not be the person who knew most, but the one who could execute the broadest range of technical functions. What, I hesitate to ask, would become of the already antiquated notion of wisdom?

I recently watched a public television special on the history of the computer. One of the many experts and enthusiasts interviewed took up the knowledge question. He explained how the formerly two-dimensional process of book-based learning is rapidly becoming three-dimensional. The day will come, he opined, when interactive and virtual technologies will allow us to more or less dispense with our reliance on the sequence-based print paradigm. Whatever the object of our study, our equipment will be able to get us there directly: inside the volcano or the violin-maker's studio, right up on the stage. I was enthralled, but I shuddered, too, for it struck me that when our technologies are all in place—when all databases have been refined and integrated—that will be the day when we stop living in the old hard world and take up residence in some bright new hyperworld, a kind of Disneyland of information. I have to wonder if this is what Perseus and its kindred programs might not be edging us toward. That program got its name, we learn from the brochure, from the Greek mythological hero Perseus, who was the explorer of the limits of the known world. I confess that I can't think of Perseus without also thinking of Icarus, heedless son of Daedalus, who allowed his wings to carry him over the invisible line that was inscribed across the skyway.

Working with the Text

1. In the course of his essay, Sven Birkerts draws important distinctions between knowledge and understanding. What is the relationship between these two terms? What role does information have in each?

2. In "Perseus Unbound," Birkerts's concern over how "the means" might "be changing the ends" centers on his view that "[i]n the humanities, knowledge is a means, yes, but it is a means less to instrumental application than to something more nebulous: understanding" (par. 8). As you reread the essay, infer his definition of "understanding" from his critique of the effects, or potential effects, of replacing books with technology. Write a brief essay in which you analyze Birkerts's concept of "understanding." What does it require? What can prevent it?

3. According to Birkerts, humanistic knowledge is "about the creation and expansion of meaningful contexts" (par. 14). His concern over access to proliferating amounts of information is that "[t]he context will widen until it becomes, in effect, everything" (par. 15). Review Birkerts's argument about context, in the second of his four reservations. Using examples from your own education and reading, write a brief essay in which you reflect on his argument. What does he mean by a "meaningful context," and why does he think it is essential? Do you consider a context of "everything" to be counter to an understanding of humanistic knowledge? Why or why not?

4. In the closing paragraph of "Perseus Unbound," Birkerts claims that "when our technologies are all in place—when all databases have been refined and integrated—that will be the day when we stop living in the old hard world and take up residence in some bright new hyperworld, a kind of Disneyland of information." In a brief essay, argue for or against Birkerts's position. Do you think technology will eventually entice us to "stop living in the old hard world"? Do you think our technologies create, or will create, "a Disneyland of information"?

From Text to Field

1. Birkerts raises the possibility that if the "field of knowledge is rendered as a lateral and synchronic enterprise susceptible to collage, not as a depth phenomenon . . . we may start producing generations who know a great deal of 'information' about the past but who have no purchase on pastness itself" (par. 12). Review the passage in which Birkert discusses this concern (the first of his four reservations). In a personal essay, reflect on your understanding of "pastness." Do you have a sense of "otherness"? If so, how does this sense color

the way you regard people, cultures, and events of the past? How do you experience the passage of time that precedes you by decades, centuries, millennia, millions or billions of years? How have books or primary documents and artifacts influenced this sense? How has computer-generated material influenced it?

2. Birkerts charges that information technologies may be responsible for tuning our sensibilities into the "flat, bright, and often affectless assemblages of materials" that he thinks characterize our culture and "mirror who we are and anticipate what we might be becoming" (par. 13). In an essay, present your own critique of the sensibility that dominates our culture. How would you characterize it? What do you think drives it? What does it say about "who we are" and "what we might be becoming"?

3. Birkerts's third reservation about information technology is that in pursuing breadth of knowledge, we will sacrifice depth. Drawing on your experience using information technology as well as on Birkerts's argument, write an essay in which you address the breadth versus depth issue from your point of view. How has this tension played itself out in one of your courses or in the college curriculum you are now studying?

4. In his fourth and final "reservation," Birkerts questions "the long-term cognitive effects of these new processes of data absorption" (par. 17). With Birkerts's discussion in mind, offer your own prediction of what the "long-term cognitive effects" might be. Consider answering one or both of the following questions posed by Birkerts:

   • "What will happen as our neural systems, evolved through millennia to certain capacities, modify themselves to hold ever-expanding loads?" (par. 17)
   • "[W]hat would be the status of knowing, of being educated? The leader of the electronic tribe would not be the person who knew most, but the one who could execute the broadest range of technical functions. What, I hesitate to ask, would become of the already antiquated notion of wisdom?" (par. 18)

Absolute PowerPoint: Can a Software Package Edit Our Thoughts?

Ian Parker

Producing and viewing PowerPoint presentations can be such a relief—difficult concepts seem comprehensible, complicated processes fall into a logical sequence, and mazes of information find form. In his 2001 article for the *New Yorker,* Ian Parker calls all of this ease and apparent clarity into question. What is PowerPoint doing to the way we think? Tracing the history of its development, Parker examines the needs and vulnerabilities that inspired, and still drive, PowerPoint and what its design helps us to avoid.

A staff writer for the *New Yorker,* Parker bases his critique on discussions with the originators and developers of PowerPoint technology as well as professionals and academics who have both used it and analyzed its influence on how we think and communicate. Since its publication, "Absolute PowerPoint" has been widely read as a source of commentary and debate in arenas ranging from business and technology to communication theory and cultural criticism. Parker's article is also frequently found on the syllabi of undergraduate and graduate courses in universities across the country.

Before there were presentations, there were conversations, which were a little like presentations but used fewer bullet points, and no one had to dim the lights. A woman we can call Sarah Wyndham, a defense-industry consultant living in Alexandria, Virginia, recently began to feel that her two daughters weren't listening when she asked them to clean their bedrooms and do their chores. So, one morning, she sat down at her computer, opened Microsoft's PowerPoint program, and typed:

FAMILY MATTERS

An approach for positive change to the Wyndham family team

On a new page, she wrote:

- Lack of organization leads to confusion and frustration among all family members.
- Disorganization is detrimental to grades and to your social life.
- Disorganization leads to inefficiencies that impact the entire family.

Instead of pleading for domestic harmony, Sarah Wyndham was pitching for it. Soon she had eighteen pages of large type, supplemented by a color photograph of a generic happy family riding bicycles, and, on the final page, a drawing of a key—the key to success. The briefing was given only once, last fall. The experience was so upsetting to her children that the threat of a second showing was enough to make one of the Wyndham girls burst into tears.

PowerPoint, which can be found on 250 million computers around the world, is software you impose on other people. It allows you to arrange text and graphics in a series of pages, which you can project, slide by slide, from a laptop computer onto a screen, or print as a booklet (as Sarah Wyndham did). The usual metaphor for everyday software is the tool, but that doesn't seem to be right here. PowerPoint is more like a suit of clothes, or a car, or plastic surgery. You take it out with you. You are judged by it — you insist on being judged by it. It is by definition a social instrument, turning middle managers into bullet-point dandies.

But PowerPoint also has a private, interior influence. It edits ideas. It is, almost surreptitiously, a business manual as well as a business suit, with an opinion — an oddly pedantic, prescriptive opinion— about the way we should think. It helps you make a case, but it also makes its own case: about how to organize information, how much information to organize, how to look at the world. One feature of this is the AutoContent Wizard, which supplies templates— "Managing Organizational Change" or "Communicating Bad News," say — that are so close to finished presentations you barely need to do more than add your company logo. The "Motivating a Team" template, for example, includes a slide headed "Conduct a Creative Thinking Session":

- Ask: In what ways can we . . . ?
  —Assess the situation. Get the facts.
  —Generate possible solutions with green light, nonjudgmental thinking.
  —Select the best solution.

The final injunction is "Have an inspirational close."

It's easy to avoid these extreme templates — many people do — as well as embellishments like clip art, animations, and sound effects. But it's hard to shake off AutoContent's spirit: Even the most easygoing PowerPoint template insists on a heading followed by bullet points, so that the user is shepherded toward a staccato, summarizing frame of mind, of the kind parodied, for example, in a PowerPoint Gettysburg Address posted on the Internet: "Dedicate portion of field — fitting!"

Because PowerPoint can be an impressive antidote to fear — converting public-speaking dread into moviemaking pleasure — there seems to be no great impulse to fight this influence, as you might fight the unrelenting animated paperclip in Microsoft Word. Rather, PowerPoint's restraints seem to be soothing — so much so that where Microsoft has not written rules, businesses write them for themselves. A leading U.S. computer manufacturer has distributed guidelines to its employees about PowerPoint presentations, insisting on something it calls the "Rule of Seven": "Seven (7) bullets or lines per page, seven (7) words per line."

Today, after Microsoft's decade of dizzying growth, there are great tracts of corporate America where to appear at a meeting without PowerPoint would be unwelcome and vaguely pretentious, like wearing no shoes. In darkened rooms at industrial plants and ad agencies, at sales pitches and conferences, this is how people are communicating: no paragraphs, no pronouns — the world condensed into a few upbeat slides, with seven or so words on a line, seven or so lines on a slide. And now it's happening during sermons and university lectures and family arguments, too. A New Jersey PowerPoint user recently wrote in an online discussion, "Last week I caught myself planning out (in my head) the slides I would need to explain to my wife why we couldn't afford a vacation this year." Somehow, a piece of software designed, fifteen years ago, to meet a simple business need has become a way of organizing thought at kindergarten show-and-tells. "Oh, Lord," one of the early developers said to me. "What have we done?"

Forty years ago, a workplace meeting was a discussion with your immediate 10 colleagues. Engineers would meet with other engineers and talk in the language of engineering. A manager might make an appearance — acting as an interpreter, a bridge to the rest of the company — but no one from the marketing or production or sales department would be there. Somebody might have gone to the trouble of cranking out mimeographs — that would be the person with purple fingers.

But the structure of American industry changed in the 1960s and '70s. Clifford Nass, who teaches in the Department of Communication at Stanford, says, "Companies weren't discovering things in the laboratory and then trying to convince consumers to buy them. They were discovering — or creating — consumer demand, figuring out what they can convince consumers they need, then going to the laboratory and saying, 'Build this!'

People were saying, 'We can create demand. Even if demand doesn't exist, we know how to market this.' SpaghettiOs is the great example. The guy came up with the jingle first: 'The neat round spaghetti you can eat with a spoon.' And he said, 'Hey! Make spaghetti in the shape of small circles!'"

As Jerry Porras, a professor of organizational behavior and change at Stanford Graduate School of Business, says, "When technologists no longer just drove the product out but the customer sucked it out, then you had to know what the customer wanted, and that meant a lot more interaction inside the company." There are new conversations: Can we make this? How do we sell this if we make it? Can we do it in blue?

America began to go to more meetings. By the early 1980s, when the story of PowerPoint starts, employees had to find ways to talk to colleagues from other departments, colleagues who spoke a different language, brought together by SpaghettiOs and by the simple fact that technology was generating more information. There was more to know and, as the notion of a job for life eroded, more reason to know it.

In this environment, visual aids were bound to thrive. In 1975, 50,000 overhead projectors were sold in America. By 1985, that figure had increased to more than 120,000. Overheads, which were developed in the mid-forties for use by the police, and were then widely used in bowling alleys and schools, did not fully enter business life until the mid-seventies, when a transparency film that could survive the heat of a photocopier became available. Now anything on a sheet of paper could be transferred to an overhead slide. Overheads were cheaper than the popular alternative, the 35-mm. slide (which needed graphics professionals), and they were easier to use. But they restricted you to your typewriter's font—rather, your secretary's typewriter's font—or your skill with **PowerPoint also has a private, interior influence.** Letraset and a felt-tipped pen. A businessman couldn't generate a handsome, professional-looking font in his own office.

In 1980, though, it was clear that a future of widespread personal computers—and laser printers and screens that showed the very thing you were about to print—was tantalizingly close. In the Mountain View, California, laboratory of Bell-Northern Research, computer-research scientists had set up a great mainframe computer, a graphics workstation, a phototypesetter, and the earliest Canon laser printer, which was the size of a bathtub and took six men to carry into the building—together, a cumbersome approximation of what would later fit on a coffee table and cost a thousand dollars. With much trial and error, and jogging from one room to another, you could use this collection of machines as a kind of word processor. 15

Whitfield Diffie had access to this equipment. A mathematician, a former peacenik, and an enemy of exclusive government control of encryption systems, Diffie had secured a place for himself in computing legend in 1976, when he and a colleague, Martin Hellman, announced the discovery of a new method of protecting secrets electronically — public-key cryptography. At Bell-Northern, Diffie was researching the security of telephone systems. In 1981, preparing to give a presentation with 35-mm. slides, he wrote a little program, tinkering with some graphics software designed by a BNR colleague, that allowed you to draw a black frame on a piece of paper. Diffie expanded it so that the page could show a number of frames, and text inside each frame, with space for commentary around them. In other words, he produced a storyboard — a slide show on paper — that could be sent to the designers who made up the slides, and that would also serve as a script for his lecture. (At this stage, he wasn't photocopying what he had produced to make overhead transparencies, although scientists in other facilities were doing that.) With a few days' effort, Diffie had pointed the way to PowerPoint.

Diffie has long gray hair and likes to wear fine English suits. Today, he works for Sun Microsystems, as an internal consultant on encryption matters. I recently had lunch with him in Palo Alto, and for the first time he publicly acknowledged his presence at the birth of PowerPoint. It was an odd piece of news: As if Lenin° had invented the stapler. Yes, he said, PowerPoint was "based on" his work at BNR. This is not of great consequence to Diffie, whose reputation in his own field is so high that he is one of the few computer scientists to receive erotically charged fan mail. He said he was "mildly miffed" to have made no money from the PowerPoint connection, but he has no interest in beginning a feud with an old friend. "Bob was the one who had the vision to understand how important it was to the world," he said. "And I didn't."

Bob is Bob Gaskins, the man who has to take final responsibility for the drawn blinds of high-rise offices around the world and the bullet points dashing across computer screens inside. His account of PowerPoint's parentage does not exactly match Diffie's, but he readily accepts his former colleague as "my inspiration." In the late 1970s and early '80s, Gaskins was BNR's head of computer-science research. A former Berkeley PhD student, he had a family background in industrial photographic supplies and grew up around overhead projectors and inks and gels. In 1982, he returned from a six-month overseas business trip and, with a vivid sense of the future impact of the Apple Macintosh and of Microsoft's Windows (both of which were in development), he wrote a list of fifty commercial possibilities — Arabic typesetting, menus, signs. And then he looked around his own laboratory and realized what had happened while he was away: Following Diffie's lead, his colleagues were trying to make overheads to pitch their projects for funding, despite the

---

Lenin: Vladimir Ilych Lenin (1870–1924), a Communist revolutionary in Russia.

difficulties of using the equipment. (What you saw was not at all what you got.) "Our mainframe was buckling under the load," Gaskins says.

He now had his idea: a graphics program that would work with Windows and the Macintosh, and that would put together, and edit, a string of single pages, or "slides." In 1984, he left BNR, joined an ailing Silicon Valley software firm, Forethought, in exchange for a sizable share of the company, and hired a software developer, Dennis Austin. They began work on a program called Presenter. After a trademark problem, and an epiphany Gaskins had in the shower, Presenter became PowerPoint.

Gaskins is a precise, bookish man who lives with his wife in a meticulously restored and furnished nineteenth-century house in the Fillmore district of San Francisco. He has recently discovered an interest in antique concertinas. When I visited him, he was persuaded to play a tune, and he gave me a copy of a forthcoming paper he had cowritten: "A Wheatstone Twelve-Sided 'Edeophone' Concertina with Pre-MacCann Chromatic Duet Fingering." Gaskins is skeptical about the product that PowerPoint has become — AutoContent and animated fades between slides — but he is devoted to the simpler thing that it was, and he led me through a well-preserved archive of PowerPoint memorabilia, including the souvenir program for the PowerPoint reunion party, in 1997, which had a quiz filled with in-jokes about font size and programming languages. He also found an old business plan from 1984. One phrase — the only one in italics — read, "Allows the content-originator to control the presentation." For Gaskins, that had always been the point: to get rid of the intermediaries— graphic designers — and never mind the consequences. Whenever colleagues sought to restrict the design possibilities of the program (to make a design disaster less likely), Gaskins would overrule them, quoting Thoreau. "I came into this world, not chiefly to make this a good place to live in, but to live in it, be it good or bad." 20

PowerPoint 1.0 went on sale in April 1987 — available only for the Macintosh, and only in black-and-white. It generated text-and-graphics pages that a photocopier could turn into overhead transparencies. (This was before laptop computers and portable projectors made PowerPoint a tool for live electronic presentations. Gaskins thinks he may have been the first person to use the program in the modern way, in a Paris hotel in 1992 — which is like being the first person ever to tap a microphone and say, "Can you hear me at the back?") The Macintosh market was small and specialized, but within this market PowerPoint— the first product of its kind — was a hit. "I can't describe how wonderful it was," Gaskins says. "When we demonstrated at trade shows, we were mobbed." Shortly after the launch, Forethought accepted an acquisition offer of fourteen million dollars from Microsoft. Microsoft paid cash and allowed Bob Gaskins and his colleagues to remain partly self-governing in Silicon Valley, far from the Microsoft campus, in Redmond, Washington. Microsoft soon regretted the terms of the deal; PowerPoint workers became known for a troublesome independence of spirit (and for rewarding themselves, now and then, with beautifully staged parties — caviar, string quartets, Renaissance-period fancy dress).

PowerPoint had been created, in part, as a response to the new corporate world of interdepartmental communication. Those involved with the program now experienced the phenomenon at first hand. In 1990, the first PowerPoint for Windows was launched, alongside Windows 3.0. And PowerPoint quickly became what Gaskins calls "a cog in the great machine." The PowerPoint programmers were forced to make unwelcome changes, partly because in 1990 Word, Excel, and PowerPoint began to be integrated into Microsoft Office — a strategy that would eventually make PowerPoint invincible — and partly in response to market research. AutoContent was added in the mid-nineties, when Microsoft learned that some would-be presenters were uncomfortable with a blank PowerPoint page—it was hard to get started. "We said, 'What we need is some automatic content!'" a former Microsoft developer recalls, laughing. "'Punch the button and you'll have a presentation.'" The idea, he thought, was "crazy." And the name was meant as a joke. But Microsoft took the idea and kept the name—a rare example of a product named in outright mockery of its target customers.

Gaskins left PowerPoint in 1992, and many of his colleagues followed soon after. Now rich from Microsoft stock, and beginning the concertina-collecting phase of their careers, they watched as their old product made its way into the heart of American business culture. By 1993, PowerPoint had a majority share of the presentation market. In 1995, the average user created four and a half presentations a month. Three years later, the monthly average was nine. PowerPoint began to appear in cartoon strips and everyday conversation. A few years ago, Bob Gaskins was at a presentations-heavy conference in Britain. The organizer brought the proceedings to a sudden stop, saying, "I've just been told that the inventor of PowerPoint is in the audience — will he please identify himself so we can recognize his contribution to the advancement of science?" Gaskins stood up. The audience laughed and applauded.

Cathleen Belleville, a former graphic designer who worked at PowerPoint as a product planner from 1989 to 1995, was amazed to see a clip-art series she had created become modern business icons. The images were androgynous silhouette stick figures (she called them Screen Beans), modeled on a former college roommate: a little figure clicking its heels; another with an inspirational light bulb above its head. One Screen Bean, the patron saint of PowerPoint—a figure that stands beneath a question mark, scratching its head in puzzlement — is so popular that a lawyer at a New York firm who has seen many PowerPoint presentations claims never to have seen one without the head-scratcher. Belleville herself has seen her Beans all over the world, reprinted on baseball caps, blown up fifteen feet high in a Hamburg bank. "I told my mom, 'You know, my artwork is in danger of being more famous than the *Mona Lisa*.'" Above the counter in a laundromat on Third Avenue in New York, a sign explains that no responsibility can be taken for deliveries to doorman buildings. And there, next to the words, is the famous puzzled figure. It is hard to understand the puzzlement. Doorman? Delivery? But perhaps this is simply how a modern poster clears its throat: Belleville has created the international sign for *sign*.

According to Microsoft estimates, at least thirty million PowerPoint presentations are made every day. The program has about 95 percent of the presentations-software market. And so perhaps it was inevitable that it would migrate out of business and into other areas of our lives. I recently spoke to Sew Meng Chung, a Malaysian research engineer living in Singapore who got married in 1999. He told me that, as his guests took their seats for a wedding party in the Goodwood Park Hotel, they were treated to a PowerPoint presentation: 130 photographs— one fading into the next every four or five seconds, to musical accompaniment. "They were baby photos, and courtship photos, and photos taken with our friends and family," he told me. 25

I also spoke to Terry Taylor, who runs a Web site called eBibleTeacher.com, which supplies materials for churches that use electronic visual aids. "Jesus was a storyteller, and he gave graphic images," Taylor said. "He would say, 'Consider the lilies of the field, how they grow,' and all indications are that there were lilies in the field when he was talking, you know. He used illustrations." Taylor estimates that 15 percent of American churches now have video projectors, and many use PowerPoint regularly for announcements, for song lyrics, and to accompany preaching. (Taylor has seen more than one sermon featuring the head-scratching figure.) Visitors to Taylor's site can download photographs of locations in the Holy Land, as well as complete PowerPoint sermons—for example, "Making Your Marriage Great":

- Find out what you are doing to harm your marriage and heal it.
- Financial irresponsibility
- Temper
- Pornography
- Substance abuse
- You name it!

When PowerPoint is used to flash hymn lyrics, or make a quick pitch to a new client, or produce an eye-catching laundromat poster, it's easy to understand the enthusiasm of, say, Tony Kurz, the vice president for sales and marketing of a New York–based Internet company, who told me, "I love PowerPoint. It's a brilliant application. I can take you through at exactly the pace I want to take you." There are probably worse ways to transmit fifty or a hundred words of text, or information that is mainly visual—ways that involve more droning, more drifting. And PowerPoint demands at least some rudimentary preparation: A PowerPoint presenter is, by definition, not thinking about his or her material for the very first time. Steven Pinker, the author of *The Language Instinct* and a psychology professor at the Massachusetts Institute of Technology, says that PowerPoint can give visual shape to an argument. "Language is a linear medium: one damn word after another," he says. "But ideas are multidimensional. . . . When properly employed, PowerPoint makes the logical structure of an argument more transparent. Two channels sending the same information are better than one."

Still, it's hard to be perfectly comfortable with a product whose developers occasionally find themselves trying to suppress its use. Jolene Rocchio, who is a product planner for Microsoft Office (and is upbeat about PowerPoint in general), told me that, at a recent meeting of a nonprofit organization in San Francisco, she argued *against* a speaker's using PowerPoint at a future conference. "I said, 'I think we just need her to get up and speak.'" On an earlier occasion, Rocchio said, the same speaker had tried to use PowerPoint and the projector didn't work, "and everybody was, like, cheering. They just wanted to hear this woman speak, and they wanted it to be from her heart. And the PowerPoint almost alienated her audience."

This is the most common complaint about PowerPoint. Instead of human contact, we are given human display. "I think that we as a people have become unaccustomed to having real conversations with each other, where we actually give and take to arrive at a new answer. We present to each other, instead of discussing," Cathy Belleville says. Tad Simons, the editor of the magazine *Presentations* (whose second-grade son used PowerPoint for show-and-tell), is familiar with the sin of triple delivery, where precisely the same text is seen on the screen, spoken aloud, and printed on the handout in front of you (the "leave-behind," as it is known in some circles). "The thing that makes my heart sing is when somebody presses the 'B' button and the screen goes black and you can actually talk to the person," Simons told me.

In 1997, Sun Microsystems' chairman and CEO, Scott McNealy, 30 "banned" PowerPoint (a ban widely disregarded by his staff). The move might have been driven, in part, by Sun's public-relations needs as a Microsoft rival, but, according to McNealy, there were genuine productivity issues. "Why did we ban it? Let me put it this way: If I want to tell my forty thousand employees to attack, the word *attack* in ASCII is forty-eight bits. As a Microsoft Word document, it's 90,112 bits. Put that same word in a PowerPoint slide and it becomes 458,048 bits. That's a pig through the python when you try to send it over the Net." McNealy's concern is shared by the American military. Enormously elaborate PowerPoint files (generated by presentation obsessives — so-called PowerPoint Rangers) were said to be clogging up the military's bandwidth. Last year, to the delight of many under his command, General Henry H. Shelton, the chairman of the Joint Chiefs of Staff, issued an order to U.S. bases around the world insisting on simpler presentations.

PowerPoint was developed to give public speakers control over design decisions. But it's possible that those speakers should be making other, more important decisions. "In the past, I think we had an inefficient system, where executives passed all of their work to secretaries," Cathy Belleville says. "But now we've got highly paid people sitting there formatting slides — spending hours formatting slides — because it's more fun to do that than concentrate on what you're going to say. It would be much more efficient to off-load that work onto someone who could do it in a tenth of the time, and be paid less. Millions of executives around the world are sitting there going, 'Arial? Times Roman? Twenty-four point? Eighteen point?'"

In the glow of a PowerPoint show, the world is condensed, simplified, and smoothed over — yet bright and hyperreal — like the cityscape background in a PlayStation motor race. PowerPoint is strangely adept at disguising the fragile foundations of a proposal, the emptiness of a business plan; usually, the audience is respectfully still (only venture capitalists dare to dictate the pace of someone else's slide show), and, with the visual distraction of a dancing pie chart, a speaker can quickly move past the laughable flaw in his argument. If anyone notices, it's too late — the narrative presses on.

Last year, three researchers at Arizona State University, including Robert Cialdini, a professor of psychology and the author of "Influence: Science and Practice," conducted an experiment in which they presented three groups of volunteers with information about Andrew, a fictional high-school student under consideration for a university football scholarship. One group was given Andrew's football statistics typed on a piece of paper. The second group was shown bar graphs. Those in the third group were given a PowerPoint presentation, in which animated bar graphs grew before their eyes.

Given Andrew's record, what kind of prospect was he? According to Cialdini, when Andrew was PowerPointed, viewers saw him as a greater potential asset to the football team. The first group rated Andrew four and a half on a scale of one to seven; the second rated him five; and the PowerPoint group rated him six. PowerPoint gave him power. The experiment was repeated, with three groups of sports fans that were accustomed to digesting sports statistics; this time, the first two groups gave Andrew the same rating. But the group that saw the PowerPoint presentation still couldn't resist it.

Again, Andrew got a six. PowerPoint seems to be a way for organizations to turn expensive, expert decision makers into novice decision makers. "It's frightening," Cialdini says. He always preferred to use slides when he spoke to business groups, but one high-tech company recently hinted that his authority suffered as a result. "They said, 'You know what, Bob? You've got to get into PowerPoint, otherwise people aren't going to respond.' So I made the transfer."

Clifford Nass has an office overlooking the Oval lawn at Stanford, a university   35
where the use of PowerPoint is so widespread that to refrain from using it is sometimes seen as a mark of seniority and privilege, like egg on one's tie. Nass once worked for Intel, and then got a PhD in sociology, and now he writes about and lectures on the ways people think about computers. But, before embarking on any of that, Professor Nass was a professional magician — Cliff Conjure — so he has some confidence in his abilities as a public performer.

According to Nass, who now gives PowerPoint lectures because his students asked him to, PowerPoint "lifts the floor" of public speaking: A lecture is less likely to be poor if the speaker is using the program. "What PowerPoint does is very efficiently deliver content," Nass told me. "What students gain is a lot more information— not just facts but rules, ways of thinking, examples."

At the same time, PowerPoint "lowers the ceiling," Nass says. "What you miss is the process. The classes I remember most, the professors I remember most, were the ones where you could watch how they thought. You don't remember what they said, the details. It was 'What an elegant way to wrap around a problem!' PowerPoint takes that away. PowerPoint gives you the outcome, but it removes the process."

"What I miss is, when I used to lecture without PowerPoint, every now and then I'd get a cool idea," he went on. "I remember once it just hit me. I'm lecturing, and all of a sudden I go, 'God! *The Wizard of Oz*! The scene at the end of *The Wizard of Oz*!'" Nass, telling this story, was almost shouting. (The lecture, he later explained, was about definitions of "the human" applied to computers.) "I just went for it — twenty-five minutes. And to this day students who were in that class remember it. That couldn't happen now: 'Where the hell is the slide?'"

PowerPoint could lead us to believe that information is *all* there is. According to Nass, PowerPoint empowers the provider of simple content (and that was the task Bob Gaskins originally set for it), but it risks squeezing out the provider of process — that is to say, the rhetorician, the storyteller, the poet, the person whose thoughts cannot be arranged in the shape of an AutoContent slide. "I hate to admit this," Nass said, "but I actually removed a book from my syllabus last year because I couldn't figure out how to PowerPoint it. It's a lovely book called *Interface Culture*, by Steven Johnson, but it's very discursive; the charm of it is the throwaways. When I read this book, I thought, My head's filled with ideas, and now I've got to write out exactly what those ideas are, and — they're not neat." He couldn't get the book into bullet points; every time he put something down, he realized that it wasn't quite right. Eventually, he abandoned the attempt, and, instead of a lecture, he gave his students a recommendation. He told them it was a good book, urged them to read it, and moved on to the next bullet point.

Working with the Text

1. Based on interviews with designers as well as critics and users of PowerPoint, Ian Parker observes that "[i]n the glow of a PowerPoint show, the world is condensed, simplified, and smoothed over — yet bright and hyperreal — like the cityscape background in a PlayStation motor race" (par. 32). Parker shares the view of one of his sources, Clifford Nass of the Department of Communication at Stanford University, that "PowerPoint empowers the provider of simple content . . . , but it risks squeezing out the provider of process . . . whose thoughts cannot be arranged in the shape of an AutoContent slide" (par. 39). Drawing on your experience with PowerPoint as well as on Parker's argument, write a brief essay in which you argue for or against his critique of PowerPoint and its effects on how we think.

2. Parker devotes part of his article to describing the impetus behind the development of PowerPoint, when advancements in technology coincided with a time when "America began to go to more meetings" (par. 13). As you reread the article, note the developments in the American business environment that created the need for more meetings. In a brief essay, analyze this development, explaining to a group of peers why it would give rise to the demands PowerPoint was designed to meet.

3. According to Parker, a sign of PowerPoint's influence over the "restraints" and "rules" of business presentations is "the 'Rule of Seven': 'Seven (7) bullets or lines per page, seven (7) words per line,'" rules created by a "leading U.S. computer manufacturer" that are now widely used in the business world (par. 8). In a small group, explore Parker's concerns by using the "Rule of Seven" to develop a PowerPoint presentation that captures his argument. At the end of the presentation, describe and discuss your experience with the "Rule" with the entire class. Did you find, as Parker suggests, that the rules were "soothing"? Were they confining? How did they influence the ways in which you thought about the article?

4. Review Parker's description of the Arizona State University experiment that asked subjects to assess the scholarship prospects of a fictional high school athlete named Andrew. Note the outcome of both phases of the experiment, as well as Parker's assertion that "PowerPoint seems to be a way for organizations to turn expensive, expert decision makers into novice decision makers" (par. 34). In a brief essay, analyze Parker's assertion. What does his assertion mean? How did he draw such a conclusion from the results of the experiment? Why did he end his account of this experiment with the story told by one of the researchers, Robert Cialdini, in which Cialdini was advised by representatives from a high-tech company to "'get into PowerPoint, otherwise people aren't going to respond'" (par. 34)?

From Text to Field

1. The use of PowerPoint has become so widespread that most of us have viewed, and even produced, a PowerPoint presentation. With Parker's critique in mind, write a personal essay in which you reflect on your experience of viewing or using PowerPoint. In what ways did it aid or constrain you? In what ways did it clarify or distort the content of the presentation or the process of your thinking?

2. In his critique of what he considers to be the limitations of PowerPoint, Parker makes a distinction between conveying simple content and capturing complex thought processes. Based on Parker's descriptions and your own experience of PowerPoint in the classroom or in other settings — such as religious organizations, athletic organizations, or clubs—write an essay in which you identify the kinds of rhetorical or communication situations in which you think PowerPoint would or would not work. Where and why would it be effective? Where and why would it be ineffective?

3. Parker points out that Bob Gaskins, the primary creator of PowerPoint, pressed for a design that "'Allows the content-originator to control the presentation.'" In spite of Gaskins's early efforts, PowerPoint became, according to Parker, a highly structured "antidote to fear." Drawing on your observations and knowledge of human behavior, as well as Parker's argument, write an essay in which you analyze the reasons for this course of development. Why would users prefer constraints rather than creative freedom?

4. Imagine that you are part of a marketing group proposing PowerPoint enhancements to Microsoft's software designers. Based on Parker's critique as well as your experience, what capabilities would you add to the program? What current capabilities would you consider changing or deleting altogether? Working with a small group, brainstorm the possibilities and agree on a brief proposal.

As a group, use PowerPoint to develop a presentation of your proposal to give to the class. To gain insight into Parker's contrast between simple content and complex process, try to incorporate both into your presentation. Be prepared to discuss your experience with the class.

Writing Culture

Jay David Bolter

As most of us focus on learning to work with rapidly evolving computer technologies, Jay David Bolter and his colleagues are asking how those technologies are shaping our minds and our cultures. For Bolter, the questions are as much historical and philosophical as they are social and cultural. How do electronic technologies of writing define cultural relationships? What are the differences between a print culture and a network culture, and what are the issues as we transition from one to the other? How are questions of intellectual property serving as barometers of this transition? Is cultural unity and stability possible—or even desirable — in the chaotic distributed system that is the new network culture? How will new technologies of writing shape culture, and how will that culture in turn shape writing?

"Writing Culture" is the final chapter in Bolter's 2001 book, *Writing Space: Computers, Hypertext, and the Remediation of Print* (an updated and revised second edition of his widely read and debated 1991 book, *Writing Space: The Computer, Hypertext, and the History of Writing*). The new edition reflects Bolter's current interest in "remediation," which he describes as "the ways in which new digital media refashion or 'remediate' older visual and verbal forms."

Bolter's education spans the study of Greek, computer science, and the classics. He is Wesley Professor of New Media in the School of Literature, Communications, and Culture at the Georgia Institute of Technology, where he also serves as director of the Center for New Media Research and Education. His primary interest is the computer as a new medium for verbal and visual communication. Other publications include *Turing's Man: Western Culture in the Computer Age* (1984), *Remediation: Understanding New Media* (1999, coauthored with Richard Grusin), and *Windows and Mirrors: Electronic Art, Design, and the Myth of Transparency* (2003, coauthored with Diane Gromala), along with numerous articles on reading, writing, and visualization in computer environments.

The Network Culture

Just as we can claim to write our minds, we can also claim to write the culture in which we live. And just as we have used print technology in the past, so we are now turning to electronic technologies of writing to define our cultural relationships both metaphorically and operationally. If, as Sherry Turkle (1995) and others have argued, electronic communication corresponds to a postmodern sense of self, it may also correspond to a postmodern definition of affiliation and community. We exploit the World Wide Web, e-mail, and chat rooms to facilitate a culture of temporary allegiances and changing cultural positions — to fashion our "network culture." The Internet and particularly the Web become for us a metaphor for the ways in which we function in our various communities by sending out dozens of links to sites of interest or contestation. We compile hot lists or bookmarks that indicate which groups we choose to belong to at any given moment, and we can erase these lists as casily as we create them.

It is a truism that American culture encourages individualism and therefore breaks with the European traditions of many of its immigrants. In the 1980s, before the explosion of interest in the Internet, the authors of *Habits of the Heart* saw contemporary, though not perhaps postmodern, individualism as the culmination of this historical process:

> [T]he colonists [to America] brought with them ideas of social obligation and group formation that disposed them to re-create in America structures of family, church, and polity that could continue . . . the texture of older European society. Only gradually did it become clear that every social obligation was vulnerable, every tie between individuals fragile. Only gradually did what we have called ontological individualism, the idea that the individual is the only firm reality, become widespread (Bellah, Madsen, Sullivan, Sundler, & Tipton, 1985, p. 276).

But if individuals become indeed "the only firm reality," this does not mean that American individuals would no longer form groups. Americans may well form more groups than ever, because they feel so much freer to associate and break off their associations as they please. Individuals now regularly join and quit jobs, neighborhoods, clubs, political parties and action committees, and even churches several times in their lives. These affiliations are all seen as voluntary, and they are usually horizontal rather than vertical. The network is displacing the hierarchy. The culture of interconnections both reflects and is reflected in our new technology of writing, so that, with all these transitions, the making and breaking of social links, people are beginning to function as elements in a hypertextual network of affiliations.

Electronic communication is increasingly the medium through which we form and maintain our affiliations. E-mail, chat rooms, and the World Wide Web have become sites for highly mediated versions of community. These new technologies join earlier ones that have promoted visions and versions of community: television, radio, and film as well as print. However, if our culture has chosen to exploit these earlier technologies largely for their ability to unify and homogenize cultural difference, we seem today to prefer to deploy electronic technologies in other ways, as interactive applications that allow individuals to talk back and talk to each other.

There is nothing inevitable about the construction of our network culture. 5 We could have chosen to exploit computers to reinforce traditional notions of community — perhaps by strengthening communication channels for existing institutional structures. What we have come to valorize in electronic communication, however, is largely the capacity to promote multiplicity, heterogeneity, and immediate, if temporary, connections. The popular writer Fred Rheingold argued in *Virtual Community* (1994) that news groups and bulletin boards could both reconstitute local communities and forge new groups from those who share common interests but are separated in space. He pointed to thousands or millions of users who have shared the vision of the virtual community since the prototype of such a community, the WELL, was formed in the San Francisco Bay area in the 1980s:

> People in virtual communities use words on screens to exchange pleasantries and argue, engage in intellectual discourse, conduct commerce, exchange knowledge, share emotional support, make plans, brainstorm, gossip, feud, fall in love, find friends and lose them . . . To the millions who have been drawn into it, the richness and vitality of computer-linked cultures is attractive, even addictive. There is no such thing as a single, monolithic, online subculture; it's more like an ecosystem of subcultures, some frivolous, some serious (p. 3).

Clearly what Rheingold values is the diversity that finds expression in these virtual environments, a diversity that is for him ultimately liberating on a political as well as personal level:

> The technology that makes virtual communities possible has the potential to bring enormous leverage to ordinary citizens at relatively little cost — intellectual leverage, social leverage, commercial leverage, and most important political leverage. But the technology will not in itself fulfill that potential; this latent technical power must be used intelligently and deliberately by an informed population. More people must learn about that leverage and learn to use it, while we still have the freedom to do so, if it is to live up to its potential (pp. 4–5).

For those, like Rheingold, who see the Internet and Web as enabling new forms of community or democratic empowerment, there remains the key problem that the technology is not universally available. Although it is called the "World Wide Web," this global hypertext system is largely limited to North America, Europe, Israel, and the developed countries of the Far East. As it continues to expand, the Web will likely remain limited to the middle and upper classes in the third world as elsewhere, so that the virtual communities that the Web and Internet mediate will remain exclusive as well. To say that these virtual communities will be exclusive, however, is not to say that they will be elite in the traditional sense. In developed countries, millions of users find on the Web expressions of their popular culture (from fan sites for film stars or country music divas to sites on weight loss or astrology) as well as their commodity culture (in online marketing and sales sites offering everything from books and CD-ROMs to fine wines or used cars). Traditional high culture is also represented, but has no special claim to the user's attention.

Cultural Unity

One consequence of this networking of culture is in fact the abandonment of the ideal of high culture (literature, music, the fine arts) as a unifying force. If there is no single culture, but only a network of interest groups, then there can be no single favored literature or music. Nor is there a single standard of grammar or diction in writing. Elizabeth Eisenstein (1979) has argued that printing was used to promote cultural unification during the centuries when the modern nation-states were being formed. "Typography arrested linguistic drift, enriched as well as standardized vernaculars, and paved the way for the more deliberate purification and codification of all major European languages" (vol. 1, p. 117). Today we are exploiting electronic writing to oppose standardization and unification as well as hierarchy. The World Wide Web is a famously chaotic distributed system, in which individuals or their organizations are free to create new pages and sites and to add them to the global hypertext without the approval or even the knowledge of any central authority. The Web offers as a paradigm a writing system that changes to suit its audiences of reader-writers rather than expecting that audience to conform to some predetermined authority or standard.

As we rewrite our culture into a vast hypertext, each of us as readers becomes free to choose to explore one subnetwork or as many as she wishes. It is no longer convincing to say that one subject is more important than another. Today even highly educated readers, humanists as well as scientists and social scientists, may know only one or a few areas well. Such ignorance of any shared textual tradition is in part the result of the specialization of the sciences that has been proceeding since the seventeenth century. But even the humanities are now utterly fragmented, so that a student of postcolonial literature may know very little about Renaissance poetry or ancient epic. The Web itself with its millions of pages is far too large and disorganized for any individual to encompass it, and the Web is still small in comparison with the verbal and visual information stored in a large research library, where the materials are much better organized but vastly beyond the scale of an individual reader.

Through the last decades there has remained some uneasiness about this situation: hence the traditionalist's plea for a canon of great authors, his call somehow to reestablish a core of textual knowledge that everyone must possess. But the specialization in the sciences and the humanities and social sciences has gone far too far to be recalled. The academic world, like the rest of our culture, is now defined by its numerous "special interest groups." Although all the groups are interconnected — some grew out of others, and each sends out runners (links) into other camps — nevertheless, an overarching unification is no longer even the goal. In *After Virtue*, published in 1981, just prior to the advent of electronic writing, Alasdair MacIntyre was already complaining about the fragmented state of moral philosophy and drew the following analogy (MacIntyre, 1981). Imagine an environmental catastrophe that causes human society to turn against modern science. Scientists are persecuted, and science texts are torn up or destroyed. Then imagine a later generation trying to reassemble these fragments ("half-chapters from books, single pages from articles, not always fully legible because torn and charred") into a single system. The result would be a mish-mash of incoherent theories and misunderstood facts. Of course, this disaster has not happened to modern science, but it is, according to MacIntyre, exactly what happened to the great systems of moral philosophy (pp. 2–3). For MacIntyre, the disaster was the Enlightenment. MacIntyre's analogy can be extended beyond moral philosophy to almost all humanistic fields today: Each is an incomplete and disorganized hypertext that no one knows how to read in its entirety.

To call this fragmentation a disaster, however, is to assume that unity is an achievable and desirable goal. In fact, the fragmentation of our textual world is only a problem when judged by the standards of print technology, which expects the humanities, including metaphysics and ethics, to be relatively stable and hierarchically organized. Postmodern culture values instead the heterogeneity and spontaneity of shifting positions — the ability to form small groups that fit local circumstances. Ironically, the global hypertext of the World Wide Web affords small groups just such an opportunity: groups with interests in dead languages, in local or national political problems, in any imaginable disease can each have Web sites. The tiniest political organization or interest group can afford to purchase space on a Web server somewhere in the world and to make that space available to its members. Hypertextual publication can and does accommodate all the mutually incomprehensible languages that the academic and political worlds now speak. Within the hypertextual libraries that are now being assembled, individual communities can retreat into their subnetworks and operate with as much or as little connection to each other as they desire.

On the World Wide Web, as elsewhere, the distinction between high culture and popular culture has all but vanished. If one click of the mouse will take a Web surfer to Project Gutenberg, a textual repository of the "classics" (www.gutenberg.net September 6, 1999), another click will take her to sites for current Hollywood movies or popular music on CD or to ostensibly marginal sites for body art or homeopathy. The ease and equality of access to all the various forms of cultural representation (including pornography) appall traditionalists, who want to see a hierarchy that reinforces the distinction between respectable literature and forbidden images. On the Web, however, none of the familiar indications of quality apply. A site on body piercing may be far better designed than the ASCII° format of Shakespeare's plays available through Project Gutenberg. An unwillingness to distinguish between high art and popular entertainment has long been a feature of American culture, and we have chosen to confirm and accelerate this trend in the Web and other new media forms.

The Remediation of Culture

Electronic forms of communication give us the opportunity to redefine cultural ideals inherited from printed genres and forms. We have been discussing one such redefinition: the breakdown of the distinction between elite and popular literature (and art in general). This breakdown was not determined or predetermined by our shift to electronic communications. It is rather that our network culture, which rejects such hierarchical distinctions, finds in the Internet and the Web media that it can shape to express its preference for popular forms. More generally, our network culture is construing new media as radical forces that disrupt the traditions of print.

For hundreds of years, we had associated with print an ideal of stability: Print was supposed to preserve and promote a stable, authoritative, and yet vital literate culture, in which tradition and innovation were in balance and in which verbal representations were of a higher order than visual. This is the ideal espoused in the late age of print by cultural traditionalists or political

---

ASCII: The acronym for American Standard Code for Information Interchange, a coding system based on the English alphabet that represents text in computer and digital devices.

conservatives from Sven Birkerts (1994) and Mark Slouka (1995) to William Bennett (1984). Just as there are many cultural constructions for electronic writing, however, there have also been many constructions for print. At various historical moments, print technology could in fact have been used to radicalize culture. The most obvious example would be the publication of printed tracts by Reformation theologians and polemicists (Eisenstein, 1979, pp. 303–450). Historian Carla Hesse (1996) has explored another historical moment, pointing out that Condorcet° and other Enlightenment thinkers also saw printed newspapers and periodicals as instruments of revolution:

> The best way to spread knowledge, according to Condorcet, was through authorless and open-ended texts, circulating freely between all citizens: He imagined the periodical press supported through the mechanism of subscription rather than through the institution of royalties to authors or monopolies to publishers. Indeed, what Condorcet conceived of as an ideally transparent mode of exchange through the deregulation of print publishing looks a lot like a mechanical version of the Internet (p. 24).

Although in the past print could be construed as radical, this is not its role today, according to either the critics of or the enthusiasts for electronic writing. In the late age of print, electronic technology defines itself as remediation, and print technology defines itself as resisting that remediation. Some enthusiasts for electronic writing still believe that it can radicalize our culture by providing that transparency that Condorcet ascribed to print publication. For these enthusiasts, the goal of perfect or authentic communication has not changed; they are simply pursuing the goal with new technological means. For them, electronic writing in chat rooms or by e-mail is more diverse and democratic, because unlike print, electronic writing can be published without the intervention of authorities (publishers and editors) who will decide on its commercial or intellectual value and therefore enforce cultural norms and biases. The traditionalists, too, still believe in authentic communication, but authenticity for them is defined differently. They favor their construction of print, with its traditions, its hierarchies, and its unidirectional form of communication. For them the authenticity of print derives from the privileged nature of the dialogue it fosters—a dialogue in which the author is necessarily dominant. As Laura Miller put it, in terms almost of sexual domination, readers in print crave "the intimacy to be had in allowing a beloved author's voice into the sanctums of

People are beginning to function as elements in a hypertextual network of affiliations.

15

Condorcet: Marie Jean Antoine Nicolas Caritat, marquis de Condorcet (1743–1794), a French philosopher, mathematician, and political scientist whose writings embody the ideals of the Enlightenment and rationalism.

our minds" (NY *Times*, 1998, p. 43). For Miller this "intimacy" is what constitutes an authentic reading experience.

To what extent do the technologies determine these different qualities that our culture is assigning? It seems clear that communication on the Internet could have evolved differently. Instead of diversity and distribution, communications systems on the Internet could have been designed to emphasize uniformity and central control. Computer systems after all can easily produce identical copies of data and establish and monitor the hierarchical control of information. In the 1980s, however, the Internet matured through the efforts of dedicated computer specialists, mostly graduate students and faculty in universities. They constructed a technology that was congenial to their culture, in which individual autonomy was highly prized. That the World Wide Web grew out of that same culture explains its distributed architecture, lack of security, and use of the hypertext model of associative linking. We can easily imagine a World Wide Web protocol in which all sites had to be registered and validated by a central authority, but that protocol would have contradicted the ethos of the Internet community at the time. By the time the Web had become a cultural phenomenon and attracted the attention of the corporate and government bureaucracies, it was too late to change its architecture radically. Control issues continue to be raised: for example, the questions of censoring pornography on the Web and of protecting intellectual property (or the economic interests of the entertainment industry). These questions are often met with the answer that the technology itself will defeat almost any method of censorship and that any means of protecting intellectual property must be evaluated in terms of what the technology, as constructed, will permit. The hierarchies of previous information technologies do not seem to be easily grafted onto the network technologies of today.

Theorists in the humanities and social sciences would, however, argue that hierarchies based on gender, race, and economic advantage remain strong in our culture. The late age of print is like late capitalism in this respect. It is a well-known irony that global capitalism is flourishing at the very time when it is being condemned by theorists to senescence. Similarly, in the late age of print, books and other printed materials are more abundant than ever: Laser printers and copying machines are largely responsible. Once again, the term "late" does not mean that print technology is necessarily about to disappear: It may continue to survive and even prosper for an undetermined future. The term refers instead to the relationship of print technology to our literate culture. The printed book is no longer the only or necessarily the most important space in which we locate our texts and images. For all our communicative purposes, print is now measured over against digital technology, and the ideal of perfect communication that our culture associated with print is under constant challenge.

That ideal is deeply ingrained, however, and may not be easily over-turned. The recent history of intellectual property shows us how tenacious the standard can be. The modern legal concepts of intellectual property and the ownership of ideas and their expression grew up in the eighteenth cen-tury and have developed since that time in the context of print technology (see Woodmansee & Jaszi, 1994). Many of these concepts fit comfortably into our current world of print, but do not seem to make sense for new media forms. In print, the words and images are determined once and for all in the process of publication, so that the expression of an idea fixed in words and images can be copyrighted. In the electronic writing space, as we have seen, words and images are not necessarily fixed; instead, they are called forth through the interaction of the author(s), the computer system, and the read-ers. Electronic documents can also be copied and altered with remarkable ease. On the World Wide Web, for example, every time a reader visits a page, she is in fact making a copy of that page, with all its images, in her computer. Although she cannot modify the page at its source (on the server), she can always save and even revise the version that she has captured on her machine.

If technologies really determined cultural values, then the notion of copy-right would already have been severely curtailed, if not abolished, at least for electronic publication. Hypertext certainly seems to suggest a different eco-nomic and social model (e.g., Samuelson & Glushko, 1991). And it could be argued that popular notions of intellectual property are in fact changing: People use copying machines, VCRs, and computer storage to make the copies that they require without much concern for legal propriety. Nevertheless, powerful economic forces (of late capitalism) are seeking to extend the notion of ownership of verbal and especially audiovisual materials throughout the realm of electronic media. They are seeking to set even stricter limits on the rights of readers and viewers to make fair use of copyrighted materials (Samuelson, 1997). Tyanna Herrington sees an ideological struggle around the question of intellectual property — a struggle between those who want to use electronic technologies to distribute information and entertain-ment for what they see as social benefit and those who want to insure eco-nomic gain for the (corporate) owners of information and entertainment. Rather than acknowledging that the notion of intellectual property is socially constructed, economic interests, with the help of the government, are insist-ing that electronic text, graphics, audio, and video are all property in a strict sense, sanctioned by a long legal tradition (see Herrington, forthcoming). Instead of withering in the electronic age, the notion of intellectual property seems to be strengthening and extending itself into new domains.

Our late age of print is characterized by such struggles, as economically   20
dominant groups and forces attempt to define the new technology to their

advantage, usually by extending definitions appropriate to earlier technologies that they already dominate. Notions of intellectual property are extrapolated from those appropriate to print and the music and film industries. Entertainment giants have been trying to "converge" new media around the model of commercial, broadcast television. Electronic commerce on the Internet has focused on reestablishing familiar genres and services: newspapers and magazines, bookstores, auctions, pornography, and so on. On the other hand, other constructions of new media are working subtly against the extension of older models of economic and cultural control. Our culture continues to find in these new forms, particularly in the Internet and on the World Wide Web, qualities of decentralization, local autonomy, and flexibility. It is for this reason that politicians from across the spectrum, at least in the United States, speak of the democratic and educational potential of the Internet: They are simply developing a rhetoric to which their constituents respond.

Thus, the reforming or remediating potential of the new writing space has probably not been exhausted. It would be foolish to doubt the power that entrenched hierarchies will bring to bear in forcing new media technologies into traditional formal, legal, and economic structures. Nevertheless, it seems likely that these traditional structures will be changed even as they attempt to assimilate new media. For example, those in the television and computer industry who are trying to promote Web television must find something to distinguish their product from pure broadcast television. So they are envisioning ways in which the Web could serve as an information resource for traditional television programs. They imagine a viewer watching a sporting event on television, having a question, and then using her browser to access a database of sports information while the television broadcast proceeds. As unimaginative as this scenario is, it nevertheless defines a changed relationship between the viewer and the viewing space. It presents an opening for the viewer to intervene in the flow of traditional television and suggests, however timidly, a myriad of other possibilities, other ways to arrange the act of communication.

It seems likely that our heterogeneous culture will choose to explore many of these possibilities — revised relationships between the media that we have known and the new media in which we are rediscovering the familiar. The future of text as a remediator of culture is uncertain, even if text (as hypertext) continues to serve a variety of functions in cyberspace. Textual forms such as e-mail, chat facilities, and even MOOs° remain popular precisely because of their role in defining electronic community. Teachers and scholars continue to promote these electronic textual forms as refashioners of the traditional

---

MOOs: An online system where multiple users are connected simultaneously.

sense of community that was (and is) mediated by face-to-face meetings and conventional mail. E-mail and chat facilities still provide most users with their best means of "talking back" in cyberspace. Although millions of World Wide Web participants now have the skills and opportunity to create their own Web sites combining graphics and text, a far larger number of the hundreds of millions of Internet users can still only be consumers of Web sites and other multimedia forms. That far larger number, however, can be producers as well as consumers of verbal e-mail. In other words, multimedia remains a somewhat privileged mode of communication within the already privileged world of the Internet.

This situation may change. Even for users at home, it is becoming easier to generate as well as receive multimedia. When most users gain fast access to the Internet and have the software and hardware needed for audiovisual communication, will they continue to type e-mail messages? Will they not seek to recapture the immediacy of phone and face-to-face conversation through real-time, video and audio conferencing over the Internet? Will they not look to other audiovisual media (television, film, and radio) as defining the authenticity of communication that they wish to capture and refashion in new media? Will written verbal communication come to be regarded as an ancillary form, to be used when microphones or cameras fail or when the Internet connection is degraded?

It is fair to wonder whether the late age of print may also become the late age of prose itself.

References

Bellah, R. N., Madsen, R., Sullivan, W. M., Swidler, A., & Tipton, S. M. (1985). *Habits of the heart: Individualism and commitment in American life.* Berkeley: University of California Press.

Bennett, W. J. (1984). *To reclaim a legacy: A report on the humanities in higher education.* Washington, DC: National Endowment for the Humanities.

Birkerts, S. (1994). *The Gutenberg elegies: The fate of reading in an electronic age.* Boston: Faber and Faber.

Eisenstein, E. (1979). *The printing press as an agent of change: Communications and cultural transformations in early-modern Europe (Vols. 1–2).* Cambridge: Cambridge University Press.

Herrington, T. K. (forthcoming). *Controlling voices: Dissonance at the intersection of intellectual property, the Internet, and humanistic studies.* Carbondale, IL: Southern Illinois University Press.

Hesse, C. (1996). Books in time. In Geoffrey Nunberg (Ed.), *The future of the book* (pp. 21–36). Berkeley: University of California Press.

MacIntyre, A. (1981). *After virtue: A study in moral theory.* Notre Dame, IN: University of Notre Dame Press.

Miller, L. (1998, March 15). *www.claptrap.com.* In *New York Times Book Review,* p. 43.

Rheingold, H. (1994). *The virtual community: Homesteading the electronic frontier.* New York: HarperCollins.

Samuelson, P. (1997, May). The never-ending struggle for balance. *Communications of the ACM 40(5):* 17–21.

Samuelson, P., & Glushko, R. J. (1991). Intellectual property rights for digital library and hypertext publishing systems: An analysis of Xanadu. In *Hypertext '91 Proceedings* (pp. 39–50). New York: ACM.

Slouka, M. (1995). *War of the worlds: Cyberspace and the high-tech assault on reality.* New York: Basic Books.

Turkle, S. (1995). *Life on the screen: Identity in the age of the Internet.* New York: Simon & Schuster.

Woodmansee, M., & Jaszi, P. (Eds.). (1994). *The construction of authorship: Textual appropriation in law and literature.* Durham, NC: Duke University.

Working with the Text

1. Jay David Bolter writes near the middle of his essay: "In the late age of print, electronic technology defines itself as remediation, and print technology defines itself as resisting that remediation" (par. 15). This observation contains two terms — *late age of print* and *remediation* — that are central to Bolter's view of how new technologies are "writing" cultural change. Reread the selection with these two terms in mind, and then in a brief essay, analyze what Bolter means by both terms. In what ways are these terms central to Bolter's argument?

2. Even as new media undermine the dominance of print media, disputes about intellectual property have become ever more contentious. In a brief essay, explain why. Why has the "remediation" of culture made intellectual property a pressing and high profile issue?

3. Bolter concludes his essay with a provocative statement: "It is fair to wonder whether the late age of print may also become the late age of prose itself." Bearing in mind Bolter's understanding of the term *late age*, write a brief essay in which you first explain and interpret this comment and then agree or disagree with it. Does Bolter mean all prose, or does he mean prose as defined or esteemed given particular values or qualities?

From Text to Field

1. Early in his essay, Bolter writes: "We exploit the World Wide Web, e-mail, and chat rooms to facilitate a culture of temporary allegiances and changing cultural positions — to fashion our 'network culture'" (par. 1). After comparing notes and observations in a small group, write an essay in which you describe

your own "network culture" or your attitude to the network culture you see around you. To what degree have you been influenced by the network culture you experience around you? How—and why—might you shift allegiances and positions? How or why might you resist such shifting?

2. Some see the fragmentation of our cultural world as disastrous. Bolter responds by asking whether cultural unity "is an achievable and desirable goal" (par. 11). Bolter continues by observing that "the fragmentation of our textual world is only a problem when judged by the standards of print technology, which expects the humanities, including metaphysics and ethics, to be relatively stable and hierarchically organized" (par. 11). In an essay, characterize the state of the textual world in which you live and study. Is it fragmented or relatively stable? What view of the textual world does your major discipline present? Do the courses you take reflect the fragmentation, or do they provide a narrative of stability and continuity?

3. Bolter asserts that "on the World Wide Web, as elsewhere, the distinction between high culture and popular culture has all but vanished" (par. 9). Can the same be said for your curriculum or for a particular course? In an essay, reflect on the tensions between and competing demands of high and popular culture. Has an interest in popular culture now become chic and an accepted part of, if not high culture, then the academic study of culture? What have we gained — and lost—through the softening of the distinction between high and popular culture?

INTO THE FIELD: Options for Writing Projects

1. **Reviewing a Hypertext or Multimedia Teaching Tool**

   Sven Birkerts's detailed discussion of the Perseus hypertext teaching tool on CD-ROM and how it affects learning (p. 632) offers the inspiration for this field project. Such teaching tools are becoming ever more commonplace, and the chances that you have or will encounter such a tool in your college courses increase each year. Your task is to evaluate a particular learning tool and its integration into a college course and, based on that evaluation, to offer recommendations regarding its future use or next edition. Bearing in mind Birkerts's reservations about such tools in certain kinds of courses, do you find that this tool enhances learning? Why might the tool be more or less effective than it seems at first? Does the tool suit certain learning styles but not others?

   The audience for this project could be either the professor of the course you are taking or have taken, the department chair in which the course is offered, the publisher of the teaching tool, or educators in that discipline. Given the possible audiences, your project could take shape as a substantive letter, a report, or a published review.

   One approach to this project is to work in teams of two or three. Even if you haven't used such a learning tool before or if you are not in the course or major where this tool is being used, your perspectives and feedback remain important. Indeed, you may be in a position to ask questions in ways not possible for someone closer to the field or to the particular tool. In addition to test driving the tool and analyzing its features, consider interviewing other students who have used the tool.

2. **Imagining a Digital Teaching Tool**

   This field project calls on your sense of the possible. It asks you to envision the application of new technology in a course you are taking or have taken recently. The course may already call on some technology as a teaching or learning tool or it may not currently use any technology at all. In either case, your task is to propose a new tool that will expand the teaching and learning in useful and productive ways.

   As you consider this opportunity, you will need to draw on your knowledge of what tools may be currently available and on your imaginative sense of what tools might yet be developed. The tool may involve the content of the course or may facilitate teaching, learning, and classroom collaboration in some way. Even as you explore a new world of technology, you will also need to pay close attention to the objectives of the course and what learning outcomes are desired. After all, what you are looking for is a tool that will enhance the course, not a tool that will create an altogether different course. You might find it useful to bear in mind Sven Birkerts's discussion (p. 632) about different kinds of knowledge (natural sciences and the sciences of culture) and the different kinds of learning involved in each.

As you develop your proposal, consider what needs, problems, or missed opportunities prompt you to offer your suggestion. After explaining the tool and its capabilities, offer a detailed rationale for its use in the course, given the course objectives. As you do so, be sure to acknowledge and respond to potential questions or reservations about your proposed tool.

3. Touching the Past

Given the glitz of new digital technologies in education, Sven Birkerts (p. 632) observes that "the dusty library stacks have never looked dustier" (par. 3). Yet for Birkerts, as for many who study and teach in the humanities, books, primary documents, and artifacts allow us a "recognition of otherness" (par. 11), a tangible sense of the course of time and the particularities of context. This sort of "depth perception" made possible through the humanities cannot be easily won through computer technologies that are largely lateral and synchronous.

This field project celebrates the pleasures of dust. It honors the old and the particular. Drawing on your major and your interests, this project begins by asking you to select an old book, magazine, or artifact. There are any number of opportunities for you to engage the past in ways that are concrete and tangible. Here are just a few possibilities:

- Visit the rare-book collection in your college library.
- Uncover old back issues of magazines (for example, *National Geographic, Life, Saturday Evening Post*) from the 1920s, 1930s, or 1940s.
- Spend time in the "heritage center" on your campus, where campus history is celebrated or archived.
- Familiarize yourself with the historical society in your local community.

Given these opportunities, what can you learn from the materiality or physical presence of these texts, documents, or artifacts that might be lost if you had simply seen them on a computer screen? What becomes tangible as you look at worn pages or encounter a time and place far removed from your own? In what ways is the "pastness" of earlier ages preserved by a print culture or by the preservation of actual artifacts, not just their digital representations? What does it mean to touch, feel, or witness in what is otherwise becoming a "virtual" age?

This field project can be developed as a substantial reflective essay or as a substantive proposal to incorporate the sort of fieldwork you have experienced into a particular course.

4. PowerPoint on PowerPoint

Having sat through more than a few PowerPoint presentations, you are most likely in a position to offer some comments on the software tool and a few suggestions as to its effective use. But instead of just enthusing or grousing out loud, or even writing a traditional essay on the tool, this field project offers the following challenge: Develop and offer a PowerPoint presentation about the benefits and possible drawbacks of using it.

The field project encourages some detailed reflection, and a good deal of self-awareness on your part, because it asks you to use the very tool on which you are commenting. Do not focus your talk on the nuts-and-bolts "how-to" issues of using the software; focus instead on evaluating the effectiveness of the tool and on some of its specific features. Here are a few questions to get you started:

- Given the various options and special effects available to you (e.g., color, sound, font and type size, animation, clip art), what are their potential contributions — and drawbacks — to a presentation? How can these features focus attention on the substance of a presentation, rather than proving to be a distraction?
- For what kinds of presentations is PowerPoint most well suited? Are there presentations whose purpose or goals do not match up well with PowerPoint? Where does your own presentation for this field project fit along this spectrum? Do some presentations have purposes or goals that would only be undermined by the use of PowerPoint?
- How can various kinds of audiences take in and use a PowerPoint presentation? How do you anticipate your current audience to use and respond to your presentation? In what ways might the use of PowerPoint constrain or limit its response?
- In many settings, the slides of a PowerPoint presentation, whether in electronic or hard copy form, become the official "document of record." That is, the presentation is often not about another document; it is the document itself. What are the advantages and disadvantages of such a practice? Does such a practice trade efficiency for complexity and nuance?
- What are appropriate strategies for connecting the text as it appears on your slides with your own verbal comments? What are the problems of reading verbatim off of the slides or of departing too far from them?

As you discuss the use of PowerPoint, you should both model best practices and illustrate common mistakes.

Because the presentation of your field project before a live audience can raise important issues or prompt new insights, follow up on your presentation with a revision of your work or, better yet, with a reflective essay in which you comment on the challenges and rewards of the project.

5. PowerPoint in the Classroom

Ian Parker's discussion of Microsoft's PowerPoint presentation software (p. 640) reminds us just how ubiquitous this tool has become. Having long dominated corporate boardrooms, PowerPoint has more recently made its appearance in the college lecture hall. There's a good chance that one or more of your professors use PowerPoint in your college courses. Your friends or roommates will likewise have a range of experiences about the use of PowerPoint in the classroom.

This field project invites you to evaluate and make recommendations regarding the use of PowerPoint in college classrooms. Here are just a few of the questions you might want to consider:

- In what type of class does the professor use PowerPoint? Is it a large class (more than two hundred students) or a moderately sized class (around fifty students)? What kind of delivery or teaching method is employed (lecture, lab, discussion, seminar, or some mixed model)? How do the capabilities of PowerPoint match the teaching and classroom environment?
- What discipline or subject matter is being taught? Is PowerPoint better suited for certain disciplines but not for others? Why?
- How is PowerPoint deployed and used in the actual teaching of the course? What relationship do the PowerPoint presentations have to the textbook and to the professor's own words and remarks? Does the professor read from the slides verbatim, or does the professor comment on them, perhaps ranging widely from what appears on the screen? What do the slides capture or fail to capture in the course?
- Are the PowerPoint slides available for printing or downloading from a Web site? If so, what effect does this have on attendance in the course? Does the presence of PowerPoint increase or diminish involvement or participation in the course?
- What role do the PowerPoint presentations have in testing and grading? What kinds of strategic decisions do you make regarding the material covered in the presentations as you study and learn?

Because you may have more than one class using PowerPoint, or you may be working collaboratively with others on this field project, you will likely have a range of classroom applications to study.

This field project draws together several avenues for research and study. In addition to familiarizing yourself with PowerPoint, you should take careful notes on the day-in, day-out use of PowerPoint in classroom teaching. You also might query or informally survey students about their responses to the use of PowerPoint in a particular classroom. Also consider interviewing the professor about his or her goals in using PowerPoint and how the tool might contribute to teaching and learning.

Your project might take shape as a substantive letter to the professor or department chair or a report to one of several offices on campus (they might go by names such as the Center for Teaching Excellence, the Office for Undergraduate Education, or the Office for Information and Technology Services).

6. Intellectual Property in the Digital Age

Because modern concepts of intellectual property developed in the context of print technology, the challenge to that technology by digital media has given issues of intellectual property fresh urgency. This field project invites you to explore some of those issues, based on your experience with print and digital media. Here are two possible ways in which you might focus your efforts:

- In the late age of print, print technologies and digital technologies coexist and compete. As a college student, you are likely submitting much of your work and writing in traditional ways, by turning in a hard copy of your writing that looks little different from something turned in decades ago. Yet your writing and research processes are shaped by digital technologies, with word-processing software and access to the Internet profoundly influencing how you write and how you use and reference the vast sea of texts that you navigate. This option for your field project has you reflect on how you use and produce text in college and on the advice and warnings you receive. What is your intellectual property, and how do you—or your fellow students —use the property of others?
- New multimedia technologies—and the ease of accessing and copying work circulated with those technologies—have given rise to everyday digital practices that can run counter to formal legal requirements regarding the use of those works. Witness, for example, the widespread practice of downloading and circulating music. This option for your field project has you explore intellectual property and everyday digital behavior. Are the two totally at odds, or have you and your friends negotiated informal rules and expectations about what is or isn't appropriate? How has life on a college campus influenced your everyday behaviors or your understanding of intellectual property? What new technologies or commercial options might help reduce conflicts in the future? How has your college campus treated the tension between intellectual property and everyday digital practice?

7. Portraits in Technology: Beyond Enthusiasts and Traditionalists

When we speak of our attitudes toward technology, it is common to express them in almost stereotypical terms. Indeed, we are fond of turning those attitudes into personalities. On the one hand, we have "the enthusiasts," who embrace new technologies and are often seen as hip and forward looking. On the other hand, we have "the traditionalists," who seem conservative and backward looking and may openly disdain technology. These traditionalists might even be referred to as "Luddites," after the bands of textile laborers who rioted in the early nineteenth century to protest how technology had changed their social and economic lives. Whatever the attitude, we are prone to attach a face to it.

This field project invites you to draw a more complex portrait, one that avoids caricature and stereotype and seeks out the mixed attitudes and reactions that most of us have about technology. For your portrait in words, you may profile either a professor or an instructor teaching on campus, a staff member working on campus, or one of your classmates.

As with any portrait or profile, your work becomes interesting insofar as you attend to detail, become aware of unexpected contradictions, and develop both a sympathetic and a discerning eye. You'll need to discover and represent the daily habits of technology use, not the recycled clichés that might be given about technology. How does the person you are profiling actually handle technology, and what might be the sources of that person's attitudes? As you look closely and write with sympathetic attention to detail, you will find a portrait emerging that avoids the extremes of "the enthusiast" and "the traditionalist."

8. University Libraries in the Late Age of Print

In the transition from the age of print to the digital age, no place on campus has felt the change quite as acutely as has your campus library. After all, libraries were developed in an age when their mission was to collect and store information in the form of manuscripts, books, and periodicals. Libraries were repositories, and the more they held, the better they were deemed to be. But the digital revolution is changing all of that. The focus is now moving to delivering materials rather than just collecting them, and that delivery can occur electronically to spaces far removed from the library itself.

These changes have raised the question of whether libraries—in their old incarnation—are even necessary anymore. Why have a library on campus when it seems that the computer in your dorm room or home can bring you a wealth of information? Clearly, we do need libraries; in the late age of print, digital offerings will by no means replace print materials entirely. Even so, libraries have been going through an identity crisis and are reassessing their roles on campus and in your education.

Given these developments, libraries on more than a few campuses are now presenting themselves as intellectual gathering places—idea cafés, as it were—

where the focus is on collaborative learning and on accessing and exchanging information, not on collecting and hoarding it. Libraries, with their hushed atmospheres, used to be places for hermits, for solitary academic experiences. Now more than a few libraries are reinventing themselves to invite students to partake in a social academic experience. Rooms for group collaboration—and even cafés—are now finding their way into library floor plans.

This field project invites you to join this reassessment of the academic library. Your ethnographic site will be your own campus library. You can frame your project either as a profile of how your library is navigating the challenges it faces in the late age of print or as a proposal for change and action.

Among the questions you may wish to ask: What does the floor plan, or any recent additions or renovations, tell you about the changing function of the library? How has the library's Web presence changed the habits and expectations of students and faculty? To what extent is your library a social gathering place or a place for collaborative work? How has the library modified its plans over time regarding the acquisition of materials? What strategic plans might the library have for the future? As you consider these questions, interview fellow students as well as librarians. Spend time in your library, and explore its physical—and virtual—spaces.

9. Writing Culture—and the Culture of Writing

Jay David Bolter (p. 654) concludes "Writing Culture" by offering the following comment: "It is fair to wonder whether the late age of print may also become the late age of prose itself."

This field project invites you to reflect on Bolter's remark. If technology helps write the culture in which we live how have digital tools changed, in turn, the culture of writing? As a student in a writing class, offer your insight on the "culture of writing" as you see it from your vantage point. What are you learning about, and how are you implementing, the new tools available to you? What promise might a writing class offer in the late age of print, and what burdens might it be under? How do you see writing treated, and practiced, in other courses on campus? If your campus has a writing center that offers student consultations, what role is accorded to technology and what stance, if only implicit, is taken toward digital tools? What are your day-to-day literacy behaviors, and how might they reflect the mixture of print and digital technologies? Is there a gap between your literacy behaviors and the formal writing class in which you participate? If so, is that gap a place for productive learning—or could it be?

This field project is an opportunity for you to assess your place, as a writer and as a college student, in the late age of print.

7

Seeing and Believing

MIND'S EYE

When we repeat, mindlessly perhaps, the cliché "seeing is believing," we are merely expressing a far more fundamental assumption that the world is "out there," ready to be perceived—and believed. And what we perceive, so this assumption goes, has nothing to do with our minds. There's much in our daily experience that, at first blush, would seem to confirm this assumption. Whether we are observing fall foliage or spring buds, artwork or photographs, we all too easily believe that what we see is what is there. Seeing is simply recording the external world; what we seek needs no composing of our own. Or so it seems.

This unit explores the connection between seeing and believing from the perspective of what the "mind's eye" contributes to our vision. Nature itself, and writing about nature, can be good starting points to question our naive assumptions about what it means to see. Close observation rarely happens by itself. To see nature, we must intervene, verbalizing what and how we perceive so that we might see all the more clearly. Yet the mind's eye in the process of observing nature can also play tricks on us, for we carry with us expectations about what we might find and how the natural world should look. Surprise and serendipity remain essential, and it turns out that we can do much to cultivate in ourselves a degree of watchfulness and readiness, a receptivity of mind.

If the natural world we see is forged as much from our responsiveness to it and readiness for it as from nature itself, the manner in which we see and respond to art offers a similar lesson. Consider crafted art objects. What we see and how we evaluate what we see are grounded in our response to art. We share in the creation, just as we appreciate art not so much for its imitation of nature as for its imitation of creation itself.

Photographs, the camera's supposedly neutral capture of the world around us, offer further cues on our role in shaping what we see. We often turn to photographs in the naive hope that they provide unbiased documentary evidence. But a cultural-studies focus on how we use photos, and how photos use us, suggests that seeing is a rather complicated act, tied not only to issues of belief but also to the role of images as a cultural commodity.

As our naive faith in what we see becomes less certain—whether it is nature, art, or photos—work in art history and the psychology of perception can teach us much about the role of culturally determined frames of reference in how we view the world.

These and related issues are explored in the four readings included here, which together help us explore the role of "the mind's eye" in what we see. Annie Dillard's essay "Seeing," from her Pulitzer Prize–winning book *Pilgrim at Tinker Creek*, invites us to see nature through the act of verbalization and written expression and to discover how such writing can send us back to nature with our eyes more open to its wonder. Using a small white wood-carved bird as his immediate example, John Berger reflects on how we respond to art and to nature and finds that the role of our own response is as telling as what we respond to. Photography, and commodified images that spring from photos, go far in defining, in cultural terms, how we see. Susan Sontag's classic essay on photography, "In Plato's Cave," explores how our culture uses photos and how photographic images shape our culture. The art historian E. H. Gombrich explores our desire for truth and accuracy in the ways in which we depict our world, yet he finds that what we draw or illustrate depends on stereotypes and schemas that help us understand the unfamiliar in terms of the already known.

Reflecting on Prior Knowledge

1. In a journal entry, recall a time when you were fascinated by observing something closely, be it in nature or in a lab. What kind of focus or concentration was required, and what kinds of insight or fruit did your sustained attention yield? What aided you in the process of close observation? Did you call upon deliberate and organized observation or general watchfulness and receptivity, or a combination of both?

2. What do you see when you look at a hand-crafted art object? If you have been astonished or pleased by that object, why was that the case? Does your response to images of nature, or to nature itself, parallel in any way your response to crafted art objects? What do you find pleasing or beautiful? In a journal entry that draws on your experience, respond to these questions about "aesthetic response."

3. Working in groups, share your early experiences with taking photos and being photographed. What do you find enjoyable or annoying about such experiences? As you share your thoughts, develop a catalog of the various reasons you or others take and circulate photos, and then share your catalog with the whole class.

4. All of us are forced to understand and explain the unfamiliar in terms of the familiar, the unknown in terms of what we already know. In a journal entry, explore one episode that captures this process. To what extent was your prior experience a useful frame of reference, and when and how might it have gotten in the way of understanding something new?

Seeing

Annie Dillard

We often segregate the senses from each other and from our mental and verbal worlds: Touching is touching; seeing is, well, seeing. We accord our senses a naive self-evidence. Annie Dillard looks more closely, more openly, and finds that "[s]eeing is of course very much a matter of verbalization."

Dillard started her writing life as a poet and spent some fifteen years composing poetry before she discovered the possibilities of seeing the world in and through nonfiction prose. Her essay on seeing is drawn from *Pilgrim at Tinker Creek*, which won the Pulitzer Prize for general nonfiction in 1974, when she was only twenty-nine years old. After nearly dying from pneumonia, Dillard began keeping a regular diary during her year-long stay in a cabin on the banks of Tinker Creek in Virginia's Roanoke Valley. Her lengthy entries would later form the basis of *Pilgrim at Tinker Creek*. A record of her observations and reflections on the natural world, the book is also a philosophical exploration.

Born Meta Annie Doak in Pittsburgh, Dillard received a BA and an MA from Hollins College. A keen observer throughout her life, Dillard has published two books of poems, *Tickets for a Prayer Wheel* (1974) and *Mornings like This: Found Poems* (1995). Her other publications include *Teaching a Stone to Talk* (1982), a collection of essays; *Living by Fiction* (1982), a book of theory; *An American Childhood* (1987), a memoir; and *The Living* (1992), a novel about pioneers on Puget Sound. In *The Writing Life* (1989), Dillard explores her life as a writer. She has taught at several universities, among them Wesleyan, and at a number of writers' workshops.

Seeing is of course very much a matter of verbalization. Unless I call my attention to what passes before my eyes, I simply won't see it. It is, as

Ruskin° says, "not merely unnoticed, but in the full, clear sense of the word, unseen." My eyes alone can't solve analogy tests using figures, the ones which show, with increasing elaborations, a big square, then a small square in a big square, then a big triangle, and expect me to find a small triangle in a big triangle. I have to say the words, describe what I'm seeing. If Tinker Mountain erupted, I'd be likely to notice. But if I want to notice the lesser cataclysms of valley life, I have to maintain in my head a running description of the present. It's not that I'm observant; it's just that I talk too much. Otherwise, especially in a strange place, I'll never know what's happening. Like a blind man at the ball game, I need a radio.

When I see this way I analyze and pry. I hurl over logs and roll away stones; I study the bank a square foot at a time, probing and tilting my head. Some days when a mist covers the mountains, when the muskrats won't show and the microscope's mirror shatters, I want to climb up the blank blue dome as a man would storm the inside of a circus tent, wildly, dangling, and with a steel knife claw a rent in the top, peep, and, if I must, fall.

But there is another kind of seeing that involves a letting go. When I see this way I sway transfixed and emptied. The difference between the two ways of seeing is the difference between walking with and without a camera. When I walk with a camera I walk from shot to shot, reading the light on a calibrated meter. When I walk without a camera, my own shutter opens, and the moment's light prints on my own silver gut. When I see this second way I am above all an unscrupulous observer.

It was sunny one evening last summer at Tinker Creek; the sun was low in the sky, upstream. I was sitting on the sycamore log bridge with the sunset at my back, watching the shiners the size of minnows who were feeding over the muddy sand in skittery schools. Again and again, one fish, then another, turned for a split second across the current and flash! the sun shot out from its silver side. I couldn't watch for it. It was always just happening somewhere else, and it drew my vision just as it disappeared: flash, like a sudden dazzle of the thinnest blade, a sparking over a dun and olive ground at chance intervals from every direction. Then I noticed white specks, some sort of pale petals, small, floating from under my feet on the creek's surface, very slow and steady. So I blurred my eyes and gazed towards the brim of my hat and saw a new world. I saw the pale white circles roll up, roll up, like the world's turning, mute and perfect, and I saw the linear flashes, gleaming silver, like stars being born at random down a rolling scroll of time. Something broke and something opened. I filled up like a new wineskin. I breathed an air like

---

Ruskin: John Ruskin (1819–1900), an English author, art critic, and social critic.

light; I saw a light like water. I was the lip of a fountain the creek filled for-ever; I was ether, the leaf in the zephyr; I was flesh-flake, feather, bone.

When I see this way I see truly. As Thoreau says, I return to my senses. I am the man who watches the baseball game in silence in an empty stadium. I see the game purely; I'm abstracted and dazed. When it's all over and the white-suited players lope off the green field to their shadowed dugouts, I leap to my feet; I cheer and cheer.

But I can't go out and try to see this way. I'll fail, I'll go mad. All I can do is try to gag the commentator, to hush the noise of use-less interior babble that keeps me from seeing just as surely as a newspaper dangled before my eyes. The effort is really a discipline requiring a lifetime of ded-icated struggle; it marks the literature of saints and monks of every order East and West, under every rule and no rule, discalced and shod. The world's spir-itual geniuses seem to discover universally that the mind's muddy river, this ceaseless flow of trivia and trash, cannot be dammed, and that trying to dam it is a waste of effort that might lead to madness. Instead you must allow the muddy river to flow unheeded in the dim channels of consciousness; you raise your sights; you look along it, mildly, acknowledging its presence with-out interest and gazing beyond it into the realm of the real where subjects and objects act and rest purely, without utterance. "Launch into the deep," says Jacques Ellul,° "and you shall see."

The secret of seeing is, then, the pearl of great price.

The secret of seeing is, then, the pearl of great price. If I thought he could teach me to find it and keep it forever I would stagger barefoot across a hun-dred deserts after any lunatic at all. But although the pearl may be found, it may not be sought. The literature of illumination reveals this above all: Although it comes to those who wait for it, it is always, even to the most prac-ticed and adept, a gift and a total surprise. I return from one walk knowing where the killdeer nests in the field by the creek and the hour the laurel blooms. I return from the same walk a day later scarcely knowing my own name. Litanies hum in my ears; my tongue flaps in my mouth Ailinon,° alleluia! I cannot cause light; the most I can do is try to put myself in the path of its beam. It is possible, in deep space, to sail on solar wind. Light, be it par-ticle or wave, has force: You rig a giant sail and go. The secret of seeing is to sail on solar wind. Hone and spread your spirit till you yourself are a sail, whetted, translucent, broadside to the merest puff.

Jacques Ellul (1912–1994): A French philosopher, sociologist, and theologian whose key concern was the threat to freedom and faith created by modern technology.

Ailinon: In classical Greek, Ailinon refers to a dirge or cry of grief. By juxtaposing Ailinon with alleluia, Dillard highlights her mixed feelings of loss and exaltation.

When her doctor took her bandages off and led her into the garden, the girl who was no longer blind saw "the tree with the lights in it." It was for this tree I searched through the peach orchards of summer, in the forests of fall and down winter and spring for years. Then one day I was walking along Tinker Creek thinking of nothing at all and I saw the tree with the lights in it. I saw the backyard cedar where the mourning doves roost charged and transfigured, each cell buzzing with flame. I stood on the grass with the lights in it, grass that was wholly fire, utterly focused and utterly dreamed. It was less like seeing than like being for the first time seen, knocked breathless by a powerful glance. The flood of fire abated, but I'm still spending the power. Gradually the lights went out in the cedar, the colors died, the cells unflamed and disappeared. I was still ringing. I had been my whole life a bell, and never knew it until at that moment I was lifted and struck. I have since only very rarely seen the tree with the lights in it. The vision comes and goes, mostly goes, but I live for it, for the moment when the mountains open and a new light roars in spate through the crack, and the mountains slam.

Working with the Text

1. Annie Dillard speaks of two ways or modes of seeing: a seeing in which we "analyze and pry" and a seeing that requires of us a "letting go." How does Dillard define each mode? How are they related? Might they be mutually dependent? Are there moments in Dillard's essay when she calls on one type of seeing and then the other?

2. Dillard's writing craft relies on both an accumulation of concrete details and on general statements or maxims. Review Dillard's essay to explore how she relates the two levels, the particular and the abstract. How is a cascade of particular observations framed by other passages? How are general statements of truth exemplified or concretized so that they ring true for readers?

3. Dillard speaks of the need "to gag the commentator, to hush the noise of useless interior babble" (par. 6). Why is this so? Nevertheless, Dillard asserts that "[s]eeing is of course very much a matter of verbalization" (par. 1). Explain this apparent contradiction. What is the proper role for words in the process of seeing?

4. At several moments in her essay, Dillard calls upon the language of religious mysticism and spiritual illumination. Why? How does she weave such references into her writing in ways that might make them compelling to readers with a range of religious beliefs?

From Text to Field

1. In a brief essay, try out Dillard's observational and stylistic techniques. After closely analyzing how she shuttles between concrete particulars and more abstract or general statements, try to render this effect yourself. You might think of this as an invitation to imitate Dillard or to write a *pastiche*—a literary, artistic, or musical work that imitates the style of previous work.

2. We are often blinded by preconceptions or assumptions that inhibit our ability to see clearly or freshly. For this reason, Dillard's essay invites us to slow down and become a scrupulous observer. Write a brief essay in which you offer and comment on an instance in which you needed to experience, or in which you benefited from, such close observation. The example may come from your connection to the natural world, or it may come from a realm seemingly far removed from Dillard's Tinker Creek.

3. In some sense, Dillard's essay is less about what she sees and more about the very process of seeing itself. Review Dillard's essay for her suggestions and comments on that process. Write an essay in which you lay out, step by step, what you see as her advice, her recommended method. Then, continue the essay by considering what might be incomplete or misleading about the very method you have abstracted. What does any "recipe" or "algorithm" for seeing succeed or fail to capture? Alternatively, instead of a conventional essay, consider offering your advice in the form of an actual "recipe for seeing." Then annotate or gloss the recipe (perhaps with side bars or hyperlinks) to comment on the shortcomings of that recipe. What are the ingredients for or steps in seeing? Can good observational techniques prepare you to see better? If so, what are the limits of such techniques?

The White Bird

John Berger

The relationship between art and society, between making or seeing and underlying cultural and social conditions, has been at the heart of John Berger's life and work. Born in London in 1926, Berger has led a distinguished and varied career as an essayist, novelist, painter, and art historian. After studies at the Central and Chelsea Schools of Art, he worked as a painter and drawing teacher. Even as he turned his attention to writing, he has continued to paint all of his life.

In 1952, Berger began writing for London's *New Statesman* and quickly became established as an influential art and cultural critic. He has published a number of books and collections of essays on art criticism, including the well-known *Ways of Seeing* (1972), which was turned into a television series by the BBC. He has also written *About Looking* (1980), a collection of essays on culturally and historically influenced interpretation; *Art and Revolution* (1969), on the role of revolutionary art in transforming society; *Keeping a Rendezvous* (1991) and *The Sense of Sight* (1992), two anthologies of essays; and *The Success and Failure of Picasso* (1965), a critical reassessment of the twentieth century's most famous artist. Berger's Marxist orientation and his own artistic background are also ever present in his four novels, among them *G* (1971), a story of migrant workers in Europe, which won the coveted Booker Prize in 1972. Berger has also written three screenplays and four plays.

For the past quarter century, Berger has lived in a small village in the French Jura alps. Fascinated by the artistic traditions and way of life of such mountain communities, he has written about them in both his fiction and nonfiction. Berger's essay "The White Bird," from the collection *The Sense of Sight,* draws on peasant art to explore the relationships among art, nature, and society.

From time to time I have been invited by institutions—mostly American—to speak about aesthetics. On one occasion I considered accepting and I thought of taking with me a bird made of white wood. But I didn't go. The problem is that you can't talk about aesthetics without talking about the principle of hope and the existence of evil. During the long winters the peasants in certain parts of the Haute Savoie° used to make wooden birds to hang in their kitchens and perhaps also in their chapels. Friends who are travelers have told me that they have seen similar birds, made according to the same principle, in certain regions of Czechoslovakia, Russia, and the Baltic countries. The tradition may be more widespread.

The principle of the construction of these birds is simple enough, although to make a fine bird demands considerable skill. You take two bars of pine wood, about six inches in length, a little less than one inch in height and the same in width. You soak them in water so that the wood has the maximum pliability, then you carve them. One piece will be the head and body with a fan tail, the second piece will represent the wings. The art principally concerns the making of the wing and tail feathers. The whole block of each wing is carved according to the silhouette of a single feather. Then the block is sliced into thirteen thin layers and these are gently opened out, one by one, to make a fan shape. Likewise for the second wing and for the tail feathers. The two pieces of wood are joined together to form a cross and the bird is complete. No glue is used and there is only one nail where the two pieces of wood cross. Very light, weighing only two or three ounces, the birds are usually hung on a thread from an overhanging mantelpiece or beam so that they move with the air currents.

It would be absurd to compare one of these birds to a van Gogh self-portrait or a Rembrandt crucifixion. They are simple, homemade objects, worked according to a traditional pattern. Yet, by their very simplicity, they allow one to categorize the qualities which make them pleasing and mysterious to everyone who sees them.

First there is a figurative representation—one is looking at a bird, more precisely a dove, apparently hanging in midair. Thus, there is a reference to the surrounding world of nature. Secondly, the choice of subject (a flying bird) and the context in which it is placed (indoors where live birds are unlikely) render the object symbolic. This primary symbolism then joins a more general, cultural one. Birds, and doves in particular, have been credited with symbolic meanings in a very wide variety of cultures.

Thirdly, there is a respect for the material used. The wood has been fashioned according to its own qualities of lightness, pliability, and texture. Looking

₅

Haute Savoie: A district in southeastern France, near the Alps and bordering on Switzerland and Italy.

at it, one is surprised by how well wood becomes bird. Fourthly, there is a formal unity and economy. Despite the object's apparent complexity, the grammar of its making is simple, even austere. Its richness is the result of repetitions which are also variations. Fifthly, this man-made object provokes a kind of astonishment: How on earth was it made? I have given rough indications above, but anyone unfamiliar with the technique wants to take the dove in his hands and examine it closely to discover the secret which lies behind its making.

These five qualities, when undifferentiated and perceived as a whole, provoke at least a momentary sense of being before a mystery. One is looking at a piece of wood that has become a bird. One is looking at a bird that is somehow more than a bird. One is looking at something that has been worked with a mysterious skill and a kind of love.

Thus far I have tried to isolate the qualities of the white bird which provoke an aesthetic emotion. (The word *emotion*, although designating a motion of the heart and of the imagination, is somewhat confusing for we are considering an emotion that has little to do with the others we experience, notably because the self here is **Art does not imitate nature,** in a far greater degree of abeyance.) Yet my defini- **it imitates a creation.** tions beg the essential question. They reduce aesthetics to art. They say nothing about the relation between art and nature, art and the world.

Before a mountain, a desert just after the sun has gone down, or a fruit tree, one can also experience aesthetic emotion. Consequently we are forced to begin again—not this time with a man-made object but with the nature into which we are born.

Urban living has always tended to produce a sentimental view of nature. Nature is thought of as a garden, or a view framed by a window, or as an arena of freedom. Peasants, sailors, nomads have known better. Nature is energy and struggle. It is what exists without any promise. If it can be thought of by man as an arena, a setting, it has to be thought of as one which lends itself as much to evil as to good. Its energy is fearsomely indifferent. The first necessity of life is shelter. Shelter against nature. The first prayer is for protection. The first sign of life is pain. If the Creation was purposeful, its purpose is a hidden one which can only be discovered intangibly within signs, never by the evidence of what happens.

It is within this bleak natural context that beauty is encountered, and the 10 encounter is by its nature sudden and unpredictable. The gale blows itself out, the sea changes from the color of grey shit to aquamarine. Under the fallen boulder of an avalanche a flower grows. Over the shanty town the moon rises. I offer dramatic examples so as to insist upon the bleakness of the context. Reflect upon more everyday examples. However it is encountered, beauty is always an exception, always *in despite of.* This is why it moves us.

It can be argued that the origin of the way we are moved by natural beauty was functional. Flowers are a promise of fertility, a sunset is a reminder of fire and warmth, moonlight makes the night less dark, the bright colors of a bird's plumage are (atavistically even for us) a sexual stimulus. Yet such an argument is too reductionist, I believe. Snow is useless. A butterfly offers us very little.

Of course the range of what a given community finds beautiful in nature will depend upon its means of survival, its economy, its geography. What Eskimos find beautiful is unlikely to be the same as what the Ashanti° found beautiful. Within modern class societies there are complex ideological determinations: We know, for instance, that the British ruling class in the eighteenth century disliked the sight of the sea. Equally, the social use to which an aesthetic emotion may be put changes according to the historical moment: The silhouette of a mountain can represent the home of the dead or a challenge to the initiative of the living. Anthropology, comparative studies of religion, political economy, and Marxism have made all this clear.

Yet there seem to be certain constants which all cultures have found 'beautiful': among them—certain flowers, trees, forms of rock, birds, animals, the moon, running water . . .

One is obliged to acknowledge a coincidence or perhaps a congruence. The evolution of natural forms and the evolution of human perception have coincided to produce the phenomenon of a potential recognition: What *is* and what we can see (and by seeing also feel) sometimes meet at a point of affirmation. This point, this coincidence, is two-faced: What has been seen is recognized and affirmed and, at the same time, the seer is affirmed by what he sees. For a brief moment one finds oneself—without the pretensions of a creator—in the position of God in the first chapter of Genesis . . . And he saw that *it was* good. The aesthetic emotion before nature derives, I believe, from this double affirmation.

Yet we do not live in the first chapter of Genesis. We live—if one follows   15 the biblical sequence of events—after the Fall. In any case, we live in a world of suffering in which evil is rampant, a world whose events do not confirm our Being, a world that has to be resisted. It is in this situation that the aesthetic moment offers hope. That we find a crystal or a poppy beautiful means that we are less alone, that we are more deeply inserted into existence than the course of a single life would lead us to believe. I try to describe as accurately as possible the experience in question; my starting point is phenomenological, not deductive; its form, perceived as such, becomes a message that one receives but cannot translate because, in it, all is instantaneous.

Ashanti: A major ethnic group in West Africa; the Ashanti Confederacy was a major state in precolonial Africa, in what is now Ghana.

For an instant, the energy of one's perception becomes inseparable from the energy of the creation.

The aesthetic emotion we feel before a man-made object — such as the white bird with which I started — is a derivative of the emotion we feel before nature. The white bird is an attempt to translate a message received from a real bird. All the languages of art have been developed as an attempt to transform the instantaneous into the permanent. Art supposes that beauty is not an exception — is not *in despite of* — but is the basis for an order.

Several years ago, when considering the historical face of art, I wrote that I judged a work according to whether or not it helped men in the modern world claim their social rights. I hold to that. Art's other, transcendental face raises the question of man's ontological right.

The notion that art is the mirror of nature is one that only appeals in periods of skepticism. Art does not imitate nature, it imitates a creation, sometimes to propose an alternative world, sometimes simply to amplify, to confirm, to make social the brief hope offered by nature. Art is an organized response to what nature allows us to glimpse occasionally. Art sets out to transform the potential recognition into an unceasing one. It proclaims man in the hope of receiving a surer reply . . . the transcendental face of art is always a form of prayer.

The white wooden bird is wafted by the warm air rising from the stove in the kitchen where the neighbors are drinking. Outside, in minus 25°C, the real birds are freezing to death!

Working with the Text

1. At the outset of his essay, John Berger notes that when he has been invited to speak about aesthetics, he has most often declined. "The problem," he says, "is that you can't talk about aesthetics without talking about the principle of hope and the existence of evil" (par. 1). How does this statement hint at the motivation behind Berger's essay and the direction that it will take? As you ponder this question, you might want to consult one or two dictionaries for definitions of *aesthetics*. To what extent is Berger's essay a response to or a corrective for such definitions? By addressing hope and evil, how does Berger enlarge our notion of aesthetics?

2. Roughly halfway through his essay, having already talked about the white bird itself, Berger raises the question of the relation of art to nature and to the world and confesses that "we are forced to begin again" (par. 8). The essay has in this sense two beginnings. How does the structure of the essay underline the argument Berger is making? Why the contrast? The very last paragraph of the essay brings the two parts together, only to highlight the difference

between the crafted white birds and the real birds coping with subzero temperatures. How does Berger's final comment reflect the structure of his argument? Likewise, how does that final comment speak to questions of hope and evil that he raises in the opening paragraph?

3. In the penultimate paragraph of Berger's essay, he addresses the complex relationship between art and nature: "Art does not imitate nature, it imitates a creation, sometimes to propose an alternative world, sometimes simply to amplify, to confirm, to make social the brief hope offered by nature. Art is an organized response to what nature allows us to glimpse occasionally." Write a brief essay in which you explore this statement in light of Berger's essay and its discussion of aesthetic response—both to art and to nature. To what extent does this statement invite us to rethink our views of both art and nature?

From Text to Field

1. Near the opening of the essay, Berger discusses the carved white bird in light of five categories of aesthetic response. To what extent can these five categories apply equally well to other forms of art, most particularly to written texts? How is our aesthetic response in the act of reading similar to or different from response in the act of seeing? Can the five categories of aesthetic response that Berger calls upon be used to inform the act of writing?

2. Berger observes that "the range of what a given community finds beautiful in nature will depend upon its means of survival, its economy, its geography" (par. 12). Although he grants that there seem to be "certain constants which all cultures have found 'beautiful'" (par. 13), Berger accords a large role for cultural factors in our aesthetic response. Choose a given community of your own—where you grew up, where you now live, or where you go to college—and explore why certain features of nature seem important and beautiful to your community. For evidence, consider the ways in which campus architecture draws on its natural setting, public art is framed in your community, or brochures link nature's beauty to the community's history, economy, and future survival.

3. Berger's essay uses as its prime example and test case a miniature carved wooden bird. What other examples or art objects might Berger have chosen? How might different art objects require some shifts in Berger's argument? How might you rewrite Berger's essay by drawing on an art object that you value or that has value in your community?

In Plato's Cave

Susan Sontag

A well-known American essayist, novelist, cultural critic, public intellectual, and controversial activist, Susan Sontag did much to define the intellectual landscape in the final third of the twentieth century.

Finishing high school at age fifteen, Sontag went on to study at the University of Chicago, Harvard University, and St. Anne's College, Oxford University. She wrote four novels and a number of short stories, most notably "The Way We Live Now," which remains a key text on the AIDS epidemic. Yet it was as an essayist and cultural critic that Sontag won lasting fame and notoriety. Sontag consistently sought to challenge conventional thinking and often explored the intersection of "high" and "low" art. Her 1964 essay "Notes on 'Camp'" helped to define the "so bad it's good" concept in popular culture. Shortly thereafter, with the publication of "Against Interpretation," she sought to make the case that response to literature was an intuitive rather than an entirely analytic process. Writing about such matters as fashion, pornography, and other aspects of contemporary culture, Sontag's essays invariably galvanized debate. In the 1970s and 1980s, she turned to examine cultural attitudes about illness and disease, which led to *Illness as Metaphor* (1978) and *AIDS and Its Metaphors* (1988). This concern was rooted in her own battles with cancer, a fight she lost to leukemia in 2004. A controversial activist and human rights advocate, Sontag made trips to North Vietnam and Cuba in the 1960s, China in 1973, and Sarajevo in 1993, and invariably saw immediate events of the day—such as the September 11, 2001, attacks—in cultural, political, and ideological terms.

Sontag's exploration of photography and media remains central to her work as a cultural critic. With her 1977 essay collection, *On Photography*, in which "In Plato's Cave" serves as the opening chapter, Sontag was one of the first to question how our culture uses images and photographs, steering the debate away from the traditional question of whether photography was an art form. Late in her life, she returned to the questions of photography and image production and consumption in her book-length essay *Regarding the Pain of Others* (2002). Here she reexamines photography from a moral perspective and explores how media coverage affects how our culture views conflict.

Humankind lingers unregenerately in Plato's cave, still reveling, its age-old habit, in mere images of the truth. But being educated by photographs is not like being educated by older, more artisanal images. For one thing, there are a great many more images around, claiming our attention. The inventory started in 1839 and since then just about everything has been photographed, or so it seems. This very insatiability of the photographing eye changes the terms of confinement in the cave, our world. In teaching us a new visual code, photographs alter and enlarge our notions of what is worth looking at and what we have a right to observe. They are a grammar and, even more importantly, an ethics of seeing. Finally, the most grandiose result of the photographic enterprise is to give us the sense that we can hold the whole world in our heads—as an anthology of images.

To collect photographs is to collect the world. Movies and television programs light up walls, flicker, and go out; but with still photographs the image is also an object, lightweight, cheap to produce, easy to carry about, accumulate, store. In Godard's *Les Carabiniers* (1963), two sluggish lumpen-peasants are lured into joining the King's Army by the promise that they will be able to loot, rape, kill, or do whatever else they please to the enemy, and get rich. But the suitcase of booty that Michel-Ange and Ulysse triumphantly bring home, years later, to their wives turns out to contain only picture post-cards, hundreds of them, of Monuments, Department Stores, Mammals, Wonders of Nature, Methods of Transport, Works of Art, and other classified treasures from around the globe. Godard's gag vividly parodies the equivocal magic of the photographic image. Photographs are perhaps the most myste-rious of all the objects that make up, and thicken, the environment we rec-ognize as modern. Photographs really are experience captured, and the camera is the ideal arm of consciousness in its acquisitive mood.

To photograph is to appropriate the thing photographed. It means putting oneself into a certain relation to the world that feels like knowledge—and, therefore, like power. A now notorious first fall into alienation, habituating people to abstract the world into printed words, is supposed to have engen-dered that surplus of Faustian energy and psychic damage needed to build modern, inorganic societies. But print seems a less treacherous form of leach-ing out the world, of turning it into a mental object, than photographic images, which now provide most of the knowledge people have about the look of the past and the reach of the present. What is written about a person or an event is frankly an interpretation, as are handmade visual statements, like paintings and drawings. Photographed images do not seem to be statements about the world so much as pieces of it, miniatures of reality that anyone can make or acquire.

Photographs, which fiddle with the scale of the world, themselves get reduced, blown up, cropped, retouched, doctored, tricked out. They age, plagued by the usual ills of paper objects; they disappear; they become valuable, and get bought and sold; they are reproduced. Photographs, which package the world, seem to invite packaging. They are stuck in albums, framed and set on tables, tacked on walls, projected as slides. Newspapers and magazines feature them; cops alphabetize them; museums exhibit them; publishers compile them.

For many decades the book has been the most influential way of arrang- 5
ing (and usually miniaturizing) photographs, thereby guaranteeing them longevity, if not immortality—photographs are fragile objects, easily torn or mislaid—and a wider public. The photograph in a book is, obviously, the image of an image. But since it is, to begin with, a printed, smooth object, a photograph loses much less of its essential quality when reproduced in a book than a painting does. Still, the book is not a wholly satisfactory scheme for putting groups of photographs into general circulation. The sequence in which the photographs are to be looked at is proposed by the order of pages, but nothing holds readers to the recommended order or indicates the amount of time to be spent on each photograph. Chris Markers's film, *Si j'avais quatre dromadaires* (1966), a brilliantly orchestrated meditation on photographs of all sorts and themes, suggests a subtler and more rigorous way of packaging (and enlarging) still photographs. Both the order and the exact time for looking at each photograph are imposed; and there is a gain in visual legibility and emotional impact. But photographs transcribed in a film cease to be collectable objects, as they still are when served up in books.

Photographs furnish evidence. Something we hear about, but doubt, seems proven when we're shown a photograph of it. In one version of its utility, the camera record incriminates. Starting with their use by the Paris police in the murderous roundup of Communards° in June 1871, photographs became a useful tool of modern states in the surveillance and control of their increasingly mobile populations. In another version of its utility, the camera record

---

Communards: Supporters of the short-lived Commune, the socialist movement that briefly ruled Paris during the period immediately following the Franco-Prussian War. In June 1871, French national forces attacked the Communards; in one week some 20,000 Communards were executed, and 7,500 jailed or deported.

justifies. A photograph passes for incontrovertible proof that a given thing happened. The picture may distort; but there is always a presumption that something exists, or did exist, which is like what's in the picture. Whatever the limitations (through amateurism) or pretensions (through artistry) of the individual photographer, a photograph—any photograph—seems to have a more innocent, and therefore more accurate, relation to visible reality than do other mimetic objects. Virtuosi of the noble image like Alfred Stieglitz and Paul Strand, composing mighty, unforgettable photographs decade after decade, still want, first of all, to show something "out there," just like the Polaroid owner for whom photographs are a handy, fast form of note taking, or the shutterbug with a Brownie who takes snapshots as souvenirs of daily life.

While a painting or a prose description can never be other than a narrowly selective interpretation, a photograph can be treated as a narrowly selective transparency. But despite the presumption of veracity that gives all photographs authority, interest, seductiveness, the work that photographers do is no generic exception to the usually shady commerce between art and truth. Even when photographers are most concerned with mirroring reality, they are still haunted by tacit imperatives of taste and conscience. The immensely gifted members of the Farm Security Administration photographic project of the late 1930s (among them Walker Evans, Dorothea Lange, Ben Shahn, Russell Lee) would take dozens of frontal pictures of one of their sharecropper subjects until satisfied that they had gotten just the right look on film—the precise expression on the subject's face that supported their own notions about poverty, light, dignity, texture, exploitation, and geometry. In deciding how a picture should look, in preferring one exposure to another, photographers are always imposing standards on their subjects. Although there is a sense in which the camera does indeed capture reality, not just interpret it, photographs are as much an interpretation of the world as paintings and drawings are. Those occasions when the taking of photographs is relatively undiscriminating, promiscuous, or self-effacing do not lessen the didacticism of the whole enterprise. This very passivity—and ubiquity—of the photographic record is photography's "message," its aggression.

Images which idealize (like most fashion and animal photography) are no less aggressive than work which makes a virtue of plainness (like class pictures, still lifes of the bleaker sort, and mug shots). There is an aggression implicit in every use of the camera. This is as evident in the 1840s and 1850s, photography's glorious first two decades, as in all the succeeding decades, during which technology made possible an ever increasing spread of that mentality which looks at the world as a set of potential photographs. Even for such early masters as David Octavius Hill and Julia Margaret Cameron who used the camera as a means of getting painterly images, the point of taking

Figure 1. Arthur "Weegee" Fellig, *Top Hats—In Trouble*, 1942. Charles Sodokoff and Arthur Webber Use Their Top Hats to Hide Their Faces, January 27, 1942. New York Daily News Photo. (Weegee/ICP/ Liaison.)

photographs was a vast departure from the aims of painters. From its start, photography implied the capture of the largest possible number of subjects. Painting never had so imperial a scope. The subsequent industrialization of camera technology only carried out a promise inherent in photography from its very beginning: to democratize all experiences by translating them into images.

That age when taking photographs required a cumbersome and expensive contraption—the toy of the clever, the wealthy, and the obsessed—seems remote indeed from the era of sleek pocket cameras that invite anyone to take pictures. The first cameras, made in France and England in the early 1840s, had only inventors and buffs to operate them. Since there were then no professional photographers, there could not be amateurs either, and taking photographs had no clear social use; it was a gratuitous, that is, an artistic activity, though with few pretensions to being an art. It was only with its industrialization that photography came into its own as art. As industrialization provided social uses for the operations of the photographer, so the reaction against these uses reinforced the self-consciousness of photography-as-art.

Recently, photography has become almost as widely practiced an amuse- 10
ment as sex and dancing—which means that, like every mass art form, photography is not practiced by most people as an art. It is mainly a social rite, a
defense against anxiety, and a tool of power.

Memorializing the achievements of individuals considered as members of
families (as well as of other groups) is the earliest popular use of photography.
For at least a century, the wedding photograph has been as much a part of the
ceremony as the prescribed verbal formulas. Cameras go with family life.
According to a sociological study done in France, most households have a camera, but a household with children is twice as likely to have at least one camera as a household in which there are no children. Not to take pictures of one's
children, particularly when they are small, is a sign of parental indifference,
just as not turning up for one's graduation picture is a gesture of adolescent
rebellion.

Through photographs, each family constructs a portrait-chronicle of itself
a portable kit of images that bears witness to its connectedness. It hardly matters what activities are photographed so long as photographs get taken and are
cherished. Photography becomes a rite of family life just when, in the industri-
alizing countries of Europe and America, the very institution of the family starts
undergoing radical surgery. As that claustrophobic unit, the nuclear family,
was being carved out of a much larger family aggregate, photography came
along to memorialize, to restate symbolically, the imperiled continuity and
vanishing extendedness of family life. Those ghostly traces, photographs,
supply the token presence of the dispersed relatives. A family's photograph
album is generally about the extended family—and, often, is all that remains
of it.

As photographs give people an imaginary possession of a past that is unreal,
they also help people to take possession of space in which they are insecure.
Thus, photography develops in tandem with one of the most characteristic of
modern activities: tourism. For the first time in history, large numbers of people
regularly travel out of their habitual environments for short periods of time. It
seems positively unnatural to travel for pleasure without taking a camera
along. Photographs will offer indisputable evidence that the trip was made,
that the program was carried out, that fun was had. Photographs document
sequences of consumption carried on outside the view of family, friends,
neighbors. But dependence on the camera, as the device that makes real
what one is experiencing, doesn't fade when people travel more. Taking photographs fills the same need for the cosmopolitans accumulating photograph
trophies of their boat trip up the Albert Nile or their fourteen days in China
as it does for lower-middle-class vacationers taking snapshots of the Eiffel
Tower or Niagara Falls.

A way of certifying experience, taking photographs is also a way of refusing it—by limiting experience to a search for the photogenic, by converting experience into an image, a souvenir. Travel becomes a strategy for accumulating photographs. The very activity of taking pictures is soothing, and assuages general feelings of disorientation that are likely to be exacerbated by travel. Most tourists feel compelled to put the camera between themselves and whatever is remarkable that they encounter. Unsure of other responses, they take a picture. This gives shape to experience: Stop, take a photograph, and move on. The method especially appeals to people handicapped by a ruthless work ethic—Germans, Japanese, and Americans. Using a camera appeases the anxiety which the work driven feel about not working when they are on vacation and supposed to be having fun. They have something to do that is like a friendly imitation of work: They can take pictures.

People robbed of their past seem to make the most fervent picture takers, 15 at home and abroad. Everyone who lives in an industrialized society is obliged gradually to give up the past, but in certain countries, such as the United States and Japan, the break with the past has been particularly traumatic. In the early 1970s, the fable of the brash American tourist of the 1950s and 1960s, rich with dollars and Babbittry,° was replaced by the mystery of the group-minded Japanese tourist, newly released from his island prison by the miracle of overvalued yen, who is generally armed with two cameras, one on each hip.

Photography has become one of the principal devices for experiencing something, for giving an appearance of participation. One full-page ad shows a small group of people standing pressed together, peering out of the photograph, all but one looking stunned, excited, upset. The one who wears a different expression holds a camera to his eye; he seems self-possessed, is almost smiling. While the others are passive, clearly alarmed spectators, having a camera has transformed one person into something active, a voyeur: Only he has mastered the situation. What do these people see? We don't know. And it doesn't matter. It is an Event: something worth seeing—and therefore worth photographing. The ad copy, white letters across the dark lower third of the photograph like news coming over a teletype machine, consists of just six words: ". . . Prague . . . Woodstock . . . Vietnam . . . Sapporo . . . Londonderry . . . LEICA." Crushed hopes, youth antics, colonial wars, and winter sports are alike—are equalized by the camera. Taking photographs has set up a chronic voyeuristic relation to the world which levels the meaning of all events.

Babbittry: Conformity to standards and attitudes of the middle class. The term comes from the character George F. Babbitt in the novel *Babbitt* (1922) by Sinclair Lewis.

A photograph is not just the result of an encounter between an event and a photographer; picture taking is an event in itself, and one with ever more peremptory rights—to interfere with, to invade, or to ignore whatever is going on. Our very sense of situation is now articulated by the camera's interventions. The omnipresence of cameras persuasively suggests that time consists of interesting events, events worth photographing. This, in turn, makes it easy to feel that any event, once underway, and whatever its moral character, should be allowed to complete itself—so that something else can be brought into the world, the photograph. After the event has ended, the picture will still exist, conferring on the event a kind of immortality (and importance) it would never otherwise have enjoyed. While real people are out there killing themselves or other real people, the photographer stays behind his or her camera, creating a tiny element of another world: the image-world that bids to outlast us all.

> **Photographs are a grammar and, even more importantly, an ethics of seeing.**

Photographing is essentially an act of nonintervention. Part of the horror of such memorable coups of contemporary photojournalism as the pictures of a Vietnamese bonze° reaching for the gasoline can, of a Bengali guerrilla in the act of bayoneting a trussed-up collaborator, comes from the awareness of how plausible it has become, in situations where the photographer has the choice between a photograph and a life, to choose the photograph. The person who intervenes cannot record; the person who is recording cannot intervene. Dziga Vertov's great film, *Man with a Movie Camera* (1929), gives the ideal image of the photographer as someone in perpetual movement, someone moving through a panorama of disparate events with such agility and speed that any intervention is out of the question. Hitchcock's *Rear Window* (1954) gives the complementary image: The photographer played by James Stewart has an intensified relation to one event, through his camera, precisely because he has a broken leg and is confined to a wheelchair; being temporarily immobilized prevents him from acting on what he sees, and makes it even more important to take pictures. Even if incompatible with intervention in a physical sense, using a camera is still a form of participation. Although the camera is an observation station, the act of photographing is more than passive observing. Like sexual voyeurism, it is a way of at least tacitly, often explicitly, encouraging whatever is going on to keep on happening. To take a picture is to have an interest in things as they are, in the status quo remaining unchanged (at least for as long as it takes to get a "good" picture), to be in complicity with whatever makes a subject interesting, worth photographing—including, when that is the interest, another person's pain or misfortune.

---

bonze: A Buddhist monk.

"I always thought of photography as a naughty thing to do—that was one of my favorite things about it," Diane Arbus wrote, "and when I first did it I felt very perverse." Being a professional photographer can be thought of as naughty, to use Arbus's pop word, if the photographer seeks out subjects considered to be disreputable, taboo, marginal. But naughty subjects are harder to find these days. And what exactly is the perverse aspect of picture taking? If professional photographers often have sexual fantasies when they are behind the camera, perhaps the perversion lies in the fact that these fantasies are both plausible and so inappropriate. In *Blowup* (1966), Antonioni has the fashion photographer hovering convulsively over Verushka's body with his camera clicking. Naughtiness, indeed! In fact, using a camera is not a very good way of getting at someone sexually. Between photographer and subject, there has to be distance. The camera doesn't rape, or even possess, though it may presume, intrude, trespass, distort, exploit, and, at the farthest reach of metaphor, assassinate—all activities that, unlike the sexual push and shove, can be conducted from a distance, and with some detachment.

Figure 2. James Stewart as L. B. Jeffries in *Rear Window*, directed by Alfred Hitchcock. (© Bettmann/CORBIS.)

There is a much stronger sexual fantasy in Michael Powell's extraordinary 20
movie *Peeping Tom* (1960), which is not about a Peeping Tom but about a
psychopath who kills women with a weapon concealed in his camera, while
photographing them. Not once does he touch his subjects. He doesn't desire
their bodies; he wants their presence in the form of filmed images — those
showing them experiencing their own death—which he screens at home for
his solitary pleasure. The movie assumes connections between impotence
and aggression, professionalized looking and cruelty, which point to the central fantasy connected with the camera. The camera as phallus is, at most, a
flimsy variant of the inescapable metaphor that everyone unself-consciously
employs. However hazy our awareness of this fantasy, it is named without
subtlety whenever we talk about "loading" and "aiming" a camera, about
"shooting" a film.

The old-fashioned camera was clumsier and harder to reload than a
brown Bess musket. The modern camera is trying to be a ray gun. One ad
reads:

> The Yashica Electro-35 GT is the space-age camera your family will love.
> Take beautiful pictures day or night. Automatically. Without any nonsense.
> Just aim, focus, and shoot. The GT's computer brain and electronic shut-
> ter will do the rest.

Like a car, a camera is sold as a predatory weapon —one that's as automated
as possible, ready to spring. Popular taste expects an easy, an invisible technology. Manufacturers reassure their customers that taking pictures demands
no skill or expert knowledge, that the machine is all-knowing, and responds
to the slightest pressure of the will. It's as simple as turning the ignition key
or pulling the trigger.

Like guns and cars, cameras are fantasy machines whose use is addictive.
However, despite the extravagances of ordinary language and advertising,
they are not lethal. In the hyperbole that markets cars like guns, there is at
least this much truth: Except in wartime, cars kill more people than guns
do. The camera/gun does not kill, so the ominous metaphor seems to be all
bluff—like a man's fantasy of having a gun, knife, or tool between his legs.
Still, there is something predatory in the act of taking a picture. To photograph people is to violate them, by seeing them as they never see themselves, by having knowledge of them they can never have; it turns people
into objects that can be symbolically possessed. Just as the camera is a sub-
limation of the gun, to photograph someone is a sublimated murder—a soft
murder, appropriate to a sad, frightened time.

Eventually, people might learn to act out more of their aggressions with
cameras and fewer with guns, with the price being an even more image-
choked world. One situation where people are switching from bullets to film

is the photographic safari that is replacing the gun safari in East Africa. The hunters have Hasselblads instead of Winchesters; instead of looking through a telescopic sight to aim a rifle, they look through a viewfinder to frame a picture. In end-of-the century London, Samuel Butler complained that "there is a photographer in every bush, going about like a roaring lion seeking whom he may devour." The photographer is now charging real beasts, beleaguered and too rare to kill. Guns have metamorphosed into cameras in this earnest comedy, the ecology safari, because nature has ceased to be what it always had been — what people needed protection from. Now nature — tamed, endangered, mortal — needs to be protected from people. When we are afraid, we shoot. But when we are nostalgic, we take pictures.

It is a nostalgic time right now, and photographs actively promote nostalgia. Photography is an elegiac art, a twilight art. Most subjects photographed are, just by virtue of being photographed, touched with pathos. An ugly or grotesque subject may be moving because it has been dignified by the attention of the photographer. A beautiful subject can be the object of rueful feelings, because it has aged or decayed or no longer exists. All photographs are memento mori.° To take a photograph is to participate in another person's (or thing's) mortality, vulnerability, mutability. Precisely by slicing out this moment and freezing it, all photographs testify to time's relentless melt.

Cameras began duplicating the world at that moment when the human landscape started to undergo a vertiginous rate of change: While an untold number of forms of biological and social life are being destroyed in a brief span of time, a device is available to record what is disappearing. The moody, intricately textured Paris of Atget and Brassaï is mostly gone. Like the dead relatives and friends preserved in the family album, whose presence in photographs exorcises some of the anxiety and remorse prompted by their disappearance, so the photographs of neighborhoods now torn down, rural places disfigured and made barren, supply our pocket relation to the past. 25

A photograph is both a pseudopresence and a token of absence. Like a wood fire in a room, photographs — especially those of people, of distant landscapes and faraway cities, of the vanished past — are incitements to reverie. The sense of the unattainable that can be evoked by photographs feeds directly into the erotic feelings of those for whom desirability is enhanced by distance. The lover's photograph hidden in a married woman's wallet, the poster photograph of a rock star tacked up over an adolescent's bed, the campaign-button image of a politician's face pinned on a voter's coat, the snapshots of a cabdriver's children clipped to the visor — all such talismanic uses of photographs express a feeling both sentimental and implicitly magical: They are attempts to contact or lay claim to another reality.

---

memento mori: A Latin phrase, "remember your death," used to refer to reminders of one's mortality.

Photographs can abet desire in the most direct, utilitarian way — as when someone collects photographs of anonymous examples of the desirable as an aid to masturbation. The matter is more complex when photographs are used to stimulate the moral impulse. Desire has no history — at least, it is experienced in each instance as all foreground, immediacy. It is aroused by archetypes and is, in that sense, abstract. But moral feelings are embedded in history, whose personae are concrete, whose situations are always specific. Thus, almost opposite rules hold true for the use of the photograph to awaken desire and to awaken conscience. The images that mobilize conscience are always linked to a given historical situation. The more general they are, the less likely they are to be effective.

A photograph that brings news of some unsuspected zone of misery cannot make a dent in public opinion unless there is an appropriate context of feeling and attitude. The photographs Mathew Brady and his colleagues took of the horrors of the battlefields did not make people any less keen to go on with the Civil War. The photographs of ill-clad, skeletal prisoners held at Andersonville inflamed Northern public opinion — against the South. (The effect of the Andersonville photographs must have been partly due to the very novelty, at that time, of seeing photographs.) The political understanding that many Americans came to in the 1960s would allow them, looking at the photographs Dorothea Lange took of Nisei on the West Coast being transported to internment camps in 1942, to recognize their subject for what it was — a crime committed by the government against a large group of American citizens. Few people who saw these photographs in the 1940s could have had so unequivocal a reaction; the grounds for such a judgment were covered over by the prowar consensus. Photographs cannot create a moral position, but they can reinforce one — and can help build a nascent one.

Photographs may be more memorable than moving images, because they are a neat slice of time, not a flow. Television is a stream of underselected images, each of which cancels its predecessor. Each still photograph is a privileged moment, turned into a slim object that one can keep and look at again. Photographs like the one that made the front page of most newspapers in the world in 1972 — a naked South Vietnamese child just sprayed by American napalm, running down a highway toward the camera, her arms open, screaming with pain — probably did more to increase the public revulsion against the war than a hundred hours of televised barbarities.

One would like to imagine that the American public would not have been 30 so unanimous in its acquiescence to the Korean War if it had been confronted with photographic evidence of the devastation of Korea, an ecocide and genocide in some respects even more thorough than those inflicted on Vietnam a decade later. But the supposition is trivial. The public did not see such photographs because there was, ideologically, no space for them. No one brought back photographs of daily life in Pyongyang, to show that the enemy had a human face, as Felix Greene and Marc Riboud brought back photographs of Hanoi. Americans did have access to photographs of the suffering of the Vietnamese (many of which came from military sources and were taken with quite a different use in mind) because journalists felt backed in their efforts to obtain those photographs, the event having been defined by a significant number of people as a savage colonialist war. The Korean War was understood differently—as part of the struggle of the free world against the Soviet Union and China—and, given that characterization, photographs of the cruelty of unlimited American firepower would have been irrelevant.

Though an event has come to mean, precisely, something worth photographing, it is still ideology (in the broadest sense) that determines what constitutes an event. There can be no evidence, photographic or otherwise, of an event until the event itself has been named and characterized. And it is never photographic evidence which can construct — more properly, identify — events; the contribution of photography always follows the naming of the event. What determines the possibility of being affected morally by photographs is the existence of a relevant political consciousness. Without a politics, photographs of the slaughter bench of history will most likely be experienced as, simply, unreal or as a demoralizing emotional blow.

The quality of feeling, including moral outrage, that people can muster in response to photographs of the oppressed, the exploited, the starving, and the massacred also depends on the degree of their familiarity with these images. Don McCullin's photographs of emaciated Biafrans° in the early 1970s had less impact for some people than Werner Bischof's photographs of Indian famine victims in the early 1950s because those images had become banal, and the photographs of Tuareg° families dying of starvation in the sub-Sahara that appeared in magazines everywhere in 1973 must have seemed to many like an unbearable replay of a now familiar atrocity exhibition.

Photographs shock insofar as they show something novel. Unfortunately, the ante keeps getting raised—partly through the very proliferation of such images of horror. One's first encounter with the photographic inventory of ultimate horror is a kind of revelation, the prototypically modern revelation: a negative epiphany. For me, it was photographs of Bergen-Belsen and Dachau° which I came across by chance in a bookstore in Santa Monica in July 1945. Nothing I have seen — in photographs or in real life — ever cut me as sharply, deeply, instantaneously. Indeed, it seems plausible to me to

---

Biafrans: People of southeastern Nigeria ravaged by civil war, hunger, and economic collapse.

Tuareg: A nomadic ethnic group, now found chiefly in West Africa, who had been involved for a millennia in trans-Saharan caravan trade.

Bergen-Belsen and Dachau: Two Nazi concentration camps.

divide my life into two parts, before I saw those photographs (I was twelve) and after, though it was several years before I understood fully what they were about. What good was served by seeing them? They were only photographs — of an event I had scarcely heard of and could do nothing to affect, of suffering I could hardly imagine and could do nothing to relieve. When I looked at those photographs, something broke. Some limit had been reached, and not only that of horror; I felt irrevocably grieved, wounded, but a part of my feelings started to tighten; something went dead; something is still crying.

To suffer is one thing; another thing is living with the photographed images of suffering, which does not necessarily strengthen conscience and the ability to be compassionate. It can also corrupt them. Once one has seen such images, one has started down the road of seeing more — and more. Images transfix. Images anesthetize. An event known through photographs certainly becomes more real than it would have been if one had never seen the photographs — think of the Vietnam War. (For a counterexample, think of the Gulag Archipelago,° of which we have no photographs.) But after repeated exposure to images it also becomes less real.

The same law holds for evil as for pornography. The shock of pho-   35
tographed atrocities wears off with repeated viewings, just as the surprise and bemusement felt the first time one sees a pornographic movie wear off after one sees a few more. The sense of taboo which makes us indignant and sorrowful is not much sturdier than the sense of taboo that regulates the definition of what is obscene. And both have been sorely tried in recent years. The vast photographic catalog of misery and injustice throughout the world has given everyone a certain familiarity with atrocity, making the horrible seem more ordinary — making it appear familiar, remote ("it's only a photograph"), inevitable. At the time of the first photographs of the Nazi camps, there was nothing banal about these images. After thirty years, a saturation point may have been reached. In these last decades, "concerned" photography has done at least as much to deaden conscience as to arouse it.

The ethical content of photographs is fragile. With the possible exception of photographs of those horrors, like the Nazi camps, that have gained the status of ethical reference points, most photographs do not keep their emotional charge. A photograph of 1900 that was affecting then because of its subject would, today, be more likely to move us because it is a photograph taken in 1900. The particular qualities and intentions of photographs tend to be swallowed up in the generalized pathos of time past. Aesthetic distance

---

Gulag Archipelago: The chain of Soviet slave labor and concentration camps. "Gulag" itself is the acronym for the Russian term "Chief Administration for Corrective Labor Camps," the camp system that, like the islands of an archipelago, spread out across Siberia.

seems built into the very experience of looking at photographs, if not right away, then certainly with the passage of time. Time eventually positions most photographs, even the most amateurish, at the level of art.

The industrialization of photography permitted its rapid absorption into rational—that is, bureaucratic—ways of running society. No longer toy images, photographs became part of the general furniture of the environment—touchstones and confirmations of that reductive approach to reality which is considered realistic. Photographs were enrolled in the service of important institutions of control, notably the family and the police, as symbolic objects and as pieces of information. Thus, in the bureaucratic cataloging of the world, many important documents are not valid unless they have, affixed to them, a photograph token of the citizen's face.

The "realistic" view of the world compatible with bureaucracy redefines knowledge—as techniques and information. Photographs are valued because they give information. They tell one what there is; they make an inventory. To spies, meteorologists, coroners, archaeologists, and other information professionals, their value is inestimable. But in the situations in which most people use photographs, their value as information is of the same order as fiction. The information that photographs can give starts to seem very important at that moment in cultural history when everyone is thought to have a right to something called news. Photographs were seen as a way of giving information to people who do not take easily to reading. The *Daily News* still calls itself "New York's Picture Newspaper," its bid for populist identity. At the opposite end of the scale, *Le Monde*, a newspaper designed for skilled, well-informed readers, runs no photographs at all. The presumption is that, for such readers, a photograph could only illustrate the analysis contained in an article.

A new sense of the notion of information has been constructed around the photographic image. The photograph is a thin slice of space as well as time. In a world ruled by photographic images, all borders ("framing") seem arbitrary. Anything can be separated, can be made discontinuous, from anything else: All that is necessary is to frame the subject differently. (Conversely, anything can be made adjacent to anything else.) Photography reinforces a nominalist view of social reality as consisting of small units of an apparently infinite number—as the number of photographs that could be taken of anything is unlimited. Through photographs, the world becomes a series of unrelated, freestanding particles; and history, past and present, a set of anecdotes and *faits divers.*° The camera makes reality

---

faits divers: French for "current news."

atomic, manageable, and opaque. It is a view of the world which denies interconnectedness, continuity, but which confers on each moment the character of a mystery. Any photograph has multiple meanings; indeed, to see something in the form of a photograph is to encounter a potential object of fascination. The ultimate wisdom of the photographic image is to say: "There is the surface. Now think—or rather feel, intuit—what is beyond it, what the reality must be like if it looks this way." Photographs, which cannot themselves explain anything, are inexhaustible invitations to deduction, speculation, and fantasy.

Photography implies that we know about the world if we accept it as the 40 camera records it. But this is the opposite of understanding, which starts from *not* accepting the world as it looks. All possibility of understanding is rooted in the ability to say no. Strictly speaking, one never understands anything from a photograph. Of course, photographs fill in blanks in our mental pictures of the present and the past: for example, Jacob Riis's images of New York squalor in the 1880s are sharply instructive to those unaware that urban poverty in late-nineteenth-century America was really that

Figure 3. Jacob A. Riis, "Room in tenement flat, 1910," from *How the Other Half Lives*, by Jacob A. Riis. (Jacob A. Riis Collection, Museum of the City of New York.)

Dickensian.° Nevertheless, the camera's rendering of reality must always hide more than it discloses. As Brecht points out, a photograph of the Krupp works° reveals virtually nothing about that organization. In contrast to the amorous relation, which is based on how something looks, understanding is based on how it functions. And functioning takes place in time, and must be explained in time. Only that which narrates can make us understand.

The limit of photographic knowledge of the world is that, while it can goad conscience, it can, finally, never be ethical or political knowledge. The knowledge gained through still photographs will always be some kind of sentimentalism, whether cynical or humanist. It will be a knowledge at bargain prices—a semblance of knowledge, a semblance of wisdom; as the act of taking pictures is a semblance of appropriation, a semblance of rape. The very muteness of what is, hypothetically, comprehensible in photographs is what constitutes their attraction and provocativeness. The omnipresence of photographs has an incalculable effect on our ethical sensibility. By furnishing this already crowded world with a duplicate one of images, photography makes us feel that the world is more available than it really is.

Needing to have reality confirmed and experience enhanced by photographs is an aesthetic consumerism to which everyone is now addicted. Industrial societies turn their citizens into image junkies; it is the most irresistible form of mental pollution. Poignant longings for beauty, for an end to probing below the surface, for a redemption and celebration of the body of the world—all these elements of erotic feeling are affirmed in the pleasure we take in photographs. But other, less liberating feelings are expressed as well. It would not be wrong to speak of people having a *compulsion* to photograph: to turn experience itself into a way of seeing. Ultimately, having an experience becomes identical with taking a photograph of it, and participating in a public event comes more and more to be equivalent to looking at it in photographed form. That most logical of nineteenth-century aesthetes, Mallarmé,° said that everything in the world exists in order to end in a book. Today everything exists to end in a photograph.

Dickensian: A reference to the novels of Charles Dickens (1812–1870) that offered fierce criticisms of poverty and social stratification in nineteenth-century England.

Brecht . . . Krupp works: Bertolt Brecht (1898–1956), a German author, dramatist, and poet known for his social criticism. Krupp works refers to the factories of the Krupp family in Germany that produced steel, armaments, and ammunition.

Mallarmé: Stéphane Mallarmé (1842–1898), a French poet and critic.

Working with the Text

1. Susan Sontag titles this, the first essay in her collection *On Photography*, by alluding to a famous passage in Plato's *Republic*, known as the "Allegory of the Cave." Plato argues that we, like cave dwellers accustomed to the dark, mistake shadows for reality, mere images for truth. Why does Sontag title her essay as she does? What attitudes or arguments in the body of the essay justify the title she gives it?

2. Sontag's essay seems to privilege the provocative statement or insight over sustained, clearly structured argument. Indeed, the essay might on a first read-ing overwhelm the reader with its range and its densely packed commentary. After you have taken the opportunity for a second or third reading, consider the question of the essay's style and structure. How would you characterize the essay's structure or its progression of argument? How might the style of Sontag's essay suit the subject that she addresses? What connection might there be between Sontag's series of insights or perceptions and photographs themselves?

3. At the beginning of her essay, Sontag asserts, "In teaching us a new visual code, photographs alter and enlarge our notions of what is worth looking at and what we have a right to observe. They are a grammar and, even more impor-tantly, an ethics of seeing" (par. 1). Drawing on the specific positions that Sontag stakes out in her essay, develop a two-page statement of her ethics of seeing. What is won and what is lost as you translate Sontag's essay into such a statement?

From Text to Field

1. Sontag's essay was first published in 1977, some thirty years ago. In the span of a generation, much has changed in how we make, circulate, and read the pho-tographic image. Writing in the twilight of the age of traditional photography, Sontag could hardly have imagined the world of the image today, with the Internet, digital cameras, and even cell phones that take photos. Write an essay in which you revisit Sontag's arguments in light of today's technology. What in Sontag's essay stands the test of time and continues to be relevant, and what might be now outdated?

2. Sontag mentions at one point in the essay that hers is a "sad, frightened time" (par. 22). Indeed, the essay is dark in tone, pessimistic in outlook. Write an essay in which you reflect on that tone or outlook from your vantage point thirty years later. You may find yourself justifying and explaining her

approach or offering an optimist's reply. Do you share Sontag's vision, disagree with her assessment, or find some alternative implications of photography as a technology?

3. The range of Sontag's essay is impressive, as she links photography and its effect on society to such issues as desire, conscience, aggression, and social ritual, among many others. Select one particular issue that Sontag raises, and explore it in some detail, drawing on your own experience with photography and on the role of photography in today's world.

4. Although the range and complexity of Sontag's essay might suggest otherwise, it invites our close consideration of individual photographs. Choose one photo that has enduring relevance in your life; it may be a personal family photo or a photo that captures a memorable or traumatic moment that you have shared with others or even a widely published photo that has special meaning for you. Write a close analysis of the photo, in light of both Sontag's arguments and your assessment of her essay. How and why might you and Sontag see the photo in similar—or different—ways?

Truth and Stereotype

E. H. Gombrich

The essay that follows is an excerpt from the art history classic *Art and Illusion: A Study in the Psychology of Pictorial Representation*. Published in 1960, the book proposed a groundbreaking theory of art that continues to serve as a springboard for inquiry into stylistic development and change. Based on scientific insights into visual perception, Gombrich's understanding of the psychology of representation suggests that even outside the realm of art, we think in terms of received models: We look at the world, literally and figuratively, through the language and images we have been given.

Gombrich was born in Vienna in 1909 and through his family and his schooling became immersed in both culture and science. An art historian, he was known for pursuing questions that could only be answered through a thorough knowledge of psychology and the history of ideas, as well as the development of styles in art. In addition to producing a number of landmark books, he taught at Oxford, Cambridge, Harvard, and Princeton universities and the University of Washington and served as the director of the Warburg Institute and professor of the History of the Classical Tradition at the University of London. His best-known work, *The Story of Art* (1950; 16th ed., 1995), was translated into twenty-nine languages and was widely read by children as well as adults. E. H. Gombrich remained active until his death in 2001, at the age of ninety-two.

Perhaps the earliest instance of [illustrated reportage] dates back more than three thousand years, to the beginnings of the New Kingdom in Egypt, when the Pharaoh Thutmose included in his picture chronicle of the Syrian campaign a record of plants he had brought back to Egypt (Fig. 1). The inscription, though somewhat mutilated, tells us that Pharaoh pronounces these pictures to be "the truth." Yet botanists have found it hard to agree on what

Figure 1. Limestone relief of botanical garden with plants and animals brought to Egypt from Syria by Thutmose III (1479–1425 BC).

plants may have been meant by these renderings. The schematic shapes are not sufficiently differentiated to allow secure identification.

An even more famous example comes from the period when medieval art was at its height, from the volume of plans and drawings by the Gothic master builder, Villard de Honnecourt, which tells us so much about the practice and outlook of the men who created the French cathedrals. Among the many architectural, religious, and symbolic drawings of striking skill and beauty to be found in this volume, there is a curiously stiff picture of a lion, seen *en face* (Fig. 2). To us, it looks like an ornamental or heraldic image, but Villard's caption tells us that he regarded it in a different light: "*Et sacies bien,*" he says, "*qu'il fu contrefais al vif.*" "Know well that it is drawn from life." These words obviously had a very different meaning for Villard than they have for us. He can have meant only that he had drawn his schema in the presence of a real lion. How much of his visual observation he allowed to enter into the formula is a different matter.

Once more the broadsheets of popular art show us to what extent this attitude survived the Renaissance. The letterpress of a German woodcut from the sixteenth century informs us that we here see "the exact counterfeit" of a kind of locust that invaded Europe in menacing swarms (Fig. 3). But the zoologist would be rash to infer from this inscription that there existed an entirely different species of creatures that has never been recorded since. The artist had again used a familiar schema, compounded of animals he had learned to portray, and the traditional formula for locusts that he knew from

Figure 2. Villard de Honnecourt, *Lion and Porcupine*, c. 1235, pen and ink.

an apocalypse where the locust plague was illustrated. Perhaps the fact that the German word for a locust is *Heupferd* (hay horse) tempted him to adopt a schema of a horse for the rendering of the insect's prance.

The creation of such a name and the creation of the image have, in fact, much in common. Both proceed by classifying the unfamiliar with the familiar, or more exactly, to remain in the zoological sphere, by creating a sub-species. Since the locust is called a kind of horse it must therefore share some of its distinctive features.

The caption of a Roman print of 1601 (Fig. 4) is as explicit as that of the ₅ German woodcut. It claims the engraving represents a giant whale that had been washed ashore near Ancona the same year and "was drawn accurately from nature." ("*Ritratto qui dal naturale appunto.*") The claim would be more trustworthy if there did not exist an earlier print recording a similar "scoop" from the Dutch coast in 1598 (Fig. 5). But surely the Dutch artists of the late sixteenth century, those masters of realism, would be able to portray a whale? Not quite, it seems, for the creature looks suspiciously as if it had ears, and whales with ears, I am assured on higher authority, do not exist. The draftsman probably mistook one of the whale's flippers for an ear and therefore placed it far too close to the eye. He, too, was misled by a familiar schema, the schema of the typical head. To draw an unfamiliar sight presents

Figure 3. Anonymous, *Locust*, 1556, woodcut.

Figure 4. Anonymous Italian, *Whale Washed Ashore at Ancona*, 1601, engraving.

Figure 5. After Goltzius, *Whale Washed Ashore in Holland*, 1598, engraving.

greater difficulties than is usually realized. And this, I suppose, was also the reason why the Italian preferred to copy the whale from another print. We need not doubt the part of the caption that tells the news from Ancona, but to portray it again "from the life" was not worth the trouble.

In this respect, the fate of exotic creatures in the illustrated books of the last few centuries before the advent of photography is as instructive as it is amusing. When Dürer published his famous woodcut of a rhinoceros (Fig. 6), he had to rely on secondhand evidence which he filled in from his own imagination, colored, no doubt, by what he had learned of the most famous of exotic beasts, the dragon with its armored body. Yet it has been shown that this half-invented creature served as a model for all renderings of the rhinoceros, even in natural-history books, up to the eighteenth century. When, in 1790, James Bruce published a drawing of the beast (Fig. 7) in his *Travels to Discover the Source of the Nile*, he proudly showed that he was aware of this fact:

The familiar will always remain the likely starting point for the rendering of the unfamiliar.

> The animal represented in this drawing is a native of Tcherkin, near Ras el Feel . . . and this is the first drawing of the rhinoceros with a double horn that has ever yet been presented to the public. The first figure of the Asiatic

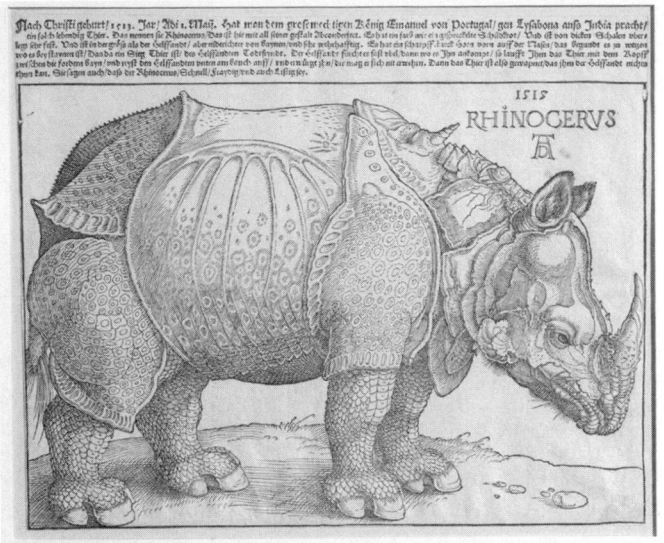

Figure 6. Dürer, *Rhinoceros*, 1515, woodcut.

Figure 7. Heath, *Rhinoceros of Africa*, 1789, engraving.

rhinoceros, the species having but one horn, was painted by Albert Durer, from the life. . . . It was wonderfully ill-executed in all its parts, and was the origin of all the monstrous forms under which that animal has been painted, ever since. . . . Several modern philosophers have made amends for this in our days; Mr. Parsons, Mr. Edwards, and the Count de Buffon, have given good figures of it from life; they have indeed some faults, owing chiefly to preconceived prejudices and inattention. . . . This . . . is the first that has been published with two horns, it is designed from the life, and is an African.

If proof were needed that the difference between the medieval draftsman and his eighteenth-century descendant is only one of degree, it could be found here. For the illustration, presented with such flourishes of trumpets, is surely not free from "preconceived prejudices" and the all-pervading memory of Dürer's woodcut. We do not know exactly what species of rhinoceros the artist saw at Ras el Feel, and the comparison of his picture with a photograph taken in Africa (Fig. 8) may not, therefore, be quite fair. But I am told that none of the species known to zoologists corresponds to the engraving claimed to be drawn *al vifl!*°

The story repeats itself whenever a rare specimen is introduced into Europe. Even the elephants that populate the paintings of the sixteenth and seventeenth centuries have been shown to stem from a very few archetypes and to embody all their curious features, despite the fact that information about elephants was not particularly hard to come by.

These examples demonstrate, in somewhat grotesque magnification, a tendency which the student of art has learned to reckon with. The familiar will always remain the likely starting point for the rendering of the unfamiliar; an

Figure 8. African rhinoceros.

---

al vifl: Literally, "from the life"; a drawing based on a live specimen.

existing representation will always exert its spell over the artist even while he strives to record the truth. Thus it was remarked by ancient critics that several famous artists of antiquity had made a strange mistake in the portrayal of horses: They had represented them with eyelashes on the lower lid, a feature which belongs to the human eye but not to that of the horse. A German ophthalmologist who studied the eyes of Dürer's portraits, which to the layman appear to be such triumphs of painstaking accuracy, reports somewhat similar mistakes. Apparently not even Dürer knew what eyes "really look like."

This should not give us cause for surprise, for the greatest of all the visual explorers, Leonardo° himself, has been shown to have made mistakes in his 10 anatomical drawings. Apparently he drew features of the human heart which Galen° made him expect but which he cannot have seen.

The study of pathology is meant to increase our understanding of health. The sway of schemata did not prevent the emergence of an art of scientific illustration that sometimes succeeds in packing more correct visual information into the image than even a photograph contains. But the diagrammatic maps of muscles in our illustrated anatomies (Fig. 9) are not "transcripts" of things seen but the work of trained observers who build up the picture of a specimen that has been revealed to them in years of patient study.

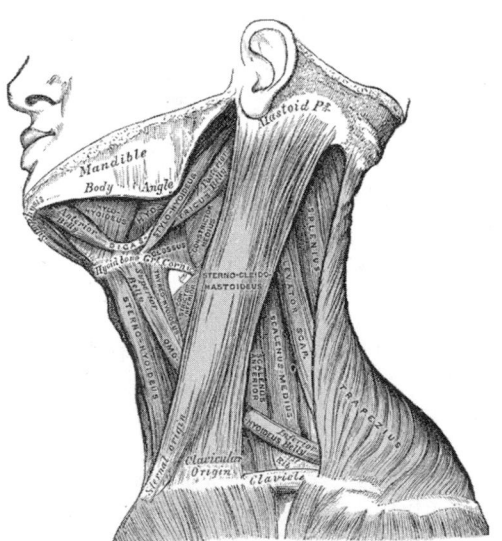

Figure 9. Muscles of the neck, from *Gray's Anatomy*.

Leonardo: Leonardo da Vinci (1452–1519), an Italian painter, sculptor, inventor, architect, and anatomist.

Galen (AD 129–200): A Greek physician whose views influenced western medicine.

Now in this sphere of scientific illustration it obviously makes sense to say that Thutmose's artists or Villard himself could not have done what the modern illustrator can do. They lacked the relevant schemata, their starting point was too far removed from their motif, and their style was too rigid to allow a sufficiently supple adjustment. For so much certainly emerges from a study of portrayal in art: You cannot create a faithful image out of nothing. You must have learned the trick if only from other pictures you have seen.

Working with the Text

1. E. H. Gombrich uses the word *schema* to designate the formulas and stereotypes artists bring to their illustrations of observable phenomena such as plants, animals, and human anatomy. As Gombrich points out, "To draw an unfamiliar sight presents greater difficulties than is usually realized" (par. 5). Inferring from Gombrich's argument and using your own insights into human behavior, write a brief essay in which you explore the challenges of artistic representation. Why would artists—even those who could observe the live phenomenon for themselves—use schemas? Where do you think schemas come from?

2. Why do you think Gombrich believes that it is difficult for close, detailed observation to challenge the formulas or schemas with which we are already familiar? Where might the difficulty lie—in our inability to see accurately, in our inability to render faithfully, or both? In what ways is it difficult to escape from the spell that schemas have over us? Why is it natural or helpful to rely on schemas?

3. As this excerpt from Gombrich's *Art and Illusion: A Study in the Psychology of Pictorial Representation* (2nd ed., 1961) draws to a conclusion, he speaks of scientific illustration as offering something more or different from photography:

   > The sway of schemata did not prevent the emergence of an art of scientific illustration that sometimes succeeds in packing more correct visual information into the image than even a photograph contains. But the diagrammatic maps of muscles in our illustrated anatomies are not "transcripts" of things seen but the work of trained observers who build up the picture of a specimen that has been revealed to them in years of patient study.

   Why might the artist, who "packs in" information and "builds up" an image, offer more information to the anatomy student than the photographer?

From Text to Field

1. Gombrich's argument assumes that the illustrators he discusses learned to draw, at least in part, by following certain schemata. In an essay, recall how your art teachers—or one particularly influential art teacher—taught you how

to draw. Did you learn to use what Gombrich would term "schemas"? If so, what were they? If not, how were you taught to render something real? How were you taught to translate three-dimensional phenomena into two-dimensional renderings? What role did observation play? What role did technique play? As a prelude to writing this essay, or as an accompaniment to it, try your hand at drawing—that is, faithfully reproducing—an animal, a flower, or a natural object. What have you learned by trying to draw, now that you have read Gombrich's essay?

2. In the chapter "Truth and Stereotype" from *Art and Illusion*, Gombrich's central assertion is that we look at the world through the language and images we have been given. To explore his assertion on a personal level, choose a stereotype you hold or have held (such as stereotypes of race, gender, or certain professions). Write a personal essay in which you describe your own psychology regarding the stereotype. What are the specific elements of the stereotype? How did you acquire it? What do you think are its origins? How do you regard it? What, in your view, does it omit or distort?

3. You might recall that as Gombrich discusses "illustrated reportage" (par. 1) he pays a good deal of attention to the captions that accompany the illustrations. In an essay, reflect on the several functions that captions have. What work do they perform? Insofar as photojournalism might be thought of as modern illustrated reportage, do Gombrich's insights still apply? What role do captions have as they accompany photographs? Consider using illustrations in your essay.

INTO THE FIELD: Options for Writing Projects

1. Seeing Your Campus Afresh

Although your college campus may seem new and unexplored during your first days as a student, you will soon have settled into a routine. You will frequent some parts of campus so regularly that you will become inured to their local details, their specific characteristics. Sheer habit of walking or biking your regular route will blind you. Other parts of campus may remain as remote and uncharted as ever, a terra incognita even after months or several years as a student.

This field project offers an opportunity to rediscover a small corner of your campus. Through close observation of a particular site and the activities that occur there, develop an essay in which you introduce fellow students and other members of your campus community to a space you all share but of which you may have become unaware. As you choose your particular site, you may want to consider the following options:

- A prominent spot on campus, often heavily trafficked, offers a chance for your readers to rediscover something they may think they already know quite well. Such a site may be layered with a rich history, multiple meanings, and various, sometimes competing, activities.
- A remote or unnoticed site on campus offers a different challenge. Here your job is to bring the site alive for those who don't know it well, or at all, and to suggest its significance. Why should members of the campus community stop and notice this little corner, this patch of ground?
- Buildings define campus geography, and yet we often don't listen well to what the walls of those buildings whisper in our ears. What would a particular building on campus want you to know about its history, about the disciplinary or residential activities that it houses, about those who inhabit its halls?
- Landmarks and memorials offer a further option and may include public art on campus, as well as benches, stones, or other markers that memorialize a teacher or a student. As you uncover the history behind such sites, and the people they honor, you will help your readers see a corner of your campus afresh.

2. Seeing to Write, Writing to See

This field project invites you to explore in some detail the complex relationships between seeing and writing, observing and expressing, envisioning and communicating. It places a premium on close attention to your writing process and the use of apt, detailed examples. Four points of departure may enrich your essay as you uncover these relationships:

- Start with the process of seeing. What is it about seeing that leads to or requires verbalization? Seeing—close observation—is often considered a precursor to writing, yet the process of writing often enables or requires us to see more deeply.
- You should also approach the relationship from the perspective of writing and the writing and revision process. How does revision invite us to see differently? As we write, how do we "envision" a text? How do we write in cues that help readers envision a text (its terrain, its structure, its progression)?
- The relationship between seeing and writing takes on different forms in particular disciplines or fields. How might the dynamic between seeing and writing differ, for example, in anthropology and sociology on the one hand and engineering and architecture on the other hand? How do seeing and writing inform work in your major?
- Even academic texts are becoming, in today's world, far more visual, as they call on not just illustrations but also forms of multimedia. How has the relationship between seeing and writing been influenced by your experience as a multimedia reader?

3. **Aesthetic Response, across the Curriculum**

We tend to think of aesthetic response as something that belongs to art and literature departments and that it has little if any relevance elsewhere on campus. Yes, aesthetic response concerns how we value the beautiful, yet we may unduly limit the range and importance of that response if we think of it in terms of paintings, sculpture, or novels. This field project asks that you consider the role of aesthetic response in fields far removed from art and literature.

To help you unpack that tricky concept "aesthetic response," let's recall that John Berger (p. 684) spoke of the wood carving of the white bird in terms of five categories or qualities that make it both pleasing and mysterious: its reference to or place in the surrounding world; its meaning, significance, or symbolic value; its respect for the material used; its formal unity and economy; and its ability to elicit astonishment at how it was made, its craftsmanship. Drawing on some or all of these qualities, consider whether and in what way aesthetic emotion plays a role across the curriculum. A few examples might prompt you to look further:

- Design, whether in engineering or in architecture and planning, involves more than building functional "things." Design also has an aesthetic dimension. What we build often depends on how users respond; function can, and perhaps must, be in some sense beautiful or pleasing.
- The best research designs in the social and natural sciences are sometimes praised as being "elegant." Is there a research aesthetic? If so, which of Berger's five qualities might be crucial to that aesthetic?

- A well-crafted analysis or argument often involves more than sheer logic and hard evidence. Is there an aesthetic of analysis and argument, one that involves its design or perhaps the author's voice? In what ways does the aesthetic of nonfiction expository prose parallel or depart from the aesthetic of fictional literature?

4. Concerned Photography

When photography is used as a means of activism of one kind or another—ecological or political, for example—we might think of it as "concerned photography." Photos can be used, as Susan Sontag (p. 690) puts it, "to stimulate the moral impulse" (par. 27). Yet she cautions that "[p]hotographs cannot create a moral position, but they can reinforce one—and can help build a nascent one" (par. 28).

This field project invites you to explore "concerned photography" through one particular case study. You might choose to examine the role of images in an environmental appeal or a fund-raising campaign or the function of images in mobilizing response to human rights abuse. Collect primary texts—brochures, Web sites, print advertisements, and the like—so that you can analyze the function of these images in some detail.

Whatever your particular case study, your task is to explore the connection between "seeing" and "believing." How do images elicit belief and spur action? What is the value of shock? And what are the dangers of repetition, repeated exposure, and cliché—in short, the banality of the image?

5. Campus Image Making

The images of college life that you find in admissions brochures and on university Web sites can influence educational and career decisions. Perhaps such images—a class held outside under a tree on a verdant lawn or a female engineering student in a lab—enticed you as well or provided a sense that you might fit in. This field project invites you to look behind the glossy public presentation of your institution to examine the process of campus image making.

The first step is to assemble a set of texts—printed and/or digital—that can serve as your primary documents. As you analyze these documents, you may wish to consider a range of questions:

- How do the images communicate a sense of your college's identity and its institutional mission? You might find it helpful to compare your images with those of similar kinds of institutions (community colleges, large state universities, private liberal arts colleges, religious institutions, and so on).
- Do the images draw on stereotypical features of college life in general, or do they capture something of the local context, the life actually lived on your campus?

- How does the making of your campus in images balance two competing demands: the wish to project the institution your campus would like to become and the need to portray the institution as it is?
- Is there truth in advertising? Have you had a class that actually met outside on a lawn? Does the percentage of female engineering students merit the portrayal it received? How does the portrayal of ethnic and racial minorities match the actual climate on campus?

To understand the behind-the-scenes work that leads to campus publications and their use with different audiences, you may find it helpful to interview admissions counselors and the editorial and photographic staff in the campus publications office.

6. Truth, Lies, and Your Life in Images

This field project uses autobiography as an opportunity to analyze the role of images in forging identity. Your source documents for this project include family albums and personal photographs, augmented by your reflection on how you and others take photos. This project can be approached from at least two perspectives:

- Consider how your life has been captured by others in images. What truths, even if unpleasant, have been captured in these photos, and likewise what lies or distortions might be apparent? Your task in this project is not merely to describe photos or assess their truth but rather to use such questions as springboards to an analysis of what has occurred to your representation through the camera's eyes and the eyes of others. For example, what is it about family photos, with their "say cheese" moments, that can be both comforting and distressing, both true and fake?
- Consider how you have captured images of others. With the miniaturization of digital cameras and with cell phones now having photographic capability, one needn't lug around a large single-lens reflex camera, or even a pocket camera. What is the story of your life as an image taker? Has technology changed your photographic habits? In what ways do you consider the truth and lies in the photos you take? Here, too, your focus in this project is not your photo-taking adventures in and of themselves; your task is to use such adventures as an opportunity to consider broader social and cultural attitudes through your own photographic acts.

7. Blindness and Insight

Our culture has organized many of its metaphors around issues of sight. For example, consider the idiomatic expression "seeing eye to eye." Likewise, stereotypes about blindness abound, as in the blind beggar with the tin cup in his hand. This field project invites you to explore and consider the consequences of such metaphors and stereotypes. Because this field project can quickly become complex and take you in different directions, consider how you might focus your efforts.

A good place to begin is to catalog as many of the metaphors or idiomatic expressions about blindness and sight as you can. Ask a classmate or a friend to help you develop such a catalog. You may also wish to interview disability counselors about how such metaphors and expressions are received by those who have issues with their eyesight.

You may also wish to focus your analysis in a particular area, such as film, literature, or cartoons and comic strips. Another option is to examine cultural icons, such as Helen Keller. To what extent do such icons dispel misconceptions about blindness, and to what extent does the very popularity of such icons make it difficult to change perceptions that are by now quite dated?

8. Pictorial Representation

In the excerpt you have read from "Truth and Stereotype" (p. 709), a chapter in *Art and Illusion*, E. H. Gombrich uses illustrated reportage and scientific illustration as examples of the psychology of pictorial representation that he addresses throughout the book. Deepen or extend your reflection on pictorial representation by choosing one of the following two options for fieldwork:

- To further explore the psychology Gombrich describes, conduct interviews or research to find out how artists learn to illustrate. How are they taught to see? How are they taught to translate what they see into a pictorial form? What role does technique play? How might schemas come into play?
- Write an essay in which you apply Gombrich's argument in this excerpt to other forms of art or other periods of art. Or apply the argument to other forms of "pictorial representation," which could range from advertising to the mental images that serve as our stereotypes for people, activities, or events. To support and enrich your analysis, pursue some research and, if possible, conduct interviews regarding the "pictorial representation" you have chosen to discuss.

9. Writing: Schemas and Imitation

The excerpt from E. H. Gombrich's *Art and Illusion* offers insights into the role that schemas play in orienting our perceptions and representations of our world. Although Gombrich confines himself to illustration, writing also involves schemas that guide our composing and reading processes. Moreover, just as pictorial representation relies in good measure on imitation, so too does writing ask us to proceed using forms and styles that we inherit. This fieldwork project invites you to consider the role of underlying schemas and imitation in the writing process through one of several perspectives or issues:

- For many centuries, writing instruction placed heavy emphasis on copying and imitating exemplary texts. What rationale do you see in that form of instruction?
- To what extent might genre—or forms of writing often meant to support certain activities—be a schema in the sense proposed by Gombrich?
- Writing instruction in school and college often proceeds on the basis of preconceived schemas or frameworks, such as the "five paragraph essay." Assess their value and limitations.
- Initiation into an academic field often involves imitating basic kinds of texts and literate behaviors. Consider how an assignment in an introductory course (such as a lab report in physics) can succeed or fail in accomplishing that purpose.

10. Received Vocabularies

Elsewhere in *Art and Illusion*, E. H. Gombrich observes that "the artist, no less than the writer, needs a vocabulary before he can embark on a 'copy' of reality." For your field project, consider the role of "received vocabularies" in an academic discipline, in teaching and learning, or in contemporary cultural and political life. Here is a short, illustrative list of the sort of projects you might pursue:

- Consider a specific field in which one term or concept, as a received "vocabulary," is now under reconsideration or has become a matter of some dispute.
- In what ways might cultural anthropology help us understand the insight offered by the art historian Gombrich: why the "unfamiliar" is inevitably understood, if only at first, through the "familiar."
- Consider how an issue of contemporary interest (gender, for example, or international conflict) is complicated by misunderstandings resulting from a "received vocabulary."

WITNESSING THE IMAGE

We live in a media culture that has saturated our lives with images. Specific purveyors of images—television, Web sites, magazines, consumer commodities themselves—all contribute to this surfeit of the visual. But it is not sheer quantity that poses challenges for us. Images have changed how we witness our world.

Our connection with images has grown more distant even as the images multiply. Chances are, the image we see is not the image we produced or the image we ourselves circulated. What the image depicts is not necessarily grounded in the world we ourselves experience. Images are now produced, circulated, and consumed in an economy of the visual that extends well beyond our experience.

We have long questioned the image—especially the photographic image—in terms of its adequacy. Does the image adequately represent what we know and have experienced, what we ourselves have seen? This question has now become secondary to a larger question about believability. Can we believe images when what we know of the world is chiefly drawn from images themselves? What happens when our acquaintance with the real largely comes by way of the image itself? What happens when we find ourselves increasingly dependent on the image yet ever more uncomprehending about what it shows?

This unit explores these issues—ones that arise as we witness the image. The belief we invest in photos seems natural enough, grounded as it is in our assumption that they capture our world. Photos seem to be the ultimate testimony about our world. And yet, we would do well to ask who is using the photo and to what end. Belief in photos must remain something that we bestow, through individual initiative and acts of conscience. Yet the larger economy of the visual would have us believe that we have already acquiesced to the image. Its very presence makes a claim on our credence.

As images become more pervasive, they have also intertwined themselves with words in ways that challenge centuries of separation between seeing and speaking. Images now speak, and words are tethered to images. In our media culture, showing and telling are no longer easily separated. With the intertwined lives of image and word come new possibilities but also challenges.

Likewise, images and our easy access to them have us question what it means to be a witness and to bear witness. What is our proximity to events, and can we trust the testimony of our eyes and ears, especially when the media function ever more frequently as borrowed eyes and ears? Witnessing has always raised difficult issues about the connections between seeing and saying, experience and language. But in an image-saturated media culture, those issues become pressing.

Our difficulties and fascination with images are nowhere made more apparent than in images that trouble us—images of war and terrorism, images of the fragility of community. Those images themselves tell a tale—about what we care to know and care to hide and about the increasingly global reach of images. As we witness images from halfway around the world, we are also witnessing profound changes in the ways we see and believe.

The four readings in this unit help us raise and explore these issues in ways that connect image and word in their own texts. David Levi Strauss asks us to question the link between photography and believability, for he is worried that belief itself may become the "collateral damage" of our media culture. In his article on "Witnessing" John Durham Peters asks us to reflect on the precarious journey from experience to words, from the seen to the said. That journey is made all the more precarious by a media culture that is happy to witness for us. We close with two essays that deal with specific images that sear into our minds and hearts. H. Bruce Franklin surveys the history of war photography and is troubled by the ways in which war images have slipped into a sanitized virtual reality. Francis A. Beer and G. R. Boynton reflect on images of terrorism in a post–9/11 world. They find that the globalization of terror goes hand in hand with the globalization of the media. The reach and speed of images brings terror into our living rooms. And terrorism itself has found a new stage: image-driven media.

Reflecting on Prior Knowledge

1. We believe in photographic images perhaps even more resolutely than we do other forms of art or texts that capture experience. In a journal, reflect on a photograph that has, for whatever reason, captured your belief. Explore why this has been the case.

2. Our culture has traditionally separated words from pictures. Working in groups, and drawing on your own reading and viewing experience, share ideas on why image and text have led isolated lives. Is this changing? If so, why and to what effect?

3. Images of conflict and war are among the most gruesome we know. They are real, all too real. And yet, images of war can often take on the quality of virtual reality, where they are, if not romanticized, at least sanitized. In a journal entry, recall and describe an image of war or conflict that has made an impression on you. What about it seems real and immediate or eerily distant and removed? How is this image used, and by whom?

4. Experience is fleeting, yet we are sometimes called upon to remember and talk about it after the fact. Have you ever been asked to talk about an event or experience that you witnessed? What was difficult about serving, if only informally, as a witness? Working in groups of two or three, develop a catalog of issues that make witnessing reliable or unreliable and always a challenge.

5. Thanks to the media, many of the images we witness have been circulated widely, often across the globe. Given the speed and reach of today's global media, how have such images affected our ability or willingness to respond to them? Writing individually in a journal or working collectively in a small group, reflect on what place images from across the globe have in your life.

Photography and Belief

David Levi Strauss

An essayist, poet, and art critic living in New York, David Levi Strauss has written provocative essays on the relationships among photography, politics, and culture. He asks his readers to look behind the apparently self-evident nature of photographs and to interrogate their place in our culture, especially in our politics.

After studying at Goddard College, Strauss worked at the Center of Curatorial Studies at Bard College and as a faculty member at the Avery Graduate School of the Arts. He has received several awards, among them a Guggenheim Fellowship. His essays and reviews appear regularly in such journals as *Artforum* and *Aperture* and have been gathered in two collections: *Between Dog and Wolf: Essays on Art and Politics* (1999) and *Between the Eyes: Essays on Photography and Politics* (2003). His essays have also appeared in monographs on such artists as Carolee Schneemann, Leon Golub, Miguel Rio Branco, Alfredo Jaar, Francesca Woodman, and Daniel Martinez.

The essay that follows — "Photography and Belief" — appears in Strauss's collection *Between the Eyes: Essays on Photography and Politics.* Here, as in many of his essays, Strauss writes about the crisis of representation, and asks us to consider the connection between what we see and what we believe. The question is pressing because, in today's world, much of what we know of the real comes by way of images. In this wide-ranging collection, Strauss tackles such subjects as photography and propaganda and the social life of the images of September 11, and he explores photographs as both social documents and as personal revelation.

They say that pictures don't lie, but that's not really true anymore.
— Advance promotion line for an interview with Fred
Ritchin on National Public Radio, February 7, 1991

> If material conditions need to be redescribed, more painstakingly
> and in novel forms, in order to be reinvested with "believability," then
> we can surely develop the form — and the means of dissemination —
> to do so.
> — MARTHA ROSLER, "Image Simulations, Computer Manipulations:
> Some Ethical Considerations"

"Seeing is believing." It's been that way from the beginning, long before Messrs. Niépce and Daguerre changed the technology of seeing by inventing photography. But photography materialized seeing in a new way, and significantly changed the relation between seeing and believing. Photography as mechanical reproduction almost immediately altered the aura of the work of art, and over the next 150 years photography acquired its own aura — the aura of believability.

Now the technology of seeing is changing again, with rapid advances in electronic imaging technologies that allow one to alter or "make up" photographs at will, and some say these new technologies are causing a tremendous crisis of believability in photography. In his book *In Our Own Image: The Coming Revolution in Photography/How Computer Technology is Changing Our View of the World,* Fred Ritchin raises a cry of alarm. In the preface to his book, he states that it was written "in appreciation of the important historical juncture at which we stand, just before the widespread adoption of electronic technology, out of a sense that we must try to take some responsibility for the future of the immensely popular *and still believable* medium of photography." (Emphasis added.) The questions raised by the new imaging technologies were discussed in *Newsweek* (July 30, 1990) under the title "When Photographs Lie: Advances in 'electronic imaging' are assaulting the meaning of the picture"; five years before that (July 1985), *Whole Earth Review* had declared with dogmatic finality that "the photograph as evidence of anything is dead." Commentators of all kinds say we are moving into a period in which the boundaries between fact and fiction, real and artificial, actual and virtual reality are going to become much more operationally porous and movable than they have been in the past.

Most of these speculations about the impact of new imaging technologies on photography have tended to be strictly materialist (unlike the more heterodox, reality-hacking, *Mondo 2000* hyperspeculations of the burgeoning cyberpunk subculture), and many are based on a series of severely restricted assumptions about how photographs are actually received and used. If we are to understand the coming changes, we must try harder to understand the present and evolving complexity of the way we look at, use, and "believe" photographs now.

Is That a Real Photograph or Did You Just Make It Up?

The word *belief* derives from the Anglo-Saxon word *geliefan*, meaning "to hold dear." The Sanskrit root for this word, *Lubh*, means "to desire, love." Belief involves the "assent of the mind to a statement, or to the truth of a fact beyond observation, on the testimony of another, or to a fact or truth on the evidence of consciousness" (*Oxford English Dictionary*). In relation to photography, this assent is influenced, but not exhausted, by the photograph's relation to "objective reality." It is also influenced and determined by its place in the complex web of subjectivities that determines how we negotiate the world.

Reputed Identities

The relation between photography and belief is especially complicated in 5
images having to do with identity, where the effect of a photograph can be decisive. When Burl Ives shows James Dean a photograph he's been holding for years of Dean's father and mother on their wedding day in the film *East of Eden*, Dean looks at it and says, "I *knew* it was true. I knew it." Sometimes,

Figure 1. Found photograph of unknown boy, believed to be the author's brother. For more information, please call 1-800-929-2323 or visit www.aperture.org. Aperture is a not-for-profit public foundation dedicated to promoting photography as an unique form of artistic expression.

the photograph doesn't need to prove anything on its own; it corroborates and confirms what we already know.

Many of us possess certain photographs that accrete believability over time. These may be photographs of family members or loved ones, autobiographical images, or other photographs that come to act as amulets or talismans, triggering certain emotions or states and warding off others. The relation of these photographs to belief is often not bound by their objective veracity. Rupert Jenkins (assistant director at San Francisco Camerawork) told me that when he was a child he picked up a photograph lying in the street and carried it around, telling everyone that this was a picture of his mother. After a while, he came to believe it *was* his mother. I had a similar experience in adolescence with a picture I found somewhere of a boy resembling pictures I had seen of my father as a child. I began to think of this found photograph as a picture of my brother who had died before I was born. In some real way, that photograph did come to represent my brother.

People use photographs to construct identities, investing them with "believability." Of course, advertisers and news-picture editors do the same thing, mimicking the private use of photographs in order to manufacture desire for products and to manufacture public consent. This has caused a great deal of confusion. The first question must always be: Who is using this photograph, and to what end?

Friendly Fire

Increasingly, those who control technology control information, and those who control information manage consent. The Gulf War ushered in a new era of information control and consensus reality in the United States, and this change can be read in the way images were used during the war. Following the successful press blackouts of their invasions of Grenada and Panama, the U.S. military was able to drop a seamless screen around the entire theater of operations in the Gulf from day one. The only images released to the U.S. public were the ones projected onto that screen by military authorities. Since photojournalists were effectively shut out of the area or relegated to tightly controlled Department of Defense pools, few of the images projected onto that screen were conventional documentary photographs. Instead, the images came from electronically manipulated and enhanced tapes; video arcade images of crosshairs floating over targets, ending in delicate puffs of smoke.

As the war progressed, most of the "photographs" printed in newspapers were actually video stills from CNN footage. These strangely attractive images of fireworks against liquid green skies, tightly composed explosions, and handsome talking heads before cold blue mosques were, literally, not to be believed. What was to believe? *This is a direct hit on a munitions dump. This is the air war over Baghdad.* The actual war information in these images was so restricted that questions of believability never really came up. What did come up, over and over, was *deniability.*

In an unusually frank piece titled "The Propaganda War" (subtitled 10 "Amid the bombs, words and pictures carry a payload on the battlefield of public opinion"), the February 25, 1991, issue of *Newsweek* stated:

> Propaganda is a broad approach to persuasion that encompasses several disciplines. So-called public diplomacy — a variation on standard public relations — involves presenting one's position in the best possible light, often on TV. Formal military psychological operations ("psyops") include broadcasting and dropping leaflets over enemy lines. Each of these mind games relies at times on "disinformation" — planting false information so as to confuse and manipulate. *Still, the most persuasive propaganda is that which is both graphic and demonstrably true.*
>
> In theory, reporters in democratic societies work independent of propaganda. In practice they are treated during war as simply more pieces of military hardware to be deployed. While the allies play it straighter than Iraq, much of the information they release has propaganda value, too. No video displays of missed targets, for instance, are ever shown. *The problem for the American press is that the American people seem to like it that way.* (Emphasis added.)

The American public had been well prepared for this type of propaganda war over the last decade. Watching it play across their screens now, they believed it because they wanted to believe it. This was war with a happy face — a "no body count" war in which the public quite clearly communicated to the press: "Don't tell us — we don't want to know. We know what we believe."

Photography materialized seeing in a new way, and significantly changed the relation between seeing and believing.

When former CBS anchor Walter Cronkite, whom the polls once named "the most trusted public figure in America," spoke out against Gulf War censorship, he was quickly given the bum's rush by *CBS News.* In a chilling piece published in that same February 25, 1991, issue of *Newsweek,* Cronkite brought up the analogy of post–World War II Germany, when most Germans claimed ignorance of the Holocaust. "But this claim of ignorance did not absolve them from blame," wrote Cronkite. "They had complacently permitted Hitler to do his dirty business in the dark. They raised little objection, most even applauded when he closed their newspapers and clamped down on free speech. Certainly our leaders are not to be compared with Hitler, but today, because of onerous, unnecessary rules, Americans are not being permitted to see and hear the full story of what their military forces are doing in an action that will reverberate long into the nation's future."

Saddam Hussein's bumbling attempts at electronic propaganda afforded no such shelter of deniability, and were about as effective as were his army and air force. Hussein's propaganda was of the old, premodern type: transparently manipulative, often verifiably untrue, and easily turned to the enemy's advantage. When the videotaped confessions of downed U.S. and British pilots hit the airwaves, they backfired famously. The tortured faces of the pilots, reproduced thousands of times all over the world, along with those of Israeli citizens huddled in sealed rooms in gas masks, immediately became emblematic of Hussein's brutality and recklessness, and made almost any action against him possible.

Even so, the Vietnam-era generals in charge of Desert Storm recognized from the beginning that modern communications technologies make it impossible to wage war in the open. Today, war must be hidden behind an impenetrable propaganda curtain—no images of death and destruction, no fields bloody with carnage, no dismembered corpses; no orphans, or gangrene, or naked napalmed little girls; and no body count. The surprise was how readily, and how completely, the American public acquiesced.

Blindsided by the New World Order

The way that images were manipulated and controlled during the Gulf War 15 makes Ritchin's warnings about the dangers of digital retouching seem almost quaint. That type of manipulation is a very small part of postmodern propaganda, and focusing on it may cause the big picture to become blurred. Take an image that appeared early in the conflict, before war was declared, in a supposedly "liberal" magazine. The cover of the September 3, 1990, issue of the New Republic featured a closely cropped, full-face photograph of Saddam Hussein. The image was slightly altered, not by means of advanced electronic imaging techniques, but in the old-fashioned way. The edges of Hussein's broad mustache were simply airbrushed away to create the universally recognizable sign for Adolph Hitler. Just to make sure the effect wasn't too subtle, the word Furor (in the headline "Furor in the Gulf") was emblazoned in red across Hussein's forehead, invoking "Der Führer in the Gulf."

Although an article inside by Edward N. Luttwak interrogates the Hitler/Hussein analogy (Iraq in 1990 was not Germany in 1935, and George Bush Sr. is not Churchill), and suggests that the cover is intended satirically, the effect of the image is unambiguous. Like Bush Sr.'s oft-repeated refrain about "Hitler revisited," the image doesn't need to be accurate to be effective, and arguing its accuracy has little relevance to this effect. Its effectiveness—the only applicable measurement of propaganda—derives from the historical amnesia of most Americans and the perennial desire to reduce the scale and significance of atrocities by attributing them to lone, monstrously evil madmen. The *New Republic*'s image contains everything one needs to know about the analogy for it to be effective, and reflects the subtle manipulations of that analogy visually. *Saddam Hussein is Hitler.* What's not to believe?

> All information should be considered false until proven true.
> — PRUSSIAN MILITARY STRATEGIST KARL VON CLAUSEWITZ

> The more crap you believe in, the better off you are.
> — FAYE DUNAWAY'S CHARACTER TO MICKEY ROURKE'S BUKOWSKI,
> IN THE FILM BARFLY

The aura of believability surrounding photographs is not all that vulnerable to new electronic imaging technologies *in themselves.* But belief itself is vulnerable to the kind of massive propaganda assault and general degradation of information that accompanied (and will certainly follow) the Gulf War. The crisis of belief we are experiencing is much larger than a simple mistrust of photographs. It involves the wholesale, active relinquishing of our public right to know. When the manipulation and control of all forms of public imaging have become this pervasive, this *complete*, it is more than ever necessary to resist, to reassert individual initiative in the production, reception, and use of images, and to find new ways to reinvest images with "believability" — before belief itself becomes part of the collateral damage.

Working with the Text

1. David Levi Strauss opens his essay with three paragraphs before turning to the connections between personal and political belief. What function do those three paragraphs serve? To what extent do they raise issues (such as digital retouching) only to redirect or reframe those issues?

2. Strauss notes near the beginning of his essay that assent or belief "is influenced, but not exhausted, by the photograph's relation to 'objective reality.' It is also influenced and determined by its place in the complex web of subjectivities that determines how we negotiate the world" (par. 4). In light of the arguments made in the rest of the essay, what does Strauss mean by a "complex web of subjectivities"?

3. The terrain explored by Strauss in his essay extends from the family photo to the propaganda photo, from the personal to the political. How does Strauss connect such disparate issues? Does Strauss's discussion of "belief" and an "aura of believability" benefit from this broad spectrum of examples, and if so, in what ways?

4. The final paragraph of Strauss's essay returns to the term *aura of believability* that he raised earlier. What role does this paragraph serve in making explicit the argument Strauss has been advancing throughout the essay? What reasoning lies implicit in his call, at the very end of the essay, for reasserting "individual initiative" and for finding new ways to "reinvest images with 'believability'"?

5. Strauss opens his essay with two epigraphs and prior to the closing paragraph offers another two epigraphs. What function do these quotes have? How do they frame and augment his argument?

From Text to Field

1. Drawing in part on Strauss's essay, write a reflection on a personal photograph that has special meaning for you. In what respect is the photo real, and in what respect is the photo infused with belief? What role does the photo play in how you construct identity—both the identity of the person photographed and your own identity?

2. Drawing on the Gulf War in 1991, Strauss discusses the use of photographs by the government and the military. Offer a brief analysis of your own that draws on a current issue involving photos by the government and the military. Does your example substantiate Strauss's insights, or does your example raise questions or perspectives not fully addressed by him?

3. Strauss's argument turns, in part, on what he sees as the responsibilities of a free press. Drawing on a current news story in which widely circulated images play a central role, discuss how you see the press fulfilling (or abrogating) its role. To what extent do you think the American public is interested in a vigorous free press? Given your news story, what challenges or constraints do the news media encounter? How do you think most readers respond to the circulation of images related to your news story? What are the limits to the readers' willingness to believe?

Witnessing

John Durham Peters

Many of the most important recent debates in the humanities seem to be tied to issues of communication—the anxieties we feel about it, its conundrums and, yes, its breakdowns. John Durham Peters has emerged as a daring, insightful, and elegant voice in the study of how and why we communicate.

Peters is interested in media and cultural history, communication and social theory, and understanding communication in its broad historical, legal, philosophical, religious, and technological contexts. After receiving his BA in English and his MA in speech communication from the University of Utah, Peters pursued his graduate study at Stanford University, where he received his PhD in 1986. He has since been on the faculty of the University of Iowa, where he serves as F. Wendell Miller Distinguished Professor in the Department of Communication Studies.

Peters is best known for his 1999 award-winning book, *Speaking into the Air: A History of the Idea of Communication.* He asks how new media and faster forms of transportation and communication can lead to increasing anxieties about miscommunication and writes to reclaim a sense of authenticity in a media-saturated world. His most recent book is *Courting the Abyss: Free Speech and the Liberal Tradition* (2005), which revisits the tangled history of free speech in light of concerns in a post–9/11 world.

In his 2001 essay on "Witnessing," Peters explores what he considers to be the fragile and complex juncture between "seeing" and "saying," experience and discourse; in so doing, he suggests that witnessing raises enduring issues regarding how we encounter and talk about our world.

Witnessing is a common but rarely examined term in both the professional performance and academic analysis of media events. Media institutions have enthusiastically adopted its rhetoric, especially for nonfiction genres such as news, sports, and documentary. Such titles as *Eyewitness News, See It Now, Live at Five,* or *As It Happens* advertise their program's privileged proximity to events. Media personae such as correspondents and newsreaders can be institutionalized as witnesses. Cameras and microphones are often presented as substitute eyes and ears for audiences who can witness for themselves. Ordinary people can be witnesses *in* media (the vox pop interview, 'tell us how it happened'), *of* media (members of studio audiences), and *via* media (watching history unfold at home in their armchairs). The media claim to provide testimonies for our inspection, thus making us witnesses of the way of the world. As a term of art, witnessing outshines more colorless competitors such as viewing, listening or consuming, reading, interpreting, or decoding, for thinking about the experience of media. What is the significance of this pervasive way of talking?

In this article, I propose to untangle the concept of witnessing in order to illuminate basic problems in media studies. Witnessing is an intricately tangled practice. It raises questions of truth and experience, presence and absence, death and pain, seeing and saying, and the trustworthiness of perception—in short, fundamental questions of communication. The long history of puzzlement and prescription about proper witnessing that developed in oral and print cultures is a rich resource for reflection about some of the ambiguities of audiovisual media. Hoary philosophical issues (such as the epistemological status of the senses) often show up in media practices in surprising ways; in turn, media practices can, if seen in the proper lighting, also clarify old philosophical worries.

An important step in this direction has been taken in John Ellis's *Seeing Things* (2000), whose lucid arguments I wish to extend and nuance. Witnessing, for Ellis, is a distinct mode of perception: "we cannot say we do not know" is its motto. To witness an event is to be responsible in some way to it. The stream of data flowing through the unaided senses already exceeds our explanatory schemata. The present moment supplies enough sensory information to outlast a lifetime of analysis. Audiovisual media, however, are able to catch contingent details of events that would previously have been either imperceptible or lost to memory. A camera can reveal the impact of a bullet in an apple; the tape recorder can fix an off-the-record comment. Such mechanical, "dumb" media seem to present images and sounds as they happened, without the embellishments and blind spots that human perception and memory routinely impose. We thus find ourselves endowed with a much amplified and nuanced record of events, a "superabundance of details" rich with evidentiary value. Though photography, sound-recording, film, and radio have all expanded the realm of sensory evidence, Ellis singles out television in particular. "Separated in space yet united in time, the copresence of the television image was developing a distinct form of witness. Witnessing became a domestic act. . . . Television sealed the twentieth century's fate as the century of witness" (Ellis, 2000: 32). Liveness is a key characteristic of televisual witnessing, including the morally problematic witnessing of violence and carnage. He advances witnessing as a key term for media analysis that, he believes, is freer of ontological baggage than other more commonly used concepts.

For Ellis, in sum, witnessing has to do with complicity; owes much to modern media of inscription; is an attitude cultivated by live television, particularly nonfiction programming; and a valuable resource for media analysis. I would concur with Ellis in everything with the exception that witnessing actually carries weighty baggage, if not ontological, at least historical. Yet this baggage is not only a burden, but also a potential treasure, at least since it makes explicit the pervasive link between witnessing and suffering and shows the degree to which media problems with witnessing are built upon venerable communication problems that are inherent in the witness as a kind of signifying act. The "baggage" has three main interrelated sources: law, theology, and atrocity. In law, the notion of the witness as a privileged source of information for judicial decisions is ancient, and is part of most known legal systems. In theology, the notion of witness, especially as martyr, developed in early Christianity, though it has resonance for other religious traditions as well. The third, most recent, source dates from the Second World War: the witness as a survivor of hell, prototypically but not exclusively the Holocaust or *Shoah*. These three domains endow "witnessing" with its extraordinary moral and cultural force today, since each ties the act of witnessing, in some deep way, to life and death. The procedures of the courtroom, the pain of the martyr, and the cry of the survivor cast light on basic questions such as what it means to watch, to narrate, or to be present at an event. Witnessing, as an amazingly subtle array of practices of securing truth from the facts of our sensitivity to pain and our inevitable death, increases the stakes of our thinking about media events.

Analyzing the Term

As a noun, *witness* is intricate. The term involves all three points of a basic   5 communication triangle: (1) the agent who bears witness, (2) the utterance or text itself, (3) the audience who witnesses. It is thus a strange, but intelligible sentence to say: The witness (speech-act) of the witness (person) was witnessed (by an audience). A witness can also be the performance itself. Thus we speak of a Holocaust survivor's witness against fascism. In African American churches when preachers ask, "Can I get a witness?", they invite audience affirmation and participation, the witness as a public gesture of faith. In religious contexts, witness can also have a more private meaning as inward conviction of religious truth, which in turn may motivate the activity of "witnessing" (evangelizing). In law, literature, history, and journalism alike, a witness is an observer or source possessing privileged (raw, authentic) proximity to facts. A witness, in sum, can be an actor (one who bears witness), an act (making of a special sort of statement), the semiotic residue of that act (the statement as text), or the inward experience that authorizes the statement (the witnessing of an event).

As a verb, to *witness* has a double aspect. To witness can be a sensory experience — the witnessing of an event with one's own eyes and ears. We are all, constantly, witnesses in this sense simply by virtue of finding ourselves in places and times where things happen. Most of what we witness is insignificant in the larger scheme of things, and vanishes into oblivion. But witnessing is also the discursive act of stating one's experience for the benefit of an audience that was not present at the event and yet must make some kind of judgment about it. Witnesses serve as the surrogate sense organs of the absent. If what we have witnessed is crucial for a judgment, we may be summoned to a formal institutional setting: a court of law, a church, or a television studio. A witness is the paradigm case of a *medium*: the means by which experience is supplied to others who lack the original.

To witness thus has two faces: the passive one of *seeing* and the active one of *saying*. In passive witnessing an accidental audience observes the events of the world; in active witnessing one is a privileged possessor and *producer* of knowledge in an extraordinary, often forensic, setting in which speech and truth are policed in multiple ways. What one has seen authorizes what one says: An active witness first must have been a passive one. Herein lies the fragility of witnessing: the difficult juncture between experience and discourse. The witness is authorized to speak by having been present at an occurrence. A private experience enables a public statement. But the journey from experience (the seen) into words (the said) is precarious. Witnessing presupposes a discrepancy between the ignorance of one person and the knowledge of another: It is an intensification of the problem of communication more generally. It always involves an epistemological gap whose bridging is always fraught with difficulty. No transfusion of consciousness is possible. Words can be exchanged, experiences cannot. Testimony is another's discourse whose universe of reference diverges from one's own. Like somebody else's pain, it always has a twilight status between certainty and doubt. A parent may bear witness to a child that a stove is hot, but getting burnt may be more persuasive. Witnessing is a discourse with a hole in it that awaits filling.

The Unreliability of Witnesses

Witnesses, human or mechanical, are notoriously contradictory and inarticulate. Different people who witness the "same" event can produce remarkably divergent accounts. Though awareness of the poor epistemological quality of witnessing is ancient, twentieth-century social science has explored it in detail. Eyewitness testimony, for instance, has been subject to intense social-psychological scrutiny (e.g., Ross et al., 1994). We now know that errors in identifying people and faces are common, with potentially devastating consequences for justice. In reports by different eyewitnesses, moustaches fly on and off of faces, blondes morph into brunettes and clothes change color like chameleons. Hats have major effects on recognition, because of the role of the hairline in identifying faces. Post-event tampering, both from inside and outside, can also alter testimony. From within, the psychological process of dissonance-reduction has the paradoxical effect of increasing confidence in accuracy of recall even while the memory of the event is fading; from without, testimonies can be shaped by the schematic constraints of narrative structure and altered, perhaps even created, by the way they are probed ("refreshed") by others. Social science methodology has noted the dubious evidentiary status of statements about even one's own attitudes and opinions. From polling, we know about acquiescence effects (the tendency of people to agree), the huge effects of phrasing on reported opinions, and the divergence between front-door and back-door measures (Webb et al., 1981). Fabrication seems inherent in the loose coupling between sentences and the world; witnesses are evidently a fallible transmission and storage medium for sensory experience.

The legal theory of evidence is also a compendium of reflections about the (un)reliability of witnesses. There is a long history of excluding people as incompetent witnesses on various grounds. Non-Christians, convicts, interested parties, spouses, children, the insane, or those standing in a relationship of professional privilege with the defendant have all been considered hindered in truth telling or as possessing special motives to fabrication. As in survey research, the law has an acute awareness about the ways that modes of interrogation (e.g., leading questions) can manufacture, rather than elicit, testimony.

Since the transformation from experience to discourse lies at the heart of   10 communication theory, witnessing entails many of the most fundamental issues in the social life of signs, especially how the raw, apparently private, stuff of sensation can have any input into the public world of intelligible words (also a fundamental question in empiricist philosophy since Locke and Hume°). The forensics of the trial, the pains of the martyr, and the memoirs

---

Locke and Hume: John Locke (1632–1704) and David Hume (1711–1776), philosophers in the empiricist tradition that emphasized the role of experience and the senses.

of the survivor are all attempts to overpower the melancholy fact that direct sensory experience—from the taste of pineapple to the pains of childbirth — vanishes when put into words and remains inaccessible to others except inasmuch as they claim to share similar experiences. Sensation is encircled into privately personal ontologies. Only words are public.

Pain and the Veracity Gap

A variety of answers have been offered to cope with the fallibility of witnessing. Devices to compensate for its inherent dubiousness are ancient. One can vouch for veracity by an oath promising to trade death or pain for truth, a practice that persists in the children's line, "cross my heart and hope to die." One may appeal to ultimate authority: "God is my witness." According to Aristotle,° witnesses in a court of law testify at risk of punishment if they do not tell the truth; he considers dead witnesses more trustworthy, since they cannot be bribed (*Rhetoric*, 1376a). To witness as if you were as dumb and indifferent as the dead is the obvious ideal, since you would be free from interest, interpretation, care, and spin. A signature is a testimony: "in witness hereof . . . ," and like all forms of witnessing, it founders on the reef of forgery. The requirement of swearing on a Bible before testifying in court is yet another device to enforce truth telling, presumably by instilling the specter of eternal consequences. A reminder of the ancient worry about corrupt testimony is the ninth Mosaic commandment forbidding false witness (not the same thing as simple lying).

From the ancient Greeks to "modern" intelligence gathering, the effort to assure the transition from sensation to sentences in testimony has involved torture—a perverse but illuminating fact. As Page duBois (1991) argues, the ancient Greek word for torture, *basanos*, originally meant a touchstone, against which you could rub golden artifacts to test if they were genuine; if so, a bit would rub off and leave a mark. From there, *basanos* came to mean any test of truth or authenticity (e.g., of friendship or fidelity), and eventually moved specifically into torture, which served as an instrument of proof in ancient Athens. In Greek ideology, torture served as a cultural line dividing slaves, who respect only bodily pain, and citizens, who speak the *logos* in freedom. Since slaves supposedly lie compulsively, torture exposes the truth by extinguishing the power to invent. (Here again we see the snobbery about who can be expected to be a truthful witness.) Torture enforces the claim that slaves are ruled by necessity (*anangke*). A slave could not appear in

---

Aristotle (384–322 BCE): Greek philosopher and a student of Plato. In addition to his writings on ethics, metaphysics, and politics, Aristotle has had enormous influence in the development of rhetoric, the art of persuasion.

court, but a slave's testimony obtained under torture was admissible as evidence. Even so, there were already doubts about the notion that pain produces truth. Aristotle (*Rhetoric*, 1377a) thought testimony obtained under torture "inartistic" and generally distrusted testimony in any case.

The shift toward the confession as a source of legal proof in thirteenth-century Europe reintroduced judicial torture. It was not understood as a kind of punishment, but, cruel as it may sound, as a kind of data gathering; that innocent people might suffer and even die under interrogation was considered an unfortunate by-product of legal investigation (Langbein, 1977; Peters, 1985). Pain was supposed to be the midwife of authenticity. Judicial torture was an attempt to assure the validity of the confession, a rather nasty way of coping with the veracity gap. In our grisly age, torture is both a method of punishment and of extracting intelligence, a fact signaled in the French term *la question*, which means both torture and interrogation, or the English phrase, "put to the question." Even a polygraph test—a "lie-detector" that circumvents discourse to tap "direct" physiological indicators—shows the retreat to the body as the haven of truth. Deathbed confessions possess special legal status, since the incentive to deceive is thought minimal. As one judge wrote, "they are declarations made in extremity, when the party is at the point of death, and when every hope of this world is gone; when every motive to falsehood has been silenced, and the mind is induced by the most powerful considerations to speak the truth . . ." (Cross, 1974: 472). Here again is the sense that death or pain impel the mind to forego the temptation to embellish.

The bodily basis of testimony is seen in a strange etymological complex. Testimony stems from *testamentum*, covenant (*testis* plus *mentum*). *Testis*, which in Latin means both witness and testicle, itself stems from *tertius*, meaning third (party). In ancient Greek, the word for witness is the word for testicle: *parastatês*, which literally means bystander. In German, *Zeugnis* means testimony, and *zeugen* means to testify as well as to procreate. The explanation of this pervasive and odd system of metaphors is obscure, but one may conjecture that the testicles, as physical bystanders to the act of procreation, were thought witnesses of paternity or virility in Indo-European culture. That knowing firsthand should be associated with the testicles may suggest an ancient preference for the testimony of men over women. This curious web of metaphors, whatever its significance, attests to some deep assumptions about the physicality of witnessing. The body serves as a sort of collateral to justify the loan of our credence. The whole apparatus of trying to assure truthfulness, from torture to martyrdom to courtroom procedure, only testifies of the strange lack at its core. Witnessing is necessary, but not sufficient: If there are no witnesses, there is no trial, but witnesses do not secure a conviction or acquittal. A witness is never conclusive or final despite the most militant attempts of martyrs or torturers to make it so.

Another ancient attempt bodily to bridge the gap between inner convic- 15
tion and outer persuasion is the tradition of Christian martyrology. As Paul
Ricoeur argues (1981: 129):

> The witness is capable of suffering or dying for what he believes. When
> the test of conviction becomes the price of life, the witness changes his
> name; he is called a martyr. But is it a change of name? — *Martus* in Greek
> means "witness." . . . Testimony is both a manifestation and a crisis of
> appearances.

To judge from appearances is the fate of all who have to rely on communication for access to other's experiences. The martyr's death proves nothing
for certain, but demonstrates the limit case of persuasion, the vanishing point
at which proof stops and credence begins. Saints Stephen or Sebastian, or
their secular equivalents, the many political martyrs whose legacies are so
powerful today, may impress bystanders with their composure under the
most gruesome abuses, but their deaths alone will not convince anyone of
the truth of their faith: One needs internal grounds for believing. To bear witness is to put one's body on the line. Within every witness, perhaps, stands a
martyr, the will to corroborate words with something beyond them, pain and
death being the last resorts.

Since the Second World War, new kinds of witnessing have been forged
in the furnace of suffering. The Holocaust has generated deep thinking about
the nature of witnessing (Felman and Laub, 1992). It is striking, by the way,
that Ellis (2000), despite his incisive comments on psychoanalytic working
through of trauma and the complicity of the bystander, hardly mentions the
Holocaust — perhaps because it is too obvious. In any case, from ashes and
hell have emerged witnesses whose task, paradoxically, is to proclaim experiences that cannot be shared and to immortalize events that are uniquely tied
to the mortal bodies of those who went through them. Elie Wiesel, for
instance, has made his career reflecting on the privilege and loneliness of the
survivor. One's responsibility to bear witness, he argues, cannot be delegated:
Testimony is unique to the survivor. It is impossible for the witness to remain
silent; but it is also impossible for the witness to describe the event. The militancy in the survivor's voice owes to the battle against oblivion and indifference. Such militancy is found no less in the martyr, who likewise uses his or
her body as spectacle of pain to convict the conscience of the observer.
Already having cheated death, the survivor seeks to save his or her experiences for others who can never have them.

Specifically, the witness has become a literary genre growing out of the
Second World War. Primo Levi, Anne Frank, Victor Klemperer, Wiesel, to
name a few, have the cultural authority of witnesses of atrocity. As survivors
of events, they in turn bear active witness which we, at one remove, can in

turn witness passively. There is a strange ethical claim in the voice of the victim. Witnessing in this sense suggests a morally justified individual who speaks out against unjust power. Imagine a Nazi who published his memoirs of the war as a "witness"—it might be accepted as an account of experiences, but never as a "witness" in the moral sense: To witness means to be on the right side. Václav Havel, Jacopo Timerman, Rigoberta Menchú, Martin Luther King, Solzhenitsyn, Mandela, Aung San Suu Kyi—those who have languished in jail all stand as witnesses against inhumanity. (*Testimonio* is a recent genre of Latin American writing which records the cry against oppression.) The prison (or prison camp) is the house of witness, a maker of moral authority, just as prison literature has turned out to be one of the great forms of twentieth-century writing. The moral privilege of the captive and martyr is a founding narrative in European civilization, as in the case of both Socrates and Jesus.° Not surprisingly, there has been something of a scramble to capture the prestige of the victim-witness, and media who speak of their role as witnesses are not immune. (A recent book on the making of *Schindler's List* is pretentiously called *Witness*, confusing the film and what the film was about.)

Witnessing places mortal bodies in time. To witness always involves risk, potentially to have your life changed. The Roman poet Ovid bemoaned his banishment to the Black Sea for seeing something in the emperor's court he wasn't supposed to. You can be marked for life by being the witness of an event. The FBI runs the evocatively named "witness protection program" providing personal security and sometimes new identities for those willing to turn state witness. Abraham Zapruder is famous (and his heirs are now rich) for a few seconds of home-movie footage of a presidential parade in Dallas on 22 November 1963. In Graham Greene's *Brighton Rock*, the gangster Pinky marries the only witness to a murder he committed in order to make her, as a wife, an incompetent witness, but of course, as usual in Greene, a sort of redemption occurs via the corruption. That simply seeing can mark your bodily fate is a suggestive way of getting beyond the idea of mere spectatorship.

In sum, the indisputables of pain and death can serve as a resource to persuade others of the truth of one's words of witness. Witnessing is a mode of communication intimately tied to the mortality of both the one who bears witness and the one who in turn witnesses that act. As Jorge Luis Borges° (1964: 243) writes:

Socrates and Jesus: The Greek philosopher Socrates (470–399 BCE) was condemned to death by the court for corrupting the youth of Athens with his philosophy. Likewise Jesus was tried by Pontius Pilot and crucified.

Jorge Luis Borges (1899–1986): Argentine writer considered one of the prominent literary figures of the twentieth century.

Deeds which populate the dimensions of space and which reach their end when someone dies may cause us wonderment, but one thing, or an infinite number of things, dies in every final agony. . . . In time there was a day that extinguished the last eyes to see Christ; the battle of Junin and the love of Helen° died with a man.

Witnessing, as we will see, not only turns on the mortality of the witness, but the contingencies of the event.

Objectivity and the Veracity Gap

A different tradition seeks to secure the validity of statements without the 20
metaphysical and moral conundrums of pain. Very roughly speaking, the effort to put testimony on a sound footing is a project of the Enlightenment, both in the effort to minimize violence and to secure trustworthy knowledge. Indeed, one of the major tasks in the rise of modern science generally, with its need for cumulative observation from many eyes and ears, was to overcome the low repute of testimony. This was first achieved in seventeenth-century England with the creation of a genteel class of scientists, whose shared social status and norms of civility established a basis for trusting each other's reports (Shapin, 1994). As one scholar quips of the epistemology of testimony in early modern English science, gentlemen prefer gentlemen (Lipton, 1998). Without trust in other's statements about sensory experiences, science as we know it would be impossible. Further, the use of scientific instrumentation was motivated in part by the desire to bypass the stains of subjectivity, fallibility, and interest that attach to our sense organs. Scientific instruments such as the microscope or telescope were thought thinglike, and hence credible, in their indifference to human interests. The camera and microphone inherit this tradition of objectivity as passivity.

John Locke exemplifies these transformations. In his *Essay Concerning Human Understanding* (1975: book 4, chs 13–16), Locke inverted the medieval notion of testimony: He maintained it was not the authority of an ancient text (such as scripture) but the report of the senses. Few things, he argues, in human knowledge are demonstrably certain. As social creatures with limited time to gain knowledge of a world in commotion, we rely on the reports of others but must find ways to test their trustworthiness. Among the various standards he offers, key is a hierarchy of testimony determined by the witness's proximity to the event: "any Testimony, the farther off it is from the original Truth, the less force and proof it has" (1975: 663–64). Eyewitness accounts lose truth (but may gain color) as they pass from mouth to mouth:

---

the battle of Junin . . . Helen: The battle of Junin (1824) was a pivotal military engagement in the Peruvian War of Independence. Helen refers to Helen of Troy, whose abduction by Paris, a Trojan prince, led to the Trojan War.

> A credible Man vouching his Knowledge of it, is a good proof: But if another equally credible, do witness it from his Report, the Testimony is weaker; and a third that attests the Hear-say of an Hear-say, is yet less considerable. (1975: 664)

Locke notes already the infinite regress in witnessing: To be an active witness requires another to witness your testimony (a passive witness).

Locke reflects the low legal status of hearsay: the reporting of statements made by someone else outside court without the opportunity for cross-examination. Any statement not made in court under oath is of dubious admissibility. Hearsay is quotation, testimony at second-hand. Each sentence is supposed to be funded by direct sensation, and in reporting another's reports, one is a passive witness of an active witness (instead of the reverse), which is dangerously derivative. The low esteem in which hearsay is held signals not only the hierarchy of the senses (the precedence of eyes over ears) but also the working epistemology of the courtroom: The act of linking experience and discourse must be done in a controlled setting in which speech is subject to cross-examination and penalties for perjury are in force. In this the law still maintains respect for death or pain as truth serums. Witness is borne under sanction—whether of pain or death or legal charges and dishonor. One testifies quite literally *sub poena* —under threat of punishment. Witnesses can find themselves bodily compelled to appear in court. It doesn't take a Foucault° to see that today witnessing is policed at its boundaries by an apparatus of pain.

Legal rules prefer a mechanical witness. A witness, for instance, may not offer an opinion (about culpability, for instance) but may only describe the facts of what was seen. The blanker the witness the better. Things, after all, can bear witness—the biblical stone of witness, trophies, or other sorts of material evidence (bloodstains). The ideal human witness would behave like a thing: a mere tablet of recording. The structure of address in testimony should be radically open and public, not varying your story for different audiences. ("Estoppel" is the legal principle that prevents altering testimony previously given.) Since a dumb witness doesn't know what's at stake, there is no motive to lend comfort to one party or the other.

In the preference for the dumb witness lies a distant origin of both scientific and journalistic ideas of objectivity: the observer as a mirror, dull as the microscope to human concerns or consequences. The objective witness is very different from the survivor, whose witness lies in mortal engagement with the story told. The objective witness claims disembodiment and passivity, a

---

Foucault: Michel Foucault (1926–1984), a French philosopher whose writings have had enormous impact on a wide range of scholarly disciplines. Foucault is known for his study of social institutions, among them prisons, as they bear on the relationship between power and knowledge.

cold indifference to the story, offering "just the facts." The hearers have to compose the story for themselves. In one sense, the claim to objectivity is simply passive witnessing idealized, that is, the dream of an unadulterated and public record of events as they "really happened." The cultural authority of mechanical recording lies in the claim to document events without the filter of subjective experience. Since witnesses were supposed to be like machines, machines are also held to be good witnesses. The conventional wisdom about film and photography today, however, is the inescapability of interest in all representation. What most irks the friends of science and reason—Locke's heirs—about this position is not so much the notion that a consensual and objective document of events is impossible, but rather its darker corollary: that pain serves as the default measure of reality and authenticity. We were, they say, supposed to have graduated from all that!

Broadcasting and the Veracity Gap

Distance is a ground of distrust and doubt. We waver about another's testi-   25
mony because of our distance from the experience they narrate. In the same way, reports from distant personae are more dubious than those from people we know and trust. The communication situation of broadcasting is analogous to that of witnessing: Experiences are mediated to an audience which has no firsthand acquaintance with them. The legitimation of the veracity gap in media followed the same path as in witnessing: using pain and the body as a criterion of truth and truthfulness. The body is authenticity's last refuge in situations of structural doubt. Perhaps the best single thing Walter Cronkite ever did for his reputation of credibility, besides the years of steady service, was to shed an unrehearsed tear on camera when reporting the news of President Kennedy's assassination. In the Gospel of Luke, Christ's disciples "were startled and terrified, and thought that they were seeing a ghost" (Luke 24:37). The resurrected Jesus assures them, "Handle me and see, for a ghost does not have flesh and bones as you see that I have" (Luke 24:39). Modern media—which resurrect and transport phantasms in optical and acoustic channels—both place us in the situation of doubting Thomas and attempt a similar reassurance: Handle me and see (Peters, 1999).

One of the most daring things in media events theory (Dayan and Katz, 1992) is the question: Just when can media be agents of truth or authenticity instead of prevarication and ideology? In other words, can the media sustain the practice of witnessing? The notion that home audiences could be witnesses is one of those apparent category mistakes whose elaboration the media events movement has made its task. It's easy to mock Ronald Reagan for confusing newsreels and his own experience: He claimed to have witnessed the liberation of the concentration camps in the Second World War when he had never left the United States. He believed in false presence: that he had really been there when he had only watched films. But presence-at-a-distance is precisely what witnessing a media event claims to offer. Critical theory has rightly highlighted the veracity gap in mass communication, the hermeneutics° of suspicion, but media-events studies seek the conditions in which the willing suspension of disbelief is justified. In media events, the borrowed eyes and ears of the media become, however tentatively or dangerously, one's own. Death, distance, and distrust are all suspended, for good and evil.

Singularity is key to the communication economics of witnessing. President Clinton came to my hometown, Iowa City, Iowa, for example, in February 1996, on a campaign stop, and spoke in an indoor arena. The whole event was to be televised locally, but the tickets were snapped up within two hours. Why the excitement to attend when one could get a better view on television at home? Because at home you can't be a witness to history. If Clinton were to be shot, or make a major announcement, people could say, "I was there." That would be a witness forever thereafter restricted to 14,000 people (if they are honest), whereas we home viewers, a much larger and potentially infinite group, would only be able to say, "I saw it on television." There's no comparison in the authority or cultural capital of the two statements! Clinton's goal after the speech was to touch as many people as possible, to spread the charisma of the king's body by working the crowd, in the apt idiom of "pressing the flesh." A live witness can shake hands with the great man, receive the torch of contagious magic, in the same way that Clinton shook JFK's hand as a teenager (luckily for him on camera). "Handle me and see" said the man we know mostly as a TV persona.

The journey from experience (the seen) into words (the said) is precarious.

"Being there" matters since it avoids the ontological depreciation of being a copy. The copy, like hearsay, is indefinitely repeatable; the event is singular, and its witnesses are forever irreplaceable in their privileged relation to it. Recordings lose the *hic et nunc*° of the event. The live event is open to unscripted happenings, chance, and gaffes. Accidents are a key part of media events—going off script. That so much of live coverage involves some sort of trauma suggests the draw of the unpredictable and of those occurrences that leave a mark in time. Media events are not always the happy social body celebrating its core values, but also the nasty stuff of degradation and disaster (Carey, 1998; Liebes, 1998).

Presence is fragile and mortal; recordings have durability that survives in multiple times and spaces. Billions of dollars in the entertainment industries

---

hermeneutics: A discipline within philosophy concerned with the study of interpretation.
hic et nunc: A Latin phrase meaning "here and now."

turn on this apparently minute distinction. Why will people pay high prices for music performed in concert whose quality and polish is often better on the CD player at home? Obviously extramusical values shape concertgoing: party, spectacle, noise, dance. Even so, live music is different. A concert is an event, not a record. A homemade bootleg tape is a souvenir, a marker of time and place, but a CD made from the tape is a commodity, even if they are musically identical. In a concert, one's mortal time line on earth is spent. Touch and eye contact with the artist are possible. So is imperfection: In the concert one may hear strains edited out in the studio, and witness the labor of the performing body. What postproduction adds musically (e.g., overdubbing) it subtracts from eventfulness, since those sounds never could have occurred in time as we know it. Recording media can do time-axis manipulation, stopping, slowing, speeding, or reversing time—one reason why audiovisual media, despite aptitude in recording, are dubious witnesses. The body, however, lives only in real time. Singing, dancing, and live performance all engage time's passage. Music can reveal the meaning of, and sometimes even provide a brief escape from, growing older.

Why Liveness?

The love of liveness also relates to the power of real time. If one sees it live, 30 one can claim status as a witness present in time if not in space; if one sees it on tape, one is no longer a witness, but rather the percipient of a transcription. Sports fans, in the case of big games, will remain glued to the television screen, even though they know that any key plays will be shown ad nauseam in the game's afterlife as reportage and video. They must be there *as it happens.* To see the big moment with even a slight delay is to be placed in a derivative role, a hearer of a report rather than a witness of an event. The fan wants to be involved in history (the happening), not historiography (the recording). The few seconds between occurrence and replay open up a metaphysical gulf in the meaning and quality of what is seen. As far as the electromagnetic tracings are concerned, the live event and its instant replay are identical, but in the psychology of the fan, one is history, the other is television. One is a window to the event, the other is its representation. Liveness serves as an assurance of access to truth and authenticity.

The hard-core sports fan sweating the seconds actually offers a profound lesson about the nature of time. Why should liveness matter? It does matter, to the tune of billions of dollars in bids for live rights. Because events only happen in the present. In a word, gambling. As Walter Benjamin° noted, gambling is a phantasmagoria of time. No one knows what the future holds,

---

Walter Benjamin (1892–1940): A German literary critic and philosopher.

and the gambler infuses the present with the diceyness of the future. There is absolutely no point in betting on a game or a race whose outcome is already known. A classic con job, as in the film *The Sting*, is to institute a small time lag in publicizing race results so that punters think they are betting on an uncertain future when in fact they are wagering on an already determined past. A few seconds do matter, and profoundly. The past, in some sense, is safe. The present, in contrast, is catastrophic, subject to radical alterations. In a single second a swerve of the steering wheel or a pull of the trigger can change history forever. Possible futures come into being and vanish with every act. In a brief moment the penalty kick is made or missed, a life conceived or taken. All history culminates in the present moment. Of course, the present is rarely so dramatic, but without a live connection its explosive possibility— its danger— is missing. Nothing quite excites like an event about to take place. In Raymond Williams's° phrase, one waits for a knock on the door. Fortuna, goddess of history and gamblers, reveals her face only in the present. In the past she veils herself as necessity, in the future as probability.

The contrast between the live and the recorded is a structuring principle of broadcasting. It replays the contrast of fact and fiction, so central to modern historiography, a field, like law and theology, whose enterprise rests on the evaluation of sources and documents—testimonies. Though theorists justly remind us of the factuality of fictions and the fictive character of facts, this contrast stubbornly resists total resolution. The division of fact and fiction, so central for historians and sports fans, as well as the structuring principle of media and literary genres, turns on witnessing. An event requires witnesses, a story only needs tellers and listeners. A fiction can be heard or told, but a fact is witnessed. Some kinds of events (baptisms, marriages) legally require witnesses. Testimony assures us—as children often ask about stories—that it really happened.

Historicity (or historical authenticity) has a similar logic to live coverage. If in visiting the Tower of London I am told that a block of wood is the one on which Henry VIII's victims were dispatched, I will act and feel differently than if I learn the block is a replica, even if it is physically identical or equally old. The block hovers in a limbo between reality and fake, its metaphysical status depending on something so slight as a caption. The caption "real" ties it to a tradition of testimony passed across the generations, an accumulation of time that links the block historically to the event. If it has the right label I can ponder edifying lessons about overweening power and look for traces of martyr's blood; I will have to work a lot harder if the caption announces that it's only figurative. Live broadcasting, like objects certified as historical,

---

Raymond Williams (1921–1988): A Welsh novelist and critic whose writing on culture, politics, mass media, and literature were widely influential.

offers the chance to witness, while recorded material stands at one remove as a representation (replica) of events. It takes about a sixth-grade education in our postmodern age to puncture the idea that history is free of representation, so that is not the point. Rather, it is to read small distinctions about what is real in cultural matters, distinctions too often written off as neurosis or fetishism, as insights into structures of history and experience. Between the historical and the verisimilar lies a small but gigantic gap, that of testimony.

Of four basic types of relations to an event, three can sustain the attitude of a witness. To be there, present at the event in space and time is the paradigm case. To be present in time but removed in space is the condition of liveness, simultaneity across space. To be present in space but removed in time is the condition of historical representation: Here is the possibility of a simultaneity across time, a witness that laps the ages. To be absent in both space and time but still have access to an event via its traces is the condition of recording: the profane zone in which the attitude of witnessing is hardest to sustain (see Table 1).

	Presence in Time	Absence in Time
Presence in Space	BEING THERE	HISTORICITY (dead not "live")
	Assembled Audience e.g., concert, game, theater	Serial Mass Audience e.g., shrine, memorial, museum
Absence in Space	LIVE TRANSMISSION Broadcast Audience e.g., radio, TV, webcast	RECORDING Dispersed, private audience Profane, witnessing difficult e.g., book, CD, video

Table 1. Sorts of Witnessing an Event.

Fact and Fiction, Pain and Time

Ultimately, the boundary between fact and fiction is an ethical one before it is an epistemological one: It consists in having respect for the pain of victims, in being tied by simultaneity, however loosely, to someone else's story of how they hurt. We may weep in reading of the slaughter of the innocents by King Herod, but we owe them nothing besides remembrance. "Live" pain is different. Simultaneous suffering forms the horizon of responsibility: Liveness matters for the living. Facts impose moral and political obligations that fictions do not. This is the ancient ethical problem of tragedy: why people take pleasure in sights that would terrify or disgust them in real life. Aristotle's 35

Poetics starts the debate about why we take pleasure in depictions of violence and human suffering. In tragedy, the representation of pain (and pain is definitional for the genre) is not supposed to excite the spectator to humanitarian service but to clarify through representation what is possible in life. The drama offers terror without danger, pity without duty. The awareness of its unreality releases us from moral obligation to the sufferers we behold. Fiction lacks the responsibility or complicity that Ellis makes definitional for witnessing. As David Hume remarked (1987), "It is certain, that the same object of distress, which pleases in a tragedy, were it really set before us, would give the most unfeigned uneasiness." Factual distress calls for our aid, not our appreciation; our duty, not our pleasure. Death is meaningful in fiction: It marks the passage of time, punishes the wicked, gives closure to events. But in fact, death is a blank, completely beyond meaning. "Nothing brings them back, neither love nor hate. They can do nothing to you. They are as nothing" (Conrad, 1921). The contrast of fact and fiction has less to do with different orders of truth than with who is hurting and when. Living people's pain is news; dead people's pain is history.

It is easy to make fun of the obsession to keep up to date with the news. Kierkegaard° suggested that if we treated all news as if it had happened fifty years ago we would sound its true importance. He is right about triviality, but misses what he is so lucid about elsewhere: the present moment as the point of decision. We have to keep up with the world because we are, in some complicated way, responsible to act in it, and we can only act in the present. We feel guilty about hurt people in news, not in fiction films. Pain separates facts from fictions. Facts are witnessed, fictions are narrated. Fictions may indeed inspire us to action, but the beholders' responsibility is diffuse. "Live" coverage of global sorrow is ethically recalcitrant: Because it is fact, we are not protected by the theater's "teleological suspension of the ethical" (Kierkegaard); because it is spatially remote, our duty to action is unclear. We find ourselves in the position of spectators at a drama without the relief of knowing that the suffering is unreal. Hence the "unfeigned uneasiness" (Hume) we face in watching the news. We feel a gruesome fascination for trauma without the exoneration of knowing it is all an experiment in mimesis. We are witnesses without a tribunal.

Finally, the curious thing about witnessing is its retroactive character, the jealousy the present has for the past. The present may be the point of decision, but it is always underinformed about what will come after. Most observers don't know they are witnesses when the event is happening: They are elected after the fact. A vast quantitative difference separates what we experience and what we are summoned to witness. There's a lot more sensation around than

---

Kierkegaard: Soren Kierkegaard (1813–1855), a Danish philosopher and theologian, generally regarded as the first existentialist philosopher.

stories. In testifying we must take responsibility for what we once took little responsibility for. We must report on events, the details of which have assumed as massive an importance as they were once trivial. What time did you catch the bus? What color was the car? What kind of shoes was the defendant wearing? In witnessing we look backwards on events we did not realize we were observing, restoring deleted files from memory. We don't know that what we notice or neglect may be the key to prison and liberty for someone. The present is blind to what the future will value. We didn't notice the butterfly that started the typhoon.°

Hence the notion, found in liberalism, existentialism, and Christian theology alike, that it is the duty of everyone to be vigilant—to be ready to stand as a witness at any time or place. Testifying has the structure of repentance: retroactively caring about what we were once careless of. A later moment revisits an earlier one in which consciousness was not fully awake. The witness's attitude to sensation (radical vigilance) goes together with the future anterior attitude to time (treating the present as if it was being witnessed from the future). To witness is to wish that the record of the past were more whole, and to grasp this lesson now is to live vigilantly, to make the present worthy as we imagine contemplating it from a future point. To cope with our fixity in the present, we can at least be awake. Every act puts one in the witness box, both seeing and saying. In Christian eschatology this attitude is dramatized by the notion of a Last Judgment that calls up the whole history of the world as judge and witness. In Nietzsche's° thought it is the notion of the eternal return, acting in the present so that the action could be eternally repeated (and witnessed) without regret. In everyday civic ideology it is the idea that citizens have a duty to be informed about the events of the day. In a phrase all broadcasters would endorse, and with apologies to Matthew 25:13, the motto of witnessing should be: "Watch, therefore, for you know neither the day nor the hour wherein the event will come."

References

duBois, P. (1991) *Torture and Truth*. London: Routledge.

Borges, J. L. (1964) "The Witness," in *Labyrinths: Selected Stories and Other Writings*. New York: New Directions.

Carey, J. W. (1998) "Political Ritual on Television," In T. Liebes and J. Curran (eds.) *Media, Ritual, and Identity*. London: Routledge.

---

butterfly that started the typhoon: A reference to the butterfly effect, in chaos theory. Small variations in initial conditions can lead to large variations over the long term.

Nietzsche: Friedrich Wilhelm Nietzsche (1844–1900), a German philologist and philosopher whose critiques of culture, religion, and philosophy—although overlooked in his own lifetime—have gained prominence since the mid-twentieth century.

Conrad, J. (1921) *The Secret Agent*. New York: Doubleday.

Cross, R. (1974) *Evidence*, 4th edn. London: Butterworths.

Dayan, D. and E. Katz (1992) *Media Events: The Live Broadcasting of History*. Cambridge, MA: Harvard University Press.

Ellis, J. (2000) *Seeing Things: Television in the Age of Uncertainty*. London: I. B. Tauris.

Felman, S. and D. Laub (1992) *Testimony: Crises of Witnessing in Literature, Psychoanalysis, and History*. New York: Routledge.

Hume, D. (1987) "Of Tragedy," *Essays: Moral, Political, and Literary*, rev. edn. Indianapolis: Liberty Fund.

Langbein, J. H. (1977) *Torture and the Law of Proof: Europe and England in the Ancien Régime*. Chicago, IL: University of Chicago Press.

Liebes, T. (1998) "Television's Disaster Marathons," in T. Liebes and J. Curran (eds.) *Media, Ritual, and Identity*. London: Routledge.

Lipton, P. (1998) "The Epistemology of Testimony," *History and Philosophy of Science* 29(1).

Locke, J. (1975) *An Essay Concerning Human Understanding*, ed. P. H. Nidditch. Oxford: Clarendon Press. (Orig. pub. 1690.)

Peters, E. (1985) *Torture*. New York: Blackwell.

Peters, J. D. (1999) *Speaking into the Air*. Chicago, IL: University of Chicago Press.

Ricoeur, P. (1981) "The Hermeneutics of Testimony," in *Essays in Biblical Interpretation*. London: SPCK.

Ross, D. F., J. D. Read, and M. P. Toglia (1994) *Adult Eyewitness Testimony: Current Trends and Developments*. Cambridge: Cambridge University Press.

Shapin, S. (1994) *A Social History of Truth: Civility and Science in Seventeenth-Century England*. Chicago, IL: University of Chicago Press.

Webb, E. J. et al. (1981) *Nonreactive Measures in the Social Sciences*. Boston, MA: Houghton Mifflin.

Working with the Text

1. John Durham Peters opens his article by referring to prior published work. How does Peters use this reference to frame and set up his own discussion? How does reference to someone else's work help to establish both focus and relevance for Peters's work?

2. Why does Peters consider *witnessing* to be a multifaceted and complex term? What are the several aspects of witnessing that readers must keep in mind as they follow Peters's discussion?

3. Issues of time and place become reoccurring themes in the essay. Track the many ways in which time and place become relevant in Peters's discussion.

4. Although much of Peters's exploration of witnessing takes us back into history, the relevance of the topic is clearly made compelling by technology and new media. How has broadcasting and new media heightened the age-old issues of witnessing? Has new media introduced new issues?

From Text to Field

1. Whether in the home, in school, or in public, you have probably served as a witness on many occasions, if only informally. In other words, you have surely seen or experienced something that you then had to talk about. Describe and then analyze one such occasion in some detail, drawing on Peters's discussion.

2. Peters wrote his article on witnessing just prior to the events of September 11, 2001. Those events, witnessed firsthand by many, became in turn a media event, in that millions more witnessed media images of 9/11. Offer an update of Peters's essay that draws on and incorporates "witnessing 9/11" as a running example. What changes or new insights, if any, do the events of 9/11 suggest for Peters's essay? Do the events and media coverage of 9/11 make the essay, and the problems it addresses, more relevant?

3. Working in teams or small groups, identify an event (such as a political, musical, or sporting event) that some of you might witness firsthand and others through media coverage. Compare your experiences of the event with how others have experienced it. What makes for reliable and unreliable witnessing? Can your witnessing differ from others and still be true or legitimate? Draw on the article by Peters to help you raise issues and refine your responses.

4. Opportunities for witnessing, and for communicating as a witness, grow with advances in technology. Choose one new technology that you believe has a potential impact on witnessing and analyze how the age-old issues of witnessing take on a particular form and salience given that new technology. Cell phones, video phones, and surveillance technology are just some of the many technologies that you may wish to consider.

From Realism to Virtual Reality: Images of America's Wars

H. Bruce Franklin

From a captain in the U.S. Air Force to a Vietnam War protester, from a Melville scholar to a scholar on the literature born in American prisons—such has been the career of H. Bruce Franklin. He won notoriety in 1972 for being the only tenured professor at Stanford University ever to be fired for his political views. Well-documented and researched, his writings (some eighteen books and more than two-hundred journal articles) position Franklin as someone who is both a scholar and an activist.

After completing his undergraduate studies at Amherst College, Franklin joined the air force, rising to the rank of captain. Upon receiving his PhD at Stanford, he joined its faculty as an assistant professor and won acclaim—and tenure—as a scholar of nineteenth-century American literature, with interests in Melville and Hawthorne. Following his dismissal in 1972, and three years of unemployment, he joined Rutgers University, becoming Distinguished Professor of English in 1980. He has also had visiting-teacher appointments at Johns Hopkins, Wesleyan, and Yale universities.

Following his early interest in Melville, Franklin turned to three other areas of research. He wrote *The Victim as Criminal and Artist: Literature from the American Prison* (1978, 1982), a seminal work that argues that prison and slave artists have created a tradition of protest against America as a prison, one that offers a vision of an alternative future. He has also written several books on the literature of the Vietnam War and is known for his pioneering studies of science fiction.

First published in the *Georgia Review* in 1994, "From Realism to Virtual Reality" surveys the role of images of warfare, arguing that as our technology has improved so too has our control over and propagandistic use of images.

The Industrial Revolution was only about one century old when modern technological warfare burst upon the world in the U.S. Civil War. During that century human progress had already been manifested in the continually increasing deadliness and range of weapons, as well as in other potential military benefits of industrial capitalism. But it was the Civil War that actually demonstrated industrialism's ability to produce carnage and devastation on an unprecedented scale, thus foreshadowing a future more and more dominated by what we have come to call *technowar*. For the first time, immense armies had been transported by railroad, coordinated by telegraph, and equipped with an ever-evolving arsenal of mass-produced weapons designed by scientists and engineers. The new machines of war—such as the repeating rifle, the primitive machine gun, the submarine, and the steam-powered, ironclad warship—were being forged by other machines. Industrial organization was essential, therefore, not only in the factories where the technoweapons were manufactured but also on the battlefields and waters where these machines destroyed each other and slaughtered people.

Prior to the Civil War, visual images of America's wars were almost without exception expressions of romanticism and nationalism. Paintings, lithographs, woodcuts, and statues displayed a glorious saga of thrilling American heroism from the Revolution through the Mexican War. Drawing on their imagination, artists could picture action-filled scenes of heroic events, such as Emmanuel Leutze's 1851 painting *Washington Crossing the Delaware*.[1]

Literature, however, was the only art form capable of projecting the action of warfare as temporal flow and movement. Using words as a medium, writers had few limitations on how they chose to paint this action, and their visions had long covered a wide spectrum. One of the Civil War's most distinctively modern images was expressed by Herman Melville in his poem "A Utilitarian View of the Monitor's Fight." Melville sees the triumph of "plain mechanic power" placing war "Where War belongs—/ Among the trades and artisans," depriving it of "passion": "all went on by crank, / Pivot, and screw, / And calculations of caloric." Since "warriors / Are now but operatives," he hopes that "War's made / Less grand than Peace."

The most profoundly deglamorizing images of that war, however, were produced not by literature but directly by technology itself. The industrial processes and scientific knowledge that created technowar had also brought forth a new means of perceiving its devastation. Industrial chemicals, manufactured metal plates, lenses, mirrors, bellows, and actuating mechanisms— all were essential to the new art and craft of photography. Thus the Civil War was the first truly modern war—both in how it was fought and in how it was imaged. The romantic images of warfare projected by earlier visual arts were now radically threatened by images of warfare introduced by photography.

Scores of commercial photographers, seeking authenticity and profits, fol- 5
lowed the Union armies into battle. Although evidently more than a million
photographs of the Civil War were taken, hardly any show actual combat or
other exciting action typical of the earlier paintings.[2] The photographers' need
to stay close to their cumbersome horse-drawn laboratory wagons usually kept
them from the thick of battle, and the collodion wet-plate process, which
demanded long exposures, forced them to focus on scenes of stillness rather
than action. Among all human subjects, those who stayed most perfectly still
for the camera were the dead. Hence Civil War photography, dominated by
images of death, inaugurated a grim, profoundly antiromantic realism.

Perhaps the most widely reproduced photo from the war, Timothy
O'Sullivan's "A Harvest of Death, Gettysburg," contains numerous corpses
of Confederate soldiers, rotting after lying two days in the rain (see Fig. 1).
Stripped of their shoes and with their pockets turned inside out, the bodies
stretch into the distance beyond the central corpse, whose mouth gapes
gruesomely.

The first of such new images of war were displayed for sale to the public
by Mathew Brady at his Broadway gallery in October 1862. Brady entitled his
show "The Dead of Antietam." The *New York Times* responded in an awed
editorial:

Figure 1. "A Harvest of Death, Gettysburg," 1863, photograph by Timothy O'Sullivan, courtesy of
George Eastman House.

The living that throng Broadway care little perhaps for the Dead at Antietam, but we fancy they would jostle less carelessly down the great thoroughfare . . . were a few dripping bodies, fresh from the field, laid along the pavement. . . . .

Mr. Brady has done something to bring home to us the terrible reality and earnestness of war. If he has not brought bodies and laid them in our dooryards and along the streets, he has done something very like it. At the door of his gallery hangs a little placard, "The Dead of Antietam." Crowds of people are constantly going up the stairs; follow them, and you find them bending over photographic views of that fearful battle-field, taken immediately after the action. . . . You will see hushed, reverent groups standing around these weird copies of carnage, bending down to look in the pale faces of the dead, chained by the strange spell that dwells in dead men's eyes.[3]

Oliver Wendell Holmes* went further in explicating the meaning of the exhibition, which gives "some conception of what a repulsive, brutal, sickening, hideous thing it is, this dashing together of two frantic mobs to which we give the name of armies." He continues: "Let him who wishes to know what war is look at this series of illustrations. These wrecks of manhood thrown together in careless heaps or ranged in ghastly rows for burial were alive but yesterday. . . ."[4]

Nevertheless, three decades after the end of the Civil War the surging forces of militarism and imperialism were reimaging the conflict as a glorious episode in America's history. The disgust, shame, guilt, and deep national divisions that had followed this war — just like those a century later that followed the Vietnam War — were being buried under an avalanche of jingoist culture, the equivalent of contemporary Ramboism, even down to the cult of muscularism promulgated by Teddy Roosevelt.

It was in this historical context that Stephen Crane used realism, then flourishing as a literary mode, to assault just such treacherous views of war. Although *The Red Badge of Courage* is generally viewed as the great classic novel of the Civil War, it can be read much more meaningfully as Crane's response to the romantic militarism that was attempting to erase from the nation's memory the horrifying lessons taught by the war's realities.[5] Crane, not subject to the technological limitations of the slow black-and-white photographs that had brought home glimpses of the war's sordid repulsiveness, was able to image the animal frenzy that masqueraded as heroic combat and even to add color and tiny moving details to his pictures of the dead:

Oliver Wendell Holmes (1809–1894): An American physician, writer, and poet, and the father of Oliver Wendell Holmes Jr. (1841–1935), who served in the Civil War and would become a Supreme Court justice.

The corpse was dressed in a uniform that once had been blue but was now faded to a melancholy shade of green. The eyes, staring at the youth, had changed to the dull hue to be seen on the side of a dead fish. The mouth was opened. Its red had changed to an appalling yellow. Over the grey skin of the face ran little ants. One was trundling some sort of a bundle along the upper lip.[6]

Other literary reactions to the new militarism looked even further back-   10 ward to project images of a future dominated by war. Melville's *Billy Budd*, completed in 1891, envisions this triumph of violence in the aftermath of the American Revolution on the (aptly named) British warship HMS *Bellipotent*, where the best of humanity is hanged to death by the logic of war, the common people are turned into automatons "dispersed to the places allotted them when not at the guns," and the final image is of a sterile, life-less, inorganic mass of "smooth white marble."[7]

In *A Connecticut Yankee in King Arthur's Court* (1889), Mark Twain reca-pitulates the development of industrial capitalism and extrapolates its future in a vision of apocalyptic technowar. Hank Morgan and his young disciples have run "secret wires" to dynamite deposits under all their "vast factories, mills, workshops, magazines, etc." and have connected them to a single com-mand button so that nothing can stop them "when we want to blow up our civilization." When Hank does initiate this instantaneous push-button war, "In that explosion all our noble civilization-factories went up in the air and disappeared from the earth." Beyond an electrified fence, the technowarriors have prepared a forty-foot-wide belt of land mines. The first wave of thousands of knights triggers a twentieth-century-style explosion: "As to destruction of life, it was amazing. Moreover, it was beyond estimate. Of course we could not *count* the dead, because they did not exist as individuals, but merely as homogeneous protoplasm, with alloys of iron and buttons."

After Hank and his boys trap the rest of the feudal army inside their elec-tric fence, Hank electrocutes the first batch, a flood is released on the sur-vivors, and the boys man machine guns that "vomit death" into their ranks: "Within ten short minutes after we had opened fire, armed resistance was totally annihilated. . . . Twenty-five thousand men lay dead around us."[8] That number of dead, it is worth noting, matches exactly the total casualties in America's costliest day of war, the battle of Antietam, and thus recalls Brady's exhibition, "The Dead of Antietam." Twain's vision is even more horrific, for the victors themselves are conquered by "the poisonous air bred by those dead thousands." All that remains of this first experiment in industrialized warfare is a desolate landscape pockmarked by craters and covered with unburied, rotting corpses.

Twain's vision of the future implicit in industrial capitalism began to materialize in the First World War, when armies slaughtered each other on an unprecedented scale, sections of Europe were turned into a wasteland, and weapons of mass destruction first seemed capable of actually destroying civilization. Meanwhile, the scientific, engineering, and organizational progress that had produced the modern machine gun, long-range artillery, poison gas, and fleets of submarines and warplanes had also created a new image-making technology that broke through the limits of still photography. Just as the Civil War was the first to be extensively photographed, the "War to End All Wars" was the first to be extensively imaged in motion pictures.[9]

World War I, of course, generated millions of still photographs, many showing scenes at least as ghastly as the corpse-strewn battlefields of the Civil War, and now there was also authentic documentary film of live action. But for various reasons the most influential photographic images from World War I, though realistic in appearance, displayed not reality but fantasy. Filmmakers who wished to record actual combat were severely restricted by the various governments and military authorities. At the same time, powerful forces were making a historic discovery: the tremendous potential of movies for propaganda and for profits. This was the dawn of twentieth-century image making.

In the United States the most important photographic images were   15 movies designed to inflame the nation, first to enter the war and then to support it. Probably the most influential was *The Battle Cry of Peace*, a 1915 smash hit that played a crucial role in rousing the public against Germany by showing realistic scenes of the invasion and devastation of America by a rapacious Germanic army. Once the United States entered the war, the American public got to view an endless series of feature movies, such as *To Hell with the Kaiser; The Kaiser, the Beast of Berlin;* and *The Claws of the Hun* —each outdoing its predecessors in picturing German bestiality. Erich von Stroheim's career began with his portrayal of the archetypal sadistic German officer in films like *The Unbeliever* and *Heart of Humanity*, where in his lust to rape innocent young women he murders anyone who gets in the way— even the crying baby of one intended victim. This genre is surveyed by Larry Wayne Ward, who describes the 1918 Warner Brothers hit *My Four Years in Germany*, which opens with a title card telling the audience they are seeing "Fact Not Fiction":

> After the brutal conquest of Belgium, German troops are shown slaughtering innocent refugees and tormenting prisoners of war. Near the end of the film one of the German officials boasts that "America Won't Fight," a title which dissolves into newsreel footage of President Wilson and marching American soldiers. Soon American troops are seen fighting their way across the European battlefields. As he bayonets another German soldier, a young American doughboy turns to his companions and says, "I promised Dad I'd get six."[10]

Before the end of World War I, the motion picture had already proved to be a more effective vehicle for romanticizing and popularizing war than the antebellum school of heroic painting that had been partly debunked by Civil War photography. Indeed, the audiences that thronged to *My Four Years in Germany* frequently burned effigies of the kaiser outside the theaters and in some cases turned into angry mobs that had to be dispersed by police.

To restore the glamour of preindustrial war, however, it would take more than glorifying the men fighting on the ground or even the aviators supposedly dueling like medieval knights high above the battlefield. What was necessary to reverse Melville's "utilitarian" view of industrial warfare was the romanticizing of machines of war themselves.

The airplane was potentially an ideal vehicle for this romance. But photographic technology had to develop a bit further to bring home the thrills generated by destruction from the sky, because it needed to be seen *from* the sky, not from the ground where its reality was anything but glamorous. The central figure in America's romance with warplanes (as I have discussed at length elsewhere[11]) was Billy Mitchell, who also showed America and the world how to integrate media imagery with technowar.

In 1921, Mitchell staged a historic event by using bombers to sink captured German warships and turning the action into a media bonanza. His goal was to hit the American public with immediate, nationwide images of the airplane's triumph over the warship. The audacity of this enterprise in 1921 was remarkable. There were no satellites to relay images, and no television; in fact, the first experimental radio broadcast station had begun operation only in November 1920.

Back in 1919, Mitchell had given the young photographer George   20 Goddard his own laboratory where, with assistance from Eastman Kodak, Goddard developed high-resolution aerial photography. As soon as Mitchell won the opportunity to bomb the German ships, he put Goddard in command of a key unit: a team of aerial photographers provided with eighteen airplanes and a dirigible. Mitchell's instructions were unambiguous: "I want newsreels of those sinking ships in every theater in the country, just as soon as we can get 'em there." This demanded more than mere picture taking. With his flair for public relations, Mitchell explained to Goddard: "Most of all I need you to handle the newsreel and movie people. They're temperamental, and we've got to get all we can out of them."[12] Goddard had to solve unprecedented logistical problems, flying the film first to Langley Field and thence to Bolling Field for pickup by the newsreel people who would take it to New York for development and national distribution. The sinking of each ship, artfully filmed by relays of

> The generation raised in video arcades and on Nintendo could hardly be more satisfied.

Goddard's planes, was screened the very next day in big-city theaters across the country.

This spectacular media coup implanted potent images of the warplane in the public mind, and Mitchell himself became an overnight national hero as millions watched the death of great warships on newsreel screens. Mitchell was a prophet. The battleship was doomed. The airplane would rule the world.

America was now much closer to the 1990 media conception of the Gulf War than to Melville's "Utilitarian View of the Monitor's Fight." Melville's vision of technowar as lacking "passion" was becoming antiquated, for what could be more thrilling — even erotic — than aerial war machines? The evidence is strewn throughout modern America: the warplane models assembled by millions of boys and young men during World War II; the thousands of warplane magazines and books filled with glossy photographs that some find as stimulating as those in "men's" magazines; and Hollywood's own warplane romances, such as *Top Gun* — one of the most popular movies of the 1980s — or *Strategic Air Command*, in which Jimmy Stewart's response to his first sight of a B-47 nuclear bomber is, "She's the most beautiful thing I've ever seen in my life."

One of the warplane's great advantages as a vehicle of romance is its distance from its victims. From the aircraft's perspective, even the most grotesque slaughter it inflicts is sufficiently removed so that it can be imaged aesthetically. The aesthetics of aerial bombing in World War II were prefigured in 1937 by Mussolini's son Vittorio, whose ecstasy about his own experience bombing undefended Ethiopian villages was expressed in his image of his victims "bursting out like a rose after I had landed a bomb in the middle of them."[13] These aesthetics were consummated at the end of World War II by the mushroom clouds that rose over Hiroshima and Nagasaki.

Bracketed by these images, the aerial bombing of World War II has been most insightfully explored in *Catch-22* by Joseph Heller, a bombardier with sixty combat missions. The novel envisions the political and cultural triumph of fascism through the very means used to defeat it militarily. The turning point in Heller's work is the annihilation of an insignificant antifascist Italian mountain village, an event which allows fascist forces, embodied by U.S. Air Corps officers, to gain total control.[14] The sole purpose of the American bombing of the village is image making. The novel's General Peckem privately admits that bombing this "tiny undefended village, reducing the whole community to rubble" is "entirely unnecessary," but it will allow him to extend his power over the bombing squadrons. He has convinced them that he will measure their success by "a neat aerial photograph" of their *bomb pattern* — "a term I dreamed up," he confides, that "means nothing." The briefing officer tells the crews:

Colonel Cathcart wants to come out of this mission with a good clean aerial photograph he won't be ashamed to send through channels. Don't forget that General Peckem will be here for the full briefing, and you know how he feels about bomb patterns.[15]

Pictures of bomb patterns were not, of course, the most influential ²⁵ American photographic image making in World War II. The still photos published in *Life* alone could be the subject of several dissertations, and World War II feature movies about strategic bombing have been discussed at length by myself and many others. Indeed, in 1945 one might have wondered how the camera could possibly play a more important role in war.

The answer came in Vietnam, the first war to be televised directly into tens of millions of homes.[16] Television's glimpses of the war's reality were so horrendous and so influential that these images have been scapegoated as one of the main causes of the United States' defeat. Indeed, the Civil War still photographs of corpses seem innocuous when compared to the Vietnam War's on-screen killings, as well as live-action footage of the bulldozing of human carcasses into mass graves, the napalming of children, and the ravaging of villages by American soldiers.

As appalling as these public images were, however, few had meanings as loathsome as the pictures that serve as the central metaphor of Stephen Wright's novel *Meditations in Green*. The hero of the novel has the job that the author had in Vietnam: He works as a photoanalyst in an intelligence unit whose mission is to aid the torture and assassination campaign known as Operation Phoenix, the ecocidal defoliation campaign originally designated Operation Hades, and the genocidal bombing. His official job as "image interpreter" is to scrutinize reconnaissance films to find evidence of life so that it can be eliminated. Not just humans are targets to be erased by bombing; trees themselves become the enemy. Anyone in the unit who has qualms about such genocide and ecocide is defined — in a revealing term — as a "smudge," thus becoming another target for elimination. The perfect image, it is implied, should have nothing left of the human or the natural. From the air, the unit's own base looks like "a concentration camp or a movie lot." The climax of the novel comes when the base is devastated by an enemy attack intercut with scenes from *Night of the Living Dead*, that ghoulish 1968 vision of America which is simultaneously being screened as entertainment.[17]

One of the most influential and enduring single images from the Vietnam War—certainly the most contested — exploded into the consciousness of millions of Americans in February 1968 when they actually watched, within the comfort of their own homes, as the chief of the Saigon national police executed a manacled NLF[18] prisoner. In a perfectly framed sequence, the notorious General Nguyen Ngoc Loan unholsters a snub-nosed revolver and places its muzzle to the prisoner's right temple. The prisoner's head jolts, a sudden spurt of blood gushes straight out of his right temple, and he collapses in death. The next morning, newspaper readers were confronted with AP [Associated Press] photographer Eddie Adams's potent stills of the execution (see Fig. 2). The grim ironies of the scene were accentuated by the cultural significance of the weapon itself: a revolver, a somewhat archaic handgun, symbolic of the American West.

Precisely one decade later this image, with the roles now reversed, was transformed into the dominant metaphor of a Hollywood production presenting a new version of the Vietnam War: *The Deer Hunter*. This lavishly financed movie, which the New York Film Critics' Circle designated the best English-language film of 1978 and which received four Academy Awards, including Best Picture of 1978, succeeded not only in radically reimaging the war but in transforming prisoners of war (POWs) into central symbols of American manhood for the 1980s and 1990s.

The manipulation of familiar images — some already accruing symbolic   30 power — was blatant, though most critics at the time seemed oblivious to it. The basic technique was to take images of the war that had become deeply embedded in America's consciousness and transform them into their opposites. For example, in the film's first scene in Vietnam, a uniformed soldier throws a grenade into an underground village shelter harboring women and children, and then with his automatic rifle mows down a woman and her

Figure 2. General Nguyen Ngoc Loan, head of South Vietnam's police and intelligence, executing a prisoner.

baby. Although the scene resembles the familiar TV sequence of GIs in Vietnamese villages (as well as *Life's* photographs of the My Lai massacre), the soldier turns out to be not American but North Vietnamese. In turn he is killed by a lone guerrilla — who is not a Viet Cong but our Special Forces hero, played by Robert DeNiro. Later, when two men plummet from a helicopter, the images replicate a familiar telephotographic sequence showing an NLF prisoner being pushed from a helicopter to make other prisoners talk;[19] but the falling men in the movie are American POWs attempting to escape from their murderous North Vietnamese captors.

The structuring metaphor of the film is the Russian roulette that the sadistic Asian Communists force their prisoners to play. The crucial torture scene consists of sequence after sequence of images replicating and replacing the infamous killing of the NLF prisoner by General Nguyen Ngoc Loan. Prisoner after prisoner is hauled out of the tiger cages (which also serve as a substitute image for the tiger cages of the Saigon government) and then forced by the demonic North Vietnamese officer in charge (who always stands to the prisoner's right, our left) to place a revolver to his own right temple. Then the image is framed to eliminate the connection between the prisoner's body and the arm holding the revolver, thus bringing the image closer to the famous execution image (see Fig. 3). One sequence even replicates the blood spurting out of the victim's right temple.

The Deer Hunter's manipulation of this particular image to reverse the roles of victim and victimizer was used again and again in the 1980s by other vehicles of the militarization of American culture from movies to comic

Figure 3. In *The Deer Hunter* (1978), General Loan's revolver metamorphoses into a North Vietnamese revolver, and his NLF prisoner is replaced by South Vietnamese and U.S. prisoners forced to play Russian roulette.

books. Take, for example, *P.O.W.: The Escape*, an overtly militaristic 1986 POW rescue movie, inspired by *Rambo* and starring David Carradine as superhero. The bestiality of the Asian Communists is here embodied by a North Vietnamese prison-camp commander who executes an American prisoner with a revolver shot to the right temple in a tableau modeled even more precisely than *The Deer Hunter*'s on the original execution of the NLF prisoner in Saigon (see Fig. 4). Then—just in case viewers missed it—this scene is replayed later as the movie's only flashback.

Toward the end of the 1980s, however, the infamous execution got manipulated incredibly further, actually shifting the role of the most heartless shooter (originally a South Vietnamese official) from the Vietnamese Communists to the photographers themselves! For example, the cover story of the November 1988 issue of the popular comic book *The 'Nam* portrays the photojournalists, both still photographers and TV cameramen, as the real enemies because they had placed the image on the "front page of every newspaper in the states!" The cover literally reverses the original image by showing the execution scene from a position behind the participants (Fig. 5). This offers a frontal view of the photographer, whose deadly camera conceals his face and occupies the exact center of the picture. The prisoner appears merely as an arm, shoulder, and sliver of a body on the left. The only face shown belongs to the chief of the security police, who displays the righteous—even heroic—indignation that has led him to carry out this justifiable revenge against the treacherous actions of the "Viet Cong" pictured in the story. The climactic image (Fig. 6) is a full page in which the execution scene appears

Figure 4. *P.O.W.: The Escape* (1986) transforms the South Vietnamese execution of a prisoner into a North Vietnamese prison commander's murder of a U.S. prisoner.

Figure 5. Cover story of the November 1988 issue of *The 'Nam*, glorifying General Nguyen Ngoc Loan and making the photographer into the villain.

as a reflection in the gigantic lens of the camera above the leering mouth of the photographer, from which comes a bubble with his greedy words, "Keep shooting! Just keep shooting!" "Shooting" a picture here has become synonymous with murder and treason. In the next panel, two GIs register their shock—not at the execution, but at a TV cameraman focusing on the dead body:

> "Front page of every newspaper in the states!"
> "Geez . . ."

One can hardly imagine a more complete reversal of the acclaim accorded to Civil War photographers for bringing the reality of war and death home to the American people.

The logic of this comic-book militarism, put into practice for each of America's wars since Vietnam, is inescapable: Photographers must be

Figure 6. *The 'Nam* images the photographer as the shooter—and the camera as the most destructive weapon.

allowed to image for the public only what the military deems suitable. Nonmilitary photographers and all journalists were simply banished from the entire war zone during the 1983 invasion of Grenada. Partly as a result of this treatment, the major media accepted a pool system for the 1989 invasion of Panama—and meekly went along with the military's keeping even these selected journalists confined to a U.S. base throughout most of the conflict. (A European reporter who attempted to report directly from the scene was actually shot to death when the military unit sent to arrest him became involved in "friendly fire" with another group of U.S. soldiers.)

The almost complete absence of photographic images was quite conven- 35 ient for the Grenada and Panama invasions, which were carried out so swiftly and with such minimal military risk that they required no Congressional or public endorsement. And for the first several days after U.S. troops had been dispatched to confront Iraq in August 1990, Secretary of Defense Dick Cheney refused to allow journalists to accompany them. The Pentagon seemed to be operating under the belief that photographic and televised images had helped bring about the U.S. defeat in Vietnam. But for the Gulf War, with its long buildup, its potential for significant casualties, and its intended international and domestic political purposes, *some* effective images proved to be essential.

To control these images, the U.S. government set up pools of selected reporters and photographers, confined them to certain locations, required them to have military escorts when gathering news, established stringent guidelines limiting what could be reported or photographed, and subjected all written copy, photographs, and videotape to strict censorship.[20] Most of those admitted to the pools, it is interesting to note, represented the very newspapers and TV networks that were simultaneously mounting a major campaign to build support for the war. Journalists were forced to depend on military briefings, where they were often fed deliberately falsified information. Immediately after the ground offensive began, all press briefings and pool reports were indefinitely suspended. In a most revealing negation of the achievement of Civil War photography, with its shocking disclosure of the reality of death, the Pentagon banned the press entirely from Dover Air Force Base during the arrival of the bodies of those killed in the war. Responding to an ACLU legal argument that it was attempting to shield the public from disturbing images, the Pentagon replied that it was merely protecting the privacy of grieving relatives.[21]

Although the media were largely denied access to the battlefields, the Gulf War nevertheless gained the reputation of the first "real-time" television war, and the images projected into American homes helped to incite the most passionate war fever since World War II. These screened images ranged from the most traditional to the most innovative modes of picturing America's wars. Even the antiquated icon of the heroic commanding general, missing for about forty years, was given new life. Although hardly as striking a figure as the commander in Leutze's *Washington Crossing the Delaware* or the posed picture of General Douglas MacArthur returning to the Philippines during World War II, a public idol took shape in the corpulent form of General Norman Schwarzkopf in his fatigues, boots, and jaunty cap.

But perhaps the most potent images combined techniques pioneered by Billy Mitchell with General Peckem's quest for aerial photos of perfect bomb patterns, the medium of television, and the technological capabilities of the weapons themselves. After all, since one of the main goals of the warmakers was to create the impression of a "clean" technowar — almost devoid of human suffering and death, conducted with surgical precision by wondrous mechanisms — why not project the war from the point of view of the weapons? And so the most thrilling images were transmitted directly by the laser-guidance systems of missiles and by those brilliant creations, "smart" bombs. Fascinated and excited, tens of millions of Americans stared at their screens, sharing the experience of these missiles and bombs unerringly guided by the wonders of American technology to a target identified by a narrator as

Figure 7. Technowar triumphs in TV sequence of a smart bomb destroying an Iraqi building.

an important military installation. The generation raised in video arcades and
on Nintendo could hardly be more satisfied. The target got closer and closer,
larger and larger (Fig. 7). And then everything ended with the explosion.
There were no bloated human bodies, as in the photographs of the battlefields of Antietam and Gettysburg—and none of the agony of the burned and
wounded glimpsed on television relays from Vietnam. There was just nothing
at all. In this magnificent triumph of technowar, America's images of its wars
had seemingly reached perfection.

Notes

1. See especially Alan Trachtenberg, *Reading American Photographs: Images as
History, Mathew Brady to Walker Evans* (New York: Hill and Wang, 1989), p. 74; and
William A. Frassanito, *Antietam: The Photographic Legacy of America's Bloodiest Day*
(New York: Charles Scribner's Sons, 1978), pp. 27–28.

2. William C. Davis, "Finding the Hidden Images of the Civil War," *Civil War
Times Illustrated,* 21 (1982, #2), 9.

3. "Brady's Photographs: Pictures of the Dead at Antietam," *The New York Times,*
20 October 1862.

4. Oliver Wendell Holmes's "Doings of the Sunbeam," *Atlantic Monthly* (July
1863), p. 12.

5. This concept is developed most effectively by Amy Kaplan in "The Spectacle
of War in Crane's Revision of History," *New Essays on* The Red Badge of Courage,
ed. Lee Clark Mitchell (Cambridge: Cambridge University Press, 1986), pp. 77–108.

6. Stephen Crane, The Red Badge of Courage: *An Episode in the American Civil
War,* ed. Henry Binder (New York: Avon Books, 1983), p. 37.

7. H. Bruce Franklin, "From Empire to Empire: *Billy Budd, Sailor,*" in *Herman Melville: Reassessments,* ed. A. Robert Lee (London: Vision Press, 1984), pp. 199–216.

8. Mark Twain, *A Connecticut Yankee in King Arthur's Court,* ed. Bernard L. Stein (Berkeley: University of California Press, 1979), pp. 466–86.

9. During the Spanish-American War, the Edison Company had recorded some motion pictures of the embarking troops but was unable to obtain any battle footage. Later the company re-created battle scenes in a mountain reservation near Edison's headquarters in Essex County, New Jersey. See "Historian Remembers the Maine, Spain-America Conflict," Newark (NJ) *Star Ledger,* 11 February 1992.

10. Larry Wayne Ward, *The Motion Picture Goes to War: The U.S. Government Film Effort during World War I* (Ann Arbor: UMI Research Press, 1985), pp. 55–56.

11. H. Bruce Franklin, *War Stars: The Superweapon and the American Imagination* (New York: Oxford University Press, 1988), chapter 15.

12. Burke Davis, *The Billy Mitchell Affair* (New York: Random House, 1967), p. 16.

13. *Voli sulle ambe* (Florence, 1937), a book Vittorio Mussolini wrote to convince Italian boys they should all try war, "the most beautiful and complete of all sports." Quoted by Denis Mack Smith, *Mussolini's Roman Empire* (New York: Viking, 1976), p. 75.

14. For extended analyses of the significance of this event, see Franklin, *War Stars,* pp. 123–27, and Clinton Burhans Jr., "Spindrift and the Sea: Structural Patterns and Unifying Elements in *Catch-22,*" *Twentieth Century Literature,* 19 (1973), 239–50.

15. Joseph Heller, *Catch-22* (New York: Dell, 1962), pp. 334–37.

16. When the Korean War began in mid-1950, there were fewer than ten million television sets in the United States. Americans' principal visual images of that war came from newsreels shown before feature films in movie theaters and from still photos in magazines.

17. Stephen Wright, *Meditations in Green* (New York: Bantam, 1984).

18. The National Liberation Front opposed the government of South Vietnam because it was allied with the North Vietnamese. [Editors' note.]

19. "How Helicopter Dumped a Viet Captive to Death," *Chicago Sun-Times,* 29 November 1969; "Death of a Prisoner," *San Francisco Chronicle,* 29 November 1969.

20. Everette E. Dennis et al., *The Media at War: The Press and the Persian Gulf Conflict* (New York: Gannett Foundation, 1991), pp. 17–18.

21. Dennis, pp. 21–22.

Working with the Text

1. H. Bruce Franklin's essay opens with a discussion of America's Civil War, and it closes with a discussion of the 1991 Gulf War. How does Franklin's treatment of images from the Civil War provide a foundation or point of reference for the rest of the essay? Are you convinced by Franklin's argument that images of the Civil War possess a reality that is largely absent from images of the Gulf War?

2. A key term in Franklin's essay is *technowar*. How does Franklin define and deploy this term? How, and to what end, does Franklin connect the technology of war with the technologies of image production and image circulation?

3. A key distinction for Franklin lies in the opposition between realism and romanticism. How does he discuss these terms? What does he mean by the "romanticizing of the machines of war" (par. 17)? How is aesthetic distance achieved in war photography? Troubling as it may be, is there an aesthetic of war?

4. The title of Franklin's essay points us to a progression from "realism" to "virtual reality." How real is virtual reality? Is virtual reality really born out of an impulse to romanticize and fictionalize?

5. Franklin concludes his essay with a discussion of the televised wars, principally the Vietnam and the Gulf wars. What is it about the medium of television that may change our relation to the image and our perception of war?

From Text to Field

1. Drawing on Franklin's essay, analyze current news broadcasts that show images of war and conflict. Do the images and the press's treatment of them support Franklin's argument, or does the broadcast raise issues not fully explored in Franklin's essay?

2. Franklin makes brief reference to video games in his essay. Drawing on your own experience or the experience of your contemporaries, discuss the relationship between video games and the virtual reality of technowar.

3. Even as he discusses photographic or video images of war, Franklin makes frequent reference to the images of war in novels and feature films. Drawing on Franklin's essay, offer an analysis of a war novel or war movie with which you are familiar. Does your "text" support, complicate, or draw into question Franklin's argument?

4. Although images of America's wars are the explicit focus of Franklin's essay, he does offer the occasional comment on what we don't see or what is censored or withheld from view (caskets arriving at Dover Air Force Base, for example). What place does the un-imaged—and the unimaginable—have in our perceptions of war? How and for what purpose are images "managed"?

Globalizing Terror

Francis A. Beer and
G. R. Boynton

Acts of terrorism and images of those terrorist acts have become, sad to say, part of our contemporary world. The images, even when taken half a world away, strike close to home. Francis A. Beer and G. R. Boynton seek to understand why terrorism, though concrete and local in its immediate consequences, has itself become globalized. They find that such globalization goes hand in hand with the globalization of the media, which has created a new public space—a stage, if you will, on which terrorists themselves have become possible actors.

A political-science professor at the University of Colorado at Boulder, Beer has focused his recent work on the cognitive and rhetorical aspects of politics and international relations. He has published *Peace against War: The Ecology of International Violence* (1981) and *Meanings of War and Peace* (2001) and has edited volumes on *Post-Realism: The Rhetorical Turn in International Relations* (with Robert Hariman, 1996) and *Metaphorical World Politics* (with Christ'l De Landtsheer, 2004).

Boynton is a professor of political science at the University of Iowa, where he pursues research in multimedia politics and communication and cognition. Among other books and articles, he has authored, with John S. Nelson, *Video Rhetorics: Televised Advertising in American Politics* (1997).

Beer and Boynton find that, just as politics and international relations have entered a multimedia domain, so too must scholarship draw on new media. They published their article on "Globalizing Terror" in *Poroi: An Interdisciplinary Journal of Rhetorical Analysis and Invention* (Vol. 2, No. 1, August 2003). As an online journal, *Poroi* afforded the authors a chance to integrate multimedia in their scholarly text, with links to actual video clips of news broadcasts. You can access their full work at inpress.lib.uiowa.edu/poroi/papers/beer030725.html.

In the aftermath of the attack on September 11, 2001, British Prime Minister Tony Blair said, "Never forget how we felt watching the planes fly into those twin towers." There is nothing extraordinary about his statement until you think about what he did not say. He did not say the people of New York City watched. He did not say the people of New York and New Jersey watched. He did not say Americans watched. He was speaking to and for the world, and he said that we watched and felt. The change in the speed of communication over the past fifty years has produced a revolution. For the first time in human history the shot was heard around the world.

Terror has existed through human history, but it has become a critical political issue since 9/11. The political use of terror, terrorism, is the subject of a growing library of work. Amazon lists almost four thousand books for terrorism and terrorists, including five encyclopedias of terrorism. There is also an extensive literature in scholarly journals and the popular press. Among other things, this work describes the psychological profiles of terrorists; the extent to which they are rational or irrational; the political, social, economic, and cultural environments that encourage them; public reactions to terrorism; possible and probable future terrorist scenarios; and strategies for controlling future terrorism (Healy et al. 2002).

The visual media have provided a feast of terrorist coverage, allowing the world to move from reading about terrorism to, as the prime minister said, watch it — in real time and in replay. The globalization of terror is something new. It goes hand in hand with the globalization of the media. The creation of new media technology has created a public space in which political actors may perform: Terrorists are some of the actors who can now play on a global stage (see Norris, Just, and Kern 2003; Greenberg and Thompson 2002; Hachten and Scotton 2002; Nacos 2002; Nelson and Boynton 1997; Alali and Byrd 1994; Livingston 1994).

We trace this change. We began in 1998 and have recorded between 200 and 250 news broadcasts a year. We started with CNN's *WorldView*. In 2001 we switched to BBC's *World News*. In this analysis we examine how the global news media handle terror — the globalization of terror. The analysis is in three parts: (1) what terror becomes in global broadcasting; (2) terror and the synchronization of global media; and (3) how terror becomes us.

What Terror Becomes

For a year the world watched the Kosovars living in terror. Finally, the world said that it had enough, a brief war ensued, the terror abated — though the hardships continued. And the world stopped watching.

The Kosovars had no monopoly on terror, of course. Today the Israelis and the Palestinians are living out mutually assured terror. The Afghans lived in terror. The East Timorese, the Eritreans, the Iraqis and the list goes on.

Figure 1. The World Trade Center, September 11, 2001, from BBC America.

The global media are there — at least for a time — making it possible for us to watch. What do they show us? What does terror become in the global media?

Kosovo is one case among many. By looking carefully at this case, one can see the elements that appear over and over in the reporting. Living in terror is told as threat and attack, fear and escape, and shock and mourning.

Here we focus on the threat of terror.

The Yugoslav government construed the Kosova Liberation Army as a terrorist organization. Fighting terrorists is war, and there are no limits on   10 what the government can do. Terrorists hide every- **Terrorists are some of the** where. The government cannot tell a terrorist from a **actors who can now play on** non-terrorist. Hence, every male is a candidate. **a global stage.** There is no limit on who can be rounded up for interrogation. The Yugoslav police went door to door searching for weapons and searching for men. It was the moment the family had dreaded. The man was taken away by the police. "Go inside, don't be afraid," he shouted to his family. But many men did not come back. The threat does not go away because there are no limits on what the government can do. At any moment the police may show up and take anybody away— never to return.

There are no limits on what the police may destroy. Any house, any structure is a potential hiding place for KLA fighters. One day, any day, they can destroy. "They came into our main street," the man said, "and then shelled

Figure 2. Street fighting in Kosovo, Yugoslavia from CNN.

our house." For everyone whose house had not been destroyed this was the threat. If they did it there, if they did it then, they can do it here and now. The threat is ever present—until you have been destroyed.

There are no limits on whom they can shoot. If anyone may be a KLA terrorist, then anyone can be shot as soon as they do something the least bit suspicious. Trying to escape from the police is definitely suspicious. So the woman was shot. The threat is not so much what they have done to you as it is what they may do to you. It is what you dread; it is what may happen. Terror is living with what may happen.

Figure 3. A shelled building in Kosovo.

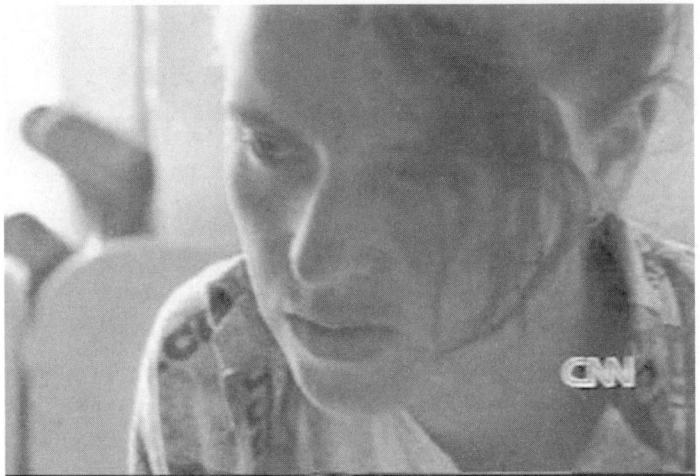

Figure 4. A woman shot by the police in Kosovo.

People tried to escape the threat by hiding in the countryside. That could work in the summer, it could work if you were willing to live without housing and without food. It could work until you were found. Then the survivors mourned.

As the global media tell the story, terror becomes threat, attempting to escape the threat, and mourning when escape fails.

On the Same Page

There are many similarities in news broadcasting around the world. For example, the anchor and the anchor desk are ubiquitous.   15

Figure 5. Escape to the countryside.

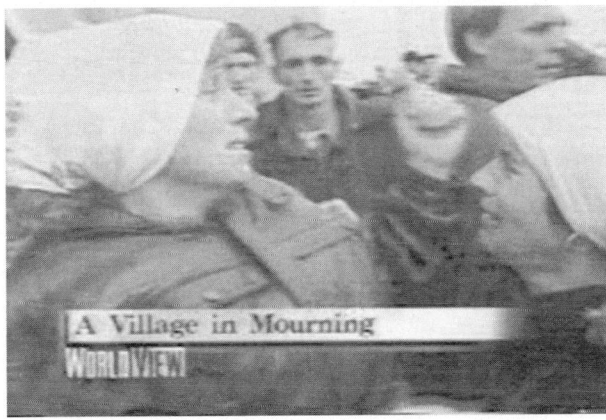

Figure 6. Mourning when escape fails.

Atlanta, Washington, New York, London—China, Croatia, Dubai, Germany, Korea, Russia, Vietnam—the anchor or anchors are managing the broadcast sitting behind a desk and in front of a map and screen display.

In addition to the other similarities, there is the story of the day—the story found in almost every media outlet. The story of the day is well known in the United States. But there is a story of the day in news broadcasting around the world, as well. The world is synchronized in what it is shown as important.

Figure 7. News anchors from around the world.

The day was April 5, 2002. The Israeli invasion of Palestine was nine days old. Around the world the story of the day was the Israeli army terrorizing Palestinians and Palestinians fighting back. Terror was the centerpiece of the news from the Middle East. There were tanks in the streets of Ramallah and Palestinian gunmen firing automatic weapons. There were helicopters attacking and destroying buildings. But the story of the day seemed to be the small arms fire as gunmen ran the length of a street. That one scene was repeated over and over in the news broadcasts we found.

Forest fires in California, flooding in Europe and Bangladesh, an election in Germany—they are all world news. But none synchronizes global broadcasting as terror does. We are all on the same page when terror is the story of the day.

How Terror Becomes Us

Tony Blair said that we watched, and we did.   20

During the first twenty-five seconds, a news reporter explains to anyone who needs explanation what we are seeing. Then we are thrust into a crowd. We are in the midst of shouting, screaming, shock, disbelief. We feel the terror when we see through the eyes of the victims.

It begins with a scream and a replay of the crash into the tower and the tower burning. The images set the story. This is where the grief comes from. The voice of a victim—a telephone message for her husband, recorded as she was waiting for death. And a wedding picture of the victim. Then the picture of a flight attendant—shown over the American flag. And her husband, sitting in front of a flag, recounting her call.

Figure 8. September 11, 2001.

Figure 9. World Trade Center

The camera moves back to show the large number of lives that have been destroyed. Then it moves in — filling the screen with the face of a wife, then a father. Pictures of searching wreckage, pictures of a victim, then the screen is filled with the face of the wife. Finally, back to the destroyed buildings. The carnage of the lives is reinforced with images of the carnage on the ground.

We cannot miss the terror. Terror becomes us when we are called upon to remember. The news media remind viewers over and over about the event. It becomes a constant point of departure for news, as the sights and sounds are repeated and repeated. And we are called to remember.

The global media brings terror to us all.   25

Figure 10. British Prime Minister Tony Blair.

Conclusion

It begins with technology. The time required to communicate from anywhere to anywhere is now measured in seconds. Global communication has
always been possible—if you were willing to wait. But waiting only seconds
brings new meaning to "global communication" and creates a new human
reality.

Kosovo, Israel-Palestine, the twin towers—terror is not a sometime thing.
Man's inhumanity toward his fellow men makes terror constant in human
affairs. Not very long ago most of the terror was hidden—beyond our willingness to wait for the news. That is no longer true. We experience the terror around the world as it happens.

References

Alali, O., and G. W. Byrd. (1994). *Terrorism and the Media: A Selected, Annotated
    Bibliography.* Jefferson, NC: McFarland.
Greenberg, B. S., and M. T. Thompson, eds. (2002). *Communication and
    Terrorism: Public and Media Responses to 9/11.* Mount Waverly: Hampton
    Press.
Hachten, W. A., and J. F. Scotton. (2002). *The World News Prism: Global Media in
    an Era of Terrorism.* Ames: Iowa State University Press.
Healy, A. F., J. M. Hoffman, F. A. Beer, and L. E. Bourne Jr. (2002). "Terrorists
    and Democrats: Individual Reactions to International Attacks." *Political
    Psychology,* 23, 3, pp. 439–67.
Livingston, S. (1994). *The Terrorism Spectacle.* Boulder: Westview Press.
Nacos, B. L. (2002). *Mass-Mediated Terrorism: The Central Role of the Media in
    Terrorism and Counter-Terrorism.* Lanham: Rowman and Littlefield.
Nelson, J. S., and G. R. Boynton. (1997). *Video Rhetorics.* Urbana: University of
    Illinois Press.
Norris, P., M. Just, and M. Kern. (2003). *Framing Terrorism: Understanding
    Terrorist Threats and Mass Media.* New York, NY: Routledge.

Working with the Text

1. Why is it telling that Francis A. Beer and G. R. Boynton begin their article with a
   discussion of the British—and global—experience of September 11? What role
   do the international press and international perspectives have in the article?

2. In the first paragraph, Beer and Boynton allude to a famous line in a poem written by Ralph Waldo Emerson about the Battle of Concord at the outset of the
   American Revolutionary War: "the shot heard round the world." In what ways
   is this a fitting line to use, given the argument advanced in the article? Are
   shots, or bombings, only now heard around the world in a way that is literally
   true?

3. Beer and Boynton refer to terrorists as global actors who can now play on a world stage, thanks to the globalization of the media. Given the article's discussion of a common narrative or dramatic structure in media broadcasts and the growing synchronization of media events, whose play is being performed? Who controls the now global media?

4. The article by Beer and Boynton is distinctive in that it calls upon multimedia technologies. How does the presentation by the authors change or enhance their ability to make arguments and elicit belief from their readers? With politics and terrorism now a multimedia domain, is it only appropriate, perhaps necessary, for the study of politics and international affairs to draw on multimedia tools?

From Text to Field

1. For their examples, Beer and Boynton draw on terrorist events during the time of their data collection, chiefly those that occurred in Kosovo, Israel, and Palestine, and those of September 11. Consider the applicability and relevance of this article to current or recent terrorist activities that you have been following in the media. Does the global media become synchronized in the fashion Beer and Boynton suggest? Is there a common or generic narrative structure to the media reports? If the media and the world are brought together on the same page, whose page is it and whose story is that page a part of?

2. Although Beer and Boynton focus on how the global media report on and thus disseminate images of terrorism, they also make it clear that terrorists are also actors on the global media stage. To what extent do terrorists use the media as a terrorist weapon—one that can be even more effective than suicide bombings? What are the ethical obligations of the media? When does covering terrorism play into the hands of terrorists?

3. If you find yourself in the midst of an event covered by nearly all media outlets — the story of the day, so to speak — do some channel surfing and catalog how similar and synchronized the coverage might be. What common devices, techniques, and angles become apparent in the coverage, even as you watch different channels?

4. If you have traveled abroad, or have access to foreign media online, comment from your own personal and viewing experience on what Beer and Boynton call the globalization of the media. Is the media really rather homogenous, or are there some cultural and national distinctions that remain? Do those distinctions tend to be erased somewhat when coverage concerns a global event like terrorism?

INTO THE FIELD: Options for Writing Projects

1. Who Is Using This Photograph, and to What End?

This field project encourages you to explore how images, especially photographs, can engender belief and consent, and the purposes to which such belief and consent are put. Speaking of old family photos, David Levi Strauss (p. 728) notes, "People use photographs to construct identities, investing them with 'believability'" (par. 7). And yet Strauss goes on to suggest that this process extends well beyond personal photos. "Of course, advertisers and news-picture editors do the same thing, mimicking the private use of photographs in order to manufacture desire for products and to manufacture public consent. This has caused a great deal of confusion. The first question must always be: Who is using this photograph, and to what end?" (par. 7)

Choose a particular photographic image—or a series of images from a brochure or media campaign, for example—and examine in some detail the ways in which desire or consent is manufactured. What are the cultural codes and conventions that come into play? What pool of experience does the image assume? Who is served by the image, and for what purpose? In what ways can the image you are analyzing develop belief and consent that text alone could never accomplish?

2. On the Cover

Images on the covers of news magazines are chosen for their impact and for their ability to elicit reaction and belief. For example, in his essay David Levi Strauss (p. 728) offers comments on a cover depicting Saddam Hussein as Hitler, published by the *New Republic,* in which he notes the role of visual analogy. For this project, choose a current or recent cover used by a news magazine (such as *Time* or *Newsweek*) and offer an analysis of how the image is meant to draw on the values and beliefs of the magazine's intended audience. You may wish to consult a range of cover images that deal with the same news item or topic. Does the same process apply to the covers of other kinds of magazines, such as publications that deal with lifestyles or fitness or celebrities? To what extent are the values and beliefs culturally determined? How are those beliefs invoked by the image? For insight into the question of culture, you might find it interesting to explore, by way of the Internet, the images and covers used by the press in other countries.

3. Auras of Believability: Images and Beyond

Although works of art have their own "aura," David Levi Strauss (p. 728) asserts that in the more than 150 years that it has been around "photography acquired its own aura—the aura of believability" (par. 1). This field project invites you to read that aura—to analyze the reasons why photos and other means of communication prompt us to believe. Three options for this project suggest themselves:

- Consider a personal photograph, perhaps from a relative who has long since died. In what ways do you invest belief in this photograph, especially since you may not have been around when it was taken? What is it about the photo, both in its material condition and in what and who it depicts, that prompts you to believe?
- Consider a photograph that depicts an event or issue in the world, perhaps as reported in the media. What is it about the image, about its caption, and about when and where it was published that prompts you to consent that this image is real, believable? How much of your belief is determined by the image itself, and how much by the circumstances of its publication and circulation?
- Consider an artifact or an instance of communication that is *not* a photograph, but instead a written text or a speech, for example. What prompts you to believe in it, to lend it credibility? How is believability won? For example, why might a newsletter from a nonprofit organization, a product brochure, a presentation before an audience, or an academic article be thought to be credible? In what ways is the "aura of believability" developed given these different (nonphotographic) kinds of artifacts or examples?

4. Images and Individual Initiative

Because many images are commodified and circulated in the mass media, they often seem beyond our control. Such images are part of a globalized media; you and I seem to have little influence on how they are produced, received, and used. And yet, individual initiative is still possible—either in terms of resisting and questioning images or bringing images to light that would have otherwise remained uncaptured or would have been ignored.

This field project asks that you consider, in some detail, an instance when individual resistance or initiative can or has made a difference. Satiric comment and criticism of the media is one route for such initiative, as in the magazine *Adbusters* or the satiric newspaper the *Onion*. Another route is advocacy, in which committed individuals seek to bring to the public's attention an image or a story that would not likely have received attention were it not for their efforts.

As you analyze and report on your particular case, ask why some images and stories are covered by the mainstream media and others are not. Why might it be important to question some kinds of images? Likewise, are there some images about which it may be difficult, if not taboo, to raise questions? What is the public's right to know, and what limits might there be to such rights?

5. **The Intertwined Lives of Image and Text**

Although often separate and judged by different standards, image and text are leading an increasingly intertwined life. Witness politics, where the ability to control one's message often depends on one's ability to control images. This field project asks you to explore the relationship between image and text in one particular arena or through one artistic medium. These arenas might include editorial cartoons, politics, advertising, graphic design, and popular culture. You may find it interesting to explore different historical periods or cultures. For example, French poster art of the 1920s and 1930s often combined image and text, as do murals of political protest in Ireland.

As you analyze image and text, ask yourself how and why they function together as they do. How has the genre that permits or invites this interaction developed? What seem to be the limits or boundaries of that interaction? Does the interaction serve aesthetic or utilitarian purposes? What is accomplished by the interaction that could not be accomplished when using text or image separately?

6. **Fast Forward: Images of Today's War**

This field project asks you to update H. Bruce Franklin's survey of war images (p. 756) from the Civil War to the 1991 Gulf War, focusing perhaps on one specific question or issue. In the years since the Gulf War, new technologies have emerged—both for fighting war and for reporting and waging that war in the media. How is today's technowar different from what Franklin describes? Do images of today's war provide additional evidence for the argument Franklin makes, or do these images call for an adjustment in his argument?

Moreover, since the 1991 Gulf War, war's face has evolved. "Armed combatants" have often replaced uniformed soldiers, and war is now characterized as "conflict." The line between combatants and civilians has grown fuzzy, and terrorism has emerged as a central tool or tactic in armed struggle. How do images of war take into account this new landscape?

What's more, the tools of and the policies regarding news coverage have also evolved. Whereas news reporters were often kept at bay during the 1991 Gulf War, the Iraq War saw the use of embedded reporters, and new technologies, such as satellite phones, made possible the filing of reports from remote areas.

A further development is the increasing globalization of the media. Is the image of war in the United States different from the image of war elsewhere? Do television networks in the Middle East, for example, understand and use the images of war differently from networks in the United States? Or does the globalization of the media tend to erase regional and cultural differences, rendering the image of war generic in its use and effect?

7. Image Ethics

The rich and increasingly complex media culture in which we live places images at the center of our world. We swim in a sea of images; we use them and are used by them. All the more reason to consider the ethics of producing, circulating, and consuming those images.

This field project invites you to explore the practical application of ethics guidelines that have been developed by leading newspapers and broadcast organizations, and by professional associations. For example, the National Press Photographers Association has developed a set of guidelines pertaining to ethics in the age of digital photography. Do you think such guidelines have influenced image making in the news? What guidelines exist or should exist for the use of images in fields removed from the news, such as advertising?

The ethics involved in image making often become the subject of discussion when ethical lines or boundaries have been crossed. Explore one or more cases, in the national press or in your own community, where images have raised ethical questions.

8. The Borrowed Eye and Ear of the Media

As John Durham Peters (p. 736) helps us understand, the act of witnessing is indeed complex, for it has us move back and forth across the threshold between seeing and saying, experience and discourse. Witnessing becomes all the more complex in our media saturated society, where we often witness through what Peters refers to as "the borrowed eye and ear of the media."

This field project has you explore the phenomenon of what might be called secondary witnessing. In what ways is it different to witness an event firsthand than through the media? Is firsthand witnessing always to be preferred? Given that we now witness so much of our world through the media, is the distinction between the two kinds of witnessing beginning to grow unclear? What are some distinctive features of secondary witnessing, such as copresence (witnessing with others or knowing that others have seen what you have witnessed)? How has secondary witnessing created a common vocabulary or a common set of cultural experiences? What problems does secondary witnessing carry with it?

As part of your fieldwork, you may wish to consider controversial events on your campus or in your community that you have witnessed firsthand and that have also been witnessed for you by the borrowed eyes and ears of the media. How widely different are the two witnessings? What might account for the difference? Can both forms of witnessing be credible?

9. Witnessing across the Disciplines

John Durham Peters (p. 736) explores the dynamics of witnessing and suggests that those dynamics speak to difficult issues in the field of communication.

This field project asks you to consider how well Peters's essay travels as it moves into different disciplinary contexts.

In one way or another, all disciplines have to confront the thorny issue of what counts as observation, and how observation becomes credible. What counts as evidence or testimony in different fields? How does your discipline or prospective major think of an ideal witness? What ground rules or conventions does your field of study establish in order to ensure the believability of any one person's observation? Are there some disciplines that seem more self-conscious or reflective about the role of the observer, or does your field seem to place the act of observation within the general scientific method? What counts as observation or witnessing in fields that focus on textual analysis? What does it mean to be a good observer of a text? How do some disciplines deal with the possibility that one might be simultaneously a participant and an observer or a witness?

As you develop your field project, you may wish to refer to exemplary or representative documents in your field or to laboratory guidelines. You may also wish to interview a professor or graduate student in one of your other courses.

10. Witnessing Global Media and New Technology

This field project invites you to develop a media journal, similar to (though on a smaller scale than) the media archiving that Francis A. Beer and G. R. Boynton developed with CNN and the BBC. Follow how one global media event plays itself out over several days.

On the basis of your journal and any taped or downloaded material, examine what role technology played in the media story. Does that technology contribute to a global media? How can that technology be used in the interests of various players on the political stage? What variations did you observe in the coverage of your story or event, or did the globalized press cover the story in similar, if not homogenous, ways?

Given the worldwide reach of new media, how does global media coverage change what it means to witness an event? How does the speed and reach of the global media affect the psychological impact events have on us as viewers?

11. Multimedia Domains

Politics and the press have surely become multimedia domains. Their activities often call upon several traditional media simultaneously and indeed seek out opportunities that are only possible at the intersection of various media. This field project encourages you to consider what other domains are becoming — or ought to become — multimedia domains as well.

You needn't look far afield. Your own classroom experience can be a rich resource for this field project. For example, does the instruction that occurs in your college classes call upon multimedia, and is the effect always positive? In what ways might scholarship become more effective and persuasive if it were pursued with multimedia tools? What kinds of scholarship or what research questions about multimedia occur to you, given its use in your classrooms?

Beyond the educational arena, what other domains are ripe for a multimedia transformation? Why might some domains be resistant to or skeptical about multimedia?

What observational skills does multimedia call for? Are there distinctive or unexpected challenges involved in witnessing the multimedia image? In what ways might multimedia affect how we think of and develop arguments? What is distinctively persuasive about the use of multimedia? Can you recall instances when multimedia tools were not handled well or failed to be persuasive?

As you respond to some of these questions, be sure to draw on concrete instances of multimedia or on specific contexts in which multimedia was used.

Acknowledgments (*continued from page iv*)

Francis A. Beer and G. R. Boynton. "Globalizing Terror." Excerpted text from full analysis at http://impress.lib.uiowa.edu/pori/papers/beer030725_outline.html. From *Poroi, An Interdisciplinary Journal of Rhetorical Analysis and Invention*, Vol. 2, No. 1, August 2003. Reprinted by permission of the authors.

John Berger. "The White Bird." From *The Sense of Sight* by John Berger. Copyright © 1985 by John Berger. Used by permission of Pantheon Books, a division of Random House, Inc.

David Berreby. "It Takes a Tribe." From the *New York Times*, August 1, 2004. Copyright © 2004 by the New York Times Company. Reprinted with permission.

Sven Birkerts. "Perseus Unbound." From *The Gutenberg Elegies: The Fate of Reading in an Electronic Age.* © 1994 by Sven Birkerts. Reprinted with permission of Faber and Faber, Inc., an affiliate of Farrar, Straus & Giroux, LLC.

Jay David Bolter. "Writing Culture." From *Writing Space* by Jay David Bolter. Copyright © 2001 by Lawrence Erlbaum Associates, Inc. Reprinted with permission of the publisher. All rights reserved.

Wayne C. Booth. "The Idea of a University—as Seen by a Rhetorician." From *The Vocation of a Teacher: Rhetorical Occasions, 1967–1988* by Wayne C. Booth. Copyright © 1988 by the University of Chicago. Reprinted by permission of the University of Chicago Press and the author

Kenneth A. Bruffee. "The Art of Collaborative Learning: Making the Most of Knowledgeable Peers." Originally published in *Change*, May/June 1994, Vol. 26, No. 3. Copyright © 1994 by Kenneth A. Bruffee. Reprinted with the permission of the author.

Alexander Calandra. "Angels on a Pin: The Barometer Story." From the *Saturday Review*, December 25, 1968. Copyright © 1968. Reprinted with permission of Martha Calandra.

Jared Diamond. "Soft Sciences Are Often Harder Than Hard Sciences." Originally published in *Discover*, August 1987. Copyright 1987. Reprinted by permission of the author.

Annie Dillard. "Seeing." Excerpt from *Pilgrim at Tinker Creek* by Annie Dillard. Copyright © 1974 by Annie Dillard. Reprinted by permission of HarperCollins Publishers.

Lisa Ede and Andrea Lunsford. "Why Write. . . Together?" From *Rhetoric Review*, Vol. 1, No. 2, January 1983. Reprinted with the permission of Lawrence Erlbaum Associates, Inc.

H. Bruce Franklin. "From Realism to Virtual Reality: Images of America's Wars." Originally published in the *Georgia Review*, 1994. Copyright © 1994, 2000 by H. Bruce Franklin. Reprinted with the permission of the author.

Paulo Freire. "The 'Banking' Concept of Education." From *The Pedagogy of the Oppressed* by Paulo Freire. Copyright © 1993 by Paulo Freire. Reprinted by permission of the publisher, the Continuum International Publishing Group

Malcolm Gladwell. "The Talent Myth: Are Smart People Overrated?" Originally published in the *New Yorker*, October 12, 2002. Copyright © 2002 by Malcolm Gladwell. Reprinted by permission of the author.

E. H. Gombrich. "Truth and Stereotype." Excerpt from *Art and Illusion: A Study in the Psychology of Pictorial Representation* by E. H. Gombrich. Copyright © 1961 Princeton University Press; renewed 1988; 2000, paperback edition. Reprinted with the permission of Princeton University Press.

Stephen Jay Gould. "Women's Brains." From *The Panda's Thumb: More Reflections in Natural History* by Stephen Jay Gould. Copyright © 1980 by Stephen Jay Gould. Used by permission of W. W. Norton & Company, Inc.

Gerald Graff. "(Hidden Meaning) Disliking Books at an Early Age" and "Other Voices, Other Rooms." Excerpted text from *Beyond the Culture Wars: How Teaching the Conflicts Can Revitalize American Education* by Gerald Graff. Copyright © 1992 by Gerald Graff. Used by permission of W. W. Norton & Company, Inc.

Beverly Gross. "Bitch." From *Salmagundi Magazine*, Summer 1994. Copyright © 1994 by Beverly Gross. Reprinted by permission of the author.

Nancy Hass. "In Your Facebook.com." From the *New York Times*, January 8, 2006. Copyright © 2006 by the New York Times Company. Reprinted with permission.

Susan Herring. "Bringing Familiar Baggage to the New Frontier: Gender Differences in Computer-Mediated Communication." Originally delivered as a speech to the American Library Association panel entitled "Making the Net Work: Is there a Z39.50 in gender communication?" Miami, June 27, 1994. Reprinted with permission of the author.

bell hooks. "Teaching New Worlds/New Words." From *Teaching to Transgress: Education as the Practice of Freedom* by bell hooks. Copyright © bell hooks. Reprinted by permission of the author.

Jamaica Kincaid. "Girl." From *At the Bottom of the River* by Jamaica Kincaid. Copyright © 1983 by Jamaica Kincaid. Reprinted by permission of Farrar, Straus & Giroux, LLC.

Perri Klass. "Learning the Language." From *A Not Entirely Benign Procedure* by Perri Klass. Copyright © 1987 by Perri Klass. Used by permission of G. P. Putnam's Sons, a division of Penguin Group (USA) Inc.

C. H. Knoblauch. "Literacy and the Politics of Education." From *The Right to Literacy*, edited by Andrea Lunsford, Helene Moglen, and James Slevin. Copyright © 1990 by the Modern Language Association of America. Reprinted with permission of the Modern Language Association of America.

Jonathan Kozol. "The Human Cost of an Illiterate Society." From *Illiterate America* by Jonathan Kozol. Copyright © 1985 by Jonathan Kozol. Used by permission of Doubleday, a division of Random House, Inc.

Thomas S. Kuhn. "The Essential Tension: Tradition and Innovation in Scientific Research." This lecture was delivered in 1959 at the Third University of Utah Research Conference on the Identification of Scientific Talent. Reprinted by permission.

George Lakoff and Mark Johnson. "Concepts We Live By." From *Metaphors We Live By* by George Lakoff and Mark Johnson. Copyright © 1980 by the University of Chicago Press. Reprinted with permission. All rights reserved.

Robin Tolmach Lakoff. "The Grooves of Academe." From *Talking Power* by Robin Tolmach Lakoff. Copyright © 1990 by Robin Tolmach Lakoff. Reprinted with permission of Basic Books, a member of Perseus Books, LLC.

Christopher Lasch. "The Lost Art of Political Argument." Copyright © 1990 by *Harper's Magazine*. All rights reserved. Reproduced from the September issue by special permission.

Hermione Lee. "Power: Women and the Word." Originally published in *The State of the Language*, edited by Christopher Ricks and Leonard Michaels, 1990. Copyright © 1990. Reprinted with permission of PFD, Ltd. on behalf of the author.

Illustrations

Pages 472, 473, 474: *Adam and Eve, Conquista,* and *Corregidor de minas,* Library of Congress.

Page 694: "Top Hats - In Trouble," 1942 photo by Arthur "Weegee" Fellig, Getty Images.

Page 698: Jimmy Stewart in *Rear Window,* © Bettmann/CORBIS.

Page 705: "Room in Tenement Flat," 1910. Photo by Jessie Tarbox Beals. Museum of the City of New York, The Jacob A. Riis Collection.

Page 710: Plants brought by Thutmose III, limestone relief from the Temple of Thutmose III, The Art Archive/The Picture Desk, Inc.

Page 711: *Lion and porcupine,* Bridgeman-Giraudon/Art Resource, NY.

Page 712: *Locust woodcut,* 1556, Wick Collection, Zentralbibliothek, Zurich.

Pages 712, 713: *Whale Washed Ashore at Ancona,* 1601, engraving; and *Whale Washed Ashore in Holland,* 1598, engraving, Muller Collection, Rijksmuseum, Amsterdam.

Page 714: *Rhinoceros* by Dürer, Erich Lessing/Art Resource, NY.

Rhinoceros of Africa by Heat, 1789, engraving, The New York Public Library/Art Resource, NY.

Page 714: "African Rhinoceros," Emil Schulthess Erben Photoarchiv.

Page 716: *Muscles of the neck,* from *Gray's Anatomy.* Henry Gray, *Anatomy of the Human Body.* Philadelphia: Lea & Febiger, 1918; Bartleby.com, 2000. www.bartleby.com/ 107/. 2006.

Page 730: Found photograph of unknown boy, Photographs, © 2003 David Levi Strauss. All images are from the publication *Between the Eyes* © 2003, 2005 Aperture Foundation, Inc.

Page 758: "A Harvest of Death, Gettysburg," photo by Timothy O'Sullivan, 1863, George Eastman House.

Page 765: "General Nguyen Ngoc Loan executing a prisoner," 1968 photo by Eddie Adams, AP/Wide World Photos.

Pages 766, 767, 771: Still from *The Deer Hunter;* Still from *P.O.W.: The Escape,* 1986; and TV sequence of smart bomb destroying an Iraqi building, H. Bruce Franklin.

Pages 768, 769: Cover story of the November 1988 issue of *The 'Nam,* and *The 'Nam* images the photographer as the shooter, *The 'Nam:* TM & © 2006 Marvel Characters, Inc. Used with permission.

Page 779: CNN World View news anchor, CNN Image Source.

INDEX OF AUTHORS AND TITLES

Need more help with writing and research?
Visit our Web sites.

We have a wide variety of Web sites designed to help students with their most common writing concerns. You'll find advice from experts, models you can rely on, and exercises that will tell you right away how you're doing. And it's all free and available any hour of the day. All of these can be accessed at Re:Writing: bedfordstmartins.com/rewriting.

Need help with grammar problems?
Exercise Central (bedfordstmartins.com/exercisecentral)

Want to see what papers for your other courses look like?
Model Documents Gallery (bedfordstmartins.com/modeldocs)

Stuck somewhere in the research process? (Maybe at the beginning?)
The Bedford Research Room (bedfordstmartins.com/researchroom)

Wondering whether a Web site is good enough to use in your paper?
Tutorial for Evaluating Online Sources
(bedfordstmartins.com/onlinesourcetutorial)

Having trouble figuring out how to cite a source?
Research and Documentation Online (bedfordstmartins.com/resdoc)

Confused about plagiarism?
The St. Martin's Tutorial on Avoiding Plagiarism
(bedfordstmartins.com/plagiarismtutorial)

Want to get more out of your word processor?
Using Your Word Processor (bedfordstmartins.com/wordprocessor)

Trying to improve the look of your paper?
Using Your Word Processor to Design Documents
(bedfordstmartins.com/docdesigntutorial)

Need to create slides for a presentation?
Preparing Presentation Slides Tutorial
(bedfordstmartins.com/presentationslidetutorial)

Interested in creating a Web site?
Web Design Tutorial (bedfordstmartins.com/webdesigntutorial)